Over The Edge:
Death in Grand Canyon

Books by Michael P. Ghiglieri

The Chimpanzees of Kibale Forest

East of the Mountains of the Moon: Chimpanzee Society in the African Rainforest

Canyon

The Dark Side of Man: Tracing the Origin of Male Violence

First Through Grand Canyon: The Secret Journals and Letters of the 1869 Crew Who Explored the Green and Colorado Rivers

Off the Wall: Death in Yosemite (with co-author Charles R. "Butch" Farabee, Jr.)

Boatman: Lessons of Survival from the Back of Beyond: (Kindle eBook)

Through the Great Unknown (fiction, forthcoming)

Books by Thomas M. Myers

Fateful Journey: Injury and Death on Colorado River Trips in Grand Canyon (with Chris Becker and Larry Stevens)

Grand Obsession: Harvey Butchart and the Exploration of Grand Canyon (with co-author Elias Butler)

The Desert Doc: A Canyon and River Emergency Medical Field Guide for the Southwest (with co-author Michael P. Ghiglieri, forthcoming)

Flipped Out for Grand Canyon (forthcoming)

Over The Edge:
Death in Grand Canyon

Expanded and Revised Second Edition

Michael P. Ghiglieri

and

Thomas M. Myers

Over The Edge:
Death in Grand Canyon

Gripping accounts of all known fatal mishaps in the
most famous of the World's Seven Natural Wonders

Expanded and Revised Second Edition

Michael P. Ghiglieri

and

Thomas M. Myers

PUMA PRESS

Flagstaff

SECOND EDITION, Fifth Printing, fourth revision, (soft cover, 53,500 copies in print)

Printing History of First Edition: twenty-six printings and sixteen revisions
  (250,000+ copies)

ISBN-13: 978-0-9847858-0-3 (Softcover)
ISBN-13: 978-0-9847858-1-0 (Hardcover 380 signed/numbered copies)
Library of Congress Catalog Number: 2011943187

Maps by Bronze Black
Book Jacket design by Bronze Black
Geology schematic by Michael P. Ghiglieri
Cover concept by Michael P. Ghiglieri, Thomas M. Myers, and Becky Myers
Front cover photographs by Connie S. Ghiglieri and the Emery Kolb Collection,
  Cline Library, Northern Arizona University.
Author photographs by Tanya Young and Weston Myers
Rear cover photograph by Ken Klementis and (again) Emery Kolb
End paper photograph by Emery Kolb Collection, Cline Library,
  Northern Arizona University.
Interior Puebloan rock art designs by Kim Besom
Book production by Mary Williams

Recycled content
Printed in U.S.A.

DEDICATION

For the millions who come to Grand Canyon in the future, that they each may walk away enriched—and in one piece.

And also in recognition of each member of every search and rescue team from Arizona and Utah and Nevada and of every guide, companion, and Good Samaritan who has risked his or her life to save those of us who otherwise never would have walked away at all.

For the want of a nail, the shoe was lost.
For the want of a shoe, the horse was lost.
For the want of a horse, the general was lost.
For the want of a general, battle was lost.
For the want of a battle, the war was lost.

TABLE OF CONTENTS

FOREWORD

"How many people die here each year?" This refrain from visitors to Grand Canyon is asked repeatedly. Who can blame them? Each of us has an underlying morbid curiosity that draws us to ask such a question, but admittedly not always openly. It may be the very reason that the title of this book caught your eye.

Although deaths and near-misses occur regularly in national parks, it is difficult for any other national park to match the range and scope found in this book. The range of drama at Grand Canyon includes the harrowing technical rescue of injured photographer Franklin Nims from Robert Brewster Stanton's 1889-1890 Expedition under conditions that today seem unsurvivable. And it expands to June 30 of 1956, when the calm of the park was shattered by the mid-air collision of TWA and United Airlines aircraft that resulted in the worst civilian aviation disaster up to that time, one so bad that it led to the creation of the Federal Aviation Administration (FAA). The scope of this book even includes the saga of the largest criminal manhunt in the history of Arizona, one which focused the spotlight of the nation on this park during the summer of 1992, when that manhunt intensified here as fugitive Danny Ray Horning eluded law enforcement for weeks with incredible cunning.

Despite the obvious dangers of Grand Canyon, a frequent observation I have made of many visitors is their tendency to have a "911 mentality." They often make the assumption that help will always be immediately forthcoming when they place themselves in harm's way. Such visitors suffer from the misguided belief that a national park is a close cousin to an amusement park. The realities are that Walt Disney did not have a hand in constructing Grand Canyon, and the inherent risks associated with this park are unbelievably real. And all too often, tragically so.

As a National Park Ranger at Grand Canyon for nearly thirty years, I have been involved in thousands of search and rescue operations. Many of the mishaps that Michael Ghiglieri and Tom Myers recount here are very vivid personal memories for myself and several other rangers who have participated in these operations. Many of us have experienced our own close calls in the Canyon and have learned personally that the margin between life and death here is narrow.

Tragically, beyond the hundreds of victims of fatal Grand Canyon accidents mentioned in varying detail here, there also exist many more unreported victims. These are the relatives and friends of those who lost their lives at Grand Canyon. In my own efforts to provide solace for the parents, friends, and companions of the victims of these tragedies I have experienced the senseless waste that such a loss of life may bring to a family. It is astonishing how suddenly a high-spirited act or a bit of high jinks can take a life.

For example, consider the tragic aftermath caused by a father pulling a practical joke on his daughter as he pretended to fall backwards off the Canyon rim down to a ledge hidden from her view. His momentum carried him beyond that ledge to a death plunge into the Canyon. That short moment in their lives cannot be reversed; it irrevocably leaves a young girl fatherless and baffled by the forces that rule our fates. Likewise is the needless loss as two companions attempt a hiking shortcut from Phantom Ranch by swimming downstream in the Colorado River, a shortcut in which one of them drowns and the other barely escapes death. The grief and suffering of the families of such victims continues permanently with an emptiness which that loved one used to fill. These families will always see Grand Canyon not as an incredible natural wonder, but as a place that stole away life. This book not only chronicles such unwarranted tragedies, it opens our eyes to preventing them in the future.

Also punctuating this book are incredible tales of survival, near misses, and rescues that fate has allowed to end on a happier note. Just one of many is the epic of David Whittlesey, who survived alone, battered and freezing, for six days in Lower Granite Gorge after losing his raft and gear and all of his food. During his rescue, I offered David my lunch. He devoured it in barely more than a heartbeat.

Traditional Canyon "lore" comes to life in these pages—in fact, some established historical legends are strongly challenged. Tom and Michael present new information which questions, for example, the originally published outcomes to the three members of John Wesley Powell's first 1869 expedition down the Colorado—William Dunn, Seneca Howland, and Oramel G. Howland—after they hiked away from the expedition at Separation Canyon. Also re-examined provocatively here is the infamous demise of the honeymooning couple—Glen and Bessie Hyde—who vanished in Lower Granite Gorge in 1928.

The many accounts of death and near-misses contained here make exceptional reading, but there exists a much greater value in compiling this research under one cover. This book analyzes recurring patterns of fatalities for commonalities in their contributing factors. And it examines ways to prevent such tragedies in the future. Hopefully, as you and other readers study the many fatal errors made by previous Canyon travelers, you will carry a valuable education with you long after you put this book down. What you learn here could truly prevent a life from being lost.

We all should keep in mind that "there are no new accidents—only new people having the same old accidents."

Ken Phillips
Branch Chief
Search & Rescue
National Park Service

ACKNOWLEDGMENTS

In executing a project of this magnitude and complexity we repeatedly relied on the good will of people who lacked the sense to just say no. Our first hurdle in writing this book was in locating reliable data and information regarding fatalities. No one source existed for these data. Even NPS records turned out to be incomplete for our needs, occasionally erroneous, and often impossible to locate. Hence, we owe a vast debt to those who helped locate (or recall) missing details. Some of these people were researchers who went prospecting for us to mine lost information from old newspaper records. Others, working for Grand Canyon National Park, searched NPS incident reports—and their memories. Yet others, who had the bad luck to be in the wrong place at the right time, simply told us what happened, from their perspectives, during fatal episodes. All of these people shared a trait: they each wanted the record to be set straight in this book, and they wanted that record to be accurate.

At the risk of inadvertently omitting the names of those who made personal contributions of time and energy in seeking out and/or providing records or details regarding several of the episodes in this book, we wish to acknowledge and thank the following people who helped (whether they knew they were helping or not) it become accurate: Bruce Aiken, Mary Aiken, Joe Alston, Ann Anderson, Martin J. Anderson, Bruce and Susan Armstrong, Dale Antonich, Jeffe Aronson, Susan Kelly Ash, John S. Azar, Bruce Babbitt, Chris Becker, Paul Berkowitz, Kim Besom, Camille Bibles, George H. Billingsley, Bob Bisson, Mary Booker, Angela Boyers, Kelly Bretta, Patty Brookins, Barbara Brotman, Ashley Brown, Garth Bundy, Harvey Butchart, Carolyn Castleman, Jeff & Laurel Casey, Dan Cassidy, Frankie Chamberlain, Chris Coder, Pat Coffey, Cyndy Cole, Jay Cole, Michael Collier, Bob Cornelius, Kim Crumbo, Jean Custer, O'Connor Dale, Peter Dale, Regan Dale, John Davenport, David Desrosiers, Aaron Dick, Brad Dimock, Becky Douglas, Jeff Drayton, Dan Driskill, Colleen Dunleavy, Michael Ebersole, John D. Edwards, Darla Ekbom, Tim Ellis, Dave Elston, John Evans, Charles R. "Butch" Farabee, Jr., Jack Fields, Chip Fleming, Dave Foster, Laura Fulgineti, Tiffany George, Cliff Hance Ghiglieri, Daniel Graber, Teresa Green, Karen Greig, Bill Grundy, Cathy and Rich Hahn, Curtis ("Whale") Hansen, Michael Harrison, Tony Hillerman, Kristin Hilton, Lois Hirst, Stephen Hirst, Bruce Hooper, Sjors Horstman, Colleen Hyde, Terry Jacobson, Daniel D. James, Teresa Janecek, Kevin "KJ" Johns, Bert Jones, Ivan Kassovic, Bruce Keller, Steve Knisely, Peggy Kolar, Kathi Koenig, Karen Kovalik, Martha Krueger, Sueanne Kubicek, Arlan Lazere, Sylvia Leimkuehler, Bruce Lenon, Tricia Lund, Lee Majure, Robert R. Marley, Scott Mascher, Paul Manwaring, George Marsik, Tom Martin, Angie Mauldin, Todd Maynard, Leah McGinnis, Chris McIntosh, Nancy Mecham, Dove Menkes, Greg Moore, Shane Murphy, Alex Myers, John Novak, Jim Ohlman, Michael Pass, James Peshlakai, Ken Phillips, Linda Popp, Dennis Prescott, Richard D. Quartaroli, Mike Quinn,

Wayne Ranney, Christopher Reynolds, Pamela Reynolds, Sheriff Joe Richards, Gary E. Robbins, William C. Roberson, John Rodriguez, J. P. Running, Elise Savage, Michael Schulte, Linda Sellers, Jean-Marc Sellier, Tim Simonds, Allison Smith, Drifter Smith, Joan Staveley, Sara T. Stebbins, George Steck, Larry Stevens, John N. Stryker, Joe Sumner, David Swickard, Barbara Theilen, Muir Thompson, Scott Thybony, Paul Toberg, Brandon Torres, Jamie Townsend, Jim Traub, Robert Vadas, Bil Vandergraff, Curtis Verploegh, Vic Vieira, Michael S. Walchle, Mike Walker, Susan Warner, Earl Weiner, Steven Wells, Robert E. White Tim Whitney, Mary Williams, Bryan Wisher, Peter Wenz, Evan Widling, Wade Wixom, Tom Workman, Mike Wynn. and Marc Yeston. Without the various contributions of these people, *Over the Edge: Death in Grand Canyon* would not be as complete a book as it is.

An onerous task once a book like this begins to assume draft form is reviewing it for accuracy, for readability, and for tone. We had helpers here too. Richard D. Quartaroli not only read an early draft for accuracy, he cross-checked the numbers of fatalities in various categories and a few river flow levels attending whitewater incidents. As an accomplished historian of the Colorado River in Grand Canyon, Quartaroli made suggestions and corrections too numerous for us to list here, but vital to improving the quality of this book. We owe him a large debt.

Likewise Canyon historian Michael F. Anderson combed a draft and found a few more gaffes and some prose offering gray instead of black and white exposition.

Several other people read working drafts of this book for readability, vital services from our point of view. Susan Kelly Ash, Hazel Clark, Daniel D. James, Tom Martin, Becky L. Myers, Sharon L. Myers, Ken Phillips, and Bil Vandergraff all made very important observations and suggestions, which again improved *Over the Edge: Death in Grand Canyon* beyond our original work. The latter two, NPS Rangers in Grand Canyon, also offered additional details on incidents during which they had responded as rescuers. Sharon L. Myers, Tom's mother, deserves special thanks for reviewing yards and yards of microfilm records in search of illusive incidents, until bleary-eyed.

Kim Besom of the Grand Canyon NPS Study Collection not only went beyond the call of duty in helping us locate missing data from hard-to-find incident reports, as a student of ancient Puebloan rock art she also designed the petroglyph elements heading our chapters. We owe extra thanks to Kim for improving the book's accuracy and also for enhancing its look and feel.

Superintendent Robert Arnberger remained interested in this project throughout; one of his most important suggestions was to incorporate several more "near-misses" than we had intended (due to space considerations). Doing this turned out not only to vastly increase the number of upbeat stories in this book—and thus improve the book's feel—it also revealed several lessons in survival, techniques of rescue, and amazing tales of both foolish adventure and heroic rescues.

We also want to acknowledge help from a source that is all too easy for a parent to forget: our children—Conan, Cliff, Crystal, Brittany, Alexandra and Weston—have provided us with daily reminders of how precious the gift of life is and that it is our duty to preserve it.

Introduction

Why A Book On Death?

W hy did we write a second edition of this book? A decade has passed since the first edition of this book hit the stores. Since then, unfortunately, about 100 more people have perished within Grand Canyon, some of them in ways new and unique, others in ways old but still tragic. This new edition analyzes *all* known fatalities. It also revises many of the older fatal episodes treated in the original book with new information. More to the point, this second edition presents scores of astonishing new episodes in detail. This new edition contains roughly 150 additional pages describing more recent fatal events and also recounting scary near misses that offer us important lessons hard won through the misadventures of the survivors.

Why a book on death to begin with? At first glance, this book's title may seem lurid, exploitative, and even macabre. Nothing could be farther from the truth regarding its contents. We are convinced that few people have died in Grand Canyon due to causes that can be assigned merely to bad luck or an unforeseeable act of God. Instead, nearly all the fatalities known within the Canyon have resulted from decisions made by the victims and/or by those responsible for those victims' safety. In short, as trite as it may sound, traumatic death in Grand Canyon is rarely an "accident" strictly as defined by Webster's Dictionary as an "unforeseeable incident."

Hence, if most "accidental" fatalities are not unforeseeable events in the true sense, but instead are what statisticians would term the "rare outcome" one would *expect* to happen given a set of specific conditions or decisions (such as not wearing a life jacket while boating the Colorado River), then many of us would benefit from learning what these given conditions and decisions are which increase the odds of being killed while visiting, boating through, hiking in, or flying over Grand Canyon.

We realize too that when we look here at decisions which contributed to some people's deaths we also may be treading on someone's toes. Our intent in this book is not to assign blame. It is instead to identify the kinds of mistakes and decision making which commonly kill people in Grand Canyon. By identifying these and sharing them, we may all be in a far better position to avoid or prevent such lethal errors in the future. Again, instead of blame, we seek understanding. It is, after all, only this sort of knowledge—combined with common sense—that saves lives.

Indeed, both of us have spent years within the Canyon, boating, hiking, bouldering, and orienteering cross-country. And we both admit that we have made decisions that we survived partly because of luck. Because luck is an undependable commodity, we admit here to a certain humility in our judgment of others' lack of it. There, but for the grace of God, might have gone either of us.

Beyond the life-saving lessons that the episodes in this book may teach us, most of its stories of Grand Canyon death and disaster are amazing, a few are truly unbelievable, some are absurd, and yet others heroic. We hope you find them fascinating as well as illuminating. But be warned: the amount of astonishing history in this book may keep you up past your bedtime.

How important are these life and death issues in America's national parks? The U.S. National Park system, if combined into one geographical entity, would be bigger than its fifth largest state (New Mexico). In 1999, for example, 287 million people visited U.S. national parks. But not all of them had a pleasant time: 4,603 of these people needed to be rescued, and about 211 of them died from falls, drownings, and other accidents. Nor has Grand Canyon been immune to this. As veteran Ranger Charles R. "Butch" Farabee, Jr. notes, in Grand Canyon in 1996 alone, National Park Service (NPS) rangers performed 482 searches and rescues (SARs) involving 377 injured or ill people, 18 of whom died. The one-day record for Grand Canyon is reputedly 12 SARs in one meltdown July day in the mid-1980s. Within America's National Park system, Grand Canyon seems a top ranking trauma zone offering a wide array of unfamiliar opportunities to make fatal errors.

And hundreds of victims have made at least one of them. Overall, the known number of traumatic fatalities inside Grand Canyon is around 700 people. The record year (not counting 1956 when 128 people died in a mid-air collision) was 50 fatalities in 1986, when twenty-five of these died in yet another midair collision. Many deaths in the Park itself over the years—carbon monoxide poisoning accidents in tents and campers, heart attacks, and motor vehicle accidents (dozens of deaths from these alone)—occur on the plateaus. The causes of most of the 700 or so traumatic fatalities below the rims are different. They occurred among a far smaller number of visitors than the millions who have crowded the plateaus above.

This tally of 700 persons who fell victim to the "larger-than-life" dangers below the rims, however, remains a bit tentative due to incomplete National Park Service records and difficult to access Coconino County Sheriff's Department records.

Indeed, until 1974, the NPS at Grand Canyon apparently did not keep a list of traumatic fatalities in the Park. Worse, some reports of fatalities before 1974 have been misplaced, lost, or even discarded to make more space. Unfortunately, NPS employees prior to 1974 are no longer available for queries on the numbers and types of fatalities during their watches. This confusion is further complicated in that, if a visitor sustained a fatal injury in the Canyon but was evacuated only to die in a medical facility elsewhere, he or she is not listed on NPS fatality lists or records. The same thing happens with Arizona Department of Public Safety medical evacuations but is further complicated by the lack in their log books (if DPS were keeping a log book during the era of the incident) of the victim's name, age, circumstances, mechanism of injury, and, again, whether or not the victim survived. Compounding all of these problems, this book is not strictly a list of fatal accidents occurring within the administrative boundaries of Grand Canyon National Park. With the exception of homicides and fatalities in aircraft and from parasites, it is predominantly about deaths inside Grand Canyon, below the rims. Why the hair-splitting? Because much of the Park is above the rims and outside of the Canyon, and because much of the Canyon itself is outside the Park and is instead on Navajo land, Havasupai land, Hualapai land, Lake Mead National Recreation Area, Bureau of Land Management land, National Forest, mining claims, and on private land. We have tried to track down all fatalities despite these complications, but we may have missed a few.

Yet another complication results from multiple reports of an incident which often are inconsistent or even contradictory regarding how or why or even where someone died. Moreover, witnesses often fail to agree on what happened. NPS rangers or Coconino County or Arizona Department of Public Safety SAR personnel focused on rescue or body recovery sometimes miss details in how these incidents happened to begin with. Moreover, some witnesses giving official reports following a fatal incident are reluctant to accurately describe their own role in the ontogeny of death. Years later these same witnesses sometimes report a far different story about what happened, and how. On top of these problems in seeking accuracy, published newspaper reports are commonly skimpy and vague. And sometimes wrong. Hence, in some of the incidents we discuss we have needed to make judgment calls to interpolate between all accounts. We have sifted the reports for what appears to be the closest fit to reality.

Again, that reality can teach us something.

We also want to say we know that there exists another danger here in our writing this book. That danger is the possible hubris accompanying our approach. We attempt here to identify the reasons why hundreds of people died as they did. Inherent in our doing this is the assumption that we know what we are talking about. We think we do. But we do not think we possess God-like omniscience. We are simply trying to do our best based on the data available and our experience.

What is our experience? One of us, Ghiglieri, has, during the last 38 years, rowed more than 160 commercial whitewater trips down the Colorado in Grand Canyon and also worked as a Grand Canyon National Park Service river ranger. The other, Myers, an accomplished backcountry hiker and route finder, worked as a physician in Grand Canyon Clinic for more than a decade, during which he saw, responded to, treated, and tried to understand the ontogeny of thousands of injuries and of all too many traumatic Canyon fatalities.

To us, this book is far more about life than about death. It is as much about preventing the great canyons that erode in the hearts and lives of families from the loss of loved ones as it is about this awe-inspiring physical canyon where these losses might occur. We empathize with the surviving family members who feel deep chasms ripped into their lives. But to save future lives, these lost lives must not be forgotten. Instead they must be remembered—and understood. Understanding, however, requires critical analysis. Such analysis can be painful for surviving family members. Unlike exploratory surgery, the only anesthesia we have to offer through our analysis here is a sense of compassion such that each death is discussed with some respect and sensitivity. It is not our intent to add humiliation to the pain of loss. But in that we are committed to exposing the true reasons for why these fatal errors occurred, we all too frequently have had to call a spade a spade. We apologize for any perceived failure on our parts to retain an attitude of respect to survivors. After all, the goal of *Over the Edge: Death in Grand Canyon* is to increase the survival of Canyon visitors—whether casual viewers from the rims or serious route-finders in the inner Canyon.

Finally, we believe accurate documentation of fatal accidents is vital to preventing future ones. Without such documentation significant details might well be lost forever or simply fade into incomprehensibility due to time, rumor, myth, and failing memories.

The bottom line here is we are convinced that the lack of prevention of preventable deaths in Grand Canyon is a serious issue. Thus we believe our analysis in *Over the Edge* is not just a leap forward in the quest to prevent future fatalities; more than this, it would be lethal not to have written this book. If, in our quest to identify exactly where that preventability might reside, we step on some emotional toes, we ask that the owners of those toes also embrace this goal and sincerely examine their own values and concerns before taking umbrage.

Having now explained our goals to give you the best we could, it's time to drop over the edge.

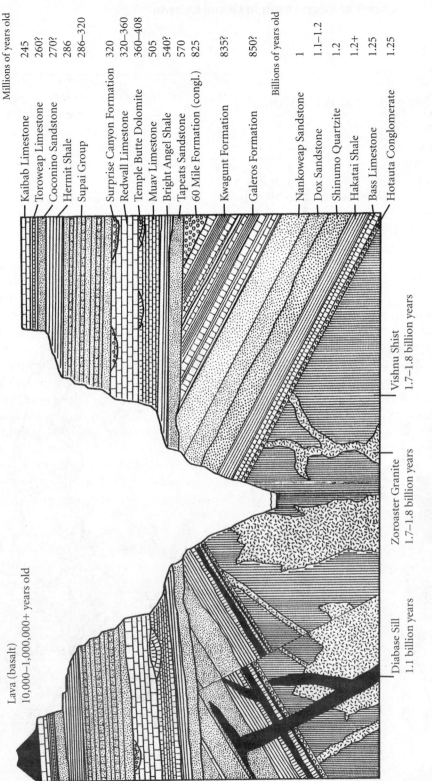

Grand Canyon Geology

	Millions of years old
Kaibab Limestone	245
Toroweap Limestone	260?
Coconino Sandstone	270?
Hermit Shale	286
Supai Group	286–320
Surprise Canyon Formation	320
Redwall Limestone	320–360
Temple Butte Dolomite	360–408
Muav Limestone	505
Bright Angel Shale	540?
Tapeats Sandstone	570
60 Mile Formation (congl.)	825
Kwagunt Formation	835?
Galeros Formation	850?

	Billions of years old
Nankoweap Sandstone	1
Dox Sandstone	1.1–1.2
Shinumo Quartzite	1.2
Hakatai Shale	1.2+
Bass Limestone	1.25
Hotauta Conglomerate	1.25

Lava (basalt)
10,000–1,000,000+ years old

Diabase Sill
1.1 billion years

Zoroaster Granite
1.7–1.8 billion years

Vishnu Shist
1.7–1.8 billion years

Map of Grand Canyon

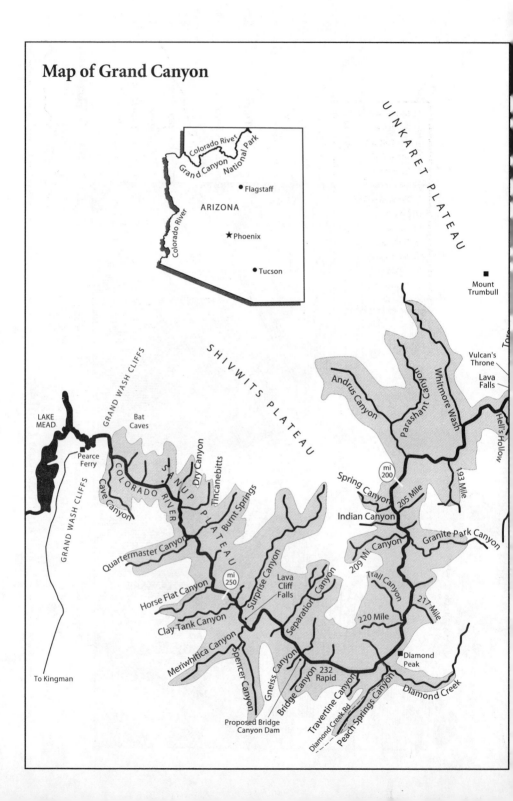

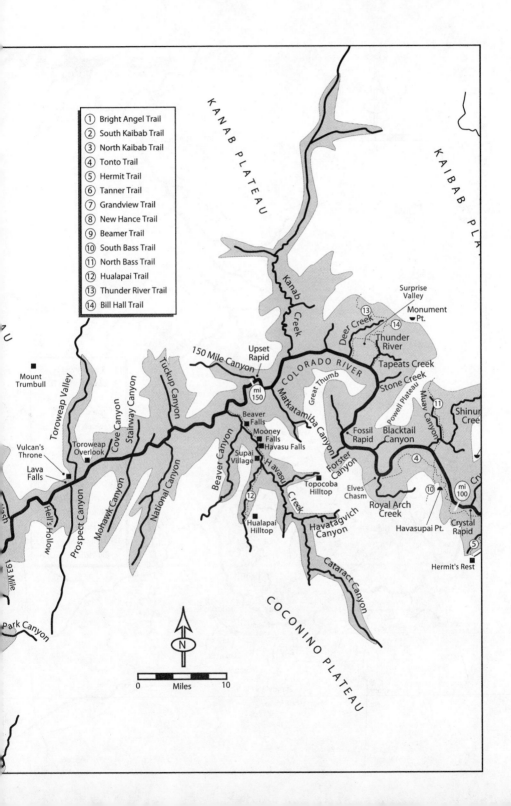

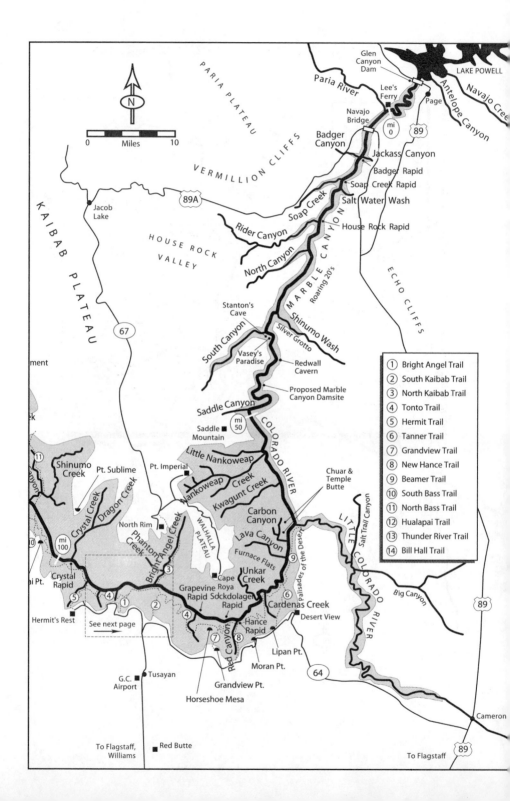

South Rim Village Area and Phantom Ranch

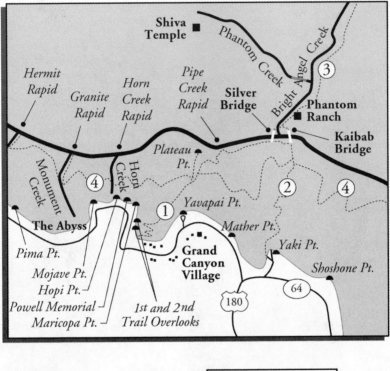

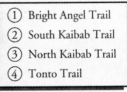

① Bright Angel Trail
② South Kaibab Trail
③ North Kaibab Trail
④ Tonto Trail

<u>Chapter One</u>

"Say, how many people fall here?"

Falls From The Rim

Get her off that wall before she falls off!" Chief Ranger Perry Brown grumbled to Ranger William Bowen as they neared the rim.

Bowen and Brown both stared in disbelief. They each had seen some stupid stunts in their careers, but this one took the cake.

It was the morning of September 15, 1946, the day when stunning Hollywood fashion designer Dee Dee Johnson, age 33, and her entourage were planning a major public relations shoot on the South Rim. They would model several new styles that they were about to market. One of these fashion blasts into the Atomic Age was "pedal pushers," skin tight pants.

Ranger Bowen and his boss, Chief Ranger Perry Brown, had just arrived out of curiosity to watch the fashion show. Hollywood was not a common visitor here. Besides, Dee Dee herself would be modeling these "pedal-pusher" things.

And there she was, the two rangers saw horrified, glamorous Dee Dee clad in a halter top and pedal pushers and posing provocatively on the parapet wall on the brink of the abyss in a death defying pose.

Brown's alarmed "Get her off that wall before she falls off" echoed in Bowen's ears as he hurried toward Dee Dee on the wall. Flash bulbs flashed blindingly. Bowen made it maybe three steps, he would later report, before Dee Dee Johnson fell off the wall and vanished into Grand Canyon....

"How many people fall here each year?" Ironically, this is the question that nearly every National Park Service ranger hears most often from South Rim visitors once they first view the shocking abyss called Grand Canyon. Questions about geology and so on emerge only after this first visual shock begins to wear off. Sometimes this prime question is phrased: "How many people die here each year?" But "die" in this context almost always means "fall." Either way, the two questions seem nearly identical.

Many NPS rangers don't know the accurate answer to either question. But most of them do know a true answer: "It varies from year to year; in some years no one falls from the rim, in other years the number can be far higher...."

Again, a fall almost always equals death. Surviving a fall from either rim is about as likely as being struck twice by lightning. Even so, a few people have survived falls. Their stories tend to verge on unbelievable. Ranger William Bowen, for example, explains what happened next with Dee Dee Johnson in her "death plunge" off the wall in front of a small platoon of photographers:

> If you know Grand Canyon you know there isn't much of anything "over" that parapet wall but a lot of scenery and open space. I quickened my pace considerably upon her disappearance, looked over and noted that she was in a sitting position, facing the Canyon, on a very steep slope and about 5' from a 300' drop. I wouldn't have regarded her as a good risk for life insurance, as the only thing holding her was some debris that had accumulated in her crotch as she slid. Perry hollered at her to sit still. I went on up the wall about 30', went over and worked my way back above her. When I got there I saw a little stunted pinyon about 3" in diameter which was so situated that if I could get a hold of it with my left hand I ought to be able to get a hold of her with my right. She was sitting very still indeed but the debris in her crotch was gradually trickling off into the void, and there didn't seem to be time for a full scale planning meeting so, much against my better judgment, I slid down the route she had just taken and grabbed the Pinyon Tree [sic]. Thank God it was well rooted or Dee Dee and I might shortly have been airborne. I reached out and got a firm grip on the seat of her pedal pushers and there we were. I wouldn't say we were comfortable, but at least we were immobile and we did have an excellent, unobstructed view of the Canyon.
>
> In a very short time Dean Dazey came over the wall on a rope and tied another rope under Dee Dee's arms and up she went. Having no further business in the vicinity I hung onto Dean and we too joined the crowd on top.
>
> There was one feature of the rescue that did cause some comment. In 1946 the "topless era" was well in the future. Pedal pushers featured a halter top. Dean had tied the rope around Dee Dee and, when the rope was pulled from above, Dee Dee arrived on the rim topless.
>
> With a half dozen photographers on hand this was well recorded to Dee Dee's intense distaste. She seemed to blame Dean.

Dee Dee Johnson, topless in her soon-to-be-wildly-successful pedal pushers (but now also with a sprained ankle and a new phobia for heights) was not unique in failing to grasp the magnitude of her error of tempting fate while standing on the rim. Since Day One, it seems, the magnitude of the dangers posed by the sheer immensity of the Canyon's cliffs has consistently failed to compute in the minds of many human visitors. Even worse, for some visitors, the immense vista holds a fatal attraction that exerts an almost magnetic pull. Right up to the edge. Then, as with Dee Dee Johnson, over it.

Half a century later, at the same wall, Fate played out a similar tableau. At half past midnight on May 11, 1997 NPS Dispatch received a frantic call from the lobby of the Bright Angel Lodge. The caller, Clifton Reeder, reported that there was an intoxicated woman outside. She was walking atop the wall behind the lodge, he said, and she was insisting that she wanted to go "climbing."

Alarmed, the dispatcher broadcasted this same message over the park radio. Ranger Keith McAuliffe responded first, hurrying into the lobby barely a minute after the dispatcher's alert. The lobby was empty. McAuliffe continued outside to the rear wall overlooking Grand Canyon. He found Reeder there standing in the dark and peering downward. Reeder turned and frantically gestured into the dark abyss to McAuliffe. "She is over the edge," he said. "You have to help her!"

McAuliffe peered down to where Reeder pointed. All he could see were the branches of a tree vibrating jerkily. Then from the depths came a very scared and clearly feminine call, "Help me!"

Still seeing no one, McAuliffe shifted his position and shined his MagLite downward, sweeping toward the chasm. The beam revealed a woman in a light blue shirt sitting precariously on a steep ledge twenty feet below him. McAuliffe recognized her as Lana Virginia Smith, age 28. McAuliffe had met Smith at a neighbor's house. She was a local Grand Canyon Village resident and an employee of the Fred Harvey Company.

"Don't move," McAuliffe cautioned her, "I'll find a way to help you."

Smith, McAuliffe now saw to his alarm, was not just sobbing; she was so upset and unstable that she was an extreme danger to herself. Smith's perch lay only a few very dangerous feet above a sheer cliff.

McAuliffe crossed the wall for a better look. Yes, Smith's position appeared sketchy in the extreme. McAuliffe wracked his brain for a safe plan to get a rope or a hand to her. The option of him descending the steep, unstable slope to her in the dark was far too dangerous without the protection of a rope. As he feverishly scanned the treacherous terrain again for a safe route to Smith, she sobbed louder and cried out again for help. Smith was so distraught, McAuliffe now realized, that whatever he was going to do, he had to do it fast.

As if to underscore this urgency, Smith tried to shift her location. She slipped downward a few feet. Rocks and debris dislodged and tumbled into a long silent free fall.

His heart racing, McAuliffe studied the terrain again and tried to calm Smith down with assurances as he meanwhile struggled to devise a plan to rescue her.

"Don't move," he advised her again. "Let me find a way to help you where you are."

"I'm really scared," Smith gasped to McAuliffe; "I want to get out of here."

Now, less than five minutes after McAuliffe had rushed into the empty lobby of the Bright Angel Lodge, Ranger Donny Miller joined him. Miller too knew Smith. The two rangers quickly agreed that Miller should assume the full-time role of talking to and calming Smith while McAuliffe formulated a plan to get to her with a rope before she tried to move again.

Miller climbed over the wall and onto the steep eroding slope. He talked soothingly to Smith as he too scanned for a safe way to get a hold of her. McAuliffe meanwhile radioed Dispatch to immediately send technical rescue expert, Ranger Michael Nash. He next radioed for Ranger Matt Vandzura to assist. Meanwhile Reeder had become so distraught and unsafe near the edge that McAuliffe had to order him away from the wall.

Minutes of waiting now ticked by as he tried to review what he would need to do to reach Smith and bring her up without casualties. Meanwhile Reeder explained to McAuliffe why Smith was such an emotional mess. At 12:30 a.m., Reeder said, the bartender at the Bright Angel Lodge had refused to sell her another drink. Smith was despondent over child custody, her ex having been switched from every other weekend to every other week. Pondering this, Smith had been drinking heavily.

The bartender had already served her three shots of Yukon Jack and two beers. But when he had said, "No more," Smith had become agitated and headed for the wall. Now her teetering above the cliff while not being in her right mind was a disaster about to happen.

Maybe, McAuliffe hoped, Miller will calm her down enough that she will stay put until they could harness her into a rope.

McAuliffe heard a scream from beyond the wall. He rushed to peer down beyond Miller, himself now inching precariously downslope unprotected by rope. Smith had again tried to move and again she had slipped and slid further toward the edge of the cliff.

Both rangers' hearts skipped a beat. They were running out of time. Running out fast. They knew it. And they still had no rope.

Smith's situation now looked even worse. She lay on her back in the dark on the steep slope now fifty feet below the wall, spreading her friction thin, and clutching loose, rattling gravel between her fingers.

"Hold on, don't move!" both men yelled to—and at—Smith.

McAuliffe thumbed his transmit button and radioed to Nash to expedite.

At 12:52 a.m., less than fifteen minutes after McAuliffe had awakened him from a dead sleep, Nash arrived with his technical gear. McAuliffe told Nash emphatically that they were running out of time and had to move fast.

As Nash secured a high strength anchor for a belay, the distraught woman lay half on her back and her side and gripped a small tree very close to the cliff. Her screams for help now merged into wailing.

Ranger Vandzura had arrived a few minutes after Nash. He now buckled himself into his rappelling harness and top roped himself from Nash's anchor.

At 1:04 a.m., McAuliffe saw their sands of time dribbling to zero. He yelled at Nash to throw him a rope. McAuliffe caught Nash's rope then tossed it to Miller, yelling at him to catch it and pass it down to Smith.

"Catch this rope!" Miller encouraged the now hysterical Smith as he yanked and gathered slack and then tossed it farther.

Instead of catching the rope, Smith screamed as she slid the last few feet to the edge. Rocky debris rattled off the edge and hissed into thin air. This time, instead of stopping, Smith kept on sliding to, and then over, the edge. At the brink of disaster Smith grabbed a stunted bush anchored in the thin soil.

Miller dared risking a scramble downslope to her a few feet farther, as had done Ranger William Bowen for Dee Dee Johnson half a century earlier. But this time, the slippery and steep terrain, far more treacherous in the darkness, stopped Miller several feet short of being able to grab Smith. Indeed, Smith had now slid partway over the edge and was almost invisible. Her wailing for help was unnerving.

All that McAuliffe could see of Smith now were her hands and head. This was as far as she could go, he realized, and still survive. Her body now seemed to be dangling off the edge in a hideous cliff-hanger.

Screaming and frantically gripping that stunted bush with both hands for dear life, Smith could neither focus on the rope Miller had tossed to her, nor was she willing to risk letting go of that bush to grab anything else.

"Hang on, hang on!" the rangers yelled again.

Smith again screamed for help.

Ranger Vandzura was still not yet fully harnessed, but he hurried over the wall toward Smith anyway.

Abruptly the other rangers' stomachs sank as they saw Smith's last visible hand release the bush. The hand vanished.

Smith called out then screamed in terror in a sickening Doppler effect. A few more rocks clattered downward and dropped off. Then silence.

Hoping for a one-in-a-million last reprieve, McAuliffe shined the beam of his MagLite along the edge of the drop-off. Still nothing. Smith was gone.

Hoping now for a true miracle, McAuliffe ordered Nash and Vandzura to execute an immediate hasty rappel over the edge. Vandzura, still not fully harnessed, immediately rappelled downward over the cliff and to the end of his 150-foot rope. He then dangled in the dark and searched the cliff face. Smith, he soon realized, had fallen a lot farther than where he now dangled. Sickened by the realization that he and his three comrades had run out of time by mere seconds and run out of space by mere inches, he slowly ascended back to the wall.

An hour and a half later Vandzura and Nash had descended farther and finally spotted Smith's lifeless body crumpled 230 feet below the edge.

Alcohol and the world's most frightening drop-off is a lethal combination whose tragic outcome few of us find surprising. Far more shocking, however, is this sort of outcome stemming from a practical joke. On November 28, 1992 Greg Austin Gingrich, age 38, visited the South Rim from Dallas, Texas with his family and friends, including a college buddy who was a former basketball player for the Phoenix Suns. They strolled along the Rim Trail between the Visitor Center and El Tovar. The group separated here with plans to meet back at their cars in the parking lot. Gingrich and his young daughter ended up walking back last.

Playing around to tease his daughter, Gingrich jumped atop the rock wall separating terra firma from the abyss. He paused precariously and dramatically atop the wall. Then, facing his daughter on the path, he wind-milled his arms comically and said, "Help, I'm falling...."

Then he jumped off backwards, toward the Canyon.

His daughter said something like, "Oh, Dad," in impatience at her father's clowning. She continued walking along the Rim Trail reluctant to fuel her father's pranks by acting shocked. Expecting her father to pop up out of nowhere any second, she returned to the parking lot for their rendezvous. Once there, however, Gingrich was the only member of the party who failed to appear.

Concerned, the entire party retraced their steps along the Rim Trail, back and forth, searching for Greg Gingrich. After an hour or two, the sun was setting. The searchers became alarmed.

They contacted an NPS ranger. The Park Service then initiated a missing-person search. They went first to the section of wall where Gingrich had been goofing around, teasing his daughter. He was not there. Fearing the worst, the search team peered over the edge of the rim looking for a body. They saw no one down below.

At this point, some of the searchers were wondering just how far Gingrich would carry his prank. NPS searchers more or less expected to find Gingrich off the beaten path somewhere and embarrassed in being caught in a joke that went a little too far.

As nightfall became a reality, the search and rescue (SAR) team suspected something far worse than a prank. They launched a helicopter equipped with infrared (heat) sensors and a powerful searchlight. They searched closely with these along the South Rim. But, yet again, they found nothing.

Finally, searchers spotted Gingrich's jacket about 400 feet below where he had been clowning around on the wall. Dropping closer near the sheer cliff, they saw the jacket was still wrapped around a crumpled body.

The morning after Gingrich's disappearance, Rangers Ken Phillips and Chris Pergiel re-examined the section of wall where Gingrich had vanished. The Canyon side of the wall was not an immediate drop-off but instead a ledge and then a talus slope that one could walk on, if one were very careful. Scuff signs on the slope revealed that when Greg Gingrich had dropped off the wall backwards while facing his daughter, he had tried to land on that 3 to 4-foot-wide ledge below the base of the wall. The scuff marks suggested that he had immediately lost his footing on contact here and had somersaulted backwards and out of control down the talus before launching off the 400-foot cliff.

Rangers Dan Kirshner, Kent Keller, and Tim Reid rappelled down the cliff that morning to retrieve the body.

Gingrich, of course, was a rare exception. Most visitors don't experience this sort of outcome. Yet all too many have. How bad does it get? Near the end of 1993's grisly, record-setting toll of falls from the South Rim, journalist Susan Trausch summed it up.

> *Chilling statistics from the Grand Canyon this week. Seven people fell to their deaths in 1993, and park officials can't remember a worse year for fatalities.*
>
> *With the exception of a tourist [in fact a local resident] who had been drinking and a drifter trying to grab coins tossed on a ledge, the lives were lost by sober, solid citizens who simply had no sense of danger standing on the rim of the mile-deep gorge. They died posing for pictures, leaning over for a better look, or strolling along rocky paths as nonchalantly as they walk through a shopping mall.*
>
> *Warning signs, guardrails, stern words from rangers, and fear did not register. They were in a park, and that meant the authorities were responsible for their safety, didn't it?*

Are such seemingly foolish deaths truly due to our having grown up in a culture so paranoically obsessed with paving the natural world that we can no longer cope with any terrain that has not been laser-leveled?

"You have to look at each one of them [the falls]," notes NPS spokesperson Maureen Oltrogge, "as a separate incident. But, in general, the falls mostly result from carelessness or ignoring warnings....we issue warnings all the time [handed to each visitor entering the park]. We talk about the dangers of getting too close to the rim. Beyond that, I don't know what else it is you can do."

Speaking also of the bonanza of foolish fatalities in 1993, Chief Ranger Ken Miller noted, "The one common thread from these incidents has been the complete lack of regard for personal safety."

"A lot of tourists approach Grand Canyon like a ride at Disneyland or some other amusement park and think it's idiot-proof," notes Tom Jensen, Executive Director of the Grand Canyon Trust. "The Grand Canyon wasn't built by attorneys and engineers."

But even Grand Canyon has been modified (however slightly) by busy engineers. At a price. In 1908, for example, a team of men was trying to pry up a tree of eight inches diameter on the edge of the South Rim at Grandview. It was spoiling the grand view.

One of the men, D. Johnson, paused for a moment. At that same moment all hell broke loose. The "problem" tree not only jerked loose from the limestone bedrock, so did the bedrock itself in which the tree had been anchored for the past couple of centuries.

As the uprooted tree and the loose rock around it all obeyed the law of gravity by toppling into the Canyon, the tree's heavy roots caught Johnson in the back. These literally catapulted Johnson off the rim and into space.

Johnson sky-dived head first into the atmosphere below. He plummeted between two narrow, projecting ledges of jagged Kaibab Limestone. Hitting either of these might have crushed his skull like an eggshell. Then, one hundred feet below the rim, and after glancing blows from sloping projections, Johnson slammed into a large clump of thick brush clinging to the thin soil above a ledge only three feet wide.

Still conscious and aware that the man-made avalanche of stones still raining down might kill him despite his miraculous survival thus far, Johnson dragged himself under a shallow ledge.

After the final stone rattled past him and whistled into infinity, Johnson risked a glimpse off his tiny ledge to the world below. This world dropped away vertically for almost one thousand feet. That patch of brush had saved his life.

A physician examined Johnson but found no broken bones. But Johnson was now sporting a colorful collection of bruises. Johnson's survival was so infinitesimally improbable that he should have limped off to buy a few lottery tickets before the clock struck midnight and ended what had to be the luckiest day in anyone's life.

Falls (and suicides, see Chapter 9) unfortunately have become a common enough tragedy at Grand Canyon's South Rim that the ranger staff has developed a series of protocols over the decades on how to effectively rescue—or retrieve—victims of falls (or jumps) in the safest possible ways. These procedures are repeatedly reviewed and refined to minimize risk, an ever-present element in SAR operations in such extreme topography.

At further risk of making light of the normally tragic denouement of a fall from either rim of the Canyon, consider Tommy Manis' sky dive. In late May of 1966, Tommy, the ten-year-old son of the assistant manager of Babbitt's General Store at Grand Canyon Village, decided to give his new bicycle a work-out.

Manis pedaled furiously as he blazed along the Rim Trail a half mile west of the Bright Angel Lodge. He was pedaling so hard that it seemed he could get that bike to fly.

And then he did. Manis came to a curve, rolling fast. He knew he had to brake. His old bike had a foot brake; but this new one had handle bar brakes, which now escaped his memory—and his feet. He launched off the rim into thin air. With no E.T. to keep him aloft, Manis and his bicycle plunged 120 vertical feet into the Canyon.

This length of fall in the Canyon has killed everyone else who has tried it. When rescuers got to Manis, however, they found him with a broken arm, scalp lacerations, multiple bruises, and several not so obvious, but potentially serious, internal injuries. His bicycle was not in such hot shape either. Manis ended up in critical condition but did okay during his long stay in the hospital. "Rescuers," the newspaper reports said, "termed the boy's survival a miracle." Just like D. Johnson's survival back in 1908. (Despite the obviously slim odds of surviving a fall into the Canyon, on May 21, 1999 motorized daredevil Robbie Kneivel deliberately launched his standard 500-cc motorcycle off a jump set on the edge of the deep upper drainage of Quartermaster Canyon on Hualapai Tribal land near the Tribal Casino. He gained 55 feet in altitude and shot horizontally a record 228 feet to the ramp on the far side—at the cost of only one broken leg.)

Sadly, however, unlike the miracles of Tommy Manis's bicycle descent or Robbie Kneivel's Canyon daredevil stunt, and completely unlike Dee Dee Johnson's topless fashion fall, during most accidental long falls from the rims, the bag of Canyon miracles has come up empty.

To understand what leads to these fatal falls, one must peruse Table 1 at the end of this chapter. This table—as does every table ending each chapter in this book—offers rewarding reading. Tables 1 and 2 (at the end of the next chapter) reveal that the conditions under which people have managed to fall into Grand Canyon are amazing, but at the same time not consistently predictable. A look at the dates, for example, in Table 1 reveals that, while common, accidental falls from the rims are not regular events. During a two-year span in 1983 and 1984, apparently no one fell off either rim accidentally. Yet millions of people visited the Canyon during those years. Earlier yet, before 1971, a decade passed when, reportedly, no one fell off either rim. In contrast (and as mentioned earlier), in 1993 seven people accidentally and independently fell to their deaths.

Why did all these 55 people listed in Table 1 (up to August of 2011) fall? Each of them was doing something that influenced their fatal outcome. The most cliché activities that many of us assume are the most common causes of "stupid" falls are posing for a photo on the edge and taking one step back too many, or else taking a photo of the Canyon from the edge of either rim and falling off while gazing absentmindedly through the view finder. Sadly, these clichés match reality.

This failure to exercise common sense has often been fatally coupled in Grand Canyon with the desire to "win" the most dramatic photographic footage. Veteran pioneers of Canyon photography, the indefatigable Ellsworth and Emery Kolb, for example, epitomized this gambler mentality. For a stunning photo, they would leap over chasms as mid-air subjects or dangle themselves above precipices by a rope to get that perfect perspective—or even to get a photo documenting their incredible daring to get that perfect perspective. But while the Kolb brothers were experienced and calculatingly competent—and frequently lucky—others seeking the most dramatic images have proved to be neither. Indeed their misfortunes arrived along with the first cameras to enter the Canyon.

This sort of mishap is now so cliché that it has its own punch line: "Take just one more step back...." An early example occurred on March 22, 1925, barely six years after Grand Canyon had become a national park. Lewis W. Thompson stood on the edge of the South Rim to pose—as millions of people by now have done—for a scenic photo proving that he actually had been to Grand Canyon. Thompson's position, however, proved less than ideal for a perfectly composed photo. So he took one more step. Into a crack.

Thompson tripped, lost his balance, tottered, then fell off the rim. He plunged hundreds of feet to his death.

Another tragic camera "killing" involved Yuri Nagata, age 21, on March 12, 1989 at the West Rim's Second Trailview Overlook. Upon arrival, the tour group leader warned everyone, including Nagata, to be careful near the rim. He reminded them pointedly about a tourist named Gesela Elixmann who only three days earlier had sat on the rim with her husband to watch the sunset. Upon standing, she had lost her equilibrium then fallen off to plunge to her death. A few minutes after being warned about Elixmann's hideous fate, Nagata of Gufuken, Japan stepped around the guardrail and sat on a lower ledge. As she dangled her feet above infinity a friend from her group asked Nagata to stand and pose for photo. When Nagata tried to stand, she, as Elixmann had done, lost her balance too. She toppled 30 feet onto a slope. Next she rolled for a second, building speed. Finally she plummeted, screaming, another 360 feet.

Another senseless fall occurred on September 8, 1993 at Mather Point. James Merriman, age 51, was a daredevil transient who haunted this particular overlook to gather "good luck" coins tossed onto small jutting ledges by tourists. Merriman, a Flagstaff resident, used to periodically ride his bike 80 miles to Grand Canyon to collect these coins. Often he would camp illegally in the woods or in a semifurnished secret cave just below the rim for days in the Park until he had harvested a sufficient haul of coinage to have justified his 160-mile round-trip bike ride. After returning to Flagstaff he would treat his buddies to a feast at Sizzlers restaurant.

Only a week earlier Merriman had gotten himself so trapped on an exposed ledge that he had to be rescued from the "zone of coins" by NPS rangers. Apparently this episode created little lasting value as a deterrent. On September 8, Merriman again climbed beyond and below the safety rail to collect "good luck" coins on ledges.

When Merriman saw tourists above watching him in horror, he hammed it up by jumping from rock to rock, inviting them to take his "action" photo (allegedly in exchange for a fee). "Watch me!" he bragged. Then he jumped. Merriman missed his footing and fell to his death.

A rumor exists that after Merriman's death a friend of his found a suicide letter written by him in his camp. The friend allegedly destroyed this letter, although his reason why never has been adequately explained.

Only two months later, on November 9, 1993, Timothy J. Rowe, age 24, botched his action photo, too. While visiting the Second Trailview Overlook on the West Rim, Rowe jumped from rock to rock to create dramatic action for the ideal photo. He missed his footing and plunged to his death.

Another "posing" tragedy occurred on August 19, 1999 at Moran Point on the South Rim. Gabriel Comerford, age 25, asked nearby tourists if they would use his camera to take his photo. These bystanders agreed. Comerford explained that he wanted to pose out on a precipice where the shot would be dramatic. The bystanders nodded in understanding.

Comerford then crossed the guardrail, climbed over a retaining wall, and walked out to his chosen, highly exposed position.

Just before arriving at his chosen spot a rock crumbled under his foot. Comerford slipped off the level Kaibab Limestone and tumbled down a rubble-strewn, bush-clumped talus chute for more than a hundred feet.

Meanwhile the bystander with Comerford's camera continued to photograph him during his battering tumble. The bystander snapped the final photo as Comerford slid to the end of the bedrock chute and as he is peering over the edge of the cliff in sheer horror into vertical air. From here Comerford fell 875 feet.

Several other people have plunged off the rim to their deaths while using the camera. On July 7, 1978 Bobbey Kay Kendrick, age 45, shuffled along the edge of a truly dizzying precipice in search of a perfect vantage point for a photo from Yaki Point. She lost her footing and fell over the edge 600 feet. Less than a year later, on April 8, 1979, Roger Sydnor, age 30, walked out on the Rim Trail near the Visitor Center for a dramatic dawn photo. Sydnor lost his footing on the rim and fell 250 feet. The next such fatality occurred soon afterward, on April 27, 1981 and in nearly the same place. But in an amazingly different way.

Essentially walking backwards while looking back toward the Bright Angel Lodge in an attempt to get an ideal photo of it, Londoner John Eric Hastrick, age 20, climbed over the rock guard wall. He continued the few feet to the rim. Again, Hastrick wanted a shot of the lodge, not of the Canyon itself. Astoundingly, while holding his camera to his face, Hastrick continued backing up toward the Canyon. He soon lost his footing, lost terra firma, and fell 330 feet. Unbelievable.

Yet another tragic attempt to get the perfect photo was caused by a crumbling ledge of Kaibab Limestone at Cape Royal. On September 7, 1993 Lori Newcomb, age 31, walked far out on the edge of a ledge to take a photo. The ledge itself crumbled under Newcomb's weight. She slipped and fell 20 feet, rolled and slid down a terrace, then plunged 60 feet farther to her death. On November 23, 2001 Fern Beuchart Shelton, age 72, asked her husband to take her photo at Tuweep Point on the North Rim. As she walked to the overlook to pose, she slipped and fell off 675 feet.

As of August, 2011 these two activities—posing for or taking photographs—account for 8 and 4 victims (21 percent) of the 55 total victims of accidental lethal falls from the rims.

What killed the many other victims of accidental falls from the rims?

Eight—all males—of the 55 victims were rock climbing or scrambling or leaping from ledge to ledge without technical protection (ropes, pitons, chocks, nuts, friends, etc.). On June 7, 1958, for example, Donald L. Mark, age 43, took a break from his job as a Grand Canyon motel clerk and climbed over the guard wall behind El Tovar. He descended partway down the cliff as a solo, recreational climber. An audience gathered above him to watch his climbing technique and to marvel at his incredible nerve above such a dizzying exposure. Mark next appeared to be "putting on an act" by "playfully jumping from rock to rock." He "continually looked up at the crowd" still gathering to watch. He had fair footing, one witness later reported, but poor handholds. On Mark's next climbing move, he lost his grip. And his balance. He fell over backwards into the abyss, plunging 300 feet.

Three other victims—again all male and most fairly young—were not even climbing but simply "goofing-off" in the most ridiculous of locations. As mentioned earlier, on November 28, 1992 Greg Austin Gingrich, age 38, jumped atop, then over, the rock wall along the Rim Trail near El Tovar. Again, he missed his landing and fell 400 feet. On September 5, 1993 Andreas Zimmerman, age 24, jumped from one ledge to another on the edge at Cape Royal just for the hell of it. He slipped and fell to his death. Two months later, on November 16, 1993 James Hyland, age 21, decided to walk atop the frosty guard wall built to separate people from the abyss below El Tovar Hotel. He too slipped and fell.

Since the first recorded falls from the rims, such reckless ones have been standard—like the following one reported in the July 30, 1920 edition of the *Coconino Sun*:

> Tourists at El Tovar hotel, Grand Canyon, came very near being treated to a thrill on Saturday that is not down on the regular schedule. A lot of them were standing near the wall in front of the hotel watching a chap about a hundred feet below the surface of the rim, who had managed to get a couple of hundred feet down the side of the cliff and was working his way back up to the top. Everyone was holding their breath and suddenly everyone lost it, for the young man lost his hold and fell. Twenty feet lower he struck on his back on a narrow ledge, by a miracle sticking there. But for the ledge he would have dropped several hundred feet. He got up, lighted a cigarette, and finished his climb to the top.

Many of the accidental falls off the rims discussed so far seem so bizarre as to beg reality. How so many people could manage to mismanage their footing on such relatively easy terrain offering a dizzyingly nearby vista that screams "WATCH

OUT, DON'T FALL!" almost defies belief. Consider the case of Richard Peña.

Late on a cold January day in 1985, Richard Peña and his family visited the West Rim to take in the view. Snow had fallen days earlier and the exact position—or edge—of the rim itself lay somewhat hidden under a few inches of frozen white fluff. For reasons known only to Peña himself, he climbed over the National Park Service safety railing at the First Trailview Overlook to get a couple of feet closer to the view.

His young son warned him, "Hey, Dad, the sign says you're not supposed to go past the rail."

Peña turned to him and allegedly said, "You gotta take some chances in life."

Then, stepping on snow which had nothing underneath it but a few hundred feet of air, Peña vanished from view and plummeted into the frozen abyss.

By a strange coincidence, NPS Ranger Rod Losson was hiking up the Bright Angel Trail at this instant. He heard Peña scream. Losson looked up and watched Peña plunge more than three hundred feet.

Meanwhile, his shocked family tried to see where he had hit. Failing in this, they hurried to find an NPS ranger. They explained to the ranger what had happened. He activated an NPS search and rescue (SAR) chopper that launched almost immediately. The SAR personnel searched the cliffs and terraces in the fading light of dusk. Minutes after launching, they spotted Peña's body 350 feet below the rim sprawled on a terrace. The body lay contorted, broken-looking, and apparently lifeless. In that the sun had set and darkness was falling and recovery of the body would be extremely risky for the rangers, the SAR team decided that it would be much safer to recover Peña's corpse in the morning during daylight.

The family was appalled. What if Peña were still alive down there? They were so upset at this perceived self-serving attitude of Park personnel that they threatened to sue the NPS. Meanwhile rumors circulated at the South Rim that a routine background check on Peña allegedly revealed that he was wanted for two counts of murder in Los Angeles County. (Law enforcement officials at the South Rim recall these rumors but, in 2000, were unable to substantiate their source.)

Park SAR personnel recovered Peña's body the next day. A post-mortem exam determined the time of death to have been upon impact.

Peña's nonchalance in the face of such a strong possibility of violent death was not unique. At least seven other victims, six of them women, revealed much the same attitude of nonchalance and seemingly were felled by their neuro-physiology. All six had either sat right on the edge, at the brink of infinity, or had approached it on foot. Yet each one, through dizziness or loss of balance or suffering vertigo— caused perhaps by each victim having lost her or his habitual visual cues of the "normal," i.e. level, world—slipped into that infinity. Some of these victims may have slipped or tripped simply because they were only accustomed to walking on artificially leveled and surfaced terrain. This is a very likely extenuating factor. For every fatal fall from the South Rim, for example, possibly twenty other victims on the rims have simply tripped on imperfections of the Kaibab Limestone and suffered injuries (some of these victims threatened to sue the National Park Service for not laser-leveling the paths perfectly).

These six fatal falls mentioned above include the July 17, 1947 episode of Fred Harvey company employee Herbert E. Kolb, age 17, again due to some sort of dizziness. Kolb had crawled through the guardrail with his girlfriend to sit on the edge of the cliff at Hopi Point. When the pair rose to leave, Kolb lost his equilibrium and slipped off the rim. He plummeted such a long distance that Park rangers could not locate Kolb's body. Desperate, they hit on a scheme taken from Mark Twain's *Tom Sawyer*. The rangers nudged a bale of hay off the exact spot from where Kolb had fallen and watched its descent. After climbing down by an old mining access route, they found Kolb and the hay scattered 950 feet below.

Many years later former Arizona Governor Jack Williams wrote a story ("*From the Ground up: Stories of Arizona's Mines and Early mineral Discoveries, 1881-1981*," published by Phelps Dodge) that two young Fred Harvey employees, male and female, were sitting on the rim in 1951 when somehow the male fell off, plummeting 1,500 feet. The Park rangers found the young man's body near the long-abandoned John Hogan Orphan Mine. Here they noted (among the scattered hay and what was left of the fallen kid) a crusty yellow mineral. Upon analysis, the mineral turned out to be high-grade uranium ore. This discovery ultimately led to the Western Gold and Mining Company acquiring the patent for the Orphan Mine (which had been grandfathered as a claim even after Grand Canyon became a national park in 1919), and it ushered in the beginning of uranium mining here during the onset of the Atomic Age. Governor Williams' story did not include an ID on the fall victim. Although some historians doubt the veracity of his story, Williams' date simply may be slightly wrong and the victim was likely Herbert E. Kolb.

To continue with this "dizzy" theme, two years later, on September 14, 1949 Minnie Edith Kindig, age 63, walked to the rim. The view was apparently so shocking to her that she fainted and collapsed to her knees. She toppled off the rim, falling 500 feet from Yaki Point. On April 12, 1971 Elizabeth Hazelhurst, age 21, was sitting on the edge of the rim with her sisters at Mojave Point. When she tried to get to her feet, she slipped and fell about 350 feet. Informal information (we were unable to verify this) from one sister instead suggests hallucinogenic drug use and a possible desire to "fly off the rim." On October 8, 1981 Maria C. Alfaro, age 23, walked to the edge, off the Rim Trail near the Visitor Center, to sit on the rim and watch the sunset. She slipped and fell 400 feet. On March 9, 1989 Gesela Elixmann, age 34, (mentioned earlier) sat then tried to stand on the edge at Mojave Point. She became dizzy and fell off, plunging 500 feet. Yuri Nagata, age 21, (also mentioned earlier as a photo-posing fatality) also became disoriented and lost her balance as she was sitting and tried to stand for a photo. She too plunged to her death.

Again, a common factor in these deaths is each victim seemingly became disoriented due to the visual shock of looking down into such an immense hole and, in seeing nothing for an instinctive reference point for orientation, lost her or his balance. Notably, all of these victims had ignored posted warning signs and also bypassed or climbed past guardrails or walls to get to the edge from whence they fell. Yet problems with depth perception and orientation are nearly ubiquitous and clearly play a role in rim falls. As mentioned earlier, falls (and suicides, see Chapter 9) unfortunately have become such a common enough tragedy at Grand Canyon's South Rim that the ranger staff has developed protocols on how to effectively rescue—or retrieve—victims of falls (or jumps) in the safest possible ways. These procedures are repeatedly reviewed and refined to minimize risk, an ever-present element in SAR operations in such extreme topography. But even the most experienced SAR personnel under highly controlled circumstances can fall prey to the Canyon's illusionary effect on depth perception. To illustrate both processes, here's a glimpse at one surprising rescue.

In fall of 2004 NPS Dispatch radioed rangers that a tourist had just discovered a body below the rim at Mather Point. Was this another fall victim? Park Superintendent Joe Alston was driving near the scene as Dispatch sent out its call. He turned his vehicle toward Mather Point.

Alston had worked his way up through the ranks, starting as a fire fighter in 1970, then as an inner Canyon ranger in 1972, then a river ranger in 1973. He had seen more than his share of mayhem during his backcountry and law enforcement years. Even though he knew he was not needed for this body recovery—happily those days were now long past—this situation offered him a chance to see his troops in action.

Even so, the Dispatch call spurred in Alston a feeling of ambivalence. Despite the gruesome nature and difficulty of body recoveries below the rim, they often offered an intriguing break from the mundane. The who-dunnit and the why, how, and when questions attending a discovered corpse always posed a mystery. And the challenge and rush of rappelling over the edge always jacked up the adrenalin. On the other hand, such body recoveries and evidence sweeps always posed danger and well, frankly, they proved disgusting. Sometimes the actual "recovery" degraded into merely scooping up bits and pieces because the victim had exploded like a watermelon on impact. Moreover, every body recovery equated to another unnecessary tragic death. The bottom line? It was never a happy task.

This time—October 15, 2004—it might be worse yet. This corpse might prove a victim of murder. Recently a 13-year-old local boy named Justin Richardson had vanished after hanging out in the woods a few miles outside the Park with friends. Several weeks of searching had turned up nothing. Searchers suspected foul play or suicide. Many people thought his body would show up below the rim.

Alston parked at the scene. There he saw several NPS personnel milling on the rim and peering over the edge. One ranger stared through a spotting scope.

Alston joined them.

"Where is it and how far down?"

Someone pointed. "Over there, a hundred, maybe two-hundred feet down. Hard to say from this angle."

Alston scanned below into the yawning chasm. Yep, a few hundred feet away and at least 100 feet straight down, a body seemed lodged in the talus. Correction: At least part of a human body seemed to be down there. A pair of booted feet protruded from beneath an orange tarp. They looked like combat boots.

Alston stared harder. This body looked like no other he had ever seen. Something here seemed not right.

The magnified view through the scope confirmed the feet were at rigid, right angles to the unnaturally stiff legs and perfectly symmetrical. Was it rigor mortis? Can a body fall such that its feet and ankles "freeze" in that position? Stranger yet, the legs and boots seemed unusually small. Maybe the victim was a child. Maybe it was the missing Richardson boy. Or maybe a small woman? But why combat boots?

No matter where one positioned oneself on the rim, every angle of view provided only a limited and unsatisfactory perspective of the body. Even so, Alston concluded, something still seemed not quite right about this body.

As the technical-rescue-trained ranger rappelled off the rim into nothingness several pairs of puzzled eyes followed his every move.

What were a pair of combat-booted feet doing down there protruding as stiff as two-by-fours from under an orange tarp? The SAR ranger reached the site after less rappelling than anyone anticipated. The open mic of his radio erupted with a chain of expletives. He almost immediately started his ascent back to the rim, climbing the difficult wall in the heat.

Everyone anxiously listening on the receiving end stared at each other. What the hell had gotten into him? Alston frowned. Well, he had gotten to see—and hear—his troops in action alright. But clearly this ranger on the rope needed a little refresher course on radio protocols.

The rescue ranger ascended the rope. It did not take him long. He arrived on the rim sweaty, fatigued, and wearing a poker face. The throng of onlookers fidgeted as they waited for him to un-harness.

Strangely, the ranger seemed to have nothing to report. The suspense was killing the crowd.

"You know your mic was open for the last ten minutes?" someone asked him.

The ranger gave an "oops" look but remained silent. He took another breath. He unslung his pack.

Someone finally blurted an impatient, "Well—?"

Now that the SAR ranger had played the crowd until it seemed poised on the verge of violence, he grinned and, with the flourish of a practiced magician, he yanked from his pack a foot-and-a-half-long G.I.-Joe doll.

"Joe," we might add, had used an orange plastic parachute for his first jump into Grand Canyon.

Sadly, Justin Richardson has never been found despite weeks of searching.

Another fatal factor in rim incidents is nightfall. Six other victims—five of them males—fell at night while camping or walking alone. A possible culprit in many of these fatalities may be the male urge to urinate off high places combined with dizziness (and possibly alcohol consumption). Other male victims (see Chapters 2 and 5) apparently have fallen to their deaths from heights within the Canyon or toppled forward into the river to drown while urinating. Following one's urine into oblivion, by the way, makes for a poor epitaph.

Surprisingly, another category for unplanned plunges involves motor vehicle accidents, usually at slow speed—or even parked. Five people have died accidentally this way. The most tragic of these is the case of James Lloyd Qualls, age 5, and Harold Frank Qualls, 15 months old, visiting with their family from Brownsville, Texas. On June 8, 1958 the two boys' father had parked the family sedan (with both boys in it) at a lookout point on the rim above the Little Colorado River eight miles west of Cameron. The father, Frank Qualls, age 28, had left the transmission in gear, but in the highest gear of "overdrive" (which offered the least resistance to the vehicle rolling). Qualls also had failed to set the parking brake.

While the adults were 200 feet away admiring the view, they sent another relative, Kenneth Dull, age 10, back to the car to fetch a camera in the glove compartment. Dull said the car started rolling as he opened the door. Dull jumped aside. After rolling only 25 feet, the car plunged over the rim 100 feet into the gorge, ricocheting off rocks, then exploding into flames.

The earliest victim of a vehicle plunge into the Canyon was Waddy Thompson Ligon, age 73. On October 29, 1925 Ligon drove his converted Ford Model T down the old, very narrow "Dugway" about 2 miles south of Lees Ferry. The wheels on the right side of the Model T slid off the narrow dugway as he backed up. The vehicle slid off the steep road and jammed into a crevasse, pinning and killing Ligon.

The only high-speed motor vehicle fatality not suspected to be a suicide was that of Elroy Ponyah, age 17. On May 1, 1971 Ponyah missed a turn and drove his newly acquired 1967 Ford sedan off Highway 64 at Tappan Springs Canyon. The vehicle leaped the gorge and hit the opposite wall 40 feet lower. Days passed before someone found him.

Bennett Hanna experienced an almost unbelievable accident on Hualapai Hilltop on August 19, 1972. Hanna had just dropped off some friends at the trailhead into Havasu. As he backed up to turn his car around, he reversed too far and plummeted backwards off the vertical edge for 500 feet.

Two victims of work-related falls include accidents while working near the edge. Philo Anderson became entangled in a rope while lowering a section of pipe on November 24, 1927. He fell 300 feet off the North Rim. Months later, on June 12, 1928, Lane McDaniels, age 42, was working on the partially constructed Navajo Bridge at River Mile 4. Despite this being the tallest steel bridge in the world at this time, the supervisors vetoed rigging safety netting under the bridge because they were sure that hot rivets dropping by accident might ignite it. McDaniels, unfortunately, missed his footing on a scaffold. He fell. There being no net, he plummeted about 470 feet into the Colorado River.

His fellow workers stared down in horror. They said that, upon impact, McDaniels' body seemed to "burst and flatten out" on the surface of the water. Four steelworkers quit after McDaniels death, not as much from fear of falling as from the dismal prospect of being swallowed up by the turbulent waters of the Colorado if they did fall, with no hope that their bodies would ever be recovered.

Some rim-falls are not merely suspected but known to have been alcohol related. Lawrence Jackson, age 24, who fell off the rim above Badger Overlook on August 14, 1993, had been drinking "heavily." As mentioned earlier, so had Lana Virginia Smith, age 28, who fell off the wall (and the South Rim) on May 11, 1997, and L. C. Hanley in 1935 did the same. It is unknown, however, to what degree, if any, alcohol may have contributed to the actions that led to the falls of other victims in Table 1.

What are the bottom lines regarding rim falls? That the 55 fatal rim-fall victims as of August, 2011 seem almost evenly divided as to their activities during the time of their demise obfuscates a couple of major risk factors. What are the truly big culprits leading to such a hideous death?

At least a dozen of the victims—and possibly more than half of them—had deliberately crossed the guardrails or walls to frolic, walk, stand on, or sit on the very edge. Some others had merely detoured off the safe trail to walk on the unsafe, loose gravel sloping toward the Canyon. Others yet had scampered even farther out, literally onto outcroppings extending from the rim itself to stand on one or to hop from one to another. Add to this mix, snow and ice. At least five, and as many as seven, victims died due to slipping on ice and snow on the rim—often after passing, or walking atop, the guardrail or wall. In short, before they fell over the edge, the vast majority of victims had behaved in an intentionally reckless manner.

A further risk factor, a glaring one, is being male. Of 55 victims, 39 (71 percent) were male. On the flip side only 16 rim fall victims were women. Table 1 (and all the other tables in this book as well) reveals in spades that men take far more lethal risks, even at the relatively "tame" lookout points on the rims, than women do. Again, all eight victims who were rock-hopping and trying to appear fearless for an audience of friends, family, or even strangers—and often doing so for someone's camera—when they slipped off bedrock to their long death plunges were men. All five victims who accidentally dropped off the South Rim in motor vehicles were male, and all died due to the actions of men. All five victims who died while rock-climbing or scrambling on the rims were also men.

On the other hand, even though "only" a quarter of accidental fatal rim falls have been of women, this is the second highest proportion of women victims in any group of people dying traumatically in any one way in Grand Canyon. In other words, for women at Grand Canyon, this is a very high level of representation (see Table 11 at the end of the book). Women, it appears, are less careful of falls from the rims than they are, as we will see in later chapters, of all other Canyon dangers except that incurred by flying with male pilots.

Youth also plays a role. As of August, 2011 half the 52 rim fall victims of known age (N = 26) were 29 years old or younger. Of these 26 people, however, only 9 were younger than age 20. This reveals that the age group at greatest risk of falling off the rims is that between 20 and 29 years old, with 13 men and 4 women having been lethally reckless.

What about kids? In our analysis we must exclude the two small Quall children as being responsible for their own demise. They were innocent, having been left trapped in their parents' car verging on a precipice with no brake set. On the other hand, some young people (7 under the age of 19 years old) have caused their own fatal rim falls. As might be expected, most of these were teen-aged boys who engaged in careless behavior.

The first known younger child to die was 8-year-old Anjanette Paya. Heeding a call by her teacher on October 27, 1973 at Hualapai Hilltop (Havasupai Reservation) to come and see the sunrise Anjanette ran along the edge but tripped over something. She slipped and fell 500 feet. Far more recently, on August 24, 2005 16-year-old Paul Stockhfs ran downslope ahead of his father at the Walhalla Overlook at the North Rim to the small peninsular, guard-railed overlook. Strangely, Paul not only ran completely out of view, he vanished utterly. Search as he might, his father could not find him. Neither could the Park SAR team. Finally Paul's father walked 100 feet laterally and spotted Paul's body 140 feet below the guardrail. It seems Paul had run into then flipped over the guardrail.

Not long after this, on October 9, 2007, 4-year-old Natali Yeargan experienced a serious misadventure just west of Mather Point. As Yeargan, daughter of a Luke Air Force Base fighter pilot, and her three siblings and parents were strolling the rim, Natali chose to walk off trail along the rim edge. Her mother led her by the hand away from the rim. Natali's mother next cupped Natali's chin in her hand and told her sternly, "Don't go too close to the edge…"

As soon as she was released, Natali rebelliously bolted across the paved trail toward the edge, lost control, and went over the edge. She fell and tumbled 450 feet. Her horrified father downclimbed to her via a seriously challenging route. Despite injuring his ankle he performed CPR on Natali. But to no avail. Rangers soon recovered him and his deceased little daughter via NPS Helicopter 368.

Despite these three tragedies, the reality of risk suggests strongly that children, especially those below the age of puberty, have proved in general to be far more cautious and capable and safe on the rims of Grand Canyon than young adults who have been infused with greater levels of testosterone. Why are children less at risk? It may be because children possess a more recent familiarity about the dangers, risks, and consequences of falling in the natural world (while many adults have been too long out of touch with vertical drops). Or, instead, it may be due to many parents exerting a double standard on their kids ("It's okay for Daddy to stand this close because he's taking a picture, but this is too dangerous for you"). Either way, this would be an interesting focus for further research. We predict the outcome of such research to be that children possess—and exercise—a far more realistic and careful appreciation of the obvious dangers of the natural world than do more jaded adults. At any rate, one cannot escape the conclusion—one hard for many parents to swallow—that children generally seem significantly smarter, when it comes to self preservation near heights, than adults.

How do we know that Grand Canyon's 55 rim falls were accidents and not suicides? Each fatal incident after 1974 ultimately generated an incident report. From these we learn that most falls were witnessed by observers who reported them as obviously unintended mishaps. On the other hand, 11 of the 55 rim falls were *not* witnessed, but the conditions surrounding most of these did not suggest suicide. Incidentally, as we'll see in Chapter 9 (on suicide) most suicidal jumps differ from accidental falls in several interesting respects. One of these is, while most accidental falls happen during summer season and its shoulder seasons, suicides are clustered in the colder seasons. Of course this difference cannot be considered definitive. Obviously the witnessed accidental falls during icy conditions did not happen during summer. On the other hand, suiciders act very differently than accidental fall victims. Suicide victims tend to leave notes, have recently experienced drastic disappointments in life, are often clinically depressed, are escaping being convicted of heinous crimes, and so on. Even with these differences, however, one or two of the falls we described in Table 1 might have been intentional. We may never know. What we do know is that more people have leapt or driven off the rims into Grand Canyon on purpose than have fallen off accidentally.

Some visitors to Grand Canyon have expressed indignantly their astonishment that the entire rim of Grand Canyon is not lined for safety with guardrails. Most of the rim just sits there as Mother Nature left it. One can walk up to Grand Canyon, then next walk into empty air. As noted by Don Lago in his interesting *Grand Canyon Trivia*, the Canyon's South Rim extends for 1,373 miles. The North Rim stretches 1,384 miles. Yes, folks, this adds up to 2,757 miles of rim. Not only would guardrails along the entire rims require enough steel (and money) to encircle half the planet (note that multiple rails are required for each foot of rim), future victims of accidental falls off the rims would climb through those guardrails anyway.

One well may wonder how anyone at all could fall off the Canyon's rim by accident or, for that matter, accidentally drive off it. After all, a more obvious visible danger posing a more obvious deadly menace but also one so easy to avoid would be hard to find elsewhere on this planet. Right? So how is it that so many people have blithely positioned themselves to topple off the rim as if sucked into some "Final Destination" movie?

For a parting perspective on this, consider the following episode experienced by Barbara Brotman in August of 1973. Brotman, age 17, and a friend had just driven to the Canyon for the first time. It was near sunset and, of course, they had to see it from the rim. Brotman's letter (July 23, 2011) to us reveals what happened next and shows all too clearly just how quickly a danger so easy to avoid turned out not to be easy at all.

> We were eager to see the sun set over the canyon, and we didn't think we had time to make it to the Visitor Center. So we just pulled over on the side of the road and bushwhacked a short distance through the woods to the rim.
>
> As we came out into the opening, we were struck by the gorgeous colors. I saw a big boulder about 15 feet from the edge, and sat down on it to take in the view.
>
> It immediately rolled. I'm unclear on exactly how—did it push me in front of it as it was rolling and then hit me?—but it broke my hip and pelvis, and then trapped my leg underneath it as it kept rolling. All this was happening in an instant, though I remember the feeling of being dragged by my leg. The boulder was much too big for me to pull my leg back out.
>
> Then somehow it stopped. I looked up and saw that it had been stopped by a skinny pinyon pine tree growing up from under the edge of the rim right where it dropped off into the Canyon.
>
> My friend was shouting, terrified. He dug in the dirt to get my leg out—it was caught in a painful position. Then he ran to get help.
>
> If he hadn't been there, I think I would have died of my injuries; no one would have found me.
>
> I don't know how long it took for help to arrive. I lay there, close enough to the edge that I could raise my head and look all the way down into the Canyon. I could feel my femur jutting out of my hip socket and pressing against my skin from the inside. I remember thinking that maybe I was so badly injured I should push myself over the edge and kill myself. I remember thinking I was mighty clear-minded to think this. I also remember seeing my favorite necklace, which had been cut off my neck during my tumble, lying in the dirt and thinking I should reach out and take it. But I didn't.
>
> When the rescuers arrived, I was so close to the edge that they wouldn't walk out to me for fear of starting a slide. They slid the stretcher at me and told me to get onto it. Which I did—because you do what you must.
>
> They put me in an ambulance and drove me two hours to Flagstaff, without so much as an aspirin. I went in and out of consciousness and thought I was

going to die of the pain.

When I got to the hospital, I remember them being taken aback at the first X-ray because my jeans still had metal tent pegs in the pockets. I remember them cutting my jeans off, but then I don't remember much.

I was in that hospital about a week. When I was stable, my parents, who had flown in from New York, had me taken to St. Joseph Hospital in Phoenix so a board-certified orthopedic surgeon could do the surgery. This time I had painkillers in the ambulance.

I remained in the Phoenix hospital, in a full body cast so heavy it took 4 people to turn me over, for about a month. Then my parents flew me to New York Hospital. I stayed there another 3 weeks or so.

I took a leave from college because I had to have another operation that February—I spent my 18th birthday recovering from the surgery there.

I was out of school for a year, on crutches for 2 years and on a cane or crutches at various times over the next 15 years. But as I got older, my hip pain actually ended, and I felt better and better, god bless Dr. Philip Wilson, Jr. at New York's Hospital for Special Surgery.

The accident taught me that cliché lesson about the preciousness of life, and I returned to school and my life with energy, gratitude and determination. I have kept in touch with Dr. Wilson, without whose skill and unusual decision to do a partial, not total, hip replacement ensured that I can walk and hike for miles today.

To this day, as I walk I wonder at the fact that I can do it.

And I never forget how lucky I was. Life is grand. I'm lucky to have it.

I saw your book on my return trip to the Grand Canyon to visit the scene of the crime, and read it holding my breath. It is still frightening for me to read it—we keep it out in the bathroom (no offense, but that's a prominent reading spot in our house)—and I see how many people have died trying to see the sunset, and how several died just before I did that summer at Grand Canyon.

Barbara

The lesson? Be *really* careful near the rim. The only genuine safety and protection for us against an accidental fall at Grand Canyon resides in our own personal common sense and careful behavior. Common sense about personal safety cannot be legislated or insured by paved paths, warning signs, or guardrails. It must reside in the mind of the visitor.

TABLE 1.   ACCIDENTAL LETHAL FALLS from RIMS of GRAND CANYON.

<u>Name, age</u>	<u>Date</u>	<u>Location on Rim</u>	*<u>Circumstances</u>*

Lewis W. Thompson, 40   March 22, 1925   South Rim
*Thompson of Denver, Colorado, who had lost his wife weeks earlier, took a side step while **posing for his own photograph** on the edge of the rim. As the camera shutter clicked, he stepped into a crack, lost his balance, and fell 700 feet. (see text) Coconino Sun, April 3, 1925.*

Waddy Thompson Ligon, 73   October 29, 1925   On "Dugway" 2 miles from Lees Ferry
*The wheels on the right side of Ligon's converted Ford Model T slid off the narrow dugway **as he backed up. The vehicle slid off the steep road** and jammed into a crevasse, pinning and killing Ligon. (see text) Coconino Sun, November 6, 1925.*

Philo Anderson, adult male   November 24, 1927   North Rim at Pipeline
*While working on the construction of the water pipeline from Roaring Springs to the new North Rim hotel, Anderson of Beaver, Utah helped lower a pipe to a ledge 50 feet below. He **became entangled in the rope used to lower the pipe** and fell 300 feet. (see text) Coconino Sun, November 24, 1927.*

Lane McDaniels, 42   June 12, 1928   River Mile 4, Navajo Bridge, Marble Canyon
*McDaniels, a construction worker from Kansas City, **missed his footing on a scaffold** while constructing the highest steel bridge in the world (in1928), bounced off several steel girders, and fell about 470 feet into river. Observers said McDaniels' body seemed to "burst and flatten out" on impact. No net had been placed below due to the worry that hot rivets might ignite it. Four steelworkers quit after McDaniels death, not from fear of falling, but of being swallowed up by the turbulent Colorado with no hope that their bodies ever would be recovered. (see text) Coconino Sun, June 15, 1928, p. 1.*

L. C. Hanley, young man   August 18, 1935   South Rim Village near Bucky O'Neil's Cabin
*After challenging a young man to a fight at a dance at the Bright Angel Lodge (his opponent declined to do battle), shortly after midnight, CCC volunteer Hanley left the dance "**drunk**" on most of a pint of gin. He "wandered along the rim" **solo** in moonlight on the cliff side of the 27-inch-high stone wall intended to keep people on the safe side. He slipped **unwitnessed** and fell 660 feet. Source: letter, "Headquarters Company 847 Camp NP-4-A, Civilian Conservation Corps, Grand Canyon, August 1935."*

Hepzibah Watkin, adult   December 2, 1939   Hopi Point
*Watkin of New Orleans, Louisiana was **walking** on the footpath (icy?) to Hopi Point. She fell off and died of a broken neck.*

Herbert E. Kolb, 17   July 17, 1947   Hopi Point
*Kolb **"crawled" under a guard rail** with his girlfriend **to sit on**

Herbert E. Kolb, *continued*

the edge. When he got up to go, he lost his balance and fell. Rangers had trouble locating Kolb's body so they nudged a bale of hay off the exact spot from where Kolb had fallen and watched its descent. They found Kolb and the hay scattered 950 feet below. (see text) Arizona Governor Jack Williams wrote a story that two young Fred Harvey employees, male and female, were sitting on the rim when somehow the male fell off, plummeting 1,500 feet. Park rangers recovering the body near the long-abandoned John Hogan Orphan Mine noted a yellow crusty mineral which turned out to be high-grade uranium ore. This discovery led to the Western Gold and Mining Company acquiring the patent for the mine and the beginning of uranium mining here during the onset of the Atomic Age. The dead teenager reportedly had no relation to pioneering South Rim photographers Emery and Ellsworth Kolb, and no I.D. was actually found on the person in Williams's story. Although some historians doubt the veracity of this story, Williams' date may be wrong and the victim may be Herbert E. Kolb. (see text) Page 28 of "From the Ground up: Stories of Arizona's Mines and Early mineral Discoveries, 1881-1981." *Published by Phelps Dodge.*

Minnie Edith Kindig, 63

September 14, 1949   Yaki Point
*Kindig of Long Beach, California "apparently **fainted**, collapsed to her knees, then toppled to her death" 600 feet from the east side of Yaki Point.* The Acting Superintendent's Monthly Narrative Report, *September 1949, offers no other details. (see text)*

Donald L. Mark, 43

June 7, 1958   behind El Tovar Hotel
*Mark (or "Lindmark"), a Fred Harvey desk clerk, had **climbed over the guard wall** behind El Tovar and a short way down the cliff as a **solo climber**. He smoked a cigarette then appeared to onlookers to be "**putting on an act, playfully jumping from rock to rock**" on edge of rim. He "continually looked up at the crowd" gathering to watch. He had fair footing but poor handholds. He lost his grip and fell over backwards, plunging 300 feet. (see text)* Superintendent's Report, *June 1958, GRCA #54734.*

James Lloyd Qualls, 5
Harold Frank Qualls, 1

June 8, 1958   Little Colorado Overlook, 8 miles W of
                          Cameron
*Frank Qualls, age 28, had parked his sedan in gear but still in overdrive, with his sons in it. Frank did not set the parking brake. While the adults were 200 feet away, another relative, Kenneth Dull, age 10, returned to the car to fetch a camera in the glove compartment. He said the car started rolling, so he jumped aside. After 25 feet the **"parked" car plunged over the rim** 100 feet into the gorge, ricocheted off rocks, and then caught fire. (see text)* Arizona Republic, *June 9, 1958.*

Elizabeth Hazelhurst, 21

April 12, 1971   Mojave Point
*Hazelhurst of Flagstaff, Arizona had **crossed guard rails to sit on the edge** with her two sisters and a friend. The other three got up to*

return to the car to make sandwiches, but turned around when they heard a scream. They saw Hazelhurst "slip" and fall about 350 feet. Unsubstantiated rumors suggest psychoactive drug use as a possible culprit. (see text) Arizona Daily Sun, April 13, 1971.

Elroy Ponyah, 17   May 1, 1971   Tappan Springs Canyon, Highway 64
*In an **unwitnessed** accidental **drive off** Highway 64, Ponyah of Grand Canyon Village sent his recently acquired 1967 Ford sedan leaping across the gorge, hitting the opposite wall 40 feet lower. (see text) Arizona Daily Sun, May 10, 1971.*

Bennett Hanna, adult   August 19, 1972   Hualapai Hilltop
*Hanna of Peach Springs, Arizona drove and dropped off friends at the trailhead. While **backing up to turn around, he drove his car off the edge**, falling 500 feet. (see text) Arizona Daily Sun, August 21, 1972.*

McCormick, female, 50s   Summer, 1973   Scenic Overlook at Navajo Bridge
*McCormick, an heiress to the McCormick farming machine company, was picnicking with her son and a friend. They **crossed the guardrail**, beyond which she lost her footing and fell 200+ feet.*

Anjanette Paya, 8   October 27, 1973 Hualapai Hilltop (Havasupai Reservation)
*Heeding a call by her teacher, Paya of Supai Village **ran along the edge** to see the sunrise, but tripped over something, slipped, and fell 500 feet. Anjanette is the first child known to die from a non-vehicular rim fall. (see text) Personal communication, Lois Hirst.*

Joseph Fielding Smith, Jr., 61 August 22, 1974   Cape Royal Overlook, North Rim
*Smith of Salt Lake City, Utah **attempted to jump from a ledge** on the rim to a dirt slope about five feet lower. He lost his balance, fell backwards, slipped, and fell 35 feet. Arizona Daily Sun, August 24, 1974.*

Bobbey Kay Kendrick, 45   July 7, 1978   Yaki Point
*Kendrick of Vero Beach, Florida lost her footing while **seeking a vantage point for a photo** and fell about 150 feet. The Saint Ausgustine Record, July 12, 1978. Incident report #78-4408*

Peter Leonard Robertson, 19 November 3, 1978   Pima Point
***Solo hiker** Robertson of San Diego, California was heavily dressed in layers of warm clothes and carrying backpacking gear, sleeping bag, etc. when he experienced an **unwitnessed** fall of 200–250 feet. His body with several broken bones was not discovered for 2 years, until December 30, 1980, by chance by a hiker. Williams News, January 8, 1981. Incident report 80-4677*

Roger Sydnor, 30   April 8, 1979   Rim Trail near Visitor Center
*Sydnor of Manhattan Beach, California **attempted a dawn photo** as a **solo** walker from edge of rim and suffered an **unwitnessed** fall of 250 feet. (see text) Arizona Republic, April 10, 1979. Incident report #79-1257*

Richard Keith Job, 26

December 27, 1979   Rim Trail near Visitor Center
Job of Hastings, New York **stood on the snow-covered edge of the
rim,** *slipped, and fell 400 feet.* Arizona Republic, *December 29,
1979. Incident report #79-6626*

John Eric Hastrick, 20

April 27, 1981   behind Bright Angel Lodge
Hastrick of Radlett-Hertz (or "Hearts"), London, England had
climbed over the rock guard wall to take an ideal photo *of the
touristed rim, not of the Canyon, from the very edge. Unbelievable
as it may seem, while holding a camera to his face, Hastrick backed
toward the Canyon and fell 333 feet. (see text)* Arizona Daily Sun,
April 20, 1981. Incident report #81-0895

Mary Lee Ranahan, 52

August 26 (?), 1981   the Abyss
Ranahan of Scottsdale, Arizona experienced an **unwitnessed** *fall
as a* **solo hiker** *of 400 feet. Body recovery of the 5' 6", >200-pound
woman took NPS personnel 6 difficult hours. Ranahan's name,
learned via fingerprints, was also recorded as "Sandi J." and
previously as "Mary Lee Manning." Because Ranahan carried
no identification: her purse was found in a trash can w/o IDs or
money. and she had fallen at a notorious suicide spot, suicide
cannot be ruled out.* Arizona Republic, *September 24, 1981.
Incident report #81-2877*

Maria Cecilia Alfaro, 23

October 8, 1981   Rim Trail near Visitor Center
*Alfaro, a Fred Harvey desk clerk at Yavapai Lodge from Miramar,
Puerto Rico, climbed past guard rail and went to edge to* **sit with a
friend and watch the sunset.** *Alfaro slipped or tripped and fell 400
feet.* Williams News, *October 15, 1981. Incident report #81-3216*

Richard Peña, 46

January 9, 1985   First Trailview Overlook, West Rim Drive
Peña of Granada Hills, California had **climbed over the guard
rail** *at dusk, slipped in 3 inches of snow, and fell 350 feet. Peña's last
words allegedly were: "You gotta take some chances in life…" (see
text) Incident report #85-0140*

Brian John Vordahl, 32

April 15, 1987   Tuweep Campground Overlook
While camping, Vordahl became a **solo hiker** *from camp and
fell 300 feet* **unwitnessed** *(possibly while urinating off the rim?).*
Arizona Daily Sun, *April 23, 1987. Incident report #87-0795*

Gesela Elixmann, 34

March 9, 1989   Mojave Point
Elixmann of Hasbergen Mazwich, Germany **sat on the edge of
the rim** *with her husband to watch the sunset. Not feeling well, she
stood. Doing so she became* **dizzy** *and fell 400 feet. (see text)* Grand
Canyon News, *March 16, 1989. Incident report #89-0507*

Yuri Nagata, 21

March 12, 1989   Second Trailview Overlook
*Shortly after being warned by her tour group leader to be careful at
the rim and being reminded of the death of Elixmann (above) only
three days earlier, Nagata of Gufuken, Japan* **stepped around the
guardrail** *and* **sat** *on a lower ledge. A friend from her group asked*

*her to stand **and pose for photo.** When Nagata tried to stand, as Elixmann above had done, she too lost her balance and fell 30 feet to a slope. She rolled then fell 360 feet farther. (see text)* Grand Canyon News, *March 23, 1989. Incident report #89-0532*

Jeremy Derron Fahl, 19

July 1, 1989   200 yards E of Verkamp's Store
Fahl of Santa Rosa, California was left by his brother sitting on the guard wall and trying to pick up girls. When his brother returned, Jeremy was 310 feet below an unwitnessed fall. *Incident report #89-2538*

Scott Awodey, 29

June 25, 1992   Francois Matthes Point
*Awodey a bicycle tour guide from Moab, Utah was "**rock-hopping**" on the edge of the rim, reportedly **hamming it up for photos.** Conflicting reports: One says a rock gave way beneath him; the other says high winds may have blown Awodey off the ledge. Either way (or both), Awodey fell 140 feet.* The Salt Lake Tribune *June 27, 1992. Incident report #92-1892*

Greg Austin Gingrich, 38

November 28, 1992   Rim Trail near El Tovar
*After jumping from rock to rock near El Tovar, Gingrich **jumped atop, then over, the rock wall** to the sloping edge of the rim while **goofing off to tease his daughter.** The Dallas, Texan slipped and fell 400 feet. (see text) Incident report #92-4185*

Lawrence Jackson, 24

August 14, 1993   Marble Canyon/Badger Overlook
*After **drinking heavily,** Jackson of Mesa, Arizona was **sitting** with a friend on the rim at Badger Overlook to watch boats floating below. The friend turned away to look at something else. When he turned back, Jackson, **unwitnessed,** had vanished over the edge hundreds of feet below. Incident report #93-2996*

Andreas Zimmerman, 24

September 5, 1993   Cape Royal
*Zimmerman was **jumping from one ledge to another on the edge.** The Bruchsal, Germany resident lost his balance, slipped, and fell 400 feet. Incident report #93-3419*

Lori Newcomb, 31

September 7, 1993   Cape Royal
*Newcomb of Houston, Texas walked far out **on the edge to take a photo.** The rock crumbled under Newcomb's weight. She slipped and fell 20 feet, then 60 more feet, eventually falling a total of 150 feet. (see text) Incident report #93-3467*

James Merriman, 51

September 8, 1993   Mather Point
*Daredevil **solo** climbing transient Merriman of Flagstaff, Arizona who often camped illegally in the woods at the Canyon during summer was **jumping from rock to rock beyond and below the safety rail** to collect "good luck" coins on ledge. He was also "**hamming" it up for cameras.** He said, "Watch me!" to the crowd then jumped, but missed and fell 360 feet. A week earlier, Merriman had to be rescued from this same "zone of good luck coins" by NPS rangers. (see text) Incident report #93-3487*

Timothy J. Rowe, 24

November 9, 1993   Second Trailview Overlook
*Rowe of Madison, Wisconsin was **jumping from rock to rock to pose for the ideal photo**. He fell 300 feet. Incident report #93-4411*

James Hyland, 21

November 16, 1993   below El Tovar Hotel
***Solo walking atop frosty guard wall**, Hyland of Sparta, New Jersey slipped and fell 300 feet. Hyland was the 5ᵗʰ person to die of a fall into the Canyon in 1993. Incident report #93-4467*

Glenn Andrew Higgins, 25

May 8, 1995   Yaki Point, South Kaibab Trailhead
*While camping with a buddy, Higgins of Stockton, California and Holden, Massachusetts became a **solo hiker at night** and fell **unwitnessed** 500 feet (possibly while urinating at night off the rim). In the morning his buddy found Higgins' clothing just off the edge, but Higgins 500 feet below. Arizona Daily Sun, May 10, 1995. Arizona Republic, May 10, 1995. Incident report #95-0985*

Daniel Sloan, 44

May 30, 1995   River Mile 1, south of Lees Ferry
*While camping with others, Sloan of Tuba City, Arizona became a **solo hiker and fell unwitnessed at night** 120 feet off the rim near camp (while urinating off the rim?). Incident report #95-1245*

Hideya Yamamoto, 73

September 25, 1996   Rim Trail near Visitor Center
*Yamamoto of Japan was **solo walking very close to the edge**. Two witnesses saw him, then heard him "slip in the dirt and scream" as he **turned to hurry away** to catch a tour bus. He impacted less than 70 feet below. Arizona Daily Sun, September 26, 1996. Incident report #96-5035*

Lana Virginia Smith, 28

May 11, 1997   behind Bright Angel Lodge.
*During late evening, after drinking at Bright Angel Bar, Smith, a Fred Harvey employee from Grand Canyon Village, walked outside with a friend and sat on a retaining wall. Her friend walked away to phone for help. Smith **solo walked atop the guard wall, slipped off**, and slid 25 feet. From there she yelled for help to people on rim. As rescuers positioned themselves, Smith became impatient, moved, and slid 30 feet farther. She grabbed a tree branch above the precipice. As rescuers set a rescue rope, Smith could not retain her hold; she fell 234 feet. (see text) Incident report #97-1689*

Michael Lawrence Hankins, 26   October 30, 1997   Yaki Point
*During a witnessed event, Hankins of Garden Grove, California **slipped** and fell 360 feet. Hankins was extremely religious, also unemployed. The witness heard an "Oh, God!" and a scream then saw Hankins falling. Incident report #97-5051*

Ignacio "Nash" Jamarillo, 36   July 4, 1998   Worship Site, Rim Trail, South Rim
*Jamarillo of Grand Canyon Village (previously Los Angeles) had been listening to an Alanis Morissette tape on his Walkman during his habitual **solo rim walk**. This time, **unwitnessed**, he apparently fell hundreds of feet. Incident report #98-2075*

Gyula Tamas Szakallas, 32   September 9, 1998   Bright Angel Point on North Rim
*Szakallas **slipped on a gravel-covered ledge**. He fell 250 feet.
Incident report #98-3034*

Gabriel Comerford, 25   August 19, 1999   Moran Point
*Comerford crossed guardrails, climbed over a retaining wall, asked
bystanders to take his photo when **he posed in a scenic spot**. A
rock crumbled under Comerford, and he slipped. Witnessed (and
multiply-photographed) fall of 875 feet. (see text) Incident report
#99-2288*

Hiroko Kawakami, 66   August 8, 2001   Mojave Point
*The guide of a sunset tour made a head count of his tourists and
found Kawakami of Kagawa, Japan missing, having been left
behind **solo**. A helicopter search found that Kawakami had fallen
mysteriously 350 feet unwitnessed. She left no suicide note nor had
exhibited any other indication of a tendency for suicide. Incident
report #01-2315*

Fern Beuchart Shelton, 72   November 23, 2001   Tuweep Point, North Rim
*Shelton of St. George, Utah asked her husband to take her **photo**;
she walked to the overlook to **pose**, slipped, and fell off 675 feet. Two
witnesses. Incident report #01-3496*

Paul Stockhfs, 16   August 24, 2005   Walhalla Overlook, North Rim
*Paul **ran downslope** ahead of his father and out of view to the
small peninsular, guard-railed overlook and vanished. His father
could not find him. Neither did a SAR team. Paul's dad walked 100
feet laterally and spotted Paul's body 140 feet below the guardrail.
Had Paul run into, then flipped over, it? Paul is the second child to
die from a non-vehicular rim fall. Incident report #05-4317*

Matthew Alexander Dickeson, 29   August 2, 2007   west side of Bright Angel Point
*Las Vegas, Nevadan Dickeson was visiting with his brother.
Witnessed, he attempted to **walk off-trail** down the northwest side
of the rock formation near the head of the Bright Angel Trail and
lost his footing. He fell 40 feet then 300 feet. Incident report #07-
6403*

Natali Yeargan, 4   October 9, 2007   west of Mather Point
*As Yeargan, daughter of a Luke AFB fighter pilot (Litchfield Park,
Arizona), and her 3 siblings and family **strolled** the rim, Natali
choose to walk off trail along the rim edge. Her mother took her
away from the rim, cupped Natali's chin in her hand, and told her
sternly, "Don't go too close to the edge…" Natali rebelliously **bolted**
across the paved trail toward the edge, lost control, and went off,
falling & tumbling 450 feet. Her father downclimbed to her, injuring
his ankle, and performed CPR. Rangers recovered father and victim
by Helicopter 368. Natali is the 6th child (<18 years old) to die from
any rim fall and also the third and youngest to die from a non-
vehicular rim fall. (see text) Incident report #07-8697*

Mian Zhang, 19

August 8, 2008   near Yaki Point
*Mian Zhang was walking the rim with a friend when he **veered off-trail onto an outcropping** where the Canadian lost his footing. Searchers found his body 250 feet below. Incident report #08-5383*

B. Holt Vaughn, 62

November 28, 2009   between Mather Point & Pipe Creek Vista
*Vaughn was walking at noon with his son, daughter-in-law, and granddaughter. Vaughn of Broomfield, Colorado **veered off the paved trail** to walk onto the talus slope. He lost his footing and fell 400 feet. Incident report #09-9010*

Andrew N. Stires, 42

October 1, 2010   off Rim Trail between Pipe Creek Vista & Visitor Center
*Stires of Burbank, California was witnessed **off-trail trying to leap from one outcropping** of Kaibab Limestone jutting from the rim to the next but misjudged and fell 500 feet. Incident report #10-6599*

Janice Wotherspoon, 64

February 9, 2011   south rim near Yavapai Geology Museum
*Janice's husband said he had gone to the restroom at late afternoon and returned to find his wife of St. George, Utah **mysteriously missing**, her fall **unwitnessed**. Her husband also said she had left her lens cap and cane on a bench. About an hour later rangers spotted her body and her Canon camera 600 feet below. An informant noted that Wotherspoon was a divorcee with more than $2 million before marrying her current husband, and the two had spent much of it on rental housing just prior to the housing bubble collapse, leading to financial problems and talk of divorce. Death to "suspicious circumstances." Arizona Daily Sun, February 17, 2011. Incident report #11-0613*

Yoshikazu Yamada, 76

October 6, 2012   The Abyss
*Yamada of Fukuada City, Japan, wearing his **photographer**'s vest and walking with a limp was last seen near Bright Angel Lodge waiting for the tour bus. After he failed to board it, an unsuccessful search was launched. Two months later, on December 7, he was discovered 4 miles away and 800 feet below the rim at the Abyss Overlook, a victim of an **unwitnessed** fall (or suicide jump?), by an NPS pilot. Case remains open. Incident Report #12-5004.*

John N. Anderson, 53

March 15, 2014   near El Tovar Hotel
Anderson of Grapevine, Texas fell 350 feet. Rumors that day from casual witnesses were that Anderson was attempting to retrieve his lost hat beyond the guard wall. SAR rangers rappelled to his body. CPR failed. CNN, March 18, 2014, National Park Service Morning Report, March 18, 2014.

This page left blank.

Chapter Two

Falls Within The Canyon

In his search for the recondite mouth of Tapeats Cave Nic Korte had forged ahead of his 29-year-old daughter Ann and her 30-year-old firefighter and mountaineer husband Ryan Leonard. Now he saw he had scrambled too far. He turned, looked back, and spotted the cave behind him. To backtrack, he bushwhacked a shortcut off the "social" trail they had been following.

—I could see the spring and cave below, but I was cliffed out here too. I headed back. Ryan and Ann were about 30 yards away. "We're too high," I yelled.

"I know," responded Ryan.

I needed to cross one face of a rock fall/ravine to get back to them....The rock fall looked ok. It was composed of big (or so I thought) pieces of Redwall apparently consolidated and cemented by mud in between the rocks. I didn't completely trust it. I needed one good step to get across and I saw what looked like a 4 by 4 foot piece of Redwall Limestone.

I reached down and tried to move/push it to ensure it was stable. It seemed ok. Then I stepped on it and it was like a "key" piece to a 3-dimensional puzzle. Pull it, and it all comes apart. The 4 by 4 piece of Redwall was actually 4 feet by 4 inches—just a thin slab—unusual. Pieces of Redwall usually stay blocky. The red mud/sand around the rocks was not consolidated but was a thin veneer with no strength. Apparently the rocks had rolled and were more or less at the angle of repose....a more or less 8 by 8 foot area released with me in the middle. I recall shouting "no, no, no, no!".... I rolled down a slope about 40 feet and then went over a 25-foot cliff onto a rock slab.

Nic Korte's Fred Flintstone style skateboard ride and fall into the pit truncated a pleasant moment of well-earned discovery. He, Ann, and Ryan had camped at the Tapeats Creek campground that morning (October 19, 2010). From there the trio had hiked up the Creek, alternately wading upstream, bushwhacking a little used trail, and route-finding off the beaten track for 2.5 hours to the confluence of Tapeats Creek and the Tapeats Fault canyon. There they had dropped their packs, turned left to follow the fault, and hiked another 2.5 hours ever upward on track-less terrain to find Tapeats Cave and Tapeats Spring. This is a subterranean copycat of Thunder River Spring but one lacking the free-falling, vertical oasis drama of Thunder. Only now they did have drama.

Ann screamed. She and Ryan scrambled down to Nic's position. His head was bleeding and he had been knocked unconscious. Not all obvious yet, but Korte had fractured his pelvis, broken both forearms, snapped his femur in two places, broken a scapula (not an easy bone to break…) and added a bevy of cracked ribs. And he had slammed his head pretty hard.

Ryan, an EMT, made a quick survey of Korte's broken, 59-year-old body then glanced at the rugged and remote terrain surrounding the trio. This imposed a cruel reality check. This situation was bad, very bad.

Ann and Ryan agreed Nic's best hope lay in Ryan hurrying southward to the Colorado River and flagging down a boater carrying a satellite phone. The rub? Almost 10 miles of rough topography, half of it nearly trail-less, separated them from the river.

Ryan rock-hopped, sprinted, and jogged downhill, essentially paralleling and sometimes splashing along within Tapeats Creek between sheer walls of Tapeats Sandstone and Shinumo Quartzite. After more than an hour he had passed the campground from which it had taken them 5 hours to hike that morning. Less than an hour later Ryan reached the confluence of Tapeats with the Colorado.

Ryan found no river runners.

So far Ryan's gamble had not paid off. He headed downstream to search beyond his current angle of view. He followed the River Trail downstream a couple of miles and upslope about 500 feet higher to drop back down into Deer Creek Grotto. Next he had to descend the NPS trail back to the river again to signal people camped with a small fleet of rafts moored on the south side of the Colorado.

After a lot of yelling and arm-waving by Ryan, a couple of boaters rowed across toward him.

Next he wrestled with the group's satellite phone. Several attempts led to no firm connection. As he tried again he knew from prior experience that the Park would not send in its helicopter after dark (the Arizona Department of Public Safety helicopter *would* do this, but Ryan did not know it). Eventually his 911 call to the Park succeeded. Yes, they would fly a helicopter to drop a paramedic team now, but no evacuation could happen until dawn.

Having jogged a half-Marathon and succeeded in his mission, Ryan collapsed on the beach.

Meanwhile Ann tried to keep her father warm. It was October. The injured man lay in broken heap at close to 5,000 feet elevation. The trio had jettisoned their gear miles downhill from here. Ann whacked the surrounding vegetation with her pocket knife. She harvested a bushel or so and spread it over her father to keep him warm.

Korte had regained consciousness and found himself wedged between boulders and feeling as if an Amtrak train had hit him. He knew he was badly injured and he also felt as if he was freezing. But as Ann added her body heat to his by lying atop her bower of foliage he realized she would prevent him from dying of hypothermia. She worried that her weight might cause his femoral artery to rupture and kill him.

At around 7:00 p.m. the Park helicopter overflew father and daughter. Nic Korte's broken arm emerged from under his heap of vegetation to wave at the chopper. To Park Paramedic Brandon Torres the oscillating appendage sticking out of the foliage looked like some primordial life form. Ann signaled the chopper with her flashlight. Then the machine vanished.

"It remained above us for awhile and then left," Korte would later report. "That silence was awful. It got dark. After some time, we heard a whistle."

Inconveniently, the closest landing spot for the helicopter stood nearly a mile down canyon. Medic Torres knew it was going to be a tough task to get back uphill to his patient. With darkness the helicopter would need to return to the South Rim. Alone, he would need all the supplies he could carry to try to stabilize his patient and keep him alive through the night. How badly this guy was hurt remained a mystery. So, rather than leave out equipment that might prove critical, Torres loaded himself up with close to fifty pounds of medical gear. He took a deep breath as the helicopter flew off. He was on his own.

The steep, rugged terrain, darkness, and the heavy gear proved a challenge. Torres divided his cumbersome load into two loads. While traversing bad sections he would carry half the load a hundred feet or so, drop it, then return for his abandoned pile, carry it a hundred feet or so past the first load he dropped, then drop it, and return again for the first load. He rigged a flashing light on each pile he abandoned so as to not lose it or lose his way in the darkness. He repeated this leap-frogging until he finally arrived at Korte's side two hours later.

Torres quickly assessed Korte. The fallen man's injuries looked serious. He injected Korte with morphine, splinted his obvious fractures, and slid a litter-carry backboard beneath him. Next he placed Korte in his heaviest piece of equipment: a twenty pound, full-body length vacuum splint. When one reverse pumps the air out from this splint it conforms to the victim's size and shape like a bean-bag straight jacket. Torres next watched over Korte all night. His positive and upbeat bedside manner provided the best care Kortes could have received.

At dawn the Park helicopter returned. The crew chief dropped a cable to attach to Korte's litter. Next the crew chief winched him up. Secured inside the machine, Korte flew three air miles to Surprise Valley. There a Classic Lifeguard aeromedical helicopter waited to transport him to Flagstaff Medical Center. Here he would spend the next 10 days. None of this was proving a great way to end his 20th hike in the Canyon. After eleven days Ann and Ryan (having been evacuated next) purchased a big inflatable mattress, installed it in the back of their GMC Yukon, and drove Korte recumbent home to Grand Junction, Colorado.

As Korte tells it:

> *I broke most of my left side: femur (two places), forearm, wrist (both major bones), ribs (4), sacrum, pelvis, clavicle—probably things I haven't remembered. Surgeons still promise a full recovery but tell me I have a year or more of healing and rehab. I spent almost four weeks in hospitals. I underwent about 10 hours of surgery over the next two days. My wrist, left leg, hip and pelvis now have permanent metal parts. I'm healing, but it is painfully slow. It will be at least 9 weeks post-accident before I'm going to be allowed to bear some weight on my left side.... Hopefully, I can write about another GC trip some time.*

Rehabilitation will be a long and difficult road, but Korte holds onto his plans to return to hiking the Canyon, admitting, "I can't imagine not."

The short but vital lesson residing in all this? Even though one must be careful while hiking any trail in Grand Canyon, once one departs from that trail onto angle-of-repose, talus terrain, every step must be evaluated for stability—and often fully tested carefully—prior to fully committing oneself.

Once one descends even ten feet below either rim of Grand Canyon, one has entered a new and different world. This world is the most convoluted, massive, and jaggedly vertical landscape on Earth, a vast complicated labyrinth carved by the vagaries of erosion as it removed 1,000 cubic miles of rock in a dendritic drainage pattern that gnaws into bedrock cliffs thousands of feet high and fractures the landscape into 600 tributary canyons. The vast majority of rock surface here is so nearly impossible to access that it may never be visited by humans. The few practical routes penetrating this landscape—most of which were pioneered millennia ago by Native Americans—are themselves fraught with precipices and pitfalls and decaying sedimentary rock that weed out the unwary.

Accidental falls within this Canyon, however, bear only slight resemblance in their conditions and their victims to the falls of tourists from the rims.

This might be because trekking into the Canyon—and then getting back out alive to tell of it—can demand a high degree of skill. But such skill can be gained only in places like the canyons of the Colorado Plateau. Canyoneering is not mountaineering. Canyoneering demands negotiating huge and lethal exposures on crumbling cliffs soaring to vast heights or plunging to even worse depths. It also requires managing this on bone-dry, 120-degree-hot traverses that lead to routes which may ultimately prove not to be routes at all, but instead heart-breaking, dead-end cul de sacs. In short, the Canyon's dangers and pitfalls tend to be larger and worse than those of normal, dangerous life.

From the beginning of recorded history, these dangers have fooled newcomers. The Canyon's very first European, would-be hikers, for example, tried for three days to climb down to the Colorado River but failed. This happened in 1540, less than twenty years after Cortez and his small army had toppled the Aztecs' huge Mexican empire to double the territory of Spain. This 1540 expedition, led by 26-year-old Francisco Vasquez de Coronado, consisted of yet another army of conquistadors assembled in Mexico. Coronado's quest was to discover—and then empty—the fabled Seven Golden Cities of Cibola located somewhere far to the north beyond a vast arid desert of shifting sands.

Several weeks north of Mexico, Coronado led his 336 Spanish soldiers and 700 Indian allies against the Zuñis of Hawikuh (in future New Mexico). After ransacking Hawikuh, Coronado's troops moved farther north along the upper Rio Grande. They looted, extorted, raped, pillaged, and murdered along their way. Despite these local conquests, those elusive Seven Cities of Gold continued to evade discovery. Coronado knew that if he returned to Mexico without having discovered the legendary gold, he could kiss his career—and maybe his life—goodbye.

Finally Coronado heard of another seven cites, those of Tusayan. These were the Hopi pueblos. Coronado sent Pedro de Tovar west to reconnoiter them. Tovar returned and reported that these pueblos too held no gold, no silver, no precious gems; they were not even surrounded by fertile lands. But, Tovar said, the Hopis had spoken of a great river to the west.

Coronado ordered Lieutenant Garcia Lopez de Cardenas and a dozen conquistadors to find that mysterious river. At Tusayan, Cardenas enlisted Hopi guides. Twenty days march to the west of the Hopi Pueblos, his reconnaissance force reached a region of low twisted pines, where, looking north, they beheld a huge canyon with a river running south and then west. North beyond and above this river was a high, barren plateau. The river down at the bottom, the conquistadors reckoned, looked about six feet wide.

The Hopis insisted that the river instead stretched half a league (1.5 miles) across.

Cardenas sent his three lightest and most agile men—Captain Melgosa, Juan Galeras, and one other man—to climb down the least difficult route to ascertain the river's true dimensions. The trio spent three days trying to find a feasible route down to the river. They failed. But they did manage to find a route one third of the way down. But at that point the Redwall Limestone cliff stopped them cold.

Even from atop the Redwall, however, they realized that the Hopis were probably correct about things here being bigger than they had looked from above. Boulders that had appeared no higher than a man from the rim, they now saw were taller than the 300-foot-high Tower of Seville. Continuing downward from the Redwall now looked like suicide.

The conquistadors' inability to comprehend the scale of Grand Canyon topography had nothing to do with the century these men lived in. Of course, Cardenas' Hopi guides knew well their own "Salt Trail" route to the river; they likely smiled inwardly even as they impassively watched Cardenas' three "agile" conquistadors struggling in vain for three days in growing thirst atop the Redwall cliffs. Hopi mirth aside, our point here is that even these tough little men in armor who toted Toledo steel and conquered empires embodied the same two failings that nearly every non-Indian visitor to Grand Canyon since 1540 has exemplified: an inability to comprehend the scale of Grand Canyon and a marked—and often fatal—tendency to underestimate it.

The earliest known deaths due to falls in the Canyon happened to men lured into its depths by hidden mineral riches they imagined must be waiting in its inaccessible nether regions. After all, God would never have built such an immense treasure room—one He guarded with a million pitfalls—unless He had hidden some very valuable treasure in it. These riches, they believed, would be claimed by the man with the greatest faith and the most grit. The Canyon attracted scores of such miners. As George H. Billingsley, Earle E. Spamer, and Dove Menkes note in their *Quest for the Pillar of Gold: The Mines & Miners of the Grand Canyon*:

> When silver was not found in abundance, copper became the number one commodity sought in the Canyon, although visions of gold veins were probably always in the minds and dreams of early prospectors. Asbestos was discovered and mined from the canyon, too, but it was not widely developed, probably because the markets were too distant. In most cases minerals were mined because they were there. It was better than nothing.

The Canyon felt the onslaught of a slow motion, "almost" mineral rush, much of which pre-dated the more organized—and more limited—official explorations of the Canyon funded by the U.S. Government. Indeed, as Billingsley, Spamer, and Menkes report, in search of riches: "By 1890, prospectors had explored virtually every side canyon in Grand Canyon."

But these 600 or so tributary canyons within Grand Canyon were not explored without casualties. Billingsley, Spamer, and Menkes note how "Old Man Snyder," for example, failed one time to make his regular pass through Paiute territory from his mine to St. George, Utah. A few of the local Paiutes checked on him. They found him dead at his mine. Before this mine was rediscovered east and north of Diamond Creek in Western Grand Canyon, it had become one of the "lost mines" that fueled dreamers' quests for lost gold. The mine itself was relocated by George and Sue Billingsley in a breccia pipe above the Redwall in the Watahomigie member of the Supai Group. Its ore contains a fairly rich concentration of copper minerals as well as arsenic, cobalt, nickel, molybdenum, and zinc. But, as usual, no gold.

Perhaps the earliest witnessed fatal fall of a prospector was that of Daniel W. Mooney. Formerly a sailor, and then a rancher in the Williamson Valley near Prescott, Arizona, Mooney too had been bitten by the lure of mineral riches. Bitten hard. Mooney and four other miners filed one of the earliest claims in Havasu (a.k.a. Cataract) Canyon. They found lead and silver, fairly common in Havasu but economically challenging to extract. Mooney and a few others among the dozen associated miners who prospected Havasu's canyon system felt teased by the mystery of what might lay below the biggest falls along the last seven miles or so to the Colorado. This mystery tortured Mooney.

The Havasupai people apparently never traveled downstream of this point, and for good reason: the falls dropped 196 feet and offered only the most hellishly exposed, expert-only climbing route.

Finally, in 1880, Mooney decided he could pull off a descent. As Billingsley, Spamer, and Menkes tell it:

> On a fateful last trip, Mooney took a rope down into the canyon and, trusting his sailor's experience with ropes and rope climbing, let himself down over the falls. Once he was over the falls, the others in the party lost sight of him and the roar of water precluded any verbal communication. Soon they felt the rope slacken and, running around to the side of the falls, they saw the rope dangling nearly half way down. Mooney lay on the rocks below. Unable to reach him, all they could do was leave.

A prospecting associate, Edward I. Doheny, described Mooney as red-headed and red-bearded, and as possessing a violent temper. Mooney was also the spokesman with the Havasupai Indians for the dozen prospectors allied in combing their canyons for paydirt. "Mooney," Doheny said, "was very reckless and did not exercise the caution that 100 percent sanity would dictate. His fall from the place where he had started to go down over a bluff on a very small rope, was not altogether unexpected by those of us who constituted the party."

A few years later, in 1883, Matthew Humphreys would blast out a descending tunnel along the creek's left side. Mooney's friends then buried him almost exactly where he had fallen. In less than four years, however, the thin sands atop Mooney washed away, as prospector William Wallace Bass noted, to reveal his "grinning teeth and eye sockets."

The next known fall victim also sought gold, but the kind to be made by selling real estate. Shortly before Christmas in 1889, Robert Brewster Stanton arrived at the Lees Ferry entry to Grand Canyon with a well-equipped river expedition to survey the Canyon for construction of a railroad within the Inner Canyon. This expedition had launched in Glen Canyon at Crescent Creek, four miles downstream of the Dirty Devil River in Utah on December 10, 1889. Shortly after Christmas, the expedition floated the Colorado into Grand Canyon.

On New Year's Day of 1890, photographer Franklin A. Nims climbed a bit higher than he should have to artfully compose—a thing Stanton had warned him not to do—a photo with the men, the boats, and the river canyon all in it.

Nims lost his footing and slipped. He fell 22 feet onto the rocks and sand below. The other men rushed over and found Nims unconscious and with blood oozing from his mouth and right ear. Nims' right lower leg had been badly broken, as had the bones of both feet.

Nims remained partly conscious but vomited repeatedly through that first freezing night and into the next morning. That day Stanton and the crew decided to carry Nims out of the Canyon. As they were only about 1,000 feet below the rims of what would soon become a mile-deep gorge downstream, such a carry did not seem ridiculous.

But it soon became insane.

The expedition splinted Nims' leg. Next they improvised a stretcher from oars and canvas. Then they pondered possible evacuation routes. Seeing no tributary canyon that looked inviting, the men decided to row Nims a few miles downstream. Near River Mile 17 they recognized what seemed an exit to the northwest via Ryder Canyon.

Stanton climbed out the 1,500-foot ascent first and fastest. Once atop the Kaibab Limestone he hiked 20 miles across the Marble Platform in the moonlight. His goal was Lees Ferry. There he hoped to fetch the ferryman and his wagon. Meanwhile the other men began a 6.5-hour, harrowing carry of Nims up nearly the same route to the Canyon's North Rim. They hauled him, still unconscious, over boulders, and they hoisted him, suspended by ropes, up cliffs. Had Nims seen and understood what his companions were doing to help him, he might have died of fright.

The evacuation team—with Nims still alive—reached the rim that afternoon, only to be forced to spend the night without blankets in a snowstorm while they waited for Stanton.

He arrived the next day by wagon with the ferryman, W. M. Johnson. Johnson hauled Nims back to Lees Ferry. There Nims lay unconscious on the cook house floor for a week. He awakened as a group of Mormons from the north passed through on their way into northern Arizona. Responding to Nims' pleas to take him to see a doctor, they agreed to take him on the 9-day, 185 mile wagon ride to Winslow, Arizona for $85.

After this ride—a hellish one for anyone in Nims' condition—the doctor in Winslow discovered several other broken and dislocated bones in addition to the obvious damage in Nims' leg. He also diagnosed Nims' skull fracture. After administering minor treatment, the doctor sent Nims to Denver for further care.

Strangely, although Stanton's crew had gone through tremendous effort and risk to get Nims out of the Canyon, as soon as Johnson arrived they abandoned Nims on the rim to return to the river. Nims was embittered by this experience. During his month and a half of convalescence, Nims wrote that Stanton's company paid none of his expenses, and cut off his "salary as of January 1, 1890, the day of the accident." Indeed, Stanton never did pay Nims another dollar.

But Nims survived. In this alone he was very lucky. Most episodes of falling off cliffs in the Canyon end fatally. Of course Nims fell "only" 22 feet. By Canyon standards, 22 feet would be considered lucky.

The identities of a few other victims of fatal falls in the Inner Canyon have been elusive. For example, commercial rafting guides commonly used to take their clients up to the Redwall caves immediately upstream of South Canyon near River Mile 31.5 to see, among other things, the "Mystery Skeleton." This was a human skeleton. And it was indeed a mystery as to whom it belonged. Courtesy of river historian P. T. Reilly, however, we have a tidbit as to how it came to lie in its niche at the foot of a Redwall cliff near the ancient Puebloan ruins. Reilly quotes the 1934 river diary of Alton Hatch:

> *July 22. Left camp at 7:30 and passed two or three bad rapids and at last we came to some that were navigable. We stopped at Vasey's Paradise and went exploring. Found pottery, rock houses, and dug up the skeleton of a man. He had dark hair, wore buckskin clothes. Had both legs broken and still had a bad odor to him. I dug back in a cave about 15 feet and found a piece of canvas and an old gun scabbard, a flour sack, and some nails. There were two caves together and this was the top cave. I had to crawl on my stomach to reach it. Bus found several little horses [split-willow figurines 4,000 years old] made out of willows and sticks. I think that they were toys for the children to play with. We camped here and enjoyed the good fresh water.*

Who the mystery man in buckskins was will likely remain a mystery (all these bones vanished by the late 1980s), although, with both legs broken, it seems fairly certain this man died in a fall somewhere in or near the sheer drops of South Canyon (a.k.a. Paradise Canyon). He may, of course, have been an Indian visiting a sacred area including the Puebloan ruins themselves. Reilly determined that Alton Hatch found the rifle scabbard and canvas inside Stanton's Cave several hundred yards downstream of the skeleton. Indeed, they may have belonged to Stanton's ill-fated crew of 1889 (see Chapter 5).

Although several other early pioneers, most likely lone prospectors, may also have met their end via accidental falls inside the Canyon, their stories are lost to us. The miners themselves were replaced in the late 1930s by a new wave of seekers. These were seekers of adventure and diversion.

A trio of these included a 30-year-old Catholic priest, Eugene A. Gavigan, and two teenage boys, John Manson Owens III, age 15, and Walter J. (Pete) Mahany, Jr., age 16. This trio arrived at the South Rim from Savannah, Georgia in late July of 1959 seeking precisely these two goals: adventure and diversion. From there they headed down the Tanner Trail. Their quest—which the two boys had begged for—was to visit an abandoned "silver" mine that Father Gavigan had said he had visited as a teenager. This mine was likely the McCormick/Tanner copper mine along the river about 13 miles from the South Rim trailhead.

Again, the three started their descent from the South Rim on a Friday in late July, the hottest month of the year, a time when temperatures in the shade below can hit 120 degrees Fahrenheit. In full sun, of course, it gets hotter yet. The distance by trail to the river via Father Gavigan's route was about nine miles. The Tanner Trail during the 1950s, by the way, was a far more recondite and rugged route than it is today. The mine itself lay another four miles upstream from the trail's foot. The round trip would be about 26 miles.

What followed evolved into a massive National Park Service and U.S. Army search and rescue effort all begun by the thinnest of threads. Father Gavigan had told no one of his plans, hence there existed no way any NPS personnel would have known anything was amiss when the trio failed to return. Almost incredibly (when one remembers just how big Grand Canyon is), however, visitors to the South Rim near the Park's East Entrance on Saturday reported hearing yells for help drift up from its super-heated, shimmering depths.

Could these visitors, a ranger wondered, have heard the real thing? He checked to see whether any cars were parked near the Tanner trailhead. There was one south of Lipan Point, not parked where he would have expected. Inside it he found a group-kept journal. The latest entry written in it stated: "Tomorrow, we are going to the silver mine."

So someone *was* down there. And in this heat it was likely to be someone in trouble. The NPS and U.S. Army began their search and rescue.

The day before this search began, Father Gavigan and his two charges had gotten a shockingly late start down from the rim. They had left the parking lot on Friday at noon—almost inconceivably bad timing given their goal to hike 26 screaming hot miles, including a vertical mile down and back up, and yet return to their vehicle on this same day. Compounding this bad planning, the three carried only one bottle of water each and a can of beans. They had left their camping gear, food, and additional water in the car. They did, however, carry first aid and snake bite kits.

Again, Father Gavigan's intent was to reach the mine and return to the rim that same day. His simple plan would fail for several reasons, most of which are spelled H-E-A-T. And, making a badly planned hike far worse, beginning atop the Redwall, Father Gavigan somehow missed the standard, NPS-maintained trail. Instead he descended at least partway on the Old Tanner Trail (possibly the same route he had taken as a teenager?). Had Father Gavigan looked a bit farther west, he would have seen the marked and maintained New Tanner Trail.

The trio consumed all of their water that afternoon as they followed trails, some false, some real. They managed to descend below the cliffs to the long slope of Dox Sandstone flanking the river. By now the trio was painfully and dangerously dehydrated.

When Walter Mahany finally saw the river only a half mile away, he panicked. Mahany ran down the slope willy nilly to the river. Neither Father Gavigan nor Owens could restrain him.

All three made it to the muddy Colorado and finally drank, but it is unclear how much. The late hour, the intense heat, Mahany's panic, and their general unpreparedness now made it clear that hiking more miles upstream to the "silver mine" was not in the cards. So the three hiked back toward the rim, toward their car, their food, and equipment.

Dusk darkened the cliffs as they trudged upward, now less than halfway up. Already their water bottles were empty again and hot to touch. The hikers themselves felt parched with thirst and, again, dehydrated. Nightfall caught them still below the Redwall cliff. In the dark they missed the all-important switchback trail at its base which allowed an ascent. This trio found themselves in the same predicament as Coronado's three would-be Canyoneers centuries earlier, but they were stuck at the foot of the Redwall instead of at its top. At this point, as Ranger Dan Davis of the search and rescue team would later explain, things went from very bad to worse.

Having lost their route in the dark thousands of feet above the river yet thousands of feet below the rim—and having made the mistake of having followed parts of the Old Tanner Trail, officially "abandoned" and unmaintained and unmarked for the previous half century—the three gave up and sat down. Unable to sleep due to thirst and raging heat, they spent a night of torture.

At dawn they started walking along the base of the 600-foot Redwall cliff again where they were stranded in hopes of finding their lost route upward. Survival was now their only priority. But after miles of wandering in the superheated oven of exposed Paleozoic sedimentary strata, they again ended up worse off than before. They still had found no trail, and now all three hikers were gripped in the throes of advanced dehydration.

They gnawed cactus pulp and wracked their fevered brains for a means of escape.

Ranger Davis explains:

They made so many fatal errors and did so much meandering around that it was almost impossible to figure out what they did and where they went by the[ir] tracks. After they missed the Redwall switchbacks when they were hiking back out at night they followed the base of the Redwall on up the west fork of Tanner Canyon almost to the head where they spent the night, then dropped into the streambed several miles up from the switchbacks in the Redwall.

Well off both the Old and New Tanner trails and hopelessly lost, Father Gavigan continued to be baffled by the location of either trail. So the boys yelled for help. Someone in the distance answered by hooting like an ape. The hikers ignored the ape calls and continued yelling for help. Finally someone who sounded like they were up on the rim responded by hollering: "Do you really need help?"

Owens yelled, "Yes." (The willingness of this Good Samaritan on the rim to tell a ranger that he had heard faint yells for help emerging from the shimmering heat waves deep in the Canyon was, again, the critical action that had set an NPS search and rescue effort into action.)

Despite having made this tenuous contact, the trio's need for water became so acute that the location of any trail upward became academic. Father Gavigan and both boys decided that, instead of searching further for a route upward, they now had to shortcut their way back down to the river for water as soon as possible.

They descended about five hundred feet then hit the same problem they had just faced at the Redwall, but now in reverse. They could not find a route downward through the 250-foot cliff of Tapeats Sandstone. Desperate from thirst and heat atop the Tapeats, the Trappist Priest found a flash-flood-polished, dry "ravine" that seemed to him to provide a route. He would, he explained, lead the way.

The heat was so intense that Father Gavigan, now possessed of diminished mental capacity due to dehydration, instructed the boys to strip off their clothes except for their pants. He also said they should discard their shoes too, and thus have cooler feet (and maybe better traction?). The three hikers tossed their shoes and clothes down the cut in the Tapeats for later retrieval.

Father Gavigan led the route down. He carried a short rope. With about one-third of the immediate cliff descent behind him, the bare-footed priest lost his footing in the Tapeats chute and fell off a high ledge about 150 feet to his death. He rotated in the air about eight times then hit his head, slammed onto yet more rock. He bounced a couple of times, then rolled to a halt on his back.

Mahany stared open-mouthed then deteriorated into hysterics. He wanted to hurry down and help "the Padre," as the two boys called him. Owens too felt appalled. But he knew they could never make it down that crevasse in the cliff to Father Gavigan. Besides, there was no question of helping the Padre; he was dead. This hike had disintegrated into a waking nightmare. One that might end their lives as well. Owens insisted that they search for some other route down to the river.

The two desperate teenagers wobbled bare-footed and woozily dehydrated across the torturously sharp, scorching rock. Fortunately they discovered a nearby route around Father Gavigan's cliff toward the river. They managed this descent on increasingly abused feet. Dehydration had taken such a toll on them that, even though they passed within a few hundred feet of their shoes and clothes, they did not detour to retrieve them.

As they struggled toward the river, Mahany grew more and more exhausted in the blistering heat. Suffering from foot injuries and severe thirst and now staggering, both boys made it to within a fairly close descent to the river. Only a fairly easy (with shoes) mile and a half slope of eroded Dox Sandstone lay between them and the river, now life itself.

Mahany, exhausted by dehydration and heat, sat down on a rock. Owens stared at him and asked, "Pete, are you coming with me or not?"

Mahany just sat in silence. The temperature in full sun now likely shimmered at close to 120 degrees.

Desperate with thirst, Owens pushed on. "That's the last time," Owens would later report, "that I saw him."

Owens reached the river. He drank his fill, went swimming, then drank some more—spending an unknown number of hours here between River Miles 68 and 69. Likely because of his seriously wounded feet and his state of dehydration, Owens never retraced his tracks upslope to assist Mahany. Owens instead decided to build a raft of driftwood by strapping logs together with his elastic belt.

Before he launched this to float downstream, Owens scrawled three desperate notes in the sandy soil. One said, "Manson Owens going on raft downriver to bridge."

The second note said, "Pete Mahany okay the last time I saw him in ravine."

Owens' third note said: "Help. One may be dead. Fall of 150 feet. Upper ravine."

Meanwhile, Mahany, shoeless and nearly naked, died of heat stroke and dehydration upslope. He collapsed where Owens had last seen him, roughly a 45-minute walk from the river.

Owens launched his raft and drifted down the Colorado. Unlike the dam-controlled Colorado of today, the river Owens was rafting had a water temperature that exceeded 80 degrees. It posed no threat of hypothermia. On the other hand, it posed an extremely serious threat of drowning. At any rate, from River Mile 68 onward he prayed, "every minute of every day. I never prayed so much in my life." He explained why:

> I hit those rapids. I like to drown. I kept praying. The water was like a washing machine. The raft turned over and I went under. I made it to the bank.

Inconveniently, after this terrifying swim through the long, huge wave-train of Unkar Rapid (River Mile 72.7), Owens swam to the side of the river where no vegetation existed.

He decided that, if he were to survive, he had to be on the opposite side, where plants grew. To get there he had to swim again, this time across the Colorado. But the river now terrified him. Indeed, despite seeing Father Gavigan die horribly in that 150-foot fall and despite having walked away from a zombie-exhausted Mahany, the only time Owens thought of his own death was in Unkar when his little raft had tipped over.

Owens now told himself: "Owens, you ain't a man unless you do it." Then, he reported, "I jumped in and swam to that sandbar."

Based on an aerial photo, allegedly of the exact beach where Owens ended up, he appeared to have "rafted" with no life jacket all the way to the beach at the foot of 75-Mile. This meant the boy had covered seven miles of river punctuated with several small rapids and one huge one. We shudder.

For these next few days Owens became an unsolved mystery. Two and three days after the three hikers had descended from the Tanner Trailhead, SAR personnel had found the bodies of Walter J. Mahany and Father Gavigan, respectively, well off the Tanner Trail and in divergent locations on Sunday and Monday. Why they had died where they had and what decisions had led to their deaths, the searchers had no idea. Nor could searchers explain the macabre trail they had found littered with Mahany's and Owens' discarded clothes and shoes.

Days passed before they found Owens' notes scratched in the silty sand. And even then, they seemed to have missed note number one about his rafting down the river. Hence the most perplexing question for the searchers remained: Where was the body of John Manson Owens III?

After a week of unsuccessful searching in the melt-down heat, most of the searchers had given up Owens too for dead. "We're just looking," searchers admitted, "for a body now."

During the end of this unsolved mystery phase of the search and rescue, doyen Canyon hiker Harvey Butchart suggested to SAR personnel that Owens might have built a raft or tried in some other way to descend the river to help. Butchart even volunteered to leap onto an air mattress and go search for Owens.

While the NPS rejected the air mattress concept, the U.S. Army chopper search crew from Fort Huachuca and a few NPS rangers, Dan Davis among them, did take the possibility to heart of Owens having gone rafting. They decided to take their huge, H-21 "flying banana" for one last run over the Canyon, again following the river but now more closely. They were pretty sure Owens was not along the river upstream of Mile 74 because the Canyon was so wide here that they had been able to fly close to the beaches and search them for Owens and for his footprints and had found none. The Canyon downstream of Mile 74, however, was too narrow in the Shinumo Quartzite for the large H-21 to fly low enough to search thoroughly.

Riding on very hot, diffuse air that gave the machine a sickeningly weak amount of lift, the crew was elated to spot a crude "H" on the beach on the left side of River Mile 75 (Nevills Rapid). The house-high letter had been built of stones on a steep, castaway beach about seven miles downstream from where Owens had scrawled his sad notes in the sand. Immediately downstream of the "H" lay 75-Mile Rapid. Below that, Hance Rapid.

The air was so hot and of such low density that the chopper felt ticklish to lower. The pilot could not land it and hope to lift off again. So he set it in a semi-landing on one wheel on the narrow "H" beach and ran his motor at full power in order to hover.

Blinking against the solar glare from behind the windbreak he had constructed, John Manson Owens, III stared at the huge machine and the sandstorm it was creating. He finally knew his ordeal was about to end...in his favor. Owens would later recount to the *Deseret News* his strange odyssey toward the head of Upper Granite Gorge:

> *After leaving my companion and arriving on the river I built a raft from three logs, strapping them together with my belt.*
>
> *I laid on the raft and paddled down the river [west] from Saturday until Tuesday. Because of the sun, I decided to stop on a sand bar. The raft was still together when I saw it float on down the river.*
>
> *I built a large letter X from sticks and a large letter H from mud along the river bank. Helicopters flew over but couldn't see my distress signals. The mud dried out and blended into the sand bar.*
>
> *Each time a `copter came over I would take off my pants and wave them, but I couldn't attract anyone's attention. That's when I decided to make a large letter H out of stones. This was on Thursday [Day # 7].*
>
> *It took a long time to make and was about thirty feet long.*
>
> *I had a knife with me and tried to flash it in the sun in the hopes a pilot would see it.*
>
> *I cut cactus plants and chewed the pulp and also found some beans on what I later learned was a mesquite tree. The beans were very hard and had to be soaked in water before they could be eaten. ["I had to search for food on my hands and knees. My feet were so sore."]*
>
> *If it hadn't been for the heat I would have stayed with the raft—and I guess I wouldn't have made it. I thought I could reach Santa Fe [hundreds of miles east and nowhere near the Colorado River] on down the canyon. I guess I drifted about eight miles.*

After nearly a week of long conversations with God and of making practical efforts at survival, Owens hobbled on his own badly bruised, blistered, swollen, and cut feet—now clad in makeshift moccasins that Owens had made from the lower legs of his blue jeans—to the semi-landed chopper. Ranger Dan Davis appeared spectral and surreal as he dropped out of the huge machine into the wild sandstorm. ("The pilots," Davis reported, "were flying on instruments as the rotors under full power were causing a regular tornado in the loose sand, and the pilots couldn't see 5 feet.") Davis hoisted Owens, now thirty pounds lighter, up into the machine. The first thing Owens asked of his rescuers was: how was his companion?

Unfortunately, Davis had to tell him that Mahany had died on Owens' same route, roughly a mile from the river.

Despite this seeming Hollywood ending to this horrific search and rescue, neither the SAR team nor Owens were out of the woods yet. In fact things looked dicey for everyone who got near Owens' "H."

"All this hovering caused some damage to the engine," Davis noted, "because it was held wide open too long...we had a heck of a time climbing out....[When the pilots finally coaxed the dying helicopter above the rim, they] landed in the local ball park because they didn't think the machine would make it to the G.C. Airport 15 miles away."

Of this incident the *Deseret News* concluded that Owens' companions, Gavigan and Mahany, were "victims of the treacherous canyon and heat."

More accurately, Owens was the lucky recipient of the actions of Park visitors who reported faint yelling from the middle of nowhere, of a ranger who had the imagination and initiative to search a vehicle and read a journal, of a hiking expert who imagined a boy desperate to survive building a raft and trying to run the Colorado to Phantom Ranch, and of U.S. Army and NPS personnel who felt it was still worth one more try after nearly a week of unsuccessful searching, even in superheated air that might crash their helicopter. True, young Owens had used his head to make the best of a very bad situation. As Dan Davis summarizes:

> Owens at times really used his head and at other times did exactly the wrong thing—of course a 15-year-old boy that's never been west can't expect to do everything the way it ought to be and I think he did better than most would in like circumstances, etc. Had he only waited on the beach at Tanner a little longer our crew would have gotten there before he took off on his log—but at the time all he wanted to do was get away from there. We were there early in the PM.

But, after all is said and done, Owens' survival ultimately had pivoted on luck and on several people having gone beyond the call of duty against the odds to try to rescue him.

Also lucky was twenty-year-old Paul Benson of Gaylord, Michigan. He hiked down the Bright Angel Trail in early October, 1963, solo—except for his faithful dog Scotty. For reasons unknown, once deep in the Canyon, Benson impulsively decided to try his hand at rock climbing. He ascended a decaying wall and terrace system. About 75 feet up, he lost his handholds and footholds.

Benson tumbled down fifty feet of 60-degree slope then launched off twenty-five feet of cliff to crumple onto the Bright Angel Trail. Another hiking tourist saw Benson's precipitous descent. He alerted rangers, who wheeled Benson out on a stretcher. In Flagstaff Community Hospital Benson was diagnosed with a skull fracture, broken wrists, a likely broken spine and ankle, internal injuries, plus multiple cuts, abrasions, and bruises. Scotty, who had not been enticed by rock-climbing at all, was fine.

As hiking within the Canyon became better publicized, casualties began increasing. In late August of 1968, for example, Rita Julie Burkhalter, age 25, left her river-running group, including two cousins, on a Western River Expeditions trip at River Mile 65.5 to hike alone up Palisades Canyon. No one had noticed that Burkhalter had hiked off on her own (she had not told anyone of her intent) but when she failed to appear in camp that evening, members of the trip began searching for her.

They found her in good spirits atop a 150-foot cliff on the south side of the creek bed. Burkhalter assured them that all was well and that she would find her way down from her high ledge. So the searchers returned to camp.

But, yet again, Burkhalter failed to show up in camp. At daybreak the next morning searchers found her body 150 feet below the ledge where she last had been seen. How she fell remains a mystery, although suicide cannot be ruled out.

The four above-mentioned victims died in fairly well-known and easy territory. Once one enters terra incognita in Grand Canyon, survival becomes far more iffy. At the end of August in 1974, for example, two students of Arizona State University (ASU) via Long Island, New York and Ohio, Frank Costa, age 21, and Edwin Heisel, Jr., age 23, decided to make one of the most beautiful hikes on Earth. They parked their car near the Big Saddle Hunting Camp on the North Rim. Then the two young men descended into the Canyon. Their goal was Thunder River flowing out of a sheer cliff face about 400 feet below a wide slump zone named Surprise Valley, itself nearly 3,000 feet below their parked car.

The note the hikers left on one of their vehicles indicated that they planned to be back out of the Canyon and be finished with their planned 5,000-foot descent to Thunder Spring then Tapeats Creek and ascent the next day, or the day after at the latest. By the way, they added, they planned to do some rock climbing. They were carrying ropes.

Even to educated neophytes in the Canyon, this plan to make a 20+-mile round trip with recreational side adventures in only two days sounds naive. And it was. Instead of following one of the two standard NPS trails off the North Rim down onto the Esplanade and then down again to Surprise Valley and then down yet one more pitch to Thunder River, the two young hikers followed a faint game trail descending somewhat easterly off Bridger's Knoll, a route neither man had ever seen before.

No one ever heard from Costa and Heisel again. Fellow students at ASU alerted the pair's parents that neither had shown up for classes.

Thirty personnel from the NPS, U.S. Forest Service, and Coconino County and Fredonia Sheriff's Departments' formed SAR teams and went to work. Because no one had a clue which route the two hikers had taken—or even whether the pair might have made it to the river and then hitched a ride out with a river trip—the search was difficult. Jeeps drove the rims. Searchers rode horses along the upper trails. Two helicopters scanned the cliffs and terraces.

Well below Monument Point and "some distance off" the standard route to Surprise Valley but on a "little-used trail near" to that standard NPS route, searchers found the two men's abandoned backpacking gear. With it were two notes. Both were dated September 2, day #3 of the pair's hike. The first note, written at 11:00 a.m. that morning, explained:

We have run out of food and water. God help us. We're trying to get water.

A second note, written 2.5 hours later, explained that the two were trying to head back down into the Canyon again (the two had stranded themselves on the then waterless Esplanade roughly 2,000 feet below the rim yet more than 1,000 feet above Thunder River). They intended, this second note explained:

—to reach a small stream. We have ropes, too. Please look for us. It looks bad, but we're tough. Don't give up looking for us. God bless whoever finds us.

Searchers—U.S. Forest Service Rangers Billy Swap, Don Mackelprang, and Tuffy Srowp—followed what remained of the pair's week-old tracks after thunderstorms had pounded their route. SAR personnel found bits of gnawed cactus, but otherwise the searchers rarely felt certain that they were following the right route. If this were the route taken by Costa and Heisel, however, the two hikers had continued to miss the nearby feasible route and had instead headed toward a thousand-foot cliff overhanging Thunder River and Tapeats Creek.

The SAR team finally found Edwin Heisel's body about 125–150 feet down this cliff, where he had obviously fallen.

Later searchers also found Frank Costa dead on a rock ledge halfway up the north side of the Canyon above the Esplanade but below Monument Point, miles away from Heisel. Apparently, after Heisel had died in the fall, Costa had changed his survival/self-rescue plan yet again to abandon the strategy of trying to reach Thunder River down the huge cliff and instead decided to hike back up to Monument Point and to their vehicle. But, without water and at temperatures exceeding

100 degrees in the shade—and on a "route" where no shade existed—Costa had died of dehydration and heat stroke.

Again, even on ground known to be dangerous, the Inner Canyon precipices seem to tempt people fatally. On May 31, 1979, for example, a recurring nightmare of most professional river guides on the Colorado came true on the second day of a Cross Tours trip. Trip leader Dick Clark and boatman's assistant Peter Weiss made an unplanned stop at River Mile 31.5 to take their passengers from a Whitworth College (Spokane, Washington) geology charter on a hike up to see that "Mystery Skeleton" we discussed earlier. Weiss led two passengers, Gordon Stanley Grace and David Olson, to a high cave/tunnel penetrating the Redwall Limestone above the skeleton. This cave is entered from its opening facing the river but also opens at its other end onto very sketchy footing then empty air at least 100 vertical feet above the floor of South Canyon and above a sheer vertical cliff. Weiss led the way out to the narrow ledge above this cliff then he returned into the cave proper.

Olson next exited the small hole onto the slim ledge for a look then returned to Weiss in the larger part of the cave facing the river corridor. Gordon Stanley Grace, age 20, was the third and last person to exit the small cave opening out to the narrow ledge perched above South Canyon.

A moment earlier, Weiss had complimented Grace on his ability to move on rock. Grace had responded by saying that he had some rock-climbing experience. Weiss had also told Grace and Olson that they should return into the cave via the same route that they had taken out, noting that any other route would be "sketchy."

Weiss and Olson waited for a couple of minutes for Grace, who was out of sight and alone on the narrow ledge. Once he rejoined them they could return together to Clark's motor rig.

Weiss and Olson heard rocks sliding from the South Canyon opening of the cave and then a long scream. And then a thump. Feeling a stomach-tightening jolt, Weiss returned through the narrow opening to check on Grace. Grace was gone.

Weiss saw a wet section of the hundred-foot-high Redwall cliff face where Grace had apparently urinated. Weiss exited the cave via its river-facing mouth and yelled to trip leader Clark below that Grace had fallen into South Canyon. Clark rushed into the Canyon. He found Grace unconscious with angulated limbs, a severe crushing injury to the back of the head, and cranial bleeding from the ears, nose, and mouth. Both of Grace's shoes had flown off, the sole of one was almost completely peeled off the shoe. Apparently Grace had contacted the Redwall with his shod feet at high speed.

Amazingly, Grace also still had a weak carotid pulse. Five minutes later Grace's pulse stopped.

As these examples suggest, and as Table 2 reveals, accidental fatal falls in the Inner Canyon are the province of young males. The patterns are consistent with one another, yet a bit different from many of the falls from the rims discussed earlier in this chapter. First, only 9 of the 55 inner Canyon fall victims were women (15 percent). Only six of these women were under the age of 49. Moreover, the average of the ages of all victims, both male and female, who fell within the Canyon (33.2 years) was comparable to the average of rim-fall victims (34.2 years). This comparison, however, may be somewhat deceptive in that 26 of the 55 (almost half) of inner Canyon falls were of young people between 13 and 28 years old. What these victims were doing in the Canyon just before they died also reveals a significant trend or risk factor.

At least 35 of the 55 victims—64 percent—were solo hikers or alone at the time and in the place of their demise. The significance of this is clear when one remembers that the vast majority of hiking and river-running trips contain multiple people. What this means is, for every solo hiker, there are many groups collectively containing hundreds of people. Statistically, for every solo hiking fatality due to falls within the Canyon, there also should be dozens of social hiker deaths. But there are not. Being solitary is the number one risk factor for these Inner Canyon falls, next to being male. As Table 2 reveals, being alone is an overwhelmingly powerful risk factor. For many young male hikers it has proved to be the kiss of death.

Why are young male solo hikers at vastly greater risk of self-destruction? At least 18 of the victims who died were "shortcutting" from an established trail or route across country in a personal cheat-route to eliminate apparently "unnecessary" distance. It is impossible to offer the percent of all victims that shortcutting accounts for because 31 of the 55 victims fell unwitnessed. Thus, while in some cases shortcutting was obvious, in others of the unwitnessed category, what the victims might have been doing prior to their falls remains unknown. All but two of these fatal decisions to shortcut were made by solo young male hikers. In several cases, these decisions were influenced by dehydration, impatience, and diminished mental capacity. The patterns in Table 2 are an eye-opener.

Young solo males are also significantly the most prone to making fatal mistakes in all other endeavors in life. Insurance companies figured this out decades ago. Indeed, the mere condition of being male and alone on a hike, with no other person to offer an opinion on the issue of whether or not a "shortcut" looks safe, is what probably killed nearly half of these 55 fall victims. As we will see in the next chapter, being young has killed yet more solo male hikers in other ways.

A further contributing factor leading to hikers' decisions—solo males or otherwise—that ultimately result in falls in the Canyon is environmental. The physiological impacts on hikers of heat and cold—especially on unprepared hikers—has played a role in dozens of deaths.

Although heat has caused far more poor decisions than cold has, hypothermia seems to have been the primary factor in Dennis E. Daboll's loss of decision-making ability on January 2, 1974. Daboll, age 27, had been solo hiking up the Tanner Trail during an increasing snowstorm. The thickening snow apparently prompted

Daboll to decide that his speed uphill was of the essence. Roughly four miles below the rim he abandoned his backpack and supplies. His decision may have been made in panic or under the diminished mental capacity that accompanies hypothermia—or both.

Either way, Daboll ascended the trail two miles higher through ever heavier snow. Approximately 2.5 miles below the rim, he slipped off the trail and fell 50 vertical feet. Then he slid or possibly crawled another 400 feet off the trail. There the storm buried him. Searchers found his body days later.

Heat has contributed to far more tragic incidents than cold for two reasons. First, more people hike the Canyon during the hot months than during midwinter. And, second, the heat in Grand Canyon is far more intense than what many hikers anticipate (see the next chapter for more on this). Hikers sometimes are taken by surprise to find themselves out of water, distant from any source of water, and seriously dehydrated—as if ambushed by some sneaky assassin. But it is a self-ambush. And, in that one's need for water is as remorseless as one's need for oxygen, dehydrated hikers frequently make bad decisions in deciding upon the shortest feasible route to a water source. We suspect many of these decisions were not simply "bad decisions;" they were instead acts of flat-out panic spurred by desperation. This is the same sort of desperation that one feels if one's head is being held under water—only in slow motion. The sad demises of Father Gavigan and Walter J. Mahany and of Edwin Heisel, Jr. and Frank Costa (described earlier) are just a few of the many examples of this.

Another such heat-driven tragedy unfolded on June 24, 1974, one of the driest and hottest days of the year. That day four men—including Gregory DeYoung, age 17, Lee Meister, age 18, and David Smith, age 31—had tackled the Grandview Trail (a trail that never nears the river). The four ran out of water roughly halfway through their hike. DeYoung separated from his companions and hiked a couple of hours ahead of them "to cut cross-country down a steep drainage to the Colorado to renew their water supply." Desperately committing themselves to a perceived shortcut, the entire group stranded themselves on a ledge with severe vertical exposure.

Even so, DeYoung continued his attempt to descend to the river. He slipped and fell off a 125-foot cliff. His fatal fall would likely never have happened had the men supplied themselves with enough water for their hike.

It was at the end of August in this same year when Frank Costa and Edwin Heisel, Jr. described earlier also made the identical error on the north side of the Canyon.

A few years later, on a very hot July 26, 1977, Charles Walter Rienecke, age 27, had hiked alone into the Canyon with inadequate food and only an 8-oz instant coffee jar of water. Rienecke, a former Fred Harvey Company busboy, had received some food and water from other sympathetic hikers. But, alone again and having run out of water on the Tonto Trail, Rienecke made a terrible decision.

Although he was only about two level miles by trail from Indian Garden with its permanent copious spring, he tried to hike down a steep drainage between Plateau Point and Horn Creek to reach the river. Arriving at a pitch that seemed too steep, Rienecke stopped and tried to dig in the stony soil for water. This yielded nothing but dust.

Rienecke tried again to descend to the river. He fell—or jumped—down a 40-foot cliff in the Tapeats Sandstone (barely missing a cushioning ponderosa pine tree that he may have been aiming for to break his fall). From there he left a 150-yard trail of blood before he collapsed at the top of large drop off. Rienecke died there from his injuries and dehydration.

Again, being young and male is a greater risk factor in falls than merely being unprepared for environmental circumstances. Notable among rim and with inner Canyon falls, however, is the small number of children who have died. How would an otherwise sensible kid fall? At 11:00 p.m. on the night of March 13, 1996 Jared King, age 14, of Bakersfield, California, decided that he had to urinate.

That day he and his companions had made a long hike from the rim to the Clear Creek Trail. Rain had begun. And King was tired. Still, he needed to urinate. Half asleep and in his underwear, he followed a typical male impulse to walk to the edge of a cliff, this one 70 feet, to relieve himself. Next he lost his footing and fell.

Waking from unconsciousness after an unknown span of time, young King screamed for help. He was alive but very seriously injured. His companions, panicky, could not climb down to him. Eventually they tossed him a tarp so he could cover himself from the rain. One of them then ran to Phantom Ranger Station for help and alerted Ranger Mary Litell.

Because a helicopter was impossible to fly in the Inner Canyon during darkness and foul weather, Ranger Bryan Wisher at Indian Garden ran with a 50-pound pack of gear down to Phantom Ranch (5+ miles) in 45 minutes. Then he jogged partway up the Clear Creek Trail to King in 20 more minutes (another 1.5 miles). Wisher had brought oxygen, an Advanced Life Support (ALS) pack, and IV fluids. He had also instructed NPS maintenance operator Frank Corey to heat water on every available stove burner in the ranger station, to fill up every available bottle with that hot water, and then to get the trail crew to help bring the hot water up to the accident site along with a backboard and yet more gear.

Using technical climbing gear, Litell rappelled down the cliff to King while Wisher climbed up to him from below. They found King perched, silent and only half under the tarp. He was naked except for his underwear. He was wet and cold—but he was not shivering. Indeed, young King was so cold he was nearly dead. Wisher inserted a rectal thermometer. The mercury failed to move up the column at all. King's body core temperature was a frighteningly low 84 degrees. Worse, the rangers felt no pulse and detected no blood pressure. They did auscultate a faint heart beat. And King did respond, albeit minimally, to painful stimuli. King's faint heartbeat and response to pain did give the rangers hope—not much hope, merely a splinter.

Wisher examined King's spine. He felt a deformity indicating a serious spinal injury. Still encumbered by working while dangling against the face of the cliff, Litell and Wisher placed King on oxygen, stabilized his spine, and started an IV line using a solution warmed by wrapping the line in the warm water bottles brought up by NPS trail crew workers. Wisher positioned more warm water bottles around King's body to try to re-warm him. Then the entire crew stayed on vigil with King for the rest of the night. The warm water bottles slowly raised King's level of consciousness. Eventually King warmed up enough to start him shivering. His core temperature inched up to 89 degrees. By dawn he was stable enough for a short haul evacuation by NPS Paramedic Tammy Keller via an Arizona Department of Public Safety (DPS) helicopter out of the Canyon.

King was flown to Flagstaff Medical Center and diagnosed with multiple spinal and extremity fractures. Ultimately, the 14-year-old made a full recovery. King was a very lucky young man.

Less lucky was 13-year-old Andrew Patrick Drugg. On June 12, 2001 Drugg was hiking on a 2-mile round trip, day hike from the Colorado River up North Canyon (River Mile 20.5). A client on a commercial rafting trip, Drugg was following his uncle and the rest of his group on a well-used but unmaintained trail. When the two reached a very deceptive portion of the route only a third of a mile from the river they took what appeared to be the safer way because it was a little farther away from a 50-foot drop-off. In reality the true safe route passed immediately next to this cliff. Be that as it may, Drugg tried to pass huggingly close against a huge, perched and outwardly leaning boulder located on sloping Supai bedrock six feet off-route from the standard, safe hiking route. The 6' 1", 255-pound teenager was witnessed by another teenager behind him to lose his balance where one must scrunch down to pass adjacent to that leaning boulder (again this location is about 6 feet off-route and 4 feet above it). Drugg slipped and silently fell backward 6 feet onto a ledge that formed the correct route. Next he tumbled off it 48 feet, touching nothing until he hit bedrock at the base of a large amphitheater. CPR by guides and later by paramedics proved unsuccessful due to the victim's severe head trauma. Drugg was the first and only "child" (being less than 17 years old) known ever to die from a fall within Grand Canyon.

As luck (bad) would have it, he would not be the only child for long. On October 3, of 2001, 13-year-old Hannah Lockwood Suzanne Stehlin of Flemington, New Jersey was day-hiking with her brother and her father down the South Kaibab Trail on an intended rim-to-river-to-rim hike. About 1.25 miles from the trailhead all three of them stopped to pet one or more of the four trail repair mules hitched to re-bar off the trail. They also took a photo. Hannah was an experienced horsewoman—her family owned four. She was also an athletic hiker and wearing good footwear. After the photo, Hannah's father and brother led onward. To ensure than Hannah was following—she loved horses and might be tempted to stay longer—her father looked back and saw her ten feet from the mules and walking in his direction. Seconds later her father, now about 70 feet from the mules, heard a "scuff" sound behind him. He looked back again for Hannah. This time she had vanished from a section of trail sprinkled with small rocks. This gravel might have been there because this short bit of trail had been dung-raked earlier that morning.

Alarmed, Hannah's father searched for her. He noted scuff marks on the rock. While he searched ever more feverishly, another group of hikers arrived. One of them, a Royal Air Force airman, helped search. He rigged some nylon webbing as protection which enabled him to climb several feet below the trail. He spotted then followed scuff marks downward. Then he saw a blood smear. He next found Hannah's hat and sunglasses. Descending a bit farther, he spotted her body below a vertical drop.

Hannah apparently had slipped all the way off the trail despite wearing ideal footwear. She had lost her footing unwitnessed. It is pure surmise to imagine that she might have been hurrying a bit to catch up to her family. Or that she slipped on the gravel. At any rate, she fell 177 feet off the 4-foot-wide trail. Hannah is the second child (under 17) ever to die from a fall within the Canyon. Trying to eliminate all possibilities, the medical examiner found no indications of Hannah having been kicked by a mule. Her tragic death remains a mystery.

One of the more memorable experiences of a river trip is the brief hike at Elves' Chasm (a.k.a. lower Royal Arch Creek at River Mile 116.5). Elves' Chasm, with its tiers of waterfalls and pools carved in the thick, ledgy Tapeats Sandstone, its beds of crimson monkey flowers, and its walls of maidenhair ferns and columbines, is a "must" stop for river trips. But seeing all of Elves' natural wonders requires serious scramble climbing on highly exposed, narrow ledges.

One of the most beautiful sets of falls and pools exists only about three hundred yards from the river. It requires only a few minutes to visit. Above this pool, however, lie eight more waterfalls, often with shallow pools below them. The problems posed by visiting these upper pools are the various necessary climbing or bouldering moves, again on exposed faces of the Tapeats.

Thousands of river trips over the decades have taken at least some of their passengers on this scary and demanding scramble to see the first seven pools (the next higher falls are far more ridiculous). And probably without exception every professional guide or trip leader who has taken people on this scramble has worried: 1. "What am I doing here with these people?" and 2. "I wonder when someone will finally peel off of one of these exposures and eat it."

Around midday on August 21, 1986 Connie Wernette, age 28, stopped with the other members of a private rowing trip down the Canyon to "hike" Elves' Chasm.

In large part due to the stunning and mysterious reputation of Elves', Wernette's party decided to make the scramble up the Tapeats Sandstone from the first idyllic pool to see the more of the hidden wonders above. At least some of the members of this group, however, had ill-prepared themselves. Some apparently did not know the correct route, and those who did know failed to ensure that those behind them followed on that same route.

Wernette apparently lagged behind other members of her group after she and they reached the first high waterfall. Her companions had made the next dangerous ascent traverse past the first large waterfall to the second waterfall. By the time Wernette decided to climb after them beyond the first falls to the second, her companions had passed beyond the critical part of the difficult ascent and disappeared from her view.

Wernette tried to solo rock scramble after them. At first she followed a correct route to where continuing upcanyon demands that the climber crawl/creep along horizontally on all fours like a lizard under a low overhang of Tapeats above a narrow ledge. Apparently deciding that this could not be the correct route—and possibly thinking the rough sandstone would abrade her knees as she crawled—Wernette decided to continue up higher. She soon climbed another thirty feet upward, alone and now on a much higher, non-route.

She next followed a small horizontal ledge yet thirty feet higher than the one she had bypassed. This too led deeper into Elves' Chasm, but it was situated sixty-five feet or so above the narrow floor of Tapeats at the first pool and thirty or more feet above the floor of the second pool area where her friends had just vanished. Wernette, wearing wet, canvas deck-type shoes, soon found herself "ledged out." She could no longer proceed upcanyon because her route had fizzled out into sheer cliff.

Wernette tried to turn around to reverse her direction and thus descend by retracing her steps. But she lost her balance or lost her friction on the Tapeats. She slipped and screamed. Two of her companions—Craig Byrne and Richard Learned—heard her.

They spun around and witnessed Wernette fall—although they did not see exactly what action of Wernette's had led to it. She fell head first to below the floor of Tapeats and into a "hole" between the huge boulders wedged and cemented on the creek left atop the first falls. The crushing impact instantly knocked her unconscious.

Wernette's companions looked at her in shock. One of them hurried back to the boats for first aid. Upon his arrival, he saw a Grand Canyon Dories trip pull to shore for a hike.

Peter Dale, a guide on this trip, said the man asked in a shocked way: "Do you have a first aid kit?"

Dale said, "Yeah, we do, why?"

The man did not answer. He simply stared at Dale.

Peter Dale and his fellow guides knew that something must have gone very wrong up in Elves' Chasm. They grabbed their first aid kits and hustled up to the scene of Wernette's fall.

The Dories guides attempted first aid, but one look at Wernette revealed she was beyond their abilities. Blood and cerebrospinal fluid now drained onto the rock from a basilar skull fracture via her nose, ears, and mouth. Wernette's neck had also broken, apparently at the third, fourth, and possibly fifth cervical vertebrae. These guides' one ace in the hole was a brain surgeon who was a passenger on their trip.

This neurosurgeon examined Wernette. His prognosis was anything but favorable. Wernette's cranial and cervical injuries were beyond what even the most skilled team of surgeons in the best facility on Earth could repair. Still he and the Dories guides tried to keep Wernette alive.

A half hour later Wernette's heart stopped.

The Dories CPR team worked to keep Wernette biologically alive—despite her neurological death—for the sake of her organ donor potential. Meanwhile, the guides also radioed an overflying aircraft to pass a fatality message on to NPS Headquarters at the South Rim. Wernette became the first Elves' Chasm fatality.

Wernette's tragic fall was re-enacted almost a quarter century later, on October 20, 2010. Hiker John Kynyk, age 52, was scrambling solo up Elves' Chasm while separated from the rest of his private river trip. Kynyk fell unwitnessed about 120 feet. His companions found him dead. Instead of leaving him in place—as required by law—they carried him to the boats and rowed his body 3 miles downriver to Blacktail Canyon where they figured a helicopter could land. The members of this private group apparently did not know NPS and Arizona Department of Public Safety helicopters are equipped with long lines and other gear for short-hauling a body (or a living victim) to a safe area for landing him.

Such tragic climbing mishaps as Wernette's and Kynyk's are not the exclusive province of amateurs. Even veteran guides fall. And the geological Siren calling them most often to climb where they should not be climbing is again Tapeats Sandstone. Many guides who work in the Canyon decide that the Tapeats Sandstone is their favorite of the Canyon's thirty or so named geological formations, or rock types. Tapeats is a ledgy, coarse-grained sandstone that typically erodes into smoothly sculpted slot canyons, such as the one at Elves' Chasm. It also erodes into cliff shelters offering shade from a remorseless sun and into wide patios of smooth stone that make wonderful picnic spots. Cracks in the Tapeats frequently erode into chimneys that can be climbed for fun via bouldering moves. The problem with this sandstone is, despite its 570-million-year age, it decays and crumbles unpredictably. In short, Tapeats is very unreliable stuff.

During the evening of September 21, 1990 on a Moki Mac River Expeditions' trip, trip leader Michael Jacobs free-climbed (without rope protection) alone in the Tapeats. He chose an ascent downstream of the trip's camp on the south side of the river at River Mile 120.25 at the head of Conquistador Aisle. Jacobs had free-climbed along several sections of bedrock during this trip. A witness said that this time Jacobs was ascending very quickly up a tall chimney next to a sandstone column.

Near the top of the Tapeats, one of Jacobs' handholds broke away from the bedrock.

Jacobs immediately lost contact with both hands and with his right foot. He fell. His left foot, however, remained wedged in a crack. As Jacobs tried to recover from this nasty slip, his left foot yanked loose. Jacobs free-fell 50 feet onto scattered blocks of Tapeats.

Jacobs sustained multiple internal injuries, including massive cranial ones. Under a tarp set up to protect him from monsoon rains, his companions, including six physicians, struggled to save him. They were desperate enough that a neurosurgeon among them attempted to relieve pressure on Jacobs' brain due to intracranial bleeding by drilling a hole in his skull. Despite every measure, however, within three hours, the 43-year-old Jacobs had succumbed to his injuries. "Michael made a courageous fight," noted Vaughn Short, "but it was not to be." Jacobs died that evening in camp.

During late summer of 2009, on September 21, Thomas Peake, age 39, of Atlanta, Georgia left his wife and set out at a late-ish 9:00 a.m. on a solo day-hike from the Esplanade to the river and back up via the remote, steep, and rugged Toroweap Trail. In a mere mile and a half this trail descends 2,500 feet down a series of eroding lava flows to the river. For his hike the 6' 1", 195-lb. Peake carried 3 liters of water, a Motorola walkie-talkie, a compass, and a camera. He carried no physical map (although he did have a photo of a map on his phone), no GPS unit, no food, nor a headlamp to afford himself the option of an evening ascent if the heat became too much or if an injury slowed him down. Nor, apparently, did Peake leave for himself a cache of water somewhere along the route to assist in his return ascent.

Soon after leaving his wife he radioed her: "Oh my God, the Colorado River is so beautiful!" (Peake previously had been on two river trips in the Canyon.)

Later he radioed to her a message of a different sort: "When you're lost here, you're really lost." Again, many victims discussed in this chapter and Table 2 eschewed physical maps. As noted above, Peake had taken a photo of a map on his phone. Whether or not he found its micro-format useful is uncertain. Yet an appropriate physical topographic map (and a compass) are musts on remote hikes. A GPS unit also might have proved helpful if pre-programmed with the coordinates of waypoints along the trail from top to bottom. Such coordinates can be transcribed from a good topographic map. Be all that as it may, for reasons unknown, Peake missed spotting the cairns marking the trail.

Peake radioed his wife that he was being forced to "rock climb" and he was lost and scrambling in the wrong ravine but he thought he knew where to find the trail. Peake next radioed his wife to report that he had re-located the trail and now was descending it again.

After 11:00 a.m., Peake's radio transmissions ceased. When, at dusk, he still had failed to appear at the trailhead, his worried wife drove 2 hours to Fredonia to phone for help.

Helicopter searchers took 5 minutes to find Peake's body sprawled near the Toroweap route about one third of the way up from the river to the Esplanade. Not only was he positioned off-trail, he also was located off feasible alternative routes. The SAR rangers assessed his situation. While ascending, they concluded, he had died from a fall of roughly 15 to 20 feet off a class 5 (= vertical) cliff marked by a "trail of crumbs" consisting of blood smears and lost clothing. This location perplexed the SAR personnel because, located only 30 feet to one side of Peake, there stood a far easier and safer class 3 (= broken and steep) route through the same cliff that required slogging up more gravelly terrain where one experiences an annoying "two steps up, one slide back."

Did he miss the safer route only 30 feet away? Was Peake's decision-making influenced by dehydration? Temperatures on the Toroweap Trail in September commonly exceed 100 degrees during afternoon. Shade does not exist there during the day. The black rock heats like an oven. This reality prompts many day-hikers to depart at dawn and return to the top before noon. Recently two separate, solo hikers here died of dehydration (next chapter). Water is vital to survival. It is so vital that drinking untreated water from the Colorado is infinitely preferable to hiking without being adequately hydrated. Had Peake re-filled his three bottles at the river? His being found only one third of the way up the ascent but with no bottle nearby suggests, but does not prove, he had not. For the lack of enough drinking water at least eight other hikers have perished in inner Canyon falls.

The memory card from Peake's now-broken camera included a video he recorded in an unidentifiable location at 2:46 p.m., close to 7 hours after having started the 1.5-mile hike down. He stood in front of his camera and stated that he had made it to the river and now was hiking back up. He also says he had "lost a shoe, sole, and a bottom but I've now got a sock with a sole on the bottom; reinforced sole because that one came off too." Peake's video shows he is wearing no shoe on his right foot, only a sock and apparently the separated sole of a shoe strapped to his foot. One wonders whether or not Peake had turned around as soon as his defective shoes had first begun to fail. Peake's missing shoe never was found: it apparently went missing well before his fall. His radio and water bottles, too, never were found.

In his video recording Peake went on to say, "…two more ravines to go and then I get up to that level and kind of boulder my way out, which is a lot easier than this loose volcanic rock. So, well, I'll be back in a couple of hours. Bye."

Peake became the 34th victim (of 55 known in total up through 2012) of a fatal inner Canyon fall to have been solo at the time of his demise. Peake also was the 34th victim to die while scrambling or climbing off-route. Upon further analysis, a whopping 30 victims of the 55 in Table 2 up through 2012 also were scrambling on semi-vertical terrain when they fell. Three more of those 55 were climbing. Five victims, like Peake, had been free-soloing.

The tragedies in this chapter underline many important lessons for future hikers. These include planning carefully with a real map (then taking it with you along with a programmed GPS unit), knowing one's own limits, carrying more than "enough" water (and knowing where to resupply), equipping oneself to orienteer yet also to hunker down during the heat or to survive a night, carrying a signal mirror and a lightweight emergency kit, and so on. But even with all that planning one must heed even more the major legacy left by several hikers who never saw a trailhead again. They posthumously emphasize one of the most important rules for all day hikers, one which also is a cardinal rule taught to aircraft pilots: **You actually do *not have to* reach your pre-determined destination, instead you may turn around and make an about face whenever prudence dictates (see pages 559–562 for survival rules and gear).**

What else can we learn from these tragic falls detailed in Table 2? Our analysis reveals nearly every inner-Canyon fall happened due to a serious lack of good judgment of the victim. "Acts of God" rank low on the list as a cause. Bad judgment by the victim or his or her guide ranks at the top. Again, the significant preponderance of solo victims (solo at the time and location of the incident)—64 percent of all victims—drives home how very important the role of a "second voice" of reason or caution is for anyone hiking or climbing in the Canyon, or even standing on its rims. The available statistics also reveal that young solo hikers who become climbers place themselves at vastly higher risk of injury or death from inner Canyon falls than do hikers with companions.

We suspect this mechanism of "social safety" works in the following way: When a hiker has a companion, that hiker normally proposes a verbal intent to try some uncertain route before tackling it. And it next seems that the hiker's companion has frequently been the voice of reason, which by merely saying something to the effect of, "It looks sort of sketchy to me," has prevented many fatal falls.

As Canyon hiking expert and author George Steck puts it, "A solo hiker often has a fool for a companion."

The lesson? If you don't possess your own Jiminy Cricket, hike with a buddy.

TABLE 2. ACCIDENTAL LETHAL FALLS WHILE HIKING or ORIENTEERING within GRAND CANYON

Name, age	Date	Location	*Circumstances*

Daniel W. Mooney, 40s(?)   January 20, 1880   Mooney Falls/Havasu

*While **descending by rope** 196-foot travertine falls, prospector and rancher Mooney of Williamson Valley, Arizona lost his grip and/or ran out of rope and fell. (see text)Bass, W.W., 1929.* Coconino Sun, *March 29, 1929. Doheny, E. I.* Coconino Sun, *August 23, 1929.*

C. F. Welch, adult   April 11, 1921   unknown within Grand Canyon

Emery Kolb photographed a grave marker within the Canyon reading: "C. F. Welch, Fell in Action." All details are otherwise lacking. This entry will not be included in any portion of statistics until more data are found. Thanks to Richard Quartaroli for this.

"Mystery Skeleton," adult   pre-1934   South Canyon (a.k.a. "Paradise Canyon")

*Dead adult male found and disinterred by Alton Hatch in 1934, with two broken legs and buried in buckskins. The circumstances of his **unwitnessed** fall remain a **mystery**. (see text)* Arizona Daily Sun, *July 21, 1950. Reilly, P.T. 1966.* The Masterkey, *40(4):126-139.*

Mary Irene Johnson, 19   August 4, 1940   near tunnel and head of Bright Angel Trail

*While chatting with a young male friend who did not follow her, former Fred Harvey employee Johnson of Glendale, Arizona veered **off-trail** to **solo scramble**. She worked her way to the edge of an exposed overhanging rock. Here, still chatting nonstop, she jumped to a new location, lost her balance, and fell 180 feet.* Coconino Sun, *August 9, 1940. Superintendent's Monthly Report, September 7, 1940.*

Lee Smith, 50   June 17, 1951   near top of Bright Angel Trail

*Fred Harvey Company guide/mule skinner Smith **rode a mule double** with Lee Roberts. Other mules crowded theirs off the trail. The mule fell and landed atop Smith. Roberts survived. Not included as a statistic in inner Canyon falls, but as animal related. (see text, Chapter 6)* Supplement to Superintendent's Annual Report, Grand Canyon National Park, *1951.*

Ronald T. Berg, 22   July 30, 1954   Old Tanner Trail

*During extreme heat, seasonal NPS Ranger Berg was a **solo hiker** who fell from a cliff. His fall likely was abetted by **dehydration** and heat. Body recovery was so difficult and hot it nearly killed rescuers. An air drop of "emergency" ice blocks, crushed gear and nearly brained the rangers, but the fragments, once gathered up, saved their lives. This incident prompted NPS Ranger Dan Davis to write his first giveaway booklet on inner canyon hiking and water needs. Farabee, C. R. "B," Jr. 1998.* Death, Daring and Disaster: Search and Rescue in the National Parks, *pp.207-208.*

Eugene Gavigan, 30

July 23, 1959   Tanner Trail in the Tapeats Sandstone
During extreme heat, Roman Catholic priest Father Gavigan of Savanna, Georgia **ran out of water,** *tried to* **shortcut** *to the river by descending a cliff/crevasse bare-footed,* **became lost** *and fell 150 feet. (see text)* Arizona Daily Sun, *July 27, 28, 29, 30 & 31, & August 1 & 3, 1959.* Deseret News, *August 1, 1959. Davis, D. 1959.* Deseret News, *August 1 & letter to Dock Marston, August 5, 1959.* New York Herald Tribune, *August 2, 1959.*

Rodolfo Marcello
  Ledesma-Vilmar, 28

April 7, 1966   near Bright Angel Trail in Kaibab Limestone
Hitch-hiker Ledesma-Vilmar of Cuba tried a **solo hike** *to* **shortcut** *his way across a cliff, by rock scrambling, from the Rim Trail to the Bright Angel Trail above the tunnel. He slipped and fell 200 feet.* Arizona Daily Sun, *April 7, 1966.*

Rita Julie Burkhalter, 25

August 20, 1968   River Mile 65.5/Palisades Canyon in sandstone
On a motor trip run by Western River Expeditions, Burkhalter of Phoenix, Arizona made a solo hike up Palisades Canyon, fell from a cliff 150 feet during attempted **solo**—*and* **unwitnessed**—**shortcut** *descent. (see text)* Arizona Daily Sun, *August 24, 1968.* Arizona Republic *August 24, 1968.*

Steven Dustin, 18

September 28, 1971   east arm of Horn Creek, The Battleship
Dustin, a novice **solo** *hiker from Hunterstown, Indiana and a swamper for a commercial river-running company, detoured off the Bright Angel Trail* **unwitnessed** *and tried to* **shortcut** *by roping down the sheer west face of the Battleship. He had "skimped on safety gear" (Bob Cornelius letter to Ghiglieri) and fell 65 feet. He was found later wedged in a narrow crack.* Arizona Republic, *September 30, 1971.*

Thomas J. Weiner, 28

April, 1972   Little Colorado Gorge tributary canyon in the Kaibab Limestone
Hitchhiking through the West, Weiner of New York stopped to **solo** *hike and gaze into the Gorge about 500 yards west of the junction of U.S. Highway 89 and Arizona 64 on Navajo Nation land. Weiner either slipped* **unwitnessed** *or the rimrock collapsed.* Arizona Daily Sun, *July 6, 1972.*

Paul Laurence Mysyk, 25

early April (?), 1973   just below Bright Angel tunnel
Mysyk, a **solo** *hiker from Illinois suffering from health and psychiatric difficulties, experienced an* **unwitnessed** *fall of 250 feet off the trail during snow. Boy Scouts discovered him during the spring melt on April 29. Possible suicide?* Arizona Daily Sun, *May 11, 1973.*

Kevin Cochran, 19

July 18, 1973   below Hopi Point in the Kaibab Limestone
Cochran, a Fred Harvey employee from El Paso, Texas, and a friend were **scrambling** *up a scree slope 200 feet below Hopi Point. Cochran slipped and fell 1,200 feet.* Arizona Daily Sun, *July 20, 1973.*

Dennis E. Daboll, 27

January 2, 1974   Tanner Trail, 2 miles below South Rim
*Returning from the Little Colorado **solo** during an increasing snow-storm, **backpacker** Daboll, a University of Arizona student in wild-life biology from Las Vegas, Nevada may have become **hypothermic in his ascent**. He had abandoned his backpack. Daboll walked off the trail 2 miles higher but 2.5 miles below the rim. **Unwitnessed**, Nevada's "Outstanding Athlete of the Year" for 1964 somehow fell 50 vertical feet then slid or crawled another 400 feet off the trail and was buried in snow. (see text)* Arizona Daily Sun, *January 26, 1974.* Las Vegas Republic Journal, *January 27, 1974.*

Gregory DeYoung, 17

June 24, 1974   below Grandview Trail
*DeYoung of Grandville, Michigan and three companions (including Lee Meister, age 18, and David Smith, age 31 and Ronald Phillips, age 18) ran out of water on their hike. DeYoung separated from his companions and descended 2–3 hours distance ahead and out of view as a **solo** hiker "to cut cross-country down a steep drainage to the Colorado to renew their water supply." DeYoung's companions stranded themselves on a ledge. DeYoung, **short-cutting**, fell off a 125-foot cliff while trying to descend to the river. Phillips made it to the river, hitchhiked a ride with a commercial trip to Phantom, and asked for a rescue. (see text)* Arizona Daily Sun, *June 26, 1974. Incident report #74-2764*

Edwin Len Heisel, Jr., 23

September 2, 1974   below Bridger Point, North Rim
*During significant heat, Heisel of Cincinnati, Ohio and partner Frank Costa, age 21, of New York, both students at Arizona State University, Tempe, were descending a deer trail "not far" from main NPS trail to Thunder River. **Lost**, they abandoned their camping gear and left notes explaining they had run out of food and water and would try to descend to a creek—Thunder River. Heisel apparently fell off a 200-foot cliff in the Redwall Limestone during this attempted rope descent **shortcut**. Costa later died of dehydration and heat exposure. (see text)* Arizona Daily Sun, *September, 10, 1974.* Arizona Republic, *September 9, 10 & 14, 1974.*

Thomas E. Velzy, 18

September 28, 1975   1.5 miles down South Kaibab Trail
*Velzy, a Fred Harvey employee and a **solo** hiker from Wheaton, Illinois, suffered an **unwitnessed** fall of 100 feet off the cliff adjacent to the trail.* Arizona Daily Sun, *October 7, 1975. Incident report #75-6793*

Douglas Pritchard, 22

June 18, 1976   Lipan Point
*Pritchard, a Fred Harvey employee from Phoenix, Arizona, at the Desert View Watchtower, was **scramble-climbing solo** below the rim on his day off. He lost his footing and fell at least 200 feet.* Arizona Daily Sun, *June 19, 1976. Incident report #76-2780*

Charles Walter Reinecke, 27

July 26, 1977   near upper Horn Creek Drainage in the Tapeats Sandstone
*During extreme heat, Reinecke of Bryan, Texas **solo** hiked into the Canyon but carried only an 8-oz coffee jar of water and inadequate*

*food. He bummed some food and water from other hikers. After running out of water, he tried to **shortcut** by **scrambling** down a drainage between Plateau Point and Horn Creek to the river (instead of hiking 1–2 level miles to Indian Garden). Next he tried to dig for water. He next fell (or jumped) down a 40-foot cliff in the Tapeats and left a trail of blood before collapsing 150 yards away at the top of large drop off. (see text)* Arizona Daily Sun, *July 29, 1977.* Williams News, *August 4, 1977. Incident report #77-4783*

Jeffrey F. Ridenour, 63   May 28, 1978   Tanner Trail to New Hance Trail
*Ridenour, a **solo** hiker on his second Canyon hike ever, vanished **mysteriously and unwitnessed** and was never found. He may have lost the trail (some sections are recondite) and fallen to his death on land, or instead have fallen in the river and drowned.* Tucson Daily Citizen, *June 15, 1978.*

Ruben D. Rodriquez, 22   June 14, 1978   below Navajo Point
*A backpacking hitchhiker, Rodriguez of DePue, Illinois and 3 friends had been **drinking alcohol**. They hiked below the rim. When Rodriguez tried to **scramble/descend** lower, he slipped and fell 200 feet. Incident report #78-3416*

Leland James Marsh, 39   September 29, 1978   North Kaibab Trail, 4 miles below rim
*Hiking after dark via flashlights with one companion, Marsh of Prescott, Arizona and his buddy Lee Prosper stopped to collect water at a seep. Marsh stood too close to the edge where **the ground crumbled away from beneath his feet**. He fell 175 feet.* Arizona Republic, *October 2 & 3, 1978. Incident report #78-7150*

Tsue Wang, 18   April 19, 1979   Havasu Canyon upstream of Beaver Falls
*Hiking with a Seventh Day Adventist group, Wang of Mountain View, California split from his party, with the leader's permission, to try an alternate **shortcut**, an unscouted trail as a **solo** hiker. 24 hours later Wang's body was discovered by an NPS and Coconino County Sheriff's Department team. He had died upstream of Beaver Falls in Havasupai land due to an **unwitnessed** fall.* Arizona Daily Sun, *May 6, 1979.*

Gordon Stanley Grace, 20   May 31, 1979   South Canyon cave/window in the
                Redwall Limestone
*A sophomore in a Whitworth College geology course on a commercial motor rafting trip run by Cross Tours, Grace of Menlo Park, California, **during or after urinating** while being left as a **solo** "hiker" on an exposed cliff face, fell off the sheer cliff more than 100 feet. (see text)* Arizona Daily Sun, *June 1, 1979.* Weiss, P. Coconino County Sheriff's Department Witness Statement, D. R. #4-0579-1371, *May 31, 1979. Incident report #79-2554*

Ronald T. Drabik, 22   August 7, 1979   ½ mile W of Bright Angel Campground
*Drabik of New Jersey, with no previous climbing experience, was apparently **rock scrambling** as a **solo** hiker to traverse a cliff of exposed and crumbling schist in an apparent **shortcut**. He fell*

unwitnessed 250–500 feet. Drabik's two companions, from whom he had separated, had hiked out of the Canyon without reporting Drabik's separation/ disappearance. Drabik's backpack left at the campground was the only clue of his mishap. Arizona Daily Sun, August 13, 1979. Williams News, *August 16, 1979. Incident report #79-4827*

Joseph Anthony Dean, 43　　November 1, 1980　　Horseshoe Mesa
While camping, Dean, an NPS Albright Training Center instructor, got up during the **night** *(due to stomach problems and/or* **the need to urinate***) and walked away from group camp as a* **solo** *hiker 200 yards, leaving his boots behind but wearing his socks. He sat down, pulled a sock off, then dropped it about 60 feet. He then walked 700 more feet down Miner's Spring Trail nearer to his lost sock. From there, Dean* **mysteriously fell unwitnessed** *more than a hundred feet. Was found with his fly zipper unzipped, belt unbuckled, and his feet badly lacerated. Incident report #80-4192*

Frank Taylor Jolly, 20　　August 31, 1982　　Yavapai Point
Jolly of Los Altos, California was **leaping from rock to rock** *while "***rock climbing.***" He slipped and fell 300 feet. (see text)* Arizona Daily Sun, *September 2, 1982. Incident report #82-3016*

Abdulla Balsharaf, 27　　November 14, 1982　　Clear Creek (River Mile 84) in the Vishnu Schist (?)
Balsharaf of South Yemen split off from a German hiking companion to **solo** *hike into Clear Creek drainage from Phantom. His size 8, Nike footprints were found by SAR personnel Sam West ascending a cliff west from the mouth of Clear Creek where he arrived after 10 miles, carrying only a daypack. No other positive evidence was found; no body. Balsharaf's death is suspected as due to a climbing fall, possibly into river, while trying to* **shortcut** *the 10-mile hike back to his gear at Phantom.* Burak, G. The Ol' Pioneer, *Spring, 1998. Incident report #82-3840*

Allen Kelling, 47　　November 22, 1982　　off old Supai Trail /Topocoba Hilltop
Kelling of Scottsdale, Arizona became a **solo** *hiker after rolling his truck while driving the road above Topocoba. He apparently decided to hike into Supai for help but slipped off the Topocoba Trail (possibly while* **shortcutting***?) at one of the switchbacks. Kelling fell 80–100 feet on Havasupai land. Incident report #82-4096*

Theodore Levin, 38　　May 6, 1984　　near confluence of Salt Trail Canyon and Little Colorado River
While **hiking** *and* **scrambling** *with two friends in Salt Trail Canyon on Navajo Nation land, Levin of Glendale, Arizona fell 150 feet.* Arizona Daily Sun, *May 8, 1984.*

Charles M. Mays, 42　　June 9, 1984　　Bright Angel Trail
Mays of Warner Robbins, Georgia was hiking up from the river with his daughter and decided to walk **solo off the trail** *onto a narrow ledge* **to take a photo** *at sunset. He lost his footing while*

preparing to take the photo and fell 300 feet. Arizona Republic, *June 11, 1984. Incident report #84-1361*

Jonathan Paul Bladel, 21   March 5, 1985   Pipeline route off Bright Angel Trail in the Vishnu Schist

*Bladel of Hinesdale, Illinois detoured as a **solo hiker** off the Bright Angel Trail, **short-cutting** between switchbacks up along the pipeline during icy conditions. He slipped and fell 75 feet. He likely died of a combination of fall and subsequent exposure. He was found the next morning.* Arizona Daily Sun, *March 7, 1985. Incident report #85-0249*

Randy V. Fischer, 22   August 17, 1985   Plateau Point/Tapeats Sandstone

***Solo hiking off** the Tonto Trail along the Tapeats Rim, Fischer of Sunnyvale, California slipped and fell (**shortcutting?**) **unwitnessed** about 600 feet.* Arizona Daily Sun, *August 21 & 23, 1985. Incident report #85-2901*

Connie Marie Wernette, 28   September 21, 1986   Elves' Chasm (River Mile 116.5) in the Tapeats Sandstone

*Wernette of Ashland, Oregon became **lost and strayed** from the scrambling/climbing route while lagging behind, and out of view of, her friends. She continued her own **solo** ascent on a non-route which dead-ended, fizzling out against a cliff face. Wernette fell **unwitnessed** 30+ feet head first onto bedrock. (see text) Incident report #86-2791*

Ronald Dwayne Hight, 47   August 16, 1989   off Tonto Trail near Boulder Creek

***Solo backpacking** a cross-country route during high temperatures, Hight of Denver, Colorado took a **shortcut** route that was a few hundred yards above the Tonto Trail. Hight, a veteran of nearly 20 Canyon hikes, fell **unwitnessed** 50 feet. When last seen (by a companion who had exited earlier) Hight had appeared ill and was spitting up blood. Other hikers found Hight's body 7 months later, on March 10, 1990.* Arizona Daily Sun, *March 12, 1990. Incident report #89-3534*

Timothy A. Burris, 39   March 17, 1990   Sheep's Head Trail, (River Mile 4)

*Burris of Flagstaff, Arizona, during a **hiking**/fishing trip to river, slipped and fell 60 feet. Incident report #90-0534*

Ronald Shortt, 21   June 6, 1990   below El Tovar Hotel in the Kaibab Limestone

*Shortt was **free-soloing off-route** in sandals in a highly exposed position not far below the South Rim. He fell 750 feet. Incident report #90-1656*

Michael Jacobs, 43   September 21, 1990   River Mile 120.25 in the Tapeats Sandstone

*Jacobs of Kanab, Utah was trip leader on a Moki Mac commercial river trip. He ascended an exposed chimney in the Tapeats as a **free-solo climber** on Class 5 terrain. He lost both handholds and his friction on one foot and fell nearly 50 feet. (see text) Incident report #90-3811*

Unknown Wescogame child   circa 1990s   S side of Ash Canyon, Havasu Canyon
A Havasupai child fell fatally. Details unclear. Stephen Hirst letter to Ghiglieri, May 1, 2012.

Beverly Ann Collins, 26   May 5, 1994   Pipeline route west of Bright Angel Trail below Plateau Point in the Vishnu Schist
*Collins, a Phantom Ranch employee from Greenville, South Caro-lina, **solo** hiked/**scrambled** the pipeline route **shortcut**. She slipped and fell 100 feet to the foot of the Tapeats Sandstone.* Arizona Daily Sun, *May 27, 1994. Incident report #94-1537*

Richard Flowers, 35   July 2, 1994   Lake Mead National Recreation Area near Grand Wash and Shivwits Plateau
*Flowers was camping with girlfriend near Twin Points off Shivwits Plateau. During the day of July 2, he had been **drinking vodka** and grapefruit juice and beer. At 7:00 p.m., he started on a **solo hike-scramble** without food or water and failed to return. On July 3, Flowers' hat was found in nearby tributary canyon. On July 4, helicopter SAR personnel located Flowers 600 vertical feet below plateau; he had fallen **unwitnessed** into a pine tree. Death had occurred upon impact. Incident report #94-2448*

Gabriel Parrish Parker, 21   October 29, 1995   North Kaibab Trail atop the Coconino Sandstone
*Parker of Portland, Oregon experienced an **unwitnessed** fall of 380 feet from the top to the foot of the Coconino Sandstone. Parker's body, equipped as a **hiker (solo?)**, was found six months later by maintenance workers. His death was ruled accidental.* Williams-Grand Canyon News, *April 24, 1996. Incident report #96-1706*

Sheryl Flack, 48   May 8, 1998   Plateau Point near Bright Angel Trail in the Tapeats Sandstone
*On a mule trip, Flack of Glendale, California was alone (**solo**) for a few minutes during a lunch break on the edge of the Tapeats. She suffered an **unwitnessed** fall of 400+ feet (possibly while urinat-ing?).* Arizona Republic, *May 10, 1998. Incident report #98-1231*

Andrew Patrick Drugg, 13   June 12, 2001   North Canyon (RM 20.5)
*Drugg of Canyon Lake, Texas was **day-hiking** as a client on a Moki Mac River Expeditions trip and was following his uncle. On a well-used but unmaintained trail Andy tried to pass close against a huge, perched and outwardly leaning boulder located 6 feet **off-route** from the standard hiking route but adjacent to the waterfall amphithe-ater ½ mile from the river. The 6' 1"-, 255-pound boy was seen by a witness close behind him to lose his balance where one must scrunch down to pass adjacent to that leaning boulder (again that location is about 6 feet off-route). Drugg silently fell backward 6 feet onto a ledge then tumbled off 48 feet, touching nothing until he hit bedrock. CPR by guides and paramedics proved unsuccessful due to the victim's se-vere head trauma. Drugg is the second child to die from a fall within the Canyon. (see text) Incident report #01-1582*

Aaron Tyree, 18   September 6, 2001   Mooney Falls, Havasu Canyon
Tyree of Mesa, Arizona was visiting with friends plus family. Pos-

sibly under the influence of amphetamines, Tyree scooted on his butt over the lip of Mooney Falls 20 feet with the intent to dive off. Bystanders talked Tyree out of diving. Next, however, Tyree tried to **solo** *downclimb* **off-trail** *next to the upper chain along descent path. He fell about 100 feet and impacted bedrock.*

Hannah Lockwood Suzanne   October 3, 2001   between Ooh-Ahh Point & Windy Ridge,
Stehlin, 13   1¼ miles from trailhead of S Kaibab Trail

Stehlin of Flemington, New Jersey and her father and brother stopped hiking to pet trail repair mules hitched to re-bar off the trail and to take a photo. Hannah was an experienced horsewoman and an athletic hiker. Hannah's father and brother led onward along their planned **rim-to-river-to-rim day-hike.** *Her father looked back and saw Hannah. She was 10 feet from the mules. Seconds later her father, now about 70 feet from the mules, heard a "scuff" sound behind him. He looked back for Hannah. She had vanished from a section of trail sprinkled with small rocks (possibly from having been dung-raked that morning) and scuff marks (possibly from a boulder moved). A Royal Air Force airman climbed several feet below the trail here. He followed scuff marks and a blood smear. He found Hannah's hat and sunglasses then spotted her body below a vertical drop. She apparently had slipped despite ideal footwear and had lost her footing* **unwitnessed.** *She fell 177 feet off the 4-foot-wide trail. Hannah is the third child ever to die from a fall within the Canyon. (see text) Incident report #01-3037*

Sabra L. Jones, 44   August 12, 2002   Havasu/Dry Beaver Creek confluence

Jones of Gallup, New Mexico was a river guide for Tour West. She broke off from her group **solo** *to belatedly follow three other crew members who had previously split then* **scramble-climbed off-trail** *a travertine cliff to visit a ceramic "protector" idol also known as "Fox Man" and "Beaver Man" tucked into the cliff facing downstream in the 1980s by Claire Donha, a passenger on a commercial raft trip. As the three other guides began descending an exposed route, Jones hurriedly climbed upward toward them. All three warned her to slow down. But to no avail. Ten feet from them Jones grabbed a ridge of travertine and used it to haul herself higher. It snapped off. She fell about 15 feet, then toppled another 35 feet. Her respirations stopped within 2 minutes. Incident report #02-2469*

Lucas Fara, 28   November 29, 2002   First Tunnel on Bright Angel Trail

Fara, a Czech citizen, made his way past an NPS sign warning "Dangerous Footing. Do Not Enter" and entered, descending **solo** *an* **exposed, off-trail** *ledge to* **pose** *for a dramatic* **photo.** *He slipped and fell 150 feet. Incident report #02-3806*

Gordon Robert Wagner, Jr., 57   September 5, 2004   North Canyon

Wagner of Jenison, Michigan, while on a private river trip, was **day-hiking** *at noon past the narrow section of the route/trail between the cuboid, out-leaning boulder and the drop-off above the dry waterfall and amphitheater located about ½ mile from the river, the exact* **off-route** *location where Andy Drugg (above) fell.*

As the 6-foot, 205-pound Wagner stepped up about 1 foot to the ledge, he tried to hug the boulder while also holding in one hand a Gatorade bottle as he stepped. He lost his "hold" and his balance and fell backwards 6 feet, bounced off his side, then toppled about 48 feet lower, identical to Andy Drugg's sad demise. He suffered cranial and spinal injuries. After this event, because the safe route only four feet away was missed twice fatally and missed thousands of times otherwise, the NPS Trail Crew radically rerouted the trail to the uphill side of the big boulder. Incident report #04-4887

Marlin Ray Lindquist, 70

September 18, 2004   North Kaibab Trail, Eye of the Needle
Lindquist of Richland, Washington was **backpacking** downhill 10 feet behind his wife at 9:30 a.m. on day #1 of a planned cross-canyon 4-day hike, the couple's first attempt, when he fell **unwitnessed.** She heard him then turned and saw him arrest his fall spread-eagled and headfirst on the steep talus about 15 feet down, near the brink of the cliff. He said, "I'm okay," then he immediately slid farther and over the cliff into a 450-foot fall. A hiker who had passed the couple minutes earlier noted of Lindquist, "The man was carrying a large, heavy pack [32 pounds before adding his water]and appeared a little unsteady," despite using a walking stick. Incident report #04-5094

Randy R. Rogers, 46

September 10, 2005   tributary off Bright Angel Trail
Rogers of Chandler, Arizona vanished on his final, ritualized **solo backpacking hike** during his last of many annual "traditional" visits to the Canyon. A large scale ground and air search for 5 days failed (the dogs used led rangers instead to the body of Texas suicider Michael Alvarado, age 37, who jumped on September 13, 2005). A year later, on August 20, 2006, Ranger Della Yurcik ascended the Pipeline route up Pipe Creek from the base of the Corkscrew. Below a big chockstone she found, partly buried in alluvial sand, glasses in a case and a damaged clipboard with "Randy R." on it. Above the chockstone Yurchik found a sleeping bag, tent, etc. scattered by run-off. This led to a focused search by foot and helicopter, which discovered 35% of a skeleton plus dentition scattered in an un-named side drainage. Forensics indicated Rogers had a **fractured tibia** sustained while wearing his Adidas tennis shoes, suggesting an **unwitnessed fall** while **solo** hiking **off-trail** and **shortcutting** followed by **dehydration.** Incident report #05-4874

Reinhard Kirchner, 61

April 1 (?), 2007   Hellhole Bend area, Little Colorado
Kirchner, a physicist from Germany, made annual **solo** visits from Germany to **scramble-explore** the Little Colorado Plateau, methodically making notes on his map of each area he covered. After he failed to rejoin his girlfriend in Las Vegas on April 9, an extensive multi-agency search coordinated by Aaron Dick of Coconino County Sheriff's SAR team found his car, camp, and annotated map—but after 1,500 man-hours by more than 50 searchers on foot, on horseback, on ATVs, in helicopters, or on rappelling ropes scouring 56 square miles—but not him. Search efforts narrowed the possibilities to abduction or an **unwitnessed** fall down a sinkhole in the Kaibab. As of 2011, he is still missing.

Alan Goldbaum, middle age   July 31, 2007   Esplanade NE of confluence of Hualapai
                                                 and Havasu canyons
*"Goldbaum, half-white, half-Havasupai, had been at a local party
that became aggressive and had left. Fearing pursuit, he ascended
the "Apache Trail" up Schoolhouse Canyon and set off along the
Esplanade trails that he knew unusually well. Hiking in the dark,
he fell." Stephen Hirst, letter to Ghiglieri May 1, 2012.* Arizona
Daily Sun *August 8, 2012.*

John Presley, 63   August 28, 2008   1.5 miles up Stone Creek trail, above wa-
                                                  terfall
*While returning to the river in the evening (6:04 p.m.) on an AzRA
river trip **day-hike** along a well-used but unmaintained trail
adjacent to severe exposure, Presley of Danville, California heard
the last words he was ever to hear: "Take your time; be careful here,
guys." Presley, an apparently fit and active skier and mountain
biker, next made a short downward jump. His Vasque low-top hiking shoes slipped on loose rock on the Shinumo Quartzite. He tried
to "**run out of the slip**." Instead he lost control as his momentum
carried him quickly to the cliff edge. In a last effort Presley grabbed
with both arms a large barrel cactus to arrest his momentum. The
cactus instantly tore loose. It and Presley fell about 50 feet onto
bedrock. Incident report #08-6073*

Thomas Peake, 39   September 21, 2009   low, near the Toroweap Trail to Lava Falls
*Peake of Atlanta, Georgia left his wife in the North Rim area of
Toroweap Valley at 9:00 a.m. and started a **solo day-hike** down the
rugged, 1.5-mileToroweap Trail, 2,500 feet to the river. The 6' 1",
195-lb. Peake carried 3 liters of water, a walkie-talkie, compass, and
camera but no map or GPS. He later radioed his wife: "when you're
lost here, you're really lost." He admitted using "rock climbing skills"
to **scramble** in the wrong ravine toward the river. After 11:00 a.m.,
his radio transmissions ceased. Helicopter searchers found his body
low, near the route, but **off-trail** and **off alternate routes, shortcutting**. Ascending, Peake had died from an **unwitnessed** fall of roughly
15-20 feet off a class 5 (= vertical) cliff marked by blood smears.
Laterally 30 feet a class 3 (= broken and steep) route led up the same
cliff. Peake had lost or discarded a shoe, his radio, and water bottles.
He had been hiking waterless up the steep, hot terrain and bouldering
shoeless instead of slogging. (see text) Incident report #09-7345*

John Kynyk, 52   October 20, 2010   Elves' Chasm, RM 116.5
*During a **solo scramble-hike** on a private river trip, Kynyk of
Goodyear, Arizona, allegedly an avid rock climber and a long-time
member of the Arizona Mountaineering Club, fell **unwitnessed**
about 120 feet. His companions found him dead, and instead of
leaving him in place—as required by law—they carried him to the
boats and rowed his body 3 miles downriver to Blacktail Canyon
where they figured a helicopter could land. The private group did
not know NPS and ADPS helicopters are equipped with long lines
and other gear for short-hauling a body (or living victim) to a safe
area for landing. (see text) Incident report #10-6997*

Barbara Evert, 77   April 28, 2011   Tabernacle route from upper Rattlesnake
                                                Camp (RM 74)
*Evert, an outdoor recreation instructor from Englewood, Colorado,
was making a **day hike** with the group on a commercial river trip
run by Hatch Expeditions. The route offers some exposure, but less
than some of the Park's main corridor trails. Evert had sat down for
a rest break. Afterward, as she stood and began to walk, she tripped
on a small rock, lost her balance and/or equilibrium, and pitched
forward into a fall of 100-140 feet. Personal communication from
J.P. Running, June 1, 2011.*

Ioana Elise Hociota, 24   February 26, 2012   Owl Eyes Canyon in Supai Group
*Hociota of Tempe, Arizona and originally from Romania was at-
tempting to complete the final 6 miles of a 15-mile section missing
from her entire record of hiking Grand Canyon's south side from
Lees Ferry to Diamond Creek, in her attempt to become the 16th
person to have accomplished this (she had logged 850 miles within
Grand Canyon). She and her hiking partner Matthias Kawski took
separate routes, out of view of one another, traversing across the
Supai **solo** within 135 Mile Bay. He heard rocks fall. He called out
to Hociota. Kawski reported that, receiving no answer and being
unable to see her or a way down, he hiked out to arrange a rescue.
Hociota had fallen 300 feet unwitnessed and due to unknown
causes.* Grand Canyon News Release, February 28, 2012. Rich Ru-
dow "Fatal Fall in Owl Eyes Canyon—RIP Ioana," March 5, 2012.

Jeffrey Klingsick, 20   May 22, 2012   Pipe Creek Vista
*Klingsick of Derby, Kansas was a U.S. Marine on his way home from
Afghanistan. He decided to downclimb from the rim to then climb
up an attached spire for a **photo**. While climbing up he slipped and
fell and was knocked unconscious upon impact. As his USMC buddy
downclimbed to help, Klingsick regained consciousness. His buddy
yelled to him not to move, but Klingsick tried to stand. He lost his
balance and fell 600 feet.* AP May 24, 2012. 5:52 p.m.

Rosa Torres Rios, 68   July 19, 2012   Grand View Trail
*Rios of Nogales, Arizona hiked a short distance down the Grand-
view, slipped and fell 300 feet.*

William Anthony Ott, 65   April-May, 2012   Mohawk Canyon/National Canyon/
                                                 Hualapai Nation
*On April 5, Ott of Cave Junction, Oregon embarked on a **solo**,
21-day, un-permitted backpacking hike, intending to explore the
Esplanade down Mohawk Canyon eastward to National Canyon
and then out in search of 3,000-year-old polychrome art sites. He
intended to rely on pothole water. There was none. Temperatures
neared 100 degrees. (In 1981, Ott had hiked the north side of Grand
Canyon, solo for 68 of the 78 days, from Lees Ferry to the Grand
Wash Cliffs, becoming the first person to hike the entire Canyon
below the rim.) 27 days of extensive multi-agency searching coordinated by Sgt. Aaron Dick of the Coconino County Sheriff's Dept.
SAR teams (1,407 person-hours by multiple teams), Arizona Dept.*

of Public Safety helicopters (96.7 crew-hours and 30.2 helicopter-hours), NPS rangers (50 person-hours and 3 helicopter trips), Hualapai Nation representatives, and Ott's friend (Scott Thybony) found few signs of Ott. Speculation is Ott became dehydrated and died due to a fall while attempting to descend a shortcut route off the Esplanade to water. Ott is not included in fall statistics due to the uncertainty of his fate. During mid- to late July of 2012, monsoon cloudbursts scoured National and Mohawk canyons and perhaps Ott.

Chapter Three

The Desert Crucible
Environmental Death Within the
"Inverted Mountain"

Polliwogs!" Paul Stryker mumbled in disgust to his wife Karen as they stared down into the bedrock pool of water in the otherwise dry-appearing bed of upper Cottonwood Creek. The inferno of late June had sucked almost every molecule of moisture from this part of the heart of Grand Canyon—except for this little bedrock pool. The tiny polliwogs in the life-giving pool now scurried for cover to escape the two huge bipeds standing over it.

"We can't drink this—"

It was late June in 1990. The weather was as hot and as dry as it gets in the Canyon. The mercury soared well above 100 degrees. Karen and Paul Stryker, both age 26 and from Pennsylvania, were making a two-day hike from Grandview to the South Kaibab Trail and then down it to the river.

Knowing that it would be hot, the couple had carried six liters of water each, three liters of water per day per person, for their two-day backpacking trip. Having never hiked before in Grand Canyon, the Strykers reckoned this amount would be adequate. Tragically, this would not be even half enough. They had also done their arithmetic on the trail. Their downhill route to the river had looked to them to be about 18 miles. Here they had underestimated yet again. In reality, the route they had tackled was closer to 26 miles.

On their first day they each drank three liters, leaving the remaining three for the next day. Having brought maybe a third of the water they should have carried for their location, season, exposure, and activity level, they were extremely fortunate to find water in the potholes in the dry bed of Cottonwood Creek.

The couple stared in disappointment at the water in the stone basin as those tiny polliwogs wriggled for cover. No amount of wishful thinking could transform this natural pool into the office water cooler back home in Pennsylvania. "I can't drink that...."

Neither Paul nor Karen overcame their sqeamishness enough to drink this water. Nor did they refill their empty bottles with this life-giving fluid "just in case" the heat became too much. This decision to favor fastidiousness over survival would become a fatal error.

The Strykers camped the first night there in the dry drainage of Grapevine Creek. Paul and Karen had backpacked before—Paul starting with Boy Scouts and both of them later across Europe and in the Rockies. But backpacking in the desert, Paul's brother John would later note, was a new thing. That night, due to the heat, Paul did not eat dinner, but he did plan to eat breakfast in the morning.

The next morning Paul did not feel like eating breakfast. The couple started hiking at 4:30 a.m., with the first faint light of dawn. Tragically, it would prove, the two parched hikers could have hiked (had they known) a mere few hundred feet either up Grapevine or down it from the Tonto and have found water in the bed of the creek. Even so, the Strykers might have refused to drink this, too.

By noon they had been hiking for several hours under full sun and now realized that they had to find shade. Paul had finally eaten: an apple, an orange, and some trail mix. The two hikers found a tiny patch of shade, but soon the movement of the sun erased it.

Karen and Paul walked on in the screaming heat of day along the disappointingly sinuous Tonto Trail under full sun. It was too hot. Finding no shade on the Tonto Trail, they stopped and set up a shade tarp. They huddled under it to try to "wait out" the heat.

Paul quickly became frustrated with the implacably radiating heat, far hotter than 100 degrees even in the shade of the tarp. "Let's go," he said. So they began hiking again.

As had been the case all that day, Paul encouraged Karen to drink more water. In so doing, he himself drank far less. Their three liters each were not enough to last either of them until noon—if they had known what to do to survive in the desert on a hike such as theirs, they each would have had nine liters for this one day alone. Instead, here it was afternoon and they were eking sips and swallows from their bottles as if to save the last water for when they might "really" need it. Meanwhile both of them were losing pounds and gallons of body moisture as their bodies battled desperately to survive the heat.

By the time they reached the upper drainages of Cremation Canyon, heat and dehydration were making it hard for either of them to make an intelligent decision. The trail that was supposed to connect with the South Kaibab Trail veered uphill. Could this uphill trail really connect with the Kaibab? Could it be right to go uphill like this when they wanted to go downhill to the river?

Of course it did connect, and it was correct, and it was only about three miles farther to the Kaibab. But neither hiker at this point thought they could walk uphill at all. They were down to one liter of water between them. Karen had swallowed the lion's share of the woefully inadequate water the two had consumed that day.

So instead of hiking the easy, though initially upward, main Tonto Trail, they decided to drop down into the Cremation drainage and make a cross-country, unknown, downhill, shortcut traverse to the river.

Scramble climbing in Grand Canyon inevitably proves far more difficult—both technically and in effort expended—than following a NPS maintained trail, especially if descending. This descent of Cremation again proved this rule. It also proved the wisdom of an even more important rule: "Do not shortcut across unknown terrain."

After a couple of hours of struggling against ever worsening terrain, Karen and Paul started shouting in hopes that someone might hear them. They next tried mirror flashes at overflying aircraft. Neither tactic seemed to alert a rescue.

At only 2:00 p.m., the sun vanished beyond a cliff. Now flashing a mirror from within the drainage became impossible.

Paul and Karen started walking downhill again. Paul stumbled and fell. Then he stumbled again. He could not seem to keep his balance anymore. Paul's loss of balance was a glaring signal of advanced dehydration.

Karen helped him up. But now Paul admitted he could not manage to descend Cremation—nor, of course, could he now ascend back up it to the Tonto Trail. Paul told Karen to "go on and save yourself."

Karen told Paul that she would rather stay with him and die with him—if he died.

They were out of water. It was barely 2:30 p.m. The afternoon would continue to grow ever hotter.

Karen stayed with Paul. He became semi-comatose and delirious, mumbling unintelligibly. Eventually Karen suspected he was dead. Soon she knew he was dead. Eventually she realized that she might still have a chance to make it to the river during the final few hours of daylight remaining. So she started down Cremation again. But after only a short distance she found the terrain too daunting. She decided to sleep then try again in the morning.

At dawn of day three, Karen awoke, grabbed one empty water bottle, and continued her hike. This time she ascended. She soon found the Kaibab Trail and hiked it west, soon passing the Tipoff emergency phone. From there she headed down the final 2 miles to the river. By 5:30 a.m., she reached the Phantom Ranger Station. In short, while Paul lay dying in a delirium of dehydration and heatstroke, he had been only 2 hours from the river by trail. Sadly, Paul Stryker died of self-induced dehydration spurring his death due to heatstroke.

During her investigative interview, Karen repeated one statement: She and Paul had no idea that the temperatures in Grand Canyon could be so hot.

Indeed. Among the fifty United States of America, Arizona is the state where the second hottest temperature ever was recorded: 128 degrees Fahrenheit on June 29, 1994, at Lake Havasu City at 420 feet elevation and 100 miles southwest of Grand Canyon. The hottest temperature ever measured officially in the USA was recorded on July 10, 1913, 178 feet below sea level at Greenville Ranch (in California's Death Valley region), a lead-melting 134 degrees. Summer temperatures in Grand Canyon have hit 120 degrees in the shade.

In the winter, however, this extreme reverses.

In the winter of 1939, for example, two young friends, Casimar Pultorak, age 22, and Paul E. Des Jardins, age 17, drove west from Detroit to Grand Canyon in Pultorak's 1937 Ford. On February 9, the young men signed the register at the Bright Angel Trailhead and descended the 9-mile trail to the river with the intent of hiking back up to the South Rim on the same day.

The soon-to-be-written *Superintendent's Report* and *Coconino Sun* article (February, 1939) both reported that NPS Ranger George Hetherington warned at least one of these hikers that their planned 18-mile hike was over-ambitious and overly-optimistic for the trail and for the season of the year (the dead of winter). Fifty-eight years later, however, Des Jardins still insisted that no one warned him that they were biting off more than they could chew.

Either way, the two hikers descended the trail dressed only in jeans, light shirts, and light jackets. They reached the Colorado River in good shape. After a lunch of crackers and pork and beans, the two began their return ascent. Now they noticed a storm coming in. The rain quickly turned to snow. In the fading, or absent, light the two wet, shivering hikers walked up past Indian Garden without even seeing it.

The two stopped at a rest house, likely at 3-Mile (measured downward from the South Rim). What happened next is as muddled as the minds of the two hypothermic young adventurers. (The original reports of this episode disagree somewhat with a letter written by Des Jardins nearly 60 years later in 1997.) According to a report in a fatalities file kept by Fred Harvey Co., amidst heavy snowfall, the two built a fire 3.5 miles below the Rim. Later, they tried to continue on up through the storm, but eventually they stopped again and built a second fire. Pultorak was so cold that he could hardly stand. He fell over into the fire, putting it out.

Des Jardins reportedly stood him against a rock ledge and tried to continue up the trail. When Des Jardins reached the next "shelter" (1.5 Mile House or 3-Mile House; which one is not clear), a small, roofed dwelling with no walls, he was so chilled that he was too confused to figure out how to use its emergency phone. He was also too exhausted to hike any farther, up or down. He climbed into the rafters to escape the driving wind and snow blowing into the hut from its open sides.

Meanwhile, Pultorak had exited the ledge where he had been left. Or else (in the other version of the story) he exited the lower, Three-Mile Rest House—or he did both—and continued up the trail. Roughly two or three miles separated him from the rim.

The next morning Wilbur Wright and his wife descended the trail on mules through heavy fallen snow. About two miles down, the mules spooked. Wright investigated. He found a hand jutting from a snowbank beside the trail. It was attached to Pultorak's frozen body.

Wright went to the nearest rest house on the trail to report his grisly find. Here Wright heard a noise from above him in the rafters. It was Des Jardins, nearly frozen, but still propped up in the rafters in the chill air.

Rangers evacuated Des Jardins first downhill to Indian Garden then up to the rim via mule litter through two to three feet of new snow. For the next five weeks in the hospital in Williams, Dr. Ewell carefully removed blackened tissue from the 17-year-old's severely frost-bitten feet. The doctor knew what he was doing. Des Jardins lost only his left big toe—instead of both feet as first anticipated.

Des Jardins' thoughts during his night of misery while cramped into the rafters of the 1.5 Mile (or 3-Mile) House—as well as his thoughts during the following five weeks in the hospital—and Pultorak's thoughts during his last few hours of life on the Bright Angel Trail were likely both haunted by the same surprising revelation: "I had no idea that Grand Canyon could be so cold."

Karen and Paul Stryker's revelation about the extreme heat of summer in the Canyon and Des Jardins' and Pultorak's revelation about how unbelievably cold the Canyon can be in winter epitomizes the single most common misconception that visitors to the Canyon share: "Lots of people hike in Grand Canyon; it can't be that dangerous."

For perspective on how naïve many visitors are when they arrive at the South Rim then stare down into that 1,000-cubic mile hole in the planet consider the following letter to us from visitor Linda Sellers:

Forty year ago (in 1969) I hiked to the bottom [of the Canyon] with my family. I was 18 and my brother and cousin were 16 and my sister was 8. My parents, August and Marge Smith, were in their late thirties. The reason we went to the Canyon was we thought we could ride the mules down. My dad is a tall man who weighed about 200 pounds and that was too much for the mules. We had no intention of hiking to the bottom, but the ranger convinced my dad it would be the thing to do, hike down the Kaibab and out the Bright Angel. You have to remember that in those days rangers were gods. If they said go for a hike, we would go for a hike.

We were so unprepared. We were a poor family from Detroit. My dad hiked to the bottom in wing tips and black dress socks. My mother had cheap canvas shoes that caused her toes to turn black for months. It took us 8 hours down the South Kaibab. My brother had cheap, slip-on canvas shoes. I had on Indian fringed moccasins, which was like hiking barefoot. To this day I remember the puddles of mule piss because they all peed in the same spot [because equines only pee when stopped, and they stop at switchbacks]. On the hike down we saw no one.

There was a pop machine at the bottom right near the ranch. My little sister was grabbing everyone's pop and guzzling them down like an animal. Then she threw it up. My God, after reading your book I realize how dehydrated we all were. We stayed that night in a tent top with a screened-in porch. It stormed like crazy and scared us all to death.

My mom thinks it took us 12 hours to get back out on the Bright Angel Trail. We did not have enough water; we only had an old army canteen. We bought a box lunch for my sister, but that's all we could afford. That walk up was misery. I thought my mother was going to die. We nick-named her Turtle Foot. On the hike up there were more people. We all remember the French girl. She was hiking in a very small black bikini and she was as white as snow. My mom told her to cover up so she wouldn't get a sunburn. She laughed at my mom.

Later at Indian Gardens she was stretched out on a table with a wet shirt on her head. She was crying. The group of American boys she was with were in a panic. I'll tell you, this is what heat does to you. None of us gave a hoot. We were so worried about getting out ourselves that we didn't care about the French girl. We just kept trudging on.

There was a group of four young men from California. They had very long hair and were definitely hippies. They kept reaching into a bag whenever we saw them. My dad called us kids to him and said stay back from those guys, they have a bag of dope. About an hour later we came around a turn and there they were. They opened the bag and asked us if we wanted some sunflower seeds, because they were salty and seemed to help. We became friendly and they encouraged us as we would pass each other on the trail. The weird part is they were going to California too. We ran into them again at Disneyland. When we saw each other again it was pure emotion. That's what the Canyon does.

When we saw the Canyon a couple of weeks ago (40 years later, in 2009). I still had that same thrill go through me. Life changes but the Canyon still moves me. I will tell you something else that moved me. There were people climbing over the barriers the minute we got there. We stopped at the tower and there was this kid over the fence and out on the cliff. His Italian mother wanted a better picture. I saw this several times. I saw kids throwing water bottles into the Canyon. Parents acted as if this were nothing. There were groups of people who would not share the sidewalk. It was crazy. Is it just me or are all our rangers old ladies? Sure, if they are Nevada Barr and can kick some ass, okay. But that's not what I saw.

The rudeness of some visitors aside, in the Canyon heat kills. And so does the

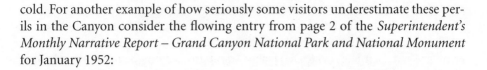

cold. For another example of how seriously some visitors underestimate these perils in the Canyon consider the flowing entry from page 2 of the *Superintendent's Monthly Narrative Report – Grand Canyon National Park and National Monument* for January 1952:

> *The superintendent and rangers had a very busy afternoon on the 29th [January, 1952] rescuing Virginia DeVore from the Hermit Trail, where she was endeavoring to hike on an exploring and prospecting expedition to Hoover Dam, following the Colorado River [250 miles by river, twice that by land]. Her supplies were six candy bars. Although Miss DeVore refused to ride the five miles out by mule, she was out on top by 8:00 p.m. The deputy sheriff took her to Flagstaff and put her on a bus for the return trip to Glendale, California, where she had been employed.*

Of course the vast majority of visitors are somewhat more savvy than "Miss DeVore." And most of them exit Grand Canyon National Park unscathed. Moreover, of those who die here, some people expire merely because the sands of their physiological hourglass have run out due to nature's normal slow course, and they happen to be in the Canyon at that moment. Yet even in many apparent cases of this sort it remains uncertain whether or not the Canyon environment also played a role in their deaths. In nearly every death, the Canyon remains a suspicious accomplice. In other cases, as with the Strykers above, it is all too clear that the Canyon—and ignorance of the Canyon environment—combined as the only cause of death.

The ways in which some victims have shattered their own hourglasses in the Canyon defy belief. For example, James Higgins, age 19, decided on a fairly reasonable itinerary for hiking the Inner Canyon. On July 7, 1977, he would park his Honda 350 cc motorcycle on the South Rim and hike down to Hermit Campground. On July 8, he would continue down Hermit Creek to the Colorado then back up onto the Tonto Trail. On the 9th, he would hike east to Monument Creek. On the next day (day #4), he would hike farther east on the Tonto to Horn Creek (which is a seasonal creek only, except during flashfloods). On July 11 (day #5), Higgins would hike to the Bright Angel Trail and Indian Garden, and then back up 2,600 feet to the South Rim. This was not a bad itinerary—except for Higgins' timing.

It was early July, the very hottest time of the year in a place that is almost unbelievably hot for five months of the year. So hot that the coolest hour of darkness may plunge only to a sizzling low of 100 degrees.

But as a long-time resident of Boulder City, Nevada, another very hot place that owes its existence only to the building of Hoover Dam, Higgins might have been expected to understand heat, what it can do, and what precautions to take so that it won't. So, even with young Higgins' admission on his permit application "Does not know the area," at least he did know heat.

On July 11, Higgins failed to appear at Indian Garden or at the South Rim.

The search began. Searchers learned that early on the morning of July 9, other hikers had seen Higgins leave Hermit Campground one day later than he had planned. From there Higgins' movements became hazy, but ended in a gruesome trail.

About midmorning of July 12, three hikers came across the first clues. As they hiked the Tonto Trail eastward toward Horn Creek Canyon and beyond, they found a set of motorcycle tools abandoned on the trail. Farther on, they found motorcycle boots. Three pairs of motorcycle boots. Next they found a receipt made out to Higgins. Next a pair of Levis. Then, far more ominous, the trio of hikers found a plastic soap dish. Inside it were Higgins' driver's license and his library cards.

When the three finally came upon Higgins himself, he was clad only in his underwear. He was unconscious, severely dehydrated, hyperthermic, and very close to death. In his backpack was only one water bottle, an empty glass jar.

One of the hikers stayed with Higgins. The other two ran two and a half level miles to Indian Garden to alert the ranger there. An NPS helicopter landed on the Tonto and evacuated Higgins. During that less-than-five-minute flight to the Grand Canyon Clinic, however, Higgins died of extreme dehydration and heatstroke.

Chalk up Higgins to a case of Canyon ignorance? Maybe. But let's not jump the gun. It is not just "outsiders" or "noncanyoneers" who succumb in the Canyon. Even men of the Four Corners' canyon country have been trapped by the Canyon's vast, complicated, waterless labyrinth. Consider, for example, this following note scrawled on the inside of a U-tah-na cherry chocolate bar wrapper and found sealed in a tobacco tin stashed below Point Imperial.

Ray Hoggan
Bert Hall
Dick Carlson
Rex   "
Sept. 29th 1929
Manti, Utah
Sanpete Co
4 days without food or water
Lost

What happened to these four men after this desperate note was sealed in the tin remained a mystery for years. But thanks to Becky Douglas, who grew up in Manti and who quizzed her grandfather, we learned all four had survived.

Again, heat is a killer, especially of the naive or ignorant. A hard lesson here is: canyoneering is emphatically not mountaineering. In any group of mountaineers, the number of potential summiteers shrinks as the mountain lets people know just how hard it really is to gain elevation solely via one's own power. In other words, mountains often weed out the unfit so early in the game that, once they realize they have bitten off more than they can chew, they can often return fairly easily downhill to their staging zone.

In complete contrast, canyons do the opposite. While descending most Canyon trails, the ease and coolness of the descent are seductive. It's a breeze even for the unfit or the unprepared. Until the time comes to hike back up. Then, when it's all too often a hot, dry, hard, agonizing, and often torturous physiological contrast to the descent, the unfit get weeded out late in the game and get weeded out brutally. Sometimes fatally.

Almost routinely—despite the Canyon's infamous heat, scarcity of water, and lethal cliffs acting as ramparts to imprison the parched hiker away from the river of life flowing within view but so far below—all too many hikers underestimate the levels of heat and thirst in Grand Canyon. That a hiker may need more than two gallons of water per day for summer day-hiking in the Canyon may seem unbelievable. But, under some conditions—pivoting on the weight of the hiker, the weight of his pack, the air temperature in the shade, the wind, and the lack of shade, and uphill versus downhill—these two gallons-plus per day may not be enough.

Table 3 lists 102 known victims through 2014—only 17 of whom (17 percent) were women—of "environmental" deaths while hiking (or simply being) in the Canyon. The predominant causes of death listed are "cardiac arrest" and heatstroke. With 43 victims known, heatstrokes account for 43 percent of all victims. The most common cause of death, with 50 victims (50 percent) listed is "cardiac arrest," often heat-related, which of course simply states that the victim's heart stopped beating. "Cardiac arrest" is often a catch-all category for trail deaths. The question of why the hearts of those particular hikers stopped beating while hiking uphill in the intense heat of the Canyon has a short list of answers. In most cases, the cause certainly includes the victim's past medical cardiac history. But the common threads connecting these cardiac fatalities were not simply that "their time was up." Instead, the hot, arid Canyon environment, the "inverted mountain" effect of an easy initial descent in cool weather followed by a very demanding ascent in hot—combined with the victims' behaviors—often severed their timelines. In fact, most of these "cardiac-arrest" victims were hiking uphill, in the afternoon, often under direct solar heat (heat that can be unrelenting even in April and October), and in the dry Canyon air. Moreover, they often were hiking without having drunk enough water. These data strongly suggest that anyone with a known cardiac risk factor get a cardiac stress test from a clinic prior to hiking into Grand Canyon. Better a clinic conduct this test than the Bright Angel Trail doing it the hard way.

The human body's methods of cooling itself demand an adequate perfusion of blood to the internal organs and to the head and extremities to operate in a "radiator" effect. Accomplishing this requires an adequate circulating volume of blood—which is mostly water. The body also requires enough water for sweat to cool the body via an evaporative heat-loss effect. Lack of adequate sweating and loss of adequate perfusion due to dehydration and/or cardiac clogging and/or cardiac muscle death creates an instant and automatic danger to the hiker's homeostatic mechanisms—similar to what happens to a car with a bad radiator or a failing water pump laboring uphill in heat. On top of these problems, a normal person requires at least a week of acclimatization in a hot environment in order to adjust in a metabolically efficient way to the high heat of summer in Grand Canyon. Acclimatization, for one thing, reduces loss of the body's electrolytes. For another, it increases the body's ability to sweat to effect its most efficient cooling, which is the only way the body cools itself at temperatures exceeding 95 degrees.

In a Canyon Catch-22, however, almost no one has that week of active acclimatization in extreme heat prior to engaging in his or her Inner Canyon hikes—unless he or she has been working as a summer construction laborer in Phoenix. Instead, many of us hiking in Grand Canyon seem more like bizarre medical experiments tossed into an alien landscape of hostile temperatures, desiccating winds, and fierce solar radiation to see how long we can walk before we collapse. An all too typical NPS "Morning Report" by Patrick Brasington on June 12, 2000 illustrates how mindless people become as the heat soaks in and the effects of ever more severe dehydration foster hallucination.

> On May 25th, rangers received a report that 61-year-old John O'Donnell had failed to return from a day hike in the canyon. His cousin advised that he planned on hiking down the South Kaibab Trail, across the Tonto Trail, and back up the Bright Angel Trail. O'Donnell had only two small water bottles, no food, no flashlight, no map, and no extra clothing. Temperatures in the canyon that day ranged from 111 degrees during the day to 102 degrees at night. Rangers established containment points at the South Kaibab and Bright Angel trailheads and swept the three trails. No sign of O'Donnell was found. An aerial search ensued on the following morning, but initial efforts were fruitless. Rangers familiar with the history of lost people in this area made a second flight of the area and this time spotted O'Donnell. He was found to be suffering from severe dehydration and was hallucinating. He had also been hiding from searchers, who he thought were "bad guys." O'Donnell had water in one of his bottles, but told rangers he hadn't drunk it because a man sitting next to him said it was bad water (O'Donnell was found alone). He was flown out and treated at a medical facility. Doctors said he would not have survived another day if he hadn't been found.

While the heat alone is bad enough, hikers with cardiac inadequacies are at far greater risk of dying on the trail in Grand Canyon from environmental challenges than are healthy hikers. And as Table 3 suggests, laboring in the Canyon environment may have precipitated these cardiac deaths on the trail. In short, "cardiac arrest" listed as cause of death emphatically does not mean a fatality independent of environmental causes. We suspect several of these "cardiac" deaths were due to combinations of dehydration, hyperthermia, and exertion on steep trails, which turn people, inch by inch, into heat zombies.

These complications are further compounded by age. The most well-camouflaged victims of dehydration/heatstroke are fairly young and athletic. Kids and young adults seem to run at full function in the heat, sweating appropriately and seemingly going strong, but abruptly, when dehydration kicks in and core temperatures spike to the point where brain function is impaired, around 105 to 106 degrees, they crash quickly and often unexpectedly. And next they die.

A classic example of this sort of run-until-you-crash mentality was embodied by Arthur Clarence "Jack" Anderson, age 19. On July 1, 1925, Anderson decided to hike down the Bright Angel Trail to the Colorado and then hike back up to the South Rim—all in one day. That day was one of the hottest days of the year. On top of his already overambitious goal, Anderson added a somewhat typical young male's macho twist: He boasted that he was "going to make a new record" on his rim-to-river-to-rim hike of 18 miles. Did he?

Anderson made it to the river quickly but was slammed into the dust by heatstroke before returning more than a few hundred feet back up. He was evacuated to the rim by a "drag out." Anderson died hours later while being evacuated homeward to Phoenix by train.

The common problem exemplified by Anderson is twofold. First, young hikers, especially athletes, often possess such a well conditioned cardiac system that they—especially males—are able and accustomed to blasting along where other people move more slowly. Second, all too many of them do not understand heat or what it does. In extremely hot climates these young men are a lot like muscle cars with big engines but undersized (unacclimated) radiators. They drive at their usual high speed, spurred additionally by testosterone-driven thinking that denies the consequences of breaking the speed limit, until they overheat. This potentially lethal overheating takes them almost completely by surprise. Meanwhile nonathletic or older people are neither capable of, nor inclined to, push themselves nearly as hard.

In complete contrast, only six of the 102 victims in Table 3 are known or suspected to have died due to hypothermia, or exposure to cold. This reflects two realities: first, and as mentioned in the previous chapter, far fewer people enter the Canyon during the cold season than the hot one. Second, people in North America understand cold better than they understand the Canyon's extreme heat, wind, and dryness; and such people are better prepared to combat cold via clothing.

Even so, as we saw earlier with Casimar Pultorak and his friend Paul Des Jardins, people hiking in the Canyon since the first trail was marked have underestimated how such a supposedly hot canyon can get so cold. In his excellent 1914 book, *Through the Grand Canyon from Wyoming to Mexico*, for example, Ellsworth Kolb notes photographing in 1911 an unidentified hiker wearing the hob-nailed shoes of a prospector and double layers of denim plus an overcoat and mittens. The body had been originally discovered in 1906 lying "halfway up the granite" in Upper Granite Gorge on river left about two miles downstream of Pipe Creek (see book cover).

> *He was lying in a natural position, with his head resting on a rock. An overcoat was buttoned tightly around him. No large bones were broken, but he might have had a fall and been injured internally. More likely he became sick and died. The small bones of the hands and feet had been taken away by field-mice, and no doubt the turkey-buzzards had stripped the flesh. His pockets contained Los Angeles newspapers of 1900. His pockets also contained a pipe and pocket knife, but nothing by which he could be identified....Such finds are not unusual in this rugged country. These prospectors seldom say where they are going, no track is kept of their movements, and unless something about their clothes tells who they are, their identity is seldom established. The proximity of this grave made us wonder how many more such unburied bodies there were along this river.*

The "unburied" part bothered the Kolb brothers. So, after photographing the peacefully reposed victim, there being no soil, they buried him under rocks. How sneaky the cold can be as an adversary is easy to underestimate. Consider the following mystery story.

"I just read your book," Superintendent Joe Alston told me (Ghiglieri). "You missed one."

Thinking it was damned unlikely that Tom Myers and I had missed a fatality below the rims after all the painstaking research work we had done, I said something intelligent like, "Oh, yeah?"

"Yeah. In 1970, I had to rappel off the rim and look for a lost kid who had fallen off."

"Did you find him?"

"No. Never did."

Now of course we had to figure out who Alston had been searching for. After all, he was Superintendent of Grand Canyon National Park, the place our book covered, and we considered him a great guy, one whom we owed the courtesy of research. Besides, just maybe he was right, maybe we had missed one.

Finding out who Alston's missing kid was and what might have happened to him, however, turned out to demand a heck of a lot of phone calls to false leads. Finally, I called Ranger Dale Antonich at Lead Mead National Recreation Area, who led me to paydirt involving some strange lost history.

The missing "kid" turned out to be 18-year-old Thomas David Carpenter from

South Dakota. He last was seen on June 15, 1970, at 5:00 p.m. while leaving the gas station at the North Rim where he worked. Even though the month was June, at 8,000 feet on the North Rim, the nights still dropped below freezing. Carpenter was known to go on evening walks. But this time he had never returned.

Ranger Jack Fields had helped organize the search. I felt amazed to be able to locate Jack 30 years later in retirement in Cottonwood. Sadly, however, Jack had since suffered a series of strokes leaving him unable to make sense of the past—to the extent of full-blown amnesia—and even more incapable of speaking about it.

Antonich, however, had also led me to Field's fellow, but "brand new" full-time ranger of that time, Vic Vieira. A U.S. Marine before becoming a ranger, Vieira told me that when Carpenter failed to show up at work the next day, Vieira had launched a search. At first this involved the standard approach of covering the immediate rim areas where someone might get into trouble. Park personnel were scarce then on the North Rim, so Vieira (and Fields) had shanghaied other personnel. One of these was Joe Alston, at the time a firefighter who had been stationed on the rim for only about a week. Vieira sent Alston down over the rim four or five times.

Vieira top-roped him as he rappelled. Alston had done nothing like rappelling since he was in Boy Scouts years earlier. Still, as Joe told me later, "I felt a lot more afraid of finding the dead guy than of falling off the rope."

Each time Alston rappelled down he spotted no body. Instead he found hundreds of discarded flash cubes from cameras scattered in the lower Kaibab. Alston wondered: "Do these people really expect one flash bulb to light up the whole Canyon, ten miles across?" Joe also found "lots and lots and lots" of table knives dating to generations earlier. He did not understand these until later when he learned one of the goofier (and more dangerous) traditions at the North Rim for people was to create "Canyon birdies" by tossing a table knife off the rim in the dark and silence and listening to the oscillating wooshing sound produced as the knife spins through the air. Flash cubes and Canyon birdies aside, however, Alston did not find Carpenter, a fact for which he privately felt grateful.

The search continued for two more days. Helicopter searches below the rim revealed no body. Jack Fields brought in bloodhounds from California. By now 55 hours had passed since Carpenter last had been seen. But the hounds could not locate a trail. Fields and Vieira now suspected that, instead of simply walking after work, Carpenter had done what a few bold young men had been doing lately, he had shortened his initial walk by hitching a ride on the Park's garbage disposal vehicle by literally grabbing the rear of the truck and jumping aboard for a ride toward the peninsula where employees hiked at times well off the beaten tourist track. Maybe Carpenter had gone as far as Widforss Point to the southwest.

Searches in these areas, however, also produced nothing. Carpenter had vanished. Carpenter's parents arrived at the North Rim from Mitchell, South Dakota and spent a month searching for him. Sadly, they found no sign.

Carpenter, Vic Vieira found, had a history of epilepsy. Carpenter possessed a prescribed medication for this condition but hated taking the medicine because it produced unpleasant side effects. A count of the pills remaining in Carpenter's bottle revealed that the 18-year-old had avoided taking them far more than he took them.

A year passed. Then, in the summer of 1973, Paul Manwaring, an employee of the North Rim Lodge, had gone hiking west-southwest with his cousin Scott Simmons toward the rim to look at Shiva Temple. West of Transcept Canyon Manwaring began to suspect they were lost. Here, wandering among the pines, he happened across a whitish object. It looked like a large, smooth white stone, or an ostrich egg. No, he soon saw, it was a human skull.

"I decided to keep the skull," Manwaring explained, "thinking it would be cool to have my own human skull."

Manwaring next looked at the setting sun to get a bearing to the west. Then he and Simons made a bee-line east. As he noted in his letter of April 27, 2005.

> I thought initially that it was perhaps an old Indian who had died in those woods a century or so before. As I examined it as we walked along, I noticed silver fillings in the upper teeth. I then began to think it was more recent than we thought. I remembered also that our brother Richard had told me of a young man who had worked at the Grand Canyon a couple of years before, while he [Richard] had worked at the lodge, who disappeared suddenly and no one ever found him. My conscience prompted me to take the skull to the rangers, which I did. The next day one of the rangers came to the dining room and asked me to accompany him in an attempt to find the location where I had discovered the skull.

Ranger Vic Vieira told a different version of this skull story. During one of his rare dorm safety inspections for fire hazards he was thinking. "Amazing what these employees have in their quarters...What's this? Hell, one of these kids has a human skull on his dresser with a candle stuck onto it!"

Both skull stories agree that Vieira asked Manwaring to take him to the place where he had found this skull. Manwaring did not quite manage to pinpoint the location. He and Vieira searched but found nothing. Soon afterward, Vieira asked Manwaring to try again. This time 70 searchers belonging to a search and rescue team from Kanab, Utah assisted. One soon discovered an organized "nice neat little pile" containing a wallet, room key, and camera stacked atop each other." Many human bones lay scattered by animals in a circle around this neat pile. The wallet held a driver's license and social security card for Thomas David Carpenter. Eventually dental records confirmed the skull as Carpenter's.

What had gone wrong? Carpenter, Vieira suspected, had experienced an epileptic seizure. When he had awakened in a weakened and dazed post-ictal state late in the evening, perhaps well after dark, he was already hypothermic. On the other hand, maybe he had simply gotten lost—as Manwaring and Simons had done in the exact same place—then slowly had succumbed to hypothermia. Either way, before Carpenter had died of exposure and hypothermia on the rim he had paradoxically disrobed and piled his clothing and possessions in a neat pile as if mentally misfiring. Again, on the night he had vanished, the air temperature had dropped below freezing. Why had Carpenter disrobed and piled his clothes so neatly? As paradoxical as it may seem, many severely hypothermic people experience a tingling sensation of feeling over-heated. This false sensation prompts many terminal victims to disrobe just before they lose consciousness.

Also either way, Carpenter had not fallen off the rim. No wonder young Joe Alston had not found him by rappelling off it.

More important, Carpenter's grieving parents wrote Paul Manwaring, thanking him. In so doing they told him something he would never forget: "It is impossible to live with what you don't know, but at least what you do know you can accept."

Carpenter died of cold four decades ago. The mystery skeleton photographed by the Kolb brothers died of hypothermia well over a century ago. Are visitors to the Canyon smarter today?

It was Superbowl Sunday. Great commercials. Sometimes even great football. In Grand Canyon a February blizzard raged during the morning of Superbowl Sunday, 2008.

Wondering if she would catch any of the game, Backcountry Ranger Lisa Hendy pounded on the door of the Cedar Ridge outhouse nearly two miles below the South Rim. She wasn't sure what to expect when—or if—someone opened that door.

Outhouses on trails within Grand Canyon had served before as life-saving havens for hikers. The sanctuary from blizzard conditions had proved worth enduring the stink. Hendy hoped this outhouse on the South Kaibab Trail would do the same. A debilitated patient, no matter what his or her aroma, usually proved better than a dead one.

Ranger Hendy had received the call for a missing person right after this early February storm had dumped a foot of snow on the South Kaibab trailhead. More than an hour ago, Michael, the leader of a 16-person hiking group of friends had reported to Park Dispatch that his group had slogged through the storm up to the rim after spending the night at a Phantom Ranch cabin. But at the five-mile mark they had abandoned one of their hikers at the outhouses here at Cedar Ridge. Because they had known they would be staying in cabins at Phantom, the hikers had gambled on their way down by carrying only minimal personal gear. Now, during their return, they found themselves without protection for the cold, wet weather. And once they reached the rim they all felt too tired to return to help her.

The woman the group had left behind had been cold and wet and unable to continue. Believe it or not, no one in the party had been willing to stay with this hypothermic victim.

Hendy thought this a pretty lame situation, to put it mildly. Maybe even criminal. Even so, Hendy had loaded up with rescue gear—food, warm clothing, a stove—and had hiked down from the rim through freezing gusts of 30 mph and blinding drifts. Less than an hour later she found Cedar Ridge cloaked in a whiteout and appearing as abandoned as a ghost town. The views deeper into the vast Canyon appeared other-worldly.

She called out again as she pounded on each of the stall doors. Finally, she heard a weak reply from a smaller stall. Hendy found the door unlocked. She opened it to discover a woman in her sixties in soggy blue jeans sitting and shivering violently. The wreck of a woman haltingly blurted, "Thank you! Please don't leave me!"

"I'm not going to leave you," Hendy said. "But I am going to move you. We need to get into the next stall and get you out of those wet clothes before you become more hypothermic."

Hendy dug out a tarp and sleeping bag. Next she shifted the quaking hiker into a larger stall. She helped strip her then re-clothe her in fleece and a down jacket. Hendry heated up a quart of Gatorade then a military MRE on a small MSR stove. A half hour later Hendy told her patient, "We could spend all night shivering in this toilet and face another foot of snow in the morning, or we could get outta here. Which will it be?"

The woman admitted she felt deathly afraid of going out into the cold wind, but she also admitted she felt even more afraid of being left alone. Hendy reassured her again. Next they started ascending the Kaibab Trail (neither a helicopter nor a mule could operate in existing weather conditions). It was 5 p.m.

Hendy broke trail, often through waist-deep drifts of snow, for her waif. She dropped back to hold the woman as they passed Ooh Ahh Point and Windy Ridge so she would not be blown off the trail to her death. Less than two hours later they arrived at a waiting ambulance. Ranger and patient both climbed in the back and warmed up. Hendy checked her vital signs. The uphill hike in dry fleece had restored the woman's vitals. Perfect. Now all they needed to do was get her back to her room at Bright Angel Lodge.

Hendy and her abandoned hiker arrived after 7:00 p.m. (Incident report #08-0608) to find her hiking group glued to the T.V. Her husband (who had not made the hike) and several of her hiking "buddies" glanced up briefly to say, "Hey, great timing! Glad you made it! The game's just started. You've hardly missed a thing!"

The final score? Indianapolis Colts: 29, Chicago Bears: 17. Negligent hike leader: one NPS ticket for creating a hazardous situation.

A pivotal factor, one clearly implicated in Inner-Canyon falls in the previous chapter, also plays a role in environmental injuries. This factor is hiking solo. There exists no question that, when it comes to appreciating and avoiding lethal dangers in the Grand Canyon, two heads are better than one. Twenty-two of the 93 environmental victims (24 percent) in Table 3 are known to have been solo hikers;

several other victims also may have been, but records are incomplete.

It is also clear from Table 3 that having passed the age of forty among men seems clearly to increase their odds of dying due to heat-related cardiac arrest in Grand Canyon. Ironically, however, being below the age of 25 vastly impacts the odds of young men in the Canyon living long enough to reach forty. Hence, neither youth nor maturity offers immunity. Nineteen heatstroke victims (half the total) were young males (N=14) or females (N=5) between the ages of 10 and 30 years old. How do these sorts of unusual deaths happen to such young men and women? Consider the following examples.

In early 1975, Charles Myers, age 20, had to get out of New York. Myers was a student in history, philosophy, and religion at Columbia University. He felt "bothered by people in New York City." To escape the crowd there, Myers hitchhiked west. He briefly visited Yuma, Arizona then spent a month living alone, fasting and walking in the woods, near Taos and Jemez, New Mexico. Myers planned to return to New York by July 4, but when someone suggested a detour to Grand Canyon, a place he had never seen, Myers veered west.

On June 28, Myers hiked alone down the Hermit Trail into the Canyon. He rested at Hermit Creek and ate all of the food he had. Realizing that, indeed, this had been all of his food, Myers decided to hike out that same day—despite the intense heat.

Fatefully, he also decided to take a shortcut off the trail during his return. "I had a topographical map of the canyon," Myers explained, "and it looked like I could take a shortcut out. It's my nature to want to do things two different ways."

Myers' decision to shortcut an established Canyon route was virtually a cookie-cut fatal error, a signature error made by the majority of young, solo male hikers in the Canyon who have ended up dying from Inner Canyon falls and/or dehydration and heatstroke. Shortcutting is the mother of most hiking errors.

You guessed it: Myers' alternate route proved not to be a shortcut. By nightfall he found himself distant from the NPS trail yet less than halfway to the rim. He slept fitfully on rock. He retackled his personal route the next morning. He walled out against a cliff that did not look overly difficult. He started climbing it. He soon lost his footing and fell about 30 feet.

The impact not only fractured a vertebra in his back, but maybe even more seriously, it also cracked one of his two canteens. The water leaked out onto the superheated rock. In pain and sweating profusely, Myers quickly gulped nearly all the little water he had remaining. Realizing that his predicament was now desperate, he decided to send up an SOS via a signal fire. One problem with this idea—other than the slim odds that anyone would see a fire—was the lack of tinder where he had fallen. In his wishful thinking about the efficacy of a fire, Myers torched his backpack.

When this short-lived blaze failed to attract a rescue helicopter, Myers stripped naked and burned his clothes.

Still no one came.

Now naked, with no backpack and very little water, and suffering a cracked vertebra, Myers continued trying to light small brush fires. Again to no avail. As the day wore on and the sun baked him dry, Myers not only ran out of faith in a signal fire, he was also down to his last few gulps of water.

Desperate, Myers discarded his knife and wallet near where he had fallen. Next he stumbled and crawled to a grassy area where he tried to sleep for the night. His night was miserable, to put it mildly. For some strange reason, Myers still believed that someone would find him. But he also knew that, before they did, the extreme heat here might kill him. So the next day, his day #3, he found a small rock overhang offering a patch of shade.

Myers stayed in his postage stamp of shade for two days. He tried to flash-signal over-flying aircraft by reflecting sunlight off a medallion he wore around his neck. He also tried to eat a little cactus. But he found the taste bitter. In pain, hot, exhausted, starving, dehydrated, and with his mouth now bleeding, he was ready to give up and die.

Instead of dropping dead, on this, his fourth day, Myers railed at his Maker by shouting a prayer-tirade. This bout with a God who had failed to equip him with common sense finally gave him the strength he needed to go on. That night and the next day, as he chewed on more cactus, he struggled back down into the Canyon. He realized finally that by being off any established route, as he was now, he might never be found.

On day #5 he found a small seep spring. He spent the night here. Eventually, he hobbled all the way back down to Hermit Creek. Now, on day #6, he had plenty of water. But he was still short on decision-making ability. He decided to head down the creek. By now, almost a week after hiking down from the South Rim, Myers was so weak and injured that he could walk only fifty yards at a stretch before needing to lie down and rest. Myers' rate of travel shrank to less than five percent of a normal person's. As he staggered through the brush and heat and boulders and cacti along the creek, he screamed like a child and he moaned and groaned.

It took Myers, still railing against the powers-that-be, five more days of stumbling down Hermit to locate his original campsite where he had gobbled his entire food supply. A normal hiker might have done this 5-day distance in two hours.

A couple of hours after Myers found his original campsite—and more than ten days after running out of food—two hikers found Myers.

Myers spent the next ten days recuperating in Flagstaff Community Hospital. He contemplated his ordeal, Native American life, religion, and his future hitchhike back to New York. To Myers, having people around him somehow had become more attractive.

The numerous baffling episodes of foolish death in the Canyon have prompted many an NPS ranger to ask herself: Are these people who kill themselves in the Canyon by hiking without enough water merely ignorant or....Or what? Journalist Elliot Almond writes in his *Los Angeles Times* article (July 23, 1995) "Summer danger in the Grand Canyon: Hikers risk heatstroke and death:"

> *Hikers have died of heatstroke after having their pictures taken next to a sign at Indian Gardens warning them not to go farther. Rangers have found people dead of dehydration who were carrying water in their packs. Rangers lament that many simply expect to be saved when in danger.*

What this "of-course-someone-will-rescue-me" mentality among some hikers can produce is tragedy. In October of 1975, for example, NPS rangers were faced with another mysterious disappearance. Arizonan Brad Riner, age 22, had planned an ambitious and challenging, solo, experts-only hike for eleven days in the heart of Grand Canyon on both sides of the river. His previous Canyon hiking experience included the Bright Angel, Kaibab, Tonto, Hermit, Boucher, Clear Creek, Hance, and Tanner trails. This is a respectable list, although it comprises only the easiest small fraction of the 500 miles of trails in the Canyon recognized officially by the Park Service and includes, significantly, all of the mere 33 miles of those trails that the NPS routinely maintains aggressively. Thus, Riner did have Canyon experience, but most of it had been on visible, well-traveled trails relatively easy for hikers of medium ability.

On September 20, Riner's father had dropped him off at the trailhead. Eleven days later, on October 1, Mr. Riner called the NPS Backcountry Reservations Office and told them that his son had failed to show up for work. Brad Riner was an "overdue hiker."

The NPS launched a helicopter search of Riner's proposed route—down Hermit Trail to Hermit Campground, then west along the Tonto Trail to Boucher Rapid (River Mile 96.7), across the Colorado in his small inflatable raft, then down to Crystal Rapid (River Mile 98.2), up Crystal Creek, up Dragon Creek toward Shiva Saddle, over Shiva Saddle, down Trinity Creek, around Cheops Pyramid, then up again to Shiva Saddle, then to the headwaters of Phantom Creek, and then down Phantom Creek to Phantom Ranch.

Although Vibram-soled foot prints thought to be Riner's were found heading up Crystal, then Dragon, creeks, the air search found no other sign of him.

On October 2, three two-person NPS search crews plus five more SAR crews from the Coconino County Sheriff's Department choppered into the Inner Canyon to search Riner's route. Meanwhile helicopter air searches continued. The day ended with one team having found tracks appearing to be Riner's around the Shiva Saddle area.

On October 3, nine crews of two to five persons each scoured the tortuous, convoluted maze north of the river in more detail. A four-person NPS crew on Shiva Saddle at the 5,250-foot contour (roughly 3,000 feet above the river) found not only footprints but also a two-inch square of blue ensolite pad snagged on a tree branch just above the Redwall Limestone cliff. They tracked this trail to the 5,600-foot level but, as night fell, they were recalled.

On October 4, a three-person NPS crew followed the previously discovered tracks. Soon they arrived at a half-acre area that had been burned by a recent fire. In it they found two expended flare tubes, then, 75 feet below the edge of a short cliff, they also found a stuff sack containing freeze-dried foods, foot powder, trash, empty water bottles, an itinerary, blue tennis shoes, a pair of old green fatigue cut-offs, two hiking books, et cetera, plus a light raft paddle. The searchers admitted that these might have rolled off the ledge accidentally rather than have been discarded. Above these, in the main burned area, searchers reported: "It appeared that RINER had spent a good deal of time in this area as evidenced by sleeping areas where he had done a great deal of rolling around."

This burned area seemed to have been undisturbed for four days. Riner's stride from here, they noted, was now shorter than it had been (Riner was 6' 2" tall), but it was still normal and strong.

All search crews now focused on this trail. Meanwhile a private boater phoned in the information that he had taken Riner from the south to the north shore across the river from Hermit Rapid (River Mile 95) to Crystal on September 21. Riner therefore had not had to use the small raft he was carrying. The NPS tracking team followed Riner's tracks for 2.5 hours, until "the tracks headed down a wash at almost the head of the Phantom Creek Drainage."

The helicopter now scrutinized this Outlet Canyon/Phantom Creek headwater area. At 10:38 a.m., chopper personnel located a body at the base of a cliff near a shallow pool in upper Phantom Creek.

Climbing crews and trackers converged here. Rangers Chase and Stan Stockton made a series of technical rappels and were first to reach the body. It was Riner's body. The NPS incident report stated that Riner:

—had apparently lowered his pack with string, then attempted to jump 30 [vertical] feet to a sandy area adjacent to a water pool. He struck his head on a large nearby boulder. Signs allude he made his way to his pack, and removed his...raft and ensolite pad. The body was found on this pad and raft lying on the left side, curled slightly with feet extending into the pool.

Chase and Stockton noticed that Riner's right leg appeared to be fractured and, worse, that blood had seeped from his nose and ears, and his eyes were blackened. Riner's glasses were found near the original landing imprint. This imprint location appeared to have been deliberately chosen and hit by a person who jumped, not one surprised by an accidental fall. It also looked like the best possible landing spot below the cliff—though, again, it was the termination point for a vertical fall of thirty feet.

An autopsy revealed that Riner had suffered a dislocated hip, a broken back and ribs, a punctured lung, and a skull fracture. Death had occurred on about September 29.

Inside Riner's pack were two, half-filled quart water bottles. Riner had carried no rope, nor hat, nor knife, but among other things (including his small raft and an inflatable life jacket) he still had plenty of food, a topo map with no route marks, plus pages torn from the *Inner Canyon Trail Guide* and Harvey Butchart's *Grand Canyon Treks*. Both these books were in the stuff sack discovered earlier above the 5,600-foot contour, which suggests that Riner had discarded everything in that sack to lighten his load. But, if he had done this, why then keep a raft when his planned route out and across the river was over a bridge at Phantom?

What went wrong here?

Riner died at the foot of a 100-foot dry waterfall the bottom thirty feet of which were unclimbable because the waterfall was fully blocked by a wall-to-wall chock-stone boulder which was undercut. Riner had tossed his sleeping bag, walking stick, and life vest down separately. He had carefully lowered his pack by a string. Then, because he carried no rope to lower himself down short pitches on which a ropeless descent might risk injury, he jumped into space.

This latter is hard to understand. Riner made the decision to jump off a cliff that guaranteed certain injury regardless of how well he (or anyone else) could have landed, even if everything went perfectly. In short, he made an impossible jump that no sane person could have expected to walk away from. Why?

For a ghost of a chance of understanding why, let's back up to his long, possibly multi-day camp above the 5,600-foot contour. Why had he stayed there so long? Why had he shot off his only two flares there? Why was the area all burned—as if ignited intentionally as a signal? And why had he abandoned roughly ten pounds of non-critical supplies and equipment only 75 feet below his sleeping spot (remember, he tore the critical pages out of the two books he had placed in that dropped stuff sack before abandoning it).

It is only conjecture, but the two most likely explanations for Riner's behavior are: a. he might have injured himself somewhat and felt that going on would be too difficult, or b. he may have, for psychological reasons, felt that he had gotten in over his head in backcountry orienteering and was worried about achieving his orienteering goals. Again, Riner's experience in the Canyon consisted only of hikes on established, visible trails. He was not experienced with Canyon orienteering, route-finding, terrain evaluation, and free-style Canyon scrambling or "boulder-ing" over serious exposures that inspire deep fear even in experienced Canyoneers. Worse, Riner had not just entered new, trackless territory whose challenges were a quantum leap above his experience level, he had done it solo, and with no back-up. Yes, he was carrying a lot of stuff, some of it useless. But on the other hand, he had not even brought a hat. Back to the bigger issue, was Riner, just before his fatal leap, worried about having pushed solo too far beyond his confidence level or, instead, was he injured—or were both true?

Either way, by his earlier time above the 5,600-foot contour he clearly had wanted to be rescued. But no rescuers had responded to his flares or fire.

Does any of this explain why, after carefully lowering his backpack so that it would not be damaged, he jumped into thirty feet of air? Was he dehydrated and thus afflicted by the typical irritable snap-thinking that accompanies it? He had a half liter of water in each of his two bottles (or had he filled these after jumping?), and he was staring down at several gallons of water in a pool. It remains unclear whether or not Riner had been drinking enough water.

Did Riner decide to commit suicide? If so, why lower his pack carefully and why choose a "soft" landing spot for himself that would guarantee a lingering, horrible death?

Our conclusion is that, days before he jumped, Brad Riner had found himself way over his head and very alone. And he had come to realize it so intensely that he may have begun obsessing about it. Hour by hour in the trackless and often terrifying route he had chosen, his fear grew, and his rational thinking declined. With the specters of failure and absolute helpless solitude lurking in every decision, Riner hurried—too panicked perhaps to believe he could re-ascend the last feeder route he had chosen—when instead he should have exercised infinite patience and contemplative judgment by climbing back up and reassessing his route.

Riner, in fact, had apparently lost his planned route after crossing Shiva Saddle shortly before his leap into space. He descended down the far left (the northern) option into his fatal "no-go" feeder wash into Phantom Creek instead of descending well to the right into Trinity Canyon as he had originally planned—and also instead of taking the more center route down the "scramble" cliff into Phantom Creek. Riner's entering a "no-go" feeder was a natural enough mistake. But when he hit that unclimbable drop at the chock stone he knew he was on the wrong route; the NPS ranger at the Backcountry Office had warned Riner when approving his proposed route not to do any exposed climbing because only scramble climbing was required. Riner knew that Trinity and Phantom creeks were both possible to enter via scramble climbing. But he apparently did not add up two and two when he was faced with an unclimbable 30-foot fall to come up with "four," that he was in the wrong drainage and on the wrong route.

The perplexing question remains: Why did Riner not turn back and spend 30 minutes re-evaluating his route (and his location) when faced with an undescendable drop-off? Only someone who had lost his ability to reason or who was inordinately worried about water (and perhaps was dehydrated due to having hoarded his water) would have refused to spend an extra 30 to 60 minutes to find a safe route that he knew must exist. Again, why did he refuse to re-evaluate his lethal predicament?

Being over his head, Riner apparently lost his head. But which environmental factors versus which psychological or physical factors were responsible for this became moot points once he leaped off that 30-foot drop.

Again, as is all too clear from a look at Tables 2 and 3, solo hiking in the Canyon proves beyond any doubt the old maxim that two heads are better than one.

Another example, a harrowing one, illustrates in Technicolor this danger of solo hiking. But this time the victim was not a stubborn young male, but a young woman.

When Mrs. O. B. Fortney of Pittsburgh, Pennsylvania, was informed that her daughter Linda had not shown up for work, she was worried. Linda Fortney, a 25-year-old nurse who also lived and worked in Pittsburgh, had sent her mother a postcard nearly three weeks earlier. It was postmarked in Arizona and dated July 31, 1975. Linda had written that she was going to hike in Grand Canyon, a place she had never been before. Mrs. Fortney knew Linda was traveling alone except for her little dog, Cocoa Gin. So when Linda failed to report to work, Mrs. Fortney immediately reported Linda as missing to the Coconino County Sheriff's Department in Flagstaff, Arizona. Mrs. Fortney's phone call set in motion the wheels of a multi-agency SAR mission.

As it turned out, Mrs. Fortney had good reason to be worried. Linda and Cocoa Gin had hiked down the trail to Havasu Canyon on August 1. But other than that postcard, Linda had left no one with specifics of her plans. Her postcard did say, however, that she was hiking to Supai Village.

Having never been to Grand Canyon before, let alone hiked it, Linda Fortney was stunned almost immediately by the heat and confused by the terrain. Temperatures soared well over 100 degrees. Worse, she had gotten a late start. Even so, she was determined to make it to the village by dark.

She never even got close.

Near sundown, still on the seven-mile trail in Hualapai Canyon, Fortney took off her pack containing her food, water, and gear. She laid it on the trail. Then she wandered off trail carrying only her purse. Becoming disoriented, she could not find her way back to the trail or to her pack—even though she and the trail and her pack were all in the bottom of the same narrow canyon. Fortney continued downcanyon without her gear. She reached the junction (or confluence) of Hualapai Canyon and Cataract Canyon in fading light.

At this point Linda Fortney had a fifty-fifty chance of turning in the correct direction. Left would take her downstream to Supai Village in a couple of miles. Right would take her upcanyon but deep into a lot of lengthy "nowhere."

Fortney veered right, up the huge side canyon called Cataract Canyon, and walked southeast.

She followed a cattle trail. This major tributary snaked miles upstream and south of Havasu Village. Again she was headed up it, to the south, in the opposite direction of Supai and the main trail and, eventually, water.

Night fell. Fortney realized that she was lost. The darkness scared her so much that she could not sleep. She had matches in her purse but she was too frightened even to light a fire. As the temperature dropped into the 50s, her halter-top and blue jeans also left her too cold to sleep. The next morning she found herself cold, foodless, and waterless—having already walked upstream past the source of Cataract (a.k.a. Havasu) Creek into the dry zone. She felt extremely anxious to reach Supai or, instead, to escape the Canyon altogether.

Again Linda Fortney had a fifty-fifty chance of going in the right direction. If she returned downcanyon, she would reach Supai Village in a few hours. If she continued upcanyon, she would be entering a desert prison and death row.

She looked both ways, then hiked farther upcanyon. En route, maybe ten or more miles upcanyon from her "bivouac," Fortney veered out of the main Cataract Canyon into Havatagvitch Canyon, a true middle-of-nowhere location.

By nightfall, once more having walked in the wrong direction, and this time, all day, she was 15 miles from Supai Village, and now 20 miles from her car.

By day three, she had become severely dehydrated—and even more desperate. Miraculously, she found a small seep up Havatagvitch. But it dripped so incredibly slowly from a cliff crack that it took 45 minutes to fill her eyeglass case. This would at least postpone death from dehydration. In fact, as pitifully tiny as this spring was, it would hold death at bay for at least 17 more days....

For the first four of those days, Fortney screamed for help. She gave up eventually when she decided that her voice was not carrying very far. The nights remained so cold and so frightening that each night seemed to last an eternity before sunrise. To fight the cold, she stood and walked around and, being Catholic, she said the rosary, or sang. When the sun finally did come up, it heated the Canyon so hot that she feared she would not be able to bear it. She still refused to light a fire, even to try to attract attention. Before she lit anything, she decided, she first wanted to be sure that someone was up there and looking down. No one was looking (she was not due back at work for two more weeks). And even if there had been someone "nearby," Fortney would not have known it.

For her first 15 days of inadvertent but self-imposed exile, Fortney kept track of the days in her address book. She also wrote dinner recipes to keep busy. But when this became too depressing, she quit. She found an old whiskey bottle. By filling this at her dripping spring, she could venture away from it for a full day at a time before fear of dehydration urged her back. This bottle alone might have gotten her to Supai had she been willing to walk downcanyon, but not long after finding this precious bottle, she dropped and broke it.

Hunger drove her to eat cactus blossoms. Cocoa Gin, weak and starving, eventually wandered off.

When finally, on August 19, Linda Fortney's mother reported her missing to the NPS, the Park and the Coconino County Sheriff's Department started a search.

They found Fortney's car parked at the Rim at Hualapai Hilltop. Cocoa Gin had already been found wobbling down in the correct direction toward Supai Village by hikers a few days earlier. The search team concluded that Fortney was most likely still inside the Canyon. But where?

On day #20 of Linda Fortney's adventure in orienteering—and the second day of the search—Hardy Jones, a Supai Indian, spotted human footprints up Cataract "where nobody should be." He returned later with his son Darrell and his friends Stanley Manakaja and Roy Young, also Supai, to follow those tracks. At 6:30 a.m. on August 20, the four Native Americans found Linda Fortney in Havatagvitch Canyon (12–15 miles upstream of the Hualapai Canyon/Cataract Canyon junction) branching to the east of Cataract.

She stared at them and cried.

After her helicopter evacuation to Flagstaff's Hospital, Linda Fortney was still 5 feet, 4 inches tall, but now, instead of weighing her normal 110 pounds, she weighed only 85. Otherwise she was in good condition—even better for having been reunited with Cocoa Gin, now nursed back to health.

Linda Fortney's near-death, wrong-way hike briefly earned her fame. Several articles capitalized on her ordeal. She was even invited to make a guest appearance on the national television game show "What's My Line?"

The lesson? Linda Fortney had lost her pack, lost her food and water, lost her bearings and sense of direction, lost her way, lost her dog, lost even her common-sensical ability to plan her own self-rescue, and lost 25 pounds. But she did make it on TV. In short, she became a modern American story.

On a more serious note, she did survive—and through her example she may have influenced other hikers not to enter the Canyon as ill-prepared as she had been. Perhaps her example has even saved a life or two.

Oddly, 19 years later, another person would exhibit an equal inability to understand basic geography in the Canyon. William Lederer, age 61, of Park Ridge (Chicago) decided to tackle the Hermit Trail in July of 1994. The devout Lederer, who attended mass daily, took time from his schedule to research for months the demands of the trip. But his research must have been a bit lopsided. He ended up planning to make the 3-day, 20-mile round-trip backpacking foray, for example, while wearing running shoes and without a sleeping bag. Friends convinced him to better equip himself and loaned him their gear.

To what avail? Lederer managed to become utterly lost in Hermit Canyon on day #1. This is a tributary canyon bisected by a marked and maintained Park Service trail, the lower end of which mostly follows the creek itself all the way to the Colorado. Somehow, however, maybe as Charles Myers had 19 years earlier (both Myers and Linda Fortney had gotten lost only months apart), Lederer deviated from this trail and never figured out how to relocate it. He wandered semi-randomly in weather of up to 110 degrees for about a week, much of it in the upper, waterless reaches of Hermit. He spent much of his time praying for rescue.

After Lederer failed to return to the rim and fly home, his family phoned the Park and reported him missing. The Park launched a search. The next day a ranger walked up to Lederer, who wondered if the ranger was an angel or instead a mere human. Upon determining the ranger's corporeal reality he hugged him.

Lederer, like Fortney, courted notoriety for his lack of competence. One can still watch a longish documentary re-enactment of Lederer's lost-in-Grand-Canyon experience (filmed at Diamond Creek on the Hualapai Nation, it seems) now and then on the Weather Channel.

Despite all the notorious mishaps, fatal and otherwise, in Grand Canyon, others would continue to enter the place ill-prepared mentally to match wits with its heat and dryness and its immense, sheer, and convoluted terrain. Another tragic but classic example of this occurred in June of 1996. A group of eight hikers from Bountiful, Utah, five Explorer Boy Scouts and three adults, hiked from near Saddle Mountain down to Little Nankoweap Canyon and the Colorado (Mile 52). The group was led by scout leader Guy C. Davis, age 44. The other two adults were Earl Pace, age 64, and his brother, Loren Pace, age 71. Loren Pace had been asked by Davis to be the group's guide. Loren Pace was in charge of all provisions and was the only person to have hiked this route before. The hike was intended to be what Davis described as "a super activity" for the varsity Scouts.

Neither Davis, who was on medication for a bronchial condition (medication which required water for him to swallow), nor Earl Pace had ever before hiked in Grand Canyon. Nor had any of the Scouts.

Davis said that Loren Pace had recommended that each hiker carry a minimum of 3, 2-liter bottles of water plus a 2-quart canteen—a total of about 2 gallons of water per boy for three days of trekking. All the boys carried only this minimum, except, Davis thought, David B. Phillips, who maybe carried only four liters plus a two-quart canteen for a total of about 1.5 gallons. Again, this amount of water was to last each hiker for three days; it was also intended to be used to prepare dehydrated food. Davis had asked Loren Pace whether these two gallons would be enough for all that. Pace had answered that they would run out of water before reaching the river, but he had done this before. Again, no one, it seems, carried more water than this minimum.

On day one, Monday, June 3, the group hiked only about two hours along the hilly plateau, maybe five miles, then camped in a flat area. During nearly all of the next morning they hiked to the end of Trail 31. The Saddle Mountain Pass to Little Nankoweap route that they were following along the Boundary Ridge area is emphatically not the traditional, more clear-cut trail route into Nankoweap near Point Imperial. It is a far more subtle route—with no trail at all—for experts only. NPS spokeswoman Maureen Oltrogge noted that the route was only for "highly experienced Grand Canyon hikers with proven route-finding ability."

That afternoon, under a scorching sun, the eight descended "The Chute." Partway down, one of the adults told the boys that they were off the correct route. The hikers spent more time in the hot sun re-locating it and then descending again. The Chute used up a lot of their remaining water. One of the boys said later that Loren Pace told them at this point that he had hiked this area before "but never once had he made it down to the river with water."

Here the adults, especially Loren Pace, had a hard time keeping up with the boys, and thus slowed them all down. The boys, one of them later said, wanted to go ahead and continue more quickly toward the river, but Loren Pace insisted that they stay together. Loren Pace "was not sure of the trail," Boy Scout Jordan Winegar later said, "and was one of the people who slowed the group down." Other survivors agreed with this.

By day's end the group was almost out of water. They now knew that none of them would make it to their destination, the Colorado River, with any water remaining. Indeed, at this point, possibly because of earlier "Canyon" stories told by Loren Pace about having run out of water during his previous Canyon hikes and about other people dying after they had lost their route, the five Scouts were already privately discussing the possibility of dying on this hike.

That night, Scout Leader Davis reckoned that each boy had 1.5 liters of water remaining. Phillips had perhaps only 1 liter. In that the temperatures had exceeded 100 degrees during most of the day, but they all had been rationing their water, everyone at this point was already dehydrated, likely dangerously so. Most of the hikers did not eat that night for fear of losing the last of their precious water by mixing it with dehydrated food.

On the morning of day #3, Wednesday, after skipping breakfast, the hikers descended another "chute." Because the adults were so slow, the boys descended ahead of them. Loren Pace yelled at them to come back up because they again had missed the route. Even the surviving boys later admitted that they did a lot of back-tracking throughout the entire hike after they went ahead but missed the routes.

Eventually everyone made it down this chute except Davis, who refused to attempt it. He was now unable to take his medication due to a total lack of water and was having trouble breathing. Trying to coax Davis down ate up more hours and more water. And in vain; Davis refused to budge.

Now the boys openly discussed the possibility of dying on the hike. They felt exhausted and unable to summon energy. But they agreed that they did not want to die here where they were. David Phillips, the most active of all, shared his water with some of the other boys.

Very soon after Davis had stopped cold, Loren Pace, their guide and the only one who knew the route, also dropped out. Now, by noon or earlier on day #3, the Scouts had not only become guideless, they also had run out of water completely. The temperature now climbed well above 100 degrees in the shade. And little shade existed.

Finally Earl Pace, the last adult still on his feet, guided the boys across another difficult area, and then traversed around a cliff. Now they were only about 1.5 miles from the river. Even so the heat next felled Earl Pace too. Too exhausted and dehydrated to take another step, he dropped out to hide from the sun under a boulder. He advised the boys to stay where they were until evening then to hike to the river in cooler air.

The five boys had been completely out of water for several hours and, worse, had been very inadequately hydrated for three days. They decided instead to continue through the blazing heat down Little Nankoweap Canyon to find water.

The river seemed very close. Other than assuring their own survival (the survivors would later say), once they reached the river they were also "supposed to" purify river water and carry it back up to the adults.

By now every boy was so exhausted and dehydrated that he could not walk straight. Phillips complained to his companions that he could not see the trail very well. Deterioration of vision is a well advanced symptom of dehydration. Phillips not only staggered, but fell several times. His loss of coordination signaled yet again an advanced stage of dehydration.

All five Scouts staggered down the bone-dry Little Nankoweap. But exhaustion and dehydration stopped all of them every few minutes. Several of them fell asleep as soon as they stopped.

Of the five boys, three fell back.

Finally David B. Phillips, age 15, and Mark Coons were in view of the Colorado, several hundred feet and only a few easy minutes away. The shade temperature at the river now was 111 degrees. Both boys stumbled on.

David collapsed. Hard. He hit his head. His eyes rolled back and his breathing became very hard and extremely fast. Although Coons likely did not know this, Phillips was gripped in the throes of exertional heatstroke.

Coons stared at him then "ran" to the river. He desperately tried to fill bottles. Then he returned to Phillips. He tried to pour some water down Phillips' throat. This did not seem to work. Next Coons poured water all over Phillips' body to cool him off. At roughly 6:00 p.m., Coons hurried back to the river for more water and saw a rafting trip. He waved frantically and yelled at them that his friend was dying.

Tom Barry, a member of this private rafting trip, said that he heard Coons yelling. So he walked downstream. Several people on Barry's trip had been hearing a faint cry for help but had had trouble locating its source. When Barry got to the beach, he found Coons looking very scared and "almost delirious and attempting to fill one or two plastic jugs with water." Barry tried to talk with Coons for about a minute as he gulped two quarts of water, sorting through the confusion about eight people in trouble and one of them, David, lying on the ground only 400 feet up a dry creek bed.

Barry hurried to Phillips then yelled for his other two companions Mark Diedrick and Dave Scalia. The two grabbed water and first aid and also sought out

David Phillips.

Scalia, a paramedic, found Phillips hatless and "all jumbled" under a mesquite tree, as if he had just fallen. While still breathing, the 5-foot, 10-inch and 130-pound boy's core temperature was higher than the 106-degree cap of the thermometer. Phillips, unconscious, was in deep heatstroke. His pulse was 180, his respirations 72 per minute, and his blood pressure was extremely low. Phillips felt dry to the touch and failed to respond to painful stimuli.

Realizing that Phillips' prognosis looked extremely bad, these rescuers, too, poured water all over him. Then they organized a bucket brigade to keep him wet. They improvised a stretcher and carried him to camp. At the risk of seeming Monday morning quarterbacks, we suggest that their efforts would have been better aimed at immediately carrying Phillips to the 50+-degree river and performing a full body immersion (while letting him still breathe) for the time necessary, even if more than an hour, for his *core* temperature to drop below 103-104 degrees (this high to avoid a risk of inducing hypothermia). This is not to denigrate these rescuers' efforts, which were heroic and well intended. It is solely to point out that reducing the temperature of any heatstroke victim requires very aggressive and immediate treatment while still proving a very slow process.

The rescuers also alerted an Outdoors Unlimited commercial river trip camped downstream of them of the emergency and asked them to radio for help. Its trip leader, Bert Jones, told me (Ghiglieri) he got on the radio and also sent up a medical doctor and two other people to help.

David Phillips died that evening, just under five hours after Coons reached the river. Phillips died of heatstroke and dehydration. Barry slept next to the body that night to make sure no animals got to it.

Melanie Miles, co-leader of the private river trip, spent most of her time with the four surviving boys. She described them:

> They were initially delirious, frantic, pale, filthy, and had assorted scrapes and scratches. Some were stumbling, most were afraid they were going to die, but within three to four hours they were all able to eat and drink and keep the food and water down without throwing it up and had definitely become more stable.

Miles added that the boys were confounded over why their leaders had let them down. The adults had, the boys told her, even asked the Scouts to carry their backpacks! Scout Leader Davis, they said, had wanted them all to wait in the shade, but "the Scouts were afraid that they were going to die and just wanted to get to the water and also wanted to do the right thing."

Around midnight, Earl Pace had been found up the wash "in very bad shape" on his hands and knees leaning over a boulder. Rescuers brought Pace to the river without his pack. He was shocked the next morning to find David Phillips dead. He said that their problems resulted from the boys having drunk their water too soon.

That night Bert Jones of Outdoors Unlimited finally managed to make radio contact with an overflying aircraft en route to Los Angeles International Airport. This aircraft relayed the distress call. The next morning an Arizona Department of Public Safety helicopter and an NPS SAR team found the two missing adults.

They found Loren Pace sitting in the shade well up Little Nankoweap. He was disoriented and swayed unsteadily when he tried to walk on level ground. Pace did not seem to know that he was dehydrated. He never asked about the welfare of anyone else in his group, but he did mention to rangers that he was fine and that he had done this hike several times and was not worried.

The searchers—Rangers David Trevino and David Desrosiers—found Guy Davis well above a cliff in little Nankoweap Canyon. Davis was "slightly confused mentally, somewhat disoriented, dehydrated, depressed, and crying." When told of Phillip's death, Davis said, "I can't believe it. Of all of us, he should have made it." Next he expressed the sentiment that he himself should have been left up on the cliff to die. He felt that, by being the weak link holding everyone back (at the lower chute) he had contributed to their prolonged and lethal exposure during the hike.

What went wrong here?

The obvious errors were:

1. No one on this hike carried enough water to make it safely (one, who died, had two liters less than the others but was allowed to do the hike under-supplied). The Scout Leader apparently had not brought to the trailhead the sixteen or so extra 2-liter bottles (old plastic soft drink bottles or whatever) of water that prudence would dictate and then "forced" each hiker to carry plenty. Given the season, conditions, and terrain, each hiker on this trek had carried barely half of the water he needed for good health.

2. Those responsible not only chose one of the very hottest times of the year to hike, but also the very driest.

3. The hiking route itself was only a "route" for experts in route-finding; it was not an established trail, let alone a maintained or marked one.

4. Only one person on this hike—a 71 year old—had ever seen the route. No one else had ever hiked anywhere in Grand Canyon. Thus, this experienced-experts-only trip was made up of novice Grand Canyon hikers.

5. The guide on the hike could neither keep up with the pace of the other seven hikers with him, nor could he easily remember each section of the unmarked route.

6. The group had no information backup: if the only person with information on the route were incapacitated, or if the group had to split up during a rescue or emergency, no one else knew the route.

7. The group did split up. And the person who knew the route dropped out.

8. The trip apparently had no emergency signaling devices, such as signal mirrors or radio.

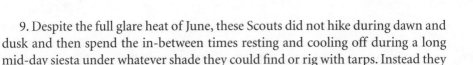

9. Despite the full glare heat of June, these Scouts did not hike during dawn and dusk and then spend the in-between times resting and cooling off during a long mid-day siesta under whatever shade they could find or rig with tarps. Instead they simply hiked all day, hatless, under full sunlight during "banker's hours."

10. The scout leaders had obtained (by mail) from the NPS Backcountry Reservations Office the legally required overnight hiking permit for a hike in the Nankoweap use area, but they had not specified their route. On the permit the NPS had written of Little Nankoweap, "Trip not recommended for 1st time hikers in G.C.— know your limits." The reservation was also for a starting date of June 10, not June 3 when they actually began hiking. Hence, no one in the Park Service would have known to look for them, or where or when. But for young Mark Coons—the only one of the eight hikers to make it all the way to the river without collapsing—having flagged down a river trip, several more of the Scouts and perhaps all of the adults might have died.

All of this may seem to clash with the motto, "Be prepared." David Phillips was at least the sixth Utahn to have died on Scouting trips in the past five years (two others drowned, one fell, and two were struck by lightning). Significantly, less than a week after Phillips died, a troop of ten more Boy Scouts and three adult leaders from Chireno, Texas, would have to be rescued after hiking beyond their abilities and their water during the hottest time of the year on yet another trail recommended only for experienced hikers, the New Hance Trail. River-runners on a hike found them and radioed out for help. The Scouts, all dehydrated in the extreme heat and spread along the trail for miles, had to be medically evacuated. All of this may sound bad, but it gets even worse.

Coconino County Detective Sergeant Kathy Palaski was assigned to this investigation. She found, from inside Guy Davis' pack, a manuscript written for, but never submitted to *Backpacker Magazine* (dated May 23, 1993) by Bradley W. Pace, son of Loren Pace. This 10-page article describes a September 1991 trail-less trek that Brad and Loren Pace and others made along this same fatal route from Saddle Mountain Pass to Little Nankoweap. Pace described a "chute," the traverse of which took twice as long as expected. Two hikers along were injured, one with a broken ankle, the other with a dislocated shoulder. The group ran short of water due to the injuries and had to carve out hollows on the 45-degree slope and then line them with rocks to bivouac so they would not fall into the abyss during the night. They hiked for 17 hours and covered only 10 miles of the 25 they needed to when they ran out of water. They lowered their packs with ropes. They stumbled and they staggered. Loren Pace and others gave up, letting the others go ahead for water. Brad Pace and another hiker made it to the river. When they returned with water, Loren Pace and another man, Ron, were in delusional states. It took Loren Pace, Brad wrote, two more days of recuperation just to begin hiking down to the river. All of this mayhem, moreover, happened during the cooler month of September.

Loren Pace explained that his son had used literary license in this unsubmitted article, combining events from more than one trip to embellish it. He also said that on the 1996 trip that killed David Phillips the boys were "like mice" running ahead and spreading out. He also insisted that he never expected or asked the boys to get water and bring it back to him.

One can conclude many lessons from this tragic hike—and we have. But one of the burning conclusions and questions which haunts us is: What might have happened had all eight hikers made it to the river without deaths or rescues and then recuperated? How many of them would have made it back out, up the much tougher uphill climb with only two gallons of water and under a blazing June sun, alive?

Clearly, when hiking Grand Canyon, water—how much to carry and where to refill—is always an issue. As we have seen, backpackers try to meet this challenge in various ways. The most novel new approach to solving the problem of resupplying water manifested itself in September, 2010. It was then, for example, when two father-son pairs from California decided to tackle one of the more challenging trails in the Canyon, the Royal Arch Trail accessed from the South Bass Trail. This rewarding multi-day backpacking route challenges hikers with the Boy Scout motto: Be Prepared. Indeed, the Park warns that the Royal Arch Loop "has a million ways to get into serious trouble" for those unprepared for the route.

How did this foursome of backpackers prepare for their late summer hike? "We never would have attempted this hike," said one of the dads, had they not been carrying a personal locator beacon [PLB]. This device taps into the U.S. military's Global Positioning Satellite System and is equipped with a panic button. The foursome's rented PLB was a SPOT "Geos" model that relays a request for "help" to the company's Emergency Response Center in Houston, Texas. Operators there alert the nearest rescue service, in this case Grand Canyon National Park Search and Rescue (SAR).

Carrying a PLB may have seemed to this California dad the apex of self-responsibility for ensuring that nothing would go wrong. In reality, its use proved the exact opposite. It turned out to be the apex of irresponsibility by fostering in these hikers a false sense of security and by encouraging the shirking of taking proper precautions to fully self-prepare to care for themselves on a hike offering a level of difficulty well beyond anything they had ever seen before.

What happened? A couple of days into their hike the four backpackers failed to find water as expected so they pushed their panic button. The hour was too late in the evening for the Park helicopter to respond. So the SAR team flew in the next morning to find that the four backpackers had moved another mile and a half and found a creek. The four now told the surprised Park SAR crew they wanted to cancel their call for rescue. They declined evacuation. They also declined water offered them by this SAR crew. Later that same day, however, long after the SAR helicopter had returned to the rim for other assignments, the four again pushed their PLB panic button.

Yet again the hour was close to dark, so instead of the Park SAR team, the Arizona Department of Public Safety (DPS) helicopter made the risky nighttime flight into the inner Canyon for rescue. Why had the hikers pushed their panic button this time? Because the water they were drinking from the creek tasted "salty." The four had moved only a quarter of a mile before deciding that their lives were in peril from dehydration due to perceived minerals in their water. It was not Evian. The DPS helicopter crew who had just risked their lives now disgustedly gave the four hikers a water supply they earlier had refused. Again the hikers declined evacuation. The DPS team then flew back to Flagstaff empty.

The next morning the four button-happy backpackers pushed their panic button a third time. Why yet again? This time it was because "their" (= taxpayers') water was running low. This time the Park SAR crew flew in and insisted the four backpackers board the chopper and evacuate back to the South Rim. There they cited the hiking leader for "creating a hazardous condition."

A huge problem with PLBs is they seem to foster among those carrying them a sense that their own responsibility for preparing adequately for a hike is not merely secondary, but unimportant. Their thinking seems to go: If anything goes wrong, I can just push this button. Indeed, journalist Tom Price has described this situation as opening the wilderness to: "any adventurer with $700 and an opposable thumb."

The head of California's Search and Rescue system calls these PLBs (marketed in 2010 for less than $100) "Yuppie 911." How grateful should we feel for this technology? Up to November, 2010, only one of the dozen previous "help" calls from PLBs used in the Canyon was used to signal an actual emergency, a broken leg. The eleven other missions, expensive ones for U.S. taxpayers, did not need to be launched. Park SAR Coordinator Ken Phillips admits PLB devices constitute questionable technology because they do not allow for any two-way conversation which might facilitate an appropriate response, one which might merely require instructions such as "continue one mile west and you will encounter a water source." In contrast, a satellite phone allows for extended communication of information both ways. Phillips wishes more hikers would consult with the Park's Backcountry Office, read guidebooks, study their maps, double check the weather, and research their proposed hikes on the web and elsewhere before stepping off the rim.

As seen above, the major strike against PLBs resides in the temptation among some people to use them irresponsibly. The act of using a PLB to call in a full-fledged SAR team who must fly through the most deadly airspace known on this planet just because one's water tastes salty, for example, must be ranked as unconscionable.

Lest any of us chortle over the above episode and shake our heads but still consider it unique, consider the next example. On September 2, 2009 Grand Canyon Headquarters received a ping from the Geos monitoring center in Houston at 1:30 a.m. This triggered a ranger hike-in at first light then later a 911 helicopter response to rescue a hiker in some sort of peril. The registered owner of the SPOT device, Park Headquarters found in their records, was hiking with a leader and permit-holder "who had extensive hiking experience at Grand Canyon National Park."

What was the emergency worthy of several search and rescue personnel risking their lives and spending thousands of taxpayer dollars?

After hustling three miles down the Tanner Trail to the Esplanade and to the GPS coordinates provided by GEOS, the now sweating ranger discovered a trio of hikers sequestered in tents and slumbering obliviously. One of them was sawing major timber.

Wondering what sort of emergency led to this scene (was it sleeping sickness?) the ranger woke the group to remind them that they had signaled an emergency.

"Oh," a groggy woman admitted, "I pushed the button."

She was new to the Canyon had become alarmed during the night in her tent when her group ran out of water. She subsequently heard "odd" respiratory sounds emanating from the hike leader's tent. Instead of waking him to ask if he was okay, she had hit the panic button of her SPOT Messenger Device. Then, her duty done, and without telling any of her companions what she had just done, she promptly dropped off back to sleep.

When the air "cavalry" landed in the rugged terrain loaded for every medical emergency other than cosmetic surgery (or a brain transplant) they, too, questioned the groggy backpackers.

The trip leader confessed, yes, he did, at times, snore.

Once this "emergency" was resolved, and the woman's use of the SPOT device was determined to have been unwarranted, the group decided that because they had not brought enough water, they would abort their hiking plans and return to the rim.

The take-home lesson here is one should never embark on any hike into the backcountry unless one has fully prepared to do that hike successfully *without* a PLB and without a sat phone. Once prepared, then okay, toss in that rented sat phone. But leave the PLB at the rental center.

Not everyone who gets in trouble by underestimating the heat and concomitantly underestimating their need for water do so on one of the more arcane of the Canyon's trails or routes. Tragedies from failing to heed, through ignorant denial, the Canyon's obvious forces of nature also occur on the main "highway" trails such as the Kaibab and Bright Angel. The most tragic of all these, however, occur when children die needlessly in the charge of adults who ought to know better. While it is true that every year in Grand Canyon thousands of hikers experience symptoms of heat injuries, in 1996 alone, six or seven of them independently died from heat. Each of these deaths could have been prevented.

Only a month after the well-publicized tragic death of David B. Phillips to dehydration and heatstroke at the mouth of Little Nankoweap, the Grim family traveled from Ohio to Arizona for their semiannual hike into the Canyon. Among their eleven members was 10-year-old Phillip. His grandmother had organized and was leading this visit, which she had decided would be during July solely because this was the only open date she could reserve for a camping spot at Bright Angel Campground. Phillip's mother felt very apprehensive about it, however, because not only was this Phillip's first plane ride, it was also his very first hike in the Canyon. In reality, only a few members of the Grim family had ever hiked in the Canyon at all, and none during a month of peak heat.

Like most ten-year-old boys, Phillip Grim seemed oblivious to his mother's worries and instead felt very excited about hiking into the Canyon from the South Rim and out via the North Kaibab Trail to the North Rim, where his mother would be waiting to meet him the next day. Phillip and the several other hiking Grims started down South Kaibab Trail toward Phantom Ranch at about 10 a.m., an exceptionally late start by anyone's book, and a deadly time in July. Adding bad luck to bad planning, this day, July 23, would turn out to be the hottest day of the year.

Consumed with excitement, Phillip started down by skipping and half running down the trail. He paid little attention to the water he carried in his backpack. Less than an hour into the hike, at Cedar Ridge, the hikers encountered NPS Ranger Peggy Kolar, who cautioned them for thirty minutes about the dangers of heat and the need to drink lots of water. Assessing these hikers against the extreme heat of this day, Ranger Kolar suggested strongly that they cancel their hike and return to the South Rim. The Grims chose not to.

The group fissioned into faster and slower hikers. Phillip, the fastest, paired off with his 50-something great uncle. Phillip complained that his backpack was uncomfortable. His great uncle offered to carry it—and the water it contained—for him. By the half way point down, Phillip looked slightly fatigued and complained of feeling tired. But his great uncle felt no concern because Phillip still was running ahead. Nor did Phillip ask for his water very often—possibly because the more-than-blood-warm fluid seemed unappetizing to an Eastern boy.

As the two hikers neared the bottom, mid-afternoon thermometers in the Inner Gorge hit 116 degrees in the shade. By now several Grims of various ages had scattered themselves over two miles. Shadeless miles. Phillip's grandmother and great aunt already were suffering severely from heat exhaustion on the trail well uphill from little Phillip.

Finally seeing the river so close, Phillip ran down to the Kaibab Bridge (a.k.a. the "Black" Bridge). Then he crossed it over the Colorado to the north side. Once there, he meandered along the gravel and sand trail against the cliff wall heading toward Bright Angel Creek. The heat was suffocating.

Abruptly, as the Kaibab Trail now failed for the first time to take him any closer to the river, Phillip likely felt psychologically defeated as well as exhausted. He sat down within roughly a hundred feet of Bright Angel Creek but unfortunately still out of view of it. His great uncle caught up with him. But he walked past Phillip saying something like, "Come on, we need to keep going." Leaving Phillip sitting alone and heat-exhausted in the hot sun, his great uncle walked a few hundred yards farther to Phantom Ranch.

Minutes later Phillip stood up and tried to walk. He collapsed face down on the trail. Hikers found him sprawled like a corpse. Alarmed, they quickly notified the closest NPS ranger. NPS Maintenance Technician Frank Corey and Ranger Marty Johnson arrived at Phillip minutes later.

Phillip, they found, was unresponsive to all stimuli. Phillip's eyes were open but glazed and covered with sand. His pulse was very weak. His breathing had ceased altogether.

The two started CPR and radioed for help. They also tried to cool Phillip with water—his rectal temperature now exceeded 106 degrees.

Meanwhile Phillip's great uncle had continued to Phantom Ranch, mixed up some Gatorade and had then returned to fetch Phillip. When he arrived, Phillip was in the throes of death to dehydration and heatstroke.

NPS rangers, Paramedic Nancy Mecham, I-EMT Ken Phillips, and EMT Bil Vandergraff arrived and performed advanced resuscitation efforts on Phillip for over an hour.

After a helicopter evacuation, the Grand Canyon Clinic staff, including myself (Myers) and my colleague, Dr. Jim Wurgler, continued resuscitative efforts on Phillip. Nothing worked. As time passed it seemed ever more hopeless. Eventually we had to pronounce him dead. It was one of the most heart-rending and saddest moments of my medical career. And not just mine. There was not a dry eye in the clinic.

Still on the South Kaibab Trail, Phillip's grandmother and great aunt— experiencing severe heat problems themselves—saw the helicopter carrying Phillip to the South Rim Clinic. They had no idea, of course, that it was transporting Phillip. Minutes later and about a quarter mile above the Black Bridge, one of these two women also plunged into full-blown heatstroke.

At roughly this same moment another hiker reached Phantom Ranch and reported that he had passed two women who seemed to be in severe heat distress. Rangers Bil Vandergraff and Matt Vandzura found both women. Phillip's grandmother looked so far gone to Vandergraff that he felt compelled to tell her, "Ma'am, I need you to drop your pants to take your temperature."

Vandergraff rolled the older woman on her side and inserted his thermometer in her rectum. Her core temperature read 105 degrees. This was, he realized, the last remaining moment in which it was still possible to save her life. Vandergraff and Vandzura cooled her down with water. Then they evacuated her by litter, hauling her by hand down the sun-blasted trail. They carried her across the Black Bridge and then down to the small flat pad for a helicopter evacuation.

About three hours after young Phillip died, the Park helicopter returned to emergency evacuate both older Grim women. They eventually learned about Phillip's death, and, at Grand Canyon Clinic, each woman was in psychological shock.

Each was also a dehydrated "mess" verging on the same lethal heatstroke catastrophe as young Phillip.

At Grand Canyon Clinic we monitored both women's intravenous fluids and started their lab work immediately. Another hour of delay in their evacuation could have meant one or even two more fatalities. The medically evacuated and emotionally devastated Grims joined the ranks of the 280 other Canyon hikers who got lost or who injured or killed themselves in 1996 and had to be rescued by NPS rangers. Two hundred of these hikers had to be helicoptered out of the Canyon. Eight of them, including poor Phillip Grim and David Phillips, emerged too late for anything but their own funeral.

Tragically and almost unbelievably, young Phillip Grim died of dehydration and heatstroke within a hundred feet of Bright Angel Creek. A few more seconds of easy walking the cold, clear water of Bright Angel Creek could have saved his life. But, then, so could having drunk the water that he, then his great uncle, had carried.

As tragedies go, Philip Grim's must rank as one of the worst ever. On the other hand, his death was due to ignorance, not malice. Consider the following lead-off from Hillary Davis' article in the *Arizona Daily Sun* for August 31, 2011:

An Indiana man has been federally charged with several counts of child abuse after allegedly forcing his three young grandsons on brutal Grand Canyon hikes this month. He is accused of beating them, making them walk on ulcerated blisters, denying them food and water, and forcing them to run up the trail under the intense sun. According to a complaint filed Tuesday by the U.S. Attorney's Office in Flagstaff, rangers and passersby took note of several instances regarding alleged abuse by Christopher Carlson [age 45], of Indianapolis, against the boys, ages 12, 9 and 8....One of these hikes, a 19-mile trek [on the Bright Angel Trail], occurred last weekend, when temperatures reached 108 degrees at Phantom Ranch along the Colorado River. Not long after, a passing hiker used the emergency phone at the Three Mile Rest House to report the group after the oldest child secretly asked for help. The children were described as hyperventilating and running, and another ranger in the area said Carlson was threatening to make them hike faster and that the youngest boy was crying.

During the final ascent of what the media termed "the hike from hell," a ranger on the rim observed Carlson through binoculars shoving the boys and whipping them up the trail with a rolled up T-shirt. Rangers arrested Carlson at the trailhead.

The boys told investigators that they had been hit, pushed, choked, pinched, squeezed and whipped during the day's hike, and that they had vomited several times, sometimes when the man forced their fingers down their throats. They also said they were not allowed to drink water until they reached Phantom Ranch and sneaked water from the Colorado River, and that they had been limited to little food....The children were placed in the care of Child Protective Services. A medical exam showed several injuries in various stages of healing, implying chronic abuse. The boys' lips had been sunburned off and they had several cuts and bruises. The eldest boy described some symptoms of potentially fatal heat stroke from Sunday's hike, including dizziness, double vision and sounds around him becoming hushed. The boys also had badly chafed groins, because Carlson did not allow them to wear underwear.

Carlson defended his actions by stating that he was trying to get his overweight grandchildren into shape and toughen them to face the world's other tough people out there. One of Carlson's alleged tactics was to threaten to push the boys over the edge if they did not keep up with him. The oldest boy also alleged Carlson not only threw rocks at them, he shoved the boy's face into a rock. Carlson later instructed the boy to hide the blood from rangers. Carlson allegedly also instructed the boys to smile at other hikers and pretend they were having a good time. Crueler still, was his denying them water while he guzzled water in front of them during temperatures nearing 108 degrees in the shade. On this same day, another man died of heatstroke in the Canyon on the Tanner Trail upstream.

"Bad Grandpa," as of this writing in September, 2011, was in the Coconino County Jail facing six counts of child abuse and child endangerment. With Carlson's 20-year history of prior arrests, this latest one—resulting in a two-year prison sentence—might prove not much more than an inconvenience.

The more than 50 deaths in Grand Canyon (Tables 2 and 3) due to a lack of water constitute more than ample proof that one should plan to drink enough if one also plans to stay alive. But should failing to drink enough water be our only concern?

On a hot June 14, 2006 night, river guide Jamie Townsend flicked the switch on his headlamp. The beam illuminated the face of his unconscious passenger. Townsend's attitude sagged even lower. The glow penetrated the Stygian blackness of 3:00 a.m. at the bottom of the Inner Gorge just enough to reveal a ghostly pale-green complexion. This woman's color alone was appalling. Added to it, however, was pair of eyes now bloodshot and glazed. The beam blazing into the woman's pupils did not seem even to faze her. Hours ago this woman had suffered a grand mal seizure. Since then she had remained unresponsive. To Townsend this 68-year-old grandmother from Wisconsin no longer even looked human. The stench of vomit and incontinence did nothing to tone down this *Night of the Living Dead* impression.

At least she was still breathing. Townsend had remained on a vigil ever since sunset to keep this woman's airway open. Challenging as this task had proved for Townsend and fellow Canyoneers' guides Angie Mauldin and Todd Maynard, it paled next to the challenge of coordinating yet another satellite phone for yet another an emergency evacuation at this un-fly-able-for-the-Park-SAR-team hour.

Finding oneself in the position of having to arrange a medical evacuation during a river trip always proves bad. But this would be this crew's third evacuation in less than 24 hours.

The guides reflected on how weird and ironic it seemed that all three of their crashing passengers were women—and were friends. They had become the apparently doomed *tres amigas.* Their odd behavior during the first few days of this trip had mimicked each other's. The three, wrapped in their dark blue rain gear, had sat together near the stern of the boat. They had eaten together, hiked together, and camped together. They had even peed in the river together, unfortunately two of them fell in and developed a phobia about the menace of the Colorado. Then, by Day Three, one by one, each had dropped into a mysterious coma.

It had started less than 24 hours earlier, on a hot June 13th. The first victim, a 67-year-old from Wisconsin, we'll call her Linda, had collapsed. She and several friends and family from Wisconsin were traveling together. They probably had chosen Canyoneers, the oldest continuously operated commercial river company in Grand Canyon, because it held a reputation for safety earned by having taken tens of thousands of people successfully down the Colorado.

Again, 24 hours ago, Linda had abruptly complained of feeling nauseous. Next she vomited. She became too weak and shaky to even walk. Next she quit urinating.

Suspecting she was dehydrated, the guides encouraged her to drink. They tried to keep her cool. By nightfall Linda had proved unable to eat dinner. Then she felt unable to sleep. Morning proved no better. Patently feeling terrible, Linda asked the crew to arrange for her a medical flight out of the Canyon. During lunch at the Phantom Ranch boat beach, the guides conferred with rangers for her medical flight.

Still vomiting, Linda boarded the Park Rescue Helicopter 368 from Phantom Ranch. Lifting off the pad would be Linda's last memory before waking up in an intensive care unit two days later.

One of Linda's buddies, a 70-year-old we'll call Francine, had been feeling nearly as terrible as Linda. The previous night she had been urinating in the river as required by NPS protocols but had slipped and fractured her wrist (though only later would x-rays would show this). Worse, she also seemed to be exhibiting early signs of the same sort of malaise that had felled Linda.

The temperature here at Phantom was 104 degrees in the shade. As Francine sipped a soda, the guides tried to talk with her about her condition and medical history. But her husband, the guides reported, had played interference with them, insisting that she was tough and would do great. Trying to avoid a preventable big problem, the Canyoneers' guides now also had offered Francine a ride out at Phantom with Linda (as per incident report #08-0608).

But Francine had declined this rescue flight. She was traveling with said husband and two adult children. She did not want to miss this long-anticipated trip.

Feeling misgivings, the Canyoneers crew agreed to not press Francine harder. It's not easy to eject a paying passenger from a trip when she seems merely marginal and when her husband is running interference.

Obeying Murphy's Law, as soon as the Canyoneers motor rig departed Phantom Ranch into John Wesley Powell's "Great Unknown," Francine started to complain of feeling weak and nauseous. She soon had trouble keeping fluids down. She barely could eat. She, as Linda had done before her, now vomited. Abruptly, she became confused. Her speech degraded into nonsensical gibberish. Her deterioration happened quickly. Suddenly she went into convulsions, seizing violently on the boat deck amongst gear, duffle, and eighteen other horrified passengers.

As guide Todd Maynard remembers, "I laid with this lady in a tarp. She was puking on me, pissing on me, and shitting on me. Then it all stopped. Her eyes rolled back into her head. They turned orange. She had lock jaw. It was horrible...."

After a subjective eternity, Francine's seizure abated. But now she remained unresponsive, in an apparent coma. Her breathing refused to rise above shallow.

Guides Townsend and Maynard continued to provide basic life support and maintained her airway. Meanwhile river guide Mauldin did battle with the satellite phone. She stood as high as possible on the deck and aimed the phone's small antenna into the narrow slice of southwestern sky. No signal. Not enough sky was exposed up there between the close walls to provide a direct line with the needed satellites. She tried again and again. Still nothing.

Seeking a more propitious bearing, Townsend ferried the big boat back and forth, shore to shore, continuing down Upper Granite Gorge. Still nothing.

Below Serpentine Canyon at River Mile 107, Mauldin finally tapped into a signal. She relayed Francine's critical condition to the Park dispatcher. The Park promised to send another helicopter and rescue crew immediately. All three crew members felt a surge of relief. Now it was up to Francine to hang in there a little longer.

Meanwhile Canyoneers motored downstream to find a shoreline big enough for the SAR helicopter to land. At Bass Camp, River Mile 108, the crew encountered a private trip. In this group was E.R. Nurse Darla Ekbom, a veteran of many Canyon trips. She assumed oversight of Francine, who remained frighteningly unresponsive and comatose. At about 6:00 p.m. the whup-whup-whup of the NPS chopper echoed between the diabase cliffs.

Wasting no time, the SAR paramedic Ken Phillips strapped the inert Francine onto a backboard and slid her into the airship. The SAR pilot lifted the helicopter off the sand then flew east.

Exhausted, the Canyoneers trip double-camped with the private trip at Bass. Dinner went mostly uneaten. The back-to-back casualties of this baffling death-like malady weighed heavily on everyone's mind. It felt too much like the beginning of a Stephen King novel.

Before nightfall the guides brainstormed on what they needed to do next to refocus the trip for the sake of the remaining passengers. At least, they admitted, both mysteriously sick women had made it off the river alive. Having managed both evacuations successfully seemed like a reprieve.

This reprieve proved unbelievably brief.

"Oh, my God! Louise is having a seizure!"

Almost immediately after the helicopter had evacuated Francine from Bass Camp, a 68-year-old also from Wisconsin, we'll call her Louise, had reported that she too did not feel well. This woman—*numero tres* of the *tres amigas*—had drunk plenty of fluids, enough to replace what she had been losing for three days, but had eaten only a small piece of banana and few crackers for dinner. Only half an hour earlier, when Mauldin and Townsend had spoken with her, she had seemed lucid but had felt ill. The crew had encouraged her to lie on the beach where it was coolest. "Sip fluids," they added, "and try to eat these salty snacks."

Louise's increasing nausea made doing the latter nearly impossible. Within minutes she became confused and restless. Next she seemed incapable of uttering a word. As the sun set gloriously in the west. Louise collapsed into convulsions "as if shot by a bullet." Next she became incontinent.

Feeling something far more intense than déjà vu, Townsend and Maynard, now with Nurse Ekbom, tried to aid the sick woman. Mauldin grabbed the satellite phone again and dialed the Park. Mauldin swallowed hard when the dispatcher informed her that no emergency flight would be made that night. The Park SAR helicopter virtually never made night flights into Grand Canyon due to the extreme hazards. (The Arizona Department of Public Safety [DPS] does make such flights in dire emergencies, but river guides are not encouraged to contact DPS.) Mauldin relayed her distressing news to crew and passengers.

The river runners were on their own.

Townsend and Ekbom now assumed assigned roles and took turns monitoring Louise. They treated her for shock and repeatedly cleared her airway. They and a friend of Louise planned to guard her all night.

The night dragged on like sludge. The sense of isolation at the bottom of Grand Canyon felt overwhelming. From their required wilderness first responder training the guides knew Louise looked sick enough to die if she did not receive advanced medical help fast. Her green color, glassy eyes, and death smell told Townsend she already had one foot in the grave. Louise's rapidly worsening condition finally became intolerable for Townsend.

"Listen," he now told his crew. "We know the Park Service doesn't fly below the rim after dark, but DPS does if it's life or death. They use night vision technology. I think Louise might die. We need to get her out now. I know a guy who works for DPS. He might be able to help us arrange the evacuation. I'm going to call him."

The crew agreed. Out came the sat phone again. Townsend dialed his contact. It was 4:00 a.m.

A groggy, annoyed voice answered, "Hello?"

Relieved, Townsend explained Louise's dire straits.

The friend's voice perked up. "I'll call our dispatcher."

The DPS dispatcher phoned the medic on call then arranged an emergency evacuation. The closest of Arizona's four rescue helicopters was parked in Page, less than an hour distant.

Within the hour the still non-responsive Louise was flying to advanced care at Flagstaff Medical Center. DPS had pulled off her evacuation perfectly. Townsend, the Canyoneers' crew, Ekbom, and DPS had just saved her life.

As dawn broke with Louise now in good hands, spirits at Bass Camp lifted.

Now, hopefully, they faced one more helicopter evacuation, the fourth in less than 24 hours. An NPS ship to pick up Francine's family members flew in near Elves' Chasm eight miles downstream at about 9:00 a.m. The Canyoneers boat, now less heavy by six passengers and infinitely lighter in mood, headed downstream,

Todd Maynard admitted later, "This was one of the worst days of my life."

Trip leader Angie Mauldin also later admitted (to Myers) that this incident with the *tres amigas* "changed my life forever."

But now, with this ordeal apparently finally over, the Canyoneers guides discussed what had happened and speculated on possible causes. Why those three women? Sure, they all appeared to be unusually anxious and out of their element. But what else had they shared in common? Was the culprit a virus? A bacterium? Was it something that they had contracted before the trip? Or was it in something they ate? Or something else altogether? It did not seem possible for the problem to be dehydration. The crew suspected a problem altogether different. Maybe loss of electrolytes? Speculate as they might, they could not pin it down.

But they were on the right track.

The *tres amigas* showed several things in common. First, the three Midwesterners were unacclimated to the heat at the bottom of Grand Canyon in June. Second, during much of their time aboard the boat they had worn rain jackets and pants to avoid splashes but had sat as far back as possible from the bow on Canyoneers' big 37-foot, C-craft rig, where splashing was minimal and sweating more likely. The guides had felt compelled to douse and spray water over the women's heads to try to prevent their overheating. Third, the women seemed to have taken to heart the advice to drink enough to avoid dehydration.

But soon their appetites for food waned. Instead of eating, they mostly drank. This is a telltale clue. They showed little interest in the salty snacks offered repeatedly by the guides. Instead, again, they drank. But as everyone knows, what goes in must come out. Yet early in the trip, when the three had tried to urinate in the river, two had fallen in. Again, one injured her wrist. Afterward the three seemed to fear the Colorado. Then, strangely, their impulses to urinate diminished. The final big clues as to what was going wrong are that, after only two days of all this, the *amigas* had begun complaining of feeling bloated, anxious, then of feeling nausea and headaches and, finally, they began vomiting the fluids they drank.

What, then, *was* the culprit here?

The baffling malady that felled these women did not come from something they ate. Instead it was due mostly to *drinking too much water.*

A ground ambulance had transported the first victim, Linda, of the *tres amigas* from the SAR heliport at Phantom Ranch to the Grand Canyon Clinic. I (Myers) was physician on duty. I first conferred with NPS paramedic Marc Yeston about her condition. He reported that she had been stable. Next I saw her.

Linda presented to me as oriented but anxious. Her blood pressure was up.

"Hello, Linda. I'm Doctor Myers."

"I don't know," she blurted, looking flustered.

Weird. She knew who she was, where she was, and today's date. But otherwise she was losing it. She kept repeating "I don't know" for no apparent reason.

Before my eyes her mental status continued to plummet. Soon she kept saying, "I can't do it. I can't do it."

I asked her, "Can't do what?"

"I can't do it."

Alarmed, I asked her name again.

"I can't do it." Acting agitated, Linda's speech soon degraded into incomprehensible gabble. Severe dives in mental status like Linda's are a late and serious sign of her malady.

During my sixteen years at the Clinic we had seen Linda's condition hundreds of times among hikers and river runners. It had become a common problem among them since the early 1990s. Based on my own calculations it now was accounting for over thirty percent of heat-related illness. Yet most travelers within the Canyon, Linda included, had no clue this menace to survival existed.

Now I knew Linda's brain likely was swelling within her skull to the point where she would be gripped in the throes of a seizure any minute. I only needed to see her lab test to reconfirm her diagnosis made by Ranger Yeston.

The new lab results confirmed it.

Linda was not *de*-hydrated. Instead she had been *over*-hydrated. She was suffering from dangerously low blood sodium, a condition also known as "hyponatremia." The diagnosis of Linda's electrolyte imbalance, also known as "water intoxication," was initially made with an "I-stat" machine kept in the tiny clinic in the Phantom Ranger Station. The check of her blood sodium there showed it was low. The repeat test at our South Rim Clinic on a more accurate machine confirmed it was dangerously low. Upon Linda's arrival at the clinic, we had set an IV in her arm and begun delivering sodium replacement.

Because she had seemed almost lucid upon her arrival here, we had hoped she could be treated at the Clinic. But her precipitous decline had presented so dramatically that I ordered her flown to Flagstaff Medical Center's intensive care unit.

Within hours helicopters would rescue Francine, then Louise, from Bass Camp to join her there. The *tres amigas* all would be monitored in the ICU and their sodium levels corrected. Done wrong, they would die. Fortunately, all three survived.

The ironic lesson in all this is, while dying of thirst in the desert may seem so obvious as to be a cliché, drinking too much water can lead to the same fate. The critical consequence of over-drinking water is the dilution of sodium in one's blood. This imbalance, again often called "water intoxication," can send one into drunken-like stupor then convulsions then death.

Not only is this true, it's far from a mere academic observation. Indeed an inadvertent "experiment" conducted not long ago "proved" it. On January 13, 2007 the *Associated Press* reported:

> *January 12, 2007, a listener named Jennifer Strange, 28, died of water intoxication hours after taking part in the "Hold Your Wee for a Wii" contest in which Sacramento, California FM radio station KDND promised a Wii video game system for the winner. In the competition, contestants were asked to drink as much water as they could without urinating. The contestant able to hold the most water would be named the winner.*
>
> *According to contest participants, 17 to 20 contestants took part in the competition in a room at KDND's studios. The contest broadcast during the station's "Morning Rave" program began around 6:15 a.m. as contestants were each handed eight-ounce water bottles to drink at 15-minute intervals. Contestants also said that as the contest progressed, they were given increasingly large quantities of water to drink. Some later remarked on the physical discomfort they suffered during and following the event.*
>
> *The* Sacramento Bee *newspaper has released audio clips from the morning show on their website. These clips indicate that the DJs of the show were aware of the [lethal potential] of water intoxication. At one point, a caller who was a co-worker of Nurse Practitioner Judy Linder called the station and informed the DJs that the contest could be dangerous and that someone could die. The DJs responded by saying "we're aware of that," and joked that the contestants had signed releases and couldn't file a lawsuit. However, according to a contestant, the waivers addressed only publicity issues and made no mention of health or safety concerns. The DJs also joked about Strange's distended belly, joking that she looked three months pregnant.*
>
> *After the contest, Strange spoke to a co-worker by telephone, indicating she was on her way home and in extreme pain, suffering from what appeared to be an intense headache. The co-worker contacted Strange's mother, who went to her home an hour later to find her daughter dead.*

Water intoxication is a layman's term to describe significant hyponatremia. My (Myers) first wake up moment with hyponatremia was as a young physician caring for a patient plagued by a compulsive desire to over-drink water. She was unforgettable. She was a physically healthy young woman suffering from psychiatric illness. Repeated lab analyses revealed puzzlingly low blood sodium levels. The data suggested her problem was due to too much intake of water. Yet she denied drinking extra water. Even so, the decision was made to restrict her fluids. The faucet in her sink was shut off. Fluids given her were monitored and kept to a minimum. Despite these precautions, her sodium levels continued to bottom out.

This baffling mystery was finally solved when a night housekeeping staff worker caught her greedily and compulsively sucking up water from her toilet bowl.

As we've seen, dehydration and heatstroke have killed people in Grand Canyon. So, too, has hyponatremia. Common in endurance athletic events, it's known as "exercise-associated hyponatremia." Both dehydration and hyponatremia are most often associated with exposure to heat, but their causes are opposites. Dehydration is caused by excessive water loss from sweating followed by inadequate replacement. This can lead to elevated body temperatures then heatstroke which, again, often proves fatal. Hyponatremia, on the other hand, emerges via the opposite mechanism: overdrinking of water which causes excessive dilution of sodium in one's blood—which may or may not be abetted by losing even more salt through sweating during exertion. In the case of the *tres amigas*, exertion was not a factor. Significantly, just as with Jennifer Strange, simple over-drinking was. How can this lead to death? Strange's salt imbalance (and those of the *tres amigas*) caused severe brain swelling ("hyponatremia encephalopothy"). Hence those headaches and mental declines.

Yet not every case of hyponatremia is a simple matter of water and salt. Hormones also play a role in the balance of both. One of the most important kicks in when one experiences pain, stress, nausea (as with the *tres amigas*), and even high temperatures. Our body then secretes antidiuretic hormone (ADH) also known as arginine vasopressin (AVP) which stops the body from peeing and fosters water retention. The downside? The extra water retained in the body dilutes one's level of blood sodium. Once this happens, a horrible negative feedback cycle may begin: Because hyponatremia itself often can lead to nausea and vomiting, it causes yet more ADH to be secreted, more water retained, then rapid brain swelling, whopping headaches, coma, and so on. Bad news....

Oddly, nearly all cases of heat exhaustion in Grand Canyon before the late 1980s were diagnosed as dehydration. Hyponatremia seemed nonexistent—or, instead, it simply may have gone undocumented. The last twenty years in the Canyon, however, have seen a shocking rise in recognized cases. Again, these account for about one third of heat-related illnesses. More than 90 percent of these victims were hikers. Two out of three were women. Lots of them ended up in the hospital. This is because, unlike treating dehydration by simply drinking water in the field, hyponatremia often demands very careful and prolonged sodium correction in a hospital.

Why did hyponatremia take an upsurge in Grand Canyon? Several reasons. First, most cases of hyponatremia are self-induced from over-drinking, again, as Jennifer Strange did in the "Hold Your Wee for a Wii" contest. Interviews with hikers diagnosed with hyponatremia in the Canyon clearly reveal they had drunk a lot to prevent dehydration. This phenomenon also has been documented among endurance athletes from the Boston Marathon. A 2002 study found 13 percent of Boston runners suffered hyponatremia ("exercise-associated") incurred by their overdrinking during the race. Six percent became dangerously low on sodium. One dropped dead.

For decades, we've been brainwashed by sports drinks advertising that we should never feel thirst because if thirst kicks in, we're already "behind the curve." People visiting the Canyon then were bombarded with warnings to drink plenty of water to prevent dehydration and avert heatstroke. But educating the public on all dangers posed by heat has proved a challenge. A "Stop! Heat Kills" campaign was designed by the Park in the mid-1990s on the heels of several deaths due to heatstroke. Their emphasis to continue to pour water down one's throat as a total preventative tactic—as if "thirst" were a dragon to be slain in advance—may have contributed to overdrinking combined with under-eating. Incidents of hyponatremia seemed to increase after these scary signs were posted. These now have been replaced with different signs that emphasize drinking only to meet (not prevent) one's thirst and also to take breaks to eat salty snacks.

"Sports drinks" do not solve this problem of diluted sodium. Because they contain, on average, less than one third the sodium we lose through sweating, you can over-drink them and still dilute your blood sodium. Worse, many people these days follow a strict low-sodium diet said to be healthy in normal environments. This can put them at greater risk in the Canyon's heat.

Also risky business is the decision by some hikers that Grand Canyon is the ideal place to go on a diet and jumpstart a weight loss. Eating little, or less than normal, is now known to increase the risk of suffering both hyponatremia *and* dehydration. Why both? Because people who eat tend not to over-drink because their belly is partially filled already. But eating does a lot more than meets the eye. This is because eating also stimulates thirst, which thus helps avoid the opposite problem of dehydration—provided one drinks only to satisfy thirst and not to match some preconceived quota. Critical here is an observation noted on page 70 of Edward F. Adolph's 1947 invaluable classic *Physiology of Man in the Desert* (discussed in more detail later). He concluded: "Men in the desert tend to become dehydrated even when water is available. This phenomenon is called voluntary dehydration... Voluntary dehydration can be minimized *if no meals are missed*." (italics ours)

What should we be eating? When hiking or backpacking in hot weather, salty carbohydrates top the list—you know, the stuff you're not supposed to eat. But foods you do like well enough to eat for certain. Whether salty nuts, trail mix,

Stackers, Pringles, peanuts, or whatever, just choose stuff you know you will eat. But whatever stuff you choose must be capable of resisting melting in the heat into an inedible mess. For a full day of uphill hiking two to three times normal calorie intake is usually needed. Think of food as an insurance policy to stay happy on the trail.

What if we do not feel like eating? Well, consider what Edward Adolph's exhaustive study (page 249) revealed: "The result is clear: less food is eaten during dehydration. Aversion to food (anorexia) is one of the most constant sequelae of dehydration."

The big lesson here? Virtually all of us are at risk when we exit a world of air-conditioned cars and homes and offices and stores to plunge into an unrelenting inferno. The prime arsenal for combating heat consists of drinking only when thirsty, taking shade breaks from your hike (Adolph found 10 minutes per hour enough to recuperate), wearing loose clothing, avoiding walking between the hottest hours of the day—10:00 a.m. to 4:00 p.m.—(or of the year), and snacking on salty carbohydrate foods. Never pass up a chance to get yourself wet, or soaking wet. Cool off, relax, grab a snack, enjoy the view. In short, chill.

So now you know. And if one is taking diuretics, the rules above still apply. Not adhering to these simple guidelines can lead to paying a very high price.

On the morning of September 4, 2008 Susan Jane Linley, age 47, of the United Kingdom had hiked with her husband and son into the Canyon via the South Kaibab Trail. They returned to the trailhead before lunch. From there the family took the shuttle bus to the visitor center. Once there Linley complained of feeling dizzy. Next she fainted onto the pavement.

Good Samaritans dialed 911.

Ranger James Thompson and another ranger arrived in Medic-1. Linley, now conscious again, told Thompson she had eaten breakfast and had been drinking lots of Gatorade. Because of her loss of consciousness and her fall, the rangers placed her in spinal immobilization then assessed her in the ambulance en route to Flagstaff 80 miles distant. The medics started an IV. Next they gave Linley Zofran to reduce her nausea.

Minutes later she sprayed the rear of the ambulance with vomit. Next she became combative and yanked out her IV.

The ranger-medics instantly requested by radio an air ambulance to meet them at the Valle Airport 30 miles south of Grand Canyon.

Soon Linley's combativeness waned and she sank into unconsciousness.

At Valle Airport Linley remained unresponsive. The medics inserted a breathing tube in her throat and put her on a respirator. The helicopter delivered her to Flagstaff Medical Center's intensive care unit.

Two days later, Ranger Thompson called the ICU to check on his patient. A nurse told him Linley suffered such severe swelling of her brain due by hyponatremia that she was brain dead. Her grieving husband later gave permission to take her off life support and to donate several of her organs.

Clearly it is far better to prevent hyponatremia long before mental or behavioral aberrancies are staring one in the face. What clues should ring our alarm bells? Lightheadedness, dizziness, fatigue, generalized weakness, chills, headache, anxiety, irritability, loss of appetite, nausea, vomiting, and muscle cramps.

How can one tell the difference between hyponatremia versus dehydration?

Distinguishing dehydration from hyponatremia early is challenging but critical because their treatments are opposite. An early diagnosis *depends* above all on an accurate history of fluid and food intake by the victim. This cannot be over-emphasized. For example, if a summer downhill hiker has drunk more than half a liter of water or other fluids per hour (depending on how hot it is) or if an uphill hiker has drunk about a liter per hour, then dehydration is unlikely. The next most important clue is food intake. If the person above has not eaten much at all, hyponatremia is more likely.

Thirst is common with dehydration but not with hyponatremia because, after all, most victims had drunk too much water.

Dehydration usually causes a rise in pulse, over 100 beats per minute while standing. In contrast, hyponatremia victims, unless anxious, tend to have a normal pulse and no elevated temperature.

If the victim is vomiting, dehydration allows very little, often dry heaves only. In contrast, hyponatremia victims vomit copious fluid, even projectile-like.

People trying to figure which problem is more likely often rely on the victim's urine output as their number one clue. But urine can be deceptive. Dehydrated people exhibit a diminishing output of urine that may be a stinky, concentrated, and dark yellow. With hyponatremia the urine at first will look copious and clear. But as time passes this output also can diminish or even stop altogether due to anitidiuretic hormone. Don't be fooled by urine. Review the victim's recent history of what he/she has been eating and drinking.

Yet another clue: Dehydrated people feel better lying flat. Hyponatremia victims, in contrast, often feel worse lying down because it tends to increase the pressure already in the victim's head due to brain swelling.

Which brings us to the next clue: as hyponatremia worsens, victims also often exhibit subtle changes in personality. They may become quiet, withdrawn, or sleepy or instead display anxiety and agitation. Either way a victim may exhibit slow thinking and poor concentration, as if drunk. Hence the term "water intoxication." Eventually, some victims cannot verbalize what they are thinking. Or, as with the *tres amigas*, they repeat the same words or phrases over and over. Canyon rangers treating hyponatremia also describe a blank, 1,000-yard stare. A few lights may be on, but no one is home. Again, as brain swelling becomes severe, seizures are common. So is erratic breathing. Then coma. Then death.

Field treatment for mild to moderate hyponatremia is simple. First, rest the person in a cool, shady place and dowse their clothes and body with water. Fanning helps too. Second, try to replace lost salt by nibbling on salty snack foods. A hyponatremia victim should avoid drinking fluids until excess fluid is peed off and symptoms improve. This may take several hours. "Sit it out, 'til you pee it out." For severe cases with altered level of consciousness or seizures, the person should be evacuated to a hospital immediately.

Fortunately, one is not doomed to hyponatremia in Grand Canyon. Again, it's easy to prevent. First and foremost—if you can't remember a darned thing otherwise—drink only enough to satisfy your thirst. Appropriate here is Tim Noakes' conclusion in his book *Waterlogged: The Serious Problem of Overhydration in Endurance Sports* (page 353): "Your body will tell you what it needs if you just listen."

On a hot May 26, 1985, for an example of not listening, 58-year-old Paul M. Christie was hiking up the Bright Angel Trail from the river during a rim-to-river-to-rim trek. His operational mode was based on something like "more water will get you there." The subsequent incident report stated Christie had gulped "extreme amounts of water" prior to his dropping dead on the trail. Likely of hyponatremia.

The upshot? Pay attention to your water intake *and* your intake of food.

And when it comes to Canyon heat, don't bet your life on blind trust.

During the spring of 2004 Margaret Bradley ran the Boston Marathon. She finished in just over three hours. The temperature had hit a sweltering 85 degrees. More than 1,100 runners needed medical attention for dehydration and other heat-related ailments. When asked by the Chicago Athlete afterward how she had managed to perform so well in such heat, Bradley responded, "I focused on keeping myself hydrated."

Born and raised in Falmouth, Massachusetts, at 24 years old Bradley had enrolled as a first-year medical student at the University of Chicago's Pritzker School of Medicine. But she remained passionate about running. During some weeks she would log 90 miles. As an undergraduate at the University of Chicago, Bradley had earned all-American status and competed in Division III national championships. Indeed, running so inspired the 115-pound Bradley that she had run a 5k race in New York then boarded a jet to compete in a 10k run in Chicago the next day. Bradley had run her 26.2-mile Boston Marathon in 3 hours and five minutes for 31st place out of nearly 10,000 female runners. Her performance motivated her to consider a shot at the 2008 Olympic Trials.

As told well by Christopher Reynolds in the *Los Angeles Times* (August 17, 2004), at around 9:00 on the morning of July 8, 2004, Bradley and a new running buddy Ryan jogged down the Grandview Trail from the trailhead at 7,400 feet. The 20-something Ryan was acquainted with Bradley from Chicago, and he had recently moved to Flagstaff. He had made a point to try to get to know some local running and hiking trails, and wanted to introduce them to his fellow Easterner

Bradley. The weather here on the rim at this hour seemed like that around Flag-staff, hovering in the upper 80s for highs, where she had been making acclimatiza-tion runs for the past few days to prepare for today's run.

At this point, however, an experienced Canyoneer would have shaken her head. This is because Ryan was carrying only a gallon of water. Margaret Bradley carried some fruit, protein bars, and a surprisingly paltry 2 liters of water. Neither runner carried a map or a headlamp or a sat phone in case something went wrong. And no one else knew exactly where they were going. Moreover, again, their timing for their start was after 8:00 a.m., 3 ½ hours after dawn. It was not a good time to begin a foray into Grand Canyon during pre-monsoon summer. The smart hour to embark on an early July penetration into Grand Canyon, any Canyoneer would advise, is dawn. Or earlier.

On the other hand, neither their timing nor water supply would have posed a problem had the two runners planned a mere hour or so below the rim. Instead, however, their intent transcended "ambitious" to emerge instead as monumental. Bradley, who never had been in Grand Canyon before, and Ryan, who had not hiked the Grandview for many years and never had hiked the Tonto, had just jogged off the rim with the goal of running what Ryan had guess-timated as 15 miles, more than a half Marathon within Grand Canyon, much of it along the Tonto Trail nearly 4.8 miles distant by foot and 3,640 feet below. Their route from Grandview to the Tonto followed an unmaintained trail hacked out by a miner many decades earlier. It offered only rugged footing. The Grandview drops 2,300 feet in a mere 3 miles. This rough and precipitous trail could transform a well-trained pair of legs during a run into quivering masses before the owner ever saw the Tonto. Worse, the route Ryan had chosen was not 15 miles. Again, he merely had guessed at that distance of this route he'd chosen. He had not carefully mapped it out. Had he taken the few minutes to do so, or to access the internet, he would have found that his route encompassed more than a full Marathon—it covered 28.7 miles.

Bradley likely figured Ryan knew what he was doing. For her, 15 miles would be equivalent to a long training run.

Again, this was the hottest time of the year in an otherwise very hot place. This is the kind of place where an active person in full sun often perspires at least 1, but up to 4, liters per hour in a physiological battle to keep cool. The temperature on the Tonto Trail was already closing in on 100 degrees in the shade at 9:00 a.m., but it would be hotter once the runners got there. And there would be no shade.

What does the Park recommend regarding this section of the Tonto Trail? "Not recommended during summer," notes the Park's free trail guide. "No water." The Park's website notes the following:

> *The Tonto Trail is notorious for its lack of reliable water sources, and this section is no exception. Do not expect the river to be a water source in this area;*

river access via side canyons in this segment ranges from extremely difficult to impossible. The combination of open, sunny country, lack of shade, many dry miles and only a single reliable water source [Grapevine Creek] makes this hike dangerous in hot weather.

Halfway down the Grandview Trail, at Horseshoe Mesa, Ryan felt a surge of alarm when he realized Bradley had not brought the 3 or 4, 1-liter Nalgene bottles of water they had discussed back in Flagstaff. Instead she had carried barely 2 liters (again, Ryan carried 4). Bradley had brought barely a quarter of the water she would need. Upon learning she had carried only two liters, Ryan should have insisted that they turn around there and then and ascend back to the rim. But he didn't.

By 1:00 that afternoon, Ryan had drunk the last drop of his water and Gatorade. Bradley also had long since polished off her mere 2 liters. Ryan already felt exhausted and over-heated. He felt that his sweating mechanism was failing, and he was verging on heatstroke. Here at the pair's 15.7-mile point (about halfway) he curled up under the scant shade of an escarpment. He hoped that after taking a break he might be able to continue to the South Kaibab then hike up to the rim.

The pair stayed here, near Boulder Creek (dry), for more than 2½ hours of "resting," while actually becoming a bit more dehydrated minute by minute because the human body *must* sweat at environmental temperatures above 95 degrees. Although they did not know it, a refill of water had been available to them a few hundred yards off the Tonto Trail, both up and down Grapevine Creek, now about 5.7 miles behind them. They had jogged unknowingly past this water source more than an hour earlier.

Be that as it may, here Ryan and Margaret sat at a crux point. Their decision making likely was based on Ryan's original 15-mile estimate. By that flawed estimate the junction with the South Kaibab Trail had to be a mere mile or so away. Maybe even less. Hence the two agreed on a quick plan. Bradley, now worried not just about their combined plight but particularly about Ryan's deteriorating condition, would continue onward alone, even though she too was out of water and even more dehydrated than Ryan.

Now, however, instead of running to the rim up the South Kaibab Trail, she would follow plan B, a detour down the South Kaibab to Phantom Ranch, two miles closer than the rim. Upon arriving there she would arrange for help for Ryan. Bradley at this point was still thinking tough-mindedly in Marathon mode. She had run 15 miles before. Several times. She could do it again even if this terrain was proving torturous.

Whatever you do, Ryan advised Bradley, don't detour off the Tonto Trail down a wash. The Kaibab Trail will be really obvious.

Most search and rescue personnel are taught that when hikers in trouble decide to split up and go separate ways under emergency conditions, the results often prove that decision to have been a bad idea.

Now in a life-or-death race, Margaret Bradley jogged along the Tonto Trail under a brutal sun. The temperature had reached a moderate 104 degrees in the shade. Even so, the hotter and shade-less landscape now radiated solar heat back into the air, making it shimmer. Bradley's body mass continued to shrink as the hot arid air sucked her dry. Again, she expected the Kaibab Trail to appear at any moment. That the distance she still needed yet to cover to reach the South Kaibab was more like 10 hard, hot miles farther likely would have astounded her.

Bradley knew what 15 miles felt like. She knew she had run at least that far by now. What the hell is wrong here? Ahead of Bradley the terrain along the Tonto became more confusing and chaotic and offered no answer. Unbroken cliffs surrounded her. She crossed the bone dry Lonetree Canyon (18.7 miles from the Grandview trailhead). From here, high on the Tonto bench, the Colorado River flowing deep in its granite gorge could neither be seen nor heard. Ryan was wrong, she now knew, about this route being 15 miles. But how far was it really? Were she and Ryan on the wrong trail? Was she lost?

Meanwhile, a couple of hours after watching Bradley run ahead for his rescue, Ryan struggled to his feet. He started following her footprints. About three hours later, he stopped because in darkness he could no longer see her footprints or even the trail itself. Again, he had carried no headlamp and no map. He gave up. He collapsed and spent the night on the trail. He lost a contact lens.

Hours earlier Bradley had covered this same ground. At some point her desperation for water would have deteriorated into panic. As dehydration claimed her, Bradley realized she was nearing the end of her own superior physical capabilities. She had to get to water as soon as possible or die. Then so would Ryan. She had to reach water....

At dawn the following morning Ryan mustered the fortitude to lurch to his feet and continue. He started walking again along the Tonto. Here and there he thought he still recognized prints in the dust left by Bradley's Reeboks. He passed the head of Cremation Creek (at mile 21.7 from the Grandview Trailhead). Amazing, he thought, she had been able to keep jogging when he himself felt so wiped out. But the temperature now felt vastly more tolerable than that of the previous afternoon.

After an hour or so spent following the Tonto, Ryan, feeling badly dehydrated and unusually weak, hit its junction with the Kaibab Trail (at mile 24.7 from the Grandview Trailhead). He would later say that he had followed Bradley's footprints all the way to this junction. In reality, for that last two or three miles, he never had felt certain that he'd seen even one definite Reebok print.

Finally, here at Tipoff, he found the emergency NPS phone. It did not work. Desperate, he started screaming, "Help!"

At 6:30 a.m. on July 9, a U.S. Geological Survey employee hiking up the South

Kaibab heard Ryan's yells. She soon spotted him. He looked whipped and dehydrated. Ryan told her he was feeling weak and in desperate need of water because he still needed to hike back to the rim. Because she was carrying too little water for both of them, the USGS worker yanked her satellite phone from her pack and called the National Park Service for advice. Phantom Ranch Ranger Ivan Kassovic on the other end directed her to an emergency water cache. But, the ranger would later note: "Nowhere in that conversation did we get the information that he [Ryan] was a runner, that he'd crossed the Tonto, or that there were two of them."

Margaret Bradley was not yet a missing person. Officially, she did not exist.

Ryan drank two liters of water at Tipoff, ate three Goos, and rested for a couple of hours. He assumed Bradley was at Phantom Ranch. Of course she was there, he thought. She was too strong a runner and too smart to be anywhere else.

Acting the Good Samaritan, the USGS worker began at 9:00 a.m. to escort Ryan the 4.5 miles up the South Kaibab to the rim over the next 10 hours. Within an hour they met a Canyon hiking guide, whom Ryan knew. The guide was escorting clients down to the Bright Angel Campground.

"Hey, can you give the ranger at Phantom message for me?" Ryan asked.

"Sure. What is it?"

"Ask the ranger to try to get a message to a woman I was hiking with. Tell the ranger to tell her I'm moving her car from Grandview to the South Kaibab Trailhead area. Her name is Margaret Bradley."

Unfortunately, Ryan did not also give details of their tortuous run to the hiking guide. Nor did he express concern about Bradley's well being.

The hiking guide agreed then trudged downward with his group. Ryan and his USGS Good Samaritan inched upward through the growing heat and dust.

Hours later, at Cedar Ridge, Ryan asked Trail Crew worker Jocelyn Pawlicki with a radio to ask about finding Bradley at Phantom to relay to her his "I-will-move-the-car" message.

At about 4 p.m. on July 9, Canyon District Ranger and Shift SAR Coordinator Marc Yeston's radio crackled to life as he patrolled the quiet East Rim Drive.

"We've got one of the Trail Crew workers on Cedar Ridge with a hiker." The Park dispatcher now explained. "She says the hiker wants to get a message to the Phantom Ranger. Can you speak with her?"

Yeston spoke briefly with Pawlicki. She told him a hiker named Ryan, who was hiking out with the help of a USGS worker, had approached her about getting a message to the Phantom ranger regarding a car shuttle.

"What's the woman's name? Margaret Bradley? Okay, got it. Anything else? Is he doing okay?" asked Yeston. "Does he need emergency assistance?"

Pawlicki replied negative on all counts.

Yeston relayed the information to Phantom Ranger Ivan Kassovic. During the next few hours, Kassovic asked around about Margaret Bradley during his campground checks. No one had seen her. No one had heard of her—except the hiking guide acquainted with Ryan. Kassovic had spoken briefly with this guide earlier in the evening. But then the hiking guide had forgotten to mention Ryan's message for Bradley. Hearing her name now, the guide remembered his promise.

"Oh, yeah! There was this guy named Ryan on the trail, who was hiking with her and wanted me to tell you to let her know he was moving her car from Grandview to the South Kaibab Trailhead."

"Anything else? Was everything okay? Do you know what she was doing?" asked Kassovic.

"I don't know. He didn't say."

That same evening (July 9) Kassovic approached the people milling around the canteen. Was anyone there named Margaret Bradley or had anyone seen or heard of her?

Silence.

At almost 7:00 p.m. that evening, twelve hours after Ryan and the USGS worker met at Tipoff, the two finally reached the rim. Ryan hobbled over to his Good Samaritan's car—then vomited on it. En route to Grandview, Ryan's nausea—and his lost contact lens—convinced him to change his plan to shuttle Bradley's car. He instructed the USGS worker, who was driving him, to turn around and head to Flagstaff. Ryan still had not told anyone that he did not actually know where Margaret Bradley was. He later would say he assumed she was at Phantom where she was supposed to arrange for his rescue.

It apparently never occurred to Ryan to wonder: If Margaret Bradley had made it to Phantom and arranged for Ryan's rescue, why then had he not heard that *he* was the focus of a search and rescue mission? And if no such mission was "on" for him, then why not?

En route to Flagstaff the USGS worker and Ryan stopped at Tusayan where Ryan could not face a burger. He did down a milkshake and a coke. Then he vomited them.

In Flagstaff Ryan offered to buy the USGS worker dinner. She declined and asked Ryan, "Are you sure your friend is all right? Don't you want to check on her?"

Ryan hosed his vomit off the side of her USGS car. He said he would call Margaret Bradley later (via the Phantom Ranch phone number). Ryan next went into his house and fell asleep on his floor. Around midnight he awoke and drank a smoothie his roommate made. Ryan still did not know where Bradley was at this point. He merely assumed she was at Phantom. Then he hit the sack.

Earlier, during the afternoon of this same day (July 9), Bradley's family arrived in Flagstaff to meet with her. Margaret failed to show up that evening. Her brother Eric Bradley called the Flagstaff Police Department at around 11:00 p.m. to report her missing.

"Where was she last known to be?" the officer asked.

Unfortunately, Eric Bradley did not know. He guessed it had to be somewhere between Flagstaff and Grand Canyon.

After midnight, systematic phone calls to lodges and motels around Flagstaff still had turned up nothing. The Flagstaff Police Department and Eric Bradley decided to contact the Grand Canyon NPS. Eric asked Park Dispatch if they had any information on Margaret. The answer was no (the new shift dispatcher had not heard of Bradley or the shuttle). An hour later Eric called again to ask whether it is possible to check local lodgings for Bradley at the South Rim.

By now, past midnight on July 10, at least 19 hours had passed since Ryan had been assisted by the USGS worker and 35 hours since he had separated from Bradley, he still had informed no one at the NPS that after they had separated on the Tonto Trail during extreme heat he did not actually know where she had gone.

Later that morning, at 4:53 a.m., roughly 38 hours after Ryan and Margaret Bradley had separated, Flagstaff Police listed her as a "missing person." After the police conversed with Park Dispatch and learned they had found a note that someone named Ryan was going to shuttle Bradley's car, the police contacted Ryan (asleep) by phone. Next a Flagstaff police officer knocked on his door.

Immediately after an acerbic interview with Ryan and now 40 hours after he and Bradley had separated, Ryan felt a surge of concern. At roughly 7:30 a.m. Park Dispatch finally learned what Ryan knew about Bradley's last whereabouts. Soon thereafter, Ranger Marc Yeston joined in a conference call with Ryan in Flagstaff. As Yeston listened, suddenly "all the dots connected."

By 9:00 a.m. the Park had twenty personnel working on the search. At 11:28 a.m. Park Helicopter 368 was flying its search from east to west over the Tonto Trail. Twenty-five minutes later the helicopter crew spotted a person wearing a white t-shirt. The person was lying in the Cremation drainage several hundred yards down from the Tonto Trail. Ryan had trudged past, but uphill from, this spot about 30 hours earlier.

The pilot lowered his machine closer and closer to the person in the drainage. Hoping to see some movement in response, he lowered closer yet. The crew now saw it was a woman down there. Her long hair whipped about in a frenzy due to rotor wash. But the woman herself did not move.

The rescuers found Margaret Bradley curled in a fetal position as if sleeping. After running a rugged and scorching 22 miles on only two liters of water, she had cradled her head on her fanny pack. The medical examiner estimated she had died of dehydration/ heat exposure roughly 12 to 24 hours earlier. The Park fixed the specific date of her death based on the longer timeline, on July 10, shortly after midnight. Again, Bradley's buddy Ryan had met the USGS worker with her sat phone about 30 hours prior to Helicopter 368's discovery of her. You can do the math, but what this means is, at that time, Margaret Bradley had been alive. Indeed, she would continue to wait and hope in Cremation for the next 7 to 19 hours or so after Ryan had walked past her, trapped above an impassible pour-off and below a shorter pour-off she had jumped down but could not re-climb.

After separating from Ryan on July 8, the specter of his extreme dehydration and danger coupled with Bradley's trained indefatigable will to win her rescue "race" had driven her to keep going under conditions that would have (and should have) stopped most other people in their tracks. She had performed for many hours as the desert version of the Energizer Bunny. But, whether one is well trained or not, dehydration remains nonnegotiable. Combined with heat, dehydration always plays out in one of two ways: the victim pushes onward, sweating at an undiminishing rate and performing, but becoming ever less capable. At 5-6 percent dehydration a person's circulatory system becomes compromised. If the victim keeps exerting in hot weather until he/she is dehydrated by roughly 10-15 percent (loss of about 2 gallons of water in a 150-pound person), this triggers a sudden death to heatstroke. If instead the victim stops and becomes inactive, that 10-15 percent level of dehydration leads to a slower, but inevitable death.

While jogging along the Tonto on the afternoon of July 8, Margaret Bradley had become vastly depleted in her total body water. Dehydration inevitably assumed full command over Bradley's will and her ability to think. It was killing her. Her instinct to survive drove her to head downhill toward water via the first apparent opportunity. This detour turned out to be a deceptively inviting but lethal feeder wash into the Cremation drainage a mere 3 miles short of where the Tonto Trail connects with the South Kaibab at the Park emergency phone and water cache at Tipoff. A half-hour walk downhill from there could have seen Bradley standing in the Colorado River. And during those minutes she would have encountered other hikers—just as Ryan would do about a dozen hours later.

Instead, operating now like a "heat zombie," Bradley, again, had detoured into, then descended that deceptive feeder wash toward water. It is the same drainage where Paul Stryker (whose story leads off this chapter) died trying to do the same thing. Bradley had committed to this route by jumping down a pour-off she could not re-ascend. She next had stared downward in shock at an impossible 130-foot, dry waterfall drop-off yawning below. She had trapped herself 500 feet above the Colorado River in a bone dry pitfall trap where the air sizzled at close to 120 degrees in the sun.

Her trap had not only looked hopeless to her, it was hopeless for someone untrained in rock-climbing techniques—unless searchers found her in time. Evidence suggests that she tried to use the flash on her camera as a signaling device that night (and maybe even the next?). The best estimate is Margaret Bradley likely stayed in this one spot at the lip of the dry fall for at least 18, but possibly more than 30 hours, alive and hoping for help, before the heat and her exertional dehydration finally took their ultimate toll. What thoughts passed through her mind while trapped we can only conjecture, but one can bet at least that she hissed,

"Fifteen miles, my ass."

In contrast, Ryan, who had hunkered down for the afternoon in shade, which incurs only 1/3 the loss of water to sweating that walking in sun would, who then had walked during twilight (walking during darkness incurs 2/3 the water loss as in sun), survived. This was similar to the situation with Paul Stryker's wife. Of course both of these survivors also had the huge added benefit of having drunk about twice as much water as had their partner who died. Sadder yet, both well-meaning hikers who pushed themselves in the heat beyond their utmost limits to assure the survival of his or her partner died of that heat and dehydration in the same drainage near the same spot.

The pattern of hunkering down in shade during heat leading to a drastically better survival prognosis than does blasting across the desert landscape during full sun was quantified during a monumental, never-repeated, three-year study during World War II (1942-1945) by physiologist Dr. Edward F. Adolph of the University of Rochester in New York and by his associates in the Rochester Desert Unit (their page 64). These researchers conducted hundreds of tests on U.S. Army recruits in southern California desert sites and in the "hot room" in the Desert Laboratory Unit in the university. Their landmark work, now considered the timeless final word (and today likely illegally dangerous to conduct, although none of Adolph's human subjects died), was sponsored by the United States Office of Scientific Research and Development and was published in 1947 as the now classic book, *Physiology of Man in the Desert*.

Adolph's second critical finding pivoted around water consumption. He marched two groups of soldiers through the desert for up to 8 hours during average afternoon high temperatures of 108 degrees. One group of soldiers was allowed to drink as much water as they wanted; the others were allowed none. The results were unequivocal: the drinkers outperformed the non-drinkers. Indeed, most of the non-drinkers failed to finish the hike (page 156). Humans, the experiments revealed, do not adapt at all, in any way, to water deficits. Adolph also confirmed a third finding, one desert dwellers around the globe had learned millennia ago: Covering up with clothing works far better for keeping the body cool; it incurs only half the water lost to sweating as experienced by men dressed only in shorts. In contrast, exposing one's skin doubles one's water loss and puts one at twice the risk for dehydration and heat problems. Wet clothing, Adolph found, worked even better yet. During the day at 80-88 degrees, without shade, wet clothing reduced water lost to sweat by 83 percent. Adolph and his colleague R. E. Gosselin conclude (pages 57-58):

> *"In any circumstances where water shortage is a possibility, the desert traveler should not remove his outer garments. This precaution is imperative if he lacks shade. By remaining clothed, he may sacrifice a little immediate comfort, but secure greater promise of survival."*

Adolph's WWII research proved that during a desperate survival situation in desert heat, it is far better to wait out the heat in shade and only walk at night, or else do not walk at all and wait for help to come to you (assuming someone out there knows you are missing and where).

Physiology of Man in the Desert estimated survival times in 110-degree desert heat (maximum daily temperature in the shade) for properly hydrated men with no further drinking of water and no walking to be as much as 72 hours. For hydrated men with no water and walking only at night, 48 hours. Walking during the day, 24 hours at the maximum. Adolph's research estimates on survival times have been borne out as accurate by several known survival times of victims trapped in earthquake debris. Therefore, it seems Margaret Bradley could have increased her odds of survival by hunkering down in the shade with Ryan then resuming her travel at twilight (or if she had carried a headlamp, at night). But thirst, the specter of Ryan's collapse being life-threatening, and thoughts of dying from thirst can supersede the logic of hunkering down, especially if panic or a sense of "duty" creeps in.

Clearly Bradley's problem was all about water. Had she found a waterhole (say, at Grapevine Creek), she could have survived there for weeks. Edward F Adolph's extensive studies (page 4) found that an average man (Adolph's World War II subjects averaged five feet eight inches tall and 152 pounds) walking during daylight at 80 degrees lost 1/2 quart of water per hour by sweating. At 110 degrees each man lost three times more water, 1.5 quarts every hour. Walking briskly in sunlight at 100 degrees exacted one quart of water per hour in sweat (page 9) Some of Adolph's subjects lost 11 liters per day at 100 degrees, 90 percent of it as sweat (page 343). For a hot, daylight hike of 20 miles Adolph recommended carrying at least 2 gallons of water, noting, too, that carrying those sixteen pounds exacts only a minor increased metabolic demand.

Again, Bradley, a trained Marathoner, had carried only about 2 liters (2.1 quarts) of water for what Ryan had told her would be a 15-mile run. Clearly, she had not wanted to be weighted down uncomfortably. So she decided to carry only the barest minimum she believed she needed before being able to tank up again at the South Kaibab Trailhead, much as a trained Marathoner grows to expect at the end of any formal race. How much water would have been enough? Bradley should have carried at least one gallon for her anticipated 15-mile run but two or more gallons for the reality of 28.7 miles under a shade-less summer sun and ending with a brutal ascent. Bradley knew her own exceptional abilities well, but she neither understood nor respected desert heat nor Grand Canyon topography. On the other hand, had Ryan's estimate of 15 miles been accurate, Bradley likely would have survived despite being seriously dehydrated.

Also, had Bradley or Ryan taken the few minutes of research time to learn that water was available to them at Grapevine Creek ten miles along the route Ryan had chosen, Bradley, refilling her 2 bottles there, might have survived her hoped-for plan B, that 26.7-mile run to Phantom.

Amazingly, many coaches and athletes even today believe they can train bodies to go without water. Many hikers also ascribe to "conserving" water by not drinking. Adolph, who was awarded the Presidential Certificate of Merit in 1948 for his pioneering heat work, would dispute this nonsense with hard data (page 350): "— the groundless notion that men ought to *drink* less water than they need should finally be laid to rest." Moreover, "It is better," wrote Adolph, "to have the water inside you than to carry it."

Doyen Canyon hiker Harvey Butchart would agree and would have informed Bradley, perhaps in different words. "You hike *from* water [meaning you load up with it before leaving], not *to* water [which you may never reach]."

As might be guessed, Ryan felt a great sense of remorse and responsibility for Margaret Bradley's untimely and tragic death.

Marc Yeston, Ivan Kassovic, Ken Phillips and the many other rangers who searched for Bradley and/or assisted in recovering her body pounded their fists in frustration over this completely preventable tragedy. Years later they are haunted by it. They still shake their heads.

Margaret Bradley's legacy remains one of trying to save the lives of future canyon hikers. Her tragic story and her photo—taken of her running—are emblazoned on posters at the trailheads of Bright Angel and Kaibab Trails. These ask each would-be hiker: "Could You Run the Boston Marathon?"

One additional lesson in this is: Betting your life on the guesswork of any unqualified "guide" can be a very risky thing to do. Another lesson is: Betting it solely on electronic technology—a major new trend these days—can prove just as bad.

After making hundreds of hits on the internet for information about Grand Canyon hikes, Bryce Lee Gillies of McLean, Virginia looked for a buddy to hike with him. No one stepped forward. The 5' 3", 130-pound, 20-year-old physics major at Northern Arizona University decided to hike solo the infamously hot but arguably most stunningly beautiful loop hike in the United States.

Gillies' intended route descends from the North Rim down to Surprise Valley. From Surprise it winds easterly then descends to Thunder River Spring. The route next plummets beside Thunder River to Tapeats Creek and to a first-night campground about 8 miles from the trailhead. On Day #2 Gillies planned to hike downstream 4 miles, passing ancient towering cottonwoods and crumbling ruins of pueblos built by Hopi ancestors a thousand years ago. Soon he would reach the Colorado at River Mile 135. From there he would trek downriver 3 miles to Deer Creek and be regaled by the famous "patio," and the astounding, sinuous "narrows," and the thundering 100-foot Deer Creek Falls. He planned to camp the night of day #2 at the Deer Creek Campground in a beautiful valley (originally named "Surprise Valley" by prospectors in 1872 before the name mysteriously migrated on maps 1,500 feet higher and a few miles eastward). On day #3 he would plod back to his Subaru, 8 miles distant and 4,750 feet up, parked at the Bill Hall Trailhead.

Gillies had perused a brief article in the on-line version of *Backpacker Magazine* titled "Grand Canyon National Park: Deer Creek-Thunder River Loop." Backpacker noted: "…spring and fall bring the most tolerable temps. Very strong hikers can manage the 27.6-mile loop in 3 days, but you'll be happier if you give yourself an extra day for the hike out."

This is fairly good advice. *Backpacker* also encourages: "Need motivation to keep those aching quads churning? Few sights are more awe-inspiring than the psychedelic sunset view from your North Rim endpoint."

One critical detail the ebullient *Backpacker* article did not emphasize is water. It said nothing, for example, about the need for stashing a cache of water 2 to 4 miles down from the trailhead for use by the backpacker when hiking back out. Nor did it even pay lip service to a hiker's huge physiological need for a large quantity of drinking water while hiking the route everywhere and anywhere uphill of Thunder River Spring and Deer Creek.

Unless one is trekking this region shortly after a snowmelt or during monsoon rains the entire area and its sculpted sandstone potholes sit as dry as craters on Mars. Moreover, even during May or September any hiker easily can become dehydrated while trekking in the greater than 100-degree temperatures of these shoulder seasons. During July—we know we have beaten you over the head with this—the heat can prove shockingly and bewilderingly debilitating. Again, *Backpacker* did not hint at this looming environmental menace.

The *Backpacker* article did provide quick directions for the U.S. Forest Service roads for the drive from Jacob Lake to the Bill Hall Trailhead. It also offered a topo map of the loop. Other than not having a buddy on his hike, Gillies' prospects must have seemed pretty good. As Gillies' roommate would later note, he often liked to be alone and sometimes felt "depressed and lonely" because his best friends lived back in Virginia.

Be that as it may, this dazzling hike also may have seemed a great way to celebrate his twentieth birthday. It had been a pretty solid year for the physics and engineering student so far. Gillies was an Eagle Scout. One does not attain that rank—or make two successful hiking stints at New Mexico's Philmont Scout Ranch—without some knowledge of outdoor challenges. On the other hand, most of Gillies' outdoor experience had been gained in or near Virginia, a place that, relatively speaking, was *wet* and offered far less drastic topographical relief. When temperatures in Virginia hit the 90s they are maligned as a heat wave. Gillies also had joined Engineers without Borders. He had very recently returned from northern Ghana where he had labored for weeks as a volunteer building—and even designing—a new medical clinic in a remote village. Again, it had been a good year.

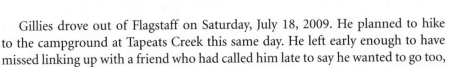

Gillies drove out of Flagstaff on Saturday, July 18, 2009. He planned to hike to the campground at Tapeats Creek this same day. He left early enough to have missed linking up with a friend who had called him late to say he wanted to go too, but otherwise Gillies' departure proved significantly late even by the standards of *Backpacker's* "very strong hiker" warning.

Gillies stopped en route at a North Rim general store to ask for directions to the trailhead. People there recall that he did not want to buy a U.S. Forest Service road map (non-topographic), but they convinced him to. The clerks noted that Gillies had never been to the North Rim before. They had to sketch for him a map to the trailhead, which stood another two hours distant.

Meanwhile the July sun poised to heat the river corridor below to 114 degrees in the shade. The catch being that virtually no shade existed.

Oddly for an Eagle Scout, Gillies had not bothered to request the backcountry permit required by the National Park Service, nor had he filed a route plan. Hence no one in the Park would know he was in the Surprise Valley area and attempting a dicey (in July) solo backpacking trip. Just weeks earlier, the Park had issued a warning to hikers not to even attempt to descend into the Canyon between 10 a.m. and 4:00 p.m. due to extreme temperatures. This warning noted: "These temperatures are beyond unpleasant or uncomfortable—they are, in fact, dangerous." The NPS warning added, "…if you fail to factor the heat into your plan, the results could be tragic."

Had Gillies requested an NPS permit, he would have received this advisory personally. Then he could have driven to the trailhead the evening before, camped there, and descended at dawn. Indeed, he should have done all this even if hiking during October.

Best estimates based on witnesses and other evidence, such as phone calls Gillies made from the North Rim, place him geared-up and ready to descend from the Bill Hall trailhead at 6,936 feet elevation no earlier than mid-afternoon or later. Indeed, early that same afternoon his aunt had phoned him to wish him a happy birthday. Hence, before he took his first step off the "chilly" Ponderosa-forested rim, the temperature where he stood was likely about 94 degrees. Below him yawned a furnace shimmering with heat waves.

This route transects and traverses the Kaibab Limestone, the Toroweap Formation, and the fine-grained Coconino Sandstone dotted with junipers and pocked with reptilian footprints from 270 million years ago. Next it cuts through the bright red Hermit Shale. At the base of the shale the erosion-resistant Esplanade Member of the Supai Group forms a broad plateau stretching a hundred miles lengthwise in the inner Canyon. Here it extends maybe three miles wide before it drops nearly a thousand feet into Surprise Valley, itself perched 2,000 feet above the Colorado River. Gillies trekked across this superlative Southwestern landscape populated by giant sculpted sandstone hoodoos from a fairy story and descended ever deeper into the Canyon. Literally with each step he took in this radiating landscape, it got hotter.

Two scorching hot days came and went. Late on Monday, Gillies' father Randy worried when he failed to call home after returning to Flagstaff as planned. On Tuesday, July 21, maybe 65 hours after Gillies had hiked into the Canyon, his father dialed 911. At this point no one knew whether one, two, or even three backpackers were missing. Gillies had informed his father by phone that he would be hiking with three buddies. He had never amended this information by explaining how he had decided to hike solo.

Coordinated by Ranger Anne Petersen, 50+ NPS searchers from Grand Canyon and adjacent parks were inserted as ground-pounders and helicopter searchers.

Clues trickled in at inchworm speed. For one thing, no clue or sign ever revealed whether, where, or even if, Gillies had made camp on his first day. Although searchers found no evidence to confirm this either way, Gillies might have camped six miles in, on the southern edge of the Esplanade just before the drop into Surprise Valley. This spot is enticing esthetically and it's a logical place to stop once darkness falls. But, again, its expanse of wind-polished sandstone is as dry as Mars. A thirsty hiker would not merely feel an urge to continue down to Surprise then to Thunder River despite nightfall, in July when nighttime temperatures remain above 90 degrees all night, he would feel a raging, irresistible compulsion.

Surprise Valley, by the way, was created a few million years ago when two cubic miles of the north rim collapsed and separated from the Kaibab Plateau then sloughed like a monster avalanche into the Canyon. This landslide shoved the Colorado River farther south and dammed it. Erosion since then has left the top portion of this slump 2,000 feet above today's river as an elongated, gentle bowl surfaced with stony soil supporting an herbarium of low desert plants. In the tortured topography of Grand Canyon, it is a surprisingly "flat" sort of place.

On July 23, Park Helicopter 368 spotted the first big clue to suggest how Gillies had gone awry. It lay in a sad heap forty yards south of the well-traveled Surprise Valley traversing trail near its eastern end. By now searchers knew they were combing this region of dissected desert for just one lost hiker. Just a few hundred yards farther east, northeast this trail offers a spectacular view of Thunder River Spring. From this edge one can not only see an astounding oasis bursting from the Muav Limestone cliff, but also hear its thunder. It is exactly the paradise *Backpacker Magazine* promised.

Again, a search team found Gillies' backpack with camping gear, iPod, a copy of Carl Sagan's *The Demon-Haunted World*, abandoned a few hundred yards from this view spot and forty yards south of the trail. Gillies' pack was minus food but contained other items he really did not need: a pack cover, towel, and extra clothes—instead of more water. Here Gillies had desperately gone to a plan B, the outcome of which he likely had never imagined.

Searchers puzzled over Gillies' discarded backpack, personal gear, and empty Camelbak and empty water bottles. Why would anyone in his right mind abandon his gear? As Incident Report #09-5519 would report: "Numerous factors led investigators to believe Gillies deliberately carried a *minimal* amount of water while hiking, perceiving he would reach an inner-Grand Canyon spring in an adequate amount of time." (Italics ours.)

The disturbing answer seemed to shout that *no one* in their right mind would abandon his gear and water bottles. Ergo, Gillies had not been in his right mind when he left his gear here.

Bryce Gillies had also carried a Magellan eXplorist 210 GPS unit. Later analysis revealed that he had plugged in only two waypoints/sets of geographical coordinates. One was the Bill Hall trailhead where he had parked his Subaru. The other he had labeled "Post." The coordinates of this latter matched the T-junction of the Surprise Valley traverse trail with the trail descending from the Esplanade. Both of these waypoints lay behind Gillies's abandoned backpack. For his intended first destination, Thunder Spring, Gillies had not pre-entered any coordinates. He would have needed a Canyon map to read the coordinates for entering them. This lack made his GPS unit almost useless once he hit Surprise Valley. The final sets of coordinates recorded automatically by Gillies' GPS unit indicated a trail of "bread crumbs" departing from that T-Junction, going east by northeast toward Thunder Spring, but then returning again to the T-junction, then leaving again toward Thunder River. In short, Gillies' GPS unit reveals that he was lost, confused, and had lost confidence in where Thunder Spring was and how to get there. Ironically, the last point his GPS unit recorded revealed that this confusion—and possible panic—and his jettisoning of his pack took place despite being on the correct trail to Thunder and being literally about ten minutes away.

By now five days had passed since Gillies had entered the Canyon. Wind had swept most of his footprints. Where, the searchers wondered anew, had he tried to go from where he had dropped his pack? Had he been carrying a topo map of the region and reading it? If so, by following it he could have reached an endless torrent of cold, clean water in a few minutes. On the other hand, for someone dehydrated from eight miles of walking mostly under full sun during the hottest part of an extremely hot day across a Mars-scape shimmering with impossible heat waves, a map in the dark may have ceased to hold meaning.

Sadly, but all too typical in today's era of relying on GPS units for orienteering, Gillies had carried no topographic map. He had not even carried a one-page partial photocopy of a topo map. He did carry a small notebook with handwritten directions on which way to go but, again, no map. Being alone in the dark and waterless and dehydrated in the unfamiliar furnace of Surprise Valley 2,000 feet above an invisible river but without a topo map…well, even nightmares rarely get this bad.

We assume that by the time—so late in the evening of his day #1 that darkness had fallen—Gillies reached this part of trail, he had lost his faith in it. It seems extremely unlikely that anyone would abandon this well-used trail during daylight. The trail allows a hiker to see that it soon heads into a deep tributary canyon (= water). But at night the same trail would appear uncertain and suspect. Maybe even treacherous and duplicitous.

Indeed the trail here leads *uphill* before it drops precipitously from northeastern Surprise Valley to Thunder River. Ironically, had Gillies walked a mere five minutes farther on the trail he would have heard Thunder River and maybe even have seen it by starlight. But Gillies knew that water is always found *downhill*. He likely had felt so unbelievably *thirsty* that he no longer could find trust in a trail that led uphill. This trail was wrong. He needed water. Water was downhill.

Downslope and southwesterly from Gillies' backpack, and running at a more than 90° turn from the trail, lies the beginning of Bonita Creek. The "creek" part of the name is strictly a monsoon phenomenon. Now, as during nearly the entire year, Bonita was dry. But the bed of Bonita's canyon in Surprise Valley consisted of smooth, hard-packed sand and gravel that likely seemed a far more inviting trail than the apparently unreliable trail Gillies had been following and second-guessing, back and forth. An even more devious detail here is someone had placed nearly in the bed of Bonita a cairn on the main traversing trail apparently to mark it as *not* going down Bonita. The confusion being that the cairn "says" nothing, it merely exists as a marker. In the dark and to a newcomer suffering from diminishing mental capacity due to dehydration the marker conceivably could be translated to mean, "Take this easy route downhill."

On July 24, NPS Helicopter 368 spotted a white plastic shopping bag near the head of the Bonita drainage. Prints from medium-sized hiking boots pocked the gravel around the bag. Gillies' had previously abandoned all his gear except his phone, GPS unit, and headlamp—and this grocery bag. He did not carry even one empty water container. The shopping bag, now raided by rodents, held several small packages of raisins and other dried foods plus a can of tuna and a can of black beans. Gillies had opened these two cans, sucked the moisture from them, left their contents uneaten, and dropped them. Bonita Creek it would be….

Bonita exits Surprise Valley and drops almost 2,000 feet to the Colorado in less than a mile. It slices first through jumbled slump material and scrub vegetation. Next it downcuts steeply through Tapeats Sandstone then through tough Grand Canyon Series formations a billion years old. At each place where the canyon hits a slightly tougher formation it forms a waterfall/cliff. Often these stand nearly vertical. Bonita's 2,000 foot drop encompasses many of these dry waterfalls. Gillies, his friends reported, was only a novice climber.

How seriously could dehydration and over-heating have affected Gillies? As noted by Kenneth Kamler in his *Surviving the Extremes,* when the human body is down even one liter, its functions become impaired. Once it's down 5 liters, fatigue and dizziness set in.

> *A loss of 10 liters disturbs vision and hearing and sets off convulsions. A deficit of 15 to 20 liters, roughly a third of the body's total amount of water, is fatal....The stomach and intestines stop digesting, and the liver stops neutralizing their toxic by-products. The blood cannot filter through the kidneys to prevent the buildup of toxins. Muscles convulse in large, violent spasms. As the brain's delicate and intricately paced chemical reactions are speeded up by the relentlessly rising temperature, the mind and body become confused. The hypothalamus loses control of itself and of the entire thermoregulatory system. The steadily rising internal heat alters proteins, cell membranes become distorted and porous; salt leaks in. The cells swell and burst, their contents exploding into surrounding tissues, where they cause more damage and inflammation, leading to more swelling and burst in an accelerating and now unstoppable fatal chain reaction.*

Again, we guess that Gillies made his desperate detour down Bonita in a diminished state of mind due to dehydration—a condition that virtually commands the victim to head downhill—and that he did this during the first night of his trek. His brutally hot hike this day had been more than debilitating enough to drastically dehydrate him and impair his judgment. Moreover, darkness also made second-guessing his GPS, the trail, and his Boy Scout education all too easy.

On July 25, a week after Gillies walked off the North Rim so late in the day, a technical-climbing, ground SAR team began a descent of Bonita from Surprise Valley. The SAR team followed a single set of boot prints. A second, similar team started an ascent of Bonita's uninviting maw from down at the Colorado River. The helicopter also inserted a canine search team halfway between the climbing teams. The dog team searched upcanyon from this midway point.

After some bushwhacking Gillies had faced those pour-off waterfalls that roar only during the monsoons. To descend to the river, Gillies would be forced to downclimb these, one after another. Each posed a different degree of complexity, texture, height, exposure, and technical difficulty. After downclimbing some of these giant stairstep falls, Gillies could hear the muted noise of Mile 135 Rapid flowing more than 1,000 feet below. From at least one spot he could have seen the Colorado by starlight.

As noted by Richard Ruelas in the *Arizona Republic* (January 3, 2010), on Saturday, July 25, a week after Gillies had entered the Canyon, technical-climbing searchers ascending via climbing gear from the river spotted Gillies high atop a pour-off in Bonita Creek a half mile from the river. The searchers found Gillies, now black and swollen, collapsed face down over a boulder. He had died of heatstroke and dehydration. In a Canyoneer's worst nightmare, Gillies had trapped himself above a narrow, funneling, 80-foot, dry waterfall in the diabase a half mile from the Colorado by his having downclimbed and jumped from difficult pour-offs of up to 30 feet high behind him. Like Margaret Bradley five years earlier, he could neither advance nor retreat from this spot in his debilitated condition. Maybe he never even considered the possibility of retreating back up to the waterless region behind him.

Again, Gillies had his headlamp when found. His hands had been lacerated by the tough spines of barrel cactus (*Ferocactus wislizenii*) that he had attempted to claw open bare-handedly for the moisture they reputedly held. Barrel cacti, however, do not load up with water until the latter part of the monsoons, and even then their "load" consists only of a half liter of alkaloid soup. This year the monsoons had not yet started.

Gillies survived in this spot for up to 24 hours before finally succumbing to heat and dehydration. He managed to leave two messages on his Blackberry cell phone while dying. "Life is good whether it is long or short," he wrote, "I was fortunate to see more than most, and for that good fortune I am most thankful."

He joked that he also felt thankful for having his Blackberry because it was so much easier to use than chiseling a farewell message into the rock surrounding him. He added that he believed in God but remained unsure as to what the afterlife might hold, "but I hope there is water."

He typed out a final sentence: "I feel like going into the wild is a calling all feel, some answer, and some die for."

BackpackerMagazine had described this "27.6-mile" hike as: "This could also very well be the toughest long weekend hike in Grand Canyon National Park, but you won't regret a single sunny mile."

NPS Preventative Search and Rescue Ranger Sueanne Kubicek had worked the Gillies search and now was assigned the task of driving his white Subaru away from the Bill Hall Trailhead. Bryce Gillies' family had requested of the Park Service a baggie of soil from where Gillies had lived his last dream before perishing. This soil-gathering was Sueanne's job, too. Sueanne opened the car door and stared inside. A gallon jug of water sat there awaiting Gillies' return.

TABLE 3. ENVIRONMENTAL DEATHS WITHIN GRAND CANYON.

Name, age	Date	Location in Canyon	*Circumstances*

W. E. or F. R. Mendenhall, adult — 1894 — near Soap Creek Rapid (River Mile 11)
A not-quite identified body was found by John Schubert of Pathe'-Bray/Clyde Eddy expedition in Dec. 1927/Jan. 1928, along with mining equipment and letters dating from 1893/1894. Personal checks on body were from a bank in Moab, Utah. Clyde Eddy, 1929. Down the World's Most Dangerous River.

Mystery Man, adult — March, 1900 — Upper Granite Gorge about 300 feet above the river near River Mile 91, south
Skeleton of a likely **solo hiker** *found by prospectors Clarence C. Spaulding and Howard Noble in 1906. Skeleton was dressed in double layers of denim and a denim overcoat with mittens. No trauma evident. Copies of the* Los Angeles Times *and* San Francisco Examiner *dated March, 1900, were in the overcoat. Death was apparently due to* **hypothermia***/exhaustion scenario of a tourist or hob-nail-booted prospector 2+ miles off the beaten track. (see text and cover photo)* Coconino Sun, *April 7, 1906.*

C. R. Moore, adult — August 7, 1903 — Bright Angel Trail 1 mile below rim
Moore was **a solo day-hiker***/tourist from Harveyville, Kansas who collapsed during a* **rim-to-river-to-rim hike** *just before completing his ascent in August heat. Likely* **heatstroke***. His body was found later.* Coconino Sun, *August 15, 1903.*

Pat Donovan, adult male — March 1905 — middle Grand Canyon
Donovan, a **solo hiker** *from Williams, entered the Canyon then vanished, likely due to* **hypothermia***.* Coconino Sun, *April 7, 1906.*

"Old Man" Snyder — After 1912 ? — Redwall/Watahomigie N of RM 213
Found dead by Paiutes, cause unknown, at Snyder Mine. Not included in statistics.

Arthur Clarence "Jack" Anderson, 19 — July 1, 1925 — Bright Angel Trail
During extreme heat, Anderson of Phoenix, Arizona, before starting his 18-mile **rim-to-river-to-rim day-hike** *down the Bright Angel Trail to the Colorado, boasted he was "going to make a new record." Anderson was stricken by heat near the river and overcome by* **heatstroke***. He was carried up by "drag out," but developed a "pneumonia" type reaction and died in Wickenburg while being evacuated by train. (see text)* Coconino Sun, *July 3, 1925.*

Casimar Pultorak, 22 — February 9, 1939 — Bright Angel Trail
Both men very ill-equipped with meager clothing, Pultorak of Detroit, Michigan and his friend Paul E. Des Jardins, age 17, attempted a **rim-to-river-to-rim day hike** *during questionable weather. 2–3 feet of snow fell during their ascent. Pultorak* **froze to death (hypothermia)** *in a snow bank on the trail. (see text)* Coconino Sun, *February 10, 1939.* Memorandum for the

Director, NPS, *February 9 & March 20, 1939. Audretsch, B. 1998, "The Death of Casimir Poltorak: A Narrative History." (unpublished manuscript).*

Lee O. Penrod, adult

July 9, 1945   Indian Garden
Penrod of Wichita, Kansas was hiking or mule riding down the Bright Angel Trail en route to to Phantom Ranch "with the regular daily party when he became too ill to continue the trip. Death followed a few hours later." **Apparent heart attack.** Chief Ranger's Memorandum for the Superintendent, *August 1, 1945.*

Ralph Stein, adult

November 2, 1947   Esplanade W of Mohawk Canyon
While searching for his lost buddy, Bill Ott, in May 2012, Glenn Rink found an inscription reading: "Stuck. No eat. Ralph Stein. Ark. 11/2/47." Not included in statistical analysis or Table 11.

Isaac D. Kriess, adult

June 9, 1950   1 mile down the Bright Angel Trail
Kriess of Santa Barbara, California collapsed while **hiking**. *Rangers that evening carried Kriess, dead of* **heart failure**, *up the trail. No other details from* Superintendent's Monthly Report, *July 1950.*

C. V. Beck, adult

June 11, 1956   Phantom Ranch
While visiting Phantom Ranch during hot weather, Beck died of **cardiac arrest**. *(Beck's was one of 5 fatal heart attacks during that June.)* Chief Ranger's Monthly Narrative Report for June, 1956.

Wilson Beigle Taylor, 59

June 6, 1956   near River Mile 44.5
a.k.a. "Necktie Willie" Taylor of Berkeley, California had a known serious heart condition and suffered a **cardiac arrest during the extreme heat** *of June. Willie's comrades wrapped him in a tarp and buried him on shore. He's still there…. Beer, B. 1994. "Willie Taylor Revisited." boatman's quarterly review. 7(4):8.*

Walter J. Mahany, 16

July 23, 1959   Tanner Trail, 1 mile from the river
Mahany of Savannah, Georgia and 2 buddies left their backpacking gear on the rim and carried minimal canteens to search for a "lost silver mine." He suffered **dehydration/heatstroke** *at temperatures close to 120 degrees in shade. (see text, Chapter 2)* Arizona Daily Sun, July 27, 28, 29, 30 & 31, & August 1 & 3, 1959. Deseret News, *August 1, 1959. Davis, D. 1959.* Deseret News, *August 1 & letter to Dock Marston, August 5, 1959.* New York Herald Tribune, *August 2, 1959.*

Bennie Tohe, 72

June 23, 1960   Beamer Trail near River Mile 65, about 25 yards from the Colorado River
Tohe, a Navajo medicine man from the Chinle area, was **solo hiking** *back from having visited the confluence of the Colorado and Little Colorado rivers on a private quest/pilgrimage and to collect herbs (the confluence is a sacred area for Navajos, in part because Salt Lady sometimes returns there). Leaving firm footprints spaced at a healthy pace, Tohe died suddenly and* **unwitnessed** *of* **heat-related cardiac arrest/heatstroke** *at a temperature of 114 degrees in the shade. (see text)* Arizona Republic, *June 23, 25 & 27, 1960.*

Alfred Milton Hillyer, 33   January 27, 1964   off Bright Angel Trail, 3 miles from Phantom Ranch
*Wearing a knee brace and using a cane, Hillyer of Centralia, Missouri, made a **solo hiking** ascent in cold weather, but wandered off-route ¼ mile and died of **hypothermia**, hidden. His body was located in May 1966.* Arizona Republic, *June 1, 1966.*

Kirk Hanson, 16   June 10, 1966   South Kaibab Trail, 4.5 miles from Phantom Ranch
*During hot weather, Hanson suffered a massive **brain hemorrhage** sustained while **hiking** with 84 other high school students from Sioux City, Iowa. Hanson's death was possibly spurred by **heat and dehydration**.* Arizona Republic, *June 11, 1966.*

Howard Mangas, 50   May 28, 1967   Bright Angel Trail
*Phoenix, Arizona Boy Scout leader Mangas, while **hiking** with his sons and other Scouts, suffered a **heat-related cardiac arrest**.* Arizona Republic, *May 29, 1967.*

Harold Murray Keller, 38   June 5, 1967   Bright Angel Trail at Mile-and-a-Half House
*While **hiking** uphill with his wife, son, and daughter in extreme heat, Keller of El Paso, Texas suffered a **heat-related cardiac arrest**.* Arizona Republic, *June 7, 1967.*

Elmer Watahomigie, 69   December 13, 1967   under ledge in tributary canyon of Cataract Canyon (Havasu)
*Watahomigie, a Grand Canyon National Park Service employee, abandoned his pickup truck 40 miles NW of Valle after it ran out of gas during an abnormally heavy snowstorm that dropped more than a foot. Next, as a **solo hiker**, he hiked 7 miles and took shelter under a rock ledge in a tributary of Cataract Canyon, wrote a note asking Be good to our grandchild, then died of **hypothermia**. Deer hunters discovered his body 7 years later.* Arizona Daily Sun, *October 29, 1974.*

Jon Herbert Freeler, 28   May 31, 1969   Tonto Trail, 7 miles from Grandview Point
*Freeler of Manhattan Beach, California was **backpacking** the Tonto with other people from the Los Angeles Sierra Club, three more of whom were affected by 110–112-degree heat and were air-evacuated out. Freeler had complained of fatigue before collapsing. He died from **heatstroke**.* Arizona Daily Sun, *June 2, 1969.*

Elmer Wallace Martin, 48   May 14, 1974   South Kaibab Trail
*Martin, a **solo day hiker** from McAllister, Oklahoma, experienced a cardiac arrest upon his return toward the rim from 3 miles below Cedar Ridge. He was found with one, 1-quart water bottle... **dehydration-related cardiac arrest**. Incident report #74-1664*

William Maxey, 60+   August 16, 1974   Phantom Ranch
*During hot weather, 110–112 degrees, Maxey, a 205-pound man, suffered a **cardiac arrest/heatstroke**. Incident report #74-5065*

Frank Costa, 21

September 2, 1974   below Bridger Point, North Rim
ASU students Costa of Westbury, Long Island, New York and part-
*ner Edwin Len Heisel, 23, of Cincinnati, Ohio were **backpacking***
to the river by descending a deer trail not far from main NPS trail
to Thunder River/Tapeats Creek region. They got lost, abandoned
their camping gear, and left notes explaining that they had run out
of food and water and would try to descend to water. Heisel, an
Army ROTC-trained ranger specializing in mountain climbing and
rescue work apparently fell off a 200-foot cliff during this attempted
descent. Costa attempted re-ascent out of Canyon and died of
***dehydration/heatstroke.** (see Chapter 2 text and Table 2) Arizona*
Republic, September 9, 10, 14 & 19, 1974.

Michael Irvin, 28

May 21, 1975   South Kaibab Trail below Cedar Ridge
***Hiking** with companion during hot weather, Irvin complained of*
*feeling ill. He died of **heatstroke.** Incident report #75-1524*

Brad Riner, 22

October 1, 1975   head of Phantom Creek
*Riner of Glendale, Arizona was a **solo backpacker** who, after a*
*week on a cross-country route, voluntarily **jumped** off a 30-verti-*
cal-foot drop. Died from impact, but was his decision induced by
***dehydration** or **panic**? (see text) Incident report #75-6727*

Raymond H. Daniel, 56

June 9, 1976   Bright Angel Trailhead below corral
After hiking down then back up the Bright Angel Trail some dis-
*tance, Daniel died of **cardiac arrest.** Incident report #76-2373*

James H. Higgins, 19

July 12, 1977   Tonto Trail, 2 miles west of Plateau Point
*Higgins of Boulder City, Nevada was a **solo backpacker** who, during*
extreme heat, carried only a 1-quart canteen but also a set of motor-
cycle tools, 3 pairs of motorcycle boots, canned food, etc. He died of
***dehydration/heatstroke.** (see text) Incident report #77-4177*

Enrico Cane, 65

April 4, 1978   Bright Angel Trail at rest house
*Cane suffered a **cardiac arrest** while **hiking,** details scanty. Inci-*
dent report #78-1456

Reed Watahomigie, 60

December 26, 1978   below Yaki Point
*Watahomigie, a **solo hiker,** was last seen on Christmas Day, but*
not reported missing until January 22, 1979. He reportedly had
been feeling sick and having respiratory trouble. On May 5, his
remains were found on a ledge below the point. He likely died of
exposure/hypothermia.

Renate Schroter, 22

August 8, 1980   North Kaibab Trail near Ribbon Falls
*Schroter of Burgergassden, Germany was **hiking** with a TrekAmeri-*
*ca guide apparently from the **North Rim-to-river-to-North Rim** in*
***one day** during very hot weather. She carried only one water bottle*
(1 liter?). She collapsed on ascent about two hours after noon. Her
body temperature reached 105 degrees. After her airlift, she died
*in the emergency room of **dehydration/heatstroke.** Arizona Daily*
Sun, August 10, 1980. Incident report #80-2974

Richard Carter Funai, 43 February 8, 1981 Kaibab Suspension Bridge
*Funai of Winston-Salem, North Carolina suffered a **cardiac arrest**
on the Black Bridge after **hiking** the South Kaibab Trail with eight
companions. CPR failed. Arizona Daily Sun, February 11, 1981.
Incident report #81-0235*

Harold Forrest Gustavson, 31 April 12, 1981 Tanner Trail
*Gustavson of Hermosa, California suffered from a thyroid condi-
tion and was on medication. While **backpacking solo** he died of
heatstroke. Arizona Daily Sun, April 19, 1981. Incident report
#80-0720*

Ed L. Agnew, Jr., 50 July 24, 1981 River Mile 229/Travertine Canyon
*Agnew of Houston, Texas was **resting** in the shade near the river
after little exertion, but in **hot weather**. At 10:30 a.m. Agnew was
found dead of **apparent cardiac arrest**. Incident report #81-2192*

John L. Herr, 50 July 25, 1981 North Kaibab Trail
*Herr **hiked** to Roaring Springs on an extremely hot day, died of
cardiac arrest/heatstroke. Incident report #81-2202*

Forney M. Knox, 56 May 26, 1982 Bright Angel Trail
*Knox attempted a **day-hike from rim-to-Plateau Point-to-rim**
during the heat. He died of **heat-related hypertension/cardiac
arrest**. Incident report #82-1172*

John E. Shakleford, 48 May 13, 1983 Bright Angel Trail at 2-mile corner
*Shakleford started his **rim-to-Plateau Point-to-rim day hike**
at 9:00 a.m. with little food or water. Although in apparent good
health, he died of **cardiac arrest/heatstroke** (?). Incident report
#83-0941*

Sheila Rowan, 26 June 4, 1984 Bright Angel Trail at Three-Mile House
*Rowan of Wausau, Wisconsin attempted a **rim-to-river-to-rim
overnight hike** during summer heat. Rowan's body core temperature exceeded 106 degrees while climbing back uphill from Phantom
Ranch during late morning. Her three companions noted that she
suddenly had leg cramps, acted disoriented, was breathing rapidly,
and her lips turned blue. She died of **heatstroke** at the Grand Canyon Clinic, but may have suffered a separate but unknown medical
condition that compromised her. Williams News, June 14, 1984.
Incident report #84-1267*

Lee C. Stern, 62 September 4, 1984 Bright Angel Trail, 3 miles below rim
*After a river trip, Stern was **day hiking up from the river** in the
heat. He suffered a **cardiac arrest**. Incident report #84-3019*

Paul M. Christie, 58 May 26, 1985 Bright Angel Trail
*Christie of Pasadena, California and his wife had **hiked** to the
Inner Gorge and back. Victim **consumed "extreme amounts of
water"** while hiking. Witnesses said Christie looked "ashen," and
was complaining of leg cramps. He suffered a cardiac arrest and
likely **hyponatremia**. Incident report #85-1000*

Father David Andrew   August 12, 1986   S of Tonto Trail, ½ mile E of Indian Gardens
Casper Gensler, 45   *Gensler, a **solo day-hiker** and Catholic priest from Cincinnati,*
                         Ohio and Calumet, Michigan was reported missing on August
                         8. Weeks after the tardy (begun 3 weeks late) search for him had
                         ended, Gensler was discovered by two NPS employees (non-
                         searchers) on October 4, 100 feet south of Tonto Trail with only one
                         *water bottle, empty. Gensler had died of apparent **dehydration/***
                         ***heatstroke** a heart-breakingly easy 5-10 minutes from Garden*
                         *Creek. His disappearance from his intended **S. Kaibab Trail-Tonto***
                         ***Trail-Bright Angel Trail** route had "set off a dispute between the*
                         Coconino County Sheriff's Office and the Park Service" because
                         the sheriff wanted a full-scale search conducted promptly while the
                         Park insisted that Gensler was merely a "missing" person, not a
                         "lost" person. Arizona Daily Sun *&* Arizona Republic, *October 7,*
                         1986. Incident report #86-3003

Frank Crowe, 70s   April 29, 1987   Bright Angel Trail near Kolb Seep, ¾ mile
                                             from rim
                         *While **hiking**, Crowe suffered a **cardiac arrest**. Incident report*
                         #87-0922

Peter E. Pastor, 76   August 5, 1987   Bright Angel Trail
                         *While **hiking**, Pastor suffered a **cardiac arrest**. Incident report*
                         #87-2756

George Lewis Ortyer, 43 May 28, 1988   River Mile 234.5
                         *After a **motorized uprun**, Ortyer of Costa Mesa, California col-*
                         *lapsed on a beach in presumed **cardiac arrest**. Incident report*
                         #88-1283

Ian Hay, 39   August 23, 1988   South Kaibab Trail
                         *Hay attempted a **rim-to-river-to-rim day hike**, down the Bright*
                         Angel then up the S Kaibab Trail. Hay collapsed 2.5 miles below
                         *the rim of **cardiac arrest/heatstroke**. Incident report #88-3694*

Ali K. Govinclan, 27   July 2, 1989   South Kaibab Trail
                         *Govinclan of India was in poor physical shape as he **hiked** down*
                         the South Kaibab Trail at temperatures exceeding 100 degrees.
                         *Resting, he became irrational and violent then died of **heatstroke**.*
                         Incident report #89-2540

Carolyn L. Guerra, 61   October 10, 1989   Crystal Rapid (River Mile 98.3)
                         Guerra of Winnemucca, Nevada, on a Diamond river trip, suffered
                         *a probable **cardiac arrest/"natural causes"** while resting on shore*
                         near Crystal Rapid during cool weather. Incident report #89-4800

Michelle Sutton, 15   May 9, 1990   North of Mt. Dellenbaugh
                         *Sutton was on a "program for troubled teens" **backpacking** trip run*
                         by Summit Quest, Inc. on its first wilderness trip. Sutton com-
                         *plained repeatedly of not feeling well. Group **carried a total of only***
                         two liters of water per person for a multi-day trip during hot
                         ***weather**. Sutton died of **dehydration/heatstroke**.*

Paul Stryker, 26

June 22, 1990   Tonto Trail/Cremation Canyon
*Stryker and his wife, Karen, from Pennsylvania, were making a 2-day **backpacking** hike during temperatures exceeding 100 degrees from Grandview to South Kaibab Trail and to the river. They planned 3 liters of water per day per person. They stopped at Cottonwood Creek to refill, but refused to drink pothole water due to polliwogs. Paul let Karen drink more water than he did. They ran out of water at the head of Cremation. After Paul died of **dehydration/ heatstroke**, Karen hiked 1–2 hours to Phantom Ranch. (see text)* Coconino County Sheriff's Department C.I. #90-1953/SAR 90-0199. *Incident report #90-1953*

Vernon Bollinger, 54

April 21, 1991   Bright Angel Trail
*Bollinger, **hiking**, died of a **cardiac arrest**. Incident report #91-0867*

George Fairchild, 42

September 3, 1991   Bright Angel Trail
*Attempting an overnight **rim-to-river-to-rim hike** in 105-degree heat with his girlfriend, Fairchild felt ill, visited the Phantom Ranch Ranger Station. The ranger recommended he stay at the little Phantom clinic. Fairchild, however, left the clinic against medical advice. He hiked but collapsed of **exertional heatstroke** four miles into ascent at the Corkscrew. His death led to a failed lawsuit against the NPS. Incident report #91-3714*

Jose Ordierez, 35

April 17, 1992   Bright Angel Trail
*Ordierez tried a **rim-to-Plateau Point-rim day hike**. While returning to the rim, he died of **cardiac arrest**. Incident report #92-0797*

Robert Kier, 62

September 11, 1993   North Kaibab Trail
*Kier **hiked** the trail during warm weather and died of **cardiac arrest** 2 miles above Roaring Springs. Incident report #93-3532*

James Cumings, 37

February 14, 1994   Visitors Entrance, Highway 67
*Cumings of Bethlehem, Pennsylvania made a non-permitted **South Rim-to-North Rim backpacking hike** and then continued, wearing a light jacket and street shoes, in up to 3 feet of snow to the North Rim. He started toward the developed area but veered away, instead passing the entrance station. He made camp nearby then returned to the entrance station where he froze (**hypothermia**) to death. Arizona Republic, February 16, 1994. Incident report #94-0307*

Gary Clausen, 47

March 24, 1994   Bright Angel Trail
*Clausen, on a **rim-to-Indian Gardens-to-rim hike** while leading a Boy Scout troop, died of **cardiac arrest**. Incident report #94-0683*

Roland Franz Kruse, 54

May 27, 1994   River Mile 250
*Kruse of Mission Viejo, California complained of being hot during a **motorized uprun** of Lake Mead. His left arm became numb and he felt dizzy. He suffered **cardiac arrest**. Incident report #94-1583*

Miloslav Hanacek, 66

June 10, 1995   Bright Angel Trail
Hanacek of Uberske Hradiste, Czeckoslovakia embarked with

*buddies on a 12.4 -mile **rim-to-Pleateau Point-to-rim day hike**.
During their ascent he collapsed suddenly in 110-degree heat. Died
of **heatstroke/cardiac arrest**. Incident report #95-1470*

Wesley S. Johnson, 63

October 16, 1995   Bright Angel Trail
*Johnson was **hiking** uphill from the **river-to-rim** after a river trip
and died of **cardiac arrest** en route. Incident report #95-3642*

Larry Selander, 52

April 14, 1996   Beamer Trail
*Selander was **hiking** the Beamer Trail in the Furnace Flats area
and died of **cardiac arrest**. Incident report #96-1638*

David B. Phillips, 15

June 6, 1996   Little Nankoweap Canyon
*Phillips of Bountiful, Utah was on a Boy Scout **backpacking** hike
down a primitive "experts only" route, ill-prepared with **less than
half the water** needed for safety in 111-degree heat. The Scouts
lacked an NPS permit for their route and date. Phillips died of
dehydration/heatstroke. (see text) The Salt Lake Tribune, June
8, 1996. Coconino County Sheriff's Department #96-06-00063.
Incident report #96-2554*

David Helmer Kruse, 57

June 14, 1996   North Kaibab Trail at Roaring Springs
*Kruse was attempting a **21-mile South Rim-to-North Rim hike
during high heat**; he died of **cardac arrest/heatstroke** shortly after
sunset. Incident report #96-2767*

Janet Katson Comela, 57

July 1, 1996   Hermit Trail, 1 mile from the creek
*During severe hot weather, Comela, while **hiking** with her husband, died of **dehydration/heatstroke**. Incident report #96-3141*

Phillip Joseph Grim, 10

July 23, 1996   S Kaibab Trail near Bright Angel Creek
*Grim of Youngstown, Ohio hiked down the S Kaibab Trail on **rim-
to-river day hike** at 116 degrees ahead of his uncle, who carried
all the water. His uncle passed him without giving him water, but
later returned with Gatorade. Grim, however, had already died of
exertional heatstroke. (see text) Incident report #96-3614*

John Holforty, 43

September 8, 1996   Tonto Trail between Mineral & Red Canyons
*Holforty of Felton, California had "considerable Grand Canyon
backcountry experience," but he died of likely **heatstroke** while
backpacking with family members. This was the fifth death to
heatstroke in 1996—a Park record for any one year. This led to the
development of the Park's Preventative Search and Rescue (PSAR)
program which since has successfully advised hikers on the main
trails on how to safely make their way. 1996 became the last year
that visitors could park at the S. Kaibab Trailhead. By requiring
a shuttle ride, the Park hoped hikers would not make unprepared
spur-of-the-moment descents. Arizona Republic, September 10.
1996. Incident report #96-4715*

Bert James Ray Mansfield, 55   November 2, 1996   Tanner Trail
Mansfield (a.k.a. "The Ranger" for his love of the outdoors and

*who holds Pittsburgh Steelers' record for the most consecutive games played [182 between 1964–76]) of Pittsburgh, Pennsylvania was troubled by a hurt ankle and, **solo**, lagged behind his son and a friend while **backpacking** down the trail. He told them to go ahead and he would catch up, or maybe even camp on the trail. He failed to catch up. The two returned in search of him the next morning. They found the 6' 3", 250-lb hiker collapsed on the trail still wearing his backpack. Mansfield had a family history of cardiac problems. He died of an **unwitnessed cardiac arrest**. Mansfield became the 7th hiker to die on a Canyon trail in 1996, again a Park record.* Williams-Grand Canyon News, *November 13, 1996. Incident report #96-5665*

John Henry James, 55

October 11, 1997   North Kaibab Trail
*James was attempting a 21-mile **rim-to-rim hike**. He died two miles north of Phantom Ranch from a **cardiac arrest**. Incident report #97-4736*

Mary Jane Beaver, 75

April 28, 1998   Havasu Canyon
*Beaver, a small but avid hiker from Phoenix on her fifth Havasu hike, collapsed in **sudden death syndrome/cardiac arrest** at the bridge over Havasu Creek about two miles upstream of Supai Village.*

Thomas A. Pacewicz, 50

April 28, 1999   Bright Angel Trail
*Pacewicz, a client on an oar-powered rafting trip, was **exiting a river trip** from Phantom Ranch. He had **day hiked** upward then detoured out to Plateau Point via Bright Angel Trail en route to the rim. He later collapsed above the 3-Mile Rest House of **cardiac arrest**. Incident report #99-0899*

Nuria Serrat, 42

June 28, 1999   Tonto Trail, 0.8 mile west of Hermit Creek
*Serrat of Las Vegas, Nevada was a **solo** female **backpacker** "experienced" in Grand Canyon. Carrying only 4, 1-liter water bottles (all of which were empty), she succumbed in 110-degree weather to **heatstroke**; her body was found the next day by another hiker less than 1 mile from the creek. (Serrat was the third Inner Canyon **heatstroke** within one week; the other two victims—both males in their twenties hiking with companions—survived after medical evacuation.) Incident report #99-1581*

Orda Seth Smedley, 48

February 6, 2000   Bright Angel Trail, 1.5 miles below Rim
*Smedley collapsed during return leg of 12.2-mile, **rim-to-Plateau Point-to-rim day hike** and died of **apparent cardiac arrest**. Incident report #00-0235*

Paul Van Hoof, 47

June 2, 2000   Tonto Trail, 2 miles west of the South Bass, 1,000 feet above River Mile 109.5
*On Day #4 of a hot, exposed Inner Canyon **backpacking** hike planned for three days from the South Rim down the South Bass Trail (River Mile 108) to upper Royal Arch Creek (River Mile 116.5) and back to the South Bass Trail and up, Van Hoof's three*

Belgian hiking partners said they had difficulty finding water. Van Hoof drank some water but rationed it during temperatures exceeding 108 degrees in the shade. Van Hoof, stumbling along in full sun, collapsed of **dehydration/heatstroke**. *A buddy had hiked ahead to the river at the Ross Wheeler (RM 108), but he refused to acknowledge waves and greetings from a passing river trip (Ghiglieri's). Two hours later, at 4:30 p.m., he reluctantly spoke to a Diamond River trip run by Leslie Diamond camping at "his" beach. She radioed for an NPS helicopter. It reached Van Hoff at 4:47 p.m. and found him dead. Hiker errors included: failing to plan for the heat, to carry enough water, and to recognize natural water as drinkable. Incident report #00-1514*

Andrianus Grootenboer, 62   October 16, 2000   Corkscrew, Bright Angel Trail
Attempting a **rim-to-river-to-rim day-hike** *Grootengoer experienced chest pain while ascending at Pipe Creek. He died during a helicopter evacuation while en route to Flagstaff Medical Center. CPR was unsuccessful.* **Cardiac arrest**. *Incident report #00-3217*

Douglas Isaia, 63   June 7, 2001   Phantom Ranch wrangler bunkhouse
Isaia, a local mule wrangler, died in his **sleep** *to unknown cause(s) but likely* **cardiac arrest**. *Incident report #01-1505*

John Rudolph Young, 68   December 5, 2002   Bright Angel Trail, ¾ miles below rim
While **day-hiking** *an ascent from river to rim, Young collapsed from* **cardiac arrest**. *Incident report #02-3862*

Elma Hickman, 74   May 28, 2003   Phantom Ranch cabin
After a mule ride, Hickman felt poorly and went to her cabin to lie down. She died in her **sleep** *from* **cardiac arrest**. *Incident report #03-2548*

John Patrick Hayton-Fawcett,   May 23, 2003   Bright Angel Trail below 3-Mile House
65   and Jacob's Ladder
On a hot **rim-to-river-to-rim day-hike** *with his brother, Fawcett of England passed unheeded the Indian Gardens warning sign to turn around there on one-day hikes—despite his recent diagnosis of hypertension and an irregular heartbeat. At noon, 6 miles into his attempted return to the rim, the 6', 210-pound Fawcett, wearing a black shirt, collapsed in sudden death from* **heat-related cardiac arrest**. *Incident report #03-2367*

Francis Joji Muramato, 60   April 10, 2004   Tonto Trail near Monument Creek
Tucson, Arizona resident Muramoto, on his 2nd day of **backpacking** *on the Tonto, died of* **cardiac arrest**. *A hiking buddy performed cardiac compressions on Muratmoto for 1.5 hours but did not perform rescue breathing (!). Muramoto was hypertensive and had been complaining of shoulder pain and insomnia for 2 weeks but apparently did not understand these warning signs, perhaps because he otherwise seemed in fair physical condition. He also stated that rest made his shoulder and neck pain subside but hiking exacerbated it. Despite all these alarming signs of cardiac distress,*

the 5' 6", 165-pound Muramoto hiked until he dropped dead. Incident report #04-1527

John A. Cosentino, 47	May 6, 2004 Bright Angel Trail near First Tunnel

*New Yorker Cosentino, of Syosset, was **day-hiking** up from Indian Gardens with an Albany school group containing his son when he collapsed ½ mile from the trailhead. Prompt CPR and then EMT interventions failed to revive Cosentino from **cardiac arrest**. Incident report #04-2043*

Margaret L. Bradley, 24	July 9/10, 2004 Cremation Creek

*On July 8, Bradley of Falmouth, Massachusetts and an all-America runner, attempted a **Marathon-length run** via the Grandview, Tonto, and South Kaibab trails to the S. Rim (28.7 miles) in a loop route during weather that hit 105 degrees in the shade. Helped by a friend Ryan of Flagstaff, the pair started late for July, about 8:00 a.m., with Bradley carrying only 2 liters of water and no map. By 1:00 p.m., 15.7 miles into their planned "15 miles" (which actually was 28.7 miles), Ryan had drunk his 4 liters and, overheated, he shaded up under a bush. Bradley's 2 liters also were long gone. At 3:40 p.m. Bradley ran on **solo** to get help for him. Dehydrated, she **short-cutted,** perhaps inadvertently, off the Tonto Trail 3 miles from the South Kaibab Trail and descended several hundred yards down Cremation drainage (dry). This was the same drainage where Paul Stryker died on June 22, 1990. Bradley downclimbed a 20-foot dry waterfall and trapped herself above a 130-footer, 500 feet above the Colorado. She curled up and died of **dehydration/heatstroke** up to 18 hours <u>after</u> Ryan had reached a USGS worker carrying a sat phone on the South Kaibab Trail. Ryan had neither reported Bradley as "missing" nor inquired as to her situation despite several opportunities. (see text) Incident report #04-3698*

Joseph Roitz, 45	June 30, 2005 North Kaibab Trail above the Eye of the Needle

*"Gung ho" Roitz of San Diego, California led Boy Scout Troop #663, including his son, uphill on a **day hike** from Cottonwood Campground. Apparently in good shape, he was the regular pacesetter for the troop. 3.5 miles and 2,200 vertical feet uphill he did an about face, walked 40 feet back down and sat on a rock. He said he felt dizzy. Next he collapsed of **cardiac arrest**. Incident report #05-3233*

Avik Chakravarty, 28	July 13, 2005 Devil's Corkscrew, Bright Angel Trail

*Chakravarty of England had been warned by his physician to avoid strenuous activity because of Avik's iron deficiency. In mid July Chakravarty and a buddy got a late start for a mid-summer **rim-to-river-to-rim day-hike**. At 7:30 a.m. the pair descended the S. Kaibab. About halfway into their 4 hour descent Chakravarty complained that his "knees felt like jelly." He also said he needed a lot of water and drank a gallon plus two cans of tomato juice. An NPS interpretive ranger at Phantom Ranch advised the pair to avoid severe heat by waiting until late evening before hiking back* *up. Instead, apparently at the insistence of Chakravarty's buddy, the two started up the Bright Angel Trail at 3:00 p.m., stopping an hour later at Pipe Creek at about 113 degrees in the shade. Continuing halfway up the Corkscrew at 5:00 p.m. Chakravarty sat down and soon began hallucinating and yelling at non-existent people to "go away." He next began seizures and vomiting. Chakravarty's "buddy" hurried 2 miles to the Indian Gardens Ranger Station for help. Meanwhile other hikers arrived to a moaning Chakravarty and tried to help by pouring water on him. He seemed to become aware of them and stopped moaning. Two minutes later (5:20 p.m.), however, Chakravarty collapsed fatally from* **heatstroke.** *An hour later the rescue helicopter parked nearby registered an air temperature of 120 degrees in the shade. Incident report #05-3577*

Darlene Buffington, 66	February 1, 2006 Bright Angel Train, Corkscrew

While **riding a mule** *to Phantom Ranch, Buffington of South Dakota became dizzy and soon died of* **cardiac arrest.** *Incident report #06-0472*

Richard Howard, 53   June 18, 2006   Escalante Creek Trail (a.k.a. "River" Trail), RM 75

As Howard of Yuma, Arizona trekked west from the Tanner Trail on day #2 of a planned 6-day, 56.6-mile **backpacking** *route during summer with his stepson, he complained of intensifying heat illness symptoms. This also had happened to him on Day #1, an overly-ambitious first day for summer. By day #2, after every 15 minutes of hiking, Howard required a rest. Upon reaching Escalante, Howard was stumbling and mumbling incoherently. His worried stepson dragged him into the shade and poured water on him. A half hour later, at noon, Howard collapsed in a 105-degree temperature and died of* **heatstroke** *600 yards from the Colorado in the Escalante Drainage. Incident report #06-3086*

Thomas Jay Nisson, 64   August 14, 2006   Coconino switchbacks 1¼ miles down Bright Angel Trail

Nisson, a Palm Bay, Florida resident, was a **solo day-hiker** *who died of* **cardiac arrest** *just before noon at an air temperature of close to 90° while hiking up from 1.5 Mile House. Found on him was a Garmin GPS unit and a 3x5-inch notebook with seven pages containing location coordinates for several GeoCache sites within Grand Canyon. Incident report #06-4733*

April Lorraine Goode, 56   May 15, 2007   junction of Tonto Trail with Ruby Canyon

On day #3 of a 6-day, 43-mile **backpacking** *trip from the South Bass to Hermit with 5 others, Goode of Salem, Oregon faltered in the 98° weather and collapsed. Three of the hikers, including Goode's husband, stayed with her. Two others tried to hike out for help at South Bass. Four other hikers found Goode then continued to the river and met an OARS trip that used its sat phone to alert the NPS. But the 5' 10," 180-lb. Goode had died of* **heatstroke** *shortly after her collapse. Incident report #073159*

Donald D. Keyes, 67   May 19, 2007   Saddle Canyon Narrows, 1½ miles from RM 47

*With "a history of heart trouble and high blood pressure," Keyes of Athens, Georgia was **day-hiking** on a commercial river trip run by Wilderness River Adventures when he collapsed on the trail after hiking uphill in 98° weather. A cardiologist friend of Keyes tried but quit CPR after 10-13 minutes and diagnosed the 6' 4," 250-lb. Keyes as dead from a sudden **cardiac arrest**. Incident report #07-3249*

Scott Craig Smith, 52   August 3, 2007   2 Mile Corner on the Bright Angel Trail

*After taking an OARS rafting trip from Lee's Ferry to Phantom Ranch, Smith of Lancaster, California was **day-hiking** with a buddy from the river to the rim when, at 10:08 a.m., he suffered **cardiac arrest**. CPR proved ineffective. Prior to hiking out, during the river trip, Smith had complained of "indigestion" (which may instead have been cardiac pain) and had taken Zantac. The possibility also exists that while hiking out, Smith felt a compulsion to hike faster than advisable to keep up with his grown—and athletic—kids hiking ahead of him. Smith's rate of hiking uphill in the heat was 2 miles per hour while gaining nearly 4,000 feet. Incident report #07-6449*

Jack Eugene Mayfield, 72   March 26, 2008   Bright Angel Trail ¼ mile below 1½-Mile House

*Mayfield was returning in an ascent from **rim-to-Indian-Gardens-to-rim day-hike** when he collapsed on the icy trail in **exertional cardiac arrest**. Good Samaritan CPR failed to resuscitate the resident of Osburn, Idaho. Incident report #08-1647*

Duane Gray, 54   June 9, 2008   15 minutes down the Bright Angel Trail

*During a **Phantom Ranch-South Rim day hike** with his wife, sister-in-law, and 14-year-old son, Gray, of Clarkdale, Arizona, who was out of shape and was experiencing health problems after an alcohol detox program a month earlier, literally sat down in the shade for a break and immediately dropped dead of **heat-related cardiac arrest**. Incident report# 08-3608*

Yvonne H. (Marie) Presley, 65 June 27, 2008   Fossil Canyon, RM 125

*Presley of Louisiana was suffering from constipation. While returning from the porta potty in camp during late afternoon at 105 degrees in the shade during a motor-powered river trip run by Arizona River Runners, she felt ill and laid down. She soon began gasping for air, became unconscious, began convulsing, and then ceased breathing due to **heat-related cardiac arrest**. Immediate CPR proved ineffective. She had a recent history of chest pain. Incident report #08-4170*

Susan Jane Linley, 47   September 4, 2008   Flagstaff Medical Center ICU

On September 3 Linley of the United Kingdom had hiked with her husband and son into the Canyon via the South Kaibab Trail and returned to the trailhead before lunch. Linley complained of feeling

dizzy then fainted. She was conscious during medical transport but deteriorated quickly into nausea, vomiting, combativeness, loss of consciousness, then unresponsiveness. After being flown to Flagstaff Medical Center's ICU, Linley was pronounced "brain dead" due to intracranial swelling caused by **hyponatremia.** *Her grieving husband gave permission to take her off life support and donate her organs. (see text) Incident report #08-5677*

Bryce Lee Gillies, 20   July 19, 2009   ½ mile up Bonita Creek from Colorado at 80-foot waterfall

After making hundreds of hits on the internet for hiking information, on July 18, Gillies of McLean, Virginia and a physics major at NAU started during afternoon and the hottest part of the day, and year, on a un-permitted, **solo backpacking** *hike into the Surprise Valley-Thunder River-Tapeats Creek-Deer Creek loop area. After he failed to return, 50+ NPS searchers were inserted. One found Gillies' backpack, etc, 40 yards south of the main trail and downslope from the "Walapai Johnnie" rock shelter west of the switchbacks to Thunder Spring. On July 25 searchers found Gillies dead of* **dehydration/heatstroke** *in Bonita Creek (dry)* **lost and trapped** *above an 80-foot, dry pour-off a half mile from the Colorado. Gillies had his headlamp when found and apparently had carried only "a minimal" amount of water for his July hike. (see text) Incident report #09-5519*

Eugene Henry Maloney, 18   August 13, 2009   Shinumo Wash route/Twenty-Nine Mile Canyon

Eight **hikers,** *mostly Navajo from the Tuba City, Arizona area and 2 dogs backpacked the old Bureau of Reclamation/Shinumo Wash route 7.5 miles and 2,800 vertical feet to the river to go fishing. The group left during late afternoon and hot weather. They brought too little water then lost two gallons in an early mishap. The route, often with no trail, proved far more difficult than expected. Maloney, overweight and not in good shape, collapsed about 3 miles below the rim. The group abandoned him then spread out downcanyon, disconnected and thirsty. They bivouacked, still scattered. The next morning some hikers began drinking their urine and trying to extract water from cacti. With Maloney still alone with nothing but a sheath knife for cutting open cactus (dry), the seven continued toward the river. One hiker's dog found a shallow pool in the wash. The group eventually collected there and sucked it dry. One hiker continued to the top of the Redwall 500 feet above the river and flagged down an NPS river trip, which requested the Park helicopter. Meanwhile Maloney,* **solo,** *had died of* **heat complications** *(= heatstroke), after having collapsed face first into a cactus. A few seep-springs existed nearby, but unknown to the hikers. Incident report #09-6261*

Andrew John Brunelli, 43   August 31, 2009   off Tonto Trail near Pattie Butte

A month after Bryce Gillies' (two above) well publicized death to dehydration in Grand Canyon Brunelli of Clayton, North Carolina set off from down the Grandview Trail on his first "ambitious," **solo**

*Canyon **1-day-mega-hike** (requiring no back-country permit) of his own design covering 28.7 miles in a descent to the Tonto Trail then west to the South Kaibab Trailhead at the rim. This was the same route which led to Margaret Bradley's death on July 10, 2004. This distance equals what the fit Bryce Gillies (two above) had planned to cover on July 19, 2009 in 3 days. The not-so-fit Brunelli vanished on his apparently waterless and undisclosed route. Six days later the Grand Canyon Inn notified the Park that Brunelli had failed to check out and was missing. Searchers found Brunelli's rental car at Grandview but failed to find the 200-pound, 5' 10" hiker within a search zone based on day hikes. On Sept. 8, a co-worker of Brunelli informed investigators that Brunelli had told him he was planning a 29-mile, 1-day hike in the Canyon. This information expanded the search. The next day helicopter pilot Mike Brinkworth spotted Brunelli's body 20 miles from his starting point and 100 yards north of the Tonto Trail at 3,700 feet elevation in a drainage below Pattie Butte, 2 miles short of the S. Kaibab Trail. Brunelli's body was sitting back against a rock shelf and now hosting maggots. His gear lay scattered below him. He had carried about 1 gallon of water and had died of **dehydration/exertional heatstroke**. The temperature on August 31 was 105 degrees at Phantom Ranch. Incident report #09-6919*

Joseph Jean Mitchell, 63   November 9, 2009   1 ¾ miles down the Bright Angel Trail
*Mitchell of Clarkdale, Arizona was attempting a **rim-to-river-to-rim day-hike** down the South Kaibab Trail and up Bright Angel with 3 family members. Mitchell became slower and slower during the ascent. About 2 miles from the rim and 12 hours after beginning the hike, he fell behind. When his family turned back to locate him, they found him collapsed on the trail in **cardiac arrest**. An autopsy confirmed a pre-existing heart disease, arteriosclerosis. Incident report # 09-8644*

Kathryn Roth, 22   July 6, 2010   0.2 mile down the Toroweap Trail to Lava Falls
*Roth had accompanied friend Dale Woods, age 24, hiking down the Toroweap Trail to launch a non-permitted solo river trip in his inflatable kayak. While **solo day-hiking (rim-to-river-to-rim)** her return up the 1.5-mile Toroweap Trail that afternoon, she apparently lost the trail during extreme heat of at least 106 degrees in the shade. On July 7, Woods was found at River Mile 231 where he hid from rangers, who arrested him for his illegal trip and his non-cooperativeness. Helicopter-based searchers next spotted Roth dead of **heatstroke/exposure** less than ¼ mile from the trailhead. Roth of Springdale, Utah died in an ascent position 40 feet laterally **off-trail, lost** at elevation 3,680 feet on a south-facing, shade-less, black rock slope of 28 degrees where climbing was required to continue upward to the top (overall, a 2,500-foot climb). Roth was found clutching an empty water bottle and had fishhook cactus spines stuck in her shoulder. 9 months later a U.S. Magistrate Court banned Woods from entering the Park for 3 years. Incident report #10-4289*

Andrzez Lara, 40   July 10, 2010   Bright Angel Trail , 200 yards up from
                                                          3-Mile Rest House
*Lara of Poland attempted a **rim-to-river-to-rim day-hike** with two buddies. During his ascent he forged ahead of them at the Corkscrew. At Indian Gardens he told PSAR Ranger Sueanne Kubicek he had hiked back to the Corkscrew but failed to find his buddies. Now, he added, he felt hot and worried. She urged him to stay at Indian Gardens until the next morning due to the extreme heat. Lara seemed extremely anxious and "on a mission" to make it to the rim that day so as to visit Monument Valley the next. He left as a **solo hiker**. 90 minutes later and 2 miles farther, he died on the trail due to **heatstroke**. Incident report #10-4369*

Gavin C. Smith, 30   September 30, 2010   100 yards down the Toroweap Trail to
                                                     Lava Falls
*Smith was one of five men who were to attend a wedding in Las Vegas within days but decided to hike the Toroweap Trail to Lava Falls first. Smith of Lawrence, Kansas had drunk significant alcohol the previous evening. He decided to quit halfway down the trail and return **solo** hiking to the parking area above. The other four continued to the river where two decided to hike back up. The other two hikers felt over their heads and decided to hitchhike a ride with a river trip. 100 yards short of the parking area at the trailhead Smith's two hiking "buddies" found him dead of **dehydration/heatstroke**. Hours later, the remaining two men hiked up, having failed to hitchhike. Incident report #10-6515*

Stephen Norman O'Keeffe, 52 August 26, 2011   foot of Tanner Trail (Tanner Canyon)
*On August 26, two backpackers descending the Tanner Trail met O'Keeffe of Flagstaff, Arizona **hiking solo** and slowly up the trail. He appeared to them to be exhausted, and he had abandoned his backpack farther down the trail. The two gave the hiker extra water and told him he should return to the river with them (where the temperature was 108 degrees). He refused, saying he wanted to continue ascending. When the backpackers returned up the trail the next day they carried an extra gallon of water for the distressed hiker and looked for him. They found his abandoned pack again but not the hiker. They recorded his permit information, spent the night on the Esplanade, then, on August 28, reached the rim and reported the missing distressed hiker. A helicopter SAR team located the hiker's body lying in the wash at the foot of the Tanner Trail. **Dehydration/heatstroke.***

Quade Uqualla, ~26   May 5(?), 2012   Dry Beaver Canyon, Havasu
On May 8, OARS boatman Ashley Brown hiked up Beaver ¼ mile and found a dead body in the bottom of the canyon, shoeless, half-clothed, and pecked by ravens. The victim, a Havasupai/Aftican American allegedly had stolen $1,200 from a Havasupai Village store and was a meth abuser. Cause of death remains unclear. Not included in environmental statistics.

Ursel Yavis, 68

June 12, 2012   Black Bridge Tunnel, S Kaibab Trail
*Around 5:15 pm, after **hiking** 9 hours from **rim to river** (with reservations at Phantom Ranch) and drinking less than 2 quarts of water, and also after earlier deliberately ignoring the advice of a PSAR Ranger at Cedar Ridge to not continue hiking into the Canyon at temperatures exceeding 100 degrees, Yavis of Bradenton, Florida collapsed near the Kaibab Suspension Bridge Tunnel of **heat stroke**. After briefly successful episodes of CPR she was transported to Flagstaff Medical Center where she died very soon with a core temp of 104 degrees. Incident Report #12-2497*

David Glen Roberts, 72

September 25, 2012   Bright Angel Trail, 2+ miles from trailhead
*Roberts of Cleveland, Tennessee was making a **South Rim-Plateau Point-South Rim day hike solo** because he suspected it would be his last opportunity to do so. During his return ascent, at about 70 degrees, and after downing 2 bottles of 5-Hour Energy, Roberts went unconscious and **collapsed on the trail, hitting his head**. He "snored" for a minute then went into **cardiac arrest due to arteriosclerotic cardiovascular disease**—only days after his physician had told him: "You have the heart of a 40-year old." CPR, AED & epinephrine failed. Incident Report #12-4767*

Sibylle Borger, 48

June 30, 2013   South Kaibab Trail, ¼ mile from river
*On a day when the National Weather Service predicted record high temperatures nearing 117 degrees, Borger of Fredericksberg, Virginia began her family **rim-to-river day hike** from the S Rim late, at 10 a.m., then stopped for an 80-minute lunch. Her group ran low on water by Tipoff Point. As her son hurried ahead to refill at Phantom she followed, but despite no complaints, collapsed of **heatstroke** ("hyperthermia due to environmental exposure") around 3:15 p.m. The temperature at Phantom was 113 degrees. CPR failed. Incident report #13-289*

Brice Henri Patricot, 63

August 9, 2013   North Kaibab Trail
*Patricot of Precy-Sur-Oise, France **day hiked** with his wife & 3 children 2 miles from the North Rim to Eye of the Needle. As he and his wife hiked back up, he became ever more "fatigued" and slow. He said his heart was "racing." At 2 p.m. he collapsed half a mile from the trailhead at 83 degrees. 66 minutes of CPR and AED use failed to reverse his **heat-related exertional stress cardiac arrest**. Grand Canyon News Release, August 12, 2013. Incident report# 13-058076*

John R. Perazzo, 62

June 29, 2014   Bright Angel Trail above 3-Mile House
*Perazzo of Cincinnati, Ohio began **day hiking** to the rim from an Outdoors Unlimited river trip at Pipe Creek at 7:30 a.m. with his family and guide. Although apparently "feeling well," he collapsed suddenly at 11:30 and at 95 degrees while ascending "ahead of everybody else" (some of his family, had hiked ahead) including his guide. At an "obese" 214 pounds, Perazzo died abruptly of heat-related "severe coronary atherosclerosis (90%)/**cardiovascular failure**." CPR by O.U. guide & Good Samaritan Canyon Exploration guide and SAR personnel for 40 minutes failed. Incident report #14-063331*

Andrew C. Sammler, 47   July 11, 2014   N Kaibab Trail ¼ mile from parking lot (elevation 8,241 feet)

*Sammler of Lancaster, Ohio, **day hiked** 3 miles from the parking lot to Supai Tunnel (at 6,800 feet) with his children, who hiked back up faster than he could. Sammler hiked up solo. Other hikers found him face down and unresponsive on the trail at 2:00 p.m. and 85 degrees. They began immediate CPR. Weighing 220 pounds, Sammler had suffered multiple previous heart attacks. CPR for 1/2 hour & AED failed. **Heat-related cardiac arrest**. Incident report #14-072279*

Michael Sperry, 46   September 19, 2014   North Kaibab Trail ½ mile below Ribbon Falls

*While hiking uphill at about 3:30 p.m. ,12 of 21 miles into his **rim-to-rim day hike** with his 2 brothers, Sperry of Valparaiso, Indiana collapsed, suddenly unconscious due to **cardiovascular failure**. Prompt CPR failed. Grand Canyon News Release, September 22, 2014.*

David Bruce Peterman, 73   February 12, 2015   Ribbon Falls, North Kaibab Trial

*During a group **day hike from Phantom to Ribbon Falls** (6 miles and 1,300 feet up), Peterman of New London, Minnesota collapsed of apparent **cardiac arrest** upon arrival. Grand Canyon News Release.*

Chapter Four

"Flash Flood!"

It's great to be back...." Roger Clubb, Sr., thought as he gazed into the Canyon after such a lengthy absence. Eighteen years had passed since 1945, when, at age 18, Roger and his father had climbed Wotan's Throne and Vishnu Temple together. These had been serious ascents, not mere plods along the Bright Angel Trail. The Inner Canyon had not only been the scene of some of the earliest triumphs of Roger's life, it was also a place of fond memories of having made these triumphs with his father, Merrel D. Clubb, Sr., doyen Canyon explorer and mentor to the likes of the legendary Harvey Butchart. Small wonder then that Roger Clubb, Sr., now age 36, would return to the Canyon and bring his own son, Roger, Jr, age 8, for his introduction to the most astounding mosaic of landscapes on this planet.

Leaving his wife, Jean, and four-year-old son, Eddie, on the rim in El Tovar, Roger, Sr., took Roger, Jr. down the Bright Angel Trail to Indian Garden. This was more than 3,000 feet below the South Rim and about halfway to the river. It was August 3, 1963. Monsoon season.

The still young veteran of Wotan's Throne and Vishnu Temple and his impressed young son made it to Indian Garden okay. Then the rain fell. As it typically does during the monsoons, it pounded down hard and fast. Nearly an inch and a half fell on the elevations above them.

Upstream of Indian Garden, in the Garden Creek drainage, much of this water funneled and cascaded in a gathering flood racing and tumbling down toward the normally peaceful oasis once farmed here by the Havasupai (until Teddy Roosevelt arrived and personally told them that the U.S. had made it a national monument for all Americans and now they would have to leave). Meanwhile several hikers, the Clubbs among them, took refuge from the rain under the giant cottonwoods of Indian Garden. No one, it seems, was imagining that the canyon above them was funneling a new river of mud, boulders, and desert vegetation in a semi-liquid monster soon to explode upon them. If anyone did imagine it, apparently no one voiced his suspicions.

The rain stopped. So, after eating lunch, father and son headed back up the trail from the Garden. This trail is one of the safer looking places in the Canyon. Deceptively so. About 400 yards up the Bright Angel Trail, Roger, Sr., heard the roar.

The deep rumble presaged the arrival of the debris flow by several seconds. Clubb saw that they would have time to rush to a safe high point on the canyon slope. As he turned to hurry his son, he saw to his horror that the boy was missing. Where was young Roger?

As a ten-foot-high wall of water and mud exploded into view from the canyon immediately upstream, Clubb saw that his young son had lagged dozens of yards downstream—and he stood in the path of the tumbling flood.

Forsaking the close, easy route to safety, Roger, Sr., made a mad dash downstream to scoop up his son before the flash flood hit. Other hikers who witnessed his desperate race against disaster reported that, although he was running as wildly as any human being could, he never made it.

The tumbling wall of slurry engulfed Roger Clubb, Sr. and then his son with supreme indifference. The two vanished in a flash of mud before the horrified gazes of the hikers who had fled safely upslope.

Searchers later found the faithful father's body about 400 yards downstream, nearly buried by debris. Five days later, after a second, much smaller flood had eroded some of the debris deposited by the first flood, searchers found little Roger, Jr., too, only about 100 yards downstream of where his father had been found.

Roger, Sr.'s brother, Merrel Clubb, Jr., flew in from Montana to assist. Later, Merrel Clubb, Sr. considered the question of what sort of memorial might be fitting to commemorate the tragic deaths of the accomplished explorer and his young son. No manmade memorial would be appropriate, he said, "After all, the Canyon is their monument."

Among the most notorious of dangers of the American Southwest, second perhaps only to dying of thirst, is its opposite: being swept into oblivion by a flash flood. The alleged danger of flash floods here is not a product of media hype or a plot device of Zane Grey potboilers, it is instead a genuine meteorological phenomenon peculiar to the geography of this region and caused by a nearly unique constellation of geographical features.

First, the northern and eastern portions of Arizona sit at relatively high elevations. The North Rim of Grand Canyon, for example, lies at 8,000–9,000 feet elevation and is part of the huge Colorado Plateau, the world's second largest and highest plateau after that of Tibet. Plateaus such as these, it is now known, actually create their own weather.

Second, the American Southwest lies in the northward monsoon "migration route" of storms, especially hurricanes, in the Gulf of Mexico and sometimes the Gulf of California during the height of summer. Prevailing winds from the ocean begin around mid-July to blow north and northeast, carrying moisture-bearing fronts onto the Colorado Plateau. As these wet masses of air are forced ever higher above sea level by the rise of topography, they cool. When they cool sufficiently to hit their dew points, they drop their moisture as rain or hail, both often violent, abrupt, and copious.

Third—and the most difficult for newcomers to believe—many of these abrupt, violent, and copious storms form and persist in very localized regions. It may rain a quick inch, for example, in one drainage, or even rain several inches for hours of downpouring, yet eight to ten miles away a similar drainage may receive virtually no measurable precipitation.

The fourth and final element in the formula for flash floods is their being paradoxically exacerbated by lack of water. The high elevations which cause these violent storms experience two or three very dry months prior to the monsoons. Hence much of the Canyon region consists mostly of desert that receives an average of less than ten inches of precipitation per year and thus lacks the soil-retaining forests and grasslands that elsewhere suck up rain like a sponge. When rain falls in canyon country, only a little is absorbed by soil. Often no soil even exists over vast areas (again due to the violence and infrequency of the rains themselves), only bare rock. All the rest of that violent rain here hits, splashes, and obeys the dictates of gravity to flow downhill.

In canyon country these flows funnel down canyons. Indeed not only do the famous "slot" canyons of the Southwest act as charmingly narrow funnels for these violent storms, these canyons are themselves the stone children of these storms. Perhaps the easiest way to visualize the power of these watery sculptors of the Southwest's stunning canyons is to imagine just how much water, carrying how much silt, sand, rocks, and boulders up to and bigger than the family sport utility vehicle, would be necessary to whack out one of these canyons from solid bedrock. Contrary to popular belief, these canyons were not carved a micromillimeter at a time by the slow passage of small streams of water in a sort of geological Chinese water torture in accordance with Lyell's "Principle of Uniformitarianism" in his famous *Principles of Geology* of the 19th century. While many canyons are polished in this gentle, insistent way, they were more often carved brutally and catastrophically by the corrasive power of rare but massive debris flows/flash floods which often contained more rock than water. Canyon country is by its very existence a warning sign that violent processes have been at work. Add a few clouds to the scene and this warning sign changes tenses to become "violent canyon carving now at work."

Knowing this alone can save your life. Do not hike narrow canyons during monsoonal weather (July through September) or during any other times of potentially rainy weather. Grand Canyon and its tributaries are nothing more than giant conduits for storm run-off. That walking the floor of a storm drain during a storm is playing Russian roulette should be obvious. What makes it less than obvious to many people (and victims) is the storm itself may be miles away, and the sky above may be blue flecked with cute white cotton balls that look like dragons, Aunt Martha, or atom bomb tests.

All of this is pretty simple, and we apologize if we are being too elementary in spelling it out. But a surprising number of nature-lovers have failed to understand this aspect of nature in the Southwest and have ended up as nature's fertilizer because of it.

One of the more recent episodes made the front page coast-to-coast. It occurred in Antelope Canyon, 20+ miles upstream of Lees Ferry and east of Page and of Grand Canyon. This example does not enter into our analysis of Grand Canyon fatalities. We include it here, however, because it offers a perfect illustration of local flash flood dynamics—and life-saving lessons.

Antelope is a six-mile long slot canyon that "ends" in Lake Powell (were the reservoir not present, Antelope Canyon would be walkable for miles farther into Glen Canyon to the Colorado River). It is one of 96 named tributaries in Glen Canyon. Because this classic, sinuous "slot" canyon carved through the Navajo Sandstone and polished to a sensuous smoothness is the closest classic one to Page, it is a seductive local tourist attraction.

On August 12, 1997, an unusually violent El Niño year, during the height of the monsoons, Ken Young, concessionaire for the Antelope Canyon Tribal Park, rescued a man. He found 28-year-old Pancho Quintana clinging to a rock near the bottom of the canyon. Quintana was battered, bruised, scratched, and stark naked. He had lost his shoes and every stitch he was wearing in a flash flood.

Quintana had also lost his grip on two of the five people he had been escorting down this beautiful canyon of death.

He had been leading a tour from a Los Angeles-based company, TrekAmerica. Quintana's tour group that day included four men and a woman, three from France and one each from Britain and Sweden. Along with this group, six other people had been hiking in Antelope Canyon. These included five from France and a man from New York.

That day rain fell about 15 miles southeast of Page on the Kaibito Plateau about 2,000 feet above the canyon. Yet while the town itself and the six-mile slot of Antelope Canyon received only trace rain, storms were visible from Page in the distance. The storm on the plateau was no freak event. Instead it was "not terribly unusual—your garden variety summer storm," noted Frank Richards, head of the Hydrologic Information Center at the National Weather Service Headquarters in Silver Spring, Maryland.

Pancho Quintana was a hired guide, but the Los Angeles welder had not been one for long. This was his third TrekAmerica trip; he was leading it after 21 days of company training. This training did not include specific operating procedures for monsoon storms: "We don't specifically define what a thunderstorm is," said TrekAmerica personnel manager Jack Aakhus. Quintana took his five clients into Antelope Canyon not only while the entire widespread region was under warning for extreme thunderstorms—but also on the very next day following a headlined mass evacuation of 100 tourists and residents of nearby Supai, in Grand Canyon, due to a massive flash flood there generated by a very quick 3 to 4 inches of rain on the Coconino Plateau (discussed later in this chapter).

After hiking for a while in Antelope Canyon, where a ten-foot-width is considered wide, Quintana says he told his five clients that it was time to climb out. He then climbed out of the 80-foot deep canyon and yelled back down at them.

No one, he told police, followed him.

Instead, a French couple still in the canyon bottom agreed to leave but said that first they wanted him to come back down and take their photograph in the narrow slot. Quintana (who refused to grant a press interview) says he climbed back down to take their photo. As he reached the bottom, a ten-foot high, chocolate-colored wall of water, mud, logs, cacti, cow manure, and other desert debris slammed down the canyon like a sewer from hell.

Quintana and his five clients heard the roar and looked up. They tried to outrun the rushing wall by scampering downstream. A few seconds later the wall of semi-liquid debris slammed into them. They struggled to capture an eddy, but the flood kept increasing its intensity. One by one Quintana's clients vanished downstream and under the mud. Quintana got a grip on one or two of his clients, he said, but the flash flood ripped them both loose from his grip.

After Ken Young rescued Quintana, a helicopter flew over the canyon searching for more survivors or bodies. They found one body. A week of searching by dog teams and SCUBA divers in Lake Powell finally unearthed eight other victims. Even after years of deeper searches armed with ultrasound equipment, the final two victims of the eleven killed have not been found.

A major take-home lesson in all this was that these hideous deaths occurred despite the Navajo concessionaires (Antelope Canyon is in the Navajo Nation and received 20,000 visitors in 1996 alone) at the head of Lower Antelope Canyon having warned the victims emphatically that, due to monsoonal storms, it was a not a safe time to enter the slot canyon. The dozen people, nearly all of whom had traveled a long distance to see the Southwest, entered regardless.

"It's really hard," explains Effie Yazzie, office manager for the Navajo Nation agency responsible for canyon tours, "to get through, especially to people who are not from this area. They have no concept of what it's like to be in a flash flood."

The conditions under which Quintana's five clients died were questionable enough for Coconino County to review the episode for possible gross negligence or manslaughter charges. "In my mind, it's clear cut as to the criminal aspect of the case," County Attorney Terry Hance concluded, dismissing criminal culpability. "Whether there is a civil liability or not will rest in another venue."

Surviving members of five of the victims' families filed suit against TrekAmerica in the U.S. District Court in Phoenix. *Trek America ultimately agreed to settle to families of the victims of the Antelope Canyon disaster for $1.8 million.*

Was this tragedy simply bad luck? Fate? Or an act of God? That none of the eleven victims included residents of any of the Southwestern states may be only the result of chance, but likely not. In short, knowledge and understanding of how slot canyons were formed and are still being enlarged are far better to possess in advance of a flash flood than is having one's surviving relatives file a suit afterward. And while education and publicity do help save lives, common sense is the last and surest defense against flash flood fatalities.

Strangely, or perhaps not so strangely after all, visitation by tourists to Antelope Canyon took an upward leap in numbers after nationwide news coverage of the 1997 flash flood disaster. As graphic as this news was, it failed to hit home with many people visiting the Southwest.

Just a few weeks after this extremely well-publicized tragedy at Antelope Canyon, for example, on September 11, 1997, three people—John and Patty Moran, age 40, and John McCue, age 36, (Patty's younger brother)—from Metaire, Louisiana, repeated Pancho Quintana's error. The trio had hiked up Bright Angel Creek during a very light, almost unmeasurable scattering of rain. Less than two miles from the river they veered off trail into Phantom Creek. Phantom, 15 to 50 feet wide, is a narrower, steeper tributary canyon of Bright Angel.

Meanwhile, on the nearby North Rim at the head of Phantom Creek Canyon less than ten miles away, a spin-off of Hurricane Linda dropped about two inches of rain in thunder showers. Just two days earlier, similar monsoonal storms had sent an eight-foot wall of water down this same canyon—after ripping through Haunted Canyon higher up—from nearly two inches of rain that had fallen then on the North Rim.

Phantom Creek, the three hikers were finding, was an amazing canyon. As deep as something in a Tolkien fantasy, it seemed like a different world. A different planet even. The hikers walked upstream in awe. Roughly a quarter mile upstream of the Bright Angel/Phantom Creek confluence, McCue helped his older sister across the creek to see a pretty waterfall ahead. This idyll was shattered by Patty's sudden scream: "Water!"

Instead of water, McCue would later explain, it was a "thick, dark, red mud." And rather than claw their way up one or the other of the 70-degree walls to attain higher ground, the trio huddled for safety on the downstream side of a boulder in the middle of the canyon bottom. Within about fifteen seconds, the five-foot high wall of water and debris careened and cascaded along the canyon floor to the trio's sanctuary. It instantly filled with violent water and obliterated the imaginary safety zone in which the three had huddled. This flood then blew all three hikers into the mainstream of mud cascading and roaring downcanyon.

This flood peaked at only chin deep—but, again, it was fast and violent and dense. As McCue felt himself tumbling out of control in the nightmare flood, he remembered some of the life-saving lessons he had learned. He now fought for his life by swimming with all of his might. The flood swept McCue about half a mile downstream before he was able to haul himself out, abraded and covered in mud, on shore along Bright Angel Creek. He painfully crawled out of the slurry like some desperate primeval amphibian caught in a prehistoric cataclysm. On solid rock again, he coughed up mud.

As a traumatized McCue struggled down the edge of Bright Angel Creek, he cried rust-colored tears from mud-caked eyelids. Search as he might for his sister or brother-in-law, they were nowhere to be found. Eventually a frantic and crying McCue found NPS Ranger Bryan Wisher, who then duplicated McCue's unsuccessful search.

Both Morans had drowned. The implacable flood carried their bodies down into Bright Angel Creek, then into the Colorado, and then miles downstream. Despite intensive searching by thirty searchers and dozens of river runners, the Morans' bodies were only discovered one and three weeks later, 30 and 46 miles downstream, by river trips.

Knowing when to and when not to hike in slot canyons is vital. I (Myers), with several years of inner Canyon off-route and remote hiking experience, had solo-hiked through the entire five-mile drainage of Phantom Creek on September 10, less than 24 hours before the Morans were killed—thereby "splitting" both flash floods. Coming off the North Rim at Tiyo Point, I had climbed Shiva Temple before dropping into the narrows of Phantom Creek. From these vantage points—as opposed to being within the blind confines of Phantom Creek—I saw no significant monsoon activity within fifty miles. Even so, flash floods weighed heavily on my mind. But what were the odds of two flash floods happening in the same drainage out of the hundreds in this neighborhood, I asked myself, on two days in a row? Low, very low, I kept telling myself. Had there been any active rain visible, though, I would have waited until it cleared or else I would have avoided the drainage altogether and detoured it by traversing along the slopes to the dry-land Banzai Route to Phantom Ranch.

But from the extremely constrained view the Morans had had in the bottom of Phantom Creek, they had possessed no way to visually check against the possibility of distant rain. Instead they had gambled blindly, perhaps even unknowingly. And they had lost big when an in-season flood had killed them.

When I reached the river after my hike, I joined a river trip run by OARS, Inc.

and led by my co-author, Ghiglieri. Within two days our entire trip was put on alert by commercial motor rigs that had passed Phantom Ranch twenty-four hours after our rendezvous. The alert? Watch the river and the eddies for bodies: two people had drowned in Phantom Creek the day after I had hiked it. This sad news and this grim duty pounded home to us yet again how important it would be to do what we could to prevent these sorts of tragedies—rather than simply search eddies for corpses. For me personally, having hiked Phantom Creek only a day before the Morans, this tragedy was a sobering experience. Two flash floods in three days....

These two fatalities were so glaringly "in-season" (as were those in Antelope Canyon a few weeks earlier), that the National Park felt obligated to conduct a criminal investigation of the Morans' demise. A post-disaster interview with John McCue conducted by NPS criminal investigator Franco Sidoti revealed: 1. McCue was acting as "trip leader" because he had been in Grand Canyon a few years earlier and thus "knew" it; 2. McCue also knew about the danger of flash floods in small canyons; 3. he had heard about the mass death episode in Antelope Canyon only a few weeks earlier; and 4. it was his idea to hike up the narrows of Phantom Creek on this occasion.

As fishy as this may sound, the investigator concluded that no criminal intent was involved.

As we have seen, being hit by a flash flood "coming out of the blue" is a hideous way to die. Its opposite, actually knowing that a flash flood is on the way, however, can produce some amazingly positive results.

Consider, for example, the outcome of Papillion Helicopters pilot Michael Moore's flight down Havasu Canyon on August 10, 1997 (two days before the Antelope Canyon disaster). While making a routine flight into Havasu, Moore had seen a flash flood ripping down Cataract Canyon into Havasu from its upper reaches. Moore knew that dozens of unsuspecting tourists were frolicking in the blue-green waters downstream. Moore veered his machine down the canyon. Flying at an illegal altitude, Moore searched for people and warned them from the air to seek high ground.

Things were going well. Everyone whom Moore had tried to warn had understood his hand-signaling to run for high ground. But when, miles downstream, Moore hovered above 23-year-old Elizabeth Nemeth and her companion, both from Tennessee, the two young women could not figure out what the pilot wanted. Nemeth and her friend were part of a group of private river runners who had scattered themselves along lower Havasu Creek that day for a big taste of Paradise. And this pilot, as friendly as he seemed, was not really improving their experience. In fact, he was becoming irritating.

Waving frantically with his hand, Moore again signaled the two women to get out of the creek where they had been swimming and to go uphill. Initially thinking that this friendly pilot from nowhere was just waving hello, they waved back.

Pleasantly—even if he was irritating.

But because Moore persisted in waving them out with ever more exaggerated gesticulations, the two young women reluctantly left the creek. Seeing this, and knowing the wall of mud upstream was now that much closer to yet more people downstream, Moore sped downcanyon to try to save yet more lives.

Once Moore's noisy machine had whomp-whomp-whomped downstream, however, and everything looked as calm as before, Elizabeth Nemeth ventured back down into the creek and its pleasantly gurgling blue-green flow.

Her companion, perhaps more impressed with Moore's gesticulations, remained on high ground. Seconds later she heard a thunderous roar. She looked upstream. To her horror, the red wall of a flash flood was bearing down from upstream like something from a computer-enhanced disaster movie.

She screamed at Nemeth to get out of the water. Nemeth, however, could not understand her screams over the noise of the creek. Nemeth turned her head to try to hear her companion's yells better. As she turned, a 6-foot-high wall of mud, water and debris slammed into her. It tumbled and somersaulted her as just one more piece of debris in the "desert batter" of logs, rocks, and trees ripped out by their roots, and liquid mud. Nemeth felt herself careen helplessly into boulders and over them as she accelerated down Havasu Creek.

Finally, several hundred yards downstream, a log pinned her against a boulder. Luckily, and this fluke saved her life, the cresting current pushed her even higher up onto this sloping rock. She clung to it with a death grip. And she kept on clinging to it for several minutes until the flood receded a bit.

Nemeth was air-lifted to Grand Canyon Clinic. There, I (Myers), found her severely bruised and battered and with a broken nose. It seemed a near miracle that she was otherwise unharmed. Strangely, despite her near brush with death and despite not having heeded Pilot Moore in his risky race against the flood to warn potential victims in time to save them and despite Nemeth owing her life only to the shape of a lucky boulder upon which chance alone had thrust her, she seemed a lot less impressed with her survival than the Clinic staff was.

But Michael Moore's desperate warning flight down Havasu Canyon was not over yet....

Downstream, the mouth of Havasu looked like a typical summer traffic jam. For river guides, the apparently dry "holes" during the monsoons prove tempting. After all, their emotional logic runs, we're here, and it doesn't look like rain, and some of my passengers may never be here again...let's hike it, at least a short way up. Again, this "lottery of death" mentality nudges people into decisions to hike slot canyons that later may seem a lot less smart.

As Moore had begun his race against death down Havasu from one group of hikers to the next, a commercial rowing trip run by Wilderness River Adventures had pulled into the mouth of Havasu Canyon. A few hundred yards downstream two other trips, motorized—Western River Expeditions and Wilderness River Adventures—had parked in the "motor" eddy in the main Colorado adjacent to low ledges of Muav Limestone. A private river trip—Elizabeth Nemeth's—was also moored in the mouth of Havasu. All these boats had stacked up to be a garden variety traffic jam.

Those who scanned the sky upstream above Havasu that morning had seen only scattered clouds. "Okie," (a.k.a. Paul Jones) leading the Wilderness River Adventures trip, however, viewed those clouds with suspicion. He changed the trip's plan from a four-hour-plus hike to Beaver Falls and back to a more prudent one-hour hike to the nearer pools.

Later, a stay-behind Wilderness boatman, Tom Janecek, heard a strange sound as he lolled on his boat in the mouth. It was a low frequency roar from up Havasu Canyon. Strangely, it sounded rhythmic. It grew louder.

As Janecek's personal alarm bells started ringing, he spotted a helicopter 100 feet above the floor of Havasu. He stared into the cockpit and saw:

—a hand making a wave-like motion much like splashing water in a pool. I screamed over the chopper's roar along with four other boatmen, "FLASH FLOOD! EVERYBODY OUT!!! OUT, OUT, EVERYBODY OUT!! NOW!"

It was mass confusion. Some people thought that we meant get on the boats to leave. Parents ran around looking for their children. One parent came up to me as I was screaming at her son, who was deep in the mouth of the pull-in spot, trying to get the vest that was blown into the water from the chopper. He finally heard the panic in our voices and left the life jacket in the water and ran across the boats.

Once the Wilderness guides had evacuated the mouth safely, they tried to figure out if they had time to rescue their boats. Was the chopper's warning a two-minute warning or instead maybe even a twenty-minute warning? "None of us," Janecek writes, "would commit to going into the mouth where there was no immediate escape route."

Even so, while wearing life jackets, they untied one boat and moved it 25 feet downstream into the Colorado, below the mouth.

While returning to move the second boat, "we heard the horrible sounds—absolutely terrifying...not of water, but of people way upstream screaming in terror and warning those downstream."

Okie and Janecek froze in the mouth of Havasu for about ten seconds listening to the screaming get even louder. Then it came, a beautiful, nearly six-foot-high wall of blue water with a 45-degree slope. It metamorphosed into a ten-foot high, nearly vertical wall of muddier water in the narrow mouth. Okie and Janecek had leaped to a high ledge. Below them the flash flood snapped all the remaining bowlines "like popcorn."

Eight boats in a vibrating mass of ropes, gyrating oars, and logs shot from the mouth into the river and under the still-hovering chopper.

Several guides hurried down to the Western rig at the lower pull-in to watch for victims shooting out of the mouth of Havasu. Every life jacket or piece of clothing popping to the surface caused at least one of their hearts to skip a beat.

As the guides at the mouth watched the river, people upstream enacted mini-scenes from a disaster movie. Not only had Elizabeth Nemeth been caught, then miraculously shoved atop her boulder, another woman as well had been caught in a pool when the flood hit. She was slammed in the ribs by a log and her halter top ripped off. A guide, Patrick, plucked her from the current. Another passenger, intent on "getting to high ground," climbed up and kept on climbing as if intent on scrambling to the rim. He finally dead-ended on a narrow ledge on a sixty-foot cliff. There he froze in fear in his dangerously exposed position. Now, he found, he felt unable to go up or down.

Matt Penrod, another guide, used climbing gear for protection to orchestrate the "trapped" man's harrowing 90-minute rescue. He painfully helped this man descend thirty feet down the cliff to a place where a harness could then be used to get him down yet another thirty feet lower to safe ground.

Many hours later and eight miles downstream, at Tuckup Canyon (River Mile 164.5), borderline chaos ruled during a monsoonal downpour. With assistance by the NPS, and with all the guides and passengers nearby working together, ninety people from the several trips visiting Havasu that day struggled, some in vain, to find their own gear, their own boats and guides, and to somehow get warm in the pounding storm. The "hole" in the weather had closed. The monsoon had become itself again. Multiple waterfalls plunged and roared off the Redwall rims surrounding the struggling knot of bedraggled humanity in awe-inspiring streamers and fountains into the inner gorge. Janecek noted that everyone was present and accounted for—and alive—due to the actions of one man:

> *The chopper pilot, Michael Moore, had saved the day. His warning was all that was needed to get everyone to high ground. Apparently he saw the flood coming upstream, and broke some rules of radio contact and flight zones, and went on the warning mission. You could easily argue that he saved a dozen lives that day.*

All in all, the above incident was an almost picture-perfect example of how to "have" a flash flood at Havasu. Unfortunately, most episodes of flash floods are considerably less than perfect; they occur with no chopper pilot present to act as knight in shining armor.

On August 6, 1988, during the peak of yet another monsoon season and again at

Havasu, the narrow, cliff-bordered mouth was again loaded with motor rigs. Tim Whitney and Richard Quartaroli were running a two-boat Arizona River Runners trip. Because it had rained lightly within a mile of Havasu as they had approached, and because the mouth was already somewhat crowded with two Western River Expeditions motor rigs and two Wilderness River Adventures motor rigs, the two boatmen opted to moor their rigs in the lower "motor" eddy along the riverside. Quartaroli next decided to take a few people up to the very first crossing only. His plan was to allow them to see the aquamarine creek plunging picturesquely over the polished boulders and waterfalls between slick ledges and walls of Muav Limestone. Quartaroli had weighed the ominous signs in the sky and vetoed going farther upstream due to the risk of a flash flood.

"Okay, everybody, here it is," he informed everyone as they arrived at the first crossing of the Southwest's most famous blue-green waters, "This is as far as we go today."

After about ten minutes of oohing and aahing, Quartaroli announced that they all would now be heading back to the boats.

As Quartaroli walked back along the route bypassing the mouth—a three minute walk—he detoured into the mouth to ask Carl McDonald and Mike Reyes, who were running the Wilderness trip tied up along side those two Western motor rigs, where they were planning to camp. As he stepped aboard and asked....

BOOM, the creek started to rise.

Pretty close timing, Quartaroli thought to himself, getting his folks out of the creek minutes before this thing hit....

Unbeknownst to Quartaroli, three of his and Whitney's passengers, a family from New York, were not as safely out of the creek as he thought. Katherine K. was a 110-pound Marathon runner about fifty years old. She was traveling with her daughter and son-in-law. As the three had followed Quartaroli and their group up and out of the Havasu drainage moments ago, Katherine's son-in-law had decided that he *had* to have a photo of the three of them in the creek. So he called his wife and mother-in-law back. The trio had quietly turned around and re-entered Havasu. As with the tragic demise of Pancho Quintana's clients in Antelope Canyon, this flash flood hit the trio as they sought the perfect family photo.

The flood caught Katherine in mid-creek above the first crossing. The wall of water whipped her off her feet, flushed her downstream, swept her over both sets of falls, rolled her down the narrows, and spurted her out of the mouth of the canyon into the Colorado and Havasu Rapid.

The flood also took Katherine's daughter. But a fellow passenger grabbed her as she flushed past. Katherine' photo-bug son-in-law ended up trapped on a pair of trees in the middle of the flood. He was rescued later via a rope extraction.

Meanwhile Quartaroli spun around and leaped off the Western River Expeditions' boat to escape the flash flood. Behind him a two- or three-foot wall of red

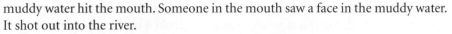

muddy water hit the mouth. Someone in the mouth saw a face in the muddy water. It shot out into the river.

McDonald tossed a life jacket into the water near the face. Both jacket and face vanished separately down the rapid.

Tim Whitney, downstream at the ledges in the motor eddy, was saying hello to small groups of his and Quartaroli's passengers as they re-boarded the boats in twos and threes. He glanced upstream and saw the flash flood disgorge from the mouth. Both Western rigs, their bowline snapped, shot out with it. The two were still tied together bow to stern and spinning out of control. He saw Darrell (a.k.a. BamBam) scrambling to get his motor started to power the boats back to shore in Whitney's eddy.

As Whitney warned everyone on the boats to brace themselves and hold on against an impending collision, Whitney looked down into the roiling muddy water. A life jacket, floating loose, bobbed past. Then a face appeared. No body, not even hair—just eyes, nose, and a mouth open and desperately gasping for air.

This was decision time. But with no time to think. Whitney jumped off his large raft into the flood. He grabbed the body belonging to The Face. The woman (he only discovered her gender later) crawled all over him as if he were an island.

"Take it easy," he told her, "relax, breathe, I've got you...." In reality, Whitney's life jacket was not doing all that well holding both of their faces out of the water. Even so, he realized, they could float safely for miles if forced to.

Then, abruptly, his view was blocked. Ahead of him the two loose Western rigs slammed into the left wall and bent into a V. He heard Darrell's 30-horsepower motor screaming as he tried to power both rigs to shore via one motor.

Whitney grabbed with his free hand for a lifeline on the nearest Western boat. But he missed it. Instantly he and The Face vanished underneath the boat into the dark and the roar. From the front of boat number one to the stern of number two lay a potential underwater swim of seventy feet. This, Whitney knew, could be like being flushed down a seventy-foot storm drain with no air and toward a whirling propeller that could slice and dice him and The Face he was trying to rescue.

Meanwhile, as Whitney and The Face bumped along under the tubes of the boats, she throttled him by the neck in a death grip.

Worried now that The Face might kill him, Whitney pried her hands off his neck.

Poof, she was gone.

Oh, my God, Whitney thought as he reached out for her in the dark, turbulent flow and found nothing. Oh, my God. She's gone. Just hold your breath, he told himself. This can't last forever.

Finally, light brown water. Then air. "Well, that was the one chance you had, bucko," he rued to himself in despair. "You're never going to see her again."

The woman with the face popped up a few strokes away. She tried to catch a breath but sank too quickly. Following her under water, Whitney stroked hard then dived as best as his life jacket would allow. He grabbed her hair. Still underwater, he shifted her to a cross-body carry across the chest. When he surfaced again, he looked around.

Still grasping Katherine K. against himself, he now found himself caught between the two Western rigs and the cliff face. One of these boats—like the closing walls of the trash-compactor in the Death Star in STAR WARS—was about to crush him and his rescued woman against the Muav Limestone.

Whitney yelled up at Darrell, "Don't run me over!"

Darrell finally spotted Whitney. He pivoted the boat to place Whitney and the woman beside it. An adult male passenger tried to help the two up, but he fell off into the river. Now he too had to be rescued. At last a goggled-eyed thirteen-year-old boy hauled the woman with the face onto the boat.

Whitney now swam to the stern of the non-powered Western boat and hauled himself out. He struggled for a while before he managed to coax its Johnson into firing up.

What impressed Whitney most about this rescue was not that he had succeeded in saving Katherine's life against serious odds—to his mind, this is exactly what professional Grand Canyon guides do. What really haunted him was that he had lost her under the boat. This reality recycled through his mind like a close-looped tape.

These two stories of successful rescues illustrate some important points about Canyon flash floods. First, Havasu—being the single most popular hike/stop for river trips in Grand Canyon—is fed by a huge drainage. While not as large as those of the Little Colorado River or Kanab or Diamond creeks, this drainage is huge. This means flash floods can, will, and do appear near the mouth with no warning at all from local rain. Indeed the source of the flood could be nearly forty miles south and be completely invisible to anyone in the Canyon. Second, the mouth is a dangerous place even when the creek is flowing as its charming, blue-green self. The mouth, circled by Muav cliffs and often with not even a shred of gravel beach exposed, feeds its swirling water directly into Havasu Rapid. So far no one without a life jacket has swum this alone and survived. Instead, at least three people have drowned here (see next chapter).

The mouth is clearly an area where life jackets should be worn by anyone on the boats or in the water. Even the several other guides, AzRA's Dave Edwards for one, who have managed truly heroic rescues (episodes of which were not covered in this chapter due to space consideration) would have been useless or suicidal had they not been wearing life jackets. A further lesson here is flash floods appear with so little warning that, if the weather appears questionable, trip leaders are serving their fellow Canyoneers' best interests if they make the difficult and unpopular—but safe—decision to not hike Havasu Canyon at all but instead go find a safe replacement activity. Go play horseshoes or something. Or sit in a safe place and read Tony Hillerman or Ed Abbey.

It may only be the luck of the draw or instead a happy product of experience and skill, but none of the half million people who have run the river in boats (as of the year 2011) has been killed by flash floods anywhere in the Canyon. A few have come very very close—some of their escapes being matters more of luck than intelligence—but, again, no fatalities of this sort have occurred to members of river trips. Sadly, and as we've seen, the same cannot be said of recreational hikers in the Canyon.

On August 24, 1992, U.S. Air Force Investigative personnel contacted Grand Canyon NPS rangers because two of their personnel were overdue in returning to Onizuka Air Force Base (the Consolidated Space Center in Sunnyvale, California) from a hike in the Canyon. Second Lieutenant Walter A. Jaskowiak, II, age 24, and 1st Lieutenant Miriam Leigh Epstein, age 26, he explained, were both "stellar performers" working on top secret projects with high security clearances. They had not returned. More ominous, they had failed to rendezvous with another hiking party as planned on August 17, day one of their hike.

Jaskowiak's and Epstein's backcountry hiking permit listed the following itinerary: On August 17 they were to hike from the rim to Hermit Creek (River Mile 95), on the 18th, Monument Creek (River Mile 93.5), and on the 19th, Indian Garden (roughly halfway up the Bright Angel Trail from the river at River Mile 89). Although these daily goals sound close to one another and therefore easy, the standard hiking route "paralleling" the river demands that hikers traverse inward and back upward, then downward and outward, within a sidewinder's posture of side canyons such as Monument or Hermit, for miles to gain about 1,000 vertical feet and the top of the Tapeats Sandstone, also known as the Tonto Plateau. The Tonto provides a safe, spacious, and relatively level hiking surface in the inner Canyon between tributary canyons. Its downside is it meanders sinuously from river-ward, immediately above the Upper Granite Gorge, to rim-ward as it follows the contours of the tributary canyons, thus multiplying the horizontal straight line distance that the raven flies from one tributary to the next. Moreover, the Tonto normally offers neither water nor shade. During cool weather, this is not serious. During summer, it is. Either way, the Tonto does offer a remarkably safe passage in a topography riddled by a myriad of extremely dangerous alternate routes.

So what happened to Walter Jaskowiak and Miriam Epstein?

For some reason, rangers found, their permit had been edited so that only the first night of the itinerary was used. Did this mean the pair had hiked down the Hermit Trail, camped, and then hiked back early but then vanished?

No. Their "plan A" was to have met two friends, Stephen and Virginia De Martini, at the Backcountry Reservations Office. From there the foursome was to have hiked together to Hermit. Jaskowiak and Epstein did not show up at this office.

The De Martinis did. And, even though their friends never showed, the De Martinis went ahead and did hike to Hermit. They next camped in the Hermit area on the 17th, as had been decided as the foursome's plan B (in the event that the two couples missed one another at the Backcountry Office). But plan B also failed. The De Martinis never saw Jaskowiak or Epstein here either. Disappointed but only mildly concerned, the De Martinis hiked back out of the Canyon and went home.

Here the plot thickens. NPS rangers found Jaskowiak's Dodge parked at the Bypass Lot on the Village Loop Drive. It was covered in dust. A background check of both hikers—seeking a motive for vanishing deliberately—revealed that Jaskowiak and Epstein were romantically involved. But it also revealed that the two normally traveled (including climbing Pike's Peak) with other people, as with the De Martinis.

NPS personnel contemplated the clues. Jaskowiak and Epstein jogged and were in good condition. Neither owed unpaid debts or had a criminal background. Nor had either seemed suicidal. Instead, both had recently appeared to their families, their roommates, and their co-workers to be in normally sound mind and body.

On top of all these positive signs, Jaskowiak and Epstein had also completed the Air Force Academy's one-week survival class.

Yet they had vanished. So completely that not even interviews with river runners camping in the general vicinity of Hermit Creek and Monument Creek turned up anyone who had seen the missing hikers.

Soon NPS rangers began uncovering small but tantalizing clues. Late on the morning of August 26, NPS Rangers Sue Cherry and Dave Chapman hiked the Tonto Trail about two miles west of Horn Creek (River Mile 90.25). The two found a cache of clothing abandoned on the Tonto Trail. Based on the rain-spattered dust on it, it appeared to have been there for roughly a week. Inside it the rangers found two or three MREs (military "meals, ready to eat"), jeans, sweatshirt, towels, a U.S. Army shovel, shorts, a book (*Catch 22*, checked out from San Jose State University, where Jaskowiak was a student), a receipt from San Jose University, toothpaste, socks, and a t-shirt.

At about this time, U.S. Air Force Special Agent Lieutenant Colonel Ron Parker phoned Ranger Keith Lober to inform him that the missing persons had possessed extremely high security clearances. Parker also told Lober that the information that Walter Jaskowiak and Meriam Epstein possessed could be sold.

An hour after Cherry and Chapman found the abandoned pack, on August 25, at 2:45 p.m., two hikers from New York City, Daniel and Linda, told rangers over the phone that on their second day out, August 18, they had met and briefly hiked with two other hikers named Walt and Miriam on the Monument Creek Trail. Walt and Miriam, they said, had been planning to camp by the river at Monument (River Mile 93.5). But they had changed their minds around noon when Daniel and Linda told them that they themselves needed a rescue.

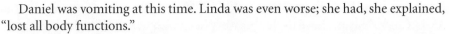

Daniel was vomiting at this time. Linda was even worse; she had, she explained, "lost all body functions."

One day before this, during Daniel's and Linda's first night's camp, they both had already felt ill. The NPS ranger at Indian Garden, Bil Vandergraff, had tried to convince them to switch their itinerary from Monument Canyon to the much easier, closer, and phone-friendly Phantom Ranch. But despite their feeling ill already from the extreme heat, Daniel and Linda had rejected Vandergraff's sound advice and instead followed their original plan.

Hence, a day later, on August 18, Walt Jaskowiak and Miriam Epstein met an even more desperately uncomfortable Daniel and Linda. Here Jaskowiak and Epstein aborted their own original plan to continue down the Monument Trail. Instead, Walt and Miriam decided to be Good Samaritans and hike out in the blazing heat to request a rescue for Daniel and Linda.

So Jaskowiak and Epstein veered from their descent and instead headed east onto the Tonto Trail. This route led past Horn Creek and continued on to Indian Garden and the ranger station, roughly seven miles from where Jaskowiak and Epstein had met Daniel and Linda. There the two Good Samaritans could alert Ranger Bil Vandergraff, who had originally warned Daniel and Linda not to hike the Tonto, that his advice had been correct: Daniel's and Linda's physiological situations had deteriorated to life-threatening.

Walt, the two heat-stricken hikers now said over the phone, was wearing a grey Australian cowboy hat. Both Walt and Miriam also wore shorts and tank tops and seemed to be in good shape. Miriam also wore a bandanna and had an ace bandage on her knee. Dangling off their packs were several water bottles, one of them a "Dromedary" type. Before veering onto the Tonto, Walt and Miriam had also told Daniel and Linda that they had missed meeting their friends at Hermit.

The weather that day, August 18, was clear and very hot. The Phantom Ranch Ranger Station recorded a high of 111 degrees in the shade. The next day soared to 113 and was hit by a severe windstorm. The next day, August 20, climbed to a stupefying 115 degrees in the shade. No measurable rain fell at Phantom Ranch (River Mile 88) until August 21, when the high temperature dropped to 110 degrees, and it rained 0.59 inches. On August 22, it rained another 0.37 inches. Aside from these specifics, the region in general had been hit all that week with scattered, severe, but unmeasured local monsoonal thunderstorms.

An hour after this phone chat with Daniel and Linda, Rangers Sandy Hand and Jesse Farias found a pack at the bottom of Horn Creek drainage well above the river's edge. Inside it they found Miriam Epstein's credit card.

That same day, August 25, at 2:45 p.m., 70 minutes after finding Epstein's pack, searchers aboard one of the three contract helicopters combing Upper Granite Gorge spotted two bodies sprawled in a dry creek bed near the foot of the extremely narrow, steep, tortuous Horn Creek drainage. The bodies lay only about

300 feet upcanyon from the Colorado River at River Mile 90.25. The topography of Horn Creek Canyon above the bodies was punctuated by several high, sheer drops. In short, it was unclimbable and undescendable without climbing gear.

One hundred horizontal feet separated the two bodies, as also did a 20-foot, sheer, vertical fall. The upper body, a woman's, was sprawled at the foot of a 50-foot, dry waterfall. It was dressed in shorts, shoes, and a t-shirt, and partially en-wrapped in a piece of plastic. Decomposition had begun. Strewn around it in the vicinity lay two military canteens on a web-belt, a large, broken flashlight, two bandannas, a "Trails Illustrated" map of the Canyon, sunglasses with a neoprene band, parachute cord, and a "Dromedary" water container still holding a quart of water. Twenty-five feet from this body, at the lip of the 20-foot falls that separated the two bodies, was a man's watch partially buried in sand.

The lower body, a man's, was also dressed in shorts, shirt, and shoes filled with red sand. The rangers found no equipment nearby, but they did find in the man's pocket a wallet containing Walter Jaskowiak's ID cards.

Upstream, roughly 350 yards up the Horn Creek drainage from the bodies and above a few more high waterfalls, sleeping bags and other camping equipment lay damaged and scattered as if they had tumbled hundreds of feet down the drainage from the Tonto Trail.

Dental charts confirmed both identities. The Coconino County Medical Examiner, Dr. Thomas Vorphal, concluded that both victims had drowned.

How?

Dr. Vorphal noted that Epstein had an abraded right knee (still wrapped in gauze) and a fractured left wrist and a skull fracture to the left side of her head which occurred well before her death. Jaskowiak himself had suffered an abdominal injury prior to death. Both autopsies concluded that no foul play was involved.

Rangers Richard Perch, David Trevino, and Keith Lober examined Horn Creek Canyon itself and concluded: "The rock on the side of the canyon was clean, with no mud, and the drainage did not appear to have flash flooded significantly in recent times."

If this conclusion were true, how then did Epstein and Jaskowiak end up where they had?

The clues were worthy of an A. Conan Doyle mystery. Investigators from the park, from Coconino County Sheriff's Office, and from the U.S. Air Force figured out that Miriam somehow must have been seriously injured in a fall while hiking—this accounted for her broken left wrist and the fracture in the left side of skull—on or near the Tonto Trail. Jaskowiak, who weighed 155 pounds, apparently carried her, possibly unconscious (she weighed 138 pounds), in a sort of fireman's carry dangling down his back. The toes of Epstein's otherwise brand new tennis/running shoes were very badly worn through, consistent with their having dragged along the abrasive surface of the Tapeats Sandstone for quite a distance. This task

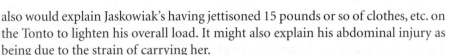

also would explain Jaskowiak's having jettisoned 15 pounds or so of clothes, etc. on the Tonto to lighten his overall load. It might also explain his abdominal injury as being due to the strain of carrying her.

It appears that Jaskowiak's first big mistake, a potentially fatal one, was not to sequester the injured Epstein in whatever protected area he could find or create near her place of injury. He could have erected a quick shade shelter and left Epstein with water. He also could have written her a note, if she was unconscious but woke up after his departure—or to inform anyone else who happened by—to tell her to stay put and to explain what had happened and where and when and how he had gone for help. Lightly loaded with nothing but a water bottle, he then easily could have reached the Indian Garden Ranger Station in a couple of hours and arranged for a helicopter evacuation in less than an hour more. If worried about Epstein's rolling while unconscious or asleep, Jaskowiak also could have tied her ankle to a large stone with parachute cord, or have built a rock retaining wall to keep her from rolling into danger.

The team of investigators concluded that Jaskowiak's second mistake—without doubt the fatal one—came next. After dragging Epstein for quite a distance along the sun scorched Tapeats of the Tonto Plateau, he was exhausted and injured and apparently sought shelter from the blistering sun, from the sand-blasting, super-desiccating wind, or from both. The flash flood-carved head of Horn Creek offered shade and a windbreak on an inviting ledge under an overhang of Tapeats Sandstone. With plenty of food, water, and now this shade, Jaskowiak, who, again, now was hurt himself, may have decided the shelter of the Tapeats was a heaven-sent haven in which to wait for Epstein to regain consciousness—and hopefully even her ability to walk to Indian Garden.

There, after being sequestered safely perhaps for three days and nights, lying on a plastic tarp, a flash flood caught and killed Jaskowiak and Epstein. The flood slammed them, then scattered their bodies and equipment down Horn Creek Canyon almost to the Colorado River.

Forensic entomological assessment (based on maggot development in tissue) placed their times of death on the evening of August 21, the date of the heaviest rain at Phantom Ranch, and four days after starting their hike.

What about the NPS rangers' initial conclusion that little mud was present in the Horn Creek drainage therefore it must not have flashed? It seems that this conclusion was wrong. Some mid-sized flash floods in the Canyon, especially in steep drainages, are fairly clear; sandy, yes, but more or less silt free. This flood had been one of these—as the piles of red sand inside Jaskowiak's shoes hinted.

A brief Associated Press article summarized this incident: "Two Air Force officers whose bodies were found in a drainage area were seeking help for another couple when floodwaters apparently swept them down a creek, authorities said Thursday."

Ironically, before Jaskowiak and Epstein were hit by the flash flood, while trying to rescue distressed New Yorkers Daniel and Linda from consequences of their poor decision making, the latter two had hiked down Monument Canyon to the river. There, on August 20, a Hatch River Expeditions trip radioed an emergency call for them, and an NPS helicopter arrived to air-lift them to the South Rim.

Again, huge flash floods are so rare that most short-term visitors to the Inner Canyon, either hiking or boating, are unlikely to witness one. Often it is only the people who work in the Canyon for many months (or years) as rangers, guides, mule skinners, and other concession employees, and so on who gain the experience to expect, fear, and predict them. Thus, many short-term visitors tend to doubt the danger that flash floods pose.

But the power of flash floods can be far more gargantuan than even what this chapter has so far spelled out. On July 26, 1984, I (Ghiglieri) was rowing on an OARS, Inc. trip with fellow guides Michael Boyle (trip leader), Craig Alexander, and Richard Haratani, and with trainees Geoff Gourley, Renee Goddard, Kelly Smith (Bretta) and my older son, Conan Michael. We stopped at Diamond Creek. We could not help ourselves. Nearly five days before arriving here, an NPS helicopter piloted by Dana Morris had materialized over us in the narrow and fantastically sculpted depths of Matkatamiba Canyon (River Mile 148). A uniformed arm had appeared and dropped us a little baggie of sand with a streamer attached. The airship then rose between the close, thousand-foot cliffs and vanished.

Like a message in a bottle, this baggie held a warning: "Diamond Creek flash flooded. Take out at Pearce Ferry."

Again, even though we could not take out our 23-person trip as planned at River Mile 225.7, we had stopped here anyway to ogle the newly scoured Diamond Creek Canyon. As we and our passengers stepped off our boats, I noticed the newly-exposed and only five-day-old Diamond Creek delta extending fifty yards farther than usual into the Colorado. Only twelve hours earlier the Colorado River had dropped for the first time in months, by about 4,000 cubic feet per second (cfs), thus exposing for the first time this new, flash-flood-created delta. Curious, I walked out onto this new landscape. Everyone else wandered up Diamond Creek.

Right away I spotted a swatch of green nylon emerging from the mud. I yanked on it, pulling up bowling-ball-sized boulders with the fabric. Cool, I thought to myself, a fly for a Eureka tent, and still in good shape. OARS used this exact same model. Having an extra fly can never hurt....But what is it doing here?

I walked farther onto the delta. No foot prints existed out here. I was the first human being to tread this tiny addition to the Inner Canyon. I saw a military rocket box lid half buried. I wiggled it hard to yank it out. A strange sensation fluttered in my stomach. The lid had been hand painted to say "COAL 2." Almost instantly I saw yet another lid. It had been painted to say "EGG 1." I knew who had painted these. Connie Walker, the OARS foodpacker, had hand-lettered both of them.

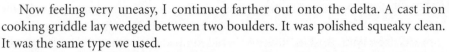

Now feeling very uneasy, I continued farther out onto the delta. A cast iron cooking griddle lay wedged between two boulders. It was polished squeaky clean. It was the same type we used.

Did our new stakebed truck carrying the trip nearly a week ahead of us drop all this stuff? Maybe the stakebed gate fell off and let this gear fall out. Or maybe.... No, that was unthinkable.

Farther out on the delta I spotted a twisted length of red-painted steel. It looked exactly like one of the steel stakes from our new stakebed. 1 tried to pull it out. It would not budge.

I stood there and gazed around me. More red-painted lengths of steel oozed twisted from the mud and boulders like giant worms caught in the act and frozen into fossils.

The answer to this puzzle seem pretty obvious now. It also seemed horrible. What the hell had happened to our truck? And, more importantly, to the crew who had been riding in it?

With a feeling of dread, I turned away from this graveyard of mud and walked up Diamond Creek to join everyone else. I saw two Hualapais with Boyle.

"You'll never guess what happened!" Boyle said to me astonished.

"Our truck got caught in the flash flood and went down the drink," I said, trying not to think about what this meant in terms of lost crew members.

He eyed me strangely, "How'd you know?"

"The delta," I explained. "Pieces of the truck are scattered all over it."

Eventually we heard the story from most of the survivors. A week earlier, when our other OARS trip had beached here to take out, it had been drizzling slightly. Our trip had been slower than usual in getting ready to leave. So too, had been the Outdoors Unlimited trip taking out here. Even slower was the AzRA trip doing the same thing. Up on the plateau to the south, near Route 66, however, it was not drizzling. It was cloudbursting from an ink-black sky in Biblical fashion.

The road that day (July 19) was already a mess because during the previous 24 hours minor monsoon storms had already gullied and slurried it, especially in the final mile or so closest to the river.

Early that afternoon, the OARS passengers and part of the crew from that trip had walked out less than a mile then rode the Hualapai school bus the other 22 miles to Peach Springs. The remaining crew—Sam West, Greg Schill, Bill Brisbin, and Charles Rau—plus the OARS manager, Mike Walker, finally got all six boats and the gear loaded into OARS' new two-ton GMC stakebed truck (OARS' previous GMC stakebed had burned to the ground not long before). Walker drove the new stakebed with the four crew up Diamond Creek.

He followed Outdoors Unlimited's Dodge Power Wagon, also hauling crew and gear. A half mile up the creek from the Colorado, the Power Wagon bogged down in the slurry of the "road" in a creekbed section of canyon between steep walls of schist called "the Narrows." Debbie Jordan, driving the Dodge as she always did for O.U., and another woman, Amy, could not get the Power Wagon moving again.

So Walker, West, Brisbin, Rau, and Schill jumped out of the GMC to help Outdoors Unlimited's guides Doug Carson and Dennis Silva to push it.

As the six men were about to push the Power Wagon, they heard a roar. Walker said the roar brought to mind a passing jet, thunder, and the Caterpillar the Hualapais used to grade the road. But the sound was not right for any of those. Simultaneously Walker looked up at the bend of the canyon two hundred yards ahead. Fingers of red-brown water five to ten feet high tumbled around the bend, rebounded as spray off the schist wall, then rumbled toward them. These fingers swelled quickly to a wall of slurry that doubled its height to about fifteen feet and filled the entire canyon from wall to wall.

"RUN!" several people yelled. As everyone scattered, Walker ran back to the new GMC. He opened the door and pulled out the ignition key, then rolled up the driver's window. Then he sprinted at top speed after the men heading for the high ground to the east.

When Debbie Jordan saw Walker rolling up the stake bed's window in her rearview mirror, she told Amy, "Don't get out, just roll up the windows."

Amy glanced through the windshield at the approaching wall of slurry, now taller than either truck, and said, "No way!" Then she yanked the door handle open.

This spurred Debbie to change her mind. Both women leapt from the Power Wagon. Now the wall of flash flood was a lot closer. Clad only in panties and t-shirts due to the heat, they sprinted for the nearest cliff. This happened to be to the west. They climbed the weathered schist like squirrels until they reached an overhanging section of slick rock beyond which they could not climb. They had trapped themselves, but turning back now would have been suicidal.

Diamond Creek, now a river of mud flowing at about 5,000 cubic feet per second (instead of its usual 1 or 2 cfs) walloped both trucks and engulfed them. Walker told me he knew the flash flood would hit both vehicles hard, but he was hoping that the GMC would stay where it was as the flood washed around it. But the wall of the red-brown debris flow picked up the Power Wagon like a leaf and tumbled it on top of the GMC two-ton. In seconds both vehicles were engulfed and rushing downstream. Due to their relative lightness and their flat-surfaced shapes, however, they continued to flow and surf half submerged on the surface, like two sinking ships dancing a slow motion fandango. Both trucks vanished downstream.

When they next heard the roar, the AzRA guides were upstream of the confluence and hauling their boats from the Colorado. They stared at the sudden flood a hundred yards downstream. For an instant the dual rear wheels of the GMC surfaced in the flood as the truck rolled end over end in a twenty-five-foot wave into the Colorado. The AzRA guides were horrified. The OARS crew, they thought, must still be inside that cab.

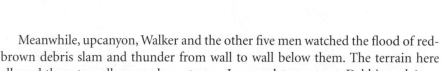

Meanwhile, upcanyon, Walker and the other five men watched the flood of red-brown debris slam and thunder from wall to wall below them. The terrain here allowed them to walk up or downstream. In complete contrast, Debbie and Amy, on the west side, could not have trapped themselves in a more terrifying predicament. The overhanging slick rock stopped them from ascending higher. Nor could they traverse laterally. The deafening flood with its thousands of boulders rolling suspended in it cascaded beneath them and sounded like an insane stone mason gone amuck. Almost malevolently, the flood yawned directly below them in a gaping hole that duplicated the famous killer hole in Crystal Rapid (next chapter).

Not only were these two women trapped, they were trapped on an awkward cliff face that they had to cling to or die. This flood would last for hours. If either woman lost her balance for even an instant during those hours, she would die.

Unable to help Debbie and Amy, Walker and the other men hiked upstream to view the flow where it entered the Narrows. Greg Schill had a hard time now. In his haste to escape the flood he had outrun his flip flops. Now he limped tenderly on bare feet on the sharp schist. Soon the others ahead of Schill sent back one of their number with another one's sandals on loan.

Upstream, the men now saw, the flood filled the much wider section of canyon from wall to wall. This was one hell of a lot of water.

And boulders, rocks, sand, silt, trees, dead animals...and now two perfectly good trucks, five river boats, two dozen oars, six rowing frames, everyone's personal gear, et cetera, et cetera. Now and then a cactus emerged from the flood, rolling to the surface as if desperate for a gulp of air. Several species of cacti swirled past the six watchers as if in some hallucinogenic vision of desert hell.

Walker stared at this flood for several seconds before the reality sank in. He reached into the pocket of his Patagonia Baggies, found the GMC's keys, pulled them out, and studied them. Then he admitted, "I guess we won't be needing these any more." He tossed the keys into the racing slurry.

About an hour later, the AzRA guides hiked upstream with ropes, wondering if they would find anyone to rescue. The six men had settled into ringside seats across from the two trapped women and were still trying to guess the volume of the flow of the now monster "creek." Debbie and Amy might as well have been clinging to a crater wall on the moon.

Near dusk, the flood ebbed. An hour or so later, Sam West strapped on two life jackets and swam across it. On the west side, West caught a rope tossed from the east. He set up a Tyrolean traverse to get both women back to the east side. After several hours of clinging to two-billion-year-old rock, West was Mister Right. He rigged each woman into the traverse. Guides on the opposite side hauled them over.

OARS' GMC 2-ton stake bed truck ended up on the opposite side of the Colorado River and partway down Diamond Creek Rapid. At very low water, it remains still visible, upside down and missing most of its parts. The nearby camp on the far side of the river over there now is called "Truck Stop."

A surprising postscript to the Diamond Creek mayhem of 1984 occurred 28 years later when boatman Doc Steve Nicholson running a Grand Canyon Expeditions dory trip spotted one of OARS' Domar "Zambezi" riverboats lost from the back of OARS' doomed stakebed. Just below Maxson Canyon, at River Mile 253, OARS' long-lost Domar "#5" lay silt-loaded and entangled in an ash tree and emerging from erosion in a cut bank. The Expedition crew struggled to liberate it. Then they towed and wrestled its ponderous weight back to Kanab.

On the other hand, after that mammoth flash flood, I never saw Debbie Jordan again.

Despite the ultrasaurus power of such flash floods, many naive hikers fail to believe that flash floods can truly wreak the unrelenting havoc that they are reputed to. One such camper, Bill Grundy, on the night of September 15, 1992, at Cottonwood Campground on the North Kaibab Trail sat in his tent and, even after noting that its floor was surging "just like my waterbed," laid down on his Thermarest.

A flashlight seemed to be bobbing in the rising flood racing past and under him. "It's flashing out," warned NPS Ranger Bryan Wisher from the dark. "You need to gather up your gear and get out of this spot."

"Since Bryan had seemed unconcerned," Grundy would later write, "I was in no hurry... [I sat] on my mattress figuring out how to pack up my gear."

Mud and water next engulfed Grundy's tent, ripped its stakes out of the ground, and started floating it away.

Grundy said, "I forced the tent down with my hands and knees...."

Earlier that evening, Ranger Bryan Wisher also had been listening to the rain. He knew that what little soil existed in this drainage was already saturated from several rains over the last week. Indeed, this very evening, he had warned campers here at Cottonwood about a potential flood. And now, as the rain fell harder and harder—the hardest rain he had ever heard in his life, he admitted to himself—he knew a flood had to be on its way.

Wisher radioed Phantom Ranch of an imminent flood. Then he yanked his boots on and grabbed a MagLite. Racing outside, Wisher stared in amazement: the eastern wall of Bright Angel Canyon appeared to be an endless sheet of cascading waterfalls. Realizing anew the extreme danger this posed to campers, he ran fifty yards downhill to the lower campground.

Wisher yelled at two campers still inside their tent. The pair was struggling to hold it down as a six-inch-deep flow of water pushed against it. "Leave your tent behind," Wisher yelled, "and head immediately to the Ranger Station at higher ground."

As the floodwater inched deeper across the campground, Wisher frantically ran to another campsite. He shouted the same instructions to its occupants.

During Wisher's scrambling, the flood rose. He found two more campers sitting on a picnic table surrounded by the flow. They were watching the flood rise and swirl around them as if the implications of the flood's final peak level were incomprehensible to them. Wisher instructed them on the run. "Get off that table and head to higher ground near the Ranger Station."

Running south, Wisher saw yet another flash flood hurtling down through the blackness of the normally dry drainage south of the ranger station. Across the flood, barely visible through the thundering rain, Wisher spotted a tent wrapped around a rock, pinned by the current. Was someone trapped inside that tent?

Trying to time his crossing so as to avoid getting hit by boulders or logs, Wisher listened for crashing rocks. What the hell? Wisher ran out into the flood, struggling to stay on his feet and angling his way downstream to the other side. The collapsed tent, he found, was empty, except for mud. Good. Now there existed only one more campsite in the upper campground that might lay in the floodplain.

Wisher recrossed the swollen new creek. Again he played a dangerous game of Russian roulette in trying mostly by luck alone to avoid being hit by rolling rocks and careening debris. He made it across. He ran to the north end of the campground. Visibility had diminished, it seemed, to about 10 feet.

Wisher strained his eyes to peer back across the wash. Penetrating the downpour, his Maglite beam caught a distorted yellow object in mid-flood.

It was Grundy's tent, now perched on a little island submerged and surrounded by racing flood waters. Inside the trapped tent a light burned. Wisher's stomach sank as he realized the implications of that light: Grundy was still inside that tent....

Again listening to the rocks crashing in the stream—as if to detect some sort of pattern—Wisher tried to time his crossing. Again he managed not to be hit by boulders or debris crashing through the waist deep flow. The flood level rose even higher as he reached the tent. Wisher screamed over the roar of the water to whomever was inside the tent, "Get out of this tent, now!"

As if in a very bad nightmare, the rising water chose this moment to engulf the yellow dome tent and float it downstream with Grundy still inside. The nylon death trap now wrapped around Wisher and pushed him downstream into deeper water and toward a six-foot waterfall that drained into Bright Angel Creek, now a river.

Grundy finally agreed to exit his tent. Desperate, Wisher and Grundy, now outside but still in his underwear, dragged it across the rising stream. Wisher dragged them both across the flood. Amazingly, the "trio" arrived on the shore unharmed.

Wisher sagged onto the bank exhausted.

"I credit him," Grundy would later write, "with saving my life."

Grundy, by the way, tells me (Ghiglieri) he is still using that same tent.

Later the following year, Secretary of the Interior Bruce Babbitt awarded Bryan Wisher the National Park Service's Valor Award for his heroic performance at Cottonwood. Wisher was credited with saving 28 lives.

Nearly three years later, on March 5, 1995, nonstop rains again pounded the Inner Canyon in the vicinity of Upper Granite Gorge. It poured all day and into the night.

Enough rain fell on the Canyon's huge north side to build the biggest flash flood since the 1966 super-monster in the upper drainages of Bright Angel and Crystal creeks. At about 11:00 p.m., the roar of this flood woke up Phantom Ranch employees as it ripped down the creek less than a hundred yards from their bunkhouse.

To everyone, this flood was a novelty. Some went outside and took pictures. Five employees—Leslie Aldrich, Julie Chaibineou, Stephanie Hettinger, Laura Tibbetts, and Wanda Woodbury (all in their mid-20s to early 30s)—walked the trail down to the bridge 200 yards upstream of the confluence with the Colorado River. They were keen to witness even more of Mother Nature's power where the great flood slammed into the river.

The creek, they saw, had already climbed to eight feet higher than normal. What a sight it must be, they agreed, where the flood pounds into the Colorado itself. The five walked to the confluence, first crossing the dry wash east of the creek. This was separated from the creek itself by a large delta-debris fan built in part by remnants of that mammoth 1966 flood. Indeed, this dry wash had been dry ever since then, almost thirty years....

The five women reached the confluence. It seemed anti-climactic. The two flows mixed with only a little turbulence and a lot of boring red foam.

Several minutes later, the women tried to retrace their route back. Now, however, the view was anything but anti-climactic. Floodwaters raged along the formerly dry (for the previous 29 years) east side of the delta. Operating under the hopeful disbelief that perhaps they were only disoriented and had walked west instead of east, the five women walked to the other side of the delta. Here the flood roared past far deeper and faster.

Suddenly all five women realized that they had trapped themselves on a shrinking island. If the flood rose much higher, the odds were that they would all die.

The rising flood had risen above and jumped the main drainage. It now cut around the delta, shrinking it. With the Colorado River to their south, the five were completely cut off from terra firma. But dredging up some optimism after finding that they had walked into an inescapable trap, they speculated that merely being stranded here for awhile might be the worst outcome of their error.

A desperate Phantom Rancher who had seen the trapped women now pounded on Phantom Ranch Ranger Patrick Suddath's door.

Suddath ran to survey their plight. Impressed, he radioed a request for assistance. Next he grabbed a throw bag and ropes from the ranger station and tried to get a rope out to the stranded women.

Several rangers were dispatched to hike down the South Kaibab Trail to help. Bryan Wisher, now the ranger at Indian Garden on the south side of the Canyon, received Suddath's distress call at 1:00 a.m. For Wisher this was deja vu, although this time the people at risk were not naive campers who refused to listen to him, but instead people he knew personally, some as friends. Maybe this flash flood would go more easily.

Wincing from the pain of a recently broken rib, Wisher gathered his gear. Next he recruited Jerry Chavez (NPS pumphouse operator and pipeline maintenance specialist), also a strong hiker, climber, and an assistant during Canyon medical emergencies and rescues. The two men ran out into the rain.

Garden Creek flowed a foot deep. The two men ran a couple of miles in the dark down the Bright Angel Trail. Wisher's rib hurt with each step. In the lead, he stopped at Pipe Creek. It now roared past them as a sluice of rocks and debris. In the worst places it flowed more than four feet deep. This, Wisher thought to himself, was not good. Not good at all.

As Wisher stood in the rain and radioed a ranger on the North Rim to check what was happening with the weather there, Chavez ran past Wisher and into Pipe Creek. The rain, this North Rim ranger told him, had begun to turn to snow. This meant that the floods in Bright Angel Creek might stabilize in the next two to four hours.

As Wisher listened he also watched in disbelief as the flood instantly swept Chavez off his feet. He disappeared into the flood. Wisher ran downstream alongside it. Chavez surfaced. Wisher helped his friend struggle out of the current. Chavez had lost his radio. Both men felt badly shaken.

But their friends' lives were still at stake, so they braced up against each other and entered the flood. For every foot they struggled across, the current shoved them several feet downstream. They finally made it across. Heading down the Bright Angel Trail again, they had to cross their own personal flood four more harrowing times.

A half hour later they crossed the big steel bridge to the north side of the Canyon. The two men found the situation at Phantom Ranch anything but improved. Rain continued to pound down. Bright Angel Creek now looked like the Colorado River. The flood slapped the bottom of the campground bridge walkway. The roar was incredibly loud as boulders crashed against one another in the current. Logs, trees and other debris flushed down in a freight train of lethal weapons. From even one hundred feet away the two men felt the ground vibrating due to nonstop concussions of rolling boulders in the flood.

The highest point of the five women's delta, normally 12–14 feet above the creek bed, now stood only three feet short of being covered by the flood. Bright Angel Creek itself now flowed at 3,000 to 4,000 cfs, much higher than many historic low flows of the Colorado River itself. The five trapped women now huddled together in the dark on an area shrunken from more than an acre to only 30 by 50 feet.

Seeing Wisher and Chavez across the flood, several of the trapped women now jumped up and down and yelled for joy. Wisher looked back at them on their shrinking postage stamp of real estate and his stomach sank.

Meanwhile Suddath had been trying to heave and float a throwrope out to the island, but with no luck. Wisher studied the horrendous, 100-foot-wide flood and decided that any attempt to have the trapped women cross this "creek" via a rope was out of the question anyway; being in that flood and fixed to a rope would spell certain death. Wisher again considered the report of snow, instead of rain, falling on the rim. According to logic and experience, this flood should be peaking, maybe even now ready to subside.

Wisher took over the operations role. Instead of extricating the women, getting life jackets and supplies to them to prevent hypothermia and maybe prevent drowning would now be the rescue team's top priority. Thus equipped, the women could maybe ride out this storm. Any attempt to extricate them—given that a helicopter would be impossible to use in the dark and in this storm—should be viewed as an absolute last resort to be tried only if the floodwaters threatened unequivocally to carry them off. For now, the five were safe on their tiny island of delta. Messing up that safety unnecessarily would not be smart. Still, Wisher instructed the trail crew to don life jackets, hike downstream of the delta, and set themselves up on shore to be ready with throw ropes in case the flood flushed anyone into the river.

Next Wisher tied a rock to parachute cord. He yelled to the women over the roar that a cord was on its way. Wisher threw the rock out to the island.

Wisher's rock clattered onto the delta. A woman grabbed it and reeled it in. Attached to it was an 11 mm rope. Wisher screamed instructions to the trapped women on how to tie the rope around the mesquite tree on their island. Next, using a karabiner attached to this rope, he sent life jackets, a radio, and a pack with food and supplies out to the island.

The women radioed that they were freezing. Wisher's crew—strengthened now by the arrivals of Rangers Nick Herring, David Trevino, Craig Patterson, and Todd Van Alstyne, who had just descended the scary South Kaibab Trail on this dark and stormy night—next sent over clothing, rain gear, a tent, sleeping bags, and a lantern. Again, Wisher was betting that keeping the five trapped people warm was far safer than risking anyone's life in trying to get them off at night. After dawn, he said, a helicopter evacuation could be safely attempted. But, again, if the flood rose much higher, the rescue team would be forced to try a risky emergency evacuation off the island across that horrendous, raging, 100-foot-wide flood.

Wisher bet right. At 6:30 a.m., a helicopter lifted all five women off their island safely. None had been injured. And, yes, after all, the women agreed, the flood, where it hit the Colorado, had been impressive.

When any of us spends enough time in any one place, the dangers of that place seem to pale over time. For some of us, some real dangers eventually vanish altogether. We are prone, given enough time, to not only saying but believing things like: "I always run this stop sign; there shouldn't even be one here at this corner." The same process of familiarity breeding contempt seems to erode the respect of some Canyoneers for the possibility of Southwestern flash floods. Consider the following example.

George Mancuso was a little guy harboring a big love affair with the Little Colorado River and its confluence with the Colorado. It was, as he would admit, the only place where he found "true peace." The 5' 5", 120-pound terrier of a Canyoneer had "discovered" the Little Colorado. As a professional photographer he had hiked into this region of Grand Canyon on dozens of backpacking trips to shoot it in its various moods. By some counts, he spent one week down here every month. For years.

Mancuso first saw Grand Canyon in 1972 at age 17 while visiting from his home in New Jersey. He began his first photo shoot in 1986 on a project he called "Granite Visions," one which would not only become his business but also seal his fate. More than 90 percent of his work would be below the rims. And as Mancuso racked up his 6,000 miles of hiking in and out of various parts of Grand Canyon, he became adept not just at meeting, but also anticipating, the challenges the Canyon poses. And maybe even discounting a few.

Mancuso looked for new angles that would make his Canyon photography more commercially viable. He sold his art to magazines, calendars, as framed prints, and for post cards. He showed slide shows at Northern Arizona University and so on. He likened himself as the spiritual heir to the redoubtable Kolb brothers, Ellsworth and Emery, whose daring and energy had fostered inspired black and white photography during the early 20th century of various arcane and recondite places of ethereal beauty within Grand Canyon. Many Kolb photos today remain the stuff of legend. Despite Mancuso's successes (and notions), however, profitability remained elusive. To fix this, he hit upon the concept of "La Femme de Grand Canyon."

Mancuso advertised on his website: "I'm looking for outdoor, athletic women and models to assist me in backpacking and photography trips inside Grand Canyon. The theme and purpose is to capture on film a unique portfolio of prints displaying the sensual, artistic, natural, and spiritual expressions of the female form within a beautiful outdoor setting."

Perhaps not surprisingly, women had not lined up and swamped Mancuso as applicants for this job. On the other hand, his ad did produce. California-born Linda Brehmer was a biologist and horse-lover and budding author of poetry and fiction with a master's degree in education. She also was a former science teacher with 17 years experience teaching at various levels. She volunteered to help Mancuso with his "La Femme" project. She "loved living things" and ultimately developed a "very close" relationship with Mancuso, notes her brother Jim Brehmer to the *Arizona Daily Sun* (August 28, 2001). Linda Brehmer became Mancuso's friend and hiking partner into the Little Colorado. Their first trip here, and Linda's first in Grand Canyon, had taken place only two months earlier in June. For Brehmer, this tributary system of the Colorado became ever more special. And the lithe 51-year-old was also a good model for photography except possibly for one tiny detail:

Brehmer had a tattoo of a badger's paw on her right shoulder.

On August 18, Linda Brehmer's two sons notified the Park and the Coconino County Sheriff's Office that Mancuso and Brehmer were 10 days overdue from their July 31-August 8, 2001 photo shoot somewhere in the Salt Trail Canyon. Coordinated search efforts launched the next day.

Why was this pair of idealistic backpackers ten days late?

Mancuso had made a career not just of Canyon photography but also in frequently returning long overdue from his forays into the Canyon. Just one year earlier he had been reported overdue. The Park launched a search for him. Ultimately he was located on a river trip on which he had hitchhiked a long ride instead of hiking out. The Park spanked him with a citation. Mancuso's normal modus operandi for his hiking trips involved skipping the entire permit process so that no searcher would have an idea of where he was. In short, Mancuso had assumed the role of a maverick whose hard won backcountry knowledge seemed to imbue in him a self-justified, rugged individualist's disdain for authority other than his own. None of this history would help in locating him or Brehmer.

On August 19, searchers located Mancuso's Isuzu Rodeo with his vanity plate "KENOBI" (for STAR WARS' Obi Wan Kenobi) parked at the head of Salt Trail Canyon, 14.3 miles west of the Gap on Highway 89. This precipitous canyon houses the ancestral Salt Trail route of Hopis to access the Little Colorado, the sacred *Sipaapuni*, and, a half dozen miles beyond, the Hopi salt mines along the Colorado itself beyond the Little Colorado. The "trail" (= route) is rough, steep, and poses significant exposure, and it is believed guarded by Hopi spiritual beings.

Coconino County Sheriff's Search and Rescue had called in dozens of personnel to help in this search. But one of the main obstacles posed against a successful search for Brehmer and Mancuso was the continued monsoonal weather. A sudden monsoonal downpour on the afternoon of August 7 had pounded this local region of Navajoland with such intensity that it filled every wash for miles, overflowed a few, and created a sheet-like flood that roared westward over the surface of Arizona State Highway 89, stranding many vehicles within its wide swath. This flood continued westerly and funneled narrowly into tributaries of the Little Colorado, one of them Big Canyon.

Most of the experienced search personnel either secretly or overtly suspected that the formula of "two hikers long overdue in a region of deep and precipitous slot canyons during August monsoons" equals "flash flood fatalities."

Wary of additional floods, searchers had helicoptered into the Little Colorado Canyon—still running at flood stage—to land at the foot of the Salt Trail. Here on high ground and tucked into a protective circle of tamarisks searchers found Mancuso's and Brehmer's camp. Their sleeping mats, food, kitchen, photo gear, seven, 2-liter, square Nalgene water bottles, et cetera, remained neatly laid out and ready to use. The two hikers' sleeping pads were positioned a few feet apart, suggesting

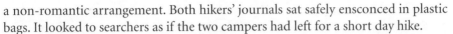

a non-romantic arrangement. Both hikers' journals sat safely ensconced in plastic bags. It looked to searchers as if the two campers had left for a short day hike.

As Ranger Bil Vandergraff entered the camp, it only took one second for the hair to lift on the back of his neck. The layers of blown sand and tamarisk needles shrouding the hikers' gear told him in a glance: There was no hope of finding them alive.

When searchers perused Mancuso's and Brehmer's diaries for clues as to where they might be, they found Brehmer's final entry (August 6) stated that tomorrow she and Mancuso planned to hike to the Emerald Pool and she wanted to wash her hair in clean water. As clues go, this one was hot. The only hitch was none of the many searchers had ever seen or even heard of this "Emerald Pool," and no one knew where it was.

The Park's search and rescue coordinator Ken Phillips now phoned Canyoneer and author Scott Thybony. Did he know, Phillips asked, where the "Emerald Pool" was?

As much as Thybony had hiked the Canyon, which was quite a bit, and as much he knew George Mancuso, which also was a lot, he had to admit (in his unpublished Field Notes) that this "Emerald Pool" remained beyond his knowledge at this time (fellow hiker Jim Ohlman, however, supposedly did know of it and later told Thybony).

By coincidence, the next morning a friend named Steve Mullaney visited Scott's wife Sandy and told her about a friend of his, Theodora Homewytewa, a Hopi curer of the Bear Clan of Third Mesa. Homewytewa, a *poosi'ytaqa* ("one who sees"), had divined the precise locations of several lost things over the years for people and for police, including a lost little girl. The next day Sandy Thybony, armed with an old 15-minute topographic map, went to visit Homewytewa.

Theodora Homewytewa did not understand the graphics or symbolism of a topo map, nor did she possess any experience with the Salt Trail or the Little Colorado (which through a U.S. Governmental screw-up more than a century past had given this sacred Hopi region to the Navajos). Sandy tried to explain what the wavy lines meant. Homewytewa had trouble orienting the map. Theodora felt extremely reluctant to "find" Mancuso and Brehmer because she knew the act of divining would leave her exhausted for days. Wiped out. Maybe sick again. She had been so sick after divining in the past that her uncle had advised her to refuse to look for any things again because things can be replaced. But people, he added, live only once and cannot be replaced. Homewytewa had moved to Flagstaff in part to escape the demands of being a seer.

Sandy encouraged her. Homewytewa reluctantly took the map. She had to wait "for permission" which revealed itself just as if she was "watching a TV set" mentally. Homewytewa returned the topo the next day with a small "x" drawn on it at the confluence of Big Canyon and the Little Colorado. Scott Thybony stared at this "x" and nodded. Although he had never been there, this was one of the locations he had suspected for the mysterious "Emerald Pool."

Meanwhile Sandy explained, "Theodora also had strong feelings that Mancuso and Brehmer had not been getting along. They had been arguing. Brehmer had wanted to leave the canyon sooner than he did." Homewytewa had explained:

She wanted to stay in camp but he wanted to go. He got angry and walked off, and she followed him. They went up. They knew it was coming. It was happening right there in front of my face, It was fear or pain—and being tumbled. There was tumbling and the taste of mud. Oh, I had to stop it and begin praying.

Scott decided to trek into the Little Colorado, to help and maybe see what went wrong. Sandy called him with Theorodora Homewytewa's advice to not go that day but to instead wait another and hike with a companion. Meanwhile, as the days had passed, the small army of searchers had found nothing beyond Brehmer's and Mancuso's abandoned camp. When Thybony suggested to searchers they consider focusing on the area revealed to Homewytewa in her vision, he was met with skepticism. A few searchers now thought Thybony had gone off the deep end by free-lancing with a Hopi seer.

Reputedly, one Park ranger suggested, "We may have to rein him in…"

Homewytewa gave Scott a small bag of *hooma*, white ceremonial cornmeal to sprinkle at the head of Salt Trail Canyon. On August 22 Scott Thybony and veteran Canyoneer Tony Williams got permits from the Navajo tribe, sprinkled the hooma, and began hiking the 2.5 miles and 2,400 vertical feet down the Salt Trail.

According to Hopi cosmology, the first War Twin turned himself to stone at the rim of Salt Trail Canyon to mark the correct spot to descend towards the Little Colorado. The two hikers espied a water jug left near the Hopi shrine of this younger War Twin. Later, just before camping atop the Supai, the hikers passed hematite pictographs, one of them a bear paw symbolizing Theodora Homewytewa's Bear Clan. The next morning they descended steeply through the Redwall Limestone, passing the cave of *Massau'u*, the Hopi death spirit and guardian of the land— the first being the Hopis had encountered once they had emerged from the Third World via the Sipaapuni into today's Fourth World. The handprint of *Massau'u's* in hematite marked the cave as his. These beings of myth turned themselves to stone at critical points in the journey to help future travelers find their way. The second War Twin chose to become a rock that served as a needed rappel anchor, just above the final cliff near the river.

Shortly beyond this, at the confluence of Salt Trail Canyon and the Little Colorado, the two met Deputy Aaron Dick of the Coconino County Sheriff's Department and Park Ranger Greg Moore who had been inserted the previous night by helicopter and now awaited additional search teams. With Dick and Moore were

K.J. Glover, Ranger Mike McGinnis, and Coconino County Crime Investigator Tom Ross. Dick and Moore had expected Thybony and Williams but considered them an unknown factor in this frustrating search. Again, no one among this expanding band of searchers had known where Mancuso's "Emerald Pool" was. But Thybony possessed a secret weapon. A map with a small "x" marking the spot.

Or did it?

At least, Thybony reflected, he was now working within the best search and rescue team he had ever seen. Aaron Dick soon impressed Thybony with his accurate observations. Maybe all this would succeed. Thybony wondered again about Homewytewa's predictions.

Had Brehmer and Mancuso been at odds with one another as she had predicted? One could not draw this conclusion from Mancuso's diary. His entries revealed he thought things were going pretty well with Linda. He seemed hopeful that Brehmer might continue to work out even better as they continued together. Brehmer's diary, however, was written by a person living on a different planet from Mancuso. Her entries revealed her thoughts that things so far had been interesting, but that Mancuso was definitely not someone with whom she wanted to continue sharing her life. This likely would be her last hike with him. She wanted to move on in a new direction.

Big Canyon debouches into the Little Colorado about one mile upstream of the mouth of Salt Trail Canyon. As photographer and journalist Elias Butler would later describe, Big Canyon is aptly named. He notes in the *Arizona Daily Sun* (January 18, 2002), 5 months later: "In places it's 3,000 feet deep and characterized by sheer walls. Big Canyon cuts a gash every bit as impressive as Grand Canyon itself. Access is difficult, and if you get into trouble here, you're out of luck."

The confluence of Big Canyon and the Little Colorado, now running pale chocolate, stands guarded by a phalanx of huge cuboid boulders, lost toy blocks of some Titan's child.

Here at the foot of Big Canyon—Theodora Homewytewa's "x" on the map—the searchers probed the muddy mayhem of a debris field of flattened horsetails and tamarisks and one dead mallard that constituted the aftermath of a mammoth flash flood.

Aaron Dick spotted a dirty rag that had wrapped around a tamarisk about eight feet higher than the streambed. He yanked it free. It proved to be a nylon T-shirt sporting a Teva logo. The photos from Mancuso's film left in camp would reveal this to be Mancuso's shirt.

Reaching Mancuso's beloved Emerald Pool and travertine waterfall less than 200 yards upcanyon past Big Canyon's boulders, clogged tamarisks, mud pits, little pools, and waterfalls demanded route finding, scrambling, and bushwhacking. All the trees had been bent downstream. Mud coated everything. The place reeked of body decomposition.

A bit more climbing revealed that the process of escaping Emerald Pool in a hurry would demand either a pair of quick wings or squirrel-like climbing prowess.

Continued searching in the debris field below uncovered nothing until about 10:00 a.m. By now the telltale rank odor of decay waxed and cloyed ever stronger in the searchers' nostrils. Thybony climbed a boulder 100 yards downstream of the Emerald Pool for a better view. His searching eye was arrested by a human body wrapped tightly around the base of a tamarisk just below him. His heart sinking and his brain wondering how the hell Theodora Homewytewa could possibly know what she knew, Scott stared at the body battered and stripped as if by miles of rushing slurry. The corpse still wore boots.

Whose body was this? Deputy Aaron Dick approached and spotted a tattoo on its right shoulder. It was the paw of a badger.

Elias Butler made a recon trek to Emerald Pool five months after the August 7th flood. There, next to the pool, Butler found Mancuso's tripod nearly completely buried in sediment. Yes, one of the last things Mancuso had done prior to being swept into infinity was take yet another photo.

The Hopi interpretation of Linda Brehmer's written intent to wash her hair in clear water carries a far more important significance than one of mere body hygiene. As noted by Canyoneer Evan Widling who has hiked the Salt Trail with Mancuso, "Hopi ceremonially wash their hair with yucca suds at birth, marriage, and death. The Hopi interpretation was that she [Brehmer] was 'washing her hair for *Massau'u.*' This applies to the locale they were in, I think, near *Massau'u's* Cave." Again, *Massau'u* is the Hopi Spirit of the Dead.

The search for George Mancuso, whom Widling noted was never very attentive to the Hopi cosmology Widling tried to impart to him, continued for days longer. On August 26, 2001 the Grand Canyon Search and Rescue team began operations on the north side of the Little Colorado. They had inserted three of the five teams planned that day by helicopter before they heard by radio Greg Woodall's news.

Woodall, a former Dories boatman and archeologist and now part of the Park's Trail Crew, had just stopped at the confluence of the Little Colorado along with the Park river trip. Woodall noticed a concentration of ravens busy on the shoreline of the large alluvial island immediately below the confluence. Curious, he investigated. As the ravens reluctantly hopped and flitted away, Woodall spotted a pair of hiking boots partly buried in a tangle of branches and other recent flash flood debris about five feet above river level. Attached to the boots were legs.

Woodall informed his fellow rangers Bil Vandergraff and David Desrosiers. They in turn advised the searchers several miles away on the rim of the Little Colorado Gorge to call off all searches. A helicopter now delivered a new team to the confluence. Using photo documentation (Mancuso might have approved...), the team excavated George Mancuso from the debris. He was all there but for a few pecks donated to the ravens and except for his mandible having separated. The team body-bagged Mancuso and transported him to the South Rim Helibase. From there, it was transported to Phoenix, following Linda Brehmer's body, for more positive identification via dental records.

How did a Canyoneer with George Mancuso's experience die this way? Could he not have predicted it? Had he noticed a forewarning to make a safer decision about where to linger? Because both victims were found with their boots on, Thybony guessed that the two might have been exploring slightly upstream of the Emerald Pool in the sheer narrows. Yet climbing above the pool would have required fording the creek, which also might have meant removing boots. To continue upward, boots or no boots, would have demanded exposed rock climbing over steep, slick and polished travertine and Redwall Limestone to ascend to the lip of the twelve-foot falls. We doubt Brehmer, as new as she was to Canyoneering, would have tried this.

Did the pair receive some forewarning of the flash flood? At the Emerald Pool the din of the nearby Little Colorado River might have muted some of the flood's roar down Big Canyon. Visual clues may have been no better. The storm arrived from the northeast, instead of the usual southwest. The bottom line? Mancuso and Brehmer may not have heard or seen any hint of monsoon activity until too late. Or instead Mancuso simply may have let his guard drop because Brehmer really wanted to wash her hair in clean water. Either way, the 40- to 50-foot high tsunami blasting out of Big Canyon would have proved an inescapable nightmare.

"I'm obsessed," George Mancuso once told Annette McGivney for the June 1997 edition of *Backpacker Magazine*: "My relationship with the Canyon is the single-most important love affair of my life." Mancuso's last big fling with the Canyon at the Little Colorado had turned out to be an 8.5-mile death tumble in a monster flash flood of 9,000 cfs that descended 1,303 feet from his Emerald Pool in Big Canyon here to this island at the Confluence. Ironically, it is a very good bet that had Mancuso been asked in life where he would like his body to come to its final rest, he would have said "the confluence of the Little Colorado and the Colorado," the region that had captivated his spirit years earlier and dominated his life ever since.

Again, friends of Mancuso agreed that he had admitted the Little Colorado confluence was the only place where he ever found "true peace." These friends want to exhume Mancuso and lay him "at peace" back where Greg Woodall found him. Let Mancuso fly with the ravens....

As a postscript, Mancuso never had deluded himself that his obsession was without risk. In the *Backpacker* article noted above, Mancuso stressed that he was never out to conquer the Canyon. "Anyone who tries to do that," he said, "will definitely get swallowed."

Indeed, he acknowledged his risk of dying in the Canyon in a July 7, 1984 letter to his hiking mentor Harvey Butchart:

> *Harvey ~ even as a young hiker/scrambler I share your thought about the possibility of ending our lives in similar fashion yet ~ if I realized I died attempting or doing something from within my inner self, I'd accept that. It's not a wish, but just a natural accepted thought.*

> *Take care ~ George*

Neither Grand Canyon nor the American Southwest in general is the only place on Earth where flash floods wreak havoc. The lesson in this is that such havoc is not merely a product of cloudbursts and canyons. It is more a product of people naive to the ways of Mother Nature voluntarily placing themselves in these canyons when Mother Nature floods them. In the Swiss Alps, for example, a relatively new sport called "canyoning" has caught on in a big way. Rather than hiking or boating down a canyon though, "canyoning" includes rappelling, jumping, sliding, clambering, and swimming down steep narrow canyons. In Switzerland alone, 50,000 people do this per year. In early August of 1999, almost two dozen international thrill-seekers on a commercial canyoning descent run by Adventure World had dropped into central Switzerland's Saxeten River Gorge and were clambering down it. From upstream a black wall of water from heavy rains cascaded into the group killing at least 21 people and injuring several others. Grand Canyon's flash flood fatalities pale in comparison. Perhaps this is due to sheer luck. Then again, maybe just enough smart people have been in the right place at the right time to prevent such mass drownings.

What are the major take-home lessons regarding flash floods? When it comes to predicting a flash flood the question most often boils down to "when?" During the monsoon season from July through September hundreds of people place themselves at risk daily. The lure of Grand Canyon's spectacular slot canyons convinces many visitors that a Canyon visit is not complete without hiking these must-sees. On hiking and river trips alike intense pressure from trip members or high-paying clients to enter slot canyons despite warning signs of potential flooding commonly supersedes good judgment by commercial guides, private boatmen, and hiking leaders. The "we may never get this chance again" mentality spurs a gambler's dilemma to risk death for a visit or photo. Unless hike leaders learn how to play those odds safely and say "no" when the danger is imminent, it seems inevitable to us that someday an entire hiking party in Grand Canyon will be tumbled and mashed into oblivion. This almost has happened already, with near misses of mass disaster measured in mere minutes. Or, as some witnesses insist, mere seconds.

Because so few people have witnessed the power of such flash floods when confined between narrow walls, the extreme menace they pose remains underestimat-

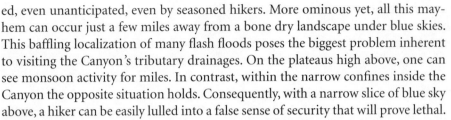

ed, even unanticipated, even by seasoned hikers. More ominous yet, all this mayhem can occur just a few miles away from a bone dry landscape under blue skies. This baffling localization of many flash floods poses the biggest problem inherent to visiting the Canyon's tributary drainages. On the plateaus high above, one can see monsoon activity for miles. In contrast, within the narrow confines inside the Canyon the opposite situation holds. Consequently, with a narrow slice of blue sky above, a hiker can be easily lulled into a false sense of security that will prove lethal.

What constitutes reasonable advice to tip the odds of the "monsoon gamble" in favor of the hiker? For starters, if black thunderheads litter the sky or it is already raining, *Stay out.*

But suppose the slice of sky above is blue or the clouds are white cotton balls? Well, all but one of the 14 known flash flood deaths in Grand Canyon have occurred between July and September. Moreover, "typical" monsoon storms are afternoon events. It usually takes a significant flash flood 1 to 4 hours to descend to river level from high up a major drainage. Although the data are limited, of 11 monsoon flash floods recorded by Sjors Horstman in Bright Angel Creek over the 12 years at Phantom Ranch beginning in the late 1980s, all (80+%) but two occurred during afternoon or early evening except for two during the middle of the night. We also know some of the biggest recent monsoon floods elsewhere in the Canyon also were afternoon or evening events, nearly catching whole groups of river runners and hikers (in Diamond Creek in 1984, for example, and Havasu in 1997 and 2008). Ditto for the eleven people killed in Antelope Canyon. *Venturing into these canyons during the afternoon or evening is significantly more risky.* In short, if one is going to enter a slot canyon during the monsoon season, one should only consider doing it during the morning—then get the hell out. If any hint of rain exists, forget it altogether.

A final complication: Flash floods can happen outside the monsoon season. Indeed, the largest, rapid-making flash floods with huge debris flows tend to be nighttime, late-winter or early spring events, where heavy rains cause abrupt melting of a snow pack. The bottom line here is, if such storms are happening, take all precautions not only to remain *out* of tributary canyons, but also to stay away from the mouth of a tributary canyon.

What if, despite everything, you are facing an oncoming flash flood? First, *always* look for potential escape routes during your hike. Second, many floods can be escaped by scrambling sideways and upwards from the drainage bottom. Sometimes only a few seconds are all one needs. Third, although this may sound preposterous, many flash floods also can be outrun—in an open field sprint—by a healthy adult. If the route downward demands tedious or tricky down climbing or boulder hopping, however, it is better to seek sanctuary laterally. As you enter any steep, long and narrow, boulder-choked drainage, ponder how those boulders got there to begin with then seriously consider not proceeding beyond any section you cannot run through or climb out of in a hurry. Above all, stay vigilant for those subtle clues we mentioned earlier: a sudden muddying of the creek, an abrupt muddy smell of clay and other minerals, or a sudden shift of wind or sound in the air, especially a distant roar. For each of the many flash floods we have personally witnessed and for those witnessed by others, a deep roar often has preceded the wall of debris flow by as much as a minute. Sometimes even longer. Such a roar— during weather that could give birth to cloudbursts—is about as close to receiving God's personal warning on a silver platter as one can get.

As now Sergeant Aaron Dick, commander of the Coconino County (the 2nd largest county in the USA) Sheriff's Department Search and Rescue Teams, concludes (in the *Arizona Daily Sun*, September 2, 2001) regarding whether or not to risk hiking in a flash flood-prone area for the sake of a hike or a photo, "If there's any doubt, don't do it. It's not worth getting a good picture if you're going to get whacked by a flood."

None of the above advice is intended to discourage canyon hiking. Indeed, exploring side canyons may be the most rewarding way to experience Grand Canyon. Our advice is intended to encourage every hiker to take the time to heed the mood of Mother Nature before playing Russian roulette. Remember and respect the natural forces that formed slot canyons to begin with. Save your real gambling for the slot machines; you have a lot less to lose.

ALL RIVER RUNNERS

On the afternoon of Thursday, September 11, a flash flood occurred in Phantom and Bright Angel Creeks. This event swept two adults, one male and one female, down Bright Angel Creek. Neither of these victims could swim, and it is possible they were carried into the Colorado. Please be aware of this situation and be on the lookout for any evidence of the victims in eddies below Phantom Ranch.

Table 4. VICTIMS OF FATAL FLASH FLOODS IN GRAND CANYON

Name, age	Date	Location	Circumstances
Lwi ("Snake"), elderly	January 2, 1910	Havasupai Village at confluence of Cataract and Hualapai Canyons	

During one of the most severe storms in 20th century Arizona, a warm rain (2.3 inches) fell during December 31–January 1 and melted a heavy snowpack. The most destructive Havasu flash flood known of many occurred as the flow breached four earthen dams built by ranchers on the Coconino Plateau to create a 20-foot-high wall of water in Cataract Canyon, filling it wall to wall at **dawn.** *A blind and feeble Supai woman, wife of deceased Chief Navajo,* **was unable to flee** *and drowned, as did about 20 horses. The flood destroyed Supai Village at a time when most Havasupai were absent (luckily) on the plateau. It also downcut Havasu Falls by 30 feet and Beaver Falls by 33–50 feet. Melis, T. M, W. M. Phillips, R. H. Webb & D. J. Bills.1996.* When the Blue-green Waters Turn Red. *USGS Water Resources Investigations Report 96-4096, pp. 14-17.*

| Claud Hallmark, 20 Claud's horse | Summer (August?), 1921 | Big Wash, 6 miles N of Bundyville | |

During an **afternoon** *monsoon storm, Hallmark* **rode his horse** *into a flash flooding wash in the evening to retrieve coats from a wagon on the opposite side for his sister and mother. This happened at the Hallmark homestead, 6 miles north of Bundyville and was bisected by Big Wash. The bodies of Hallmark and his horse were found the next day. Nellie I. Cox. 1998.* Footprints on the Arizona Strip *(with Accent on Bundyville).*

| Gwe Gthgwaya, 78 | August 2, 1928 | Havasupai Village (present location) | |

A monsoon storm sent yet another destructive flash flood down Havasu at **noon.** *Gwe Gthgwaya, wife of Chief Manakaja,* **fled the flood** *but was* **pinned** *by the current against a* **barbed wired fence** *and drowned. Melis, T. M, W. M. Phillips, R. H. Webb & D. J. Bills.1996.* When the Blue-green Waters Turn Red. *USGS Water Resources Investigations Report 96-4096. p. 20.*

| Roger Clubb, Sr., 36 Roger Clubb, Jr., 8 | August 3, 1963 | Bright Angel Trail, 400 yards uphill from Indian Garden | |

During **afternoon,** *a ten-foot wall of water and mud exploded from the canyon immediately upstream engulfing the Clubbs of Vancouver, British Colombia, killing both father and son* **as they hiked.** *(see text)* Arizona Daily Sun, *August 5 & 7, 1963.* Arizona Republic, *August 4, 6, 7, 1963. Memorandum for the Superintendent, August 1, 1945.*

| Walter A. Jaskowiak, II, 24 Miriam Leigh Epstein, 26 | August 21, 1992 | Horn Creek Canyon (River Mile 90.25) | |

The bodies of Jaskowiak of Mountain View, California and Epstein of Sunnyvale, California were found in the bottom of lower Horn Creek Canyon. They and their gear had been deposited by one or two flash flood(s), most likely on August 21 and/or 22, when significant rain fell on days whose temperatures reached 110 degrees in the shade. Reconstruction of this incident suggests that Jaskowiak had dragged Epstein, possibly unconscious from a fall on the Tonto Trail, to **seek shade under the ledges of Tapeats Sandstone** *in upper Horn Creek Canyon* **during afternoon**, *where the flash flood hit them. (see text)* Arizona Republic, *August 28, 1992.* Coconino County Sheriff's Department #92-08-00315. McGibben, S. E. 1992. Forensic Entomology Report, AFOSI Comunication, file #921815D6-S719048, September 14. District 18/RFC, Norton AFB, CA 92409. *Incident report #92-3020*

Patty Moran, 40   September 11, 1997   Phantom Creek
John Moran, 40

The Morans of Metairie (New Orleans), Louisiana, plus Patty Moran's brother, John McCue, age 36 of Chicago, were **hiking in the narrow canyon** *during* **afternoon** *when they were hit by a chest-high wall of "thick, dark, red mud." Both Morans drowned. (see text)* Arizona Daily Sun, *September 12, 1997.* Williams-Grand Canyon News, *September 24, 1997.* Arizona Republic, *September 13 & 14 & October 5, 1997.* The Times-Picayune, *September 14, 16 &19, 1997. Incident report #97-4142*

George Lamont Mancuso, 46   August 7, 2001   Little Colorado/Big Canyon
Linda Brehmer, 51

On August 18, NPS SAR personnel found that Mancuso and Brehmer of Flagstaff, Arizona had left their gear in camp at the confluence of Salt Trail Canyon and the Little Colorado. Major flash floods scoured the Little Colorado and several tributaries on the **afternoon** *of August 7 during the pair's un-permitted hike for Mancuso's "La Femme de Grand Canyon" photo shoot. Mancuso was an "expert" remote Canyon hiker with a passion for the Little Colorado Gorge. 2 weeks later, on August 23, Scott Thybony found Brehmer's body, identified by Deputy Aaron Dick, wrapped around a tamarisk below Emerald Pool, in Big Canyon, a steep, narrow, boulder-choked drainage offering limited high ground. Days later NPS boatman Greg Woodall found Mancuso's body on the island at the confluence of the Little Colorado and Colorado rivers. (see text)* Arizona Daily Sun, *August 21, 22, 24, 25, 27 & 28, September 1 & 2, 2001 & January 8, 2002. Personal interviews with Aaron Dick, Evan Widling, Scott Thybony & Bil Vandergraff. Incident report #01-2535*

Melvin Pesata, 39   August 10, 2001   Hualapai Canyon/Havasu
Denice Cooper, 40
Aaron Pesata, 2

During **evening**, *en route to the Havasupai Peach festival, Pesata and Cooper and their four children Aaron, Christa Cooper, Drey Pesata, and Yvonne Cooper of Dulce, New Mexico, became separated* **as they hiked**; *the latter three going ahead and linking up with a Boy Scout group. Boy Scout leader Jim Furgo gathered all the kids onto a high ledge because of a storm. The 7 scouts had been planning to hike up Hualapai Canyon that night but got nervous due to storm signs and instead backed a mile downcanyon to a much wider area. Meanwhile the three hikers behind in Hualapai Canyon's narrows were hit by a flood that Furgo described as a 20-foot-high wall of water that "sounded like a 747 jetliner." The three victims' bodies were recovered 3.5 miles upstream of Supai Village.* Arizona Daily Sun, *August 14, 2001.* Arizona Republic, *August 18, 2001.*

This page left blank.

Chapter Five

The Killer Colorado

I never want to see it again anywhere. Near the Grand Cañon it probably will remain unvisited for many years again, as it has nothing to recommend it but its general desolation as a study for the geologist....What I have seen of Arizona I do not consider worth settling. As a disgusted woodchopper put it: "The whole damned Territory is a Bilk."

John Colton Sumner confided this appraisal of the Colorado River to his journal on August 31, 1869. Sumner had only one day earlier fulfilled his contract as head boatman for John Wesley Powell on the first-ever river trip of deliberate exploration down the Canyons of the Colorado in 1869. Upon exiting Grand Canyon after 98 days of exploration beginning in Green River, Wyoming—and also having survived one of the most harrowing journeys in the annals of North American exploration—Sumner had earned the right to express an opinion. Nor was his opinion formed in haste. He had just spent 26 days thoroughly convincing himself that nothing of material worth could possibly exist in this 1,000-cubic-mile hole in the ground that some fool (it was not named by John Wesley Powell, by the way) had named Grand Cañon.

Nor was Sumner merely a grumbling boatman disgusted with having been welshed out of what he expected as his due financial reward, one he never did receive (for more on this see Chapter 10 and M. P. Ghiglieri's *First through Grand Canyon: The Secret Journals and Letters of the 1869 Crew Who Explored the Green and Colorado Rivers*). Instead Sumner was simply measuring the arid Southwest with the eye of a man born in the green Midwest. Indeed, Sumner's assessment echoed that made by U.S. Lieutenant Joseph Christmas Ives eleven years earlier on April 18, 1858. After struggling upstream by boat from Mexico to the head of Black Canyon, well downstream of Grand Canyon, and then riding and hiking overland into western Grand Canyon, Ives, in his 1861 *Report,** also concluded regarding the Coconino Plateau:

> *Ours has been the first, and will doubtless be the last, party of whites to visit this profitless locality. It seems intended by nature that the Colorado River, along the greater part of its lonely and majestic way, shall forever be unvisited and undisturbed.*

Yes, time would prove both Ives and Sumner wrong. And for reasons they both would have denounced as demented. Grand Canyon's desolation and immensity—the very same hideous qualities that Sumner and Ives condemned as being so inhospitable and worthless—would soon sound as the song of a Siren to those seeking their fortunes from railroad projects, from publicizing their adventurous exploits, or from wresting precious metals from the hidden rocks themselves. Yet not even these fortune-hunters ever suspected that eventually millions of people would seek the Canyon's unfriendly depths in search of spiritual solace—or to experience the euphoria of adventure. After all, not much more than a century ago, nearly anything anyone did in Arizona often proved an adventure. Furthermore, "adventure" was best avoided if you didn't want to cash in your chips before you were ready to play your last hand.

At any rate, long before the first tourist would hazard the taxing journey across the Coconino Plateau to the South Rim, the Colorado River in Grand Canyon had seduced its first known victims. The river's reputation quickly became that of a killer. And for years this reputation was well-deserved. But exactly how well-deserved—and why—has long been shrouded in myth and hyperbole.

Strangely for such a reputedly deadly river, during most of the Colorado's length between its headwater regions in Wyoming's Wind River Range and in Colorado's Western Rockies, the river appears deceptively calm. Even most of its 277 miles in Grand Canyon appear harmless. Between Lees Ferry at elevation 3,107 feet and Lake Mead (River Mile 238 or so) at 1,221 feet, the river descends less than a mere eight feet per mile. Those who run technical whitewater rivers elsewhere tend to smirk when they hear this eight-feet-per-mile gradient. For example, rowers and paddlers on California's Tuolumne River routinely navigate whitewater plunging almost sixty feet per mile. One of us (Ghiglieri) has run an exploratory first descent of the Alas River in Sumatra, a river that drops for three of its miles at 165 feet per mile. How dangerous could a mere eight feet be?

---

*Report upon the Colorado River of the West, Explored in 1857 and 1858 by Lieutenant Joseph C. Ives. Corps of Engineers, Under the Direction of the Office of Explorations and Surveys, A. A. Humphreys, Captain Topographical Engineers, in Charge, by Order of the Secretary of War.

When it comes to the power of a river to grab a human being and exert total control over him or her, descent is only one part of the equation for danger. The Amazon River during its final couple of thousand miles to the sea drops only one foot per each thirty miles. Yet the Amazon's tremendous volume, more than the next three largest rivers in the world combined, exerts immense power.

Overall, the Colorado River flowing within Grand Canyon gobbles people because of a constellation of hydrodynamic features. First, while it ranks only 26th in size in the U.S., it is still a respectable-sized river. Before Glen Canyon Dam went on line in 1963, the Colorado fluctuated in an average year between an average low of 1,000 to 4,000 cubic feet per second (cfs) during winter to an average peak of about 86,000 cfs in June, when the spring run-off from the northernmost of its 244,000 square miles of catchment rushed past Lees Ferry (River Mile 0, the head of Grand Canyon). In all the years since 1927, its highest peak runoff was 126,000 cfs on June 12, 1957. Since 1959, when construction of Glen Canyon Dam began, the highest peak within Grand Canyon was about 97,300 cfs, on June 30, 1983. And this high flow was strictly "accidental."

The next factor in the equation of danger is the river's gradient. Half of those eight feet of drop per mile happens in about 160 rapids of varying size. These constitute only 9 percent of the river's 240 miles downstream of Lees Ferry. This means that for 21.6 of its miles, the Colorado drops an average of 45 feet per mile. And, since passage of the Grand Canyon Protection Act by Congress in 1992, it usually descends with an average flow of roughly 8,000 to 25,000 cfs. Beyond its flow and gradient, the Colorado used to possess yet one more deceptive feature that spelled doom for those trapped in it.

This third factor was most obvious prior to the 1963 completion of Glen Canyon Dam, which created a huge sediment settling "pond" (also known as Lake Powell) upstream of Grand Canyon. Before the building of Navajo Bridge in 1928 at River Mile 4 of the Colorado, livestock were driven across the calm stretch of river at Lees Ferry. Oral history has it that many animals never reached the other side. It was not the cold that drowned these animals. True, the Colorado did once run cold as ice in winter then up to 80+ degrees in summer instead of today's 47–55 degrees at Lees Ferry. Instead, the problem lay in what the river carried.

"Too thick to drink but too thin to plow" used to be the wry description for the water quality of the Colorado. During high flows or periods of monsoonal runoff from the Painted Desert and the spectacular regions adjacent to it, the Colorado River seethed and sizzled and hissed with silt and sand. At flows of 100,000 cfs, about half of what flowed down the Canyon was sediment, the other half water.

So what? Stories have been told for years that when sheep tried to swim across the river under these conditions, their wool captured so much silt that the animals sank. Stockmen watched their animals plunge in the muddy flow and bravely swim across with heads held high and noses aimed at the rimrock of the cliffs. Slowly those heads sank deeper and deeper until only the animals' nostrils protruded from the silty river. Then nothing. Likewise, it would turn out, for men.

Lethal Errors Made While Running the River

The first recorded mishap attributed to the Grand Canyon Colorado may have instead occurred downstream of its mouth. We may never know for sure. It happened during a classic Western adventure, the stuff of Zane Grey thrillers. On September 8, 1867, at Callville, Nevada, (now submerged under Lake Mead) a couple of men saw what looked like a person lying on a crude log raft on the Colorado River. They waded out and snagged it as it drifted near shore. Aboard it was an emaciated, bruised, half-naked, severely sunburned wreck of a 30-year-old human being who gave his name as James White. White's story of how he came to be where he was—and in the state he was—has been disputed and debated almost since the moment he told it.

In a letter White wrote to his brother on September 26, 1867 he explained what had happened to him. He had been prospecting since April with Captain Baker and George Strole in the San Juan Mountains in southwestern Colorado. In search of better prospects, the three headed down the San Juan River about 200 miles. They crossed over to the Colorado River. But the argonauts saw that they could not travel down it with their horses. So they decided to turn back.

On August 24, while ascending the tributary out of the canyon, identified much later by anthropologist Bob Euler as Moki Canyon, 15 to 20 Indians—Utes, White guessed—attacked them.

Baker was shot to death almost instantly. White and Strole gathered their guns, four ropes off their horses (losing seven head to the Utes), and a ten-pound sack of flour. They fled on foot fifteen miles downcanyon back to the Colorado River. They reached it at night and built a driftwood raft in the dark.

Then they escaped downriver. They had smooth floating for three days. On the fourth, however, they ran a small rapid and capsized. Here Strole saved White's life by grabbing him by the hair. The two men next built a new, bigger raft. Bad luck, though, in the next rapid Strole fell off it and drowned in a whirlpool.

Fearing he would be next to die, White pulled off his boots and pants (so he could swim) and tied himself by his waist to the raft with part of his fifty-foot rope. Given his situation, this was a good decision. His raft floated over 10- or 15-foot falls and flipped upside down three or four times per day. Seeing no sign of civilization, not even a road, White stayed on the river.

This float was no picnic. The remains of that sack of flour had been lost even before Strole drowned. For seven days White ate nothing. Gaunt with hunger, he finally ate his rawhide knife scabbard. After eight days, he found some honey mesquite beans and ate them. On day nine his raft disintegrated, and he had to rebuild

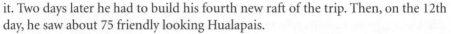

it. Two days later he had to build his fourth new raft of the trip. Then, on the 12th day, he saw about 75 friendly looking Hualapais.

A few of them waded out and pulled him to shore. A squaw gave him a bit of honey mesquite loaf. Meanwhile other Indians stole one of his revolvers and a hand axe. When they would give him nothing more, he set sail again. The next day he traded his last revolver to another group of Indians for the hind quarters of a dog they had butchered. He lost one hind quarter accidentally in the river.

The following day the men at Callville grabbed his raft. Ever since, White's claim of having been first to traverse the entire Grand Canyon by river has been doubted, disputed, or, by a few, believed.

After interviewing White in 1907, Robert Brewster Stanton, in his role as historian (see his *Colorado River Controversies*), takes a highly skeptical, superior, even supercilious view of the suggestion that White had floated through Grand Canyon: "It is my conviction that at the time White wrote his letter he knew neither where he had been, how far he had come, or how long he had been on the river—only that he had been on a raft, somewhere on the Colorado."

Instead of floating for 500 miles of the Colorado, Stanton concluded from White's own testimony of passing 300-foot walls of sandstone on his float, and seeing only one tributary (from the north), and running only one really huge rapid, and never seeing extremely high canyon walls at all, that White instead had floated only 60 miles from Grapevine Wash near the Grand Wash Cliffs (River Mile 277 and 330 miles downstream from the San Juan River) to Callville.

On the other hand, White's mention in his letter to his brother of having seen a very high tributary waterfall suspiciously resembling Deer Creek Falls (at River Mile 136 in Grand Canyon), would seem to suggest that he indeed did float through the Canyon. The most comprehensive saga of James White's hegira down the Colorado is told by his granddaughter Eilean Adams in her *Come Hell or High Water: James White's Disputed Passage through Grand Canyon 1867*.

The primary—indeed only—valid criticism of James White's story resides in the argument that it is not possible for a person on an unpowered (no paddles or oars) raft to make it all the way down the Colorado through half of Glen Canyon and all of Grand Canyon in a mere dozen days or so. Despite a current speed of 3-5 miles per hour, critics say, the river's many eddies and whirlpools would detain a drifting raft so often and long that they would make such a journey impossible in such a short time. This critical argument, often assumed to be devastatingly true (especially by those with limited personal experience observing the Colorado), was in fact demolished many decades ago. We will see more on this in the next chapter (If Looks Could Kill: Death from the Air), but here's a pertinent preview.

"Grave robber" John Billingsley demonstrated an inadvertent re-enactment of the tough part of James White's journey. On July 19, 1957 witnesses watched Billingsley put in at Lees Ferry on a small, home-made raft whose floatation consisted of two inner tubes. He stopped for a long time to explore and loot the TWA crash site (next chapter) on Temple Butte at Mile 62. He next had planned to stop at Phantom Ranch at Mile 88 to end his trip, but he had felt so weak and sick at that point that he failed to fight his way out of the current into the eddy there. He continued downstream on about 50,000 cfs. Still feeling ill, he stayed on a beach for two days. Then he had resumed his journey.

On July 31, guano miners for the Bat Cave spotted him about a dozen miles short of Pearce Ferry and offered him a ride to Kingman.

The short story here is: Billingsley drifted unpowered down the Colorado for about nine-plus days yet traveled at least 267 miles, for an average of about 30 miles per day. Hence, James White's claimed drift of 500 miles on a raft over 12 days, an average of 41.7 miles per day, also seems to have been do-able. White's one-third greater mileage was perhaps attributable to his high motivation to keep going by staying on the river from dawn to dusk because he was starving and escaping hostiles by floating a canyon of unknown but great length. Billingsley, in contrast, was feeling ill and floating through a well-known and well-mapped national park. In summary, White would only have needed to drift 14 hours per day at three miles per hour to accomplish what he claimed. The bottom line? One of us (Ghiglieri) thinks it likely that White did make the 500 mile float. Meanwhile the other (Myers) doubts he could have pulled it off.

Playing Devil's advocate, Myers points out that White ran on low flows typical of late summer, which were likely one quarter of the flow that Billingsley saw. The speed of the White's current flowed significantly slower. A later experiment of this sort was conducted by Harvey Butchart in August, 1960, who floated through Marble Canyon on a buoyant air mattress. Butchart's speed through most of Marble Canyon averaged 12-14 miles per day, during which he also portaged the big rapids on foot. This prompted Butchart to write in his logbook (August 1960): "Even if James White had come through shooting all the rapids, he couldn't have done any better, since he couldn't have paddled the raft forward or even enough to take advantage of the best current."

Admittedly waterlogged logs do travel downriver more quickly than an air mattress. Logs track in the current far better due to their inertia and exhibit little tendency of being caught in eddies, as Harvey on his air mattress repeatedly was.

Regardless of all this, even if White could have made Billingsley-like time on his log raft, Myers also suggests, he most likely would have drowned in one of the rapids, as had happened with Strole and with other known boaters not wearing a life jacket while being dumped into the Colorado. Therefore, Myers suggests, White likely did not float Grand Canyon but did float the section beyond its foot.

This, however, does leave a huge open question as to how White, Strole, Baker, and their horses made their way west unknowingly across about 400 miles of arid plateau lands to beyond the foot of Grand Canyon, especially when the Coconino

Plateau offers no water sources for over a hundred miles.

Much earlier yet—squirmingly early for many river historians for whom only John Wesley Powell could have been first through the Canyon—"Captain" John Moss claimed to have floated the entire Grand Canyon Colorado solo and nonstop in the summer of 1861. As reported much later by the *San Francisco Call* (April 9, 1877) Moss says he did this by poling a 16-foot long by 5-foot wide wooden raft constructed by soldiers at the site of future Lees Ferry. He admits he lost everything in the first huge eddy downstream, however, including his pole.

But he continued drifting because he considered climbing out of the Canyon impossible. Moss says he continued to drift nonstop, night and day, and retained a terrified death grip on his raft every time it capsized in rapids. After 3½ days of drifting he was spotted by Indians upstream of Fort Mohave. They towed Moss to shore.

Moss's very brief description of Grand Canyon does not inspire confidence in his tale. On the other hand, he says nothing drastically incorrect about the place. Moreover, witnesses allegedly saw him at each end. Was Moss' trip possible? You can double double-check the math: 3½ days equals 84 hours. At 4 miles per hour (the speed many lost boats in Grand Canyon have demonstrated over the years as they floating freely over night), the hypothetical distance Moss could have drifted would be 336 miles of the 400 he claimed. Was this even possible? Some oddball data suggest it was. On June 1, 1933 Ida Rusk committed suicide by leaping into the Colorado (see Table 9) at Hermit Rapid (River Mile 96). Workers at Hoover Dam spotted her body 3 or 4 days later, more than 250 miles downstream. Dead, she had floated 65 to 80+ miles per day. Hence, Moss's story does seem remotely feasible—and drastically faster than James White's hellish journey. Even so, most experts conclude Moss had sold his story as a tall tale to the *San Francisco Call* either for money or for fun, maybe both.

A further comparison reveals what sort of speed is known to be possible in the Canyon. The record speed run for a boat being *rowed* is 36 hours and 38 minutes for the 277 miles of river through Grand Canyon set on June 27, 1983 on about 70,000 cfs by Kenton Grua, Rudi Petschek, and Steve Reynolds in Kenton's dory the *Emerald Mile.*

After all is said and done, the whitewater death of James White's rafting buddy George Strole, as tragic as it was, may not have happened in Grand Canyon. The odds, however, seem better and better that it did.

Ironically, the firm honor of the first certified whitewater boating deaths in Grand Canyon go to the trip on which Stanton himself became its leader.

This chapter of the Great American Dream to trick the West into laying eggs like those of the proverbial golden goose began in late 1870. In that year, a prospector, S. S. Harper, alone and down on his luck, became desperate as his store of flour and bacon dwindled to zero. Harper came across a small band of men driving a herd of cattle north from east of the San Francisco Peaks. The men offered Harper a piece of the action if he would help them with the herd. Harper agreed.

Harper noticed, however, not only that the herd did not shrink due to losses, daily it grew. And the cows' brands were mixed. Harper added up two and two and came to the conclusion that he had fallen in with a band of rustlers intending to sell their stolen stock to Mormons in southern Utah. Harper knew that, were a posse to catch them, if he was not shot immediately, he would be hanged with these rustlers.

The men and cattle reached the south side of the Colorado across from what soon would be Lees Ferry. That night some of the stock strayed back south. Harper volunteered to round them up so that no posse would find them and thus back-track the cows to find the rest of the herd. Harper's "partners" agreed to this. Harper immediately rode south and kept on riding as fast as his bronco would carry him—stray and stolen stock be damned.

Harper's day and night on the Colorado and his glimpse of it flowing down-stream from the Lees Ferry area, however, had planted in him the seed of a grand idea to build a railroad from the Colorado Rockies to San Diego via a route that followed the river itself—within its canyons.

Many years later, after Harper had finally struck serious paydirt in Colorado, he confided his plan to another member of Denver's new rich upper crust. The man was lawyer Frank Mason Brown, a real estate and mining magnate. Brown was captivated by the grandeur of Harper's scheme—and also by its potential profits. He immediately formed the Denver, Colorado Cañon and Pacific Railroad and launched a survey expedition from Green River, Utah, down the Green and Colorado rivers. Brown hired as his chief surveyor, Robert Brewster Stanton.

Stanton notes that Brown was optimistic to a fault. For example, though Brown met for an hour with John Wesley Powell, who had commanded the explorations of the Colorado in 1869 and 1871–72, Brown had somehow walked away from that meeting with little sense of what would be necessary as equipment to survive the river. Stanton listed three main faults in Brown's planning.

First was the boats themselves. While Powell had used one 16-foot Whitehall hauler built of pine plus three, 21-foot-long Whitehall haulers constructed of oak and double-ribbed, Brown chose five cheaper, 15-foot-long canoe type boats only 40 inches wide, a mere 18 inches deep, and built of thin planks of brittle red ce-dar. On top of being far too small to carry sixteen men plus the several months of provisions and equipment they needed, Brown's tiny, fragile boats were round bottomed and easy to capsize.

Next was Brown's choice of boatmen. Stanton asked Brown to hire four men who knew moving water. Brown said that professional boatmen would not be nec-essary; two of his own friends, fellow lawyers, would come along as his "guests" and they would row the easy stretches. And the men would line or portage the boats around the rapids themselves, just as Powell's crew had done.

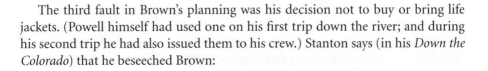

The third fault in Brown's planning was his decision not to buy or bring life jackets. (Powell himself had used one on his first trip down the river; and during his second trip he had also issued them to his crew.) Stanton says (in his *Down the Colorado*) that he beseeched Brown:

> *Then came up that much vexed question of life preservers. I urged President Brown to provide them for all of the men....I could make no impression upon Brown, and called my friend S. S. Harper, the real father of the enterprise, to help me. We both urged more caution and better preparation for the journey. It was no use, even though the air grew blue as Harper tried to convince Brown that he was going into dangers that he knew nothing about. Harper and my other friends urged me to take a life preserver myself, because...in my early childhood, I had had a battle with my Irish nurse, and, I suppose, getting the better of her while in her arms, she dropped me on the pavement and so smashed up my left arm that it has been of little use to me since; hence...I could not swim a stroke, especially in the whirlpools of the Colorado. No life preservers were gotten for anyone....*

Brown's survey expedition put in at Green River, Utah, on May 25, 1889. Three days earlier, Stanton had been aghast when he had stared into the railroad car hauling Brown's five boats. Two of them had already split almost end to end. Brown's crew had repaired the injured boats and then added a sixth boat, a flat bottomed scow/dory they purchased locally, as the cook's boat.

The necessary provisions failed to fit into the bow and stern compartments of Brown's fleet of six. So the men built a raft of zinc-lined boxes to tow the food down the sluggish waters of Labyrinth and Stillwater canyons where the gradient is only about 1.5 feet per mile. A week later Brown's crew rowed their boats onto the Colorado River flowing into Cataract Canyon. Cataract immediately introduced itself as a 40-mile nightmare that would last more than two weeks.

For starters, the men lost that towed raft of food. Next they pinned a boat underwater and lost almost everything in it. A day later, another boat flipped upside down. Then, soon afterward, the cook's boat was pinned against boulders. Although the men finally did rescue some of the cook's equipment, most of the mess ware and yet more food were lost. On top of this, the river utterly destroyed the cook's boat.

After these first few days of poor boating decisions, Stanton's surveying crew began openly criticizing the "management" by Brown and his lawyer buddies.

Only a day after this open criticism began, yet another boat was badly smashed. Luckily, it was salvageable. Four days after criticism began, with all five boats now leaking and as most of the men openly muttered their disgust of the situation, the cook's "new" boat flipped upside-down—losing all the rest of the expedition's plates, et cetera.

Yet another boat was sucked into the vortex of a whirlpool to half sink in a nose-stand. Three days after this, the men lost a boat altogether (recovered intact four days later). As more days passed, each day had its crashes, and each lost yet more food and gear.

Finally, on day #14 in Cataract, Stanton suggested to Brown that, since the expedition now had less than a week's rations, Stanton and five of his surveyors should hike the rest of the canyon on half rations, while Brown tried to get the boats and nine other men several miles down to Hite where a re-supply could be arranged. Brown agreed. The expedition prepared to split in half.

Unfortunately, Brown's crew promptly demolished yet another boat—permanently—before the division could even take place.

Discontent now boiled over into mutiny. Stanton ordered the cook to cook every last bit of food remaining and divide it into sixteen shares, one per man. Discouragingly, each small pile now added up to only one day's ration.

At this point, on day #17 in Cataract, everyone but Stanton and four of the men loyal to him headed downstream in three of the four surviving boats to float ten miles to Hite. In their first rapid that morning—the last rapid in Cataract—one of Brown's three boats immediately lost most of their remaining food and clothes.

Meanwhile Stanton and his tiny crew toiled on, hiking and surveying the walls of Cataract and Narrow canyons. Lunch on these hikes was three lumps of sugar plus as much Colorado River as one cared to drink. Three days later, Peter Hansbrough, having rowed a few miles up the Colorado from Hite into Narrow Canyon, met Stanton with a load of fresh supplies.

What, you might ask in all fairness, do all of the trials and tribulations of this amateurish expedition, with its almost slapstick river-running mistakes, have to do with death in the Grand Canyon? Plenty. The "can-do" and "brave-but-ill-advised" actions of the principal men during this first month of the Brown Expedition explain their otherwise nearly unbelievable decisions next in Grand Canyon. These decisions set the record, still unbroken, for boating deaths on one trip in Grand Canyon.

Brown decided that he and Stanton and a half dozen of the crew who had proved their loyalty—oarsmen Peter M. Hansbrough and Henry C. Richards, engineer and surveyor John Hislop, photographer F. A. Nims, carpenter Harry McDonald, and cook George W. Gibson—should continue their survey down Grand Canyon in three of their surviving original boats. Brown planned to eyeball and photograph the inner canyon, rather than run time-consuming transits.

Many people still wonder today why Brown made this decision "merely" for a railroad bed. The answer is, Brown and Company had far more in mind than just two lengths of steel rail connected by ties. As written in its Articles of Incorporation, Coconino County, Territory of Arizona (Recorder's office, Flagstaff), the Denver Colorado Cañon and Pacific Railroad's stated purposes were: "the opera-

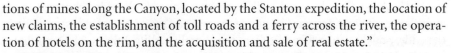

tions of mines along the Canyon, located by the Stanton expedition, the location of new claims, the establishment of toll roads and a ferry across the river, the operation of hotels on the rim, and the acquisition and sale of real estate."

Stanton agreed to Brown's plans, he says, because "I considered it my duty to remain with my superior officer."

On July 9, 1889 Brown's party of eight headed downstream in their three repaired and heavily resupplied boats. They portaged Badger Creek Rapid (River Mile 8), then did the same at Soap Creek Rapid (River Mile 11+), and camped at its foot. For the first time during the entire survey, Brown, that night, dreamed of rapids. The next morning, at 6:20 a.m., Brown's boat, with McDonald steering and Brown at the oars, pulled away from shore. The next two boats took a few minutes longer to get off shore and to break into the current. They lagged behind.

Several hundred yards downstream, Brown and McDonald passed through a narrow "gateway" of Esplanade Sandstone bracketing the Colorado. Next they entered a series of haystack waves bisecting a sudden widening of the river where the Supai-Esplanade bedrock has been carved into a deep cove by debris flows from Saltwater Wash and by the river itself. The river here widens into a massive, powerful eddy system walled on the left by low cliffs. The standing waves of the downstream current raced past the eddy's very powerful upstream current on the left side of the river with a few feet of "eddy fence" whirlpools between them.

Brown yelled to McDonald, "Mac, we want to make this eddy and look at the rapid below—this is where Stanton wanted to stop and look at the rapid which he could not see."

"Alright," McDonald said, as he steered the boat left. Instantly a heavy wave erupted from the eddy fence. As the upstream eddy current grabbed the bow, the round-bottomed hull rolled over in an instant upstream flip.

This capsize tossed McDonald from the stern into the main current. He emerged to see Brown to his left, already on the surface. As the rush of warm, silty water carried McDonald and the boat downstream, he "hallooed" to Brown to "Come on!" Brown cheerfully answered "Alright!"

The river swept McDonald through a series of small haystack waves for two hundred yards and toward the left shoreline. McDonald gasped for air. Then he swam like a madman for that left shore. He grabbed solid rock and hauled himself out. Next he looked for Brown.

Brown had hit the river farther left, more toward the bow of the boat. This was not a good location. Brown had plunked into a whirlpool in the eddy fence swirling between the rushing downstream flow and the powerful upstream eddy current. Brown probably saw the left shoreline of smoothly sculpted Esplanade Sandstone only a hundred feet away and decided to swim for it—instead of trying to follow McDonald's route down the river. To a whitewater novice, McDonald's downriver swim would have looked anything but enviable.

As Harry McDonald raced back upstream along the boulder-cluttered sandstone ledges, he saw Brown. The would-be railroad magnate was still struggling in the eddy, now less than fifty feet from the shoreline cliffs. Brown, McDonald saw, was slowly being swept back upstream. At this same instant, McDonald also saw Stanton's boat, with Henry Richards and Peter Hansbrough rowing, only 200 feet upstream of Brown.

Stanton and his crew, however, could not yet see Brown. But Stanton did see McDonald frantically waving. He also heard him yell, "Mister Brown is in there!"

Stanton's crew steered into the eddy and searched the muddy surface. But they saw no one. Brown's notebook suddenly shot to the surface in the eddy. Stanton saw it and yelled. Hansbrough grabbed it. Brown himself, however, had vanished. Stanton's boat had arrived just seconds too late.

The seven survivors spent the day rowing around the eddy and walking miles of the shoreline below in hopes of rescuing Brown's body. But Brown had vanished. The men did find their missing boat a mile downstream. That afternoon, Nims would later report, Hansbrough carved an epitaph in inch-high letters in the black desert varnish of the Esplanade a few feet above the racing eddy:

> *F. M. Brown Pres. D.C.C. & P.R.R. Co*
> *was drowned July 10 1889*
> *opposite this point*

"Thus it was," Stanton writes, "that President Brown sacrificed his life, which could so easily have been saved if he had had a life preserver to keep him afloat one-half minute longer. A noblehearted man and a true friend, he had won the love of everyone associated with him."

It was at this point that this strange and tragic trip became irrational—and soon far more tragic. The seven survivors camped here at the mouth of Saltwater Wash. In a bit more than an hour they could have hiked the easy thousand feet up the wash to the plateau above. Another three hours of walking could have returned them to Lees Ferry, where friends, food, and transportation to the outside world could have been had.

Instead, as Stanton would write:

> *It was a day of terrible experience....[But] In this world we are left but little time to mourn. We had work to do, and I determined, if possible, to complete the whole of that work. That such a determination at that time was unwise, I can freely admit, as I look back upon it today, but neither Hislop nor I ever thought of leaving the river then. That we did not sufficiently appreciate the difficulties, even after such a warning, knowing the outfit we had, is also clear as I see it now, but who is there that can say our decision was culpably wrong?*

Remember, however, that Stanton himself had beseeched Brown on the issue of life preservers:

> *I urged President Brown to provide them for all of the men....It was no use, even though the air grew blue as Harper tried to convince Brown that he was going into dangers that he knew nothing about.*

Indeed Stanton's actions from this time after Brown drowned make little sense except in light of his own vision of what marvels—and economic remunerations—the Denver Colorado Cañon and Pacific Railroad Company might still yield. As Stanton wrote in his *Down the Colorado*, in addition to mineral wealth, he also envisioned within Grand Canyon "each cove with its picturesque Swiss chalet, and its happy mountain people with their herds of sheep and mountain goats, developing a local business for our future railroad."

Stanton now led the survey expedition deeper into the Marble Canyon section of Grand Canyon. They were now so careful about whitewater that they portaged everything with a wave in it, thus making only three miles of progress per day. Four days downstream, as the crew rested on Sunday, both Hansbrough and Richards, Stanton reports, independently expressed deep worries over drowning in the Colorado. Each man also discussed the possibilities of life after death.

The next day, July 15, at 25-Mile Rapid, the crew lined their three boats halfway downstream on the left. Then, stopped by a cliff face in the Redwall Limestone, they had to run the rapid's large tailwaves.

The first boat, rowed by McDonald and Gibson, after a false start, tried again and made it. They beached on a strip of sand a few hundred yards downstream.

The second boat, Stanton's, rowed by Henry Richards and Peter Hansbrough, followed. The two (Stanton had decided to walk around this rapid, atop the low Redwall cliff) failed to row far enough to the right to enter the downstream current. The river swept their boat back to the left, into the cliff face, which was slightly undercut. The current here was mild enough that Hansbrough and Richards could use their oars and hands to push back away from the wall. But, in so doing, their narrow, round-bottomed canoe abruptly flipped upside down.

The river sucked both men under. Both were good swimmers. Even so, no one ever saw Hansbrough break the surface. Richards, however, did appear in midstream where he swam hard to save himself.

McDonald and Gibson pushed out from shore to row upstream to intercept Richards. But the man sank forever in the thick Colorado before their horrified eyes.

What killed these two men was a series of bad decisions to continue running the river at all, inadequately equipped and untrained as they were. These and the river itself, which might have been flowing at about 25,000 cfs, more or less. On top of these, however, the Colorado was living up to its name. Two days earlier the monsoon rains had started with a vengeance. Countless tributary canyons had dumped millions of tons of mud, silt, and sand into the river. Both Richards and Hansbrough were fully dressed, as had been Brown. Their clothes, like the wool of those sheep at Lees Ferry, may have loaded ever heavier with sediment with each passing second in the river to the point where neither man could remain on the surface regardless of his swimming ability. If so, they might as well have been wearing weight belts loaded with lead.

A bit late in the game, one concludes, Stanton finally believes his own and Harper's admonitions about life jackets:

> *Then I realized fully what it meant to be without life preservers....*

At last fully realizing that he and his four survivors were on a suicide mission, Stanton resolved at this point to abandon the survey. But now the convenient exit of Saltwater Wash was—Stanton thought—at 14 miles upstream, too far behind them to use. So, paradoxically, the five survivors continued downstream, with eyes peeled for a tributary canyon to the north that might offer them deliverance from this river that "seldom gives up its dead."

Two days later—having passed five other potential routes by which they might have exited the Canyon downstream of where Brown had drowned—they found a route labeled almost in neon. Tipped off by ancient Puebloan Indian ruins at South Canyon (River Mile 31.5), they decided that, if Indians could get in and out here, so could they.

The next day, after the most awful monsoonal symphony of lightning and thunder Stanton had ever witnessed, the survivors cached their gear in a cave in the Redwall and readied themselves to hike out. At the last moment, however, Stanton spied Brown, identifiable by the coat he was still wearing, floating down the river.

McDonald and Hislop scrambled to get a boat off shore and back into the water in time to snag Brown. Not only was this the Christian thing to do, Brown had had all of the expedition's money in his pockets when he had drowned. But Brown drifted past his few surviving crew members too quickly to be intercepted.

On July 18, the five survivors hiked up South Canyon through "solid sheets of water" dumped by the monsoons. Four vowed to return and complete the survey.

And those four (Gibson, the cook, had had enough) did return just before January of 1890. One, Nims—told in Chapter 2—was badly injured in a fall only five days into this second expedition. On this second trip, however, Stanton had brought good life jackets and suffered no fatalities during his 86-day survey of Grand Canyon.

Many more people would seek their fortunes in the Canyon. In the winter of 1895–1896, Al Marsh took his string of burros with supplies into the upper end of Grand Canyon in search of paydirt. As noted in the *Coconino Sun* (January 8,

1896), Marsh reckoned that he prospected nearly one hundred miles of the Canyon without finding good prospects before he ran out of food. Deep in the Inner Canyon, Marsh found it impossible to climb out. After some disappointing non-routes on snow-covered cliffs, Marsh abandoned his burros and his outfit and headed downstream on a raft he built from driftwood.

Marsh reckoned he had drifted down about fifty miles of river before being stopped by his fear of a huge rapid. He abandoned his raft and started hiking to the South Rim again. This was likely a smart move even though days passed as he wandered and struggled along the high cliffs searching for breaks that might allow him to escape the Canyon walls. Finally, during early January, 1896 Marsh, half-starved, frozen, and footsore, found a break in the wall. A few days later he reached Aubrey Valley (near present day Seligman) and the railroad.

"He will not attempt to regain his burros or camp outfit," noted the staff writer for the *Mohave Miner*, "as he has seen enough Grand Canyon to last him a lifetime."

Almost forty years passed after Brown, Hansbrough, and Richards drowned during their attempted railroad survey before the river claimed new known victims trying to navigate (rather than cross, see next section) the Colorado. The most famous of these victims died during a romantic bid for stardom.

The pivotal event of this epic took place one day during early summer in 1927, when a shy, twenty-one-year-old woman named Bessie Haley embarked with a girlfriend, Eraine Granstedt, on an overnight trip by ship from San Francisco to Los Angeles. Bessie had come west a year earlier from Parkersburg, West Virginia, to attend the California School of Fine Arts. Weeks earlier, in Kentucky, she had secretly married her high school sweetheart Earl Helmick. But after living with him for less than two months, their marriage had failed. After Bessie vanished to the West, however, Helmick had allegedly wired her money for an "operation." Some historians conclude that Bessie was pregnant. The money, they say, was either for an illegal abortion or for the medical costs of childbirth coupled with adoption. On the other hand, this "operation" story may be a false rumor.

Once in San Francisco, Bessie attended classes, worked in a large local bookstore, and she also wrote poetry. She shared a room (on Hyde Street...) with a nineteen-year-old nude art model, Eraine Granstedt (a.k.a. Irene Granstedt, a.k.a. Greta Granstedt). Bessie's roommate was not only a young and beautiful blonde, but also an ambitious one. And perhaps a very persuasive one as well. After less than a year of studying art, Bessie and Eraine purchased one-way tickets south to the City of Angels on that overnight ship. Eraine's goal was to make it big in Tinsletown. Bessie's goal was, well, a mystery.

Fate, however, placed on this same southbound ship a tall young adventurer named Glen Rollin Hyde. Glen was the son of a boom-and-bust-cycle rancher and builder, Rollin C. Hyde, from Twin Falls, Idaho. Glen had run a few Idaho and British Columbian rivers—the Salmon, the Fraser, and the Peace—and had learned "drift," or "sweep" boating techniques from veteran boater Harry Guleke. (Idaho drift boats were built like gigantic horse troughs thirty or more feet long. Riding on the steeper gradient of Idaho rivers, the boatmen rarely found the need to power their boats downstream. They simply drifted. They positioned their long sweep oars off the bow and stern srictly to be able to move their boats out of the way laterally of obstacles in the river.)

Electricity must have flowed between Bessie and Glen. On that short voyage down the California coast to the City of Angels, their destiny became the stuff of a Hollywood fantasy. When Bessie disembarked in Los Angeles she and Glen had already become inseparable. Eraine stepped off the gangway with Bessie and Glen—and legally vanished. As pods of grey whales near their ship had spouted geysers onto Pacific waves, she had assumed a new identity; Eraine was now Greta Grenstedt. Greta, as river historian Brad Dimock notes in *Sunk without a Sound*, "went straight to Hollywood for thirty-some years of bit part roles."

Bessie, in contrast, left Los Angeles with Glen for Idaho. She married him several months later, in April of 1928, one day after her uncontested Nevada divorce from Earl Helmick. Glen had a dream that had captivated Bessie: to be the first man and woman team to run the Colorado River through the Grand Canyon. Glen also wanted to maximize their publicity, fame, and money for having done so.

Bessie could draw and write poetry. Glen too could write. Glen's grand plan incorporated her talents as well as her gender. They would run the river, the two of them. And they would run it in a boat Glen built. They also would set a speed record for traversing the canyons. On top of all this, like trapeze artists defying death without a safety net, Glen and Bessie would run the treacherous Grand Canyon Colorado without life jackets—just as Idaho boatmen had been doing for decades.

Not only would all of this make them famous, it would open the door to the lucrative vaudeville lecture circuit and also land them a book contract. Bessie and Glen could write the book and illustrate it with her drawings.

It seemed a perfect plan.

In October, 1928 Glen and Bessie arrived at Green River, Utah. Here Glen spent $50 on materials to hammer together an Idaho drift boat, a flat-bottomed scow of the type that the legendary Harry Guleke had taught him to build on the Salmon. Two days later, Glen's scow measured twenty feet long by five wide by three deep. He equipped it with a pair of long sweep oars off the bow and stern. He also installed conveniences such as bedsprings and a stove consisting of a metal box of sand into which kerosene could be poured, then burned. These would free the honeymooners from any need to camp on shore. Speed was the thing.

Harry T. Howland, a Green River local who possessed significant river experience and had helped the two with facilities for building, stared at Glen's boat. Howland appraised the poorly angled cuts of the boards and the imperfect vertical rows of nail heads holding Glen's big box together and remarked to Bill Reeder, "It looks like a floating coffin."

Reeder, for his part, had no luck getting Glen to reconsider his design. Hyde, according to Reeder, was "surly, conceited and stoopid."

On October 20, Glen and Bessie set off down the Green in their scow. After 100 miles of flat water they struggled through the 28 rapids of Cataract Canyon. One ejected Bessie from the scow, sans life jacket. Glen somehow retrieved her. The two arrived unscathed at Lees Ferry in mid-November on 14,000 cfs. They had named Glen's scow "Rain-in-the-Face" because of how the squared-off bow snowplowed into waves and ricocheted huge splashes instead of slicing through them.

Here at Lees Ferry boatman Owen Clark, veteran of the 1927 Pathé-Bray Expedition down Grand Canyon, warned the Hydes they needed a second boat and also should be wearing life jackets for safety. Clark had run the river to Mile 95, also told them that the worst rapid they would encounter would be Soap Creek (River Mile 11). Glen ignored Clark's safety warnings then he and Bessie continued downstream.

Days later, Earl Boyer and some companions would hike down Soap Creek Canyon to retrieve the body of Royce E. Dean, who had drowned on June 7 in a tragic accident during the last cross-river run of Lees Ferry (discussed later in this chapter). Boyer and company were surprised to find a man's and a woman's foot prints heading up Soap Creek Canyon for three miles from the river then reversing to return to the river.

Apparently, after Glen and Bessie Hyde had scouted Soap Creek Rapid, which never had been run at low water, they had decided to abandon the trip and hike out of the Canyon. But, after walking miles up Soap, the Canyon walls either frightened them or their own sore feet convinced them that continuing downriver remained their best option after all. Either way, the honeymooners returned to the Colorado and managed to get their scow past this rapid.

How navigable was Glen Hyde's scow? In 1996 Brad Dimok and Jeri Ledbetter ran a precise replica scow through Grand Canyon. Ledbetter noted of the generally terrifying experience: "When it [the scow] started hitting the big waves, it was so violent, the sweep oars would just fly around, and we would dive on the floor and hide." Further, and eerily explanatory: "We just got slammed—especially at [Mile] 232, we were completely out of control, dead sideways, right over the fangs. If the water had been lower and the fangs had been out, we'd have crashed in a huge way. The boat sank twice." (boatman's quarterly review, December 2013, vol. 26 (4):29-30.)

Later, in Sockdolager Rapid (River Mile 79) or Grapevine Rapid (River Mile 81.5), a big wave beguiled Glen. His sweep oar thumped him in the chin and knocked him out of the scow. Bessie grabbed the sweeps and kept the scow straight. Next, once Glen grabbed a gunwale, she hauled him back into the scow.

Twenty-six days—a record time—and 424 miles downstream of Green River, Glen and Bessie tied up their scow near Phantom Ranch (River Mile 88). From there they hiked up to the South Rim Village. This stop had multiple purposes.

First, it was a perfect way for the world to learn that Glen and Bessie Hyde were alive and well in their conquest of the Colorado. Second, the honeymooners had run out of food. The rim offered them a chance to resupply—if only Glen had brought enough money to buy the food they needed.

On the rim the couple was treated as royalty. But quickly, Emery Kolb, an inspired photographer and an experienced Grand Canyon boatman who had rowed the entire Canyon twice, swept Bessie and Glen out of the limelight and into his studio. There, perched on the South Rim overlooking the Bright Angel Trail, Kolb tried to convince Glen to take Kolb's own life jackets. Glen refused, saying, "We don't need any artificial aids."

Emery, who had done his share of unplanned swimming in the Colorado, beseeched Glen to at least buy an inner tube or two to keep on the scow as throwable life preservers. Glen refused, this time, more angrily, announcing in a letter from the rim, "I am going to do it without life jackets, or else."

Ranger Bert Lauzon met the Hydes on the rim and reported, "The little woman was sick of it when she reached this far. He wanted to make a record—taking the first woman thru—she would have quit long before if she had her way—she just had no enthusiasm—she was dejected…Mrs. Hyde had enough of the Canyon and went on only because Mr. Hyde insisted."

Before hiking down the trail to their scow, Bessie accompanied Edith Kolb, Emery's 20-year-old daughter. Then she gazed longingly at Edith's new pair of shoes. "I wonder," Bessie mused, now sobered by Emery's warnings of the dangers awaiting the honeymooners downstream, "if I shall ever wear pretty shoes again."

A San Francisco businessman, Adolph Sutro, solved Glen's other problem of not enough money to resupply on food by offering Glen a trade. If Sutro could ride along in the scow for seven miles from Phantom Ranch to Hermit Rapid, Sutro would provide a couple of weeks of food—to be delivered at Hermit Creek by mule. Glen agreed.

Sutro rode with the Hydes for those seven miles, including through Horn Creek Rapid (River Mile 90.25). They camped one night en route, likely at River Mile 91. Sutro would years later report to river historian Dock Marston, however, that he had never seen a boatman as indifferent and irresponsible to boating techniques as Glen Hyde—nor one as consumed with his own feat and the money it might get him. Glen seemed slipshod. He had, Sutro said, the habit of jamming an oar into the sand and then securing the scow only with one rope tied to that oar. Indeed, Sutro's impression at this point was that Bessie was both tired of the trip, terrified of the rough water, and fearful of continuing, even while Glen mostly discussed the possibilities for making money by cashing in on their fame. "It was," Sutro wrote, "the most inadequately equipped outfit I have ever seen. I couldn't understand how they got to Bright Angel. [But] it was obvious that [the] whole object of the trip was to make money in show business."

On November 18, at a Hermit Rapid now flowing well under 10,000 cfs, they found Sutro's mules with food. After loading the scow, however, the Hydes' bid for stardom took an ominous twist.

One account told to mule packer Bob Francy, who wasn't looking at the time, by other men present has it that Bessie refused to get back into the scow to continue the trip. Glen, the men said, physically picked her up and placed her in the scow. Although the story of Glen carrying Bessie may be apocryphal, Sutro himself did note that, once Bessie was back in the scow, "Her face registered stark terror."

The last and final photo taken of Bessie and Glen (at Hermit Camp) prior to their launch onto the River at Hermit Rapid reveals body language shouting despair and lack of confidence—or worse.

Either way, Glen and Bessie ran Hermit Rapid at low water—then vanished.

Glen's 69-year-old father, Rollin C. Hyde, waited at Needles to pick up Glen and Bessie on December 6. When the honeymooners still had not appeared by December 16, R. C. Hyde reckoned that the scow had somehow escaped his son and daughter-in-law and marooned them. He called the governor of Idaho and requested an aerial search by the U.S. Army of the river corridor. On December 19, L. G. Plummer and H. G. Adams, piloting a Douglas O-2 airplane out of March Field, California, spotted what appeared to be the scow floating in an eddy at River Mile 237.

On December 21, Emery Kolb, his brother Ellsworth, and Chief Ranger Jim Brooks, along with R. C. Hyde and Deputy Sheriff John Nelson of Yavapai County, borrowed a Hualapai wagon and saddle horses to get down Peach Springs Wash to Diamond Creek and the Colorado (Mile 225.7). The Kolbs and Brooks re-hammered together a skiff abandoned by the James Girand Dam Site Survey party several years earlier. On a bitterly cold Christmas Eve, the three put in at Diamond Creek.

The three Christmas boaters found the Hydes' scow in the same eddy as where the search plane had located it. Its bowline seemed to have caught underwater between boulders. But searches up and down the river—initially, by the Kolbs and Brooks below Diamond, and by R. C. Hyde and Deputy Sheriff Nelson upstream of Diamond, and then later by the Hualapais, by cowboys, and by the NPS and Fred Harvey personnel enlisted by R. C. Hyde (who had lost his other two sons as infants and was now 100-percent dedicated to rescuing his only surviving one)—discovered no other definite signs of the missing honeymooners beyond an abandoned camp several miles upstream of Diamond Creek near River Mile 212 or 213 containing empty tins and a jar from Idaho. They also spotted Glen's footprints while scouting Mile 217 Rapid.

Aboard the scow sat virtually all of the Hydes' possessions: their coats, Glen's long-barreled, .30-.30, lever action rifle, Bessie's camera, diary, and even her purse. But, oddly, no sketchbook. Glen had carved forty-two notches, including crosses for Sundays, in the gunwale of the scow, one per day. The last would have been incised on November 30. Bessie's diary, a skimpy document often written in a simple code of dashes for quiet stretches and circles for rapids and with few words, placed the honeymooners three days downstream of Lava Falls (River Mile 179.5) on this date, floating on about 8,000+ cfs. This translates to the area of Diamond Creek (River Mile 225.7) or beyond. Whatever had happened to the Hydes had occurred on November 30 or on December 1. But what had happened?

Five miles upstream of the self-moored scow, 232-Mile Rapid was pouring its entire narrow sluice of Colorado into a carnivore's gleaming dentition of jagged fangs of Precambrian metamorphic bedrock. The Kolb brothers and Brooks had experienced the devil's own time figuring a way around it in the rickety old boat they had re-hammered together. They finally had to line the boat along the shore. What, they had wondered, had Glen done here? (Remember the out-of-control near disaster experienced in the replica scow by boatmen Brad Dimok and Jeri Ledbetter here in 1996 {page 229].)

The three found no footprints, which suggests the Hydes ran 232-Mile un-scouted. This rapid, all three men figured, was the likely culprit—that and Glen's obdurate refusal to bring life jackets.

If Glen simply had run the scow in the main current, flowing at 8,700 cfs on December 1, it would have collided with those surprising fangs sieving the main-stream. It easily could have jarred and ejected Glen and/or Bessie into the cold rapid. Without life jackets.

Indeed the scow did show minor collision damage to its hull and also had a foot of water in the bilge, though it otherwise remained ship-shape. After searching both shorelines at River Mile 237 and finding no sign of humanity, the Kolbs and Brooks off-loaded the Hyde's possessions into their small boat, sliced the scow's bowline, then rowed downstream. About three miles downstream, the searchers capsized their own little rig in Separation Rapid. Jim Brooks was trapped under the upside-down boat with one of the upright standards caught in his overalls. He finally got loose. But at least he had a life jacket. With only two jackets for the three men, Ellsworth had strapped an empty five-gallon can to his back for safety.

Ellsworth now struggled in the icy flow to keep his face above water. All three men escaped alive but now were freezing. Ice formed on them and on and in the boat itself. The three shivering, would-be rescuers continued to Spencer Canyon (River Mile 246). From there they rode out on horses with Deputy Sheriff Nelson of Yavapai County, R. C. Hyde, and some Hualapais. This ride on horseback avoided their otherwise being forced to run 30 more miles of the freezing Colorado and, more important, Lava Cliff Rapid, then considered by those who had run the entire Grand Canyon to be the worst rapid on the entire Colorado (Owen Clark and the Pathé-Bray Expedition had quit the river at River Mile 95; hence his warning to Glen Hyde at Lees Ferry that Soap Creek would offer the worst challenge).

Glen and Bessie Hyde were chalked up as victims of drowning (or maybe even murder, see Chapters 9 and 10). But no matter how she died, Bessie Hyde had become the first woman to run the rapids of the Colorado from Cataract Canyon through Grand Canyon to somewhere near River Mile 232, for a total of 565 miles. Bessie is rarely credited with this "first-woman-to-do-it" because she did not make it past River Mile 237 to the foot of the Canyon at River Mile 277—alive and in a boat, that is. The women normally credited as having been the first, Elzada Clover and Lois Jotter, were designated thus by the self-appointed "bean counter" of who had "really" boated Grand Canyon—"Dock" Otis R. Marston (who perhaps eliminated 150 names of those who did not run all 277 miles in order to include himself among the first 100). Clover and Jotter, however, descended the river a decade later, in 1938, as paying passengers on one of Norm Nevills' early commercial trips. This was during a time when, ironically, the rapids below River Mile 237 had been drowned by Lake Mead. Moreover, Nevills portaged or lined many of the rapids that Bessie and Glen ran. In short, Bessie Hyde was the true "first," a woman who also, for many miles, manned one of the sweeps, thus "rowing" the Hydes' boat downriver. The next two women to follow her ran only a couple of minor rapids beyond what she had but ran far fewer big ones before River Mile 237 than Bessie and, of course, did no real Canyon rowing whatsoever.

The Grand Canyon Colorado took its next river-running victim less than three years later, during the depth of the Great Depression, a time when a steady job, no matter how back-breaking, was life itself.

This next amazing story became known—in part, anyway—at about 8:00 a.m. on June 23, 1931, when James R. Ervin walked up to a Hualapai ranch house about five miles from Peach Springs, in Peach Springs Canyon. Ervin was pin-cushioned with cactus thorns, exhausted, and had lost twenty pounds off his normal 130. He had eaten no food for four days. And he had just traversed a landscape offering little water.

Ervin fell under the Hualapai's artesian water hydrant and gulped like a dying man. Then he vomited. Charles McGee, the young Hualapai owner of the ranch, dragged Ervin away from the hydrant and forced him instead to take small sips.

Ervin explained to McGee that he had a partner, Bill Payne, somewhere in the Canyon behind him, to the west, in Lower Granite Gorge. But his partner, Ervin added, was exhausted and probably had been unable to follow him out.

How Ervin and Payne had gotten themselves into the mess they had comprises an odyssey of non-planning and poor decision-making that would make Custer's Last Stand look clever.

Bill Payne of Hollywood, California, and James R. Ervin had been working for Anderson Brothers Boarding and Supply Company, which housed and fed construction crews on site at the Boulder Dam project. Payne (whose true name was reportedly William Talmadge but who said that he used the alias "Payne" to avoid possible bad publicity for his famous sister, Hollywood actress Constance Talmadge) held the job of checking the men's names as they entered the mess hall at the foot of the thousand-foot canyon wall. Ervin was a waiter. Both men—and hundreds of others—considered the 120-degree-hot dam project a boiling "Hell-hole" (nor were they wrong; 110 men would die building Hoover Dam, as computed from J. E. Stevens' *Hoover Dam*).

In late May, Payne suggested to Ervin that they drive Ervin's stripped down Model T to Denver, Colorado, and work instead on a dude ranch run by some friends or relatives of Payne's. Ervin agreed. Not even waiting for payday, the two arranged for their final checks to be mailed to them in Denver. Then they drove east. Ervin was thirty years old, Payne twenty-seven. The two were an odd couple. Ervin had worked physical jobs all of his life, had served a stint with the Coast Guard, and was an excellent swimmer. He described himself as in "perfect condition physically" and probably was. In contrast, Payne had never resorted to physical labor in his life and was, in Ervin's opinion, what today would be called a wimp.

In Denver, Payne could not find the people who were supposed to offer them employment. Nor could the duo find other work. Worse yet, the two men's final paychecks also failed to arrive. The pay steward in Boulder City, Nevada, it would turn out, had "forgotten all about it."

So the pair drove south. Ervin's Model T broke down in Cobero, New Mexico. With no money to pay for repairs, the pair abandoned it and their luggage in a Navajo garage in hopes of retrieving it all later. They hopped a freight train on the Santa Fe line with the goal of picking up their old jobs—and their paychecks—in Boulder City, Nevada.

Railroad guards tossed the two off. Multiple times. Finally Ervin and Payne gave up on the rails. They hitchhiked west. By the time they reached Peach Springs on Route 66, roughly 150 round-about miles short of Boulder City, they had gone two days without food. Desperate in an era when bumming food was a tough go, they perused their road map again for inspiration. The map showed the Colorado River flowing past them only 23 miles north.

To Ervin, the river distance from the mouth of Diamond Creek to Boulder City seemed to be far fewer miles than overland by road. Besides, Ervin reasoned, because this western half—133 miles—of the Grand Canyon Colorado was not within the national park boundaries (it was not included in the Park until 1975), it must not include any of the rough rapids that made the river so famous. "I assumed," Ervin admitted, "the river to be rather calm from there on down." So, thinking it was smooth sailing—and, perhaps more importantly, that it would not require them to hitchhike or to hop trains—the two men narrowed their dire straights by walking 23 miles down Peach Springs Canyon.

Neither man carried food or water. Payne, exhausted, sat down to rest. Ervin continued downcanyon. He scooped the mud out of a wet burro track and drank what seeped into it, missing the clear spring nearby. From there he made it to Diamond Creek. After drinking his fill of clear water, Ervin headed back upcanyon with an old coffee pot he had found and filled with water for Payne. Ervin soon

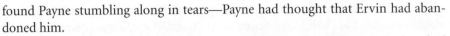

found Payne stumbling along in tears—Payne had thought that Ervin had abandoned him.

The two walked the last mile to the Colorado River. The Colorado had peaked that year on June 17 (measured at Phantom Ranch) at a mere 32,000 cfs. Now, on June 21, it had dropped by 8,000 cfs. Ervin walked along the new clean beach, then he poked his nose into the bushes and buildings higher up from the river. "Imagine my elation," Ervin later would write, "at finding an old boat pulled up with boards and pipe rollers."

At Diamond Creek in Lower Granite Gorge, Ervin and Payne found their shortcut to the Boulder Dam site assured in the form of this serviceable riverboat, the *Bright Angel*. It was one of six wooden boats built in California with watertight compartments of galvanized steel, and painted white. The 1927 Pathé-Bray expedition had used these six boats during the dead of winter to film a movie in Grand Canyon. Due in part to an undecided screenplay and a hideously bad lead actress, Rose Blossom (who never entered the Canyon), this movie flip-flopped in both its title and concept from being "The Bride of the Colorado" to "The Pride of the Colorado." It had no woman on the expedition; instead, one of the boatmen dressed in drag. The film was never released. Pathé-Bray had abandoned their filming and the expedition itself, including the *Bright Angel*, 130 miles upstream of Diamond Creek at Hermit Rapid (River Mile 95). Soon afterward, Bob Francy, a handyman at Phantom Ranch, had enlisted some friends to help him row, line, winch, drag, and portage the *Bright Angel* seven miles back upstream to Bright Angel Creek (River Mile 88) and Phantom Ranch.

Months later, Rollin C. Hyde had implored Francy with the lure of a $1,000 reward to use his hard-won *Bright Angel* to search for Glen and Bessie—or at least to find firm information on what might have happened to them. Francy had enlisted Jack Harbin to help him. Assistant NPS Superintendent P. P. Patraw had ridden with the two for the first twenty miles—until social friction drove Patraw to hike out alone up the South Bass Trail to the Coconino Plateau (where he got lost in the snow for two days). Francy's search and rescue expedition in the dead of a very nasty winter had been a truly horrible experience for all three men, the *Bright Angel* having flipped once, wrapped once, and frozen the men constantly.

Worse, it had uncovered nothing that R. C. Hyde defined as "firm." Hyde, who had mortgaged virtually everything he could to raise search money, refused to pay the two men any of the $1,000 reward he had promised. Francy, now had had no choice but to abandon his dearly-won *Bright Angel* in the early winter of 1929 at Diamond Creek. He felt disgusted with R. C. Hyde. Finally, Francy threatened to sue. Hyde settled for $700. At any rate, this serviceable, though anything but lucky, boat sitting on shore at Diamond Creek with a good pair of oars and one cork life jacket eliminated Ervin's and Payne's need to build the raft that they had planned to build (without tools or supplies).

Before they shoved off the next morning, Ervin quipped to Payne that the boat might be called the Dark Angel before they got out of the Gorge. Payne answered, "Yes, it will be a great story to tell your grandchildren if you live to tell it."

Shortly after dawn on June 22, the duo set off downriver. For the past couple of days the river had been flowing an almost steady 23,600 cfs. While this was a low flow for a normal June, relatively speaking, it was a very serious high flow in the Lower Gorge, especially for a novice boater. In fact, it would prove to be nuts.

In the first six rapids, by Ervin's count, they capsized the Bright Angel an amazing five times. But, in that sixth rapid, Ervin lost one of the oars. (A packrat had nibbled through its tether, and, despite having extra rope aboard, Ervin had not bothered to replace this tether.) Even before this loss, however, Ervin admitted that he could not control the boat at all in the rapids. But now, upside down yet again, he leapt off the boat's hull toward the wall on the south side, swam the warm river, and made it. This fifth swim without a life jacket—Payne was wearing their only one—had taxed even his "excellent physical condition."

The duo tied up the *Bright Angel*, still upside-down, above a large boulder in the south side somewhere near River Mile 234. Evidentially trusting the seals of the hatches of its watertight compartments to allow no water to leak in that might sink it—or, more likely, not even thinking that the boat might leak—Ervin decided to leave the Bright Angel upside down and to hike out of Lower Granite Gorge.

By now, mid-morning of June 22, both men were weak and starving after more than three days without food. Ervin, believing it would be impossible for Payne to climb out, told him to wait there with the boat. He would come back, he promised Payne, when he found help.

Roughly a thousand feet up, Ervin found a spring. He drank his fill, wetted his face and shirt, and climbed higher. He hit the Redwall. It looked sheer and unclimbable. Ervin searched along its base but could not find a breach. Finally he gave up and walked back down to his spring. From there he walked over to the edge of the Tonto to see what Payne was doing. Payne, he saw, had started up the first sloping wall of Vishnu Schist. Payne looked up and saw Ervin. He yelled to him, "Hey, wait for me!"

Ervin explains how things continued to go wrong:

> *This is where I made another mistake. I yelled back, "Go back and stay there." If I had told him to come on up and also about the spring, he might have, just might have, stayed there, as he might have been too exhausted to go back down to the boat from up there. However, I knew that if I saw him fall it would unnerve me to the point that I would be unable to climb out, granting I had a chance at all.*

Now late morning, Ervin searched again for a breach in the Redwall looming so high above him. He finally found a chimney crack extending upward hundreds

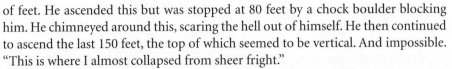

of feet. He ascended this but was stopped at 80 feet by a chock boulder blocking him. He chimneyed around this, scaring the hell out of himself. He then continued to ascend the last 150 feet, the top of which seemed to be vertical. And impossible. "This is where I almost collapsed from sheer fright."

But, continuing up, he found a small bench to the right with a barrel cactus growing on it, the only one he had seen. He hacked it open for the pulp. He reached the rim about a half hour before sundown on what was one day short of the longest day—and one of the hottest—of the year. That night, under a half moon, he walked southeast, pin-cushioning himself with cactus thorns. Ervin got so woozy before dawn that, as he descended a wash littered with round boulders, he was afraid he would fall and bash his brains out.

So he laid down and fell into a tortured sleep while awaiting the dawn. When it finally came, Ervin awoke to see only trackless desert. The absence of any evidence of human presence, even in the far distance, almost sent him "into a tail spin again."

A half-hour of walking, however, brought him to a barbed-wire fence. At about 8:00 a.m. on June 23, Ervin walked up to Charles McGee's ranch house and guzzled madly from his faucet. Then retched.

Ervin had hiked out of Lower Granite Gorge, from roughly eight miles downstream of Diamond Creek, possibly twenty or more miles and thousands of feet of elevation, including scaling the dreaded Redwall Limestone. The soles of his new shoes were worn completely off.

John Nelson, deputy sheriff at Peach Springs, led a six-man search party, including Ervin, back to the head of Bridge Canyon (River Mile 235.3).

Descending into it, they picked up Ervin's tracks coming out of the canyon and the Inner Gorge itself on the Tapeats Sandstone, the Tonto Plateau. On June 24, they reached the spring Ervin had first found on the 22nd and saw more of Ervin's tracks. The party then descended into Lower Granite Gorge. There, however, they could find no sign at all of Bill Payne or the *Bright Angel*.

A hard rain set in and likely obliterated the possibility of finding at least some of the tracks. Ervin showed Nelson the exact spot where he and Payne had tied up the boat at River Mile 233.6. Nelson, however, saw no sign of anything and remained unconvinced that a boat had ever parked there (Nelson, incidentally, had been the person who had originally dragged the *Bright Angel* above high water back at Diamond Creek after Bob Francy had abandoned it in disgust. Hence, Nelson now may have been annoyed with Ervin not just for all the hassle he was causing, but also for having hijacked the *Bright Angel* to begin with and then losing it).

Ervin also explained to Nelson how Payne had started to follow him. But the search party found no signs of that having happened either. At this lack of material evidence—no boat, no Payne, no foot prints, no boat drag marks, nothing at all—Nelson, again possibly already irked at Ervin for "stealing" his *Bright Angel*, began to doubt Ervin's story. Nelson reports in June 1931:

> *Camping at a spring on a bench that night that [over-] looked the Coun-*
> *try after looking a while Ervin seemed to be satisfied and started back toward*
> *bridge [sic] Canyon by him Self. After looking around a while longer we all*
> *decided from Ervin's actions, that they had an accident at this point Ervin get-*
> *ting to shore and he was not sure whether his partner had reached shore or not*
> *but after making this search around 2 miles in vicinity of where he came out*
> *he was satisfied in his own mind he was drowned, which he would not admit.*
> *After we reached the head of Bridge Canyon Ervin was in camp. I accused him*
> *of being doubtfull [sic] of his friend getting out of the river. He still maintained*
> *that he started to follow him out of the Gorge after they tied up boat being up*
> *side down at the time. After making the search from Point of Accident to bridge*
> *[sic] Canyon I still believe his partner never reached the bank of the river and*
> *was drowned.*

But Ervin's explanation is different. "I think he [Payne] must have taken the boat and gone on the day I left him or not later than the next morning."

Maybe so. But muddying this mystery even more, the river had spike-flowed another 500 cfs during Ervin's hegira through the desert, possibly raising the river enough to float the *Bright Angel* loose and to erase any marks made by its bow on shore.

Ironically, only three miles downstream of the place where Ervin had left Payne a cabin stood in a camp left by the Bridge Canyon Dam surveying team. Its shelves lay stocked with $75 worth of canned food, a large larder in 1931. "You know," Ervin wrote later, "it took me three months to get over my hunger."

So what happened to Bill Payne and the *Bright Angel?* A week of searching found no trace of either man or boat or even the life jacket. Nor was the boat or body ever seen by anyone downstream beyond the Grand Wash Cliffs. Likely Bill Payne drowned in the Colorado and the *Bright Angel* sank, but, even more likely—and as with the unsolved mystery of Glen and Bessie Hyde (more on this one later)—we will never know exactly what happened. But when, back in 1931, Ervin had tried to retrace William Payne's Hollywood connections to inform his relatives of his loss, he allegedly found no firm record that William Payne was related to Hollywood's famous Talmadge sisters. He did find instead that William Talmadge had quit his restaurant job in Hollywood prior to arriving at Hoover Dam. And when Talmadge had left, the restaurant proprietor informed Ervin, he had absconded with the entire day's till, a whopping $700. So, after all, William Talmadge may have become William Payne for reasons other than what he had disclosed to Ervin.

Even so, Payne's mysterious disappearance would haunt Ervin for the rest of his life. So much so that, in 1965, Ervin returned to Lower Granite Gorge with Harvey Butchart to retrace Ervin's harrowing, 1931 escape route out of the Canyon. Ervin considered his tragic adventure so gripping that he tried to sell it as a Hollywood screenplay. While the route was every bit as difficult and frightening as Ervin remembered, Hollywood passed on Ervin's saga of survival.

Far more river runners in Grand Canyon would die. Some of them would be unsuspecting passengers who trusted in the expertise of their guides; a few would be fortune hunters; some would be partiers who mixed too much alcohol with their river, or vice versa; some would be quixotic wayfarers, unrealistically prepared and living, then dying, a fantasy. Yet others would apparently be suicidal.

In October, 1938, members of the Amos Burg-Buzz Holmstrom-Willis Johnson trip down the Grand Canyon Colorado spotted a boat half-sunk and half filled with the sand on the north shore immediately downstream of Lava Canyon Rapid (River Mile 65.5). The boat was a 16-foot punt, square at both ends, built of new pine lumber. It was 4-feet wide and had 3-foot-high ends. Holmstrom reckoned that it was Jack Aldridge's boat.

Aldridge had put in at Green River about two months ahead of them. Aldridge, Holmstrom thought, had planned to manage the punt with a sweep oar off the stern. The boat was a very rough copy of the earliest boats that Norm Nevills had used on the San Juan River, the prototype of which was constructed from planks from an old horse trough and a privy, whose knotholes and cracks were patched with tin and caulked with old undershirts. At any rate, nothing remained in this derelict boat now wrecked below the Little Colorado but sand.

Upon investigation by the NPS they learned that in Glen Canyon just downstream of California Bar at Hansen (roughly Mile 100 upstream from Lees Ferry and one of the few Glen Canyon tributaries passable by a wagon or Model T off Highway 276), two Japanese visitors reported seeing Jack Aldridge. Aldridge had explained to these two tourists that he was planning to row through Grand Canyon all the way to the newly completed Boulder Dam (roughly 430 miles downstream). As bad as Holmstrom thought Aldridge's boat to be ("impossible to control in heavy rapids"), Aldridge had somehow navigated it in one piece through the forty difficult miles of Cataract Canyon.

But no one had seen the boat float past Lees Ferry. This could have been because Aldridge had passed at night, or during the day but was not seen (and in neither case had Aldridge stopped, which would be surprising), or because the boat passed without Aldridge aboard, either afloat, or half afloat. In any case, Aldridge's fate was a mystery. Did he drown in Glen Canyon, drown in Grand Canyon, or had he hiked out somewhere?

River sleuth Dock Marston pursued the mystery further in December of 1948. He tracked down an acquaintance of Aldridge (who was normally a painter in San Diego) named Waldo Watkins. Watkins wrote back, "Regarding Mr. Jack H. Aldridge. Met him last as I remember in late Spring 1940 at Palm Springs, Calif., have not seen or heard of him since that time, have inquired of others who also knew him to no avail. It seems he quietly disappeared." [punctuation added.] If

Watkins' memory was accurate, then somehow, somewhere, Aldridge escaped the Colorado and abandoned his boat only to vanish yet again from civilization. We include Aldridge's incomplete saga here only because, if Waldo Watkins' memory had instead failed him over the years as to the last date he had seen Aldridge, and if all of Aldridge's other friends' memories were correct in recollecting their not having seen him, then Aldridge may indeed have drowned in the Colorado River or died while trying to hike out.

Aldridge may seem eccentric, but a far more bizarre example of an eccentric lone boatman exists in the *Superintendent's Monthly Report* for October, 1946:

> On Oct. 24 one man in a rubber raft was sighted passing the mouth of Bright Angel Creek. Subsequent investigation revealed the man, who refused to give his name, had been put into the river near Lees Ferry on Oct. 19 by employees of Marble Canyon Lodge. The man, who may be Charles Roemer, of 353 E. 19th St., New York City, started without adequate food or equipment, and the success of his mission seems doubtful, although his knowledge of the river, obtained by extensive reading, was complete and accurate. On Oct. 26 Chief Ranger Perry E. Brown chartered a plane, and with Ranger Lauzon and Deputy sheriff John Bradley, flew over the river from Havasu Creek to the Bright Angel without sighting either man or raft. Subsequent investigation discloses that if the man is Chas. Roemer; he is a retired engineer from Hungary but recently arrived in the United States. The New York Chief of Police states that the man has no known friends or relatives in this country. [punctuation added]

Roemer's one-person attempt to traverse the full Grand Canyon Colorado in his small inflatable—allegedly without oars or paddles—was the first such attempt to run the entire river in five years and also the only try of the first 198 miles below Lees Ferry in 1946. A solo run had been done before Roemer, by Haldane "Buzz" Holmstrom in 1937. Holmstrom, however, had built a fine boat, knew how to row it, and he had worn a life jacket.

At any rate, Roemer was not a recent immigrant as the report above stated. He had emigrated from Hungary shortly after World War I, abandoning his wife and three children in Budapest. He then had lived in New York City for more than twenty years. Months before arriving at Lees Ferry he had quit his job and planned to move to California. En route, he also planned a solo run of the Grand Canyon Colorado. To get ready for this, he memorized the rapids from a book. He named off to Art Greene, owner of Marble Canyon Lodge, which rapids he could run and which he would have to line.

While preparing for his descent, Art Greene tried to dissuade the fifty-something-year-old Roemer. But to no avail. Even if things went wrong, Roemer insisted, he was a good swimmer and could simply swim to shore. On top of this level of confidence, Roemer impressed people as a stingy man. He bargained hard with Greene for two loaves of bread, two Bermuda onions, and five small packages of raisins, apparently as his only provisions for the entire 277-mile (ten-day) journey. Roemer's crash diet alarmed Greene even more. "Even if you just rub the onions on your belly," Greene warned Roemer "and don't even eat them, they still will be gone by the end of the trip."

We likely will never know whether Roemer failed to provide himself with a life jacket because he was miserly or because he was so self-confident in his swimming ability. Maybe it was both.

Roemer floated past Bright Angel Trail (River Mile 89) on 7,100 cfs at 3:20 p.m. on October 24, in his little "five-man" inflatable. He waved and called out to a surprised tour guide on shore. At this point, the guide said, Roemer seemed to be in fine spirits. Horn Creek Rapid, very nasty at this medium low water level, awaited Roemer less than two miles downstream. Indeed, Roemer was never seen nor heard from again.

The following June, despite searches by air and by water on Lake Mead by Harry Aleson, still no sign had been found of Roemer. A "memo to [Park] director" concluded, "The fate of this adventurer is still unknown, but he is presumed to have perished in the treacherous rapids below Bright Angel Creek. This incident emphasizes the need for better control of river parties, although the mechanics of such control are uncertain."

Only three years later, the Grand Old Man of the Colorado, Bert Loper, ended his rowing career in 24.5-Mile Rapid. Albert Loper was an enigma of sorts. No doubt he loved the Colorado River system. Since the late nineteenth century, he had worked as a boatman on the river's upper tributaries: the San Juan River, the Green River, and the Colorado in Glen Canyon. And he had worked in as many capacities as it was possible to do: as a mining employee, a free-lance prospector, and as head boatman on the 1922 U.S. Geological Survey expedition on the Green River. He had also worked as a Boy Scout leader in Glen Canyon. He built his stone cabin in Glen Canyon and lived for a while as a sort of protégé of Henry David Thoreau. For Loper, the Colorado River system seemed to be life itself. Then his exit from life.

Despite being known as "The Grand Old Man of the Colorado," Bert Loper had only rowed his first Grand Canyon trip in 1939, at the age of nearly seventy. That trip had worked out so well that Loper had built a new boat, the *Grand Canyon*, for his second Grand trip: a July, 1949 reunion trip with Don Harris and a few other friends with whom he had run in 1939. Loper made this trip, notes Dock Marston, "against the advice of four doctors who warned him that his proposed traverse of the canyon at the oars would be an excessive strain on his weak heart."

On July 8, three weeks short of his eightieth birthday, Bert unwisely rowed well ahead of Harris and company and entered 24.5-Mile Rapid with DeWayne Nichol riding on his deck. Both men wore life jackets. 24.5-Mile is a respectable rapid at all flow levels. At super-high flows, it is hideous. Bert Loper had entered this rapid in a solo boat at 51,500 cfs, an unforgiving flow.

As waves now filled their view, Nichol turned around. He was startled to see that Loper was not rowing. Nichol turned to Bert and allegedly uttered an admonition which today is cliché for Canyon boatmen: "Look to your oars, Bert!"

Instead Loper stared glassy-eyed at 24.5-Mile Rapid and let his oars lay idle. Speculation has it that, at this moment, he was either in the grip of yet another heart attack or instead was experiencing his first stroke. Either way, the *Grand Canyon* capsized. Bert floated out of sight into 25-Mile Rapid—itself a killer since Hansbrough and Richards had drowned there in 1889. Meanwhile Nichol clawed his way to the bottom of the upset boat. The current shoved it toward shore. Nichol leaped from it onto shore. But without the bowline. Now, as the boat drifted after Loper, Nichol wondered what to do next.

Reunited with Harris, Nichol explained how Bert Loper had vanished downriver. And "vanished" unfortunately turned out to be an accurate description of Loper's demise. Until a quarter of a century later. In 1975, hiker Curtis Verplegh of Socorro, New Mexico found what was decided to be Bert's skeleton on the south bank in the driftwood near the mouth of Cardenas Creek at River Mile 71. Despite Bert's expressed last wishes that if he died on the river, he wanted to be buried on shore, Loper ended up buried in Sandy, Utah. Even so, Bert Loper's own words still ring down to us from his diary written while he was leading the 1922 U.S. Geological Survey trip down the Green River. Indeed, Loper's words comprise the most succinct explanation for most boatmen's decisions today to keep running the river. Right after portaging Hell's Half Mile in Lodore Canyon, Loper wrote, "Who in the hell wants to be a white collar sissy when one can enjoy such grandeur and beauty such as this?"

Months later, by 1950, only about 345 people had traversed all or part of the Grand Canyon by boat since James White's float in 1867 and John Wesley Powell's first expedition in 1869. From 1950 to 1954, the number of new river runners per year averaged only 31 (the average was 62 per year for the entire 1950s decade) for completing first-time, full traverses. Commercial river running remained in its infancy. Such operations were polarized at one end with exclusive and expensive trips on small, plywood cataract boats modeled after the ones used by their commercial innovator, Norman Nevills (Nevills had run the first commercial Grand Canyon river trips in 1938 and had invented the profession of river-running in the Canyon). In the 1950s, these small hard-hulled boats were often run by Frank Wright, by Jim and Bob Rigg and their associates, and by Gaylord Staveley.

At the other end of the spectrum were large inflatable boats, often rigged together and pushed by outboard motors. These operations were epitomized during

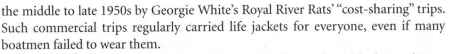

the middle to late 1950s by Georgie White's Royal River Rats' "cost-sharing" trips. Such commercial trips regularly carried life jackets for everyone, even if many boatmen failed to wear them.

Ironically, it may have been none of these types of boats that kicked Grand Canyon river-running into third gear. Instead it was running with no boats at all. The biggest single boost to the numbers of clients demanding river trips came directly from Bill Beer's and John Daggett's painful 26-day swim of the Grand Canyon Colorado begun in April 1955. Although poorly equipped due to lack of funds, they were smart enough to wear swim fins, long johns, neoprene jackets, and most importantly, Mae West life jackets. They also took movie footage. Good enough footage to support their future lecture circuit.

Beer and Daggett swam and shivered in the cold river. They ate and breathed flying sand (occasionally they wore swim goggles to see what they were eating). They bled through cracked hands and feet. Meanwhile, newspapers in the outside world printed headlines of their deaths in the Canyon. This odd odyssey is recounted beautifully in Bill Beer's engaging book *We Swam the Grand Canyon the True Story of a Cheap Vacation that Got a Little out of Hand*.

Soon after surviving this cheap vacation, Beer's and Daggett's movie aired on television. The two also ran their lecture circuit. Public awareness of the magnificence of the river corridor in Grand Canyon grew in leaps.

In 1955, the year Beer and Daggett swam the river, only 70 people ran it in boats. The next year, however, 135 people ran it. In the five years following Beer and Daggett's big swim, the number of people running the entire Grand Canyon portion of the river per year averaged 92. Also in 1955, Georgie White began running triple "G-rigs" of surplus U.S. Army ten-man rafts. These—plus her huge triple inflatable bridge pontoon rig—played a large role too in increasing numbers of tourists carried. In 1962, 372 people ran the river. The demand for river trips grew exponentially for years after that. In the 1990s, for example, every year saw more than 25,000 people run all or part of the Grand Canyon Colorado—in boats, and with life jackets. Since 1972, more than half a million people have run this river.

The pioneer era of running the Grand Canyon Colorado in boats began with John Wesley Powell's expedition in 1869 and lasted nearly 70 years, until 1938, when it was ended by Norm Nevills taking women clients who paid him for a Canyon river trip. But even by the end of 1955, when Beer and Daggett swam the Canyon, a grand total of only 570 people had run all or part of the river (101 of them by 1914).

In July of 1955—only two months after Beer's and Daggett's epic swim—yet another "river runner" drowned. George D. Jensen, age 28, embarked on a copy-cat swim down the Colorado. Instead of starting at Lees Ferry (River Mile 0), however, Jensen started near Furnace Flats (somewhere between River Miles 68 and 72, near the Tanner Trail) on a flow between 20,000 and 36,000 cfs. Jensen had no life jacket and is thought to have embarked on the river on a driftwood raft. His body was discovered near Hermit Rapid (River Mile 95) on July 13.

Despite ever heavier traffic, the Colorado claimed no new victims from among river runners for a decade. When it did, its next victim was an NPS ranger.

It happened on a chilly February 21, 1965, when two NPS rangers paddled their canoe out from Lees Ferry for fun. Phillip D. Martin, age 27, had been stationed at Lees Ferry for about five months. His paddling partner, Don Pledger, was a ranger in Great Smokies National Park. The two drifted downstream of Lees Ferry into Paria Riffle flowing at 9,000 cfs. They capsized. Fortunately, both men wore life jackets.

But it was February, a cold month, and the river itself was only 47 degrees. Pledger and Martin tried to right their boat, but failed. Next they discussed swimming for shore. Pledger stroked for shore and made it. Martin, however, stayed with the canoe, clinging to its limited buoyancy.

Phil Gentless, an NPS maintenance man, hauled Martin out of the river an hour later about 1.5 miles downstream of the Paria. He was still floating but had died, perhaps from drowning, though Page physician Dr. Ivan Kazan suspected that hypothermia had taken Martin's life.

As Grand Canyon grew bigger on the tourist map, more people got in trouble. On a relatively warm November 5 or 6, 1966, three young teenage hikers from Flagstaff camped near Phantom Ranch. They decided that riding a driftwood log on the Colorado sounded like a good idea. David Rider, age 14, Harold Lindstrom, age 15, and Peter Scott Le Brun, age 14, launched their log from the Boat Beach at River Mile 88. Very soon the 9,000 cfs current grabbed the log and hurried it downstream. As their log romped into Bright Angel Rapid, all three boys got nervous and swam toward shore. Peter Scott Le Brun never made it.

The next tragic whitewater death was a boatman. Moreover, he was a good, thoughtful boatman. And he was wearing a life jacket. In fact, this was what killed him.

Shorty Burton's tragic death was enigmatic in many ways. First, he was not even short. He was nearly six feet tall. Second, he was a very careful, organized boatman who developed techniques in the early 1960s to cover nearly every aspect of a Grand Canyon trip from cooking great food over a driftwood fire, to repairing and rigging a boat to make it tight and safe, to caring for passengers as if they were his own family, and, of course, to running rapids. Shorty Burton was mentor to a small legion of green boatmen for Hatch River Expeditions, all trying to learn the profession.

So what went wrong in Shorty's thirteenth year as a guide?

On June 14, 1967, one day after Shorty's 44th birthday, he powered into the top of Upset Rapid (River Mile 150) on 12,750 cfs. Shorty hated Upset. He had talked of it during this trip even 150 miles upstream at Lees Ferry. Moreover, in his previous

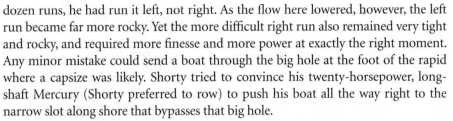

dozen runs, he had run it left, not right. As the flow here lowered, however, the left run became far more rocky. Yet the more difficult right run also remained very tight and rocky, and required more finesse and more power at exactly the right moment. Any minor mistake could send a boat through the big hole at the foot of the rapid where a capsize was likely. Shorty tried to convince his twenty-horsepower, long-shaft Mercury (Shorty preferred to row) to push his boat all the way right to the narrow slot along shore that bypasses that big hole.

He did not make it.

Shorty's boat was sucked into the steep hole, very likely at some angle other than straight-on. It flipped upside down in a flash. His passengers, more than half of the thirteen on the trip, scattered like jetsam and raced downstream willy nilly.

Shorty's fellow boatman, Clarke Lium, also ran the hole behind him, but punched through it. He gave chase, picking up swimmers en route. He hurried because, not seeing Shorty, he suspected Shorty was trapped under his boat. When, close to ten minutes later, he finally pushed Shorty's upside down boat to shore and re-flipped it right-side-up, Shorty was indeed underneath, but already dead.

The new style life jacket that Ted Hatch had talked Shorty into wearing on this trip had caught on one of the open eye-bolts suspending a floor board. Lium reckoned that, as cool under stress as Shorty was, had he been conscious he would have tried to use his knife to extricate himself. Hence, Lium suspected that Shorty had been knocked out during the flip.

But the causes of 44-year-old Shorty's last run may have been more complicated. Shorty was a diabetic and he smoked, both of which put him at risk for early heart disease. And, as will become clear in this chapter, traumatic immersion in cold water can trigger a quick cardiac arrest in such people at risk. Be that as it may, three hours of CPR failed to resuscitate Shorty.

After Shorty's death, new victims of Grand Canyon Colorado River running belong to what we think of as the "True Modern Era." In this era professional boatmen would no longer be the Colorado's predominant victims.

Some of them would continue to be Tom Sawyer-type amateurs. On April 23, 1971, for example, two young men at the boat beach at Phantom Ranch (River Mile 88) would be inspired like Rider, Lindstrom, and Le Brun had been five years earlier, to raft downriver. Bruce Allen and John Zombro, buddies from Massachusetts in their early 20s, found an abandoned "raft" of driftwood combined with an air mattress. The two young men tightened up their salvaged rig and launched it onto 15,000 cfs. Two other companions—Joseph Tomaselli and Steven Anderson—watched them from shore.

The two Huckleberry Finn rafters made it almost a mile before hitting the area above or in Pipe Creek Rapid (River Mile 89). This moderate whitewater disintegrated their raft. Zombro and Allen swam successfully to the north bank. But the hiking "route" back upstream along shore on this side cliffs out. So both men tried to swim across the Colorado to the south bank of the river to join their companions waiting on the river portion of the Bright Angel Trail. Allen dived in and made it across. Zombro dived in too but was never seen to surface at all.

But the modern era of surviving boatmen and drowning passengers finally had begun. On July 10, 1972, one of Georgie White's (a.k.a. Georgie Clark) G-rigs piloted by one of her guides flipped on day #1 in House Rock Rapid (River Mile 16.8). These rigs, used seriously in Grand Canyon for decades only by Georgie's company and, less so, by Dick McCallum's Grand Canyon Youth Expeditions, consisted of three inflatable U.S. Army, ten-man rafts roped side by side in a triple rig powered by a small, 10-horsepower outboard motor astern the middle boat. The outer two boats were rigged with one oar each. Georgie invented these rigs in a flash of insight in 1954, as a means of avoiding so many flips experienced when running the ten-man rafts as individual boats through big rapids. She considered them safer than the more flip-prone single boats. But she never managed to upgrade them to be adequately powered. She called them her "thrill boats" because, in part, they were so under-powered that they could not be finessed around the worst dangers in certain rapids. Instead, they just slammed into or through the worst hydraulics the rapid offered, creating unavoidable thrills. Adding to the thrill, Georgie often "hired" fairly inexperienced boatmen, whom she sometimes paid, sometimes not (depending on her end-of-the-season profit margin) to run these G-rigs. Georgie herself ran a much larger boat (discussed later).

Mae Hansen, age 64, rode one of these G-rigs during this July 1972 trip. Hansen was an annual passenger with Georgie—she had run the river 14 times in 14 years—though she had ridden only once before on one of these small triple rigs. The other times she had ridden with Georgie herself on her huge boat.

Hansen's G-rig flipped upside down in House Rock Rapid in 14,000 cfs. Hansen and two other passengers became trapped beneath it. Although many boatmen today shudder at the thought, Georgie used to instruct her passengers to stay under the boat when the boat flipped—Georgie admitted, "Having a boat flip in a rapid was just a way of life for me, and an enjoyable one at that." By staying under, or at least with, the boat, her passengers would not be scattered from hell to breakfast up and down the river. It is unclear whether Mae Hansen and her cohorts were thus instructed on this trip. But Georgie's "cardinal rule" for all passengers throughout her Canyon career did remain that everyone should stay with the boat if it flipped, instead of swimming the rapid independently or swimming to shore.

The other two people in Mae Hansen's predicament in the 47-degree water under the G-rig found air pockets. Mae Hansen apparently never was able to find enough air under the vast floating carpet of heavy rubber boats. She cardiac arrested in a laryngeal-spasm, "dry" drowning. Mae Hansen became the first commercial passenger to die as a river-running casualty in the history of river-running in the Canyon.

Curiously, Georgie excluded Mae Hansen from this category of dying due to a river-running mishap. Only a few years after Mae Hansen's death, Georgie, who believed that our lives and deaths are ruled by Fate, would write in her 1977 autobiography of river running, *Georgie Clark: Thirty years of River Running*:

> *Fortunately my trips have few major problems and I have the best safety record on the Colorado River. I have never had a fatal accident on any of my boats or even a minor one. Over more than thirty years of rapid running however, two people with me have suffered fatal heart attacks, including my very good friend, May [sic], who went with me for years.*

Interestingly, a passenger who did die of a heart attack on one of Georgie's trips was a 70-year-old man who collapsed—apparently due to natural causes—while taking photos from the back of her rig while running the Salmon in Idaho. Despite his natural and thus innocent demise, Georgie quickly hid his corpse under a tarp. After a prompt evacuation, she told her remaining passengers that the man had become ill and had to leave.

Georgie, who was unique in a number of her stylistic decisions on how a Grand Canyon trip should be run, was also known for her tendency to respond to tragedies with denial. Mae Hansen's and the unnamed 70-year-old's deaths are examples. But this was standard for Georgie, whose mother had insisted to Georgie as a girl that she never cry nor feel sorry no matter what went wrong. As the years passed, Georgie, who, again, believed that Fate (and luck) ruled all, took her mother's injunction to heart. As one biographer, Richard E. Westwood, wrote of Georgie's response to one of her passengers having sustained serious skull and spinal fractures in a fall while trying to assist others of her passengers who had gotten stuck on a high rock at Elves' Chasm, "Georgie's reaction to all of this was to pretend it hadn't happened."

Ironically, this seriously injured victim, Vernon Read of Milwaukee, Wisconsin, became—once he was evacuated from Elves' Chasm after his fall—another first. Read's evacuation was the first ever by helicopter of an injured river-runner in Grand Canyon history. The year was 1959. (Boater Ed Hudson, age 43, had been evacuated by helicopter from the Canyon nine years earlier, but not due to injury. Hudson of Paso Robles, California was piloting his 26-foot Chris Craft-type inboard motorboat on a seven-person trip with Dock Marston running second. Seven days into their mid-June, 1950 trip Hudson had capsized his boat, which next was essentially destroyed by colliding with boulders. Dock Marston's wife, due to an attack of "woman's intuition," overflew the river and discovered Hudson's predicament. Pilot Edwin Montgomery of Tucson not only evacuated Hudson, his son and two others, he also rescued a second pilot from Tucson, Elmar Carson, who wrecked his helicopter during the same rescue operation.)

While Mae Hansen was the first commercial river passenger to drown or suffer hypothermia-induced cardiac arrest in the Colorado in Grand Canyon, by no means would she be the last. On April 27, 1973, for example, on a research trip run by the Museum of Northern Arizona, Charles Lyon, age 25, drowned or died due to hypothermia due to flipping while running Sockdolager Rapid (River Mile 78.7) at 34,000 cfs in an inflatable kayak. Other members of the research trip did not catch Lyon, who apparently was unable to recover his boat or swim to shore in the 47-degree water despite his life jacket and a loose-fitting wetsuit.

Ranger Stan Stockton, standing on the Phantom boat beach spotted Lyon drifting in midriver and singing to himself. Stockton sprinted to the Ranger Station, retrieved a rope then ran across the Silver Bridge. From there he tried to calculate where the hypothermic victim might pass beneath the bridge so he could drop the rescue rope in the correct place. Stockton lined up for the interception then sent the rope down as Lyon drifted into the left eddy above the Silver Bridge (a.k.a. "the Devil's Spitoon"). Sadly, Lyon was too far gone with hypothermia to recognize Stockton or the rope as something of importance. He pawed the rope away, kicked backward out of the eddy back into the current, and drifted into oblivion.

Four years would pass before another boater would drown in the Canyon. And it ultimately happened for the first time in Lava Falls, the most infamous, hyped, and dreaded Grand Canyon rapid of this century.

At 8:45 a.m. on August 22, 1977, George "Butch" Hutton, ran his Sanderson 33-foot motor rig down the notorious Right Side of Lava on 23,000 cfs. Almost immediately, in the V-wave, water swamped Hutton's motor. Out of control like this, a 33-foot rig still might float through okay. Then again, it might turn sideways and flip. This had already happened to another big, motor rig here a few years earlier, earning a prize-winning photo in LIFE Magazine (and our rear cover).

Hutton turned around and pulled the start cord of the motor. The T-handle at the end of the cord broke off. Hutton tried pulling the rope. His pulls refused to coax the drowned motor back to life. Meanwhile, the mere four or five seconds that a boatman is allotted to accomplish anything in the Right Side of Lava elapsed.

The big boat slammed up onto the big Black Rock near the right shore and near the foot of the rapid. Still powerless, the boat rode up on the left side of the rock like Godzilla emerging from the ocean. The left side tube sucked under and submerged. The boat slid into the main waves immediately to the left of the rock. As the left tube of the rig had submerged the powerful waves had stripped a half dozen passengers and the boatman's assistant off the boat.

Hutton and his still-on-the-boat passengers, including a future AzRA boatman "hitchhiking" just for Lava Falls, Drifter Smith, scrambled along both sides of the boat hauling passengers back in. In less than a minute everyone was aboard. They thought.

Then the real nightmare began: someone spotted an empty life jacket floating near the boat.

Hutton had been running boat number two. Downstream, just below "Son of Lava Rapid," Sanderson's first boat had already pulled to the beach. Many of its passengers had walked back upstream to photograph Hutton's boat. In short, the boat ahead was not a safety boat, it was a "helpless" witness boat tied to shore.

Two of the passengers swept off the left tube when the rig slid off the Black Rock were 118-pound Andalea Buzzard, age 49, and her husband, Forrest. (Ironically, Forrest Buzzard was the liability insurance agent for Sanderson River Expeditions and had been invited on this trip many times by Jerry Sanderson before he finally agreed to go.) Forrest said he had gotten a hold of Andalea's ankle in the rushing water with one hand. He also had grabbed a front D-ring of the boat with his other. In the immediate vicinity of the Buzzards at this moment, the force of the current rushing away from the stalled rig was so powerful that the D-ring in Forrest's hand ripped off the boat. Next Forrest lost his grip on his wife's ankle.

Speculation has it that it was during this moment of being held by Forrest as he held the D-ring that Andalea's life jacket, a Holcomb Industries type 5, though apparently securely fastened before the rapid, failed to remain strapped to her body. Being held by the ankle against the current would have whipped her head-first downstream and also have caused her life jacket to act as a "parachute." This situation was worsened by her also wearing a rain jacket beneath the life jacket. It too acted like a parachute. The force of current on the lower hem of the jacket and life vest likely yanked both garments over her head and off her arms and then down the river.

People on the now drifting motorboat heard a faint scream. At least 100 feet upstream of them and slightly left of the main current, Andalea's head emerged briefly from the waves. She screamed for help.

Because the boat was still unpilotable due to lack of motor power, the boatman, Hutton, did the next best thing he could: he leaped into the river and swam upstream toward Andalea, who he knew to be a nonswimmer.

But she sank life-jacketless in the eddy fence whirlpools on the river left before he could reach her. Hutton continued swimming. Andalea surfaced briefly a half dozen times. Yet, each time, she emerged too far away for Hutton to grab her. At last, she sank and was not seen again.

Drifter Smith witnessed all of this in amazed horror. He said that the entire rig had now drifted into Son of Lava. As the rig exited this and floated past the right beach, and as the swamper tried to get the motor started, Drifter dived off the rig into the river. He swam to shore and to the other Sanderson rig. There he informed the other Sanderson boatman, trip leader Armand-Didier "Frenchy" Cadol, what had happened.

One of Andalea's and Forrest's two children had witnessed this mayhem from Hutton's boat, the other from Cadol's on shore.

As Drifter jogged back upstream along broken columns of black lava to rejoin his own river-running party, he saw Hutton on the opposite side of the river. By now he had escaped the river via the tiny beach by the warm springs. He was, Drifter saw, retching his guts out behind a bush.

Andalea's life jacket was found floating six miles downstream. When recovered, the straps needed to secure the back portion of her jacket were missing. Without them it could not have remained cinched onto her or anyone else in the water. Ironically, Andalea had worn this jacket, assiduously fastened in front, even on shore, because she was a non-swimmer. Andalea's body was discovered by boatman Perry White eight days later, on August 30, ten miles downstream, floating in an eddy at Whitmore Wash.

Years would pass before yet another river-running tragedy happened. And this time it would happen in a huge rapid on a phenomenally high flow. On the morning of June 25, 1983, Lane Jackson Parmenter piloted a 33-foot Tour West motor rig into Crystal Rapid (River Mile 98.5) on a horrendous flow of 69,000 cfs. Parmenter's job on the rig was boatman's assistant. Parmenter had run the Idaho Salmon 38 times, but he had been on only two Grand Canyon trips before.

Tour West's assigned boatman was Darryl Roberson. Roberson and Parmenter had scouted Crystal for at least 30 minutes. They had then decided that the latter should make a hard right run. This meant starting his cut to the right very early to avoid plowing into a now monstrous Crystal Hole at center left. It also meant, Roberson explained (to Parmenter, and later to Ghiglieri), continuing to motor their rig so far toward the right shore that they should "try to ram the trees."

Parmenter, however, missed his cut. He later complained, "the boat didn't have enough power."

Other guides who watched this run in stunned disbelief (personal, private communications from witnesses), however, alleged that, as Parmenter was running the boat in his entry to Crystal, Roberson was sitting in front of Parmenter and gesticulating to him via emphatic gestures of his right arm pointing to the right side of the river, signaling, "GO TO THE RIGHT NOW." Roberson continued gesturing like this throughout the entry and into the wave train of rapid, signaling Parmenter to steer to the right side of the rapid, away from Crystal Hole.

Parmenter, however, seemed unable to—or was unconvinced that he should— steer his boat into an aggressive angle to the right early during his run. He committed a double-error: he entered Crystal far too near the middle of the tongue instead of well to the right to begin with, and then he began his break-out move late instead of early. A haunting series of 14 photographs taken by Dick Kocim from shore of Parmenter's run (and later published in Tom Myers' *Fateful Journey: Injury and Death on Colorado River Trips in Grand Canyon*) shows his too-far-left entry in the main flow of the tongue—and next shows that his boat stayed in the tongue. Worse, Kocim's photos also reveal a very weak downstream right ferry angle, one that vanished two or three seconds into Parmenter's entry to become a nearly straight downstream angle and mainstream run.

By the time the Tour West rig dropped into the sixty-foot-wide Crystal Hole, Parmenter had angled the rig directly downstream into it. Then he yelled, "Oh God, we're going to hit the hole!"

Kocim's photos at this point show the 33-foot Tour West rig buried almost three-quarters and nose first in Crystal Hole and vanishing into and under the 25-foot-high standing wave. This 3-ton boat quickly pivoted to the left. Next it surged up, vibrated, then slid back down into the hole fully sideways. The next frames show the boat standing vertical on its left tube, then flipping. The rig stayed in the hole a few more seconds as its metal frame bent, nylon straps snapped like cotton thread, and the boat itself partially de-rigged while contorting like a pretzel. Meanwhile everyone who had been aboard flushed into Lower Crystal at blurring speed.

William R. Wert, age 62, was one of those passengers. He "drowned" in 69,000 cfs despite wearing his life jacket and despite having been in "reasonably good" physical condition. Two other passengers injured their legs during this mishap but were rescued in time. Both had to be evacuated.

On November 10 of this same year, a bizarre and mysterious boating tragedy occurred. It began when a pair of fishermen, next-door neighbors from La Mesa, California, drove most of the day from San Diego to Lees Ferry. Dick Benjamin Roach, age 71, and Richard Bruce Sheperski, age 50, then launched their Monarch 16-foot aluminum motorboat at the Ferry. For November, the river was flowing an unusually high 23,000 cfs. The two men intended to power upstream into Glen Canyon to "Camp 9" via their 10-horsepower motor, an ambitious goal considering the high flow and their low horsepower.

Four days later, after this pair of fishermen was overdue to return, the NPS initiated a search and rescue. A fixed-wing overflight spotted a small aluminum boat and a blue tarp on the north side of the river in an eddy below Soap Creek Rapid (River Mile 11.25). Rangers Tom Workman and Joe Evans landed in a helicopter to investigate. The boat, the two rangers found, was badly damaged. It also appeared to have been pulled up onto shore by hand. Had Sheperski and Roach survived and then abandoned this stuff?

While Evans overflew the river at 50 feet, Workman hiked up the nearby, four-mile Soap Creek Trail toward the rim. He found footprints, but as this was a hiking route for fishermen, they could have been anyone's.

Meanwhile Evans landed at River Mile 52 to talk with a four-person private river trip led by Ron Stark, which also had put in at Lees Ferry on the 10th, the same day that Sheperski and Roach had intended to motor upstream.

Stark's group had camped that night below Badger Rapid (River Mile 8) on the left shore. After dark, at 7:30 p.m., one of the group, Fred Stasek, noticed a light

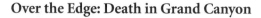

coming downstream. The four campers had a campfire blazing and—to celebrate their first night of finally making it onto the river—had been drinking wine. Now the four stared at the approaching light. Why anyone would be boating through Badger Rapid at night and on 23,000 cfs puzzled all of them.

The mystery light drifted into Badger Rapid but remained pointed at the campers and their fire. Stark's group aimed their flashlights into the rapid to try to see what was happening in the peek-a-boo wave train. They saw what looked like a low-floating boat. They yelled questions over the roar of the waves.

Fred Stasek said that, through the "pitch dark" they saw:

—a long narrow object riding the center of the current. It cleared the water by less than a foot, and a dark irregular shape appeared near the leading edge of it—apparently a person, holding on. I yelled, and I believe I heard a response— "Hello!" or "Help!" barely audible over the roar of the river.

Ron Stark reported, "I yelled 'Hello' and I heard someone on the boat yell back something like 'Help!' I was not willing to go downriver at night to try to catch them."

The light grew brighter and still aimed at them. Then it passed them and continued downstream beyond the rapid's tailwaves. None of this made any sense to the four on shore unless: a. someone who really knew the river well was running it in the dark to make up lost time (this has been done by several deadhead [passenger-less] trips running empty to Phantom Ranch); or b. someone was in real trouble and could not start his motor, could not use his oars or paddles to go to shore, and could not even lean over the gunwale of the boat and use his hands or another paddle-like object to paddle to shore; or c. someone was in even worse trouble: their boat was already upside down.

Stark's party knew that if some variation of "b" or "c" was the true answer, then whatever was happening was unsafe. So the group set off three or four aerial flares toward small planes they saw. Meanwhile two of the four campers, Stasek and Nigel, walked downstream over the boulders in the dark about a mile "in hope that the person(s) had eddied out or swum to shore." But the two men saw nothing, not even the drifting light.

Downstream the next morning Stark's group found a Monarch 16-foot boat upside down in the eddy below Soap Creek Rapid. The hull had holes punched through it. A large blue tarp and some other items floated nearby. But they found no footprints on shore. The four dragged the boat onto shore and spread the tarp as a signal. When they turned the boat right-side-up they found two life jackets and another flotation device bundled and tied to its bow. Stark's group left a note of explanation of their discovery wrapped in a brown rain poncho weighted down with a rock. Then they rowed downriver to puzzle over this tragedy for days.

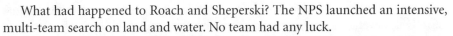

What had happened to Roach and Sheperski? The NPS launched an intensive, multi-team search on land and water. No team had any luck.

What went wrong here? This is not an easy mystery to solve. Roach and Sheperski's boat had a ten-horsepower outboard, a three-horsepower backup engine, and a pair of oars. The ten-horsepower engine was still mounted on the boat when Stark and friends found it. But when the boat drifted into Badger Rapid, they had heard no motor noise. Again, a ten-horsepower motor provides a very limited thrust when traveling upstream against 23,000 cfs unless the boat is piloted by a savvy river boatman.

On March 23, 1984, more than four months later, Walter M. Gregg found most of Dick Roach's badly decomposing body (an arm and lower leg were missing) in an eddy near Vasey's Paradise (River Mile 32).

On August 28 of that same year, nine months after Roach's and Sheperski's mishap, Skip Bell, a boatman for Grand Canyon Expeditions, reported that one of his passengers, Wayne, had discovered a human skull with soft tissue still attached. The skull was under a honey mesquite tree and next to mule deer bones and an antler. The mesquite was 75 yards from the river, well above the historical fluctuation zone, and 150 yards downstream of Nankoweap Creek (River Mile 53).

Obviously some person or animal had placed the skull in this location. Despite diligent searching, no other human body parts were found nearby. Mountain lions do frequent the Nankoweap drainage. And these predators sometimes cache kills or scavenged carcasses. Dental charts identified this skull as Richard Sheperski's.

Yet how these two fishermen drowned remains an unsolved mystery. Capsizing a 16-footer on the quiet water of Glen Canyon is uncommon, but it would have been easy had they allowed their underpowered boat to lodge against a projection of shoreline that was being hit by downstream current. Capsizing also would have been easy in Paria Riffle (River Mile 1) at 23,000 cfs, had the two accidentally drifted downstream past Lees Ferry in the dark. That neither man had donned his life jacket may suggest they had experienced an abrupt and unexpected capsizing, wherever it took place.

Once they began drifting, with their boat upside-down and out of control, hypothermia would have set in quickly in the 47-degree water, well before reaching Badger Creek Rapid and then floating past the river-runners camped there. Rapid hypothermia and psychological shock might also explain why neither man retrieved and donned his life jacket from under the bow. These scenarios seem to be the only ones that make sense.

Except that all four people in Stark's party camped at Badger that night apparently thought they had witnessed (albeit in the dark) a boat floating right side up and with a light aboard it being aimed at them by a person inside that boat, not in the water.

Indeed these four witnesses were nonplussed in trying to imagine a realistic scenario to explain what they saw. They spent days afterward trying to make sense of it. Only several months later did they learn that one of the two fishermen had had a serious heart condition which may have lead to cardiac problems during that first afternoon on the swollen Colorado. Had he experienced a cardiac arrest, and if the other man was unfamiliar with the river, or with the boat's motors, or with the location of unlit Lees Ferry in darkness, or all of the above, this second man could have allowed the boat to drift downstream for hours in the expectation that Lees Ferry would be well illuminated—and thus noticeable—and that it would offer them help in the form of an NPS ranger.

The alternate possibility also exists that the pair may have, after driving several hundred miles from San Diego that morning, arrived at Lees Ferry so late that they launched their boat at twilight or after dark. Next, in the darkness and against the surprisingly powerful current, they may have ended up going downstream instead of upstream without noticing it. Why no motor was heard running at Badger, however, remains a mystery—unless it was drowned out by the roar of whitewater. In any case, perhaps only upon pounding through the huge waves of Badger did either fisherman realize their serious error. Stark and his three companions had neither the confidence nor state of mind to abandon their camp in the dark at a moment's notice and then risk their lives giving chase on the ink-black river downstream of Badger to rescue someone from what may or may not have been an emergency.

As the many examples discussed thus far reveal, life jackets are aptly named. Being on the river or *in* the river beyond chest level without a life jacket is the primary situation in which nearly all drowning victims above had drowned. Indeed 17–18 people (Jack Aldridge's drowning remains questionable) who were originally in boats or rafts in Grand Canyon drowned after mishaps because they wore no personal flotation devices. Eleven other victims discussed later in this chapter drowned from Lees Ferry without flotation devices. Eight to eleven more victims yet without life jackets drowned while trying to cross the river via a boat, raft, or air mattress—or just by swimming. These bring the total number of "boating" mishap deaths associated with a lack of life jackets to 36–39.

To these we must add 22 other victims, nearly all hikers, who deliberately decided to enter the river without jackets, usually for a swim, and drowned plus yet 13 other involuntary swimmers—including eight disappearances from a river-running camp or hike plus hiker Jody Mack and four fishermen who fell from shore—who also drowned without life jackets.

The total number of known drowning victims not wearing life jackets in all situations on the Grand Canyon Colorado is somewhere between 71 and 74 of a total of 93. In contrast, thousands of other people wearing personal flotation devices have been tossed into the river—and serious whitewater—via mishaps or have entered it voluntarily and survived.

Two other victims drowned despite having been dumped into the Colorado

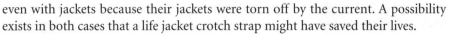

even with jackets because their jackets were torn off by the current. A possibility exists in both cases that a life jacket crotch strap might have saved their lives.

Many passengers these days wear a rain jacket—or worse a rain poncho—while riding a boat through dangerous rapids. A poncho should be avoided altogether because almost certainly it raises the risk of drowning if the wearer is dumped into the rapid and the poncho material wraps around the head of the wearer. If rain gear is worn in serious rapids, it is best worn *under* a life jacket and should allow for tight wrist/cuff closures.

Due to the obesity epidemic now characterizing Americans, many passengers on river trips are wearing life jackets that, even though strapped snugly, will not remain on these people's pear-shaped bodies in serious hydraulics but instead can be yanked over their heads by the river itself or by a rescuer trying to haul them back into a boat. The solution? Life jackets equipped with crotch straps for rotund people.

If only one thing is to be gained from this chapter, it should be: *Never enter the Colorado more than waist deep and never allow yourself to be in the position to accidentally enter the Colorado without wearing the best personal flotation device available, Coast Guard approved, and fastened securely on your body.*

The wearing of a life jacket even on dry ground adjacent to fast water while scouting rapids is a good practice. Many rescues of swimmers by on-shore boaters have been facilitated by their still wearing their life jackets. Conversely, without them, conducting a rescue may become either impossible or overly risky.

Only seven months after Dick Roach's decomposing body surfaced, yet another boater drowned. On June 7, 1984 a private boatman, Tom Pillsbury, a 66-year-old from El Cerrito, California and an heir to the famous Pillsbury flour and baking mixes company, rowed his inflatable boat on a private trip into Crystal Rapid (River Mile 98.5). Pillsbury had erred, as so many boaters have done here, by entering too far left to make the cut to the right. Not only was Pillsbury rowing against a very difficult flow level, according to trip member Carolyn Marley (now Carolyn Castleman), he was trying to identify his critical "landmarks" in the rapid with one bad eye and very poor vision otherwise. Perhaps this helps explain why trip members on shore—Bob Finkbine and Jeff Jackel—were surprised to see Pillsbury entering the rapid out of sequence, unprotected by a companion boat, and also making no solid attempt to execute a break-out-of-the-tongue cut toward the right shore. In spite of his previous trips down the Canyon (on lower flows), on this very challenging flow of 43,500 cfs, Pillsbury allowed his raft to be sucked down the center of the wave train toward Crystal Hole.

Pillsbury had been told to run last of six boats. But he had ignored this and entered, carrying two passengers, Pauletta Davis and Monica Corella, as a surprise third boat late in the first, planned "pulse" of two boats. This trip had split its boats during this run so that some of the boatmen could take photos instead of running

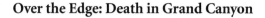

all the boats in one tight pulse for mutual support. This 43,500 cfs level was so difficult and dangerous at Crystal that many commercial rowing trips during this period and flow level routinely walked their passengers around Crystal Rapid on shore as they ran their boats through empty in one pulse on a conservative "cheat-" run hugging the right shoreline. Those who walked would reunite in the boats below the first half of Crystal. After having watched NPS rangers successfully run the right side of Crystal in oarboats, however, members of Pillsbury's trip had decided not to use these tactics.

When Pillsbury failed to cut to the right, a large wave near the top of Crystal swept him off his rowing seat and flipped his fifteen-foot inflatable upside-down. Next he and his passengers Pauletta and Monica swam the rapid.

To complicate matters, ahead of Pillsbury, the number-two boat behind Marley had also capsized. Luckily, the three people aboard it—boatman Scott Berry, trip permit holder Susan Groth, and passenger Linda—swam to the right shore.

As the NPS incident reports and letters from Bob Marley and from Carolyn explain: Bob Marley had rowed the lead boat with his son Scott, wife Carolyn, and Don Johnson aboard and had kept it right side up, but swamped. By the time Pillsbury, his passengers, and his upside-down boat washed downstream unexpectedly, Marley was already "engaged in securing boat number two and its crew" by tying multiple ropes from the boats—one swamped, the other upside down—to shore.

One of Pillsbury's two passengers, Monica, swam to the right shore well upstream of Marley's position and unseen. Meanwhile, as Carolyn reports, Pauletta did not try to swim to shore but instead held onto the bowline of Pillsbury's upset raft such that Marley and the others did not see her. She would not grab terra firma until a mile later, after abandoning Pillsbury's boat, below Tuna Rapid. (She was so hypothermic and traumatized by this swim, Carolyn noted, that she almost could not continue with the trip).

Pillsbury, separated from his boat, floated past the Marleys but on the opposite (left) side of the river and close to the far shore. Members of this trip had earlier seen Pillsbury, with his low body mass, become hypothermic quickly. Now, as Bob and Carolyn and other witnesses interviewed in the NPS report indicate, Pillsbury waved his arm to attract attention and yelled out to Marley as he passed, "Help, Bob!"

Carolyn said that she and the others yelled back to Pillsbury, "SWIM OUT! SWIM OUT!"

Pillsbury yelled back, "Help! Help, I can't!" Indeed, although Pillsbury drifted close to the left shore, no witness saw him try to swim toward it. On the contrary, as Pillsbury drifted downriver from here, Don Johnson saw him instead simply hold both of his arms across his chest in a "gripping-your-life-jacket" position suggesting hypothermia and/or to hold his life jacket snugly preparatory to entering Tuna Rapid.

With two of the first three boats upside down, and two of the people who had been riding in them scattered in the river downstream, Marley says he made a "triage decision" to continue his "commitment to the previously overturned raft [boat number two] and its crew."

The next boats to arrive were part of the group's second planned pulse through Crystal, delayed after Pillsbury's episode, and were rowed by Jeff Jackel and Bob Finkbine. Both boats had emerged from Crystal right side up. When Jackel caught up with Marley, as Carolyn notes, Marley told him there were two people who had swum into Tuna Rapid and to try to catch them.

Jackel picked up Pauletta below Tuna Rapid (River Mile 99.3 to 99.8) where she had self-rescued. Jackel tried to combat her hypothermia then continued to row downriver in hopes of catching Pillsbury, now downstream with a lead of unknown distance.

Meanwhile, four miles downstream, the NPS river patrol that had already run Crystal ahead of Pillsbury's party and parked for lunch near River Mile 103 (Shady Grove). At noon they saw Pillsbury's upside-down boat drifting toward them. Ranger Dennis Haskew rowed out to capture it. Ranger Becca Lawton paddled her kayak out to help. To her alarm, she spotted a person floating in midriver face down. At Becca's call, Haskew abandoned the drifting boat in an effort to rescue the victim.

It was Pillsbury. His pupils were fixed and dilated. He was not breathing. He showed no pulse.

The rangers initiated CPR immediately.

The time was 12:57 p.m., 57 minutes after Pillsbury had flipped his little boat. The river rangers radioed for assistance. Ranger Paramedic Sherrie Collins arrived with Ranger Larry Fredricks at about 3:00 p.m. Pillsbury had been on shore in 105-degree heat for two hours as the river rangers performed CPR. Yet now Ranger Collins found his core temperature to be only 78 degrees. Even so, he still had heart activity, albeit only ventricular fibrillation. Unfortunately, despite a prompt (at this point) evacuation to Flagstaff Medical Center with advanced life support en route, Pillsbury was finally pronounced dead at 5:39 p.m.

Pillsbury had been wearing a kayaking-type life jacket, one that does not orient a swimmer face upwards. Ironically, he also had a farmer-john wetsuit offering both warmth and more flotation, but instead of wearing it, he had packed it while rowing into Crystal. He had "drowned," likely due to cold shock syndrome (discussed a few pages below) as he careened downstream below Crystal, despite his U.S. Coast Guard-approved life jacket.

One of the cardinal rules of river-running is: The welfare of people always comes before that of equipment. During runs of the Colorado between April through October, for example, even if boaters—as a result of chasing people downriver as a first priority—lose one or more boats or other critical gear, they remain safe in their decision that people must be rescued first. This is because it's nearly impossible to be stranded along the Colorado during prime time for more than 24 hours without another trip arriving to render assistance. This "people-first-gear-second" rule should be followed regardless of season.

Only a couple of months later—on August 25, 1984—the legendary Georgie White had her own out-of-control ride. On Georgie's personally-guided Royal River Rats' raft trips, she used a boat that some guides had nick-named the Queen Mary. Georgie simply called it her "big boat." Some of her boatmen called it "Mama's boat." The Queen Mary title came naturally because the boat was so huge. Georgie invented it in 1955 with the twin goals of increased safety and high passenger capacity in mind. She simply rigged together three "donut" military bridge pontoons, each about 33 feet long but with the center donut staggered sternward about four feet. This giant triple rig, filled internally with yet more "sausage" tubes, was about 37 feet long by 27 feet wide. Georgie considered this mammoth rig unflippable. She probably was right. Yet staying aboard this big rig in some of the routes Georgie chose through big rapids was problematic for some of her passengers.

Georgie's technique at Lava Falls (River Mile 179.4), for example, was to raise her passengers' expectations to a frenzy of anticipation of impending whitewater mayhem. While we other boaters stood and scouted Lava from the basalt boulders above, we could hear Georgie's boat approaching (Georgie herself rarely scouted Lava). Even over the roar of Lava Falls, we could hear her passengers screaming like maniacs as the Queen Mary drifted into the rapid. Sometimes nearly twenty passengers would be seated, facing outward and wildly kicking their legs in the air.

Georgie normally instructed her passengers to keep their feet up and off the boat so they would not become entrapped between the strapped-together tubes of her hybrid rig during its convolutions in the radical whitewater that Georgie ran. At Lava Falls, Royal River Rats' tradition had evolved this feet-in-the-air, safety position among some passengers into a two-footed kicking-into-the-air frenzy.

Then, immediately upstream of the center of the rapid, Georgie would yank her 20-horsepower motor out of the river, cut it, and don her construction hard hat (if she were not already wearing it). Next she would slip down into her "hidey hole," a semi-private compartment forward of the motor well where she had rigged two high wrist straps. She would slip her wrists through these. Then, in a crucifixion position, she would ride out whatever the Ledge Hole of Lava Falls dished Mama's Boat.

In 1955, Georgie had christened her Big Boat by running the center Ledge Hole (a run no other company makes on purpose). Everyone aboard had survived that experiment. So the Ledge Hole too had become tradition. Running the Ledge Hole, however, normally entailed gut-wrenching gyrations of Georgie's entire boat. Once the Queen Mary hit the tail waves, Georgie would drop her motor back into the river and frantically yank its start cord.

Again, this was her standard run. And by August 25, 1984 she had run Lava Falls at least 150 times.

Passengers on this wild ride knew they had to hold on tight. Norine Abrams, however, was 58 years old and weighed 240 pounds. And at 11:00 a.m., when Georgie arrived at Lava, she had let the Queen Mary drift well off center. As she motored into view above Lava, a Moki Mac commercial river trip already stood on the left shore scouting. They wanted to be dead sure they had their entry to the left route figured out to safely run left of the dangerous Ledge Hole. One of these witnesses, river guide John Davenport, reported Georgie's—to him—astonishing approach to Lava Falls:

> She [Georgie] was pretty far left in her entry. It looked like she was going to run left. But then I saw her stand up and look toward the Ledge Hole. As soon as she saw she was going to miss it, she fired up her motor and powered over to the center of the river. She was too late to reach the Ledge Hole and also straighten out. So she entered the Ledge Hole at a 45-degree angle. It was the worst example of gross incompetence I have ever seen.

As Georgie dropped her *Queen Mary* powerless and nearly sideways over the center Ledge Hole, flowing at 24,500 cfs, the boat stalled in the reversal water. The 33-foot donut in the upriver section of the Ledge Hole submerged and folded under the center donut. One of Georgie's passengers at that moment, 15-year-old Robert Bisson, (in a letter to us on April 4, 2008) explains what happened:

> Norine [Abrams] was not happy about being on this trip. From the start at Lees Ferry, she was cranky....During the trip, myself and my younger brother, and another girl about our age learned to kind of stay away from her. She didn't like the noise, the temperature, the lack of service, etc. Her husband was pretty cool...She was overweight and shouldn't have been there and she usually needed help getting situated on the Big Boat each day.
>
> The big boat's construction had us seated in two groups, facing each other and alternating spaces along the two joints where the outer donuts were connected to the center donut. When we entered the rapid [Lava Falls] at a 45-degree angle, I ended up being able to essentially face angled forward as we went over and into the hole. I felt like I was going straight down and then straight back up again.

Bob Bisson added (to Ghiglieri) that Norine had been so nervous that morning about running Lava Falls that Georgie had offered to tie her to the Big Boat. But Norine had declined. Bisson continues:

My brother was seated with Norine and her husband and at least one of my parents in the other group on the Big Boat. They were in the rear, due to our entry to the rapid, and when the rear donut folded up under the center section, their seating area was immediately exposed to the river and 4-6 people, including my brother and Norine, were forced overboard UNDER THE BIG BOAT.

As Norine Abrams had slid off the *Queen Mary*, her husband Ray Abrams had grabbed her. Soon, however, the force of the current was injuring his arm and he had to let go. As Bisson continues:

The river caught them and took them underneath for quite a while. My brother remembers this too, and vividly describes how he knew he was going in, and under, and he held his breath for a very long time. He attempted to surface, and remembers the fear when he came up to find the bottom of the Big Boat and everything was dark. He and I have been swimming, including the ocean, since we were in diapers, and he kept his calm and held his breath until he finally surfaced with the assistance of a big arm that reached down and pulled him up. He rode out the main rapid while under the boat. Norine went through this same physical trauma. When we cleared the second rapid set (Son of Lava, I think) everyone began counting heads, grabbing people clinging to the boat, and trying to reset the buckled section. It was then we saw Norine bobbing in the water ahead of us and appearing unconscious.

The other boat, the thrill boat [a motorized triple rig of Army 10-man boats], is the one who was able to catch up to her, not Georgie.... We almost lost Norine down the river, considering we were scheduled to pull over and camp at the helicopter pad just below [3 miles from] Lava Falls. The small thrill boat motored to her, passengers grabbed on and held, and then motored slightly against the current to get back to the sand bar where we camped that night. When the guides pulled her out of the river to begin CPR on the beach, the force of the rapid on her body was obvious: her jeans, her underwear, and her shoes had been completely removed from her body. She was naked from the waist down....

I stood there for a long time while the guides (one was an L.A. firefighter) made their best effort at CPR [for 35-40 minutes]. Her husband cried the whole time and I felt really bad for him. My parents didn't really shelter us from the whole scene, we were a tight group by now [after a one-week trip], my brother and I had proven ourselves and we just stood by and watched the CPR attempt....

Neither Georgie nor anyone else made a big commotion about what was going on, and I think this is because it was obvious. She was dead, nothing was going to change that, and we had to wait until the next day to inform anyone about it.

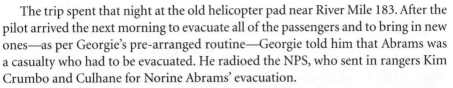

The trip spent that night at the old helicopter pad near River Mile 183. After the pilot arrived the next morning to evacuate all of the passengers and to bring in new ones—as per Georgie's pre-arranged routine—Georgie told him that Abrams was a casualty who had to be evacuated. He radioed the NPS, who sent in rangers Kim Crumbo and Culhane for Norine Abrams' evacuation.

Crumbo explained to me (Ghiglieri) that same day in frustration that 73-year-old Georgie had been exhorting him in irritation to hurry up before anyone else arrived and saw Abrams' body bag. Crumbo, who now injured his back moving the heavy victim, responded, also in irritation, "Georgie, you just killed this woman, now you want me to hurry up and hide the body?" Georgie stared Crumbo in the eye and said, "You're damned right I do. Now get her out of sight before you scare these new people."

For several years after the June 1983, 97,300 cfs flood of the Colorado remodeled Crystal Rapid, this rapid would prove to be not only The Scary One in Grand Canyon—eclipsing the terror of Lava Falls hands down—but, far more sinister, The Lethal One. At 1:30 p.m., on June 14, 1989, for example, Martin M. Hunsaker, the 54-year-old pilot of a 33-foot motor rig, entered Crystal as trip leader for a Georgie's Royal River Rats trip. He lost motor power in the second tail wave after entering the rapid on 13,250 cfs. Hunsaker had aimed for the wild left run, standard at that flow level for many motor companies.

Every effort Hunsaker made to restart his motor in those five seconds above the Hole and the left wall failed. Tellingly, as that brief time ran out, passenger Kjeld Harris heard Hunsaker exclaim, "Oh, shit!"

Hunsaker's 33-foot "baloney" rig slammed directly into the left cliff wall of schist downstream of the mouth of Slate Creek and to the left of Crystal Hole. The rig inched up the wall, stood on edge, sucked a lower side tube, then flipped upside down.

More than a dozen people aboard flew, dropped, or were slam-dunked into the Colorado. In the ensuing several hundred yards of whitewater, nearly all of them but Hunsaker swam to the upside-down boat. They held onto it, or climbed up it, or were dragged aboard by Hunsaker's two other crew members who had already clambered aboard.

Other swimmers agree that Hunsaker did not try to return to the upside down boat. Assistant boatman Paul Semerjian reported seeing Hunsaker not far upstream of it. Hunsaker gave Semerjian a "thumbs-up" signal "indicating that he was alright." As Semerjian pulled more passengers aboard, he lost sight of Hunsaker, who he thought might be swimming after yet another passenger downstream of them.

Even after Semerjian managed to tie the capsized rig to shore immediately above Tuna Rapid (River Mile 99.3), he said he was not worried at Hunsaker's absence. Only after Semerjian motored the rig downstream (the rig was still upside down; the crew simply reversed the motor mount, et cetera, and ran the boat upside down) to join Georgie at her camp at River Mile 107.8, did he learn that Hunsaker was missing in action.

At 6:30 p.m. that evening, a Hatch River Expeditions trip led by Curtis "Whale" Hanson found Hunsaker. Steve E. Hatch spotted Hunsaker floating "mostly submerged" in the main current below Tuna Rapid (River Mile 100.1). When Hatch pulled Hunsaker aboard, he was pulseless, without respirations, and his pupils were fixed and dilated. Whale told me (Ghiglieri) that a physician aboard checked Hunsaker's core temperature then pronounced him dead. An autopsy concluded Martin Hunsaker had "drowned" in Crystal Rapid despite his life jacket, an Extrasport, "shorty" type III with 22 pounds of floatation displacement. Hunsaker was the fourth victim to "drown"/cardiac arrest due to cold shock syndrome in Crystal Rapid while wearing a life jacket.

Whale, in tears, and Steve Hatch stopped in Georgie's camp to deliver Hunsaker's body and to inform her that her number-one guide and trip leader had just drowned. Georgie, Whale said (to Ghiglieri), just stared at him as if he were speaking Greek then walked away. Eight of Hunsaker's passengers decided to leave the river due to this Crystal flip. An NPS helicopter evacuated them to the South Rim.

A pattern began at Crystal. On April 27, 1990 Gene Elliot Stott, age 54, rowed his 13.5-foot Miwok into Crystal as a member of a private trip but flipped and died shortly afterward on shore due most likely to cardiac arrest spurred by cold shock syndrome—despite his having worn a life jacket and despite three hours of CPR. On March 30, 2007 Marc Allred, age 62, rowed his Cataraft in a private party but flipped. Allred quickly succumbed, despite CPR, in an apparent cold shock/cardiac arrest "drowning" despite wearing a life jacket and other protective gear. Stott, Allred, and their four deceased predecessors at Crystal embody the clear lesson shared in common. Crystal, with its 33-foot drop and rock garden halfway, holds the record as the most lethal rapid in the Canyon due to its violence, boulder field, and its great length of cold water. Of the six victims who died in Crystal, William R. Wert was 62 years old, Tom Pillsbury was 66, William B. Blair was 65, Martin M. Hunsaker was 54, Gene Elliot Stott was also 54, and Marc Allred was 62. Hence Crystal is also the most dangerous rapid to run for older people aboard (whether as guide or passenger) in any manner beyond the most conservative run possible.

The last three drowning victims in Hance Rapid with its 30-foot drop and boulder-choked upper half were all private boaters with demographic profiles very similar to victims in Crystal Rapid. (On March 16, 2008, for example, 45-year-old Randall Johnson rowed his private raft into Hance on low water, flipped and drowned during inclement weather, and on June 9, 2011 48-year-old James J. Waring, Jr. entered Hance at 23,500 cfs as 1 of 6 people on a 2-oarboat private trip. His boat flipped. Waring became the 4th victim and 4th private boater to die in Hance Rapid.) This pattern suggests similar care and caution should be exercised in Hance and most other rapids as well.

High flows of the Colorado through Grand Canyon have been presumed, and then claimed, to be more dangerous than "normal" (dam-controlled) flows. In 1983, for example, the river peaked at more than 97,000 cfs and otherwise ran at "high" flows for the entire commercial, "high-use-summer" boating season. Despite a nearly full summer boating season and despite many boating mishaps on this spate, however, only one river-runner drowned, a commercial passenger on a boat whose boatman had not yet run the, then, minimum NPS-required three trips down the river required of Grand Canyon river guides (the NPS changed the minimum to six trips after this incident).

There exists no evidence in the patterns of fatalities observed in the past century of boating in Grand Canyon to demonstrate that high flows are more dangerous than other flow levels. If anything, high flow incidents analyzed by Tom Myers, Chris Becker, and Larry Stevens in their book *Fateful Journey: Injury and Death on Colorado River Trips in Grand Canyon* reveal that medium water levels correlate with more drownings. This again suggests that boatman competence and flow temperature (see below) are more important than flow level.

Interestingly—and as mentioned above—the temperature of the Colorado River may play a far more serious role in fostering fatalities than its level of flow. During the extreme high flow summer season of 1983, for example, hundreds of people were tossed involuntarily into the river. Indeed, hundreds were dumped involuntarily just into Crystal Rapid alone, the record-holding "killer" rapid, and were forced to swim for their lives often for long distances in treacherous flows. Yet only that one river fatality occurred during 1983's summer season. The river that year, however, flowed significantly warmer than usual for post-dam times because all water above 48,000 cfs was coming over the spillways from the warm surface of Lake Powell, not from 250 feet under it, as penstock water does.

So what about cold water? Loss of body heat can be up to 100 times faster in calm water than in air of the same temperature. In a rapid this lethal process proceeds far more quickly yet due to the constant stripping away of warmer water molecules adjacent to a swimmer's skin. Worse, the sudden immersion in cold water spurs an abrupt involuntary physiological response known as "cold shock."

This syndrome sets a cascade of potentially lethal, maladaptive reflexes into motion: several huge involuntary gasps, lethal heart stoppage, or heart attack or rhythm irregularities (especially in predisposed people and the elderly). Elevations in blood pressure also occur, as do lightheadedness, palpitations, and air hunger. A person's breath-holding capacity also is reduced to one third of normal. Conversely, hyperventilation and panic may occur. All of these problems will be followed by muscular loss of coordination and increasing weakness.

After less than 10 or 15 minutes, swimmers in the now cold Colorado experience muscular dysfunction with uncontrollable shivering and weakness. Hence one's ability to swim or self rescue degrades. An average person is unlikely to remain capable of swimming more than half a mile in moving water of 50 degrees. After 15 to 20 minutes, a diminished level of consciousness becomes likely, further increasing the risk of drowning.

The data reveal a situation far worse than the above-mentioned physiology. Most people who have drowned in Grand Canyon rapids since 1963 have died in a mere few minutes, often before exiting the foot of the rapid, despite wearing a life jacket.

Those several victims who died within those very few minutes succumbed due to a combination of all these cold shock, water immersion-caused events. In short, all six victims in Crystal and three more in Hance may be primary victims not of whitewater per se but of the deep penstock feeders in Lake Powell.

A take home message here: Age plays a role in who lives and who dies in cold water. Older victims of whitewater mishaps are at greater risk of dying. This is due to at least four factors: the higher susceptibility of older people to become quick victims of cold shock syndrome, the greater metabolic susceptibility of older people to suffer quick hypothermia from the river's 46- to 55-degree water, the greater propensity of older people for cardiac arrest when plunged into such cold and turbulent whitewater, and the lower ability of older people to self rescue. Moreover, anyone afflicted with known cardiovascular disease (a prior heart attack, high blood pressure, being a smoker, having high cholesterol, diabetes, and/or being over the age of 50, or having a family history of heart disease) should submit to a heart stress test in a clinic before leaving for the river and possibly being dumped into a nasty rapid. The last thing anyone wants is his or her "stress test" being conducted by Crystal Rapid itself.

Ironically, instead of making whitewater boating "possible" or "safe" as claimed by some pro-dam publications, Glen Canyon Dam may instead be killing far more people—including boaters, swimmers, and accidental fall-ins from shore—than the pre-dam river would have due to the river's now extreme and unnatural cold even during summer. Second, the proposed but perhaps infinitely delayed future release of warmer water from Lake Powell via the installation of redesigned penstocks may be a matter of life and death for human visitors to Grand Canyon, not solely a mechanism for the survival of endangered native fish species.

Running the Colorado River conservatively is a good idea in general. Even so, many boatmen tend to be seduced into complacency by their success or by the increasing state of the art of the equipment they use—or by both. On top of this complacency, some professional guides succumb to pressure from clients to go for the biggest possible rides. After all is said and done, commercial boating companies in the Canyon all hire their boatmen to run safely, not wildly. Still, passengers, especially naïve passengers, tend to push their guides to make their rides more exciting. We doubt these same passengers did this with their pilots during their jet rides to

Arizona. Perhaps this is because these folks are slightly more savvy about the risks in the air than about those aboard a raft or dory in whitewater. Hence, boatman decision-making to enforce (or instead not to enforce) safety rules/behaviors based on all the above factors also may have played a role in some of the observed patterns of fatalities. Compounding all of this, many people entering Grand Canyon at the beginning of the twentieth-first century also assume that recent triumphs of human technology—especially in improved communication devices—render the consequences of human error in the river corridor far less dire. Indeed the scariest words I (Ghiglieri) have ever heard a passenger utter (and I've heard plenty) happened as I was piloting our raft into Horn Creek Rapid at low water, which is about as violent a place as one can find in Grand Canyon. After warning my two brand new passengers in the stern to hold on tight with both hands and to hunker against the load, I heard one whisper to the other: "They would not even let us do this [rafting] if we could get hurt."

A more inaccurate assessment of their situation would be tough to find.

Dead is, after all, still dead. A good example of the "maybe not," during which a Canyon voyager was reduced to the most helpless mammal on Earth, comes from a fascinating 1991 incident. As with most tragic episodes in the wilderness, this one started off looking like good clean fun.

Perhaps the most effective way to tell this story is to begin when Grand Canyon Dories' guide Chris McIntosh and the rest of the crew tied up their boats above 232-Mile Rapid to scout it on November 2, 2000. "I hadn't run 232-Mile left, and it was flowing at low water [about 10,000 cfs]," McIntosh explained to us, "and I was nervous because I knew it could destroy our boats if we hit the fangs at the bottom right." McIntosh and company scouted for several minutes, then "We all ran it down the left side."

Several minutes downstream of the Dories' uneventful run of 232-Mile they encountered a tiny private trip. One of its two boatmen, David Whittlesey, age 54, had just suffered a far less pleasant outcome at 232-Mile. He and passenger Darla Ekbom, age 44, had spent ten minutes sitting in Whittlesey's 14-foot raft above and out of view of 232-Mile Rapid while they waited for the second boat in their two-boat, four-person trip to catch up with them. As Ekbom tells it, Whittlesey sat there that long but elected not to scout this dangerous rapid. Next, with the goal in mind of getting splashed as little as possible, Whittelsey rowed down the right side of the rapid. His boat slammed into those fangs of sculpted schist near the right shore that likely had killed Glen and Bessie Hyde in late 1928.

Whittlesey's boat now pivoted sideways and began climbing to vertical. Whittlesey and Ekbom "high-sided" frantically. The boat flipped, however, almost in slow motion. So slow that Ekbom was in the river already when it slammed down, she said, and hit her on the head. She inhaled water as she fought her way to shore.

Whittlesey ended up making a fifteen minute swim with his boat, one which ended only when that missing boat number two finally caught up.

When, several minutes later, boatman McIntosh next caught up to Whittlesey and his three companions, he was flabbergasted to learn what had happened. He had, as you'll see, good reason to be. On an earlier commercial trip on which McIntosh had been a guide and Whittlesey a trainee, the latter had pointed out to McIntosh several critical sites between River Miles 232 and 234 where a heart-rending struggle for survival had unfolded on and after November 17, 1991, a struggle against pain and endurance and disappointment that would scar most of us....

David Whittlesey, then age 45, from Prescott, Arizona, had made two previous Colorado River trips down the Canyon, both with other people. On October 28, 1991 he next launched his 14-foot inflatable boat from Lees Ferry on a three-and-a-half-week solo voyage.

As insurance against loss, Whittlesey had supplied himself with provisions for six weeks. Whittlesey was concerned about food. Being hungry in the middle of nowhere in cold weather is not what he considered a good time.

For 232 miles he enjoyed "a wonderful trip," having safely navigated all rapids. Then, as it likely had with Bessie and Glen Hyde, 232-Mile Rapid, in its low-water, demonic form, took control.

Shortly before noon on November 17, with only five rapids (of 160+) and a half-dozen miles left to run before hitting Lake Mead, Whittlesey entered 232-Mile on about 10,500 cfs. The guide book rated this rapid lower than many of the upstream rapids that had turned out to be not so difficult to run. Besides, floating down toward 232-Mile, it appeared harmless (just as it likely had to Glen Hyde).

Whittlesey's boat rollicked over the standing waves just fine. Then it slammed up onto a large cluster of sculpted knobs and fangs of bedrock semi-hidden in the main current. The boat pivoted, stern into the current. Whittlesey tried to maneuver his raft off the rock. It flipped upside down.

The good news was Whittlesey was uninjured. He clung to the overturned raft as the river swept it into an eddy flanked by a wall of schist. For an hour Whittlesey tried to right his capsized raft in the cold river. Unsuccessfully.

Desperate to get the thing right side up and then unload his gear, especially some warm clothes and shoes, Whittlesey got careless about the current. His raft floated into the riffle below 232-Mile. He tried to stay on its slick floor. But waves in this riffle washed him off.

Whittlesey clung to the side of his raft. He narrowly avoided being crushed against or dragged over rocks in the riffle. By now hypothermic, he tried again to drag his raft to shore as quickly as possible, even while in the riffle. As Whittlesey scrambled onto shore, he lost his grip on his boat. The raft pulled away and drifted downstream.

As Whittlesey stared at it in disappointment, it floated away serenely. Then it disappeared around a bend.

Although being safely on shore was an improvement over freezing to death in the river, the shore quickly metamorphosed from salvation to prison. The rock here inclined steeply, with numerous cliffs. And having lost his shoes along with everything else, Whittlesey realized that he needed to either find his boat or at least get to a safer place to wait for help to happen along. With these two options in mind, he started walking downstream.

While traversing a cliff ledge twenty-five feet above the water, his handhold crumbled off. Whittlesey fell backwards. He slid head first down an incline. His jaw struck a rock. The blow knocked him unconscious. He somersaulted into the river. The cold water revived him. He scrambled out. His chin, he now found, had been punctured by that impact during his fall. Four of his teeth were now broken. The pain became intense.

Still, he had to get farther downstream. Whittlesey started walking again. While perched precariously on another cliff, a loose boulder rolled onto his bare foot. It broke two of his toes.

Desperate, cold, and in insistent pain from multiple sources, he finally hobbled to a beach on the right bank above 234-Mile Rapid. (This is about where James R. Ervin had left Bill Payne back in 1931, never to see him again.) En route to this patch of beach Whittlesey had also found a can of beer wedged in a crevice by the high water of 1983.

That eight-year-old beer—along with one lizard and one grasshopper—would constitute Whittlesey's provisions for the next six days.

As each day passed, the seriousness of his plight impressed Whittlesey ever more deeply. This being November, and river trips being vanishingly rare in November, he might not see anyone on the river in time to be rescued. Without a rescue, he now knew he would die. He was stranded, crippled, and without food. His outfit consisted only of a life jacket, t-shirt, and shorts. On the positive side of the list, however, he was carrying a Bic™ lighter and a knife.

Whittlesey dug a pit in the sand and bivouacked under sand and grass. To keep warm, he heated rocks by burning driftwood and grass then used them to warm the sand in his pit. The days became unending. "When I was thinking rationally," he admitted, "I knew help would come. But when I was thinking emotionally, I'd never been so scared."

During one bout of despair, when he believed he would die, he used his knife to carve his farewell letter into a piece of driftwood.

"David Whiitlesey Stranded
11/17/91 Days 11111 11   Mother
Sorry, Friends, Prescott, AZ
I will miss you, Love to All."

Five days after losing his boat, a friend of Whittlesey informed the NPS that he had failed to arrive at Pearce Ferry (46 miles downstream) on November 21, as planned. The NPS launched a search and rescue effort. On November 22, the sixth day after Whittlesey had watched his capsized boat float away, NPS Rangers Susan Cherry and Ken Phillips spotted Whittlesey from a helicopter. He was still alive. And hungry.

Phillips offered Whittlesey his lunch. Whittlesey almost inhaled it.

Perhaps now you understand how and why boatman Chris McIntosh found Whittlesey's re-enactment of this, the worst time in his life, nine years later, flab-bergasting.

Other private boaters would be less lucky than wrong-way Whittlesey. In late afternoon of November 15, 1994 a private rowing trip stopped at Hance Rapid (River Mile 77) to scout their "low" water run on 9,000 cfs. John Littels rowed first down the right tongue. Mark Miner followed, rowing a new "Protar" raft with two passengers aboard, Emilio X. Solares, a 26-year-old from Nederlad, Colorado, and Lisa Abell.

Miner miscalculated the flow and entered too far right. Abell, an experienced kayaker, warned him during his entry that he was heading for "the hole." Miner, she added, had acted very nervous as he had scouted Hance. A raft had already cap-sized during this trip and another had been badly ripped. And Hance had looked worse than anything they had encountered thus far.

Solares, meanwhile, was holding onto Miner's boat with one hand, having jammed his leg between the frame and the boat for stability, so he could operate a video camera with his other hand.

Two oar strokes after Abell's warning, Miner's boat dropped into a large hole near the top of the rapid and capsized. Littels, well downstream, rescued both Min-er and Abell at the distant foot of the lengthy, 30-foot drop.

Solares, meanwhile, stayed with the boat, even grabbing one of its oars. The upside-down boat had snagged on a boulder in the rapid itself. Witnesses on shore said they could see Emilio Solares still with the raft. Through binoculars it was apparent to them that at least one of Solares' legs or feet was somehow trapped in the boat's rigging.

Solares struggled violently for several minutes to get out from under the raft. Failing to extricate himself, he continued to lay on his back under the water with his head aimed downstream. At least one of his feet, it still seemed, remained trapped under the overturned raft.

Those on shore watched in dread as Solares struggled frantically to keep his face above water and gasp for air.

Abell later said that, as they had pulled away from shore, she had noticed a loose rope trailing. But it was then too late, she thought, to have secured it.

Mark Miner, who had kayaked for three years but had purchased his "Protar" raft only four months earlier, reported that he had told Abell and Solares that Hance "was powerful—and, if they went over [capsized]," he advised them not to try to highside but to "just go with it."

Amazingly, two more video cameras were operating from shore. Tapes from these two, however, failed to show Solares in his struggle. Solares' own videotape recovered later shows Mark Miner rowing as Lisa Abell warns him in the background that he is heading for the hole. Miner shouts "Oh Shit! Hang on!" as his raft flips in this hole.

Solares' camera continued to film for several ghastly seconds under water before it shut off.

Those on shore now groped for a way to get out to Solares before it was too late. They made several attempts to paddle kayaks from the right shore—with a rope—to Solares' position in the rapid. But they failed in this even as they watched Solares still clawing at the water and the boat to escape. Apparently Solares was not carrying a knife with which to cut a line, if such had snagged his legs. Or else his leg or foot was trapped in some other way, perhaps still wedged between the frame and the boat.

In the end, the boat's lodged position in the river proved too challenging for his would-be rescuers. Finally, after Solares' face vanished under water a last time, his companions gave up. Two of the kayakers paddled eleven miles downstream to Phantom Ranch to seek NPS ranger assistance.

The weather had turned so foul that a helicopter landing was deemed too dangerous. Rangers Jim Traub and Bil Vandergraff hiked down the New Hance Trail after dark through a blizzard to reach the river. Of course they were not able to do much at this point except collect statements and try to avoid hypothermia themselves. When the NPS finally recovered Miner's boat, which drifted off the rock that night, they saw the boat had been rigged with a frightening "spiderweb of loose netting" that all too easily can trap a person's arm or leg instead of with safer, tight straps. They also found several stashes of marijuana aboard in Miner's personal gear.

On January 8, 1995, 45 days after Solares' drowning, NPS Ranger Marty Johnson spotted Solares' body floating past River Mile 88 at Phantom Ranch. A Glen Canyon Environmental Studies trip recovered it at River Mile 100.5.

Until Solares' nightmarish death, Hance Rapid had not yet been an accomplice to homicide. Strangely, however, it would soon carve notches to become the second fastest gun in the Canyon, taking down a total of four separate private boaters. On November 22, 2004, for example, a private trip of firefighters from the Phoenix area entered Hance on 32,000 cfs during a beach-building flow. Also aboard this trip was Leonard Gentry, a stocky 5' 5", 195-pound, 61-year-old African American who lived in a warehouse in Maricopa County, Arizona. He had been "cajoled" onto this four-boat trip of mostly Phoenix firemen by two, well-meaning brothers.

The trip's boatmen knew they were at Hance, but the rapid seemed so easy to them from above that the firefighters decided to enter Hance without bothering to stop and scout it.

Three boats made it right side up. The fourth ran over a pour-over, was captured by the reversal water behind it. The raft recycled then capsized. Two of the rafters aboard swam and made it to shore in about "7 minutes."

Number three, Gentry, had been riding in this ill-fated raft. As the cold rapid propelled him downstream he yelled for help. One of the other two swimmers grabbed him. Seconds later a big wave yanked him loose. The two separated.

As the other two, "seven-minute" swimmers were picked up by the boaters ahead, Gentry drowned in an apparent cold shock syndrome/cardiac arrest despite his wearing a life jacket and neoprene gear. CPR by the firemen for 30 minutes failed.

The terrified survivors next spent a rainy night aboard their three boats (the capsized raft had escaped them) in an early section of Upper Granite Gorge. With no beach available, the group attached their three boats to a cliff by jamming an oar into it and mooring their bowlines to the oar. Their experience at Hance so unnerved them that they all abandoned their trip at Phantom Ranch via emergency helicopter evacuations and hiking.

Some of the bodies of other river fatalities have proven nearly as elusive to recover. A case in point happened at one of Georgie White's favorite stopping spots in Grand Canyon, below the cliffs soaring upward with almost unearthly grandeur near River Mile 53. Nankoweap Camp was one of Georgie's very favorites. The place offers one of the most spectacular settings in Grand Canyon. But in the summer of 1958, Nankoweap impressed Georgie in a different way.

It began when one of Georgie's Royal River Rats ran anxiously in camp to her yelling, "Hey, there's a grave!"

The grave, six feet long and lined with rocks, had been built several days earlier by Gaylord Staveley's Mexican Hat Expeditions trip. 18-year-old Earl Weimer, a boatman rowing for Mexican Hat Expeditions (now Canyoneers), had followed his nose and found a dead beaver (*Castor canadensis*) here during the high water year of 1958. Because the carcass was big, several days old, and stunk to high heaven, Weimer and Staveley decided the beaver warranted a burial. Weimer interred it in the beach on June 15, 1958 by dumping several buckets of sand over it. After due consideration, Weimer next decided the beaver deserved a burial marker.

With the huge decaying rodent buried and its stench no longer permeating the camp, Staveley's group now could camp here.

Georgie's problem arose from this later decision by Staveley's group, the one about the deceased beaver needing a small wooden grave marker. Weimer had fashioned one and inscribed it: "Here lies D. Beaver, died June 15, 1958." (The "D." was short for "dead.")

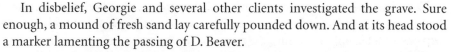

In disbelief, Georgie and several other clients investigated the grave. Sure enough, a mound of fresh sand lay carefully pounded down. And at its head stood a marker lamenting the passing of D. Beaver.

It damned well looked like a grave. But maybe, Georgie suspected, it was just a joke. She knew Staveley had passed here only a few days ahead of her. But if not a joke, Georgie realized, she would be smart to find out now. So she started digging. Soon the stench and sight of rotting flesh was unmistakable. No question now that a corpse had been buried here! Disgusted, she stopped digging and covered up what she had exposed.

Georgie later called the NPS from Phantom Ranch and asked to be transferred to John McLaughlin, Superintendent of Grand Canyon National Park. "Staveley lost a passenger," Georgie told him. She next explained that she had found a Mr. D. Beaver buried at Nankoweap.

As bureaucrats are wont to do when they have been left out of the loop, this NPS official became irate. Absolutely, McLaughlin said, Staveley should have reported this fatality. Unable to contact Staveley to verify who D. Beaver was and what sort of tragic accident had taken him, however, NPS officials instead checked the trip itinerary from Staveley's launch at Lees Ferry. Unhelpfully, the itinerary listed no "D. Beaver."

This was worse yet. Staveley had been carrying a passenger whom he had failed to list. Here was yet another violation!

National Park headquarters put out the word to the rangers at Lake Mead National Recreation Area, to the Arizona Department of Public Safety, and to the Coconino County Sheriff's Department to apprehend Staveley as his trip exited across upper Lake Mead into Pearce Ferry.

This army of law enforcement officials somehow missed Staveley's trip.

Because this was too early in Grand Canyon Park history for a helicopter reconnaissance of the grave, too early for beach sanitation rules, and too early even for good interagency communication, Mr. D. Beaver detonated an explosion of rumors and bizarre ideas as to who the dead person really was and what dastardly fate had placed him in his hideously isolated grave. Had a murder been committed? The Coconino County Sheriff's Department wondered. This explosion of weird hypotheses proved a nagging thorn in the side of NPS headquarters for weeks. Park authorities were worried that "D. Beaver" was actually Gilbert H. Hansen, a wealthy easterner who suspiciously vanished under water at Music Temple in Glen Canyon on May 17, 1957, while on a river trip.

Meanwhile the Arizona Game and Fish Department was worried that Mr. D. Beaver was not a human at all. Instead, they feared, it was one of their recently transplanted desert bighorn sheep. They were dismayed at the prospect of having lost one of their vital transplants because the new population they hoped to restore to Paria and Marble canyons was so precarious.

Later, Gaylord Staveley drove to Grand Canyon National Park Headquarters for his routine check-out for the season. To his surprise, he found himself in very hot water. McLaughlin read him the riot act over the seriousness of not reporting dead bodies.

Staveley told him it was a dead beaver stinking to high heaven and he had simply wanted to camp there…

So far, as of July 2011, a total of 35 people (only four of them women) have drowned because of boating mishaps in Grand Canyon. As revealed in Table 5A, the early drownings (ten men and one woman) occurred universally to victims not wearing life jackets. Since the closing of Glen Canyon Dam in 1963, however, and the consequent artificial shift of summer water temperatures of the Colorado from around 80 degrees to around 47-55 degrees, all but four of the others have been victims who did wear life jackets (17 men and 3 women) but died anyway of various manifestations of a cold shock syndrome "drowning" or instead due to other freak circumstances, despite having worn those life jackets and other protective gear.

Interestingly, yet of course subject to change at any moment of bad luck in the future, of all those 35 victims of drowning, none had been aboard a commercially rowed oarboat during the entire history of professionally-rowed trips dating back to the very first trips run by Norm Nevills in 1938. Every other type of craft thus far (including Georgie's triple rig thrill boats equipped with a pair of oars and a 6-horsepower motor), however, has produced fatal casualties including private oarboats and kayaks, and commercial paddleboats and motor rigs. As most people realize, though, this clean record for commercial oar boats is subject not only to the skill of boatmen but also to luck.

River Crossers Who Didn't

The early days of Anglo-Canyon relations resembled a geological cat and mouse game. The Anglos were the cat. The mouse was gold—or at least silver—hidden somewhere in the unfathomable vastness of Grand Canyon. That this gold must exist somewhere in the Canyon many men were dead certain.

Hence, it is no surprise that the strange saga of the first certain historical death in the Colorado in Grand Canyon was that of a prospector positive that gold lay hidden here, in God's own secret treasure room. His story begins with this passage from the reminiscences of prospector Edward Schieffelin:

> *About the hardest trip I ever took was in the spring of '72 when I, with four others, went up the Grandest of all canyons, the Grand Canyon of the Colorado River. Although it was short, less than a month, it was a hard one.*

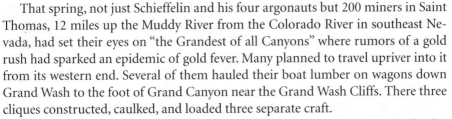

That spring, not just Schieffelin and his four argonauts but 200 miners in Saint Thomas, 12 miles up the Muddy River from the Colorado River in southeast Nevada, had set their eyes on "the Grandest of all Canyons" where rumors of a gold rush had sparked an epidemic of gold fever. Many planned to travel upriver into it from its western end. Several of them hauled their boat lumber on wagons down Grand Wash to the foot of Grand Canyon near the Grand Wash Cliffs. There three cliques constructed, caulked, and loaded three separate craft.

One young man, Bush Dulin, had done the lion's share of the work for his group, only to see all of them change their minds once the time came to row upstream. Ultimately Dulin convinced four others—Edward Schieffelin, George Magin, George Goodnow, and Oliver—to abandon their own smaller boat and instead use his own large pride and joy, the *Lady Jennings*.

In late March, 1872, these five men headed upstream in company with another group, all Irishmen, using a similar boat, the *Shamrock*.

Attrition among these argonauts continued at a high rate. The *Lady* had just entered the Grand Wash Cliffs when downstream of them, not quite inside Grand Canyon, the *Shamrock* wrapped, sank, then emptied itself of all of its cargo in a minor rapid. Its crew salvaged the boat itself. But now destitute, they decided to give up and float forty miles downstream and then head up the Virgin River then the Muddy River back to St. Thomas.

Now only five prospectors of that potential 200 rowed and hauled their boat upstream. They struggled, prospecting along the way, for ten days. Their only other companions were two ravens who dived on their camp each morning once they abandoned it. By April 10, the four had progressed possibly thirty miles upstream in Grand Canyon when they encountered a rapid that required them to haul their boat around a twenty-foot-long granite boulder projecting into the current.

As they tried to tow their unloaded boat around this rock, the current grabbed it. The sudden jerk yanked everyone off his feet and jerked them into a pile. The rope hissed through their hands and flew into the air. The *Lady*, freed, zipped downstream.

Thoughts of being marooned here "in hostile Indian country" (the Hualapais had been defeated by now by the U.S. Cavalry but were dribbling back into their traditional lands in small groups) flashed through each man's mind.

Abruptly, the large knot at the end of the *Lady's* bowline caught between two boulders. The rub was that the *Lady* had "moored" herself close to the opposite side of the river.

Dulin had hurt his knee in the dogpile when the *Lady* had leaped loose. As the other men grabbed the oars with the intention of building a hasty raft to row out and recover the Lady, Dulin said, "It might tear loose at any time and as soon as my knee gets well, I will go up the river somewhere and swim over."

Dulin and two others walked a mile and a half upstream to find a safe crossing.

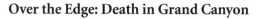

The first man in, George Magil, swam across successfully. Dulin and Oliver tried to follow him while carrying the oars. But they soon realized they could not make it. They turned back. Ashore again Dulin felt such urgency that, instead of retracing the shoreline upstream to follow Magil's route exactly, and instead of waiting until he had warmed up, he walked only part way upstream and dived into the river while still cold from his previous swim.

Dulin made it three-quarters of the way across before the Colorado became a rapid racing against a cliff face on the side of the river he had been swimming toward. At that point Dulin vanished under water.

His four horrified companions never found his body. Magil, however, did recover their boat by severing the bowline from shore. He used a knife lashed to a long driftwood pole. The four survivors now possessed their boat again. But without its rope they could no longer tow it upstream. So the four prospectors instead used the *Lady* to escape the Canyon.

Even as they floated safely downstream, the specter of Bush Dulin's death haunted Schieffelin, who wrote:

> *And to lose a comrade in that out of the way, wild, terrible, dismal place was too horrible to think about. And I imagined I could hear him calling not to leave him. Friends may die surrounded with comfort of Brothers or Sisters where they can see the flowers and trees or at least fields of level country and cause us a great deal of grief. But to die in that dark and life forsaken place and be left there was more appalling I believe than it is possible for it to occur in any other way or place.*

A far more mysterious pair of drownings occurred nearly twenty years later. During the summer of 1890 (uncertain date), John Fuller and Harry MacDonald were working as herdsmen on the Kaibab Plateau. Harry MacDonald was very likely the same "Harry McDonald" who, as mentioned earlier, had been steering F. M. Brown's boat when it overturned fatally for Brown at Salt Water Wash in 1889. Six months later, McDonald had returned to the Colorado River with Robert Brewster Stanton on his 1889–1890 Grand Canyon surveying expedition and worked as head boatman. But in February of 1890 he had quit in disgust at the men having destroyed in Horn Creek Rapid one of Stanton's three boats, the *Sweet Marie*, that he, McDonald, had just spent five days rebuilding. Fed up, he had hiked out to the North Rim and beyond through horrendous snow.

Now, in summer, Fuller and MacDonald rode and led their horses down Bright Angel Fault before the North Kaibab Trail existed along it. They were on a mission in search of the remains of a man whose identity was not mentioned, but who likely was Frank Mason Brown himself or, less likely, Henry Richards (the body of the third casualty of Brown's trip, Peter M. Hansbrough, already had been discovered in January of 1890 at River Mile 44 by McDonald and the rest of Stanton's crew).

Fuller's and MacDonald's descent down the treacherous deer trail following the Bright Angel Fault from the North Rim was hideous. Both men lost their horses to fatal falls. They ended up carrying their salvaged gear to the river. McDonald and Fuller trudged into a macabre mystery, a fully equipped but unoccupied camp set up along Bright Angel Creek near the confluence. The tent stood well set up and in ship shape. Inside it stood two cots with the blankets pulled back as if just vacated. Two rifles and two revolvers lay next to them. An expensive gold watch (run down and no longer ticking) hung from the tent pole. A Dutch oven sat outside on cold coals and held half a loaf of bread baked about three days earlier. Tracks on the ground indicated that two adults had saddled horses and rode them to the Colorado—then entered it as if to swim across.

Also standing in camp, waiting dutifully, was a gelding donkey, "Brighty" (named after Bright Angel Creek) of the Grand Canyon, made famous 60 years later in a book by Marguerite Henry, who read about Brighty in a 1922 *Sunset Magazine* article by Thomas Heron McKee.

The two missing men, Fuller learned later, were never seen again, but they originally had been seen passing through Flagstaff with their gelding donkey—"Brighty"—en route to Grand Canyon. People on the South Rim also told Fuller that the pair with the donkey and horses had descended the early version of the Bright Angel Trail to the region of this mysteriously abandoned camp. Again, the two missing men were never seen to exit the Canyon—and, of course, had they been planning to do so, they never would have abandoned their valuables, even if they might have abandoned their set up camp. The identities of these original owners of Brighty of the Grand Canyon remain a mystery, though their fate seems very likely to have been one of drowning during an attempted crossing of the Colorado. Like Brown and Richards, McDonald's lost companions, these two men too were never found.

In the early years of human presence historically in Grand Canyon, the river took those most available to her. Hence, the most common drownings were at Lees Ferry because it was by far the most accessible crossing point of the river for more than four hundred miles. Every one of the eleven victims of drowning here while the ferry was in operation started out in some sort of boat. But every one of them shared two elements in common: mishandling of the boat and not wearing a life jacket.

The first such victim was Lorenzo W. Roundy, who drowned trying to cross the river on May 24, 1876. Not long after this, around 1880 or 1881, two unnamed Navajos drowned here. And soon after them, in June or July of 1884, Henry Rosely and his twelve-year-old son, Al, drowned while trying to cross. Two more Navajos, brothers, tragically drowned here while operating the ferry incorrectly in 1889. Next, Preston Apperson, a crewman with Charles Spencer's huge, but failed, mining promotion

drowned here on March 9, 1911, along with a team of horses when the entire ferry sank in midriver. The most gruesome of incidents at Lees Ferry took place on its last attempted crossing.

All three people aboard the ferry's last journey across the Colorado on June 7, 1928—passengers Royce Elliot Dean, age 25, and Lewis Nez Tsinnie, age 26 (and their wire-cage Ford truck), plus substitute ferryman Adolpha Johnson, age 26— became victims of an apparent freak gust of wind on very high water. The ferry successfully crossed the river to the east with all three men and the Ford. But as Johnson tried to tie it up, a gust of wind hit. The ferry began drifting hard, back out toward midriver. Johnson dug in his heels to try to stop it, but found himself dragged to the river anyway.

At the river Johnson climbed hand over hand onto the ferry as the powerful current relentlessly shoved it back out toward midriver. Johnson needed to crank the forward windlass to change the ferry's angle so that the current would shove the boat back to the east shore again. Either of the two passengers still on the ferry might have done this quicker than Johnson. But neither Dean nor Tsinnie did so— either from lack of understanding or from fear.

When Johnson reached the ferryboat, the upstream beam was dipping into the relentless 86,500 cfs current. The entire deck listed upstream at a precarious angle.

As Johnson's wife, Marva, and their small son, Milo, watched from the west shore, the cable broke loose. The entire ferry tipped over and hydroplaned under. Horrified, Marva watched as "everything went out of sight." She never saw her husband nor Dean (nor the Ford truck) again. After several minutes of searching, Marva Johnson did see Lewis Nez Tsinnie floating downstream apparently motionless.

Dean's body was discovered two months later embedded in a sand bank twenty feet above the water near Soap Creek (as mentioned earlier, along with the Hydes' footprints). These final three fatalities hold (but now share) the record for the highest known number of deaths for drowning victims not attempting to travel downstream. They also heralded the last gasp of the ferry service. After more than fifty-five years of service—and the "deaths" of 14 different ferry boats and 11 people—Lees Ferry became simply a place along the Colorado at the head of Grand Canyon. It also became River Mile 0, as designated by the Colorado River Compact of 1922. The completion of Navajo Bridge about four months later replaced the ferry function at Lees Ferry altogether.

Aside from tragic mishaps at Lees Ferry, crossing the Colorado River in Grand Canyon has all too often been like playing tag with the Devil.

The next known victim of an attempted crossing well downstream of Lees Ferry was yet another prospector. On June 9, 1899, a party of prospectors from Williams—George H. Gibson, George D. Roberts, Henry B. Clifford, William F. Russell, Henry Sellers, and T. A. and George Fleming—descended from the South

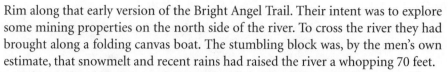

Rim along that early version of the Bright Angel Trail. Their intent was to explore some mining properties on the north side of the river. To cross the river they had brought along a folding canvas boat. The stumbling block was, by the men's own estimate, that snowmelt and recent rains had raised the river a whopping 70 feet.

It being already 5:00 p.m., the seven hastily set up their canvas boat. T. A. Fleming and William F. Russell paddled the frail craft onto the racing spate. The river sped them downstream. The men's efforts to power their boat across the flood to the north side failed. As Russell shifted position in the boat, it capsized. True to form for those days, neither man wore a life jacket—even though they had been invented decades earlier. Fleming, a good swimmer, stroked back to the south bank. Russell, instead, clung to the capsized boat. The two raced hundreds of yards into the rapid below and vanished.

Half of Russell's companions hurried along the shore in the twilight, hoping to assist him. They never saw him again.

They camped that night then hiked back up to the South Rim the next morning, counting Russell as dead.

On June 16, William Wallace Bass, pioneer asbestos miner and tour operator, along with John Waltenberg and R. M. Bleak, launched a search for Russell's body near River Mile 108. All they found during their four days of strenuous efforts was an inordinate number of rattlesnakes. On day #4 the two lowered Bleak off a short cliff to ascertain whether something in the river below was Russell's hat. The rope broke. Bleak fell and was knocked unconscious. The trio gave up their search. Bleak recovered days later.

Roughly a year and a half later, in January of 1901, Frank M. Friessell and David W. Barter launched a winter prospecting trip through the Canyon. "Several miles below Bright Angel, Barter shoveled a hole in the sand to create a dry bed and hit a skeleton believed to be Russell's." The duo boated to Yuma—minus most of their gear lost during upsets of their boat.

Again trying to wring money out of the Grand Canyon Colorado, in 1903 the Grand Canyon Electric Company conducted surveys deep within Upper Granite Gorge for good locations to harness the river. Surveyor P. T. McConigle, age 37, who was quitting the company, was aiming to show his successor, surveyor Charles McLean, age 44, the company's camp on Bright Angel Creek. McConigle then planned to exit the Canyon with his personal effects.

The two men hiked down from Indian Garden on the morning of July 27. Two days later, launch marks in the sand from the company's aging pine scow showed that the two men had launched to make their crossing. The mystery arose in the lack of landing marks on the opposite side of the river.

Several days of laborious searching by Niles J. Cameron, Louis D. Boucher, and others found not only no boat marks on the opposite side of the river, but no footprints nor any other sign that either McLean or McConigle had ever crossed the river, safely or otherwise, or ever reached the company's camp.

Yes, the river was running high, but McConigle had crossed the river only ten days earlier in the same boat. All parties agreed, however, that this boat was weak from exposure to the elements and could have disintegrated if the men in her had inadvertently run a rapid. Exactly what went wrong to drown McLean and McConigle—a lost or crabbed oar, a man overboard, a shipping of too much water, disintegration of the boat itself—remains a mystery. It is only certain that the two men were not wearing life jackets and they had vanished.

It also has been rumored for years that the skiff the two had used dangled a chain for a painter. The rumor continues that the dangling chain was found later by searchers, perhaps Godfrey Sykes and Harry Hussey, caught between two boulders, it having ripped the stern of their scow clean off when it caught.

Despite such notorious deaths during attempted crossings, not even NPS personnel were immune to repeating the fatal errors that caused them. On February 20, 1929, less than two months after the large-scale search for the vanished "Honeymooning" Hydes, three NPS personnel attempted a crossing below Phantom Ranch near Horn Creek Rapid. The three were Naturalist Glen E. Sturdevant, age 33, Ranger Fred Johnson, age 30, and Chief Ranger James P. Brooks (who, with the Kolb brothers two months earlier, had searched for Glen and Bessie Hyde). For nine days, they had been exploring the Tonto Plateau atop the Tapeats Sandstone to conduct an inventory of natural history and archeological sites on the north side of the river, more than 1,000 feet above the Colorado. Meanwhile Rangers Michael Harrison and Carl Lehnert had explored the corresponding South Tonto across the river.

Once the trio on the north had completed their recon work, they wanted to cross to the south side to return to the South Rim. They had been congratulating themselves on the fact that, although they had been in some rather dangerous places, the trip had been completed without the slightest accident. And they now had only to go on out, the expectation being that they would reach home that afternoon. The trio had earlier portaged their 12-foot, 10-inch folding boat about 100 yards upstream of Horn Creek Rapid. At about 8:00 a.m., they started across the river. Sturdevant, who was wearing a kapok-filled life belt, Brooks later would explain, had insisted on rowing. Johnson, a weak swimmer, was standing up in the boat and wearing a larger, kapok-filled life vest. Brooks, too, wore a life belt. As might be guessed, this attempt at crossing stumbled quickly.

According to Brooks' somewhat muddled statement at the coroner's inquest:

> *Mr. Sturdevant was rowing, Fred in the bow, and I was in the stern. The boat swung around, and I told Glen to pull and I would try to turn it. We began to lose distance. The shore current swung the boat around...and drifted us towards the rapids, and we could see then it was impossible to do any more*

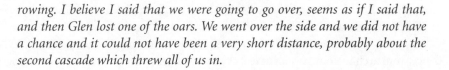

rowing. I believe I said that we were going to go over, seems as if I said that, and then Glen lost one of the oars. We went over the side and we did not have a chance and it could not have been a very short distance, probably about the second cascade which threw all of us in.

The trio and their little boat had dropped into Horn Creek Rapid flowing at 5,700 cfs, a horrible level for this rapid.

Park Superintendent M. R. Tillotson's account written on February 28 notes that Brooks saw that Johnson, having lost his buoyant life vest (apparently this happened almost instantly, which suggests Johnson had not fastened it properly), was now in peril. Brooks tried to rescue him. But he never did catch him. Meanwhile the rapid swept all three "swimmers" into the incredibly violent maelstrom of crushing hydraulics and boulders that Horn Creek Rapid becomes at low water.

The racing current sucked Brooks under almost instantly. He thought he had caught one of his companions by the hair for a moment, but did not know whose hair he might have held. Brooks later found himself cast to the shoreline on the north. He looked around for his companions but saw neither them nor the boat.

Hypothermia already had taken a toll on Brooks. It took him minutes to marshal the strength simply to drag himself out of the river onto dry land. Once out, Brooks climbed the low cliffs to search the shorelines and river for two hours for his companions. But he saw nothing. He shouted, but also heard nothing.

At last giving up, he scrambled upstream along the broken schist and granite in his soggy, freezing clothes and reached Phantom Ranch at nightfall. Brooks next hiked across the Kaibab Bridge, then up the South Kaibab Trail to the South Rim, and finally to Park Headquarters to make his report.

Superintendent M. R. Tillotson ordered several search parties into action. Brooks, in an early version of the Iron Man Competition, returned to the river with one of them, logging about 25 hard miles of hiking since the accident. Tillotson ordered Harrison and Lehnert to hurry to the mouth of Monument Canyon (River Mile 93.5) to join a party of Fred Harvey personnel searching the river by coming upstream (alternatingly rowing, towing, and portaging) from Hermit Rapid (River Mile 95). They were using a sawed-in-half-then-reassembled boat abandoned recently by the Pathé-Bray expedition.

These searchers soon found a body wearing a life belt floating in the large eddy below Granite Falls at the foot of Monument Canyon. Near it floated several other items belonging to the three swimmers, including Brooks' leather coat, which "now weighed 75 pounds." Harrison immediately identified the body as Sturdevant by a once-broken but still stiff finger on the corpse's hand. Despite his life belt, Sturdevant had either drowned or succumbed to hypothermia.

Four more days of searching, including the use of hard-core tactics, failed to find Johnson. As Michael Harrison recalled: "We dynamited the head and foot of

Horn Creek Rapid....We threw in...a full case of dynamite." But the searchers never did find Johnson, who had lost his life vest.

As might be guessed, crossing the river likely always has been a problem. Evidence from archaeology reveals at least casual visits from as early as 4,000 years ago by people of the Desert Culture. It also hints at visits as far back as 10,500 years ago by Folsom people, who likely were here to hunt North America's last giant ground sloths, Harrington's mountain goats, or other huge creatures of the now-vanished Pleistocene megafauna still lumbering within a Grand Canyon that was far more lush than today. Since 850 AD or earlier, Puebloan Indians lived in various sections of the Canyon at least seasonally, if not semi-permanently. They grew corn, squash, beans, chilies, and cotton. They also hunted and gathered. Their stone pueblos and metates, elegant potsherds, and flaked stone tools still litter the Canyon's deltas and creek courses. All of these people up to our highly technological "now," however, have faced the same problem when they hit the Colorado: How do you get over to the other side?

No one today knows how prehistoric Native Americans or PaleoIndians did it. They left no paddles, boats, rafts, or inflated bighorn sheep bellies behind for us to puzzle over. Nor did they leave pictographs painted on, or petroglyphs etched in, the cliff faces depicting river crossers that might give us a clue. Your guess as to how they did it, other than by fording shallow places at extreme low water during winter, may be as good as anyone's. In some parts of the world in which primitive cultures face crossing good-sized rivers without a boat, they do use floats. Natives of Ethiopia's upper Omo River, for example, use inflated bladders or skins of animals such as goats or sheep. By contrast, some natives of the 1950s Southwest use inflated air mattresses.

Unquestionably the doyen of Grand Canyon hiking is Harvey Butchart. This former professor of mathematics at Northern Arizona University (NAU), logged 12,000 miles of hiking during 1,025 days in the Canyon on 560 hikes. And Butchart's routes were anything but routine. He found 116 different approaches from the rims to the Colorado River, climbed 83 of the Canyon's named peaks, and logged 28 first ascents. (For a look at some of Butchart's achievements and adventures we recommend Elias Butler's and Tom Myers' *Grand Obsession: Harvey Butchart and the Exploration of Grand Canyon*.) Butchart's avocation to know the Canyon's maze consisted of brilliance flirting with obsession.

On May 26, 1955, only a month after Bill Beer and John Daggett swam the entire Grand Canyon Colorado, 48-year-old Harvey Butchart tried to talk his best hiking partner from the NAU hiking club, 22-year-old Carlton Boyd Moore, into following in Beer and Daggett's wake on air mattresses. Moore responded, "no way."

So, instead, they hiked down the Nankoweap Trail from Point Imperial, reaching the Colorado near River Mile 53 and walked downstream.

Butchart wanted to cross the river somewhere upstream of the Little Colorado

River (River Mile 61.5). At first he picked a quiet stretch of river about a mile upstream of Kwagunt Rapid (River Mile 56) to practice their mode of transport parallel to shore—the intent being to paddle across via an inflated air mattress later—with no other sort of personal flotation device. Moore, who was almost a nonswimmer, had been leery of the Colorado, so Butchart tried to aid him by lightening his pack and even towing him with a short rope. While towing proved futile, Moore seemed to catch on and was ready to continue, warily remarking, however, that he could see that once they were on the river, they were strictly on their own.

After safely landing back on the same side where they had started, the two portaged around the huge Kwagunt Rapid. Below it the pair launched back onto the cold, swiftly flowing river, heading downstream along the right bank before attempting a crossing near 60 Mile Rapid.

Butchart started paddling across on his air mattress first, while Moore elected to watch. To Butchart's surprise, once beyond the eddy, the 26,000 cfs flow of the river swept him through a small rapid and back to the right shore, downstream and out of view of his starting point and of Moore. Butchart climbed out of the river onto a ledge to signal Moore not to try it.

It was too late. Moore already had launched and now raced past him down the middle of the river on his own mattress.

Butchart quickly jumped back into the river and paddled furiously to catch up with him. He chased Moore for more than two miles. He might never have caught him were it not for Moore getting stuck in a large eddy a mile downstream of the Little Colorado River, nearly three miles downstream of their attempted crossing point. Moore at this point was hanging upside down with his arms and legs wrapped around his air mattress from underneath. He was gripping the inflated rubber for dear life while he swirled around in circles in an eddy whirlpool.

As Butchart tried to get to Moore, the current whipped Moore into another eddy on the opposite side of the river. Here Butchart finally reached him. Moore's face had drawn pale, almost white. Butchart saw that Moore was "not thinking clearly." Butchart tried to get him to shore by first telling Moore to shrug off his waterlogged backpack and to climb atop the mattress. Moore did both.

Butchart then tried towing the panic-stricken Moore by having him hold onto Butchart's feet. But Butchart found himself unable to tow Moore against the current. Next, as Moore seemed to try paddling himself to shore, he was swept back into the main current and rushed pell-mell downstream again.

Butchart frantically paddled after him in the darkening twilight. The big flow swept both men toward Lava Canyon Rapid (River Mile 65.6). Butchart thought Moore had too great a lead on him for Butchart to be able to catch him before the rapid, so he made the mistake of paddling to shore and climbing out among the willows on the left bank. Then he jogged downstream.

But Butchart never saw Boyd Moore alive again. No one did. But according to a

July, 1955 letter from P.T. Reilly to Dock Marston, "Moore's body was finally located above the suspension bridge, traced downstream, and recovered by Moki Mac's crew below Hermit [RM 95] on July 5 or 6." Earlier, in June, Reilly himself had found Moore's backpack, split open and empty, on a beach above River Mile 72.

Only after this tragedy did Butchart learn that when Moore was 3 or 4 years old he had experienced a near drowning from which he had never recovered psychologically and which had left him too fearful of water to learn to swim.

Swimmers Who Drowned between Phantom and Pipe Creek

The combination of brutally hot weather and a steep dustbowl of a trail winding for mile after mile under an unblinking desert sun has beguiled thousands of hikers who have descended to the foot of the Bright Angel Trail. The surprisingly intense heat and amazingly fast process of dehydration have sapped the mental acuity of many otherwise intelligent hikers like a brain vampire. This combination of heat and dehydration has made fools out of thousands of summer hikers, some of whom have literally walked off the trail and into the river fully dressed like zombies from a bad B-movie. Even NPS rangers have done this in uniform, radio and all.

The heat is that unnerving. Even veteran Canyon hikers can attest to this without embarrassment.

This sort of "cool off" swim, however, has often turned fatal. On July 20, 1935, for example, on a day about as hot as it gets in Grand Canyon, three teenage trail workers for the Civilian Conservation Corps (C.C.C.) hiked to the foot of the Bright Angel Trail. They camped there all night. The next morning two of them decided to cool off. This location, only a few yards upstream of the head of the lethal whitewater of Pipe Creek Rapid (at River Mile 89), has tempted thousands of hikers. And even though it was only 9:30 a.m., a cool hour in many parts of the world, here, now, it was already torrid.

After splashing a bit in the 80-degree water, Robert Demeree and Kenneth E. Curtis, age 18, of Kingman, Arizona decided to swim across the Colorado (no life jacket) to the north side as the third CCC volunteer, Wilton Cox Bryan, photographed them. The river was flowing 21,000 cfs.

"I thought it would be easy to swim across but we hit the main force of the river in a strong current," noted Robert Demeree. "I was immediately in distress."

Demeree swam Pipe Creek Rapid and barely managed to regain the same, south, shore. Curtis had proved a stronger swimmer and, fatefully, it would turn out, made it 30 feet farther out into stronger downstream current. He never made it back.

Demeree and Bryan climbed and headed farther downstream over the talus. They spent the rest of the morning searching the shorelines. But they found no sign of Curtis. A later search of 3 miles of shoreline by field glasses also failed. No one ever found a sign of Curtis.

Two years later, on August 7, 1937, Wallace Peshlakai, a Navajo interpreter of the Christian Reformed Church Mission, of Rehoboth, New Mexico, also hiked down with several others to the foot of Bright Angel Trail. Here he decided to ease himself into the Colorado to cool off.

As his hysterical eight-year-old step-son, Tommy Atchinson, reported, Peshlakai disrobed at the foot of the trail, just above Pipe Creek, and entered the warm river flowing at 9,500 cfs. A few moments later he saw Peshlakai, a horrified expression on his face, sucked into the swirling current and carried downstream. Peshlakai too was never seen again.

While it was once commonly said that the Colorado never gives up its dead, this is not exactly true. More true perhaps, is the Colorado frequently packaged its dead in mysterious circumstances. During their mid-April Easter vacation in 1968, for example, two Northern Arizona University students—Bruce Mitchell and Jan Jensen—hiked from the western North Rim area into Parashant Wash (River Mile 198.5). While admiring the grandeur of the western Canyon they were shocked to find a human skull protruding from the sand bar above the river. Upon returning to civilization, they alerted the National Park Service.

NPS personnel then hiked into Parashant and searched the area. They too found the skeleton, still clad in a woman's one-piece blue bathing suit, buried in the river sediments of the bank. The skeleton, forensic investigators concluded, was that of a young woman, 5-feet, 7-inches tall. The young woman's skeleton showed no indications of trauma. Nor did it possess any identification.

The investigators, however, suspected murder. Nearby in a recently abandoned mine were a woman's clothes and also expensive mining equipment. It seemed fishy. As in a mystery novel, something sinister seemed to have happened here.

Ultimately someone remembered that nearly three years earlier, Carol Goldman, age 18, of Albuquerque, had stepped from the hot beach into the 17,400 cfs river near Phantom Ranch for a quick dip—on August 24, 1965. She had been careful, her 17-year-old companion Jeanne Putnam later had explained, because Goldman could not swim. Yet despite her care, Goldman had slipped into an unexpectedly deep hole and had been swept away. Searchers had never recovered her body. Forensics in 1968 now indicated that the skeleton found 107.5 miles downstream of Phantom was that of Carol Goldman. The women's clothes with the mining equipment at Parashant were apparently an unexplained coincidence.

Thankfully, despite three additional drownings of young men attempting to swim the river during the 1970s at Pipe Creek, nearly two decades passed before someone else committed this same fatal error. On June 25, 1995 a pair of hikers, Tom Snashall and Gerald Deyo, arrived at the foot of the Bright Angel Trail at Pipe Creek and met Louis John Stano, III, age 21, from Tennessee. The three men talked for a few minutes. The pair noted that Stano, with a dirty blond ponytail, scruffy beard, and torn clothes, was a rough looking specimen. He had been badly sunburned, they said, and had old broken blisters on his face and shoulders. At age 21, he looked worn out.

Stano told them he was traveling across the U.S. to California to see the San Diego Zoo and that he had just been hiking in Colorado. This morning he had lost track of his traveling partner on the Bright Angel Trail. Unknown to Stano, his partner, who had not been carrying any of their water, had drawn an unnoticed message to him in the dust of the trail several yards above the trio's heads, and was now awaiting Stano at Phantom Ranch.

Snashall and Deyo mentioned they were about to do some work in Tennessee, but Stano, they said, seemed distant and uninterested. He asked them for a match. They did not have one. Stano bummed a match from one of the six other hikers nearby and lit up a cigar. He then stood knee-deep in the river and smoked it.

During their conversation, Snashall and Deyo reported, Stano had asked the pair several times their opinion of the river, how deep it might be, and so on. The two said there was a sign that said swimming was illegal. They also said they thought the current was dangerous. They recommended against trying to swim in it.

After Stano smoked his cigar, the pair was surprised to see him walk behind a bush, strip naked in the 106-degree heat, then run to the shore and make a shallow dive into the river. Stano swam out into the Colorado, flowing at 17,800 cfs, as if to cross it immediately upstream of Pipe Creek Rapid.

The current funneled Stano into the 51-degree rapid. Witnesses say Stano kept swimming the whole time while in view, never disappearing more than briefly. Even so, as Stano vanished out of sight, the eight others on the beach felt shocked. A woman from Denmark asked, "Why would anyone do something like that?"

An Hispanic man said, "They'll find him in Yuma."

But Stano never got close to Yuma. Three weeks later a Western River Expeditions' trip led by Bill Skinner spotted Stano's body twenty miles downstream of Pipe Creek Rapid and floating near Shinumo Creek Beach.

Later that year, on November 25, eight day-hikers from Los Angeles descended the South Kaibab Trail with the intent of returning to the South Rim via the Bright Angel Trail. At 1:00 p.m., two of the eight, Frederick Zernik, age 29, and Troy M. Fortney, age 26, decided to eliminate the nearly two-mile walk along the River Trail that connects the South Kaibab with the Bright Angel Trail. These two accomplished body surfers would swim instead of walk.

Ignoring the sign they had just passed saying "Dangerous Currents Swimming Prohibited," both men waded into the river, found it shockingly cold, then exited back to shore in a hurry. The only way to get into such a cold river they decided, was to leap in from a high rock with full commitment. Zernik and Fortney jumped into the cold Colorado immediately below the Mile 88 Boat Beach. Mere seconds in the cold water convinced Zernik that he had made a serious mistake.

It did even worse to Fortney.

As the two entered Bright Angel Rapid, flowing at 14,000 cfs, Fortney was already hyperventilating and panicking in the cold water. He climbed on top of Zernik. Zernick pushed Fortney off. Fortney crawled atop Zernick again.

The other six hikers ran downstream to the Silver Bridge in hopes of helping, but they arrived too late to do anything but witness the tableau unfold.

Zernick knew both of them were about to drown. And probably he would be the first. He fought his way free of Fortney again and stroked for the south shore. He swam into a tight eddy. Fortney followed him. After cycling around and around in the eddy with Fortney close behind him for a minute or two, and getting colder by the second, Zernick managed to self-extricate onto dry, but nearly vertical rock. At his precarious haul-out on a cliff face, Zernick perched, self-trapped, just upstream of the Silver Bridge. From here he would require a technical rescue via ropes.

Meanwhile the eddy swept Fortney out into the downstream current again.

Zernik became irrationally combative due to panic and likely hypothermia. He was no plum for his rescuers. Indeed Zernick was so cold and scared by the time that Rangers Mary Litell and Patrick Suddath dropped a rope to him that when he harnessed himself into it, he also looped it around his own neck.

The common propensity for panic and for hyperventilation upon sudden immersion in cold water presents a big risk factor for victims, especially those not wearing a life jacket. In turbulent water this syndrome increases the swimmer's risk of aspirating water then drowning. Merely knowing this information in advance can make the difference in a swimmer's mental state and ability to self-rescue. This is important for accidental swimmers wearing a life jacket because, forewarned, a swimmer now knows that he or she must combat the urge to panic and instead take an active role in his or her own rescue. With this sort of knowledge and a personal flotation device a swimmer vastly increases his or her odds of experiencing a non-traumatic adventure.

Be that as it may, Fortney never again escaped the current. It swept him under the Silver Bridge into Bright Angel Rapid. His body was found two weeks later at River Mile 95.25.

We would love to be able to write that the NPS warning signs posted near the river and all the above-mentioned avoidable tragedies have left such a powerful legacy of caution that no one else since has repeated the fatal mistakes at the feet of the Kaibab and Bright Angel Trail. We'd love to. But we cannot.

Instead the worst was yet to come. On April 30, 2009 a group of 18 hikers from the Tri-City Baptist Church of Tempe, Arizona descended the South Kaibab Trail on a planned rim-to-river-to-rim day-hike. While riding in the van before ever reaching Grand Canyon, however, three of the hikers—Joey Merrill, age 22, Mark Merrill, age16, and Saif Savaya, also age16—had discussed and expressed their strong desire to swim across the Colorado. Saif Savaya had not only told his father (earlier, at home) that swimming across the Colorado was on Saif's "bucket list," he also had brought swim goggles and trunks from home.

Once the group headed down the South Kaibab Trail the trio's talk of swimming the Colorado continued. No one, it seems, convinced the three to give up their plan. Neither the specter of extreme danger nor the illegality of the swim carried enough weight to prevent their attempt. Nor did any other adult in charge take charge by preventing them.

Near the tunnel to the Black Bridge and near the foot of the South Kaibab Trail the two Merrill brothers and Saif walked past the NPS "Swimming not permitted" sign. They veered westward here off the trail to scramble downstream of the Black Bridge to the small beach across from the Phantom boat beach at River Mile 87.4. The three stared at the 12,500 cfs flow of the Colorado moving swiftly past them toward the Silver Bridge. This was their challenge. How hard could it be?

As others of the Baptist hiking party watched from the Black Bridge, the three dived into the 52-degree river. The three swam onward (without life jackets). As do so many people possessing little experience with rivers, the three swam "across" with an incorrect, downstream ferry angle into the current (swimming in an upstream ferry as a deer would do being required to cross a river). The cold river swept the three hypothermic swimmers screaming into the Devil's Spittoon eddy just upstream of the Silver Bridge, the same eddy from which Frederick Zernick had been rescued years earlier but Charles Lyon not.

All three drowned: a record for a swimming party in Grand Canyon.

Mark Merrill's body was found 1 mile farther downriver on May 1. On May 14, Savaya was found near River Mile 99 and Joey near River Mile 100.

The dean of Joey Merrill's International Baptist College said: "We can only pray that the Lord will raise up more young men like Joey."

What was learned from this highly preventable tragedy? We have shown that this short stretch of river between the Black Bridge and Pipe Creek Rapid has proven to be the single most lethal place in all of Grand Canyon.

Testosterone is an accomplice. As with fatalities to falls, the primary and most numerous hiking-swimming-drowning victims were young men or adolescent boys. Of 73 victims of known age, at least 42–44 were at or under 28 years old. Aside from age, of all 93 known or suspected victims, 84 (90 percent) were males. In short, again the main factor in these drownings—besides lacking a life jacket— is being male. Worse yet, a young male. The signature error such victims most often make is failing to respect the magnitude of the power of the river. And the number one manifestation of this lack of respect is denying their need to wear a life jacket or denying the power of the river.

Especially applicable to hikers, ignorance is bliss only if "bliss" is the Hereafter.

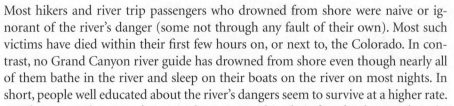

Most hikers and river trip passengers who drowned from shore were naive or ignorant of the river's danger (some not through any fault of their own). Most such victims have died within their first few hours on, or next to, the Colorado. In contrast, no Grand Canyon river guide has drowned from shore even though nearly all of them bathe in the river and sleep on their boats on the river on most nights. In short, people well educated about the river's dangers seem to survive at a higher rate.

The preponderance of victims drowning within their first few hours of reaching the river shows that means of advising caution cannot be overdone. In other words, there may be no such thing as too many warnings. For example, the high death toll of hikers drowning between the Black Bridge and Pipe Creek exists despite several warning signs posted on trails. Perhaps additional signs should be posted right on the beaches themselves. And these signs should not read "Swimming not permitted," which may be translated to "One does not need a permit to swim here." Instead the signs should read "Swimming prohibited: No swimming allowed." These signs might also list the names of all the victims who have drowned in the Colorado between the Black Bridge and Pipe Creek Rapid in the order in which they drowned, followed by the words, "they all thought they were good swimmers."

Swimmers Who Drowned Elsewhere in the Colorado

As we have seen, swimming in the Colorado to foil the heat waves shimmering from every square yard of exposed surface in Grand Canyon is all too tempting, even to those who should know better. On April 19, 1931, for example, 22-year old Iven Bundy and his cousin, Floyd Iverson, were grazing the family's sheep along the Colorado River near Whitmore Wash (River Mile 187.5). Floyd decided to swim across the river for fun, a thing both young men had been forbidden to do by their families.

Floyd swam alone across the 9,700 cfs current and made it to the other side. He called back to Iven that the swim was not all that hard.

Iven followed Floyd into the Colorado but was sucked under by a whirlpool. He vanished. Floyd searched for him desperately, but never saw a trace of him again. Floyd then faced the swim back across the Colorado and, after that, the long hike up to the family ranch at Mount Trumbull to explain how Iven had died—or had he merely been swept downstream?

Iven's father, Roy Bundy, had been crippled by arthritis. He asked his brother, Chester Bundy, to help search for Iven—or his body. Chester and Floyd plus Pat and Ensign Griffiths returned to the river. They searched in the rain, but found nothing. They plodded back up to Mount Trumbull to get a better outfit for searching properly. They next dragged a 180-pound, galvanized iron boat with watertight chambers fore and aft down to the river and loaded it with supplies, including a box of dynamite "for fishing." Chester, Floyd, and Pat now began their search for Iven in earnest.

During the first twenty miles or so of river they found no sign of Iven. But they did manage to flip their metal boat in a rapid "south of Parashant" (River Mile 198.5). This may have been 205-Mile Rapid. They also managed to lose most of their supplies, including their dynamite. Fortunately, no one else drowned.

The searchers continued downriver for five days in total to Diamond Creek (River Mile 225.7). Dissolute and hungry, Chester Bundy sat down in the old blacksmith's shop which had been built at Diamond by a government survey camp nearly a decade earlier. Chester sat on a bedspring under a two-foot wide plank that had been a tool shelf. As he looked up he read penciled on the wall, "Glen and Bessie Hyde, November 31st [sic], 1928."

This inscription, assuming it was genuine, helped pinpoint where Bessie and Glen had vanished, i.e., downstream of Diamond on December 1, but upstream of 237-mile. But it did nothing to help the searchers recover Iven, dead or alive. Nor did it help fill the three searchers' empty bellies.

They continued searching downstream. They portaged their small boat around rapids. On day eight, they reached Separation Canyon and Separation Rapid (River Mile 239.5). Although none of the three had even been here before and thus did not know where they were, they were smart enough to realize they could not run this rapid and emerge from it alive. Nor could they portage it.

So they resorted to "ghost-boating" it with a log tied onto the tow rope as a float in the hopes that two of them could swim out below the rapid and rescue the empty boat. The searchers shoved the empty boat into the slick, silky vee feeding the already notorious rapid and watched from shore.

The rapid gulped the boat. The craft ruptured an air chamber, filled, and half sank. The searchers waded into the river downstream and rescued it, but the boat was a mess. On top of this, the three men were out of food. So out of food that the whole enterprise of boating down the Colorado now seemed insane.

The trio gave up. They hiked up Separation Canyon, taking the east fork. They shared a one-quart canteen. They ate tiny birds' eggs right out of the nest. Chester shot a jackrabbit with his six-shooter. This was like Thanksgiving. Up on the plateau, many hours later, they found an old mining road. From there they hiked from ranch house to ranch house, finding most of them unoccupied. Eventually they made it home.

Much later, the Bundys learned that Iven's body had been discovered by two prospectors while fishing at Gregg's Ferry, west of Grand Canyon, and was buried there.

During more modern times, other swimmers would drown (see Table 5). For example, on August 7, 1983 at River Mile 2.5, another mishap occurred. Less than an hour into an OARS, Inc. rowing trip, the group stopped for lunch. After the trip leader's safety talk, and as the guides cleaned up lunch, three young passengers on the trip, Jeffrey Kaplan, age 16 of Massachusetts, Jeff's younger brother Rick, and Kenneth Richard Kleeburg played a sort of "follow-the-leader" game sliding down the sand dune bank toward the eddy. Abruptly, Jeff, without a life jacket, jumped into the water about twenty yards downriver of the boats.

He swam with the eddy current up past the sterns of the boats. Rick, also wearing no life jacket, followed. Rick reported that the cold water took his breath away. Kenneth, still on shore behind the two brothers, decided not to enter the river.

Jeffrey, Rick saw, was doing a slow-motion breaststroke ahead of him. Then Jeffrey submerged out of sight. When Rick reached the upriver end of the boats, he still could not find Jeffrey. Rick looked around for a few seconds. He poked his head in likely hiding places. He suspected that his brother was trying to trick him. But as his searches continued to come up zero, he finally asked, "Where is Jeff?"

The last person to see Jeff was a fellow passenger and Kenneth's father, Richard Kleeburg, on this father-son trip. Jeff, Kleeburg said, had been twenty feet from the boats. He was floating "in the eddy face down, moving his arms, then his face came up and went down. These were gentle motions and Jeff appeared to be OK." Kleeburg did not watch Jeff after seeing this.

But at Rick's worried question, the boatmen now scoured the eddy. They looked in, stepped in, then checked under the boats. That done and nothing being found, they rowed around the eddy and probed its depths with oars. But still they found nothing. Later, neither did NPS divers, land searchers, nor helicopter searchers.

What happened to Jeffrey Kaplan?

His medical history included his experiencing an epileptic (petit mal) seizure a year and a half earlier. He was on the medications Dilantin and Tegretol to control a recurrence. Despite these, while swimming the cold water of this eddy, he had apparently suffered yet another seizure anyway. And none of the guides, three of whom were on their boats stowing food away at the time, had seen him. The chilly Colorado, it was surmised, had triggered a seizure in Jeffrey despite his medications, and he had silently sunk out of sight into a powerful flow of 36,000 cfs at a moment when no one was looking.

On August 30, 23 days later, a motorist stopped atop Navajo Bridge (illegally) to treat himself to the inspiring view into Marble Canyon from 470 feet above River Mile 4.3. This tourist, however, saw more than he had hoped to. Below him floated something that looked all too much like a human body. It was, it turned out, Jeffrey Kaplan's body, floating barely two miles downstream from where he had vanished.

On March 22, 1990, Boy Scout Matthew Cranny, age 13, hiked with his Arizona LDS Troop 189—14 boys and 8 adults—down Saltwater Wash. The troop camped at River Mile 11.5. The next morning, Cranny and another scout, Scott Dillon, and his father, Steve Dillon, walked a mile or so upstream to a few hundred yards upstream of Soap Creek Rapid.

Steve Dillon saw Cranny sitting despondently on a rock. Steve asked him how he was doing. Cranny answered that he was not doing too well and that he probably would not catch a fish during the whole trip. Steve asked Cranny to come upstream and join him and Scott where they were fishing and to use their bait instead of salmon eggs.

Cranny walked upstream and baited his line with the Dillons' worms (illegal bait in Grand Canyon at this time). After baiting it, Cranny set his pole down and walked to the water. Steve Dillon thought Cranny was just going to wash his hands. But Cranny waded into the cold Colorado. Dillon yelled at him, "It's no wonder you don't catch anything, you just screwed up a good fishing hole."

Cranny, only two merit badges short of Eagle Scout rank, looked at Dillon but said nothing. Then he continued walking into the river. When he was chin deep, Steve Dillon yelled, "Matt, come on out."

As Jeffrey Kaplan (above) had done, Cranny dunked over his head and swam, sort of, upstream. Cranny surfaced, and looked directly at Steve Dillon. Dillon said, "Matt, get out!"

Cranny looked away. Frustrated at Cranny's lack of response, Dillon watched him tread water for "a short time" while drifting upstream. Then, speaking loudly of Cranny's lack of etiquette, Dillon turned away from Cranny to pick up his own tackle, preparatory to moving to yet another fishing spot. (Every member of this hike had been briefed that there would be no swimming.)

Steve Dillon's son, Scott, then told his father, "He's gone."

Concerned, Dillon ran up the beach 25 feet. Both father and son saw Cranny surface. Young Scott said Cranny was struggling and could not stay above the surface. But Steve Dillon later said, "not knowing exactly how long he had been under, I was undecided as to whether to attempt a rescue."

Steve Dillon turned away for a moment to remove his vest and hat and toss them to higher ground. When he turned around, Cranny had vanished yet again into the 11,500 cfs current. Now finally alarmed, Dillon dived into the water but each time found a boulder instead of Cranny. Meanwhile Scott yelled for help. After 45 minutes of searching by Troop 189, two adults hiked out to notify NPS rangers at Lees Ferry.

Troop leader John R. Whitmer reported to NPS Ranger Lenore Grover that Cranny had a history of epileptic seizures—and that indeed he had just had one only 3 or 4 months earlier on a troop bicycling trip. Scott Dillon then described how Cranny's petit mal seizures manifested themselves: he "would walk around as if he were in a trance, he would just stare off and not say anything. After a while he would fall down."

Much like Jeffrey Kaplan, Matthew Cranny had drowned apparently as a victim of a seizure. This would happen again to another fisherman (see below). Indeed, the susceptibility of some epileptics to experiencing seizures when they watch flickering lights—such as the bright reflections of sunlight dancing on the rippling surface of the water—may put epileptics at higher risk of drowning than other people.

NPS divers from Glen Canyon National Recreational Area scoured the nearby eddies but failed to located Cranny. Dog teams on shore also failed. The next day Glen Canyon Dam operators lowered its outflow to 1,000 cfs, dropping the river level by about ten vertical feet. Divers still could not find Cranny. A few months later a leg wearing his style of and size hiking boot washed ashore at House Rock Rapid almost six miles downstream.

On August 28, 1992 Boy Scout Troop 17 from Mankato, Minnesota, started their backcountry hike into the Inner Canyon. George Fischer led the troop. Accompanying him was his grown son, Paul. Four 15-year-old Scouts from Troop 17 were on this hike. The six descended the South Kaibab Trail and made their way west on the Tonto, descending into Hermit Creek Canyon on September 2. They camped at Hermit Creek (River Mile 95).

That same afternoon, one of the Scouts, Christopher Guetschow, dived into the Colorado without a life jacket about 100 yards upstream of Hermit Rapid. The investigation by NPS rangers into this incident revealed that Guetschow had been socially "outcast" by his peers in the troop. Being odd man out in a tiny group of three other peers could become nightmarish after a few days in a place as isolated—and isolating—as Grand Canyon. Guetschow may have been trying to redeem or prove himself by showing that he had the guts and the ability to swim across the Colorado.

Indeed, Guetschow's intent did seem to be to swim across the river. But only halfway across, the slick tongue of water funneling into Hermit Rapid gripped Guetschow and accelerated him into the rapid. His companions last saw him above the surface in the upper swells of the rapid.

Two weeks later a Grand Canyon Dories trip with Kenton Grua and John D. (a.k.a. "D5") Edwards aboard lassoed Guetschow's decomposing body in the eddy near River Mile 104 and towed it to shore. Here Kenton double rolled Guetschow's body inside a pair of tarps and secured it on the beach for the rangers to pick up. Edwards hated the idea of continuing the trip and leaving the body unattended. Kenton continued his efforts to contact the Park via radio transmission to overflights. Later that day the Park helicopter retrieved the body.

The common thread in these nineteen drownings of deliberate swimmers is that the victims (who mostly were young men) all vastly underestimated the power of the current in the Colorado, and, after 1963, its coldness as well. Driven by heat and the promise of cool relief in the river, they had entered the flow. Their outcomes, however, would have been much the same had they stepped off the South Rim into a thousand feet of vertical air. Hopefully, if future visitors understand this, they will approach the Colorado River as if it were a hungry man-eating crocodile.

Accidental Swimmers Who Fell In From Shore

Although accidentally falling unseen and unheard into the Colorado while being surrounded by people then never leaving it alive may seem like a pretty unlikely chain of events, several people have done exactly that. A few of these victims were witnessed as they slipped into the river, or else heard as they cried for help. But more victims have vanished unseen and unheard.

On May 17, 1919 two young male hikers from the Eastern United States, of surnames Van de Bunt and Betts, arrived at the South Rim by train. Next they hiked down the Bright Angel Trail. They camped halfway down but then lost the trail. Confused by the weave of trails left by feral burros, the two hikers followed a wrong route, the old Wash Henry Trail (unused at this time for about twenty years, but likely following the unusually steep "Miner's Route" leading to today's river trail between the South Kaibab Trail and Pipe Creek). Then, near the river, they deviated from this trail too.

The two found no trail along the river at all. The trail was supposed to be here somewhere, they reasoned. But not only was the trail not where it was supposed to be, neither was the cable (put in place a dozen years earlier by David Rust) visible that was supposed to cross the river to Roosevelt's Camp (which would become Phantom Ranch three years later, in 1922).

The two young men decided to walk along the river and find the missing trail and cable. They felt certain that they would eventually reach both in a short distance. Soon, however, the banks of the river became almost vertical walls of Vishnu Schist. And still neither a trail or a cable was in sight. Betts started climbing this wall. Behind Betts and unseen by him, Van de Bunt tried walking in the water against the cliff face.

Betts turned around and saw Van de Bunt in the water. Alarmed, Betts yelled at him to either wait where he was or else back up onto dry land.

As Betts turned around to backtrack himself off the cliff to rejoin Van de Bunt, he slipped and fell at least twenty feet. Battered, Betts pulled himself together and checked on Van de Bunt. To Betts' added consternation, Van de Bunt had vanished. Searching failed to locate any trace of him.

When Betts later showed Emery Kolb the place where he had fallen, Kolb wondered aloud how Betts could even have survived. Betts next showed Kolb where he had last seen Van de Bunt. Kolb nodded. Van de Bunt, Kolb noted, had been walking on a ledge about two feet underwater. Kolb knew this area at lower water. Van de Bunt's ledge dropped off a vertical twenty feet almost directly in front of where he was last seen by Betts. The missing man, Kolb concluded, almost certainly had taken one step too many, a fatal one. Then the hugely swollen current of late May in the steep gradient of Upper Granite Gorge had swept Van de Bunt downstream and underwater as if he were no more than a mouse.

How quickly the unwary can be swept into oblivion by the Colorado can be nothing short of appalling. On April 29, 1983, for example, the San Diego Nomads, a Sierra Club hiking group of 44 people, hiked from Hualapai Hilltop down to the Havasupai Campground and camped. The following day some of the Nomads, including a woman, Jody Mack, M.D., age 31, hiked up Carbonate Canyon. The next day, May 1, again several of the Nomads, including Mack, whom everyone agreed was in a very positive mood and in excellent physical condition, reached the mouth of Havasu Creek at the Colorado River (River Mile 156.8). There the group ate lunch.

The air temperature was below 70 degrees. Mack had goosebumps as she talked briefly with boatman Bruce Simbala of Grand Canyon Dories, whose boat was tied in the mouth of Havasu.

One of the Nomads, Jerry Herrman, later saw Jody Mack 30 to 40 feet away and crouching on a low ledge of polished Muav Limestone jutting into the river about 150 feet downstream of the mouth of Havasu Creek and along the edge of Havasu Rapid. Mack, Herrman said, was leaning out and seemed to be trying to put her hand in the river. Abruptly, Mack's feet slipped (she was wearing Sierra Sneakers). Mack kerplunked feet-first into the swift current. Herrman immediately yelled, "Jody's in!"

The 19,000 cfs current instantly swept Mack into the mainstream. She seemed, however, to remain in control. Even without a life jacket, she kept her head up and faced downstream. But she continued to funnel down the mainstream instead of swimming back toward the left shoreline. Horrified onlookers watched her until she floated out of sight a few hundred yards downstream between cliffs of Muav.

Upon hearing Herrman's yell, Bruce Simbala grabbed several life jackets and one of the hikers. He sliced his bowline and rowed into the river to give chase. Despite his relatively quick response time of less than five minutes and despite his rowing hard for more than half an hour, Simbala never saw Mack again. Her hundreds of yards of lead plus her submersion into invisibility cut her odds of rescue drastically. Sixteen days later, a river trip found Jody Mack's body floating in the river forty miles downstream near River Mile 196.

Jody Mack's demise illustrates at least two other lessons. First—and all too obvious—the river is a very dangerous place. Second, life jackets are vital while on or in the water. In our opinion, life jackets are a good idea even while fishing in the Colorado from shore. A fisherman at Lees Ferry—Robert Wiel on July 24, 1988—fell into a flow of 11,000 cfs without a life jacket. Wiel drowned in his waders. The wide rubber legs acted like two huge buckets of water. No other fisherman could reach him. On January 29, 2000 Jamie Padilla, age 22, suffered a petit mal seizure while fishing without wearing a life jacket above River Mile 8 near the mouth of Jackass Canyon. Despite his companions witnessing the seizure (caused perhaps by sunlight flickering on the water), they could not reach Padilla in time. He drowned in the rapid. So too did fisherman Todd Strickland, age 49, on May 30, 1999, when he fell in below Nevills' beach at River Mile 75 in search of a good fishing spot, again without wearing his life jacket.

At times the Colorado River seems almost treacherous. On June 14, 1989, the same day that boatman Martin Hunsaker flipped his 33-foot rig in Crystal Rapid and drowned, only an hour downstream the river took yet another victim.

Things had started off well enough for Karl Sebastian Jacobi. The 21-year-old from Germany had been touring the U.S. on a motorcycle. He had motored down between the soaring Triassic cliffs framing Lees Ferry for a look at the Colorado River. There, on the launch beach, was a private party with gear scattered across the beach preparatory to loading for a three-week trip. Jacobi chatted with them.

Having been required to wait for several years after their application to the NPS for the actual issuance of a permit to launch a private float trip, this trip's members—like many others—had lost many of its originally-intended fellow boaters. To finally use their long-awaited permit, the surviving original members of this intended trip had patched it back together to a dozen members by adding several people who neither knew one another nor understood one another's abilities in whitewater. Several of these new people, the group was now finding out, had little to no experience on big rivers. And now, as Karl Sebastian Jacobi walked up, several members of the trip's paddle crew were already very worried about being able to paddle their boat safely. Consensus at this moment was that they needed at least one more strong, aggressive paddler to complete a safe crew.

The group of worried boaters stared at the youthful, athletic Jacobi and could not believe their ears when he asked if he could go along with them.

Almost instantly, Jacobi, a total stranger, became a last minute, but unlucky thirteenth member of this trip and was assigned to its paddle crew. He did not remain a stranger for long. Other members of the trip found him a very positive addition: he was young, quiet, self-confident, undemanding, optimistic, and enthusiastic. On the flip side, he was over-confident, did not seem to appreciate the danger of the Colorado, and frequently had to be reminded to put on his life jacket while boating. Indeed, Jacobi's "I-can-do-anything" attitude may have set the stage for tragedy on day nine.

That morning, the trip was camped near River Mile 103.8. At 11:00 a.m., Jacobi had asked the trip leader if he could hike alone from camp upstream along the shore. The trip leader said yes, but for no more than 40 minutes.

Jacobi failed to return by 60 minutes. One of the women in camp said she thought she heard someone call for help. Several of them listened and searched the slope with binoculars. Three of the trip members began searching for Jacobi. One, Frank Leuthold, hiked upstream and uphill hundreds of feet above the river. He looked down and, to his shock, saw Jacobi shouting and breast-stroking toward shore in an eddy bordered by vertical cliffs about 40 yards upstream of camp.

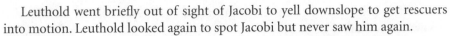

Leuthold went briefly out of sight of Jacobi to yell downslope to get rescuers into motion. Leuthold looked again to spot Jacobi but never saw him again.

Meanwhile a second searcher, Esther Graw, had also climbed high upslope, thinking too that the original calls for help were coming from up there. Graw too now heard frantic shouting from the river. She saw "a white person in the middle of the river with arms outstretched, head out, and shouting." As Graw ran back down to the shore, she too lost sight of Jacobi, who likely entered 104-Mile Rapid flowing at 13,250 cfs. Neither Graw, nor anyone else, ever saw him again.

Helicopter searches that afternoon failed to locate Jacobi. Twelve days later, a commercial river trip found his body at River Mile 105.5. An autopsy revealed death by drowning.

Although several people involved assumed that Jacobi had somehow fallen into the river from a short cliff while hiking, at least one member of the trip, Arlan Lazere, thinks it may have been otherwise. "He may have jumped into the river, planning to swim back down to camp," she reflected. "He was that kind of guy, really confident, but he did not understand the power of the river."

Mysterious Disappearances Who Drowned From Camp

As is all too clear by now, the Colorado River is far more deceptively lethal than many people guess. Yet no single type of fatality seems quite as bizarre and puzzling as when a person vanishes unseen and unheard into the Colorado at night —even while "surrounded" by other people.

On June 8, 1973, Desi Baca led a party of eleven children backpacking down from the South Rim to Indian Garden. The party dropped off their camping gear there then Baca took his eleven charges miles farther down the Bright Angel Trail to the Colorado River at Pipe Creek. This hike took longer than he expected. Now the hike back to Indian Garden would require traversing the trail at night. Baca next found his flashlight was not working right. So he told the boys to bivouac at the mouth of Pipe Creek for the night.

Baca made a head count at midnight. Two boys, Kenneth Baca, age 9, and Marcos Ortega, age 11, had disappeared. Worried, Baca yelled for the boys. Kenneth, Baca's son, answered from the other side of the creek where he was stranded for unexplained reasons on a rock ledge above "camp." But no amount of yelling or searching located Marcos (Mark) Ortega, whose shoes were still in his sleeping spot. Nor did a six-hour ground search or seven hours of searching by air by NPS rangers on the next day (June 9) turn up further clues. Additional searches continued for a week. They too found nothing.

None of the boys seemed to know what events had led up to Ortega's disappearance. But young Mark, it turned out, had a history of sleepwalking—hence his bare-footed disappearance into a flow of 11,000 cfs that night. On June 26, 18 days later and six miles downstream, river runners found Ortega's body in the river just below Hermit Rapid.

Sleepwalking aside, "drunk" drownings have proved a more common culprit in cases of mysterious disappearances. On July 8, 1981, for example, a 58-year-old male passenger, Charles Robert Hunter was a client on a Diamond River Adventures motor trip camped at River Mile 19. Hunter had been drinking alcohol heavily that evening—having started with four beers at lunch—before going to sleep on the motor rig with the crew at about 10:30 p.m.

Amazingly for only an 8-day trip, Hunter had brought along a full case of twelve one-fifth bottles of Seagrams 7 and yet another case of twelve one-fifth bottles of vodka. He had broken out several bottles that first evening for general consumption.

Hunter, whom all of the guides reported as having a positive attitude, drank bourbon by mixing it in a Sprite can and also straight from the bottle. Trip leader Daryl Diamond told Hunter, who was a local teacher at Page High School and had taught some of the Diamond guides as teenagers in his classes, he could sleep on the boat if he wanted to. Hunter laid out his sleeping bag on the bow of the downstream boat, removed his shoes, and reclined atop his bag in the July heat. That was the last thing anyone saw him do.

An hour before dawn, Diamond boatman Max Hamblin (a.k.a. Garn) came down to the boat from shore. Still drunk (by his own admission), Hamblin saw an empty sleeping bag. Cold, he crawled into it. After he awakened later, he realized it was Hunter's bag. That morning, Daryl Diamond found Hunter's cigarette case in the wet sand of the fluctuation zone (the river had dropped after midnight) under the front pontoon of his rig.

Hunter, as several victims before him, may have been urinating into the river off the edge of the boat, lost his balance, and fallen into the Colorado flowing at about 15,000 cfs and drowned.

All tolled, the Canyon has claimed at least 7 drunk drowning victims as of August, 2011. Moreover, probably 13 victims have died, some from falls, others from drowning, while urinating into the Canyon and losing their balance. The Canyon's several "drunk drownings" pinpoint alcohol consumption in significant quantity as their most common single precipitating factor. It is no secret that alcohol consumption reduces alertness and common sense—drinking alcohol has caused millions of fatalities while driving cars, hunting with firearms, arguing in bars, and, yes, boating. Consider the summary findings of the BOAT/US Foundation (*Foundation Findings #31: Alcohol and Boating—January 1999*. Alexandria, VA: The BOAT/US Foundation for Boating Safety.):

> *Most boaters think of collisions as the greatest threat when drinking on the water. Yet, according to BOAT/US Foundation for Boating Safety research, an*

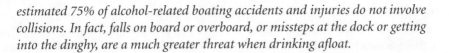

estimated 75% of alcohol-related boating accidents and injuries do not involve collisions. In fact, falls on board or overboard, or missteps at the dock or getting into the dinghy, are a much greater threat when drinking afloat.

This research concludes that drinking afloat is even more dangerous than while driving a car. Having drunk alcohol was a factor in 46 percent of 586 U.S. boating fatalities in 1997 and in 37 percent of such fatalities in 1998. The U.S. Coast Guard also reported that a boat operator with a blood alcohol concentration above 0.10 percent (the legal threshold in 38 states) is ten times more likely to be killed in a boating accident than one with zero blood alcohol concentration. "No matter what the activity," the BOAT/US Foundation for Boating Safety added, "alcohol affects balance, vision, coordination and judgment. But in boating, stressors like wind, sun, noise, motion, and vibration can magnify the effects of alcohol and even accelerate impairment."

Eerily, one of the most common—and striking—errors people make after even imbibing only one drink (when tested in a field situation) was failing to fasten their life jackets correctly. Little surprise then that adult disappearances involved alcohol consumption.

But, again, the act of urinating into the Colorado while visiting or camping in its corridor, as required by the Park, also can prove deadly. On July 16, 2006, for example, 19-year-old Iryna Shylo, a concession employee at the rim but from the Ukraine hiked with a new buddy down the Hermit Trail to the Colorado at River Mile 95. There at 6:00 p.m., the 5' 10," 120-pound woman took a "bathroom" break. Earlier, at the Park's backcountry permits office a ranger had advised Shylo that the rule was to urinate only in the river. Shylo, complying, separated from her male hiking partner at 6:00 p.m. to visit the shoreline at the top of Hermit Rapid.

When Shylo failed to return, her buddy began searching for her. Other than finding her footprints mixed with the prints of several other people who had scouted Hermit Rapid, he had no luck. What might have gone wrong here?

The air temperature that afternoon was a sweltering 110 degrees. This opens the possibility that Shylo had decided to dunk herself during her break. Even though the river looks innocently calm above Hermit, it actually flows deep near shore and moves relentlessly into the rapid. On the other hand, Hermit Creek also flows very nearby and offers perfect, clean water for cooling oneself off. Hence there exists no need in that immediate area to dunk in the river. So instead of dunking in dangerous water, Shylo may simply have lost her footing and fell in. Her yell for help would have been difficult to hear due to the incessant roar of the rapid.

Because Shylo's disappearance looked highly suspicious as "the perfect crime," the Park investigated her new hiking buddy. He turned out to be an older man and truly nothing beyond a new and last minute hiking buddy who had no prior relationship to her. Because investigators found no reason for suspicion, they concluded Shylo indeed had suffered a mishap in the river during her pee break.

Two weeks later, on July 30, a private river trip found Shylo floating in an eddy 10 miles downriver near Ruby Rapid (River Mile 105). An autopsy found drowning but no signs of foul play or sexual assault. Again, prior to this hike, Shylo had been instructed by a ranger in the Park's backcountry permits office to urinate in the river. One wonders if this ranger in the permits office also cautioned Shylo about how to safely accomplish peeing in the river. At least six victims of the Colorado were urinating just before they drowned. Moreover, many people, women especially, have fallen into the river while trying to adhere to this Park rule. Some were rescued only by slim chance. The act of urinating into the river while intoxicated may be (this is an untested hypothesis) a concomitant cause of drunk-drowning.

In this regard, the use of a "pee" bucket in each camp's porta-potty set-up will likely save a life or two in the next decade or so. Indeed, some companies now provide a 1-gallon plastic pee bucket per each passenger for their entire trip. The bucket is later discarded in recycle back at the warehouse. At less than one dollar per bucket these comprise incredibly cheap life insurance and also ensure the Park's rule against peeing on the ground at or in camp is easily adhered to.

The lessons from the 94 drownings discussed above are many. Perhaps it would be trite to simply say that the Grand Canyon Colorado is a dangerous river. Even after hearing this, however, many people would mentally answer, "Yes, of course it is, but I am a good swimmer." It well may be this thought alone that killed half the victims discussed above.

Table 5–A. RIVER TRAVELERS (upstream or downstream) WHO DROWNED IN THE GRAND CANYON COLORADO (most incidents are discussed in text unless noted otherwise). River flows in cubic feet per second (cfs) for dates of incidents are from the U.S.G.S. Historical Streamflows Daily Values Data Base, from Stations #09380000 (Lees Ferry) and #09402500 (Phantom) at wwwdaztecn.wr.usgs.gov/index.html.

Name, age	Date	River Location / Flow	*Circumstances*
George Strole, adult	August 29, 1867	Maybe in Grand Canyon or, instead, downstream of the Grand Wash Cliffs	

*Strole of Colorado and Wisconsin native James White built a log raft and headed down the Colorado from a now unknown put-in point fleeing from hostile Indians. Although White made a 14-day journey, Strole, wearing **no life jacket**, drowned on day four. Adams, E. 2001.* Come Hell or High Water. *Logan, Utah: Utah State University Press. Stanton, R. B. 1932.* Colorado River Controversies. *New York: Dodd, Mead & Company.*

| Frank Mason Brown, 43 | July 10, 1889 | Saltwater Wash (River Mile 11.8) | |

*As Harry McDonald steered it into the left eddy, Brown's small round-bottomed boat/canoe rolled and flipped. McDonald and Brown of Denver, Colorado **wore no life jackets**. McDonald swam to shore a few hundred yards downstream. Brown drowned trying to swim directly to shore across the eddy. Stanton, R. B. 1965.* Down the Colorado. *Norman, Oklahoma: University of Oklahoma Press.*

| Peter M. Hansbrough, adult | July 15, 1889 | 25-Mile Rapid | |
| Henry C. Richards, adult | | | |

*After lining, then running most of 25-Mile Rapid, Richards' and Hansbrough's boat was pinned against the left cliff. As the two men stood to try to free it, it flipped. Hansbrough of Ashley, Indiana, wearing **no life jacket**, never surfaced. Richards, an African-American from Kentucky, also wearing no life jacket, surfaced, swam strongly toward a downstream rescue boat, but sank in the silty water. Stanton, R. B. 1965.* Down the Colorado. *Norman, Oklahoma: University of Oklahoma Press.*

| Bessie Hyde, 22 | December 1, 1928 | 232-Mile Rapid (?), flow: 8,700 cfs | |
| Glen R. Hyde, 29 | | | |

*Precise circumstances of the demise of the Hydes of Twin Falls, Idaho remain an unsolved mystery, but the most likely scenario is that the couple drowned in 232-Mile Rapid. Both wore **no life jackets**. Neither body was ever recovered. Coconino Sun, November 16, 1928. Norm Tessman, 1986. Sharlotte Hall Gazette. Vol. 13 (1). Brad Dimock, 2001.* Sunk without a Sound. *Flagstaff: Fretwater Press. Personal communications to Ghiglieri from Martin J. Anderson, George Billingsley, O. C. Dale, Regan Dale, Michael Harrison, and Scott Thybony in 1990.*

| Bill Payne, 27 | June 22–24, 1931 | 234-Mile Rapid (?), flow: 23,600 cfs | |
| (a.k.a. William Talmadge) | | | |

Payne of Los Angeles, California and James R. Ervin, age 30, tried running the Colorado from Mile 225.7 to Hoover Dam in the Bright Angel, one of six wooden boats abandoned by the 1927 Pathé-Bray Expedition. They launched on the ebb of the peak flow *of the Colorado. They capsized several times, losing their oars in rapid "number six." Both men swam to the south side. Ervin hiked out. Upon returning on June 24, Ervin and the Deputy Sheriff found that Payne (**no life jacket?**) and the boat had vanished forever. Nelson, J. (Sheriff). 1931. "Notes RE: Ervin and Payne (Talmadge) Experiences of June 1931." (Report sent on September 3, 1931). Irvin, J. R. 1966. "Experiences in Grand Canyon." (with corrections by Otis "Dock" Marston, 10 VII 1966).*

Jack H. Aldridge, adult

October, 1938   Marble Canyon?

*Last seen by two Japanese visitors just downstream of California Bar at Hansen (roughly 100 miles upstream of Lees Ferry), Aldridge, of Palm Springs, California, told them he was planning to row solo through Grand Canyon all the way to Boulder Dam. Aldridge's boat was found at Mile 65.5 by members of the Amos Burg-Buzz Holmstrom-Willis Johnson trip. Aldridge had worn **no life jacket**. One friend claimed to have seen Aldridge in 1940, but no other acquaintance did. Excerpt from letter by Acting GCNP Superintendent Lon Garrison, October 20, 1938 in "Excerpts from files—Grand Canyon National Park. Oct. 31, 1938."*

Charles Roemer, 50+

October 24–26, 1946   Inner Gorge beyond River Mile 88, flow: 7,100 cfs

*Roemer, a Hungarian immigrant from New York City, made a solo attempt to fully traverse Grand Canyon in a small, "five-man" inflatable while wearing **no life jacket**. After passing Mile 88, Roemer was never seen nor heard from again. An air search on October 26 and an upriver search by Harry Aleson both failed to locate him.* Arizona Daily Sun, *October 25, 1946.* Arizona Republic, *October 25, 1946.* Superintendent's Monthly Report for October 1946, #54706 (364).

Albert Loper, 79+

July 8, 1949   24.5-Mile Rapid, flow: 51,500 cfs

*Loper of Green River and Salt Lake City, Utah rowed well ahead of his companions into 24.5-Mile Rapid at flood level and may have suffered a heart attack or stroke, which led to flipping his boat and not surviving his swim **despite his life jacket**.* Arizona Daily Sun, *July 11, 1949.* Brad Dimock. 2007. The Very Hard Way. *Flagstaff, Arizona: Fretwater Press.*

George D. ("Dave") Jensen, 28

June–July 1955   between River Miles 68 and 72, flow: 20,000–36,000 cfs

*Jensen of Imperial Beach, California launched a driftwood raft in the Furnace Flats area and wore **no life jacket**. He had done a previous trip with two buddies in April, 1950. His body was discovered near Mile 96 on July 13 and identified by the shoes he was wearing.* Arizona Daily Sun, *July 13, 1955.*

Phillip D. Martin, 27

February 21, 1965   Paria Riffle (River Mile 1), flow: 9,000 cfs

*Lees Ferry Ranger Martin and a fellow NPS ranger capsized their canoe in Paria Riffle. Both **men wore life jackets**. A native of Los Angeles, Martin stayed with the boat and died of apparent **hypothermia**.* Arizona Daily Sun, *February 22, 1965.*

Peter Scott Le Brun, 14   November 5, 1966   Phantom Beach (River Mile 87.8), flow:
                                               9,000 cfs
*Le Brun of Flagstaff, Arizona and two other teenage hikers rode
a driftwood log down the Colorado. Upon entering Bright Angel
Rapid, all three boys got nervous and tried to swim to shore. Le
Brun, wearing **no life jacket**, drowned.* Arizona Daily Sun, No-
vember 8, 1966.

Jesse "Shorty" Burton, 44   June 14, 1967   Upset Rapid (River Mile 150), flow:
                                              12,750 cfs
*While motoring toward the right cut in Upset, Burton of Vernal,
Utah ran the steep hole and flipped. **His new life jacket caught
on one of the open eye-bolts** suspending the floor and by trapping
him underwater, drowned him.* Arizona Republic, June 19, 1967.
Al Holland, 1998. "Shorty's Back" boatman's quarterly review
11(3):14-23.

Mae Hansen, 64   July 10, 1972   House Rock Rapid (River Mile 16.8), flow:
                                   14,000 cfs
*Hansen and two other commercial clients were **trapped beneath
one of Georgie White's triple, ten-man rigs** after it flipped in
House Rock. The two others found air pockets. Hansen of Santa
Monica, California apparently did not and drowned and/or cardiac
arrested **despite her life jacket**.* Arizona Daily Sun, July 29, 1972.
Clark, G, White and D. Newcomb. No date. Georgie Clark: Thirty
Years of River Running. *San Francisco: Chronicle Books. pp. 13,
15, 46, 53, 103, 104 & 114-115.*

Charles Lyon, 25   April 27, 1973   Sockdolager (River Mile 78.7) or Grape-
                                      vine (River Mile 81.5), flow: 34,000 cfs
*Lyon of Yakima, Washington became **hypothermic** while **wearing a
life jacket and a loose wetsuit** after flipping an inflatable kayak in
Sockdolager or Grapevine during a research trip run by the Museum
of Northern Arizona. He floated past Phantom Ranch in a stupor unable to assist in his own rescue before drowning.* Arizona Daily Sun,
April 30, 1973. Letter to Ghiglieri from Bob Cornelius (undated).

Michael ("Mike") Koenig, 29 May 21, 1973   217-Mile Rapid, flow: 17,200 cfs
*Koenig and fellow Southern Californian, Tony Burdick, put in a
motorboat at Diamond Creek (Mile 225.6) to power upriver in an
illegal run. Both men wore **no life jacket**. They capsized. Koenig
drowned. (not in text)* Arizona Republic, May 22, 1973.

Steve Brunette, 16   August 17, 1974   Gneiss Rapid (River Mile 236), flow:
                                         21,000 cfs
*While riding in a motorboat from Lake Mead up the Colorado
during an illegal upriver run, Brunette, a University of Arizona
student, fell out dressed in heavy clothing and hiking boots but
while wearing **no life jacket**. He sank instantly and drowned. Ten
days later, a river rafting party found Brunette's body more than
30 miles downstream in Lake Mead. (not in text)* Williams/Grand
Canyon News, August 30, 1974.

Andalea Buzzard, 49

August 22, 1977   Lava Falls (River Mile 179.4), flow: 23,000 cfs

*Buzzard of Scottsdale, Arizona was a client on a Sanderson 33-foot rig motoring down the right ride of Lava. The boat lost motor power, rode up the big Black Rock, slid back in, and the left tube submerged stripping off six passengers including Buzzard, a non-swimmer. She reappeared later having **lost her life jacket**, a Holcomb Industries type 5. Buzzard resurfaced but no one could reach her in time to rescue her. She drowned. When recovered, **her life jacket was missing its vital rear straps**. Drifter Smith (witness) personal communication to Ghiglieri. Incident Report #77-6184*

Terry D. Evans, 26

December 2, 1981   Bridge Canyon Rapid (River Mile 235.3), flow: 10,500 cfs

*Evans, a chief water quality researcher and graduate student of the University of Nevada, Las Vegas, was riding in an open, 25-foot, Duckworth aluminum boat in an attempted uprun during a Bureau of Reclamation research trip. The boat pilot nosed it into a hole. The boat swamped instantly and sank. A Waco, Texas native, Evans was wearing **no life jacket** (although eight life jackets were on board, none of the three persons aboard was wearing one), grabbed a Coleman cooler for flotation as he floated toward Mile 237 Rapid. Evans drowned. His body was found 27 days later near Spencer Canyon (River Mile 246). (Not in text) Incident report #81-3636*

William R. Wert, 62

June 26, 1983   Crystal Rapid (River Mile 98.5), flow: 69,000 cfs

*Wert of Carbonvale, Colorado was a client on a 33-foot, Tour West motor rig piloted by a trainee/swamper with very limited experience running on flood flow. The rig flipped upside down and disintegrated. Wert died (**cold shock drowing/cardiac arrest**) in Crystal Rapid **despite his life jacket**. Incident report #83-1592*

Dick Benjamin Roach, 71
Richard Bruce Sheperski, 50

November 10, 1983   Soap Creek Rapid (RM 11+) at 23,000 cfs

*Fishermen Roach and Sheperski, both of La Mesa, California launched their Monarch 16-foot aluminum motorboat at Lees Ferry and headed upstream but that night floated possibly upside-down but possibly alive through Badger Rapid. Both wore **no life jacket** (but had them aboard); neither survived Soap Creek Rapid. Coconino County Sheriff's Department #5-1183-2620. Incident report #83-3887*

Tom Pillsbury, 66

June 7, 1984   Crystal Rapid (RM 98.5) at 43,500 cfs

*Pillsbury from El Cerrito, California, was rowing a 15-foot inflatable on a private trip and carrying two passengers, entered too far left in Crystal Rapid at flood flow, flipped, and died (**cold shock drowning/cardiac arrest**) despite wearing a life jacket, after floating past other members of his trip. Incident report #84-1327*

Norine Abrams, 58

August 25, 1984   Lava Falls (RM 179.4) at 24,500 cfs

Abrams of Rosemead, California was a client on a Georgie's Royal River Rats motor trip. As Georgie ran her triple rig into the Ledge

*Hole at a 45-degree angle of entry, the 33-foot donut on Abrams'
side folded under the boat in the Ledge Hole. Abrams and other
passengers were stripped off the upstream tube. Abrams was **held
underwater under Georgie's boat for many seconds** and drowned
despite her life jacket. Letter from witness Robert Bisson to M.P.
Ghiglieri, April 10, 2010. Witness account by John Davenport,
July 3, 1999 to M.P. Ghiglieri. Personal communication from Kim
Crumbo to Ghiglieri, August 26, 1984. Incident report #84-2832*

William B. Blair, 65

September 21, 1986   Crystal Rapid (RM 98.5) at 27,800 cfs
*Blair was a client on a Friends-of-the-River-chartered paddleboat
on one of the last trips run by Wilderness World after the sale of the
company to Canyon Explorations. The heavy-set Blair of Ellen-
wood, Georgia who had survived heart surgery, died of a **cold shock
drowning/cardiac arrest despite wearing a life jacket** seconds
after the paddleboat missed its intended run and flipped upside
down in the main wave train. Blair's body was yanked lifeless from
the foot of Crystal by Ray Interpreter, Jr. Sadder yet, Interpreter
would later drown (1993) in the Salt River. (not in text) Incident
report #86-3237*

Martin M. Hunsaker, 54

June 14, 1989   Crystal Rapid (RM 98.5) at 13,250 cfs
*Las Vegas, Nevadan Hunsaker was pilot and trip leader for a
Georgie's Royal River Rats trip. He lost power in his 33-foot motor
rig in the second "tail wave" after entering Crystal while aiming for
the left run. The boat flipped upside down against the schist wall.
Hunsaker was found dead (**cold shock drowning/cardiac arrest**)
at the foot of Tuna Rapid (Mile 100.1) by Curtis Hanson (a.k.a.
"Whale") and Steve Hatch. He died in, or due to, Crystal **despite
wearing a life jacket**. Personal communication by Curtis (a.k.a.
Whale) Hansen to Ghiglieri, June, 1989. Incident report #89-2092*

Gene Elliot Stott, 54

April 27, 1990   Crystal Rapid (RM 98.5) at 10,250 cfs
*Stott of Eugene, Oregon rowed his 13.5-foot inflatable Miwok on a
private trip, missed the right cut, and flipped in Crystal Hole. After
Stott was rescued and his boat re-flipped, he suffered **cold shock/
cardiac arrest** and died **despite wearing a life jacket**. Incident
report #90-1018*

Emilio X. Solares, 29

November 15, 1994   Hance Rapid (RM 77) at 9,000 cfs
*While on a private trip, Solares wedged his lower body against
the rowing frame of a "Protar" raft to video tape the oarsman's
run through the large, turbulent Hance Rapid. The raft flipped in
the top hole on the right. Solares, of Nederlad, Colorado, became
trapped in the frame and/or the cargo netting securing dunnage.
Rescue efforts by the trip's kayakers failed. Solares drowned **despite
his life jacket**. Incident report #94-5066*

James M. Mehegan, 52

July 29, 2004   205 Mile Rapid
*Mehegan of Riverside, California, was on a private river trip and had
just paddled his kayak through 205 Mile Rapid. He paddled toward
his buddy on a raft and told him, "I am having a heart attack."*

Mehegan then lost consciousness and his boat rolled upside down. Despite 1.75 hours of CPR performed on him, he died of a massive **heart attack. He had worn a life jacket.** *The Arizona DPS helicopter evacuated his body. (not in text) Incident report #04-4102*

Leonard Gentry, 61

November 22, 2004   Hance Rapid (RM 77) at 32,000 cfs
Gentry, at 5' 5" & 195 pounds, lived in a warehouse in Maricopa County, Arizona. He was "cajoled" onto a private rowing trip of mostly Phoenix firemen by two well-meaning brothers using 4 rented boats. The trip boatmen knew they were at Hance but the rapid seemed easy to them, so they entered **un-scouted.** *3 boats made it. The fourth ran behind a pour-over, recycled, then capsized. Two rafters made it to shore. Gentry yelled for help, was grabbed by a swimmer but yanked loose and separated in a big wave. As the other two swimmers were picked up, Gentry* **drowned in an apparent cold shock drowning/cardiac arrest despite his wearing a life jacket and neoprene gear.** *CPR for 30 minutes failed. The terrified survivors spent a rainy night aboard their 3 boats, attached to a cliff by jamming an oar into it. They all quit the trip at Phantom via emergency helicopter evacuations and hiking. Incident report #04-6029*

Marc Allred, 62

March 30, 2007   Crystal Rapid (RM 98.5) at low water
Wearing a type III pfd, wetsuit, and spray jacket, Allred of Salt Lake City, Utah rowed his Cataraft last, aiming for the right run. He missed, hit the first hole, washed off his boat, swam Crystal, and, below, was rescued by his private trip buddies alive. But he quickly succumbed, despite CPR, **in an apparent cold shock/cardiac arrest despite wearing a life jacket.** *Incident report #07-1886*

Randall Johnson, 45

March 16, 2008   Hance Rapid (RM 77) at low water
While rowing his boat during inclement weather, private boater Johnson of Grand Junction, Colorado complained of shortness of breath then flipped. Minutes passed before his buddies on his trip hauled him out lifeless **in an apparent cold shock drowning/cardiac arrest despite wearing a life jacket.** *Incident report #08-1382*

Scott Foster, 42

January 10, 2011   President Harding Rapid (RM 44.5)
Bend, Oregon resident Foster, rolled his kayak over in the rapid at noon on low water, did not roll back up, and stayed under. His buddies on his private trip looked back, failed to spot him, then did spot him, and after a bit of a delay, retrieved him. Foster died of **cold shock drowning/cardiac arrest despite wearing a life jacket** *and receiving CPR efforts soon after his retrieval. (not in text) NPS Grand Canyon News Release, January 11, 2011.*

James Joseph Waring, Jr., 48

June 9, 2011   Hance Rapid (RM 77) at 23,500 cfs
Waring of Lexington, South Carolina was part of a 6-person, 2-oar-boat private trip which capsized a raft in Hance. One person from his boat stayed with the boat, another swam to shore, but Waring **cold shock drowned despite wearing a life jacket.** *His body was found shortly downriver by a Hatch River Expeditions Trip. CPR for 45-60 minutes failed. Waring was the 4th victim and 4th private*

boater to die in Hance Rapid. *Rafting Grand Canyon/River Runners for Wilderness Internet Group, June 15, 2011, 9:36 a.m.* NPS
Grand Canyon News Release, *June 10, 2011.*

Gary Aus, 64   September 18, 2011   Lava Falls (RM 179.4) at 14,500 cfs
*Aus of Leavenworth, Kansas was washed off a raft on a private river
trip in "Son-of-Lava." He grabbed a second boat but had trouble
hanging on. Meanwhile his buddies aboard did not pull the 200-lb
Aus in. He told them he was okay and would swim to shore. His
group lost him for 2 miles and finally found him face-down, **his
lifejacket pulled up over his head**, drowned at mile 181. Twenty
minutes of CPR failed.(not in text)* Grand Canyon Regional Communications Center, *September 19, 2011.*

Mary Phyllis Simpson, 67   September 25, 2013   Mile 209 Rapid
*At noon Simpson of Flagstaff, Arizona was aboard an 18-foot inflat-
able boat rowed by her husband Robert well behind boat #1 due to 15-
25 mph winds. Robert, with a shoulder injury, entered Mile 209. His
boat flipped in the hole in view of boat #1, which had trouble slowing
down. With no flip line for re-boarding, Mary, medically compromised
by emphysema, stayed in the river "10 minutes" floating down to Mile
210+ and died in it due to respiratory failure resulting from exacerba-
tion of her **severe chronic obstructive pulmonary disease** caused
by excessive exertion in extreme cold water (= **hypothermia**). 20
minutes of CPR by lead boaters failed. Incident report #13-079572*

Curtis Van Alen Joyce, 31   March 18, 2014   Lower Whitmore Rapid (RM 189), 8,000 cfs
*Arriving later at camp, at 3 p.m., a buddy of expert kayaker Joyce of
Portland, Oregon pulled his kayak spray skirt on the eddy line to check
his map but took on so much water that he exited. Joyce paddled away
from six other private trip members on shore at Whitmore to chase the
now runaway kayak plus drifting gear. Yet another buddy, however,
also paddled ahead and rescued the runaway boat and swimmer. Not
noticing Joyce, this rescuer then chased gear a half mile beyond. Later
the first buddy (allegedly "obviously drunk") repacked his recovered
boat on river left then paddled across to check on Joyce's now upside-
down boat, which he'd seen capsized 20-30 minutes earlier. He found
Joyce still inside it, having died **unwtnessed**. 2 hours earlier, at Tequila
Beach, Joyce had drunk "5-7" drinks ("a lot") of tequila and whiskey.
Afterward he drank cinnamon Fireball whiskey while floating. Just
before reaching Whitmore he had uncharacteristically "missed five or
six roll attempts" in an "easy" situation. Very late CPR for 5-10 minutes failed. Joyce's blood alcohol content was 0.27%. Coroner's report
concluded drowning. Incident report # 14-018508*

Hans Uhl, 43   June 11, 2014   Badger Rapid (RM 8), 11,000 CFS
*At 2 p.m. Uhl of Augsburg, Germany capsized his kayak during a
kayaking charter supported by Hatch River Expeditions. He exited
his boat. When helped by a safety paddler, he spoke incoherently then
lost consciousness and died. CPR for 90 minutes failed. The medical
examiner reported a massive coronary attack and, allegedly, off the
record, noted that Uhl's arteries were so clogged he was a "walking
time bomb." Incident report #14052004*

Table 4–B. RIVER-CROSSING TRAVELERS WHO DROWNED IN GRAND CANYON.

Name, age	Date	River Location / Flow	Circumstances

Bush Dulin, adult male   April 10, 1872   approximately River Mile 246–250
*While trying to travel upriver into Grand Canyon 30 miles from its western end, Irish prospector Dulin and his four prospecting comrades lost their boat. Dulin, **wearing no life jacket,** drowned trying to swim across the Colorado to retrieve it. Schieffelin, E. 1996.* Destination Tombstone Adventures of a Prospector. *Mesa, Arizona: Royal Spectrum. pp. 51-61.*

Lorenzo W. Roundy, adult   May 24, 1876   Lees Ferry (River Mile 0)
*Roundy of Kanab, Utah drowned (**no life jacket**) while trying to cross the river by ferry. P.T. Reilly, 1969. "How Deadly is Big Red?" Utah Historical Quarterly 37(2):244-260.*

Navajo (unnamed adult male)   1880 or 1881   Lees Ferry
Navajo (also unnamed male)   *Both of two unnamed Navajos (**no life jackets**) drowned during an attempted river crossing when the skiff overturned. P.T. Reilly, 1969. "How Deadly is Big Red?" Utah Historical Quarterly 37(2):244-260.*

Henry Rosely, adult   June or July 1884   Lees Ferry
Al Rosely, 12   *During an attempted crossing the Roselys' (**no life jacket**) skiff overturned. The Roselys of Provo, Utah area were reportedly part of a Mormon emigrant party called to Arizona. Neither death was officially substantiated, possibly because of uncertain name spelling. P.T. Reilly, 1969. "How Deadly is Big Red?" Utah Historical Quarterly 37(2):244-260.*

Navajo (unamed adult male)   1889   Lees Ferry
Navajo (brother of above)   *Both of two unnamed brothers, Navajos, "mismanaged" a ferry crossing (**no life jackets**) and drowned. P.T. Reilly, 1969. "How Deadly is Big Red?" Utah Historical Quarterly 37(2):244-260.*

unidentified man   1891 ?   Roosevelt Camp area at River Mile 88
second unidentified man   *John Fuller and Harry MacDonald (or, more likely, McDonald), descended Bright Angel Creek in the summer of 1890 or 1891 to search for the remains of a man who had drowned the previous year (possibly Frank Mason Brown or Henry Richards). They arrived to find an equipped but unoccupied camp with a tent set up with two cots, two revolvers and rifles next to them, a gold watch (run down) on the tent pole, bread baked three days earlier in a Dutch oven, and evidence that two adults had saddled horses and rode to the Colorado—and apparently entered it **to swim across.** Standing in camp, waiting, was a gelding donkey, "Brighty" of the Grand Canyon. The two missing men, Fuller learned, were never seen again, but had originally passed through Flagstaff en route to Grand Canyon and were known to have descended Bright Angel Trail to the region of this mysteriously abandoned camp. T. H. McKee. 1922. "Brighty, free citizen: How the sagacious donkey of the Grand Canyon maintained his liberty for thirty years.* Sunset*

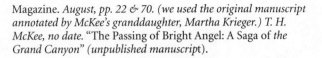

Magazine. *August, pp. 22 & 70. (we used the original manuscript annotated by McKee's granddaughter, Martha Krieger.) T. H. McKee, no date. "The Passing of Bright Angel: A Saga of the Grand Canyon" (unpublished manuscrip*t).

William F. Russell, adult

June 9, 1899   above Pipe Creek Rapid (River Mile 89)
*Syracuse, Nebraska resident Russell, and George Fleming from Williams, Arizona were among five prospectors attempting a two-man crossing, with **no life jackets**, of the Colorado during flood stage via a folding canvas boat. It capsized. Fleming swam to the south bank. Russell clung to the capsized boat and drowned. 1.5 years later prospectors found Russell's body "below Bright Angel."* Coconino Sun, *March 9, 1901.*

P. T. McConigle, 37
Charles McLean, 44

July 27, 1903   probably above Pipe Creek Rapid (River Mile 89)
*While trying to cross the Colorado at high water, with **no life jackets**, to visit the Grand Canyon Electric Company's camp in Upper Granite Gorge in a boat weak from exposure to the elements, both McConigle, a native of Pennsylvania, and McLean, a native of Scotland, and the boat vanished forever.* Coconino Sun, *August 8, 15, 22 & 29, 1903.*

Preston Apperson, adult

March 9, 1911   Lees Ferry
*Apperson, a crewman with Charles Spencer's mining promotion, while wearing **no life jacket**, drowned with a team of horses when the entire ferry sank in midriver. P.T. Reilly, 1969. "How Deadly is Big Red?"* Utah Historical Quarterly *37(2):244-260.*

Royce Elliot Dean, 25
Lewis Nez Tsinnie, 26
Adolpha Johnson, 26

June 7, 1928   Lees Ferry, flow: 86,500 cfs
*As the ferry made a successful crossing to the south in the afternoon, a strong wind blew all three men (with **no life jackets**), two from Cedar Ridge, Arizona and the ferry back into the mainstream of a very silty flood flow of the river. A cable broke. The ferry overturned. All three men, including Johnson, the Lees Ferry operator, drowned. 2 months later Dean's body was found at Soap Creek.* Coconino Sun, *June 22, 1928.*

Glen E. Sturdevant, 33
Fred Johnson, 30

February 20, 1929   Horn Creek Rapid (River Mile 90.2), flow: 5,700 cfs
*NPS Rangers Sturdevant, Johnson, and Chief Ranger James P. Brooks attempted to cross the Colorado to the south in a **12-foot-10-inch folding boat** about 75-100 yards upstream of Horn Creek Rapid. A Lacyville, Pennsylvania native, Sturdevant was rowing and wore a kapok-filled life belt. He lost an oar in an unexplained way. Brooks also had a life belt. Johnson of Kanab, Utah, a weak swimmer, had worn a larger, kapok-filled life jacket but lost it almost instantly as all three swam Horn Creek Rapid. Only Brooks survived. Searchers found Sturdevant's body at RM 93.5.* Coconino Sun, *March 1, 1929.* Tyler R. Sturdevant and Michael Harrison, Ranger: The Journal of the Association of National Park Rangers, *Summer, 1998.* Tillotson, M. R. Our sorrow, Grand Canyon Nature Notes, *February, 1929.*

Carlton Boyd Moore, 22　　　May 26, 1955　　　near Lava/Chuar (River Mile 65), flow:
27,000 cfs

Recent graduate of Arizona State College in Flagstaff, Moore and his mathematics professor Harvey Butchart, hiked from Point Imperial down to the Colorado near River Mile 53 and walked downstream. The two tried to cross the high flow **without life jackets** *but with air mattresses. Moore, who hailed from Berrian Springs, Michigan, harbored a phobia of drowning and lost control for seven miles of floating, mostly upside down. He drowned below Mile 65.6. A Moki Mac crew found Moore's body below Hermit Rapid (RM 96) on July 5th or 6th. Letter from P. T. Reilly to Dock Marston, July, 1955. Elias Butler and Thomas M. Myers. 2007.* Grand Obsession: Harvey Butchart and the Exploration of Grand Canyon. *Flagstaff: Puma Press.*

Table 5–C. SWIMMERS, VOLUNTARY OR OTHERWISE, WHO DROWNED IN THE GRAND CANYON COLORADO (all discussed in text). River flows in cubic feet per second (cfs) for dates of incidents are from the U.S.G.S. Historical Streamflows Daily Values Data Base, from Stations #0938000 (Lees Ferry) and #09402500 (Phantom).

Swimmers Who Vanished Between Phantom Beach (River Mile 87.8)) And The Foot of Bright Angel Trail at Head of Pipe Creek Rapid (River Mile 89)

Name, age	Date	River Location / Flow	*Circumstances*
Kenneth E. Curtis, 18	July 21, 1935	foot of Bright Angel Trail/head of Pipe Creek Rapid. Flow: 21,000 cfs	

*At about 8:00 a.m. after camping all night, CCC volunteer and Kingman, Arizona resident, Curtis, and Robert Demaree, took a break from a CCC trail project and jumped into the eddy to cool off. Demaree and Curtis tried to swim across the Colorado (**no life jacket**) to the north side as CCC volunteer Wilton Cox Bryan photographed them. "I thought it would be easy to swim across but we hit the main force of the river in a strong current," noted Demaree. "I was immediately in distress." Demaree swam Pipe Creek Rapid and barely managed to regain the same, south, shore. Curtis, a stronger swimmer who made it 30 feet farther out, never made it back. A search of 3 miles of shoreline by field glasses failed. Headquarters CCC Company 819 Camp NP-2-A, Grand Canyon, Arizona. Letter on hearing and interviews, July 23, 1935.*

| Wallace Peshlakai, adult | August 7, 1937 | foot of Bright Angel Trail/head of Pipe Creek Rapid, flow: 9,500 cfs | |

*Peshlakai, a Navajo interpreter for the Christian Reformed Church Mission of Rehoboth, New Mexico, was hiking with his step-son, eight-year-old Tommy Atchinson, and five other Navajo missionaries following a Bible conference in Flagstaff. They hiked to the foot of the trail where Peshlakai (**no life jacket**) dunked into the eddy above Pipe Creek Rapid. A hysterical Atchinson told authorities that his step-father disrobed before entering the water. A few minutes later he saw Peshlakai with "a horrified expression on his face," sucked into the swirling current and carried downstream and drowned. Arizona Republic, August 8, 1937.*

| Harold William Nelson, adult | June 20, 1955 | Phantom Beach, flow: 29,000 cfs | |

*Nelson of San Diego, California drowned in a high flow. As the Park Superintendent's Report 1955 stated, "Assistant Chief Ranger Lehnert and Ranger Davis made a trip into the Canyon to drag the Devil's Spittoon with a grapnel hook to locate the body of Harold William Nelson who drowned in an attempt to swim (**no life jacket**) across the Colorado at the suspension bridge. Their efforts proved to be fruitless and they returned to the top on June 21." "Jim Rigg recovered the body of Ed Nelson who was drowned attempting to swim, nude, across the river below BA. I understand he was found about Mile 126." –P.T. Reilly letter to Otis "Dock" Marston, July 1955. P.T. Reilly, 1969. "How Deadly is Big Red?" Utah Historical Quarterly 37(2):244-260. Superintendent's Monthly Report for June 1955, #54134 (p. 14).*

Dwight L. Miller, 26   June 3, 1970   foot of Bright Angel Trail/head of Pipe Creek Rapid, flow: 16,000 cfs
*Miller (**no life jacket**) leaped into the river, was swept away, and drowned. The Dallas, Texan's body was discovered downstream 13 days later.* Arizona Daily Sun, *June 30, 1970.*

John Zombro, early 20s   April 23, 1971   Pipe Creek Rapid (River Mile 89), flow: 15,000 cfs
*Zombro and Bruce Allen of Lynnfield, Massachusetts found a drift-wood and air mattresses raft combo. They launched it from RM 88 while **wearing no life jackets**. Two other companions—Joseph Tomaselli (Rochester, New York) and Steven Anderson (Milbury, Massachusetts)—watched. The raft disintegrated above RM 89. Both men swam to the right shore near Pipe Creek Rapid. To return to Phantom, both had to swim across the Colorado to the river-left trail. Allen dived in and made it. Zombro dived in but never surfaced.* Arizona Daily Sun, *May 7, 1971.*

Julian Griffiths, 21   August 4, 1973   foot of Bright Angel Trail/head of Pipe Creek Rapid, flow: 11,500 cfs
*Griffiths of London, England and a U.S. student, ignored the sign warning against entering the river and tried to swim (**no lifejack-et**) across the Colorado to the north side. He failed. 25 days later, a commercial trip found his body at RM 102.* Arizona Republic, *August 7, 1973.*

Aparicio Gil, 26   April 8, 1977   foot of Bright Angel Trail/head of Pipe Creek Rapid, flow: 2,000 cfs
*San Francisco, Californian Gil also ignored warning signs and tried to swim (**no life jacket**) across the river on Good Friday on a near-record low flow and was swept downstream to his demise. 16 days later an air search found Gil's body 4 miles downstream.* Incident report #77-1106

Louis John Stano, III, 21   June 25, 1995   foot of Bright Angel Trail/head of Pipe Creek Rapid, flow: 17,800 cfs
*Stano also ignored warning signs and swam out (**no life jacket**) as if to cross the Colorado against a high flow through Pipe Creek Rapid. The Brentwood, Tennessee resident's body was recovered three weeks later near Shinumo Creek, 19 miles downstream.* Incident report #95-1747

Troy M. Fortney, 26   November 25, 1995   Phantom Beach, flow: 14,000 cfs
*Frederick Zernik, age 29, and Fortney, both experienced surfers from Los Angeles, California, descended the South Kaibab Trail intending on returning that day to the South Rim via the Bright Angel Trail. They ignored warning signs and decided to swim (**no life jacket**) nearly two miles between the two trails. Zernik aborted and self-extricated, panicked, from the river but trapped himself on a ledge. Fortney was swept into Bright Angel Rapid. His body was found 2 weeks later at RM 94.25.* Grand Canyon News, *November 29, 1995.* Incident report #95-4005

Joey Merrill, 22
Mark Merrill, 16
Saif Savaya, 16

April 30, 2009   S shore below Black Bridge, across from
                        Phantom boat beach, RM 87.4, 12,500 cfs

*The Merrills of Chambers and Savaya of Gilbert, Arizona descend-
ed the S. Kaibab on a Tri-City Baptist Church of Tempe trip of 18
hikers on a **rim-to-river-to-rim day-hike**. The group segregated
into faster and slower hikers with the younger hikers walking 15–20
minutes ahead of the adult leader walking "sweep." Roughly an
hour above the Black Bridge, Savaya said he wanted to swim across
the Colorado River and invited the Merrill brothers to swim with
him. (Prior to leaving home Savaya alegedly told his cousin that
swimming across the Colorado was on his "bucket list.") Savaya
had packed his water shoes and swim trunks for the hike. Near the
tunnel to the Black Bridge, Savaya and the Merrills diverted off
trail and walked past the NPS "Swimming not permitted" sign but
did not see it. In haste, they next dived into the 52°river. The three
swam (**no life jackets**) with an incorrect, downstream ferry angle
into the current (swimming in an upstream ferry as a deer would
do being required). As other hike trip members watched from the
Black Bridge, the river swept the three swimmers screaming into
the Devil's Spittoon eddy just upstream of the Silver Bridge. All
three drowned: a record for a swimming party in Grand Canyon.
Mark Merrill's body was found 1 mile farther on May 1. On May
14, Savaya was found near RM 99 and Joey near RM 100. Incident
report # 09-2705*

Deliberate Swimmers Who Drowned Elsewhere along the Grand Canyon Colorado

Iven Bundy, 22   April 19, 1931   near Whitmore Wash (River Mile 187.4), flow: 9,700 cfs
Iven's cousin, Floyd Iverson, swam across the Colorado from the north shore then called to Iven of Bundyville, Arizona that the swim was not hard. Iven (with **no life jacket**) *tried to follow but was sucked under by a whirlpool and drowned. Fishermen discovered Iven's body at Gregg's Ferry west of Grand Canyon. N. Cox. 1994.* Boatman's quarterly review *7(2):9-11.*

unknown young adult male   August, 1973 ?   Mouth of Havasu (River Mile 156.8)
second young adult male   *Mike Wynn on an ARTA trip noted 2 of 4 young male hikers waded upstream across the mouth of Havasu during a flow of about 5,000 cfs to see what lay upstream. When they returned the river had risen. The two tried to swim without* **no life jackets** *downstream across the mouth and into the eddy. The first swimmer missed the mouth and was pulled toward Havasu Rapid. The second tried to help him but failed. Both unidentified swimmers vanished into the Colorado. (not in text).*

Minoru Oda, 31   August 5, 1976   Pearce Ferry (River Mile 280), on reservoir
Oda, a Japanese male passenger on a motorized Hualapai River Runners' trip, tried to swim, **with no life jacket**, *200 yards from the boat to shore. Oda drowned four feet from a buoy near shore. 8 days later Oda's body surfaced at the bouy. (not in text)* Arizona Daily Sun, *August 7, 1976.*

Jeffrey Kaplan, 16   August 7, 1983   River Mile 2.5, flow: 36,000 cfs
About one hour into an OARS, Inc. rowing trip, Kaplan of Framingham, Massachusetts, **without a life jacket**, *jumped into the eddy at high water 20 yards downriver of the boats and swam with its current up past their sterns. Kaplan submerged out of sight. Possibly the cold or flickering water had triggered a* **petit mal seizure**. *23 days later, Kaplan's body surfaced beneath Navajo Bridge. Incident report #83-2449*

Matthew Cranny, 13   March 22, 1990   upstream of Salt Water Wash (River Mile 11), flow: 11,500 cfs
During an Arizona Boy Scout Troop 189 hike sponsored by the Gilbert Ray Ward of the LDS Church, Cranny of Tempe, waded into the 46-degree Colorado and ignored instructions to come back out. ("No swimming" was this troop's rule.) Cranny struggled **without a life jacket**, *unable to stay above the surface, and drowned. Cranny had a very recent history of* **petit mal seizures** *and seemed to suffer one here. Months later a leg wearing Cranny's boot washed ashore at RM 16.5. Incident report #90-0610*

Elmer Meredith Akers, 40   June 21, 1990   Diamond Creek Rapid (River Mile 225.7), flow: 17,500 cfs
Akers, a Cherokee from Gainesville, Florida had been drinking alcohol and had bragged to river runners that he was a "strong

*swimmer," claiming that earlier that day he had swum across the Colorado and back. Next he swam (**no life jacket**) into Diamond Creek Rapid and drowned. His body was recovered at River Mile 269 a week later. (not in text) Incident report #90-1955*

Bert Francisco, 28   July 26, 1990   Diamond Creek Rapid (River Mile 225.7), flow: 16,000 cfs

*After eating chicken and drinking multiple beers starting at 8 a.m., Francisco, a Navajo woman from Wingate, Arizona jumped in the river to cool off (**no life jacket**). The current swept her into Diamond Creek Rapid. A Mark Sleight trip found her the next day below 234-Mile Rapid. (not in text) Incident report #90-2669*

Christopher Guetschow, 15   August 28, 1992   Hermit Rapid (River Mile 95), flow: 14,900 cfs

*Guetshow, on a Boy Scout Troop 17 (from Mankato, Minnesota) hike that had forbidden swimming, dived into the Colorado (**no life jacket**) with the apparent intent of swimming across the river. Halfway across, he was in the slick tongue carrying him into Hermit Rapid. 2 weeks later his body was found at RM 104. Incident report #92-3169*

Accidental Swimmers Who Fell In From Shore, Witnessed or Mysterious

Van de Bunt, young adult male May 17, 1919   Upper Granite Gorge on south side
across from Phantom (RM 88)
*Van de Bunt, an Eastern tourist, hiking with a friend, lost the trail
but made it to the river. While trying to locate Roosevelt's Camp,
he tried wading in the river at high flow against a cliff face. Van de
Bunt (**no life jacket**) vanished.* Coconino Sun, *May 23, 1919.*

Carol Goldman, 18   August 24, 1965   Phantom Beach (RM 88) at 17,400 cfs
*Goldman of Albuquerque, New Mexico, who could not swim, entered
(**no life jacket**) the Colorado to cool off. She slipped into an unexpected hole (deep section) and was swept away. 3 years later hikers
found her skeleton 110 miles downstream at Parashant.* Arizona
Republic, *August 25, 1965.* Arizona Daily Sun, *April 26, 1968.*

Anthony Krueger, 20   March 24/25, 1971   Phantom Beach (RM 88) at 9,000 cfs
*While camped with friends under a rock shelter near Phantom
Ranch, Krueger of Bell Lake, Minnesota, drank a brew of* Datura
*blossoms. Many hours later, after several inappropriate behaviors
such as trying to lift impossible boulders, talking to nonexistent
people for hours, and eating dirt, he (**no life jacket**) entered the river
unwitnessed and **mysteriously** drowned. Death was mitigated by
Datura poisoning. Hikers found his body weeks later and 6 miles
downstream at Hermit, washed ashore.* Arizona Daily Sun, *May 7,
1971.* Arizona Republic, *August 24, 1971. (Not counted in drowning
statistics, but counted in Chapter 8, Critters, see text & Table 8).*

Marcos Ortega, 11   June 8, 1973   foot of Bright Angel Trail/head of Pipe
Creek Rapid (RM 89) at 11,000 cfs
*Ortega, a sleep walker from Santa Fe, New Mexico, vanished
mysteriously from a bivouac at Pipe Creek and (**no life jacket**)
drowned. His body turned up 18 days later, 6 miles downstream.*
Arizona Daily Sun, *June 12 & 27, 1973.* Coconino County Sheriff's Department Case #0673-2441-4.

Teresa Rainey, 25   July 18, 1974   Trail Canyon (RM 219.2) at 23,000 cfs
*While camped with Fort Lee Co., Rainey, intoxicated (and wearing
no life jacket), fell off one of their 33-foot motor rigs into the river
at night **mysteriously**. (not in text)* Incident report #74-? *(not on
GCNPS fatality list)*

David Bret Lasater, 19   August 4, 1980   River Mile 22.5 at 22,500 cfs
*While camped at night with a motor trip run by Canyoneers,
Lasater of Overland Park, Kansas, heavily intoxicated (and wearing
no life jacket), vanished **mysteriously** and drowned. 17 days later
a river trip found Lasater's body at RM 37. (not in text)* Arizona
Daily Sun, *August 5 & 21, 1980.* Incident report #80-? *(not on
GCNPS fatality list)*

Charles Robert Hunter, 58   July 8, 1981   River Mile 19 at 15,250 cfs
While camped at night with Diamond River Expeditions, Hunter, a

schoolteacher from Page, Arizona, heavily intoxicated (and wearing **no life jacket**), *vanished* **mysteriously** *off their 33-foot rig and drowned. Incident report #81-1947*

Jody Mack, 31	April 29, 1983 Havasu Rapid (RM 156.8) at19,000 cfs

Mack of Escondido, California on a San Diego Nomads, Sierra Club hiking trip, crouched on a low ledge jutting into the river 150 feet downstream of the mouth of Havasu Creek. As she leaned out, trying to put her had in the river, her feet slipped. She dropped into the swift rapid and, with **no life jacket**, *drowned. 16 days later a river trip found Mack's body near RM 196. Incident report #83-0795*

Robert Wiel, about 40   July 24, 1988   Lees Ferry, 200 feet downstream of launch ramp, at 10,500–11,000 cfs

*While fishing with a buddy, Wiel (**no life jacket**) stepped into the river, slipped on a rock, and fell in at moderately low water. He grabbed another rock and screamed for help. This rock was too slippery to hang onto. Wiel yelled for help again, slipped off his rock into the current. His waders swamped. He sank and drowned in the current. Wiel's buddy seemed unable to render assistance. NPS Ranger Tom Workman injured his back during a retrieval of Wiel's body. Incident report #88-? (not on GCNPS fatality list)*

Karl Sebastian Jacobi, 21   June 14, 1989   River Mile 103.8 at 13,250 cfs

*Jacobi, while solo hiking upstream from a private river trip, either fell into the Colorado or jumped in (**no life jacket**) to swim back down to camp. He was swept into midstream and drowned. A commercial trip found his body 12 days later at RM 105.5. Incident report #89-2093*

Robert Walker, 21   August 6, 1997   Diamond Creek Rapid (RM 225.7) at 24,000 cfs

*Walker, a Hualapai, had been with friends hanging out on Hualapai River trip boats drinking alcohol at night. He (wearing **no life jacket**) disappeared* **mysteriously** *that night. His body was found the next day on the gravel bar about a mile downstream. (not in text)*

John Anthony Frye, 43   September 13, 1997   River Mile 220 at 24,000 cfs

*While camped at night with a Diamond River Expeditions motor trip, Frye, heavily intoxicated (and wearing **no life jacket**), vanished* **mysteriously** *from camp and drowned. 8 days later an OARS trip found Frye's body at RM 260. (not in text) Incident report #97-4193*

Todd Strickland, 49   May 30, 1999   Nevills' Beach (RM 75)

*Strickland, **fishing solo**, fell (**no life jacket**) into the Colorado 300 yards downstream of the camp chosen by the commercial motor rafting company, Wilderness River Adventures, and drowned. Rescue and CPR efforts by AzRA river company crew proved unsuccessful for the Tucson, Arizona firefighter. (not in text) Arizona Daily Sun, June 1, 1999. Incident report #99-1233*

Jamie Padilla, 22

January 29, 2000   Jackass Canyon (RM 8)
*Padilla of Flagstaff, Arizona stood next to swift water upstream of Badger Rapid and baited a hook as he suffered an **epileptic seizure** (perhaps caused by flickering sunlight on the water). Padilla's two friends, upstream, witnessed this and saw him slip into the river (**no life jacket**). His two companions tried to, but could not reach Padilla in time to prevent his drowning. Searchers found his body the next day 3/8 of a mile downstream, below Badger Rapid.* Arizona Daily Sun, *January 31, 2000. Incident report #00-0194*

Paul Smith, 48

September 8, 2004   Mile 118 Camp at 7,500 cfs
*Smith of Newcastle, Washington was on a Tour West trip and on his 14th wedding anniversary. He complained to his wife of radiating pain in his left arm but attributed it to paddling. The two camped 75 feet from a broad shallow eddy flowing 7,500 cfs. At 10:00 p.m., a passenger heard faint calls of "Help!" from the eddy. He alerted the sleeping crew. Within 3 minutes everyone began a 2-hour search of the 118-Mile eddy (wading it) plus eddies downriver on both sides. Smith had admitted he was a non-swimmer and had promised the trip leader to never get near the river without a life jacket, but this time he wore **no life jacket**. Smith's family and personal history included early cardiac problems; he may have entered the eddy diaphoretic during a **cardiac episode**. Six days later Dr. Michael Collier noticed that a river trip had jettisoned a load of French toast into the eddy at Mile 122.5. Collier then saw Smith's body amid the debris. Collier, who had experienced the tragic death of Gordon Robert Wagner earlier that trip, now stabilized Smith's body for 4 hours before the Park extracted it. (not in text) Personal communication from Bruce Keller to Ghiglieri, Sept. 14, 2004. Incident report #04-4945*

Iryna Shylo, 19

July 16, 2006   shoreline of Hermit Rapid (RM 95) at 13,000 cfs
*A hiking partner reported that Canyon concession employee Shylo of the Ukraine (**no life jacket**) **mysteriously** failed to return from a short, toilet break at 6:00 p.m. at the top of Hermit Rapid at an air temp of about 110°. On July 30, a private river trip found the body of 5' 10", 120-pound Shylo in an eddy 10 miles downriver near Ruby Rapid (RM 105). Prior to this hike, Shylo had been instructed by a ranger in the Park's backcountry permits office to urinate in the river. One wonders if this ranger also cautioned Shylo about how to safely accomplish this. Incident report #06-3878*

Kaitlin Anne Kenney, 21

January 11, 2013   Tapeats Creek downstream camp, 13,000 cfs (RM 134.5)
During a double-private trip "pretty wild party" on a very cold evening (29 degrees at Phantom), Kenney of Englewood, Colorado was described as happy but undergoing a striking personality shift: she was abnormally "slurring," "obviously stumbling drunk," "intense," "irrational" and "flirtatious" after drinking whiskey, eating 4 stems of her magic mushrooms and eating marijuana butter. She said, "I am so high." Around 11:00 p.m., she walked away from the fire pan unnoticed and with no headlamp. (No "designated driver" or "Jiminy

*Cricket" system was practiced.) It snowed 2 inches that night. Missing
Kenney in the morning, her dozen fellow boaters plus the nine other
kayakers searched. They found her boot prints, then sets of 1-boot-
plus-1-bare-foot prints, and hand-prints at the cut bank/river. These
led 1/4 to ½ mile downstream from camp. An extensive NPS search
found no other clues. 70 days later, on March 22, her body was spotted drifting, fully dressed but barefooted, near Mile 164 by another
private river trip. Toxicology yielded a blood alcohol content of 0.11
percent. Because Kenney normally peed nearby, next to the boats,
her fellow boaters felt mystified. One suspected foul play by trip #2
kayakers. (not in text) Tom Martin, personal communication. April
26, 2013. anonymous member of adjacent private trip, personal communication, February 6, 2013.* Grand Canyon News Release, April
1, 2013. Incident Report #13-0116

Victor Tseng, 68

June 27, 2014   lower Havasu Rapid, (RM 157) 11,000 cfs
*At 3:10 p.m. one day after his 43rd wedding anniversary, Tseng of
Phoenix, Arizona was hiking in about 100-degree heat with his
group back to their Hatch River Expeditions motor rig parked in the
lower eddy. While descending "two lobes of [Muav] rock which slope
gently down towards the river" and to a cove 100 yards upstream
of 5 moored big rigs, Tseng, not wearing a life jacket and possibly
hurrying to catch up, stumbled. He tried to recover on one foot but
hopped off the ledge. He fell 15 feet. Current swept him onto a foot-
deep ledge 50 yards closer to the boats. He sat up then slid back into
deep water. Seeing this, Canyoneers boatman Ethan Dyer raced to his
most upstream rig. He extended a hand down to Tseng, who seemed
dazed and did not grab at it. Tseng next was swept under the middles
of 3 boats. He popped to the surface 10 yards beyond them. A pfd
tossed to him was diverted by wind. As Dyer started his engine and
backed from shore, a Hatch passenger who failed to secure his own
pfd dived in carrying a second pfd and tried to swim to Tseng, now
40 yards farther downriver. As Tseng's head bobbed lower and lower
then vanished, Dyer rescued the floundering would-be rescuer then
roared after Tseng, but seconds too late. On July 4, a Grand Canyon
Expeditions trip reported Tseng's body at Mile 184.* Incident report
#14-062039

Chapter Six

If Looks Could Kill: Death From The Air

Bombardier Lieutenant Charles Goldblum had just made an emergency parachute drop into an ink-black Grand Canyon. His long and terrifying night descent had jerked to a sudden halt on a three-foot-wide shelf of bedrock. What lay below this ledge was invisible. Goldblum now had a choice: he could dangle where he was and hope that his chute did not slip loose, or, instead, he could unclip from his chute and take his chances. Again, everything around and below him was imperceptible in the darkness. Directly below Goldblum, it turned out, yawned a 1,200-foot vertical drop.

In both Europe and the South Pacific, World War II was a raging storm claiming millions of lives. Mid-1944 was a pivotal time in this worst struggle known in human history. The United States would ultimately emerge victorious from this war by putting 17 million Americans in uniform and by training them as well as possible—though often in a hurry—for their military missions. But in June of 1944, this victory was less clear than it is now via hindsight.

In the European Theater, massive daylight bombing of Germany had exacted a horrible toll on Allied bombing crews. Tens of thousands of U.S. airmen were dying. More yet were dying as the U.S. Army turned its bomb sights on Japan and its now crumbling, short-lived "Empire of the Rising Sun" with its thousands of *kamikaze* pilots. "Replacing" these lost U.S. airmen with trained flyers was a struggle of titanic proportions.

On June 20, 1944 the five-man crew of a B-24 had just completed a routine celestial navigation exercise at 28,000 feet somewhere over a Grand Canyon shrouded by nightfall. Now the pilot banked the bomber around to fly back to the Tonopah Army Airfield several hundred miles to the west in Nevada. As told in the *Coconino*

Sun (June 30, 1944) and by Butch Farabee in his *Death, Daring and Disaster: Search and Rescue in the National Parks* (pp. 162-165), things went wrong fast.

The B-24's engines sputtered, then went dead. Knowing that no one could survive a crash landing into the tortured terrain below where they now were, its pilot ordered the crew to bail out. At 12,000 feet, three men made it out of the B-24's bomb bay door. Seconds later each man deployed his chute.

The three jumpers never saw each other in the midnight air, but they did see distant lights nearly one hundred miles away. Abruptly these lights were eclipsed as the three jumpers glided below an unseen Canyon wall.

This fairytale descent eventually had to come down to Earth. And it did. The navigator, Flight Officer Maurice J. Cruickshank, Jr., smashed into a steeply sloping cliff. He broke a bone or two in his foot, but amazingly, he otherwise "landed" in one piece. After skidding to a halt in the darkness, Cruickshank stayed right where he lay and waited for the light of dawn.

Instructor Aerial Engineer Corporal Roy W. Embanks waited four seconds to pull his rip cord. By his estimate, he then descended for fourteen minutes before landing uninjured.

Again, Bombardier Lieutenant Charles Goldblum found himself ricocheting from rock to rock in the darkness. Goldblum reported, "I came down within the arms of death when my chute was caught by a jagged cliff." Goldblum's landing on an invisible three-foot-wide shelf against a 1,200-foot cliff where he dangled all night in his harness was a cliff-hanger of the first order. Very fortunately, his decision not to unclip until dawn revealed his options. They turned out to be survivable. But only by climbing upward.

Meanwhile, up in the air at 8,000 feet, a mere thousand feet above the South Rim, after the "malfunctioning mechanism controlling the propeller's pitch" corrected itself, the B-24's engines re-started. The pilot and copilot, sweating bullets, nursed their bomber to those distant lights of Kingman only one hundred miles away.

At dawn Embanks awoke to see himself alone and surrounded by soaring cliffs and terraces in the heart of Grand Canyon. Being of sound body and sound mind, he decided to pack his chute and start climbing. No one, he knew, could ever rescue him this deep inside the Canyon. He climbed 1,200 feet up to a plateau. There he deployed his 24-foot canopy as a distress signal.

Cruickshank and Goldblum had both landed somewhere on the Tonto Plateau, also on the north side of the Colorado but about 1,000 feet above it. They both headed down instead of up, into Tuna Creek (River Mile 99.3). They spotted each other almost immediately and linked up. Cruickshank fashioned a makeshift crutch from a tree limb and hobbled with Goldblum down toward water a vertical mile below the North Rim.

The first squadron of twenty search planes roared over Embanks. Standing beside his deployed chute, he waved at them like a maniac. The planes passed over Embanks as if he did not exist. "That," he admitted, "was probably the most disheartening sight I ever saw."

Cruickshank and Goldblum eventually made it to the tiny creek. There they expropriated (this was wartime) a bobcat's den for shelter. Goldblum scanned the walls for a break where it might be possible to hike out. Still climbing about and searching for a way out on day three, Cruickshank and Goldblum spotted Embanks' chute. They painfully hobbled and climbed to his plateau to join him.

A day or two later, another plane finally roared by and dropped smoke bombs signaling that they had spotted the trio on their mile-long, half-mile wide plateau. On day six, another plane came by and dropped K-rations, water in canteens, blankets, a walkie-talkie, cigarettes, bottles of Old Overholt whiskey, and a note reading: "Greetings, you are in the Grand Canyon."

Once the three castaways had drained the canteens, however, they were forced to resume their previous, inconvenient climbs off the plateau for water. Each day, sometimes a few times, one of them would descend for four hours to a small spring that Embanks had found early on during his first ascent. There he would refill the canteens. It being June, the two able-bodied survivors were forced to engage in a lot of very hot exercise.

Meanwhile, two rescue parties descended from the South Rim. To cross the river, one man shot a cable across it. There being no one on the other side to catch it, this failed. They next brought from the South Rim to the river a dismantled, hard-hulled boat. But after staring at the ten-foot waves in the rapid at the foot of the trail, the team gave up the idea of boating across the river. It was, they decided, too much like suicide.

Colonel Donald B. Phillips, commander of the Kingman Air Field, flew around the stranded trio's location for two hours photographing the region. Upon studying these aerial photos, Phillips thought he had identified a breach in the cliffs that would allow a descent from the North Rim. The Army set up a base on the North Rim at Point Sublime and enlisted the aid of the veteran Toroweap Ranger Ed Laws and the veteran Inner Canyon hiker, Professor Alan A. McRae (future mentor to Harvey Butchart), in strategizing a rescue descent.

Laws and MacRae—who had just been hiking in the Canyon with his bride on their honeymoon—teamed up and pioneered a descent. It turned out, however, not to be the one that Phillips thought existed. Balked by a 150-foot cliff in the Redwall Limestone on Phillips' route that had not been visible in Phillips' aerial photos, MacRae and Laws backtracked to search the Redwall the hard way, from afoot atop it. Zeroing in on some greenery on the far side of this tributary canyon, they circled around it. On the far side they found a spring and a rare break in the Redwall. They followed a deer trail down this break. It led, after a total of ten miles and 20 hours of hiking, almost directly to Embanks', Cruickshank's, and Goldblum's position on the plateau.

Had this happened in the 1950s or later, the story would have ended differently—with a helicopter ride. But this was 1944. Men had to be men and they had to use their feet, broken or not. Hence, all five men climbed out in a quasi-"self-rescue." Even Cruikshank with his crutch. All that the downed fliers had really needed to rescue themselves was knowledge of the location of a climbable route out.

After successfully exiting the Canyon, the three fliers proposed naming their ten-day camp spot EMOGO Point (for Embanks, for Cruickshank's nickname, "Mo," and for Goldblum). Sadly, after surviving their unplanned night drop into Grand Canyon, then surviving their ten-day "camp-out" in the heat, and finally surviving their demanding, trail-less hike and climb a mile up and out of the Canyon during the blazing heat of late June, one of these three airmen, Goldblum, would die in 1944 in an aircraft accident in the Pacific War with Japan.

Painful though it was for both the rescued and their rescuers, the story of this B-24 crew's "rescue" recounts one of the happiest air mishaps ever to occur over Grand Canyon. Indeed, these mishaps are so common and so lethal that unsuccessfully trying to fly over the Canyon has killed more people than have died by drowning in the river, by falling off cliffs in the Canyon or from its rims, by being killed by flash floods, and by dying from the heat, combined. The airspace over the Grand Canyon region is likely the most dangerous peacetime airspace in the world.

The worst episode happened in 1956. At 10:01 a.m. Mountain Standard Time, on a reasonably clear morning of the last day of June, Trans World Airlines Flight 2, a four-engine Super Constellation L-1049 named *Star of the Seine*, took off with 70 people aboard, six of them crew, from Los Angeles International Airport. It was en route to Kansas City. Flight controllers told 42-year-old Captain Jack Gandy (with nearly 15,000 hours flight time) to fly at 19,000 feet. This would his 178th repeat of this route.

Three minutes later, a faster United Airlines DC-7 named *Mainliner Vancouver*, Flight 718, took off with 58 people, five of them crew, aboard from the same air strip en route to Chicago. Air Traffic Control told its 48-year-old captain, Robert Shirley (with 16,000-17,000 hours of flight time), to fly America's newest, fastest civil aircraft at 21,000 feet.

Both pilots had filed flight plans that deviated from standard, monitored "airways" (TWA 2's would have been via Albuquerque; UA 718's via Salt Lake City) in favor of more direct flight routes that would intersect near Grand Canyon but with 2,000 feet of vertical distance between them. An important issue to clarify at this point is that the flight environment immediately over the merely 15-mile-wide Grand Canyon provides a rougher, not smoother flight. Both pilots, we submit, deviated north and south and chose this narrow and lengthy bit of rough airspace instead of a nearby parallel but likely smoother route strictly for the view into Grand Canyon. Hence these flights became, in their own way, scenic flights.

Well into his flight, Captain Gandy asked for permission to move his Super Constellation up to 21,000 feet to avoid turbulence. Los Angeles Air Traffic Control denied his request. There was, they noted, already another large aircraft overtaking him at that elevation.

Captain Gandy later asked again for permission to fly higher, this time for "one thousand on top." This was a request to rise one thousand feet above cloud cover, which apparently TWA 2 was in. About half of Gandy's passengers (30 plus) were TWA employees, some of them high-level employees, or their dependents. This unusual situation makes it all too easy to speculate that Gandy did not want his TWA bigwigs aboard to libel him as a poor pilot because he was taking them on one of the bumpiest rides of their lives, hence his request to lift above the weather. Had Gandy been granted his request, he could have moved TWA 2 to about 21,000 feet, based on wherever the tops of those clouds extended.

Surprisingly, the Los Angeles air controller for TWA this time said yes. But he also warned Gandy again about United Airlines Flight 718 at 21,000 feet in the same region, overtaking him, and flying in the same direction. Once Gandy gained his two thousand feet he would be much closer to this United flight than before. And now flying on visual flight rules, it would be his responsibility to avoid it—and to fly only in clear sections of sky so that VFR actually was possible.

A half hour later, TWA 2 made its second routine call-in: "TWA 2, over Lake Mojave at 10:55, one thousand on top at twenty-one thousand, estimating Painted Desert eleven-thirty-one."

An air traffic controller in Salt Lake City heard this and noted to himself that TWA 2 and United 718 were now at the same altitude and in the same neighborhood of roughly a hundred-mile-wide airspace and heading over Grand Canyon. But because this sort of situation was not unusual, he turned his attention to other tasks.

It is important at this point to note that in 1956 air traffic control operations were specific to a single company. United controlled United. TWA controlled TWA. Air traffic controllers were company men who generally used a slip of paper to keep track of each flight. The controllers stacked or pinned these slips on vertical boards, positioning them based on each flight's altitude. This system normally worked pretty well. But not perfectly. Moreover, Air traffic controllers were not required to inform controllers of other companies' flights of changes in their own planes' flight paths that might influence other companies' flights. It made sense to communicate such changes, but no law mandated it.

In the 1950s it also was not only common for a pilot to modify his flight plan away from established airways, but to also alter his course to offer his passengers (and himself) this spectacular overview. On this day Grand Canyon weather offered "a reasonably clear sky" dotted with billowing thunderheads up to 35,000 feet.

Air Traffic Control next heard from United 718 at 11:28 a.m. as they "neared"

Tuba City (roughly fifty miles east of Grand Canyon). Four minutes later, a west-bound United flight heard a broken transmission from United Airlines Flight 718: "We are going in...." Then brief static. Then nothing.

Three separate tourists, Eugene J. Sieffer, Blanche England, and Frederick Riley, saw something happen in the sky. Sieffer was driving near Flagstaff. He told Civil Aeronautics Board (CAB) investigators that he saw the two planes converge and then "fly as if stuck together." Seconds later they disappeared "behind some mountains."

Blanche England, driving many miles away near Winslow, reported:

> All at once I saw a great puff of smoke, something came out of the sky like a parachute, then something came down with smoke following after it. The smoke spread out just like a parachute opening up. The object that came down didn't come straight down. It came down at sort of an angle.

Frederick Riley, driving along Highway 64 on the South Rim, saw the collision through his windshield much closer, only about ten miles ahead.

> This plane here peeled right off and went over like this...it looked to me as if it had bent—broken....It didn't glide at all. It tipped over and went right straight down. The other took off at a gliding angle....It looked like it possibly kept on the same general flight, and then it tipped over and went down....

Riley feared the scene he had just witnessed was a hallucination or a visual trick played by the shimmering light. At first he did not even report it for fear of being laughed at.

Before 1:00 p.m., both United and TWA authorities were worried. Neither east-bound flight had checked in. And both failed to respond to radio hailing. Search planes took off and unsuccessfully scoured the regions farther east toward Tuba City. Meanwhile a tourist at Desert View at the national park's east entrance noticed a column of smoke near the confluence of the Little Colorado and Colorado rivers.

Hearing about this smoke (and the missing aircraft), Bill Deaver, a 20 year-old reporter for the *Arizona Daily Sun*, hired a Cessna 180 owned and piloted by Beth Wright to search for the smoke's origin in Grand Canyon. To get aerial photos, Wright explained to a terrified Deaver, just get rid of the airplane's door. At the last minute, a *Los Angeles Times* reporter, Jerry Hulse, jumped aboard with Deaver.

As Deaver tried to shoot pictures, he worried that his ill-functioning seatbelt would disintegrate and dump him into a free-fall into the Canyon. So Hulse held Deaver inside the plane with a death grip.

The trio spotted the huge Super Constellation, down and burning in pieces, on the east shoulder of Temple Butte. A mile north of it, they also saw the United

DC-7 exploded into fragments against the south face of 6,400-foot-high Chuar Butte, less than a mile from the confluence of the Little Colorado River with the Colorado (River Mile 61.5).

Early the next morning, Clarke Cole, the 46 year-old undersheriff of Coconino County, flew his own small Ercoupe single engine plane to confirm for the Coconino Sheriff's Department where the crashed planes were. "I started down into the Canyon from the lower end," Cole explained, "and it was a rough day."

Cole too spotted the DC-7 disintegrated against Chuar Butte. Next he slowed to 80 mph to view the Super Constellation wreckage. Strong turbulence bucked his small plane. No way could anyone have survived either crash, Cole saw as he dropped as close as he could to survey the damage. Then, as Cole pulled up to escape the Canyon, he hit worse turbulence. Cole explains:

> When I hit that turbulence, after I saw those two planes, my own plane flipped over and I was flying upside down. Gas spilled out on me. God, I thought I was a goner. But the next batch of turbulence flipped me right back over again.

These overflights confirmed everyone's worst fears: 128 people had just died in a mid-air collision that sent both aircraft hurtling into Grand Canyon. The odds of anyone surviving either of the high impact collisions with the unyielding faces of Paleozoic rock were infinitesimal. Even recovering the bodies would be a very dangerous proposition. This collision was the worst peacetime civilian airline disaster in all of commercial aviation history (until it was exceeded in 1960). Indeed the carnage of this accident was so hideous that it spurred Congress to investigate America's air traffic controlling industry and to formulate a better, more fail-safe system. This quest ultimately led to the formation of the Federal Aviation Administration (FAA) and to today's universal air traffic control system.

Be that as it may, the result of these 1956 errors—the United pilot had deviated 25 miles south of his route; the TWA pilot had climbed 2,000 feet higher than was prudent and also had deviated five miles north off his own route—more than doubled the total number of people killed in Grand Canyon up to 1956 from all other causes combined since its recorded history began.

So how, exactly, did this disaster happen? Analysis of that final United 718 transmission received by Salt Lake and San Francisco revealed two voices over the radio. One, in the background, was saying, "Pull up! Pull up!" The other voice was that of United 718's First Officer Robert W. Harms: "Salt Lake City from United Seven One Eight...uh...we're going in!"

Reconstructing what went wrong would have to wait until chief investigator Jack Parshall could examine the surviving fragments of the downed aircraft.

Almost instantly, coordination and control in recovering bodies and debris became a shambles. Every agency remotely connected with the incident—TWA and United Airlines, the Civil Aviation Administration, the Civil Aeronautics Board, the National Park Service, the Federal Bureau of Investigation, the U.S. Air Force, five separate bases of Army Rescue teams, and the Coconino County Sheriff, Coroner, and Attorney—all tried to make something useful happen. As Ranger Butch Farabee notes, "Finally, on the afternoon of the third day, Park Superintendent McGlaughlin and Chief Ranger Coffin got a top official from each agency together in one room and somehow orchestrated the chaos to calm."

The position of the Super Constellation wrecked on Temple Butte at 3,400 feet allowed fairly easy access. It had hit at a steep angle and upside down. Mixed with its debris was the left wing tip of the United Airlines DC-7. Fabric covering this wing tip matched the interior ceiling fabric of the Super Constellation. Later examination of the TWA wreckage, notes a collision report, "indicated that the left wing of the United DC-7 had slashed sideways and downward across the rear of the TWA plane, ripping off the latter's tail [and rear fuselage]." The TWA plane, tail-less, probably dropped like a lead Frisbee spewing coats and pillows and other cabin appointments over miles of desert landscape. No passenger had ever been killed on board a Super Constellation before. This incident, however, proved a jackpot in the casino of death.

The most likely collision scenario was reconstructed by investigator Jack Parshal to place the DC-7, flying at 345 miles per hour, overtaking the TWA "Super Connie" at 308 mph, from behind as each plane veered around, or blindly through, a large anvil-shaped thunderhead. Captain Shirley had no time to fully avoid the Super Constellation suddenly appearing ahead of him at a speed 37 mph slower, but he tried to by veering hard to the left and diving, slicing off the Super Connie's tail section from its right side. Each pilot's considerable blind spot may have conspired here. A pilot's field of vision from a Super Connie's cockpit is only 17.2 percent of an unencumbered person's. Worse, that from a DC-7 is an extremely narrow 13.8 percent. As veteran pilot, TWA Captain John Carroll, noted with respect to this collision, "The fact is a pilot often finds it almost impossible to see another airplane even when it is right beside him—particularly when its paint job camouflages it against the sun or sky, or when the sun glare is bad, as it often is at high altitude."

Making a bad long-shot worse over Grand Canyon, Captain Robert Shirley of the DC-7 had no idea that anyone else was up there near 21,000 feet in his airspace. Air Traffic Control—for reasons discussed earlier—had not advised him of TWA 2's new 21,000-foot altitude.

Three days after the crash, Larry Wren, Deputy Coconino County Attorney, flew by helicopter to within 50 yards of the wreckage of the TWA Super Constellation. He was horrified.

There could be no one left alive. Blackened charred bodies dotted the ground

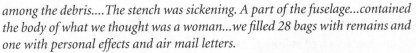

*among the debris....The stench was sickening. A part of the fuselage...contained
the body of what we thought was a woman...we filled 28 bags with remains and
one with personal effects and air mail letters.*

*During the afternoon, two paramedics [sic] left for the treacherous peak
where the United plane was down. They reported they had found only one
body—the only body—that was not burned.*

*Some of the bodies crumbled to ash as we lifted them. Aluminum parts of
the plane had melted and run in rivulets between the rocks....We found a baby's body across the arms of a woman....We found a toy boat that wasn't even
scratched.*

The TWA Super Constellation was a horrible mess. Yet the wreck of Shirley's
DC-7 was a nightmare. It was painted across the southern face of Chuar Butte atop
a nearly inaccessible cliff of Redwall Limestone.

"Leave them where they fell," advised Flagstaff editor-publisher Platt Cline,
who explained that the risk to rescuers of trying to salvage bodies from the pulver-
ized DC-7—the first ever of that model to crash—veneered against the cliffs of
Chuar Butte was unconscionably high. "Grand Canyon is not an inappropriate
resting place for these tragic crash victims."

Instead, officials dropped off climbers at the river at 2,700 feet elevation with
orders to ascend Chuar Butte. They trekked up newly named "Crash Canyon" and
began the final, challenging 800-foot ascent of Chuar Butte to the DC-7 at 4,050
feet. But after two days of sweltering technical climbing during early July and after
hammering hundreds of bolts into the weathered, decaying wall, the climbers still
had not reached the impact site. They had, however, thoroughly terrified themselves.

Determined, TWA, owned and operated by legendary aviator Howard Hughes,
flew in a crack mountain climbing team of Swiss air rescue personnel and their
2,000 pounds of equipment from their training program in Colorado. U.S. Army
Captain Walter Spriggs landed them, one by one, with his helicopter in a very hairy
location on a narrow ledge—deemed impossible by the experts—about 30 feet
above the wreckage of the United DC-7. The Swiss rescue team set up their base
camp on this ten-foot-wide ledge.

For the next several days they pried from the crevasses and vertical cracks
corpses and fragments of corpses that had been pressure injected into fissures and
then subjected to six days of scorching desert heat.

In one of the most hazardous operations the U.S. Army had ever undertaken,
their pilots brought their H-21 "Flying Banana" helicopters down through the superheated and treacherous air to evacuate these bodies. Only 30 of the 128 killed
were ever identified, most of them from TWA Flight 2. The majority of the twenty-

nine bodies recovered from the DC-7 were buried unidentified in the Grand Canyon Cemetery. Sixty-seven of the TWA victims were buried in Flagstaff. Strangely, the monuments placed at both mass graves, however, contain most of the names of the victims of each flight, but not all of them.

Both the Hopi and Navajo tribes recognized that all these people had died on the sacred grounds surrounding the Little Colorado Confluence. Both tribes held 24-hour prayer vigils for the victims. The entire city of Flagstaff and all of its businesses closed down in respect to the deceased.

But not everyone was paying respect to the dead. A prime example of one who did not was 39-year-old Robert Billingsley of Ajo, Arizona. He set off down the flooding Colorado on July 19, 1957 from Lees Ferry. Billingsley on his home-built raft, whose flotation consisted of two inner tubes. His plans called for stopping at Phantom Ranch to phone his wife and let his family know he was okay—and then to hike out. He failed to do this because "It was impossible to stop at Phantom; there was no backwash [eddy], and I had been sick and was very weak."

Billingsley later admitted he had not brought along enough food and, again, he felt sick, perhaps because he had been dining on cactus he had found growing on shore. Green prickly pear cactus fruit will lay anyone low who eats it.

Billingsley's having missed the eddy at Phantom led to a long and risky and hungry float. It also spurred an expensive search and rescue effort in the Canyon. This included an air search by U.S. Air Force pilots, and it involved yet another boat trip his brothers Paul and Joe who soon contracted with a professional guide and launched from Lees Ferry to look for Robert along the length of the Canyon.

There exists a big eddy at Phantom at all flow levels that makes stopping there possible. But in July, 1957 the Colorado was running unusually high, 50,000 cfs, making an escape from the main flow a challenge, especially for someone ill and riding on a crude raft lacking yare.

More to the point here, Billingsley, however, *had* managed to stop his makeshift raft 26 miles upstream at Crash Canyon. Indeed he later admitted that visiting this 1956 crash site was his primary motivation for having launched his planned 88-mile raft trip (which became a 277-mile trip). As the *Arizona Daily Sun* reports (August 8, 1957):

> *Six days later, Billingsley had reported to a Phoenix radio station (KOY) that during the course of his trip he had come across the wreckage of the TWA Super Constellation which collided in flight with a United Airlines DC-7, June 30, 1956. The 128 persons aboard the two planes were killed. He said he found a large quantity of human remains and removed some coins, a spoon and two rings from the scene. He said he took the rings off the mummified hand of a woman. Billingsley said he had not reported his find to authorities at Kingman because "I wanted to keep it from the relatives of the victims. I knew they'd be*

hurt if they thought remains of someone might still be in the canyon instead of being buried in the cemetery at Flagstaff."

Instead of informing anyone in authority about human body parts and valuables emerging from the tortured ground via erosion and now being scattered near the crash site, Billingsley thoughtfully filed the dead woman's initials off her wedding ring. Indeed, he later admitted, "I guess there's a little larceny in all of us. I had thought of maybe selling this ring."

Billingsley emerged from his adventure 28 pounds lighter than when he had launched on the river. He had felt so sick at one point that he remained on a beach for two days and eschewed rafting. All tolled, he had spent nine or ten days drifting on the current of the Colorado for nearly 277 miles. Appropriately perhaps, as his raft had neared Pearce Ferry on July 31, Bat Cave guano miners snagged him and gave him a ride to Kingman.

Back in civilization someone informed Billingsley that he had broken the law by looting the site of the Super Constellation crash. At this he had gone to see Attorney General Robert Morrison and confessed.

Since Billingsley's "raid" on the TWA crash site, it has been revisited thousands of times by the curious. In 1976 the Park superintendent insisted to TWA and United Airlines that they remove their wreckage, then twenty years old. The airlines hired an independent salvage contractor who dumped a lot of it on nearby Navajoland, later recycling some of the aluminum. As of June 30, 2006 the small bits of wreckage remaining in Grand Canyon abruptly were protected by the Federal Antiquities Act. On April 23, 2014 the site became a National Historical Landmark.

How odd was this collision between TWA 2 and United 718? This disaster was the 131st mid-air collision of civil aircraft to occur between 1947 and 1956. But it was drastically worse in casualties than all previous collisions. As mentioned above, it was the worst commercial air crash in U.S. history prior to 1960. And it was bad enough to spur U.S. Congress into action.

Congressional actions included a $250 million safety investment and new flight rules to: 1. fly on Instrument Flight Rules (IFR) above 18,000 feet, 2. to achieve better and wider air traffic control of airspace, and 3. to form a new regulatory, investigatory, and advisory entity, the Federal Aviation Administration, today's FAA.

Despite all improvements in flight control, when it comes to Grand Canyon, the cliché "lethal beauty" unfortunately has been all too accurate all too often. Even if one has no interest in geology, planetary history, or just mere scenery, the quest to see the sheer dazzling phenomenon of Grand Canyon from the air can be a killer.

By the 1990s, Grand Canyon Airport was Arizona's third busiest, reportedly handling up to more than 1,000 take-offs and landings daily. By 2000, it sometimes was Arizona's second busiest airport, handling yet more take-offs and landings. Yet some of those landings were made nowhere near the airport. On July 7, 1980, for example, Willis L. Woods, age 35, piloted his Piper Comanche from Page to the Grand Canyon Airport. With him were three passengers. Woods did not top off his fuel tanks in Page because "fuel was unavailable." Neither did Woods re-establish touch with reality by waiting at the airport for more fuel to arrive—or even by leaving by vehicle to go get some fuel himself.

Instead, undaunted by the inconvenience of not enough fuel in his tanks, Woods flew on toward Grand Canyon Airport. During this flight, he was fueled by determination.

Dozens of miles short of this destination, near Grandview Point below the South Rim, Woods ran out of aviation gas. This was the moment of enlightenment: Woods found that determination does not at all affect the thrust vector in heavier-than-air flight.

Woods crashed onto an Inner Canyon plateau. His Piper rattled and banged along a rare stretch of semi-level terrain, denting and abusing the fuselage, but otherwise leaving the aircraft in one piece. With no fuel at all aboard, at least the possibility of an explosion was low. Miraculously, Woods and his three passengers survived and were rescued.

Others would not be so lucky. Less than twenty years after Glen Canyon Dam went on line 15 miles upstream of Lees Ferry in 1963, for example, before the passage of the National Environmental Policy Act, the Bureau of Reclamation decided to rewind and upgrade their generator turbines to produce more kilowatt-hours of electricity per hour during daily peak, or "spike," releases. Since now, in 1981, this upgrade would widen the difference between daily high spike flows of 31,500 cfs and nightly low flows as low as 3,000 cfs from the dam even more disparately by raising the highs to 33,200 cfs during the day and lowering the lows to even less than 3,000 cfs at night, it would change yet again the flow regime of the Colorado River in Grand Canyon National Park.

The reason for such fluctuations was that a kilowatt-hour of electricity sold during the day generally brought in twice the money as a kilowatt-hour sold at night. But these existing drastic daily fluctuations, many ecologists suspected, were already wreaking havoc with several native species inside the Park. Some species— river otters (*Lutra canadensis*), the giant Colorado squawfish (a.k.a. pike minnow, *Ptychohelius lucius*), roundtail chub (*Gila robusta*), and bonytail chub (*Gila elegans*)—had become extinct in the Park due to the dam's operations. These lost species, however, formed barely the tip of the iceberg. Greater daily fluctuations yet, ecologists and conservationists worried, would cause even worse damage.

This being 1981, well after passage of the Federal National Environmental Policy Act (NEPA), the Bureau of Reclamation now was required to perform an Environmental Assessment before upgrading turbines then increasing daily flows of the Colorado (and also reducing nightly flows). The Bureau did this, but only in the most perfunctory way. They wrote it up in an office as bureaucratic paperwork without even looking into the river corridor in Grand Canyon to see what their fluctuating flows were actually doing to the Park. Not surprisingly, the Bureau decided that their upgrade would produce no significant effect in Grand Canyon and issued a "finding of no significant impact."

Environmentalists sued the Bureau in 1982 for "bypassing" the NEPA process. In response, on December 6, 1982 the Bureau launched what would become one of the most expensive and protracted environmental studies on Earth, the Glen Canyon Environmental Studies (GCES). GCES has since evolved newer names as the decades have passed, and it cost a truly incredible number of hundreds of millions of dollars spent. Be that as it may, GCES was aimed at determining the effects of dam operations on the resources—both living and nonliving—within the river corridor in Grand Canyon. Because of vested interests among all the main players in this research, it may continue without conclusive results until hell freezes over.

One of the most obvious resources being damaged at this time were beaches. They were shrinking drastically. Hundreds had vanished altogether since 1963. To investigate this situation, the Bureau set up five stations in the Canyon to measure sediment transport by different flows of the Colorado, high versus low, and so on. This was necessary because, due to the damming of the Colorado, the natural sediment loads entering the Canyon—a million tons every two or so days on average—had decreased to a very small fraction of maybe 2 or 3 percent. Most of what did exist in Grand Canyon was being slurried and deposited downstream in Lake Mead and was not being replaced.

One of these stations was installed upstream of National Canyon (River Mile 166.3). It consisted, as the other four did, of a steel cable stretched across the river about 35 feet above the water. This allowed researchers to cross above specific sections of the river in a cable car to collect water samples at various flows and depths. These samples provided sediment load data. GCES researchers were often poorly paid. Some were even unpaid volunteers. They were dropped off in the Canyon by boat and then, because the NPS had forbidden non-emergency helicopter traffic in the Canyon, the researchers were resupplied and/or relieved at multi-week intervals by other boats.

During summer months, these researchers experienced an idyllic life in the Canyon frequently punctuated by social visits from river-runners. During winter when river-running dropped to almost zero, however, those "trapped" at now sunless National Canyon were cold and monotonously lonely, experiencing an Inner Gorge version of cabin fever.

On the evening of December 8, 1983, two researchers, Heidi Herendeen and John Pittman, were readying their little cart at the National Canyon site. They were about to dangle above the river and collect the last sediment load samples of the day. Abruptly they both heard the echoes of a helicopter approaching low within the limestone walls of the Inner Gorge. This, to them, here, was a unique sound.

As they looked upstream, a Bell-206 swiftly rounded the bend and raced downriver thirty feet above the water. Again, helicopters—and all aircraft at this time—were requested to remain above 2,000 feet of this elevation except for search and rescue (SAR) missions. Even SAR missions rarely screamed down the corridor buzzing the river. This racing chopper was a novelty. Moreover, this BLM flight was breaking yet other Federal regulations by deviating off its official route.

It was also in the wrong place at the wrong time.

Its pilot, William J. "Doc" Holliday, had two passengers: Bill Lamb, the District Manager for the Bureau of Land Management in Utah, and Charlie Houser, age 50, a BLM congressional liaison from Washington, D.C. These two federal bureaucrats had been comparing two regions of the plateau thousands of feet above the river and miles away to the north of Grand Canyon as candidates for wilderness designation. Once done up there, at least one of the two bureaucrats had convinced Holliday to buzz the river in a joy-ride (again, against federal regulations and at taxpayers' expense).

As Herendeen and Pittman stared in disbelief, the Bell-206's engine-cowling, then rotor mast, slammed into their one-inch cable. The 2,500-pound airship stretched the cable like a bowstring then stopped on a dime. It flipped upside down as it dropped into the river. As it drifted downstream it began to sink slowly in the 15-foot-deep water near shore.

Herendeen dived out of the way as the cable snapped. The cart that she had been about to step into launched up in the air then crashed back down one foot away from her. All of this had been very lucky. Had Holliday's helicopter hit this cable a minute or two later, all five people involved likely would have been killed.

Pittman jumped into the cold river and assisted Pilot Holliday in his struggle to shore. Herendeen jumped in too. She grabbed the chopper's skid in one hand and a shoreline bush in the other, trying to stop it from drifting into National Rapid with people trapped underwater inside it.

Meanwhile, half underwater, Bill Lamb extricated himself from his harness. Next to him, Charlie Houser was unconscious, still strapped upside down, with his head underwater. Lamb pulled Houser's head out of the water by his helmet but then fumbled unsuccessfully with Houser's seat belt release buckle.

Pitman entered the sinking chopper and made several dives to release Houser's buckle. Finally Lamb pulled Houser out and onto the belly of the Bell-206 and gave him cardiopulmonary resuscitation (CPR). Everyone made it—or was towed—to shore.

Secretary of the Interior Donald P. Hodel awarded Department of the Interior Valor Awards to Heidi Herendeen and John Pitman—and, strangely, in view of the flight's regulation-breaking, joyride nature, also to Bill Lamb. Despite CPR, Charlie Houser died due to "delayed" drowning/lung complications several days later.

As we have already seen, the Canyon's stunning beauty combined with pilot error led to a major disaster in 1956, one so horrific it became midwife to the FAA. Almost exactly 30 years later, the beauty of the Inner Canyon would yet again combine with pilot error to produce such tragic results that U.S. Congress would feel compelled yet again to re-attack the lethal problem of regulating commercial flights over the Canyon.

It was mid-morning, about 9:30, on June 18, 1986. The boatmen of a commercial river trip were scouting Crystal Rapid (River Mile 98.5). A few of their passengers heard a strange sound. As they looked downstream and northward, a fixed-wing Twin-Otter and a Bell Jet Ranger helicopter had just collided above the drainage of Tuna Canyon (River Mile 99.3). Now both plummeted down to Earth.

Meanwhile an emergency call came over the radio. NPS helicopter Pilot Dana Morris heard it. Morris detoured away from his route to a noncritical river medevac injury. Within five minutes he flew Rangers Ernie Kuncl and Charles Peterson to the smoking wreckage.

The twenty-seat plane, a DeHavilland Twin-Otter operated by Grand Canyon Airlines, Inc. had indeed crashed. The three rescue personnel saw people still strapped in their seats in this aircraft, dead and burning. All twenty of the passengers and crew of the sight-seeing plane had died.

Twenty minutes later the NPS searchers also spotted the debris of a crashed Bell-206 helicopter owned by Helitech, Inc. strewn over a mile across the Tonto Plateau. All five persons aboard it too had been killed.

Why?

"Three good men died," a ground crew member said of the pilots, "for no fault of their own. They died in an accident that couldn't be avoided. It was an act of God."

Whether or not God had been complicit in creating this disaster remains questionable. Humans were piloting the aircraft. It seems more appropriate to ask: What had these humans been doing?

By informal agreement between air tour operators, helicopter tours were to stay below a ceiling of 6,500 feet while fixed wing flights were to stay above 7,000 feet, the intent being to create 500 vertical feet of airspace as a margin of safety between the two types of aircraft. Hence a crux question is: Where had these two aircraft been flying?

A tourist on that rafting trip scouting Crystal had taken three photos from the river of both aircraft in the air. Using photogrammetric reconstruction analysis, federal investigators bracketed the collision at between 6,401 and 6,613 feet. More than two months after the collision, the National Transportation Safety Board (NTSB) ballparked the collision as having occurred at about 6,500 feet. Years earlier, the FAA had issued an advisory urging pilots not to fly lower than 2,000 feet above the rim (7,000 feet elevation). Hence, the fixed-wing Twin-Otter and the helicopter had been flying well below their advised airspace (as many scenic pilots habitually did during the 1980s). But the fixed wing also was apparently flying 400–500 feet below its informal, conventional airspace. In contrast, the helicopter had been flying at the ceiling of, but most likely within, its informal, conventional airspace.

Weeks later, however, the cause of this midair collision still had remained unexplained. Even after combing through and removing most of the wreckage, and after evacuating the 25 burned bodies, the FAA and the National Transportation Safety Board still could not figure it out.

Two months after the midair collision, the helicopter pilot's brother, Scott Thybony, hiked to the crash site on the shadeless Tonto Plateau. In the emotion of his quest, Thybony outwalked his water. He soon experienced classic symptoms of advanced dehydration: narrowed visual field, cramping stomach, tingling scalp, loss of judgment. Having made hundreds of Canyon hikes before, Thybony knew he was in trouble—enough trouble to now begin imagining the effect of his death upon his wife and son and the rest of his family so soon after his brother's death. How could he have been so stupid, he wondered now, as to not have filled up his canteen at that last pothole a few hours back? It had held at least two gallons of rainwater.

Thybony looked toward the ridge above where, he reflected, he should have been walking. He thought ruefully about how distant that water was.

Then I saw it. On the slope lay a piece of wreckage overlooked by the search parties. They hadn't expected to find anything this far north. It was the missing rotor blade from my brother's helicopter, scarred from the impact of metal on metal. Later retrieved, it turned out to be the critical piece of evidence used in reconstructing the moment of collision. In the final instant, it's likely that neither aircraft could have seen the other as the airplane overtook the helicopter from above and behind.

Scott Thybony had just found the key to understanding what had gone wrong. But he still had to survive to hand over that key to the ones who knew how to use it. Still in agony for that waterpocket a mile and half away, he finally found a ledge in the Tapeats Sandstone that offered a scrap of shade. He gave up his quest for water and hid under this shelf from the sun.

Lying there on the rough sandstone he hallucinated an old Indian, maybe Apache he thought, grim and unsmiling, sitting next to him. After what seemed like a long time, his new companion spoke: "Yes, we wait here, sun go down." Minutes later, the phantom Indian departed.

Five hours later, after Thybony had dredged up the energy and good sense to pull the cactus spines from his boots, the sun set. An hour later he reached that tiny waterpocket, life itself. Too burned by thirst to continue by foot in the twilight—or even to swallow any food—Thybony bivouacked under a nearby ledge where, by eerie coincidence, he and his brother John Thybony had camped a dozen years earlier. The firewood they had gathered then still sat nearby stacked neatly. Deja vu.

Haunted now by his brother's stories then of the many terrifying sorties he had piloted during the Vietnam War, Thybony kindled a small fire. Despite his deja vu—and everything else—Thybony felt relieved to be alive. He reflected on how his brother had decided after returning from Vietnam to quit flying. Many years had passed after this decision before John changed his mind recently and agreed to pilot a tour helicopter. To have survived so many sorties in Vietnam against blizzards of enemy fire only to die in peacetime airspace simply because another pilot decided to fly lower than normal....

Later, Federal investigators would conclude from Scott Thybony's discovery that the rotor mast of the helicopter piloted by John Thybony at roughly 6,500 feet had been hit by the left landing gear of the fixed wing Twin-Otter piloted by Bruce Grubb and Jim Ingraham. Each aircraft had been in the blind spot of the other.

What is the overall tally of fatal air crashes in and around the Canyon? Unlike the media-blitzed airline crashes that populate our nightly news on television and win cover photos on U.S. news magazines, most of the 64 fatal crashes in and around Grand Canyon as of August, 2011 have received relatively little public attention. No aura of sensationalism surrounds the deaths of most of the 379 people who have died during these 64 fatal crashes (multiple additional nonfatal crashes have occurred which we have not tabulated) that we have determined to have occurred in and near to Grand Canyon. Nonetheless, as Tables 6–A and 6–B show, these 64 disasters caused 259 deaths from 32 aircraft crashing in the Canyon and another 120 deaths from yet another 32 aircraft in the environs around it. Together these Grand Canyon air deaths comprise a stunning total.

How could so many aircraft go down forever in one region?

Grand Canyon is not the Devil's Triangle, but somehow it has gobbled up more aircraft victims than that infamous Bermuda "hole" in so-called reality. One possible explanation may be that too many inexperienced private pilots fly over the Canyon's extreme turbulence and through its very changeable and dynamic weather from those same monsoonal systems that create flash floods and from those same winter storms that close the North Rim all winter. Some of these pilots, some critics say, are overcome by these challenges when matched against their own experience. This argument, as we will see, holds merit when matched against what is known about the causes of these crashes. These 64 aircraft that crashed fatally did include 37 under the control of private pilots. But of the other 27 aircraft down, 26 were piloted by men with commercial licenses (the April 1, 1999, helicopter crash is the only one known to have been piloted by a woman, and she was in training). These 26 men possessed commercial pilot licenses and were trained in some way to anticipate the challenges posed by the airspace over and within Grand Canyon. Yet, within the Canyon itself, 18 commercial pilots have gone down in fatal crashes, while 14 private pilots have done so. In these within-Canyon crashes, 217 people died inside the Canyon from commercial flights, 42 people died from private flights.

The causes of these tragedies—involving both private and commercial pilots—do show some common threads. The discernable causes for these 64 fatal crashes are summarized in Table 6–C. Of these crashes, causes were not determined (or not available to us) for eleven. Of the remaining 53 crashes for which at least one cause is known or strongly suspected, mechanical failures and/or inadequate maintenance accounted for thirteen or fourteen (about 25 percent).

On June 25, 1977, for example, George Lutteum was flying a private twin, piston-engined Piper Navajo on the Kaibab Plateau a half dozen miles south of Hermit's Rest on the South Rim. He lost one engine and crashed. Four of the nine Californians aboard (George Lutteum was not among them) fled the crash site before the plane exploded. Those four survived. The other five aboard died. On July 21, 1980 Richard T. Mierhouse, age 33, piloted a Scenic Airlines Cessna 404 twin, piston-engined aircraft on its takeoff for a scenic flight with seven passengers aboard. Almost immediately upon takeoff, metal fragments from incomplete repair work were sucked into the left engine, freezing it. The Cessna crashed shortly after takeoff and killed all eight people aboard, mostly Nigerian and Japanese tourists. On May 13, 1991 all seven people aboard an Air Grand Canyon Cessna 207 died due to a cylinder-head explosion freezing up its one engine (piston-powered) a few minutes after take-off. On June 19, 1992, ten people died on an Adventure Airlines Cessna 402 twin immediately after take-off. It too had lost its right, piston engine due to a maintenance problem. On February 13, 1995, a Las Vegas Airline scenic flight crashed killing all eight aboard. The Piper PA-31 Navajo twin had also lost one piston engine. In summary, at least 60 people died in a dozen crashes due in part or in whole to mechanical failures, some associated with faulty maintenance of their piston engines, some not.

We looked for a pattern of fatal crashes that implicated certain models of aircraft. Nearly 40 different models have crashed in these 64 known fatal incidents. We have not determined any specific "killer" model among them (although five Cessna 172s did go down fatally. But with 40,000 172s built, it is the most common model in the air). On the other hand, a pattern does exist. First, among scenic commercial crashes single-engine aircraft seem less implicated in fatalities than twin-engined craft. Only four single-engine tour flights have gone down fatally, killing 21 among crew and passengers. Meanwhile eight twin-engine craft have crashed, killing 81 passengers and crew (more on this below).

To compare the numbers of scenic helicopters down fatally compared to scenic fixed-wing flights, a fairly high number of a dozen fatal helicopter accidents have occurred. Of these dozen, two crashed within the Canyon while filming commercial movies and while flying too close to bridges or cables (described below). Three more crashed as "workhorses" while hauling equipment for pipeline or other construction. A sixth one, a joy-riding chopper on a BLM contract but on non-government business (described earlier) went down when it too hit a tram cable at River Mile 166. A seventh machine became fatal when the pilot in training crashed in 1999 at the airport, possibly due to moisture in the intakes.

Of the five scenic helicopter flights down, John Thybony's helicopter (also described earlier) was hit in mid-air by a fixed-wing scenic tour plane flying below the floor of its informal conventional airspace. Four other scenic flights have crashed—one due to engine failure, one other to unknown causes, and two to pilot error, when the pilots were basically "hot-dogging" their machines and lost control. These last crashes killed a total of 21 passengers and all five pilots. Table 6-A describes the two worst helicopter disasters after the year 2000. Both proved terrifying and infuriating.

Even so, instead of aircraft type, and also instead of aircraft design or mechanical or maintenance failures (which we admit are important), a more lethal problem has caused a far greater number of the 53 fatal crashes due to known causes. As Table 6–A reveals, and as Table 6–C tabulates, pilot error of some sort has been implicated in 40 to 43 of these 53 crashes, or roughly 75 percent. Unsurprisingly, this approximate 75 percent figure matches the proportion of all crashes of jet transports in the United States determined to have been due to pilot error. For an unsettling example of how some of these might happen, half of all commercial pilots in a 2010 survey admitted to having fallen asleep at least once while flying.

Pilot errors take many forms. The most common, it turns out, seem to occur in the actual flying ability or flying/maneuvering decisions of the pilot. These errors—analogous to the sorts of driving errors made by a driver of a car that mishandles the vehicle as road conditions change and crashes—accounted for about 25 of the 53 crashes and comprised 40+ percent of the total. Interestingly, these 25 flying errors are closely split between commercial and private pilots, with at least a dozen each.

A clear example of pilot error occurred on April 19, 1982. Glenn Miller of Santa Barbara, California flew his Hughes 500 helicopter low and fast along the river near Lees Ferry. He had three passengers aboard, the members of an EMI Productions TV crew from Los Angeles and Tucson who were filming an "American Eagle" adventure film for CBS. Miller failed to see the tram cable across the river. This cable had been there for decades. The rotor hit the cable. The aircraft skidded across the water for one thousand feet. Only one of the four people aboard, Laurie Gere, survived, rescued by the quick actions of river guide Dale Whitmore.

Doing a similar sort of job only about four miles downstream, on July 12, 1985, pilot Don Nasca, age 50, met a similar fate. Nasca of Page, Arizona was flying his helicopter as a motion picture "bad guy" airship during the filming of the Italian action/science fiction film, "Hands of Stone." As the hero of this film dangled from Navajo Bridge, Nasca's aircraft rattled off blanks from a machine gun at him. For drama, Nasca maneuvered closer (for the camera) to the bridge. Too close. On his second pass, Nasca's rotor struck the bridge. The helicopter plunged 470 feet into the Colorado and sank. Both Nasca and his actor-passenger Claudio Cassinelli, age 47, of Bologna, Italy died.

Slightly less dramatic, but even more lethal, Keith Crosson, age 42, was co-piloting a Grand Canyon Airlines DeHavilland DHC-6 Twin-Otter with 21 people aboard, when he mishandled his landing at Grand Canyon Airport on September 27, 1989. Only eleven people survived. Some of these were injured due to seat belt failures and were also trapped in the plane for an hour as rescuers worked feverishly—worried that the aircraft might explode—to free them.

Yet another incident of pilot error was made by private pilot John C. Walker, age 23. His piston-engined Cessna 172 had been experiencing power problems periodically on September 4, 1988. But because he and his three passenger-friends could not find a room for the night at the South Rim and he was "anxious to get home," Walker decided to fly without fully correcting his engine problems. The heavily loaded Cessna 172 stalled after takeoff and crashed. All four aboard died.

Additional types of pilot errors in decision-making that led to fatal crashes included flying into dangerous weather systems. Ten pilots, four commercial and six private, did this fatally (accounting for nearly 20 percent of all pilot errors).

After 600–700 flights over the Canyon, for example, pilot Wayne Leeth, age 47, flew a Scenic Airlines twin, piston-engined Cessna 402 with 9 passengers aboard on a tour flight on October 16, 1971 into an early winter snowstorm. Other pilots in the area said the storm was characterized by "clouds down to the ground." Fifteen miles south of Mount Trumbull, Leeth's Cessna hit the ground in Parashant Wash below the rim.

For many pilots accustomed to flying on visual flight rules (VFR), being inside a cloud can be instantly disorienting—despite the altitude indicator (AI), automatic direction finder (ADF), horizontal situation indicator (HSI) gauge, altimeter, and other instruments intended to allow an instrument-rated pilot to fly "blind." Whatever went awry with pilot Wayne Leeth's situation, all ten aboard were killed. In total, three commercial pilots committed the error of flying during, and into, cold, dangerous weather and consequently iced up or otherwise crashed fatally. A half dozen or more private pilots, however, made this same mistake.

Another fatal error made by three or four private pilots—but not by commercial ones—include attempting to take off and fly an overweight aircraft. Three pilots, private ones, ran out of fuel fatally. For example, on June 28, 1978, Arthur D. Meyers, age 28, committed the same error made by Willis L. Woods (described earlier), but without the happy ending. When Meyers ran out of fuel, he crashed his Cessna 170 into the Canyon near Cape Royal, killing all three aboard.

The upshot? While a known quarter of aircraft crashes and fatalities within and near Grand Canyon were due to mechanical problems and/or to faulty maintenance, the vast majority of crashes and fatalities were caused by pilot error. This high proportion of fatal errors—as opposed to acts of God or unforeseeable malfunctions of aircraft—prompt a few questions.

The first might be: how are pilots trained before they fly over the Canyon? The answer for private pilots is: they were trained by whomever, wherever they got their ground school and in-flight training. In short, their in-the-air training was/is likely random and in no way uniform with regard to preparing them or honing their abilities to successfully meet the challenges posed by the dynamic air masses over the high canyon country of the Southwest. Not much will likely change in this situation. Hence it remains likely that future private pilots will crash in and around the Canyon in the same ways as their predecessors have done.

What about commercial pilots, especially the ones making multiple short, scenic flights each day, again and again, over the same itinerary? This is a tougher question. Just as we saw in the previous chapter analyzing Inner Canyon fatalities on commercial river trips—deaths to witnessed and unwitnessed drownings and disappearances and to fatal falls—the companies' safety records differ drastically. Some whitewater companies, for example, have been in business for decades and have experienced no fatalities. Others of similar operational size have had as many as four separate fatal incidents. The same holds true for scenic air tour companies flying for hire over Grand Canyon but with far higher stakes. Some have had no fatalities. One has had three fatal crashes. Yet another air tour company has had five fatal crashes involving 44 fatalities. Of these five crashes, one occurred due to unknown causes, one to mechanical failure, and three flights went down (killing at least 36, but possibly as many as 43 of those 44 people) due to pilot error.

Several dangers and conditions specific to the Grand Canyon scenic environment conspire to make flying over it more iffy than flying over another American wilderness of comparable size and elevation, say, Yellowstone National Park. First, flying over the uneven and unstable air masses created by the superheated hard rock maze of Grand Canyon necessitates repeatedly exiting updrafts and downdrafts. In addition to flying, pilots' take-off and landing environments often must be made at high density altitudes. "Density altitude" means the air density at an elevation and its prevailing local temperature and pressure compared to the density of air at sea level under the international standard atmosphere defined as being at a temperature of 59 degrees (15 degrees Centigrade) and a barometric pressure of 29.92 inches Hg (1013.2 millibars). Why is this important? Because conventional prop-driven aircraft fly "on" or "in" air much like ships sail on water. They gain their lift, thrust, and maneuverability based on how dense the air is. In general, the denser the better. Based on each aircraft's specific design, it possesses diminishing performance capabilities and ceilings in increasing density altitudes. Too high an actual altitude or too high a density altitude due to a combination of low air pressure and high air temperature can make some aircraft unflyable. Commercial jetliners sitting on the tarmac at Sky Harbor in Phoenix, Arizona, for example, have been grounded en masse at low elevation simply because the air temperature exceeded 122 degrees in the shade and because this air was so "super-empty," or diffuse. At such high temperatures of dry air its density and pressure are so low that even a low elevation mimics the thin air found at high altitudes. Such air is so diffuse that the wings of the aircraft provide insufficient lift to get them safely off the runway and into the sky.

The problem over Grand Canyon is the take-off elevation is at nearly 7,000 feet. Everything in the air above is higher yet. Air pressure drops by about one inch of mercury for each thousand feet of elevation gain. So at take-off the air pressure is already 23 percent less than at sea level. Add summer heat to this equation and the air pressure plummets even more. On top of this, over Grand Canyon the air masses are often unstable, superheated, rising, falling, and unequal even when adjacent to one another. This also means that any aircraft flying a straight course from one air mass to another—as in off the edge of the Coconino Plateau to over Grand Canyon—may abruptly shift performance environments, sometimes drastically. To control an aircraft in such conditions, a pilot requires not only experience but thrust, or power.

Yet at above 7,000 feet on a "standard" day a prop plane has only 75 percent of the engine power that it would at sea level. At 95 degrees at that same 7,000 feet, that power drops to the equivalent of flying at 11,000 feet, with only 63 percent of sea level power.

During the monsoons things get worse. The added humidity may further cut operational power during take-offs by another 1 to 10 percent. Far more hair-raising during monsoons, however, are microbursts of weather that consist of intense localized downdrafts. Often clues of these airplane-busters consist of streamers of vanishing rain called virga, or of expanding dust rings on the ground. But the vertical and horizontal wind shears within microbursts may instead be completely invisible, like mile-wide downdrafts (or "downbursts," see next paragraph) that can slam some flying aircraft onto the ground.

Monsoonal thunderstorms—which occur during the prime tourist season—pose the worst wind shear hazards pilots face. These abrupt changes in wind speed and/or direction over very short distances can be horizontal or vertical (as in microbursts). The alchemy of thunderstorms spins off "first gusts" and "downbursts" (a.k.a. microbursts). The abrupt winds of first gusts can shift direction up to 180 degrees and blast at over 100 miles per hour as far as ten miles from the storm. Downbursts adjacent to the storm can not only reach speeds dropping at 720 feet per minute but, in so doing, may also exceed the climb capabilities of aircraft caught in them. Even high performance U.S. Air Force jets have augured into the ground due to such downbursts. The bottom line here is that such fierce winds can and do alter an aircraft's lift and indicated airspeed so drastically and also escalate the thrust requirements for escape so much that they can exceed the pilot's capability to recover. Such atmospheric phenomena may help explain fatal crashes during the monsoon season in or near Grand Canyon on July 26, 1967 (7 killed), August 3, 1975 (3 killed), August 21, 1981 (6 killed), August 5, 1983 (3 killed), August 17, 1983 (10 killed), August 1, 1984 (3 killed), August 2, 1996 (1 killed).

Clearly a vital performance element of all aircraft flying over Grand Canyon is thrust. Thrust allows for speed and lift. Lift makes airplanes go up. And engines provide this thrust. Increasing density altitudes, increasing humidity, and the possibility of microbursts and first gusts all demand reliable thrust for safety. Engine designs, of course, differ in thrust capacity and, significantly, in their price. Knowing that the Grand Canyon flight environment will predictably put aircraft abruptly into air masses demanding high thrust in order to retain a safe margin of lift and maneuverability, one might assume that all eleven companies of the air tour industry purchase aircraft powered by the most efficient and powerful motors, gas turbine engines, not piston engines, which provide poorer thrust and/or less reliable performance. Gas turbine engines, as used in helicopters and in the DeHavilland DHC-6 Twin-Otter fixed-wings, which some companies use, provide far more thrust. To reduce the cost to the consumer/operator of the initial purchase, aircraft manufacturers install piston engines, but increase their thrust by also installing turbochargers. The problem here is turbochargers add to the aircraft's weight yet may not match the performance of the more expensive, reliable, and quiet gas turbine engines. Of course the faster a plane is traveling, the better its lift and gliding capabilities. But at what speed do most piston-powered air tour planes fly? Slowly. So that tourists can best see the sights below. Add to this piston-powered equation this low air speed and the plot thickens.

It thickens even more because many air tour companies have gone to twin, piston-engined planes. While this may sound promising, the reality is that most of these aircraft in most of the Canyon's summer flight environments cannot fly on only one engine. Instead, with only one working piston engine, they often can only descend in a controlled "glide." And the steepness of these "glides" may be exacerbated by increasing density altitudes. This "glide" capability has apparently seduced some pilots via a sense of added security which has prompted them to fly into air masses that pilots of single-engine craft have avoided through greater savvy and caution. Indeed, a look at Table 6–A reveals that some of the most serious fatal crashes of commercial flights here have been of twin, piston-engine planes "flying" on only one engine. Table 6–A also reveals that single-engine commercial planes seem to have a better record. As discussed earlier, among scenic commercial crashes only four single-engine tour flights have gone down fatally, killing 21 among crew and passengers. Meanwhile eight twin-engine craft have crashed, killing 81 passengers and crew.

With such variable and difficult flying conditions, one might conclude that the very best pilots for the job would be the very best pilots around. And one might further guess that the air tour industry would be preferentially hiring them. Instead, however, as local pilots have explained to us, many of the pilots who gain employment in the air tour industry around Grand Canyon are relative newcomers to the commercial scene; many are "flatland" pilots who are willing to accept the relatively low pay offered by scenic air companies and to endure the challenging flying conditions and back-to-back flights here in order to get their hours in to improve their resumes and flight experience record, and to thus make themselves more competitive in applying for more desirable commercial piloting elsewhere. Meanwhile many pilots fresh out of military training are trying to do the same thing. In short, many air tour companies flying over Grand Canyon do not pay enough to attract and hold most top notch pilots possessed of solid mountain-flying experience. Nor do many potentially high-earning pilots want to live in the small, remote community near Grand Canyon. This is not to say that all air tour pilots are bad pilots; this is emphatically not true. Instead it is to point out that many of them stand on a low rung of the appropriate experience ladder.

What can be done to improve this situation? Tellingly, the NTSB investigator and author of accident report NTSB/AAR-93-01 on the fatal crash of a Scenic Air Tour's Beech E18S on Maui on April 22, 1992 analyzed this crash against similar—and more numerous—crashes in and near Grand Canyon. He concluded (on his page 31) that some tour operators inadequately screen and train their pilots due to the lack of FAA requirements to do so—and that some of these pilots' flying errors prove lethal because of this weak screening. He further concluded:

> *I also agree with the majority that no single management action, no screening program, no training program can absolutely guarantee passengers freedom from risk. In the real world, one can realistically only alter probabilities; failure to take reasonable action to positively manage these risks also causes accidents. Since every pilot hired by an operator must ultimately pass through a sieve whose mesh size is set by management policy and practice, pilot screening and training programs effect real leverage on system safety. In my opinion, this Board ought to take every opportunity to bring its considerable moral authority to bear on the operators who are responsible for the conduct of such programs. I believe that we have missed such an opportunity.*

Knowing these rudiments of safety requirements, one can see the wisdom of air tour companies that either pay for expert training to create "mountain pilots" or else pay well enough to attract well-trained mountain pilots to begin with.

One example of how this pays off is revealed by the air record of the Arizona Department of Public Safety and Grand Canyon National Park Service. Their helicopter pilots—who fly search and rescue missions and maintenance runs—fly into the same scenic environment as the scenic flights above. But the NPS and DPS pilots also must drop into the Canyon, often in extremely challenging weather, and land their machines on frequently dangerous and unforgiving terrain. The NPS does this almost a thousand times each year. DPS pilots even do this at night. Tellingly, during the past 40 years from 1970 to the present, they have experienced no fatal accidents. Extensive pilot training prior to flying in/over the Canyon, NPS and DPS SAR personnel say, is what is responsible for their 40+ year, fatality-free flight record.

What has happened to improve the commercial scenic flight pilots' decision-making protocols and abilities and to improve the air tour industry's choice of aircraft type, maintenance protocols, pilot-hiring standards, and pilot training?

Closer federal examination of some of these issues was prompted in part by the June 18, 1986, incident (discussed earlier) in which that Grand Canyon Airlines DeHavilland Twin-Otter on a scenic flight collided with that Helitech, Inc. Bell 206 Jet Ranger helicopter over Tuna Canyon (River Mile 99.5), taking 25 lives. The NTSB and the FAA looked at this and several other crash histories recounted above and went to work to reduce their recurrences. That horrendous 1986 midair collision above Tuna Canyon led directly to Safety Recommendation A-87-91 and also to a congressional mandate sponsored by Arizona Senator John McCain. This passed as Public Law 100-91 on August 18, 1987, imposing flight restrictions at Grand Canyon and also at Yosemite and Haleakala (Hawaii) national parks.

Public Law 100-91 also spurred the FAA in 1987 to issue Special Federal Aviation Regulation (SFAR) 50-2. While prohibiting scenic flights below the South Rim—in most of eastern Grand Canyon—this complex regulation prescribed rules for operating aircraft specifically in the vicinity of Grand Canyon National Park in a Special Flight Rules Area (SFRA) between Page, Arizona, and Lake Mead National Recreation Area, Nevada, and up to 14,499 feet elevation in flight free zones. Again, these new rules were spurred by the high numbers of crashes and fatalities mentioned above (and listed in Tables 6-A and 6-B) and were issued only for the Grand Canyon region, but the FAA intended SFAR 50-2 to examine and reduce the effects of aircraft noise on visitors and Park resources, not to increase safety. To reduce noise, SFAR 50-2's Grand Canyon National Park Special Flight Rules Area restricts pilots to specific flight zones to allow other zones to remain quiet. Guidelines for these new rules were published in FAA Handbook 8400.10 Bulletin 92-10 to specify surveillance of the tour operators themselves. Despite all of this bureaucratic "control," however, an NTSB reviewer added, SFAR 50-2 "does not relieve the pilot-in-command from the responsibility to see and avoid other aircraft."

SFAR 50-2 also requires Grand Canyon operators to now hold 14CFR Part 135 certification, which, while restrictive, actually allows Part 135 commercial pilots to fly 2,000 feet lower than general aviation pilots may. Flight standards inspectors also mapped out and published new visual flight rules describing these companies' airspace, routes, and reporting points above the Canyon. The FAA next got to work to create automated weather reporting for the Canyon to help pilots avoid lethal environments.

One of the administrative problems in all of this is that scenic air tour flights— by definition—can only function in a VFR (visual flight rules) environment. With the exception of specifying even altitudes plus five hundred feet to fly west and odd altitudes plus five hundred to fly east, VFR flying is essentially open or "free-style" within the tour-flight routes allowed. Nor does the FAA directly monitor the inter- action of VFR air traffic between the various operators and aircraft.

Sadly, as Tables 6–A, 6–B, and 6–C reveal, while the airspace in and around Grand Canyon seems to have proven to be as lethal as any peacetime airspace any- where on Earth, the causes for its air fatalities remain all too mundane and all too human. And maybe too complicated to fully solve via FAA rules.

How serious is all this? Many of us have heard the oft-quoted "statistic" which says something like "you're far safer statistically to fly commercially than to ride in a car." Many of us instinctively respond to this assertion with, "It depends on who is driving that car." Admittedly, aircraft have become far safer, only partly because jet engines are safer than prop engines. What is the reality here?

Between 1964 and 1997, for example, the fatality rates on commercial air car- riers in the U.S. fell dramatically from 28 dead to less than 3 dead per 100 million miles flown. How do cars stack up safety-wise? The U.S. Department of Trans- portation concluded in 1997 that cars have a fatality rate of 1.44 persons per 100 million vehicle miles driven. As of 2009, according to the U.S. National Highway Traffic Safety Administration, road fatalities had declined to the year 2009, a year when the fatality rate on U.S. roads dropped to 1.13 fatalities per 100 million miles driven. The figure for 2010 was somewhat less.

Airplanes, meanwhile, produced a fatality rate of 2.8 deaths per 100 million aircraft miles flown prior to the year 2000. Over Grand Canyon the aircraft fatal- ity rate appears much higher yet, but the full statistics on total miles flown by all aircraft are not available and may never be. One statistic quoted by the *Arizona Daily Sun* (August 25, 2001) is a passenger aboard a scenic flight over Grand Can- yon faces a risk of being killed via an aircraft accident that is 40 times greater than the odds faced of being killed while flying on a standard commercial air carrier between U.S. cities.

On another tack entirely, as hinted before, aircraft noise is now considered by many people to be the auditory equivalent of DDT pollution in the natural sounds of Grand Canyon wilderness. As one traveler of literary bent wrote:

> *From the river, another change is more wrenching. It floods the system with a kind of panic that in other animals induces nausea and sudden evacuation of*

the bowels; it is the descent of helicopters. Their sudden arrival in the Canyon evokes not jeers but staring. The violence is brutal, an intrusion as criminal and random as rape. When the helicopter departs, its rotor-wind walloping against the stone walls, I want to wash the sound off my skin.

Since the 1987 legislation, scenic flight helicopters no longer legally drop deep inside the Inner Canyon as they once did in the 1970s, so routinely and obnoxiously and by the dozens, as when the one above so disturbed Barry Lopez in his 1978 *Crossing Open Ground*. But when they did do this, even most lovers of helicopters honestly would admit that they and their noise were heavily intrusive—even if not the equivalent of "rape." Indeed, the noise of low, overflying aircraft within the Canyon was not merely "intrusive," in some of the most scenic places it was virtually nonstop during daylight. These flights were so irritating that by 1981, Southwestern curmudgeon Ed Abbey joked:

> *The prevalence of airplanes and helicopters in and above the Grand Canyon is a distracting, irritating nuisance which should no longer be tolerated by anybody. I look forward to the day when all river runners carry, as part of their basic equipment, a light-weight portable anti-aircraft weapon armed with heat-seeking missiles.*

Ed Abbey's grumbling in his introduction to Kim Crumbo's 1981 *A River Runner's Guide to the History of the Grand Canyon* aside, restrictive changes in flight zones and altitudes in the Canyon, as intended by the FAA to increase passenger safety, were also intended to reduce levels of aircraft noise. Was such noise a genuine issue to more people than literary curmudgeons Abbey and Lopez? Prior to 1987, Grand Canyon NPS headquarters received one thousand visitor complaints about intrusive aircraft noise. So it does seem to have been genuine.

By 1999, U.S. Congress called specifically for a "substantial restoration" of natural quiet in Grand Canyon National Park to take place by the year 2008. This "quiet" is defined as 50 percent of the Park being naturally quiet—no motor noise at all from aircraft or motor boats or vehicles—for at least 75 percent of the day (the "day" being defined as the 12 hour period from 7:00 a.m. to 7:00 p.m.). Based on these criteria, only 32 percent of the Park in 1999 was "quiet." Even so, in 1999, NPS headquarters at the Canyon received only thirty complaints of intrusive aircraft noise. So, many visitors, at least, were less aware of non-quiet despite some aircraft noise carrying twenty miles. Yet even if the flight zone rules of 1987's National Parks Overflights Act were adhered to strictly, only 41 percent of the Park on an average day would be "quiet." And on a day of peak use, only 19 percent would be. The arguments on both sides of this issue have continued up into 2011 with no firm resolution as to a compromise solution.

Aside from this degree of "quiet" or lack of it, however, the bigger question remains: By crowding more tour planes into smaller legal airspace, will safety improve? The answer to this remains unclear even in the year 2011, when the draft Environmental Impact Statement regarding air travel restrictions and natural "quiet" remains un-finalized.

This is because achieving "quiet" may be incompatible with safety and with current air tour businesses over Grand Canyon growing at 3 percent per year—up to 88,000 flights during the one year between 1997 and 1998. This computes to an average of 241 flights per day, or about 20 flights for every daylight hour of every day of the year over the Canyon. One new flight every three minutes! Predictably, in 2001 several air tour companies, some of which are based in or near Las Vegas (and elsewhere), objected to being limited to a quota of only 88,000 flights per year. When the FAA added up all flights over Grand Canyon, it became clear that merely addressing the operations of tour companies would not achieve "quiet." On average, the FAA found, one type of flight or another crossed some part of Grand Canyon during every 24/7 period every minute around the clock.

The question remains: Are tour flights a gold rush or instead are they a vital service for people who could not afford to see, or are physically unable to see, the Canyon in any other way? Thirty percent of the nearly 900,000 tourists these flights carry (for about $120 to $2000 each) are over fifty years old, and hence, by some standards anyway, they may be less capable of seeing the Canyon on foot, from muleback, or by raft. Twelve percent of air tour clients, the air tour industry claims, are handicapped in some way. Overall, however, the issue of overall flight numbers, limitations on those numbers, and the rationale of what sectors of the public actually "need" versus simply "desire" such flights remains murky.

Finally, in spring of 2000, the FAA "slapped" Grand Canyon air tour companies hard enough to leave a red bureaucratic handprint. The FAA released new rules included in FAR 93 (Subpart U), to be enforced alongside the National Parks Air Tour Management Act. This additional FAR increased the "no-fly" zone from its existing 45 percent of the park to a far more restricting 75 "no-fly" percent. The FAA also raised the ceiling under which these rules apply to a new higher altitude of 17,999 feet (up from 14,499 feet). Again, these new rules were less aimed at safety than at restoring natural quiet to the region. Even so, perhaps the most significant specific restriction in FAR 93—beyond shrinking the available airspace from 55 to 25 percent of that above the park—is the FAA rule to limit and freeze Canyon scenic flights to 48,000 per year, although a 2011 environmental impact "preferred alternative" specifies 65,000 tour flights per year. (This rule applies only to scenic flights, not to the 30,000 Canyon overflights per year by civil air transportation, NPS maintenance, repositioning and training, and Grand Canyon West.) This rule limiting commercial tour flights went into effect in May, 2000. Although the rafting industry, the mule riding industry, and backcountry use in general has been limited by the NPS under a quota system for decades to prevent overuse of the Park, the air tour industry has heretofore enjoyed limitless tourist loads in the sky. No surprise, several air tour companies discussed fighting FAR 93 in court with the claim that these new FAA regulations would drive them out of business. As of 2011, the new scenic flights *higher* daily cap is 364 flights. If spaced evenly over 12 hours, one new scenic flight takes off every two minutes.

In short, the $350-million-per-year (in 2001) Canyon air tour industry is a difficult enterprise to manage.

But for safety even more than quiet, managing it remains vital. In that more people have died flying in and around Grand Canyon during their quest (or their pilot's) to see it from the air than have died from all the other hundreds of mishaps in the Canyon combined—including falling from the rims or cliffs inside it, drowning in the Colorado, suffering fatal doses of heat or cold, being swept into oblivion by flash floods, hit by lightning or falling rocks or falling tree limbs— should remain a wake-up call.

But to be fair we should ask: Is the air fatality rate for the Grand Canyon region really all that high for an Arizona landscape? To try to answer this, we compared the air crash records for the Grand Canyon region with three other appropriate high use regions. We first compared the Grand Canyon region against that encompassing Phoenix, the sixth largest city in the United States. Phoenix not only has the busiest airport by far in Arizona and is #8 in the USA, Sky Harbor International, it also holds several other private and commercial airports. Using all data on crashes posted on the Web by the National Transportation Safety Board, available only from 1983 to 2000, the Phoenix region experienced 16 fatal aircraft crashes resulting in 21 deaths. Meanwhile, during the same time span, the Grand Canyon region experienced 28 fatal crashes, 16 of these by private pilots and 12 by commercial, resulting in 43 private passengers and pilots killed and in 82 commercial passengers and pilots killed. This grand total of 125 people killed, which does not include the 1956, 128-fatality crash of TWA and United, over the Grand Canyon region is six times higher than the fatality rate during the same time period in the much busier Phoenix airspace.

Admittedly, the Grand Canyon region is larger than Phoenix. So, in fairness, we should also ask: Is the large Grand Canyon region's overall grand total of 379 air fatalities really all that high a tally for such a large chunk of wilderness landscape? Lee H. Whittlesey reports in his exhaustive 1995 book *Death in Yellowstone* that from the time of the first fatal air crash in May 23, 1943, when a U.S. Army Air Force B-17 crashed killing 10 crew members, until 52 years later in 1995, the grand total of all air crash victims in the huge, but similar-to-Grand-Canyon-region-sized Yellowstone National Park (2,222,000 acres, 3,272 square miles) is only 20 fatalities from a mere half-dozen crashes. During the same time span, through 1995, the Grand Canyon region experienced 53 fatal air crashes resulting in 345 fatalities, a rate more than 17 times higher than that in the Yellowstone region during this 52 year span.

A skeptic might object that comparing the Grand Canyon region's airspace with that over Phoenix is unfair due to its non-scenic nature and its being a radar-controlled environment—despite Phoenix's huge air traffic load. One might further object that comparing Grand Canyon with Yellowstone is unfair too, despite the two park regions' similar sizes and similar beauty, because Yellowstone experiences fewer scenic overflights. Hence we offer one more comparison. This one is with all flights, commercial-scenic or otherwise, over the Big Island of Hawaii (4,035 square miles) including Hawaii Volcanoes National Park. This region not only poses unstable and severe weather conditions and other flight hazards that challenge pilots, during times of impressive eruptions every aircraft of all of the ten or more companies offering scenic flights are swamped with clients. Indeed these island pilots have a reputation among some Grand Canyon pilots as being "cowboys" who are "15 years behind the times" in terms of safety. How deserved is this?

To compare crash histories we again perused NTSB records. As with NTSB records for Phoenix, those posted on the Web began on January 1, 1983. We looked at the records for flights from all scenic airports on the island—Hilo, Kailua-Kona, Waikoloa, Kanuela, and the Volcano golf course. For the nearly 18-year period between January, 1983 and August, 2000, the NTSB lists a grand total of 12 fatal crashes with 27 victims killed, including those on flights ditched into the Pacific. Comparing this to the grand total of 125 people killed over the Grand Canyon region during the same recent time period reveals that Canyon air crash fatalities are nearly five times higher than those over Hawaii.

So, yes: based on far less lethal air histories of these three other large, busy, challenging regions, the overall grand total of 379 people killed in 64 air crashes in and around Grand Canyon is high.

Perhaps this is an esoteric question, but some people wonder whether such a high fatality rate is worth that slightly different scenic vista. If an aerial perspective is so important to nearly a million foreign and American tourists each year, perhaps they might be better off if, instead of flying over the Canyon, they spent less money and simply bought the video and viewed its aerial footage. No one has been killed (so far) while watching a Grand Canyon video.

Significantly, few people who have been on the ground in Grand Canyon would agree that staring at the Canyon landscape from the window of a plane equals the experience of spending a few hours visiting it on foot. Indeed, many on-foot visitors to the Canyon have experienced profound revelations, even life-changing ones. This is not to say that flying a few thousand feet above the rims and over the Canyon does not offer one hell of a view. It does. That's why 25 percent of all scenic air tours in the United States are ones that fly over Grand Canyon. But in that it also is the one type of look that is most likely to kill, it also seems a far more risky view than any other. As one veteran Grand Canyon NPS/SAR pilot with 25 years in residence admitted, "I've often thought that the advertising phrase 'the trip/flight/ view of a lifetime' was, sadly, too often true."

While these final words on air fatalities may be taken as cynical to the American dream of making a buck at every opportunity, they do address a very important issue. One of lives or deaths. No question exists that the greatest single cause of traumatic human deaths in Grand Canyon has been due—up until the present— to crashing while flying over or near it for the purpose of an "easy" viewing of it. But what about that important question of whether the new, more restrictive flight rules contained in Safety Recommendation A-87-91, Public Law 100-91, and in Special Federal Aviation Regulation (SFAR) 50-2 of 1987 actually improved air safety over and adjacent to Grand Canyon once they went into effect in 1988? A final look at Table 6–A reveals that, while new FAA regulations and decisions may have helped reduce noise, the "safer" decade from 1988 to 2003 still saw seven more crashes of commercial scenic tour flights within and adjacent to Grand Canyon. These seven commercial crashes killed 53 more people. Meanwhile, from 1988-2006 a dozen more private pilots crashed in or near the Canyon, killing 32 more people. This total of 85 fatalities for the post SFAR 50-2 years seems no lower statistically than the average air casualty rates during the previous three decades before SFAR 50-2 went into effect though, admittedly, more scenic flights flew, and did so in less airspace, during these later years.

A look at Table 6-A will reveal a somewhat hopeful trend that since 2003 to 2011 no one else has been killed on a commercial scenic flight. Still, the question of what safety repercussions will result next from the FAA's year 2000 FAR 93, which will crowd those same 48,000–65,000 scenic flights per year into only 25 percent of the airspace over Grand Canyon, remains open.

Again, when all types of flights—scenic tour, private pilot, NPS maintenance and SAR, Coconino County DPS or Sheriff, U.S. military, and commercial passenger and freight transport—are considered, it turns out that the airspace above Grand Canyon on an average 24-hour daily basis for years on end is penetrated by some type of overflight at least every minute! Making the Canyon below this level of traffic "quiet" is one big challenge. Making the airspace itself safe is a bigger one.

Because the blizzard of statistics we blasted at you in this chapter may produce an effect of numbness regarding the deep impact such crashes can produce in peoples' lives, we now offer you a poignant parting story....

"Would you marry me?"

Milena Stanoycheva, age 26, stared down at the ring Albert Glenn Howle now tried to fit onto the ring finger of her right (= wrong) hand. The stunningly gorgeous Bulgarian tennis player wrestled for the right words in English to answer him. She finally settled on a word to match Glenn Howle's choice.

"I would," Milena said.

Howle had been head over heels about the 5' 11" brunette, whose extreme intelligence and beauty and essential kindness had captured him almost immediately. Now more than two years later, standing in a Southwestern canyon, he had finally popped the question. Yet, after all his careful planning, he somehow managed to mess up both the wording of his proposal and the choice of the brunette's right hand for her engagement ring.

Glenn, a successful entrepreneur, had tried to show Milena America for the last two years during their extended courtship. Milena had worked so hard and such long hours in Bulgaria on her high school and university studies and during her focus on tennis that she had been denied the normal "worldly" education most people take for granted. Milena was delighted at America, taking in each new wonder as if a child.

When Glenn had driven Milena to Las Vegas to meet his friends and to propose to Milena, his friend's wife had said: "He's the most romantic man I've ever seen in my life."

After proposing and accepting, Howle and Milena drove north to Reno to visit his father, a psychiatrist who worked there. The lovebirds were surprised when Milena's best friend and tennis team mate Ania Dolinska Warszawa, age 22, of Poland flew in to join them. There the couple bought a "perfect" wedding gown.

Glenn's father Jerry A. Howle added a surprise: He would pilot the four of them on a sight-seeing flight over Grand Canyon before flying them to Las Vegas where they were to be married the next day. Jerry owned a single engine, "amateur-built" experimental plane, a Bachman Lancair IV-P (N299SD).

Glenn and Milena and Ania climbed aboard.

At about 5:30 p.m. that day a small group of visitors who had driven two dusty and rattling hours off the pavement to enjoy the famous sheer-walled view of the Colorado River near Lava Falls from Tuweep (a.k.a. Toroweap) stood and gazed at a flaming sunset. They next spotted Jerry Howle's Lancair flying northwest toward Las Vegas.

The aircraft they watched, however, was descending steeply from 16,000 feet.

With its engine gearing up ("revving high") then slowing down repeatedly and "spinning or moving in some strange way", the Lancair plowed into the bedrock before their eyes high on the Hualapai Indian Nation side (south) of the river. The Lancair disintegrated on impact and burned in a mushroom cloud. Father and son, lovers, and two best friends all died on impact. The National Transportation Safety Board could not figure out what had gone wrong.

Several days later Jessica Curlee, Glenn's mother and Milena's future mother in law, received a small package mailed from Grand Canyon by Milena. It contained a packet of seeds labeled "Flowers of the Grand Canyon." On the packet's other side Milena had written: "I know flowers is [sic] a hobby of yours and maybe sometimes we can experience this together.

Love, Milena and Glenn."

Table 6–A. FATAL AIR TRAFFIC CRASHES IN GRAND CANYON AND ON ITS ADJACENT PLATEAUS. Codes for each category of flight are as follows: "C" designates a commercial flight; "P" designates a private flight; "Ca" designates a crash within the Canyon; "Pl" designates a crash on the plateaus or rims near the Canyon. Fatality totals for each crash within the Canyon are underlined. Fatality totals for air crashes atop the plateaus are not underlined. Probable cause(s) for crashes are discussed in "Accident Details;" symbols (pe) indicate "pilot error" and (ppe) indicate "possible pilot error."

Name, age	# Killed	Date	Location	Accident Details

C/Ca

United Airlines #718 (58) **128** June 30, 1956   Chuar Butte & Temple Butte

TransWorld Airlines #2 (70)   *TWA Super Constellation Flight 2 entered the vertical airspace of UA DC-7 Flight #718 at 21,000 feet. Both were bound east out of LAX on a reasonably clear day dotted with cumulonimbus clouds. Pilots of both aircraft were 5 miles and 25 miles off plotted course, respectively, to purposely fly over Grand Canyon. The mid-air collision—both aircraft flew in the blind spots of each other—was witnessed from ground when the DC-7 overtook and collided with the Super Constellation. The DC-7's left wing sliced off the Super Connie's tail. Both aircraft crashed in the Canyon. All 128 aboard were killed. This crash was the worst commercial, civilian air line disaster in history until 1960. (see text). Arizona Daily Sun, June 30, 1956; June 30, 1971; June 29, 1986; June 30, 1996. LIFE, April 29, 1957. Farabee, C. R. "B", Jr. 1998 & 2005. Death, Daring and Disaster: Search and Rescue in the National Parks.* **(pe) x 2.**

United Airlines DC-7, Flight #718 Crew & Passengers:

Captain Robert Shirley, 48   Flight Engineer Girardo Fiore, 39
Flight Attendant Nancy Lou Kemnitz   Flight Attendant Margaret Ann Shoudt
First Officer Robert W. Harms, 36

John A. Barry, Lt. Col. C.E.A.U.S.   Christopher Balsat
Phyllis G. Berman, 45   Rosemary Bishop
Stephen Bishop, 3 mo.   Gertrude Coyne Book, 62
Frank C. Caple   M. Barry Carlton
Carol Jean Church, 6   Frank H. Clark, 46
L. David Cook, Jr.   Elizabeth Crider
Jeffrey Crider, 5   Elizabeth Francis Doering, 63
Thomas W. Doyle, First Lt.   Walter M. Fuchs, 75
Stella Blum Fuchs   Noel Gottesman, 30
Jack Groshans   James Hadfield
Lillian Ruth Hahn   Eugene B. Hoffman, 26
Russell Charles Huber   Frances Robert Johlie II, 31
Donald F. Kiel, 46   Dee D. Kovack
Ted M. Kubineck, 37   R.O. Lasby
Sally Lou Laughlin   Joseph M. Lewis, Jr., Lt. U.S.M.C.
Theodore Henry Lyman   Carl G. Matland, 39
Dwight B. Mims   John J. Muldoon
Gerald Murchison, 51   Floyd A. Nixon
Elsie W. Osterbock, 60   Hugo Pekruhn, 80
John George Reba, Lt. U.S.N.R.   Alexander Eugene Rosenblatt

Russell A. Shield, 31
Fred Staeckler, 11
J.P. Tobian, Jr. Captain, U.S.M.C.
Stanley Jerome Weiss
Albert C. Widdifield, 50
Donald L. Winings, 32
John E. Yeager

Carl J. Snyder, 59
Thomas J. Sulpizio, 30
Albert Vogt
Peter White, 15
Roberta E. Wilde
Weslau G. Wright

TWA Lockheed L-1049 Super Constellation, Flight #2 Crew & Passengers:

Captain Jack Silvetus Gandy, 42 (pilot)
Co-Pilot James H. Kitner, 31
Flight Engineer Forrest Dean Breyfogle, 37

Flight Attendant Tracine Elizabeth
　Armbruster, 29
Flight Attendant Beth Ellis Davis, 24

Harry Harvey Allen
Robert Vernon Beatty
Stephen Robert Bishop
Esther Ellen Braughton, 9
Lois Klein Brock
Lawrence Zay Chatten
Chester Arnold Crewse
Selma Louise Davis
Donald Lloyd Elentie
Virginia Elizabeth Goppert
Mildred Rogene Crick Hat
Janice Mae Heis
James Joseph Jang
Sidney Roland Joslin
Linda JoAnn Kite
Peachie Marie Kite
Lois Marie Laxton
Mary Lytle
Howard John Maag, infant
Donald K. MacBain
Rosalie Maude McClenny
Andrew Jackson Nasalroad
Marietta Thompson Noel
Richard Darling Payne
Monica Jean Payne
Robert Farley Perisho
Neal Alan Power
James Henry Ritner
David Karn Robinson
Robert Earnest Sanders
Robert Frank Sontag
Bessie Whitmen
Elizabeth May Young

Thomas Edward Ashton, Jr.
Martha Ann Beck
Connie June Braughton, 6
Linda Kay Braughton
Lillian Estelle Carple
Sally Ann Cressman
Helen Colleen Crewse
Robert Earl DeLonge
Mrs. A. Evans
Janice Tracy Haas
William Wallace Hatcher
Harry Robinson Holman
Wayne Gardner Jeffrey
Joseph James Kite
Sharon Marie Kite
Marie Jane Klemp
Michael Anthony Laxton
Claire M. Maag
John Otto Maag
William H. Markey, Jr.
Alice Emma Meyer
R. Nelson
Richard Curtis Noel
John Walker Payne
Richard Michael Payne
Dennis Joseph Phelan
Edward Merrill Reaves
Jeanette Karn Robinson
Geoffry Brian Robinson
Esther Fair Sharp
Gloria Kathleen Gipson Townsend
Carolyn Ruth Wiley

C/Ca

Jack Pittman, (pilot)　　①　April 12, 1966　　"The Box," 4 miles N of Phantom Ranch
A Bell G3B helicopter used for cross-canyon pipeline construction by the Halvorson-Lents Construction Company of Seattle crashed and burned due to unknown causes. Pittman of Orange (Los Angeles), California was the sole casualty among the 3 aboard. Arizona

Daily Sun, *April 12, 1967*. Arizona Republic, *April 13, 1966*.

C/Ca

Tom Rumore, 24 (pilot) ⑦ July 26, 1967   10 miles E of Village at "Duck on the
Charles Wilhelm, 38   Rock," 200 feet below the rim
John Wilhelm, 12   *A Grand Canyon Airlines scenic flight in a single piston-engine,*
Steven Wilhelm, 8   *Comanche Six (noted elsewhere as a Piper Cherokee 6) crashed*
Carolyn Wilhelm, 34   *into a cliff during "relatively clear" weather due to unknown*
Herbert Roscoe, 42   *causes (possible mechanical failure) and burned. Pilot Rumore*
Scott Roscoe, 17   *was from Tucson. The Wilhelm family was from Washington*
    Courthouse, Ohio. The Roscoes were from Suffern, New York.
    The survivors of the two victim-families sued for "negligent and
    careless management." Arizona Daily Sun, *July 27, 1967.* Arizona
    Republic, *July 28, 1967.* **(ppe)**

P/Pl

Stephen Eugene Pritchard, ⑤ November 1, 1967   ½ mile W of Grand Canyon Airport
   27 (pilot)   *The NTSB concluded the pilot misjudged his altitude while circling*
Carol L. Pritchard, 27   *his piston-powered Cessna Skylane (N3555Y) in a landing pattern*
Patricia A. Burnes, 28   *at 8:50 p.m. (after dark), then crashed, killing his Fort Worth, Texas*
Jeffrey Pritchard, 4   *family and "hitchhiker" Burnes.* Arizona Daily Sun, *November 2,*
Stephanie Pritchard, 19 mo.   *1967.* Arizona Republic, *December, 1967.* **(pe)**

P/Ca

Paul McDonald, 24 (pilot) ④ May 6, 1969   Western Grand Canyon
Mrs. Paul McDonald   *Pilot McDonald had 80 hours of flight time. He had not filed a*
David Wilson, 31   *flight plan. He flew his piston-powered Cessna 172 out of Las Vegas*
Mrs. David Wilson   *and vanished short of Kingman. All 4 aboard were from Redwood*
    City, California. Arizona Daily Sun, *May 8, 1969.* Arizona
    Republic, *May 7, 1969.* **(pe)**

P/Pl

Wilfred Dugan, (pilot) ② July 5, 1969   North Rim 18 miles SW of Jacob Lake
Mrs. Wilfred Dugan   *Piston-powered Piper Cherokee Arrow crashed and burned due*
    to unknown causes. The Dugans aboard were from California.
    Arizona Republic, *July 6, 1969.*

C/Ca

Joe E. Savage, Jr., 31 (pilot) ② July 29, 1969   Yaki Point
James D. Savage, 18   *As the Bell 206 Helicopter took off, its sling load of fuel caught in a*
    ground obstruction. The cable failed to disengage and the aircraft
    was yanked to the ground and caught fire, killing both brothers of
    Lake Whitney, Texas hired for cross-canyon pipeline construction.
    Arizona Daily Sun, *August 6, 1970.* Arizona Republic, *July 30,*
    1969. **(pe)**

C/Pl

John Harper, 29 (pilot) ③ July 30, 1969   3 miles S of Grand Canyon Village
Richard H. Hamblin, 24   *The Scenic Bell 47G Jet Ranger helicopter run by Grand Canyon*
Wayne W. Wright, 20   *Helicopters crashed due to one engine failing during final approach*
    to the airport and burned. Hamblin and Wright were cousins from
    Silver Spring, Maryland. Arizona Daily Sun, *July 31 & August 1,*
    1969 & August 6, 1970.

C/Ca

Arthur Ranger, 45 (pilot) ① December 15, 1969　Along Bright Angel Creek
A Halverson-Lent Construction Company pipeline construction helicopter crashed in Bright Angel Canyon when a cable used to haul pipe was left dangling and became entangled in the tail rotor. Pilot Ranger of Silver City, New Mexico was the sole casualty. Arizona Daily Sun, *December 16, 1969.* Arizona Republic, *December 16 & 17, 1969.*

C/Pl

Russ Marsh, 51 (pilot)　⑥ March 26, 1970　near Wolf Hole, Mojave County
Frederich Meir　　　　*The Grand Canyon Airlines flight, a piston-powered Piper Chero-*
Helga Grueger　　　　*kee 6 crashed, the NTSB concluded, due to the pilot's decision to*
Karl Schwartz　　　　*continue "VFR (visual flight rules) flight into adverse weather"*
Klauss Spann　　　　*combined with pilot "spatial disorientation." The flight took off*
Austrian stewardess　　*during a "budding snowstorm" and went missing for four months. It was found 50 miles north of pilot Marsh's planned route with the five European passengers long dead.* Arizona Daily Sun, *March 30, 1970.* **(pe)**

P/Pl

Merrill Shepro, (pilot)　⑤ April 16, 1971　1 mile S of Grand Canyon Airport
Margaret C. Nejdl　　　*Twin-engine, piston Beechcraft, 257 pounds overweight, crashed*
William Vickers　　　　*shortly after take-off. NTSB attributed cause to "inadequate preflight*
Martin Rutsay　　　　*planning by the pilot." The victims were from Riverside, Oak Park,*
Robert Kostro　　　　*and Legrange, Illinois.* Arizona Daily Sun, *April 17, 1971.* **(pe)**

C/Ca

Wayne Leeth, 47 (pilot) ⑩ October 16, 1971　5,500–6,000 feet in Parashant Wash,
James E. Allen, Jr., 60　　　　　　　　　　15 miles S of Mt. Trumbull
Florence Allen　　　　*This Scenic Airlines' twin-engine, piston Cessna 402 tour flight flew*
Dr. R. Lynch　　　　*into an early winter snowstorm with "clouds down to the ground"*
Mrs R. Lynch　　　　*and crashed. Pilot Leeth of Las Vegas, Nevada had flown 600 or 700*
Walter Pilgram　　　*previous trips over Grand Canyon. NTSB concluded no structural*
Paul Haack　　　　*problem with the Cessna. Instead the crash was due to the pilot's*
Mrs. Paul Haack　　*error of having flown too far into the storm.* Arizona Daily Sun,
P. Dosmond　　　　*October 18, 1971.* **(pe)**
Mrs. P. Dosmond

P/Pl

Priscilla Diane Ryan, 29　② July 11, 1974　immediately at the end of Grand
Ibey Teresa Spurlock, 20　　　　　　　　　Canyon Airport Runway
The piston-powered Piper Cherokee 150's pilot (Thomas Ryan) encountered difficulty on take-off due to his apparently overloaded plane. He tried to turn around, stalled, and crashed, augering in. The pilot plus two other passengers survived. The fatal victims were from Escondido and San Diego, California. Arizona Daily Sun, *July 12, 1974. Incident report #74-3560* **(pe)**

P/Ca

Curtis V. Gwynne, 42　④ January11, 1975　Dragon Creek, 1,600 feet below the North
  (pilot)　　　　　　　　　　　　　　　　Rim

Patrizia Feretti, 20
Renata Feretti, 41
Nicola Feretti, 17

The rented piston-powered Cessna 182 crashed during windy but clear weather while the pilot attempted to turn inside a narrow section of canyon and struck a wall. All 4 aboard were from Bergamo, Italy. Arizona Republic, *January 14, 1975. Incident report #75-0072* (**pe**)

P/Ca
Edward E. Sedwich, 33 (pilot)
Cecil C. Allen, 40
Janet Allen, 33

(3) August 3, 1975   South Canyon, a side canyon in Marble Canyon
Piper Arrow (piston-powered) crashed due to unknown causes. Incident report #75-4798 (**ppe**)

P/Pl
Phillip Creese, 59 (pilot)
Patricia Creese, 52

(2) April 23, 1976   Old Grand Canyon Airport
The cause of the crash (auguring in at 45 degrees and upside down) of this twin, piston-engine Beechcraft was unknown, but it may have been mechanical failure. Pilot Creese attempted to land but seemed to have decided to abort his landing. The aircraft was witnessed to pull sharply up, stall, then fall. The Creeses were from Seal Beach, California. Arizona Daily Sun, *April 26, 1976. Incident report #76-1072*

P/Pl
Bonnie Watts, 28

(1) September 21, 1976   Old Grand Canyon Airport
Four people in a single-engine (piston-powered) Cherokee Warrior were on approach to the airport when the pilot over-corrected for an off-approach position. The plane stalled and crashed. Three of the 4 aboard survived. Watts was from Smithfield, Utah. Arizona Daily Sun, *September 22, 1976. Incident report #76-6905* (**pe**)

C/Pl
Saax Bradbury, 33

(1) November 13, 1976   ½ mile S of Park south entry station
Four people were aboard a Beechcraft Muscateer (piston-powered) when its carburetor iced up on take-off. Three people survived. Bradbury of New York City died. Arizona Daily Sun, *November 15, 1976. Incident report #76-7781* (**ppe**)

P/Pl
George Lutteum, 50 (pilot)
Henry Lutteum, 20
Lois Jean Garcia, 46
Stephen Eisel, 16
Michael Eisel, 7

(5) June 25, 1977   6 miles S of Hermit's Rest
This rented twin-engine Piper Navajo (piston-powered) lost one engine and crashed, flipped over, and exploded in flames. Four survivors fled before the plane exploded. The victims all were from California. Arizona Daily Sun, *June 27, 1977. Incident report #77-3210*

P/Ca
Arthur D. Meyers, 28 (pilot)
Waldo C. Cross, 33
Debra R. Nelson, 26

(3) June 28, 1978   near Cape Royal
Meyers of Florence, Colorado tried to fly his Cessna 170 (piston-powered) from the North to South Rim but ran dry of fuel. He apparently tried to emergency land on a nearby mesa but crashed into the side of a "mountain." Cross was from Lakewood, and Nelson of Colorado Springs. (see text) Arizona Daily Sun, *June 29, 1978. Incident report #78-3919* (**pe**)

P/Pl

Nancy R. Day, 39   (2) July 4, 1978   North Rim
William C. Post, 48   *This piston-powered Cessna 195 was overweight and crashed due to failure of pilot to compensate for high altitude take-off. Incident report #78-4181* (**pe**)

P/Pl

Ernest P. Buntz, 42   (3) December 4, 1978   South Rim
   (pilot)   *Pilot Buntz radioed that his aircraft was "icing up," then crashed.*
June Buntz, spouse of pilot   (**pe**)
Ferdinand E. Buntz, elderly

P/Pl

no fatality yet   (0) February 12, 1979   House Rock
    Herbert and Anna Redd of Salt Lake City, Utah crash-landed their 1967 Piper Cherokee 140 in 2 feet of crusty snow and managed not only to walk away from the crash with minor injuries but also have dinner at El Tovar that night. The Redds would return 2 years later with Herbert piloting again, this time flying a Piper Colt, and crash again. In upper Nankoweap fatally. Incident report #79-0453

C/Pl

none   (0) November 16, 1979   2 miles N of Grand Canyon Airport and
                       100 yards W of Highway 64
    A Nevada Airlines Martin 404 crashed with 44 passengers and crew aboard. The plane burst into flames promptly suppressed by tankers. All 44 persons aboard escaped via hatches and windows. Paramedics cleared each passenger. This incident involved more passengers aboard than any other Grand Canyon aircraft crash except for the biggest one in 1956, but without fatalities. Incident report #79-6291

P/Ca

Lloyd Weir, 59 (pilot)   (4) February 19, 1980   West side of Powell Plateau
Mary Wier, 58   *Leonard Grayson's piston-powered Cessna (N2350R) crashed due to*
Leonard Grayson, 61   *possible icing. Two witnesses in the Canyon noted hearing and seeing*
Lucy Grayson, 56   *it as it descended and circled in overcast and heavy rain and snow conditions. The Cessna crashed into the ground and accordioned. All four aboard (from Montana) were killed on impact. Arizona Daily Sun, February 28, 1980. Incident report #80-0415* (**ppe**)

C/Pl

Richard T. Mierhouse, 33 (8) July 21, 1980   near Red Butte, 2.5 miles S of Grand
   (pilot/Las Vegas)   Canyon Airport
William Calhoun, 31   *A Scenic Airlines Cessna 404 twin, piston-engine sight-seeing*
M. Parab   *tour plane crashed shortly after takeoff and burned, killing the*
D. Parab   *pilot, mechanic Calhoun of Grand Canyon, and all passengers*
L. M. Parab   *(from Nigeria and Japan). Investigation revealed intake of metal*
B. M. Parab   *fragments into left engine from earlier error in maintenance/repair.*
Haroko Miazawa   *(see text) Arizona Daily Sun, July 22 & 25, 1980. Incident report*
Sawaka Minato   *#80-2626*

P/Ca

Gregory A. Mathes, 26 ⑥ January 12, 1981   5 miles SE of Fraziers Well (S of Havasupai
(pilot)   Canyon)
Daniel Bolware, 18   *Pilot Mathes radioed that single-engine (piston) BE-36 Beechcraft*
(co-pilot)   *Bonanza was icing up badly. Next he crashed into a 200-foot-deep*
Michael Bailey, 39   *canyon, a tributary of Havasu, while seeking a lower elevation less*
John Bailey, 17   *prone to icing.* Arizona Daily Sun, *January 15, 1981.* (pe)
Mark Bailey, 15
Matthew Bailey, 11

P/Ca

Herbert Redd, 51 (pilot) ② March 1, 1981   upper Nankoweap Canyon/Brady Peak (?)
Anna Redd, 51

*Redd, with 500 hours of flight time, reported his Piper Colt (piston-
powered) had trouble 15 miles south of Page while heading into bad
weather, including snow. The Piper crashed about 50 miles farther
south. This was the Redds' second crash in the Canyon Area. The
Salt Lake City, Utah couple had survived their first one, crash landing a Piper Cherokee 140 into 2 feet of snow in the buffalo range
in House Rock Valley 2 years earlier.* Arizona Daily Sun, *March 3,
1981.* Tucson Daily Citizen, *March 6, 1981. Incident report #81-
0380* (pe)

C/Ca

Joseph Horace Baldwin, 68 ① May 24, 1981   below Horseshoe Mesa, 3,000 feet below
                                                South Rim, 12 miles E of Village
*The pilot of Grand Canyon Airlines scenic flight Cessna T207 with
7 passengers aboard lost its only engine (piston-powered) and
crash-landed. Six were injured. Baldwin of Romford, Essex, England, however, had unclipped his seatbelt to turn around to inform
his deaf sister seated behind him that the plane was going to make
an emergency landing. The plane slammed atop the inner Canyon
before he re-buckled.* Arizona Daily Sun, *May 25, 1981.*

P/Pl

Barton T. Watson, 47   ⑥ August 21, 1981   1.5 miles W of Desert View Ranger Station
(pilot)   on East Rim Drive
Doris Watson, 43   *The single-engine (piston-powered) Piper Lancair "shredded"*
James R. Brady, 40   *during a crash landing into trees due to unknown causes. Incident*
Kelsey Ann Brady, 39   *report #81-2634*
Deanne Hulett, 35
Larry E. Hulett, 38

C/Ca

Glenn Miller (pilot)   ③ April 17, 1982   Lees Ferry
Diane Doherty, 27   *Miller of Santa Barbara, California piloted the Hughes 500 helicop-*
Frank Novak, 49   *ter 30 feet above the river at Lees Ferry with an EMI Productions
TV crew from Tucson, Arizona and Los Angeles, California aboard.
At high speed the airship impacted its rotor with a tram cable while
filming a CBS adventure film "American Eagle." The aircraft disin-
tegrated as it skipped for nearly 1,000 feet across the water. A third
passenger, Laurie Lee Gere of Tarzana, California, was rescued by*

river guide Dale Whitmore. (see text) Arizona Republic, April, 19 & 20, 1982. **(pe)**

P/Ca

Bob Wakeman, 60 (pilot) ③ August 5, 1983   Western Grand Canyon
James Huffman, 41   *Wakeman's Mooney 231 turbo (piston-powered) aircraft vanished*
Grant Huffman, 5   *during his flight plan to overfly the Colorado River over Western Grand Canyon.*

C/Ca

Wallace S. Gustavson, Jr., ⑩August 17, 1983   below South Rim near River Mile 209
  48 (pilot)   *This Las Vegas Airlines' scenic charter in twin-engine (piston-*
Enrico Annibali, 49   *powered) Piper Navajo Chieftain crashed over the Hualapai*
Maria-Vittoria Magnani, 48   *Reservation during a "severe" thunderstorm then "disintegrated*
Giancarlo Annibali, 15   *and burned" 70 feet below the top of a Canyon wall at the 5,800-*
Luciano Annibali, 45   *foot contour. The tourists aboard were from Italy. (see text) Arizona*
Guliana Ranieri, 44   *Daily Sun, August 22, 1983. Arizona Republic, August 18 &19,*
Francesca Annibali, 16   *1983. Incident report #83-2718* **(pe)**
Federica Annibali, 13
Stefano Annibali, 22
Daniele Vernava, 19

C/Ca

Charles L. Houser, 50   ① December 8, 1983   River Mile 166
    Two Bureau of Land Management officials were illegally (by breaking Federal regulations) joy riding down the Colorado River corridor at Mile 166, less than 30 feet above the water. The Bell-206 helicopter's rotor impacted a tram cable at a sedimentology research site and slowly sank. The pilot and other passenger were rescued by researchers. Houser died of delayed-drowning several days later. (see text) Incident report #83-4003 **(pe)**

C/Ca

David Bauer, 23 (pilot) ③ August 1, 1984   Grand Wash Cliffs
Richard E. Reed, 50   *An unknown possible mechanical problem or pilot error (?) caused*
Linda Sue Reed, 38   *the impact of scenic tour Fairchild-Hiller FH1100 helicopter with the treetops then the cliff. Of the Reeds' (of Scottsdale, Arizona) two sons, Bryan, age 12, suffered serious injuries and remained at the crash site. Kevin, a 14-year-old Boy Scout with a broken wrist and facial injuries, walked six miles from the site of the Boulder City Bauer Aviation crash, overnight, to Meadview to seek help.* Arizona Daily Sun, *August 1 &2 , 1984.* Arizona Republic, *August 1 & 2, 1984.* **(ppe)**

P/Pl

Davis Baumann, 42 (pilot)④ December 15, 1984   near Dog Lake on North Rim
Michael Corey, 23   *This piston-powered Mooney single-engine plane developed*
Debra Jean Radez, 21   *problems during a heavy snowstorm. Pilot Baumann reported the*
Peter Van Horn, 25   *plane "was icing up and going down". The plane disintegrated upon impact.* **(pe)**

C/Ca

Don Nasca, 50 (pilot)   (2)   July 12, 1985   Navajo Bridge, Marble Canyon
Claudio Cassinelli, 47   *During a film shoot for the Italian science fiction movie,* Hands
of Stone, *actor Cassinelli of Bologna was simulating machine gun
fire from the aircraft at a "hero" hanging from Navajo Bridge.
Nasca rose too high from under the bridge and allowed his rotor
blades to hit it. His Bell 206 (?) Jet Ranger helicopter plunged 470
feet into the Colorado River and sank upside-down 12 feet, 20 feet
from shore. (see text)* Arizona Daily Sun, *July 14, 1985.* Arizona
Republic, *July 13, 1985. Incident report #85-2057* (**pe**)

P/Ca

Willard K. Martin, 55 (pilot) (2) September 17, 1985   Crazy Jug Canyon near North Rim
Eric Martin, 25   *Martin's vintage piston-powered 1940s Piper Cub crashed after
clipping off a wing tip on a cliff face. The aircraft's low altitude (flying within the Canyon) was due to unknown causes. Both persons
aboard (from Oregon) were killed.* Arizona Daily Sun, *September
25 & October 3, 1985.* Arizona Republic, *October 1, 1985. Incident
report #85-3612* (**pe**)

P/Pl

Ben Blecher, 34 (pilot)   (3)   January 8, 1986   ¼ mile W of Grand Canyon Airport
Steven C. Tabbert, 41   *Rented piston-powered Cessna 172 with three Michigan men
Jim Elton Bobinson, 49   aboard vanished after refueling at Grand Canyon Airport and
taking off just after nightfall and after the airport tower had closed.
Arizona Civil Air Patrol searchers found the Cessna 5 days later
almost hidden, having crashed nearby in heavy timber and rough
terrain. The aircraft had crashed less than a minute after takeoff in
the dark.* Arizona Daily Sun, *January 15, 1986.* (**ppe**)

C/Ca

Bruce Grubb, 27 (pilot)   (20)   June 18, 1986   Tuna Canyon, River Mile 99.5
James Ingraham, 27 (pilot)   *A Grand Canyon Airlines' gas-turbine-powered DeHavilland
Mr. G. Tholenaars   Twin-Otter on scenic tour with 18 passengers apparently entered
Mrs. H. Bek   the ceiling of the informal conventional airspace (between 6,401–
Mrs. K. Mulder   6,613 feet) of Helitech, Inc. Bell 206 Jet Ranger helicopter carrying
Mrs. K. Vandeelen   4 passengers—both aircraft were flying in the blind spots of each
Mr. D. Feiters   other. Midair collision killed all 25 people—from 4 nations plus the
Mrs. D. Feiters   USA—aboard. The Schlegels of Switzerland had been married only
Mr. Kleinjans   18 days and were on their honeymoon. The combined law suits to-
Mrs. Kempin   taled about $12 million paid by insurance companies, who in turn
Heinz Schlegel   sued the Federal government and the Park for negligently managing
Beatrix Schlegel   its air space. (see text)* Arizona Daily Sun, *June 19, 21 & 23, 1986
Mr. Pigi   & March 18, 1987.* Arizona Republic, *June 28, 1986 & January
Mrs. Pigi   6, 1990. Farabee, C. R. "B", Jr. 1998 & 2005.* Death, Daring and
Mrs. Pakkert   Disaster: Search and Rescue in the National Parks. *Thybony, S.
Mrs. L. Meissner   1997.* Burntwater. *Incident report #86-1512* (**pe**)
Marcus Christian
Katrina Christian
Sherry Goss
Jay Whittenburg

C/Ca

John Thybony, 39 (pilot) ⑤ June 18, 1986   Tuna Canyon, River Mile 99.5
Rudolph Held   (see previous crash)
Wolfgang Banmann
Wern Geibold
Henietta Pearl

P/Ca

Don D. Safely, 34 (pilot) ② August 14, 1986   River Mile 19
Gentry D. Safely, 4   *Pilot Safely (a.k.a. "Smedley") of Page, Arizona "buzzed" a rafting*
party at low elevation in his vintage 1948 piston-powered Luscomb
monoplane to "wave his wings." As he tried to pull up into a turn,
his plane stalled and fell into the Colorado upstream of the rafters.
Don drowned inside the plane 30–85 feet deep (found later via
sonar). His son drowned in the river and was found 3 months
later, 32 miles downstream. Arizona Daily Sun, *August 25, 26 &*
November 11 & 21, 1986. Incident report #86-2659 **(pe)**

P/Pl

Edward Vernon Brown, ② August 24, 1986   Grand Canyon Airport
   Jr., 42   *Douglas Pound piloting a single-engine piston-powered Cessna 172*
Aaron Brown, 14   *carrying four persons crashed on take-off. He and his son survived.*

P/Pl

Renato Ricci, 47 (pilot) ④ November 11, 1987   ½ mile S of Grand Canyon Airport
Glenda Jewel Ricci, 43   *Trying to make emergency landing due to engine troubles during*
Paul William Lasley, 46   *an attempted landing, the single-engine, piston-powered Mooney*
Goldie Ruth Lasley, 45   *aircraft struck a tree short of the runway and crashed but did not*
burn. All 4 victims were from Campbell, California. Arizona Daily
Sun, *November 16, 1987.*

P/Ca

Charles Frederick Arnold, ② May 17, 1988   Vista Encantadora 100 feet from rim
   Jr., 62   *The Cessna 182 was under full piston power, but at very low alti-*
Wesley Frensdorff, 61   *tude 500 feet below FAA minimum altitude. At 10:00 p.m. (after*
dark), it crashed through treetops onto the rim at full speed at 8,400
feet due to unknown causes. Both victims were from Tucson, Ari-
zona. Arizona Daily Sun, *May 19, 1988.* Williams-Grand Canyon
News, *May 26, 1988.* Arizona Republic, *May 19, 1988. Incident*
report #88-1088.

P/Pl

John C. Walker, 23 (pilot) ④ September 4, 1988   Grand Canyon Airport
Christopher Watson, 23   *After not being able to find a motel room near the park, private*
Jeff D. Yardman, 25   *pilot Walker took off at night "anxious to get home." Hours earlier*
Charles Sivils, 23   *this plane had been plagued by engine power failures. On this last*
take-off, Walker stalled his still heavily loaded, piston-powered
Cessna 172, 200 feet above the runway. It crashed, killing all four
aboard. (see text) Arizona Republic, *September 5, 1988.* **(pe)**

C/Pl

Keith Crosson, 42 (co-pilot) ⑩ September 27, 1989 Grand Canyon Airport
William Welch, 47 (pilot)
Lorraine Lou Murphy, 75
Joyce Anne Jones, 52
Barbara Ann Marchand, 61
Eugenia Sheehan, 78
John Sutton, 65
Donna Sutton, 63
Helen Zuckerman, 64
unnamed Scottish woman

The Grand Canyon Airlines gas-turbine-powered DeHavilland DHC-6 Twin-Otter scenic tour airplane crashed as "co-pilot" lost control during his landing attempt. FAA concluded "pilot error" by co-pilot had "botched the landing." Both pilots and 8 passengers were killed. Eleven more were injured as several seatbelts failed. During its first impact with the runway, the aircraft sustained damage to the right wingtip, possibly making control of plane problematic. Rescuers required more than an hour to remove trapped victims. Survivors sued for damages in excess of $9.3 million. (see text) Arizona Republic, *September 29, 1989. Incident report #89-4633* (**pe**)

P/Pl

Chris Jones, 22 (pilot) ④ February 16, 1991 12 miles SW of Jacob Lake, on the Kaibab
Tim Jones, 21 Plateau, north of Grand Canyon near
Terry Dewayne Williams, 21 Kaibab National Forest
David Ross Bennett, 21

During a flight from Bryce Canyon, Utah, to Grand Canyon, the single-engine, piston-powered Piper Archer II encountered large pockets of bad winter weather. Radar tracking reports indicate the aircraft made several abrupt and drastic course changes, including about-faces, and attained a surprisingly high altitude of 13,000 feet. An onboard video camera recorded full cloud-cover weather, leading to the suspicion that the heavily loaded plane iced up. The aircraft ultimately went into a flat spin, in a possible emergency landing or fuel-less descent, and "pancaked" into the ground relatively undamaged. The landing gear remained intact. All four aboard (from Torrance, California) were killed by the impact. Personal communications to Ghiglieri from Sandy Chris Cancro, January 24 & February 1, 2000 and from Jean Louise Custer, February 3 & 4, 2001. (**pe**)

C/Pl

Robert R. Matthews, 26 ⑦ May 13, 1991 National Forest near Grandview, 4 miles S
(pilot) of rim, 10 miles E of Airport
Gabriela Erikas Hoerler, 26
Max Johann Krucker, 28
Doris Maria Kaelin, 26
Franz Lueoend, 29
Paul Lipscombe, 26
Gitta Lipscombe, 27

The Air Grand Canyon single-engine, piston-powered Cessna T207A scenic flight crashed minutes after takeoff due to engine cylinder head melt, cylinder explosion, and subsequent engine seizure. The plane burned, killing all 7 aboard. Pilot Matthews was from Chandler, Arizona. 4 were newlyweds from Switzerland, and 2 were from Germany. (see text) Arizona Daily Sun, *May 14, 1991. Incident report #91-1139*

C/Pl

Perry Smallwood, 44 (pilot) ⑤ December 10, 1991 25 miles W of Grand Canyon and ½ mile
Daisy Boukobza S of Indian Pass, Lake Mead NRA
Yardena Solal Cohen
Marie Sarfati
Ester Suid

The Las Vegas Airlines scenic charter in a twin-engine, piston-powered Piper PA31-350 Navajo Chieftain was returning from a scenic overflight tour of Grand Canyon. It crashed while flying through a thunderstorm. All 4 passengers aboard were from France.

Williams-Grand Canyon News, *December 19, 1991. Incident report #91-3860* **(pe)**

C/Ca

Boris J. Orent, 61 (pilot) ⑩ June 19, 1992   Hualapai Reservation 25 miles E of
Frederick Klenger, 23   Meadview near Lake Mead
Sylke Klenger, 21   *The heavily loaded Adventure Airlines Cessna 402 lost its right*
Rico Thieleman, 23   *piston-powered engine, then lost control, went into a right spin,*
Kevin Scully, 37   *and crashed 1 mile from the airstrip on Hualapai Tribal land. The*
Janet Scully, 35   *NTSB concluded the scenic tour pilot erred in not maintaining*
Rolando C. Valdez, 36   *minimal airspeed, but also due to maintenance shortfall in fuel*
Dahlia Valdez, 29   *tank plumbing. (see text)* Arizona Daily Sun, *June 20 & 21, 1992.*
Jerald Strnad, 54   **(pe)**
Jane McNitt Strnad, 41

P/Pl

Ralph Murray, 70+ (pilot) ② November 29, 1992   about 10 miles SE of Grand Canyon
Clara Murray, 70+   *Piston-powered Cessna 182 crashed due to unknown causes (it had*
                                            possibly iced up).

C/Pl

Alivia W. Moore, II (pilot) ⑧ February 13, 1995   2.5 miles NE of Tusayan
Wei Chen Chang, 22   *A Las Vegas Airline scenic charter in twin, piston-engine Piper*
Mei Chi Tseng, 40   *PA-31 Navajo crashed after losing one engine. To return to the*
Chen Chuan Chang, 25   *airstrip, pilot Moore banked into higher, not lower topography, pos-*
Hui Chuan Chen, 22   *sibly lessening the odds of survival. Seven people killed were from*
Chiang Yu Hsuan Tseng, 48 *one family. Mechanical failure was possibly compounded by pilot*
Hsiao Chi Tseng, 17   *decision-making. (see text)* Arizona Republic, *February 14 &15,*
Hsiao Fen Chen, 24   *1995. Incident report #95-0266* **(ppe)**

P/Pl

Jason Evan Cook, 25 (pilot) ② November 22, 1995   ½ mile S of Grand Canyon Airport
Sondra Schuler, 23   *Cook had earned his pilot's license 1 month prior to crashing and*
                                            had bought his piston-powered Cessna 210 one week before. With no
                                            instrument rating, Cook took off from a runway at night flying south
                                            into total darkness with no horizon visible. He may have overesti-
                                            mated his angle of attack and eased off too much during "correction"
                                            while having lost his horizontal orientation. The Cessna nosed into
                                            the ground. Grand Canyon News, *November 29, 1995.* **(ppe)**

P/Ca

Paul Capek, 39 (pilot)   ① August 2, 1996   below Pima Point
                                            Capek of Manhattan Beach, California crashed his piston-powered
                                            Mooney 20 doing loop-de-loops (witnessed) in a restricted air-
                                            space. He had apparently deviated around a thunderstorm before
                                            performing for an audience on the rim then crashing and burning.
                                            Arizona Daily Sun, *August 3, 1996.* Arizona Republic, *August 4,*
                                            1996. Incident report #96-3892 **(pe)**

P/Pl

Dedier Brullemans, 29   ④ October 6, 1996   On Highway 64, 1.5 miles inside Grand
 (pilot)   Canyon National Park

Olivier Brullemans, 25
Savine Lory, 25
Yves Krier, 30

The rented piston-powered Cessna 172's wingtip hit a tree during the pilot's attempt to make an emergency landing on the highway as he veered away from vehicular traffic, which failed to yield to him. The Cessna crashed and burned. All 4 victims were from Belgium. Arizona Daily Sun, *October 6 &7, 1996.* Las Vegas Sun, *October 7, 1996. Incident report #96-5234*

P/Ca
James Eldredge, 56 (pilot)② April 2, 1997
Darla Eldredge, 53

head of Fuller Canyon near 8,800 feet and Point Imperial
Pilot Eldredge of Salt Lake City, Utah reported "having trouble" with his piston-powered Cessna 210 during increasingly bad weather and diminishing visibility. Then he crashed. Darla Eldredge's body parts were not found for 18 days, 100 yards from crash. The government search for this lost plane and body in 4 feet of snow used 102 people, took 5,814 man-hours, and cost $130,000. Arizona Daily Sun, *April 16, 1997.* Navajo-Hopi Observer, *April 9, 1997. Incident report #97-1063 (**ppe**)*

C/Pl
Colleen Littlefield, 31 ① April 1, 1999
(pilot)

Grand Canyon Airport
Littlefield, a Papillon scenic helicopter pilot on a training flight, had phoned a friend that morning and asked, "Wish me luck, I'm doing my training flight today." Unfortunately, Papillon's helicopter had been parked outside without engine inlet covers installed. Inches of snow accumulation in both engine inlets likely were incompletely removed. Several attempts and battery packs were required to get the engine started. Engine failed quickly at 150 feet elevation. Descended in nearly silent auto-rotation, it hit nearby pine trees (which were mandated in 1994 by the FAA to have been cut) and crashed before reaching a landing site. The sole passenger survived in critical condition. Incident report #99-0680

P/Pl
Michael Regli, 39 ② August 3, 1999
Christine Hostettler, 21

100 yards from Highway 64 and 2 miles from rim
The piston-powered Cessna 177B took off at Grand Canyon Airport but failed to gain enough elevation to clear the pines (engine problems?) and crashed. One survivor (pilot?). Incident report #99-2092

C/Ca
Kevin Innocenti, 27 (pilot)⑥ August 10, 2001
David Daskal
Shiya Lichtenstein
Avi Wajsbaum
Barbara Wajsbaum
Aryeh Zvi Fastag

Grand Wash Cliffs at elevation 3,700 feet on 5,600-foot cliff on BLM land 5 miles E of Meadview
The Papillon Grand Canyon Helicopters' American Eurocopter AS350-B2 skimmed the Grand Wash Cliffs then crashed (the fifth Papillon incident in 2 years). A local rancher, Floyd Dwiggens, three miles from the crash site, noted how tour helicopters had been "nose-diving" there as a "thrill-seeking type of thing." "There have been a load of them doing it," Dwiggins said. "They kick through here 100 feet off the deck." Sole survivor, New Yorker Chana Daskal, age 25, suffered a fractured spine and burns over 80% of her body. She told

paramedics, "It got quiet and fell from the sky." NTSB preliminary mechanical evidence indicated the engine and rotor were turning during a puzzling, almost vertical, straight down descent to impact. An NTSB report concluded in June 2004 the probable cause of this crash was the pilot's decision to descend too fast and too close to the cliff. A settlement reached on behalf of Chana Daskal totaled $38 million. Arizona Daily Sun, *August 11, 12, 14, & 15, 2001 & June 4, 2004.* Las Vegas Review Journal, *August 11, 13, & 22, 2001.* (**pe**)

P/Pl

George Howard, 71 (pilot) ① September 8, 2002   Platinum Tank near Cataract Canyon
En route from Bullhead City to Liberal, Kansas, Howard of Palm Desert, California crashed his piston-powered Beechcraft Bonanza A-36 single engine turboprop near the rim of Canyon about 21 miles west of Grand Canyon Airport. The wreck was spotted by a Scenic Airlines flight diverting around a severe thunderstorm. Coconino Sheriff's Dept. SAR supervisor Aaron Dick fought his way through miles of mud to find the aircraft intact but Howard deceased. The crash was due to unknown causes but occurred in dangerous flying weather. Williams News, *September 8, 2002.* (**ppe**)

C/Ca

Takashi Mezaki, 45 (pilot) ⑦ September 20, 2003   "Descent" Canyon near Quartermaster
Joseph Hanna, 52   Canyon, Grand Canyon West
Nouhad Hanna,   *After an unusual 30–45-second hover during radio silence, the*
Masami Kato, 24   *French Aerospatiale AS-250 Helicopter run by Sundance Helicop-*
Makiko Hatano, 23   *ters made a routine descent from Hualapai Grand Canyon West*
Julia Hueyng, 33   *Airport toward an inner canyon landing pad to deliver tourists for*
Wolf-Diter Mueller, 46 *a boat ride. But it crashed into a cliff face. The aircraft had been serviced the previous day for problems with its main rotor—an apparently recurrent problem. No survivors. In October 2006, a jury awarded Makiko Hatano's mother $3.2 million in damages due to negligence by Sundance in not firing pilot Mezaki for his previously reported reckless flying as determined by NTSB interviews of previous passengers, some of whom had complained to Sundance.* Arizona Daily Sun, *September 23, 2004.* Las Vegas Review Journal, *September 24, 2004.* Las Vegas Sun, *September 2, 2006.* (**pe**)

P/Ca

Jerry A. Howle, 57 (pilot) ④ May 15, 2004   1 mile from Vulcan's Throne on the
Albert Glenn Howle, 34   Hualapai Nation
Milena Stanoycheva, 26   *Jerry Howle, a Reno psychiatrist with 1,900 hours flight time,*
Ania Dolinska Warszawa, 22 *flew his single engine, "amateur-built" experimental Bachman Lancair IV-P (N299SD) equipped with a 350-horsepower Teledyne Continental Motors TSIO-550-E1B engine out of Las Vegas to view Grand Canyon and climbed to 16,500 feet. 11 minutes later it disappeared off radar. Visitors at Tuweep 2 miles distant saw the Lancair steeply descend to the ground and explode on the Hualapai side of the Canyon. Howle's son Glenn of Greenville, South Carolina and his fiancé Milena Stanoycheva of Atlanta, Georgia had experienced a fairy-tale courtship and were to be married in Las Vegas the next day. Cause of crash remains unknown but the*

aircraft had a history of scores of maintenance issues. (see text)
The State, Columbia, South Carolina, *May 23, 2004..* NTSB #
LAX04LA213 *&* # 20040602X00714.

P/Pl

Thomas Redgate, 42 (pilot) ② September 2 or 3, 2004 1 mile SSW of Marble Canyon airstrip
Marianne Redgate, 40   *As discovered on September 4 by another pilot, Redgate, piloting*
his Redgate "Europa Classic" experimental aircraft (N912EE)
from Long Beach, California apparently ran out of fuel during an
approach to the Marble Canyon airstrip then augured into the roll-
ing desert terrain. The plane gouged a 75-foot swath and stopped
at a 45-degree angle, destroyed. Being fuel-less, no fire started.
Redgate had designed and built the plane. Marianne was a Boeing
safety officer. Yet amazingly, not only did the couple run out of fuel
and crash, neither victim had fastened his/her seat belt. NTSB #
LAX04LA313. (**pe**)

P/Pl

Luis "Lucho" DeCastro, 44 ④   October 25, 2006   25 miles NE of Meadview at 4,520 feet
(pilot)   msl "on rugged terrain" near Lake Mead
Laura DeCastro, 41   *DeCastro flew IFR his single-engine, parachute-equipped Cirrus SR-*
Nadia DeCastro, 7   *22 (N121LD) from Lake Tahoe, violating military airspace, en route*
Trevor DeCastro, 4   *to Grand Canyon and tried to deviate around a cell of weather but*
into clouds during NTSB warnings of severe turbulence, icing, and
low-level wind shear in his area. His final transmission to L.A. Center
was a panicked "we got an ice…ice everywhere." Las Vegas Now,
April 26, 2007. NTSB #LAX07FA021. (**pe**)

P/unlocated

Joseph Radford, 47 (pilot) ① March 11, 2011   unknown location W of Scorpion Ridge
Radford of Glendale, Arizona flew his "experimental" homebuilt
(from a kit) RV-6 (N650RV) from Grand Canyon Airport at 8:30
a.m. westerly for a couple of minutes. Then he manually turned off
his transponder, cutting the ability of radar to track him. He next
made a hard right, north turn to fly into a no-fly zone over Grand
Canyon. Radford's RV-6 next turned westerly and was seen by hik-
ers flying illegally low over Scorpion Ridge. Next it vanished. Two
days later a commercial pilot reported hearing transmissions from
an ELB (emergency locator beacon) nearby and about 30 miles
northwest of the airport. The following day Radford was reported as
a missing person, spurring a coordinated Coconino County Sheriff's
SAR and Grand Canyon NPS search. By now the ELB had stopped
transmitting. (Background: Radford allegedly had seemed upset
that his illicit girlfriend in Washington state would not change her
plans to meet him.) Various tactics for the air search continued for
three weeks but found nothing. Not included in air crash statistics.
Instead included in suicides stats.

This page left blank.

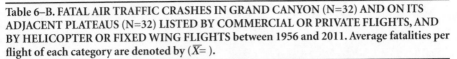
Table 6–B. FATAL AIR TRAFFIC CRASHES IN GRAND CANYON (N=32) AND ON ITS ADJACENT PLATEAUS (N=32) LISTED BY COMMERCIAL OR PRIVATE FLIGHTS, AND BY HELICOPTER OR FIXED WING FLIGHTS between 1956 and 2011. Average fatalities per flight of each category are denoted by ($\overline{X}=$).

Type of Flight	Crashes in Grand Canyon Aircraft crashed / Fatalities		Crashes on the Plateaus Aircraft crashed / Fatalities	
Commercial Fixed-wing: (after 1956)	6	58 ($\overline{X}=9$)	7	45 ($\overline{X}=6.7$)
Commercial Helicopter:	10	31 ($\overline{X}=3.1$)	2	4 ($\overline{X}=2$)
Subtotal:	16	89 ($\overline{X}=5.6$)	9	49 ($\overline{X}=5.5$)

[Subtotal of all Commercial Crashes after 1956, both in Canyon & on Plateaus: **25** aircraft & **138** fatalities ($\overline{X}=5.5$)]

June 30, 1956 collision:	2	128 ($\overline{X}=64$)		
Subtotal of all Commercial Crashes in Canyon:	18	217 ($\overline{X}=12.1$)		

[Total of all Commercial Crashes in Canyon & on Plateaus: 27 aircraft, **266** fatalities ($\overline{X}=10$)]

Private Fixed-wing:	14	42 ($\overline{X}=3.0$)	23	71 ($\overline{X}=3.2$)

[Subtotal of Private Crashes in Canyon & on Plateaus: **37** aircraft, **113** fatalities ($\overline{X}=3.1$)]

Subtotal of all commercial & private crashes:	32	259 ($\overline{X}=8.2$)	32	120 ($\overline{X}=3.9$)

GRAND TOTALS: 64 aircraft in fatal crashes in and around Grand Canyon, **379** fatalities.

Table 6–C. PROBABLE OR KNOWN CAUSES OF FATAL AIR CRASHES BY COMMERCIAL AIRCRAFT (N=27) AND BY PRIVATE AIRCRAFT (N=37) IN GRAND CANYON AND ON ITS ADJACENT PLATEAUS between 1956 and 2011.

<u>Types of Pilot Errors</u>

Type of flight	Unknown cause	Mechanical failure	Flying error	Ran out of fuel	Flew into bad weather	Icing of aircraft	Overweight aircraft
Commercial*	4	8	12-13	0	4	1–3	0
Private	9	4	12	3	4	6	5
Total:	13	12	24–25	3	10	6–8	3

* Total causes for 26 commercial flights exceeds 26 because two crashes were deemed by NTSB to have been due both to mechanical failure and to pilot error.

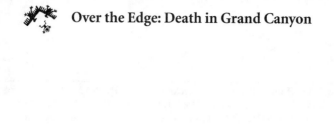

Chapter Seven

Lightning Never Strikes Twice: Freak Errors and Accidents

"Last piece of nature's handiwork he should ever behold" reads the title of a century-old article that records the first known death in Grand Canyon caused by lightning. On July 25, 1895—monsoon season—Blachley H. Porter, age 18, from Connecticut, hiked several miles with his brother, Louis, and their friend Arthur Renton, from the Tolfree Camp (formerly Hance Ranch, three miles east of Grandview) to Bissell Point (now called Comanche Point). Although the day had been cloudless and unusually clear that morning, a sudden rainstorm set in.

The three hikers sought shelter in the Canyon under a projecting rock. Lightning flashed "all around them." Abruptly a blinding flash exploded in the three young men's faces. It hurled Louis Porter and Renton downslope and unconscious. Renton regained consciousness first. Still very disoriented, he dragged Louis upward and behind a log to prevent him from falling off a nearby cliff. Finally Louis, too, regained consciousness. It took both young men a while longer to regain their wits and to even realize where they were and why they were there. The two at last climbed back up to the rock where they had been "hiding" from the storm.

The two young men found Blachley Porter lying dead with his face turned toward an impressive view of the Canyon.

Almost a century later, on late Sunday evening of June 14, 1987, the NPS emergency rescue team was called to the Maswik Lodge. They found Robert Plsek, age 71, without pulse or respirations. This seemed a routine case of cardiac arrest. But the family soon explained that during that afternoon Plsek had been thirty feet from a man who was struck by lightning while photographing the Canyon. The man who had been struck directly survived. But Plsek himself did not.

As ideal as the north and south rims seem—if being struck by lightning is one's goal—lightning has taken fewer victims here than one might guess. Overall, lightning strikes somewhere in the United States an estimated 40 million times per year. A bolt lasts less than one tenth of a second, strikes without warning, heats the air around it to 20,000 degrees Fahrenheit, and hits with up to 2 billion volts. An average bolt of lightning emerges from 15 million volts of electrostatic charge created by the friction of water droplets condensing on millions of specks of dust rising higher into the atmosphere and racing through clouds. The 500 megajoules of energy produced in an average strike can boil 250 gallons of water instantly (and thus explode trees). This electrostatic charge grounds out into the Earth as does a charge gathered by the friction of walking on a synthetic carpet grounds out when one touches metal. Worldwide, lightning proves to be the most lethal weather event (greater than floods, tornados, et cetera). Yet as we have seen, flashfloods have killed more people in Grand Canyon than lightning strikes, including those on the rims. Otherwise, these vital statistics seem to imply that most people in America are doomed.

But in fact, while lightning does ignite about half of U.S. forest fires, it kills only a few people: During the past decade in America about 40 per year. The worst states are Florida, with 10 per year, and Texas with 4 per year. Ninety percent of strike victims survive but often with profound physical, mental, and even personality changes and deficits. Again, people struck fatally at Grand Canyon have been men. Men account for 80 percent of fatal strikes in the U.S., and most victims are between 20-45 years old.

On May 13, 1993, for example, Daniel Mark Caesar, age 21, was struck by lightning and killed while hiking the Tanner Trail within the Canyon. CPR by his two companions was ineffective.

On September 11, 1997, a mere hour or so after a flash flood killed the Morans while hiking in Phantom Creek—and almost in view of the flood that killed them—lightning struck two people on the South Rim. The two visitors, Heinrich Parvicini, age 26, and Jasmine Mischke, age 24, were from Germany. The two were sitting on a rock at Mojave Point, west of Grand Canyon Village. Weather throughout that day had been cloudy with scattered thunderstorms.

The German couple had chosen a perch that was too exposed. Lightning struck Parvicini directly, causing instant cardiac arrest. Mischke was hit indirectly, causing first- and second-degree burns over ten percent of her body. Bystanders performed CPR on him until NPS rangers arrived to provide life support. Happily, he regained cardiac function. Emergency medical personnel evacuated him to Flagstaff Medical Center. The next morning, he was listed in fair condition.

Less than a year later lightning struck another visitor. On July 11, 1998 Stuart Wire, a 44-year-old tourist from London, stood and gazed over the Canyon as millions had done before him. It was 4:00 p.m. Wire stood at the guard rail at Lipan Point Overlook near Desert View. Wire peered at a tiny rectangle of Canyon within the field of view offered by his video camera. Then he panned the Canyon to videotape his experience of "the Canyon during a thunderstorm."

Wire's wife stood beside him. Three other people also stood next to the same guardrail.

When the lightning bolt struck, the blast knocked everyone off their feet. Each person landed jarringly several feet away. The good news was that no one had been blasted over the rim into the abyss. The bad news was that the bolt of lightning had struck Wire directly on the top of his head.

It burned his hair and ruptured his eardrum, filling his ear canal with blood. The bolt traveled down the left side of Wire's face, causing first degree burns down to his neck. Crossing the left side of his chest, it next blew open his shirt to leave a long gash of burnt fabric and melted or missing buttons. It next singed the hair on his chest and burned the underlying skin. The bolt exited through the left front pocket of Wire's shorts, blowing a hole through the pocket, melting the zipper, and causing second degree burns to the skin beneath.

Wire collapsed onto the Kaibab Limestone as lifeless as the stone itself. His wife, trying to collect her senses, saw him lying motionless. She looked and listened for respirations. There were none. Panicked, she started CPR. Wire quickly woke up, as if in a CPR training film. But he seemed stunned.

Bystanders notified EMS officials. All the victims were taken to the Grand Canyon Clinic for examination. Amazingly, none of the victims was seriously injured.

On June 11, 2005 lightning struck fatally again on the rim. Ben Bernal, age 55 and from California, was walking with a woman companion along the South Rim Trail near the outdoor worship site. As thunder shook the Earth, the pair took refuge under a tree from lightning.

As we have just learned, the tactic of hiding under a tree (= lightning rod) is not a wise one. Lightning struck the walkers' chosen tree and grounded through both people. Bernal collapsed in cardiac arrest with several burns. The crotch of his trousers had blown out, as had one shoe, leaving serious burns to soft tissue. Park rangers appeared nearly ten minutes later and managed to resuscitate Bernal and assist the woman with him. Both were transported to Flagstaff Medical Center. She survived, but Bernal died there five days later from complications due to the millions of volts having passed through him.

Six years later lightning killed another tourist on the rim. On August 4, 2011 64-year-old Sabrina Hamann of Bradenburg, Germany was struck fatally on the West Rim Trail near Mojave Point. Again CPR proved ineffective.

How likely is it to be struck by lightning in Grand Canyon? Arizona is not in the top twenty states for lightning-caused human fatalities. In the 41 years since 1959, 62 people have been struck and killed by lightning in the entire state of Arizona. In the Inner Gorge of Grand Canyon near the river none have been struck and killed—although, granted, Daniel Mark Caesar was killed while hiking an open section of the Tanner Trail, miles from the river. By standing on open, exposed salients near or on the Canyon's rims, people inadvertently act as lightning rods. And the risk of being struck in such places during thunderstorm activity is predictably higher. Just as some people do win the lottery, some people are struck. Unlike players in the lottery, however, a person who chooses to stand as a potential lightning rod on open, projecting points in the higher elevations of Grand Canyon can definitely increase his/her odds of "winning." Otherwise, the odds of being struck are about one in 615,000 lightning events—but, again, one can change those odds dramatically by doing the right or wrong things. One of those wrong things would be to stand or hunker under an isolated tree during a lightning storm. Hunkering elsewhere (even in the open), however, is reputedly a good idea.

Rock Falls

One of the most commonly asked questions by first timers floating the Colorado River at the base of miles and miles of cliffs and slopes littered with a trillion tons of loose rock lying at its angle of repose is, "Have you ever seen a rock fall?"

The honest answer given by most veteran guides is "yes, but not very often." This is usually followed by an explanation of why rocks fall, spalling, flash flooding, animals (humans included) setting a fall in motion, or, a favorite, frost-heaving. This is a process in which water in cracks or in spaces between rocks freezes, expands, thaws, and freezes and expands again in a cycle that ultimately wedges rock off a face or pushes boulders off their balancing points, making them fall. Sometimes they roll and fall for thousands of feet during which they convince other rocks to join them.

Of course, in the back of many peoples' minds is the second question: "Aren't rock falls dangerous?"

Although it is possible to spend six months in the Canyon and see nothing inanimate but solid and larger than a grain of sand move, rocks frequently do fall somewhere in Grand Canyon, and more so during winter due to frost-heaving. Indeed, at least 1,000 cubic miles of rock over the past 20 to 30 million years have fallen here in one way or another—otherwise no Grand Canyon would exist. But what are the odds of being in the wrong place at the wrong time so as to be hit by a rock fall? Incredibly low—but not nonexistent.

As Table 7 shows, the earliest known fatality due to a rock fall was of a miner. Prospectors William H. Ashurst, age 57, and J. Marshall both had worked in the 1890s in mining ventures with the colorful "Captain" John T. Hance, the first permanent white resident of the Canyon's South Rim (Hance was also a hosteller and a teller to tourists of the tallest Canyon tales ever told.) On January 18, 1901, after having discovered rich copper ore near Number Seven copper mine, Ashurst went prospecting yet again with the idea that he and Hance might still haul even richer paydirt out of the Canyon.

This time, alone near a mineral claim three miles downriver from Lone Tree Canyon (River Mile 84), Ashurst's keen eye roved the mineral deposits that he and Hance had thought promising in the general vicinity of River Mile 87 (near Cremation Canyon). Out of the blue, a rock fall, not mining related, caught him.

Hance did not find Ashurst until 49 days later, pinned to the ground by a slab of Vishnu Schist. Hance was appalled to see that his partner had apparently suffered a hideously prolonged death.

Interestingly, Ashurst's son, Senator Henry Fountain Ashurst, played the key role, along with Senator Carl Hayden, in obtaining national park status for Grand Canyon. The two men introduced numerous bills—in the 63rd, 64th, and 65th congresses—to gazette the Canyon as a park. Not inclined to give up on this, Ashurst kept trying, eventually introducing S-390 on April 4, 1917. This legislation finally passed in 1919 (this success was ironic in that so many miners opposed national park status for Grand Canyon).

Hance buried William H. Ashurst's body near where he had found it. Ashurst's body remained there until 1908, when it was exhumed and buried at the top of Bright Angel Trail. Around 1934, it was moved again to the Grand Canyon Pioneer Cemetery.

Again, the odds of being killed in the Canyon by a rock fall appear far lower than of dying by other causes. This is because during a random rock fall a rock must hit an otherwise "well-behaved" victim. In most other fatal incidents in the Canyon the victim himself or herself normally contributes to his or her demise to some degree. Indeed, it is the very helplessness and randomness of lethal rock falls that make them a terror for some people. That one rare rock fall happening at the right time could smash a hapless victim in that tiny, unpredictable, billion-to-one place smacks of Fate and the vengeance of an angry God.

Yet, as minuscule as the odds are of such an event happening in the few hundred square miles of Grand Canyon actually visited by people, when people are visiting, rock falls do kill people.

On October 20, 1968 Masayuki Konno, age 24, was visiting the Canyon from Tokyo, Japan. He and his fiancé Junko Morimoto hiked down the Bright Angel Trail. Konno was to wed Morimoto in a few days. The two young lovers were walking about a mile below the South Rim. A recent rockslide had occurred just above this point on the trail. The two hikers also had seen a mule deer moments earlier.

Acting all too much as an agent of cruel Fate, a volleyball-sized boulder rolled abruptly from above the pair and hit Konno in the head. He died hours later. This one in a million type of accident, recalls Ranger Vic Vieira, was precipitated by kids on the rim, throwing rocks off, "trundling," to try to create a larger rock fall/ avalanche. Apparently, this worked all too well.

On August 6, 1982 57-year-old Ralph R. Voss was acting as boatman's assistant on a Hatch River Expeditions' trip. Mr. Voss' son, Jeff Voss, was one of the two Hatch boatmen on this trip. While escorting a group of passengers up the trail to Deer Spring, one of the two source-springs of Deer Creek (River Mile 136.2), at noon, Ralph Voss became separated from them. Fifteen minutes later, when next he was seen, he was lying pulseless on the trail. Although at first Mr. Voss's demise was assigned to a cardiac arrest, a subsequent autopsy revealed multiple broken ribs, a punctured lung, and tension pneumothorax—all consistent with death to an impact from a large falling rock. No additional evidence clarified exactly how this incident happened.

Fatalities from rock falls, like those from lightning bolts, are random but eerily spooky. Certainly in the tragic case of Masayuki Konno, the boulder that took his life seemed like something out of fiction, or even from mythology. The same is true of the agent of Tom Gregory Standish's demise. Standish, age 32, of Boulder City, Nevada, had hiked down the trail into Havasu Canyon with his fiancé, Jody Pollins. The couple had set up their small tent near a ledge in the Havasu Campground downstream of Havasu Falls.

Heavy monsoonal rains during the afternoon of July 21, 1990 prompted the couple to seek refuge inside their tent. At about 3:00 p.m., a boulder peeled off the cliff above and plunged meteor-like into their tiny tent. It struck Standish in the head, killing him instantly. Pollins was unscathed by the rock itself but she plummeted into deep psychological shock.

On May 19, 1992 Rosalee Heaney, age 33, from Australia was hiking with three friends along the upper Bright Angel Trail, below Mile-and-a-Half House. Shortly after 2:00 p.m., Rosalee and others heard the loud thunder cracks of a large rock loosened by recent heavy rains as it dislodged and fell from far above. Rocks tumbled and bounced into space for hundreds of feet above the hikers and sounded like cannon fire. One rock the size of a grand piano whistled through the air, witnesses said, then hit Rosalee.

It crushed her chest and knocked her down hard. Her respirations stopped almost instantly. Ranger Paramedic Keith Lober and Ranger I-EMT Ken Phillips noted that had she been standing even ten inches to one side, she would have been unscathed.

On October 15, 1994 members of a private river trip camped about three miles upstream of Phantom Ranch on a small beach on the left, upstream of Zoroaster Canyon (River Mile 84.4). The weather had turned foul. A very early winter storm had dropped a foot of snow on the South Rim. Nearly half an inch of rain fell on the Inner Gorge. Everyone on this trip camped along the river and huddled in their tents hoping for the weather to clear.

Amid a heavy rain in the pre-dawn light, Rhesa Collins, age 25, of Buena Vista, Colorado, lay sleeping on her stomach in her tent. Well above her a loud crack echoed off the cliffs. Rocks began bouncing down the steep walls of schist. One small boulder ripped through Collin's tent, and smashed her pelvis. Three other people in this camp were hit as well. Their injuries included a broken arm, crushed feet, and a bruised thigh. While extremely painful, none of these injuries was life-threatening, except Collins'. With her pelvis crushed and large wounds over her buttocks, she now bled heavily both internally and externally.

In severe pain, she quickly passed into hypovolemic (low blood volume) shock. Her companions recognized how serious her condition was. But they had launched from Lees Ferry with no radio. Attempting to flash a mirror to an overflying aircraft was impossible during the storm. Collins' companions sent a fast raft to the Phantom Ranger Station (River Mile 88) to ask for medical assistance when the slower one behind arrived with Collins.

Collins' companions had placed her on a table as a stretcher. They loaded it and her onto a raft. They rowed her downstream almost four miles, through two rapids and in a drizzling rain to Phantom Ranch. Every motion of the boat spurred excruciating pain.

NPS personnel Patti Thompson, Frank Corey, and Katie Gaines on the scene reported that, upon arrival, Collins was pale, lethargic, and had a low blood pressure and a rapid pulse. Internally, she was bleeding to death. Even so, Thompson would say of Collins, "She was a little fuzzy, but she was a great patient."

The paramedics started Collins on intravenous fluids and oxygen. NPS personnel also tried to arrange a helicopter evacuation for her. But a flight into the Canyon cloaked by near-zero visibility from snow mixed with rain was too unsafe. For nearly six hours at Phantom, Collins' condition deteriorated, despite additional help by Rangers Todd Van Alstyne and Bil Vandergraff. In a few more hours, all these rangers knew, Collins would die.

With the first good break in the weather, the NPS helicopter succeeded in evacuating Collins to the South Rim. But the weather again became so foul that direct air transport to the nearest hospital 80 miles away in Flagstaff was again unsafe. A quick re-assessment of Collins at Grand Canyon Clinic revealed anew that she was in critical condition. X-rays revealed her pelvis had been broken severely in nearly a dozen places. A blood count showed she had already lost nearly fifty percent of her blood volume. Unable to provide blood transfusions, Clinic staff gave Collins more intravenous fluid to keep her blood pressure up, morphine for pain, and intravenous antibiotics to prevent infection. Clinic facilities at the South Rim were far better than at Phantom, but they did not include what Collins needed to save her life.

EMS personnel transported Collins along those eighty miles of road to Flagstaff. Once there, she received multiple blood transfusions and surgical repairs of her vascular damage and pelvis fractures. Amazingly, after some touch and go post-operative complications, Collins did recover.

As hideous as Collins' odyssey was after that rock fall, she was lucky. She survived. Around 9:00 a.m. on February 26, 1996 49-year-old Randy Thompson was working on the NPS trail crew in the Tapeats Creek Drainage (River Mile 134). The crew had scattered itself vertically in the first very steep ascent chute that hikers take when hiking upstream through the diabase intrusion into Tapeats Valley from the Colorado River.

A trail volunteer levered a prybar to maneuver a 400-pound, rectangular slab of rock to be used as a stair in the trail near the top of a chute. Abruptly he lost control of it. As the slab dropped down the chute, he yelled "Rock! Rock! Rock!"

Two other members of the trail crew working with Thompson below the chute heard the warning. They immediately moved to a safe location. Several people echoed the "Rock!" warning. Witnesses said that Thompson, positioned low in the chute, hesitated, as if in indecision about which way to move (he was not wearing his prescription glasses). He first moved to the left then he changed his mind and moved back to the right. Then he crouched down.

The falling block impacted another boulder and split into two equal-sized fragments, each weighing about 200 pounds. One of these continued down the chute, the other deflected onto a trajectory about 45 degrees to the right.

The deflected slab hit Thompson's back in the right scapula, inflicting a severe crushing blow.

At first, Thompson, still conscious, told his companions, "I'm hurt bad." Thereafter he lost consciousness. Later he regained consciousness and reported that he felt no sensation below the nipple line and could not move his legs. He complained too of having trouble breathing as he coughed up blood.

Fellow crew member and NPS Wilderness Ranger Nick Herring climbed a mile up and out of the Tapeats drainage to place himself in radio line-of-sight with NPS traffic. Even so, calls to NPS headquarters proved frustrating. A snowstorm on the South Rim prevented the NPS and the Arizona Department of Public Safety (DPS) helicopter from completing a rescue run. The helicopter did lift off and began flying toward Tapeats, but the rotor iced up and nearly crashed the aircraft.

Herring looked around him for inspiration. If the South Rim was now out of the question as a source of rescue, did another option exist?

The North Rim was overcast, but no snow yet. Winds gusted around Herring in changing directions in a "squirrelly," undecided way. He continued his emergency calls, hoping that someone from somewhere could penetrate the storm.

Meanwhile Thompson's fellow trail workers strapped him to a backboard for stability then hauled him down to the Tapeats Creek camp to get him into a tent and out of the snow. Though warmer, Thompson was very seriously injured. His heart stopped beating. Immediately his companions began CPR. Almost miraculously, Thompson responded with a renewed heartbeat. His breathing remained very labored as he coughed up more blood. Eerily (to put it mildly), a couple of days before this rockfall happened, Thompson had said to fellow trail volunteer

Brian Hansen at Tapeats, "This is not such a bad place to die."

Eventually, after 11:00 a.m., a Blackhawk helicopter from Nellis Air Force Base in Las Vegas piloted by Captain Paul Youngblood (unfortunately killed later during another flight) dropped into the Tapeats Creek drainage. At 12:42 this aircraft evacuated Thompson to North Las Vegas Hospital one hour away. Thompson coded twice, but CPR brought him back. Yet despite this heroic extraction by Youngblood, one Grand Canyon Clinic nurse Karen Vandzura aboard described as a foul-weather nightmare flight, Thompson died from his serious injuries within two days. Youngblood, Vandzura, and crew were awarded Sikorsky Aircraft Rescue Awards.

The Occupational Safety and Health Administration (OSHA) issued three willful safety violation citations against the National Park for Thompson's death. The trail crew, OSHA alleged, "allowed risky work practices, had an insufficient communications system, and had inadequate rescue and evacuation plans." "The situation," said Frank Strasheim, OSHA regional administrator, "could have been avoided with reasonable planning."

Grand Canyon National Park administrators made changes to improve safety. These included supervisor "hazards analysis," satellite phones, EMT-trained crew members, and restrictions on participation by VIPs ("Volunteers in the Park").

Although this book so far has revealed that most fatal episodes in Grand Canyon result far less from Fate than from the decision-making of the victim and/or his or her guide, several spooky episodes have occurred. Consider the following one of August 8, 1912.

Charles Bell and several other workers were blasting the face of the limestone cliff on the Bright Angel Trail to open a tunnel. Just before noon the crew set off five strategically located blasts. Only four exploded.

The crew waited about fifteen minutes. The fifth charge still failed to detonate. Finally, noon rolled around. Charles Bell volunteered to go get dinner ready. Inconveniently, the crew had to pass by the location of the hangfire charge to do so. They plodded up the trail with Bell in the lead.

Just as Bell reached the vicinity of the charge, it exploded.

The blast blew Bell into the air and off the edge of the cliff face to plummet about eighty feet. The impact broke both of Bell's legs and badly fractured his skull. Bell survived the errant blast for an hour.

This kind of tragedy happened again in the line of duty a decade later. In 1922, trail foreman Rees B. Griffiths was working as part of a team building the South Kaibab Trail. On February 6, Griffiths decided to remove a large projection of rock blocking what he considered the perfect route near the suspension bridge. The crew detonated an enormous charge of dynamite here, blowing the offending bit of Canyon wall to smithereens. The placement of explosives had been perfect.

Minutes later, as Griffiths climbed to the top to inspect the blast excavation at close range, a "mammoth" boulder loosened by the blast rolled down on Griffiths, carrying him down to the rocks below half crushed. Griffiths died six hours later in Camp Roosevelt (now called Phantom Ranch). After careful consideration, NPS rangers and trail crew gave him a proper Mormon burial, interring him "about five hundred yards west of the bridge in an alcove in the Archaean rock which forms the Canyon wall."

A memorial plaque near Kaibab Suspension Bridge on the north side of the Colorado River states:

> *Rees B. Griffiths*
> *Trail foreman, National Park Service.*
> *Born October 10, 1873. Died Feb. 6, 1922 in Grand Canyon he loved so well, as a result of injuries received near this spot while in the performance of his duty in building of Kaibab Trail.*

Other Freak Accidents

Again, many of the "freak" accidents people experience often prove to be not so much freak as instead the statistically unlikely outcomes of having made risky decisions. These decisions seem particularly easy for people naïve to the desert Southwest to make. Consider, for example, some of the weird accidents that have occurred to outsiders visiting one of the most beautiful creeks in the American Southwest.

On June 27, 1965 Otis Brown, age 40, swam in this idyllic creek behind its most famous waterfall, Havasu Falls. Brown's two swimming companions said he was trapped in a "whirlpool" (reversal water) under and behind the falls. Unable to swim beyond the falls downstream into the expansive and nearly placid pool, Brown exhausted himself in the reversal current and drowned.

On a screaming hot July 10, 1972 Frenchwoman Christiane Haag, age 22, paused from her hike and eased herself into Havasu Creek. As her entry point she chose the foot of Navajo Falls, a beautiful location by anyone's standards. Haag, however, went swimming alone. Caught by current that proved more powerful and rock-strewn than it may have appeared, Haag lost control and drowned.

Toward the end of her day at Havasu with a Western River Expeditions motor trip on July 26, 1998 Sylvia Ann Leimkuehler, age 18, from Ohio—and ironically a lifeguard—also made a fatal misstep. She had just hiked with an 18-year-old male friend, Derek, and a 50-year-old friend, Kim, on the very hot, eight-mile round trip from the Colorado River to Beaver Falls and back (or almost back). At 3:00 p.m., right on time, the trio finally arrived, after a hurried and likely dehydrating march, at the rendezvous point of their Western River Expeditions' motor trip where they reunited with the guides, families, and several other members of the trip.

This shallow ford so near the river is a rendezvous zone for members of many such trips. It offers shade, ledges, a small pool to dunk in, and a beautiful view. Downstream of the ford is a waterfall. Not a 196-footer such as can be found upstream at Mooney Falls (higher than Niagara Falls), but a mere less-than-ten-footer. This picturesque falls, however, funnels the creek between two boulders long cemented in place by travertine. The creek here narrows to five feet wide. From this gap it plunges straight down to pound into a re-circulating eddy pool then feeds into a millrace toward another, smaller falls.

Leimkuehler now followed Derek and Kim across the ford. Havasu was flowing murky. The bottom was hard to see. Both males plodded across the ford ahead. Behind the trio, Western River Expeditions' guide Tiffany George sat and chatted with another guide. When she glanced back at Leimkuehler, George could not believe her eyes. George saw Leimkuehler floating face down, her feet aimed downstream, toward the waterfall. Leimkuehler explains:

> *Derek and Kim crossed over and I followed. As I was walking the water was cloudy and I stepped on a large rock or something. My ankle turned and I fell down into the water. The current was pulling me and I could not stand up. I tried as hard as I could to stand but the water was too strong. I managed to grab hold of a rock at the top of the waterfall and held on for a few seconds. I was looking across at my family and the others on the trip yelling for help but I could not hear them. The rock I was holding on to was very sharp and the water was rushing over my body with my legs hanging over the waterfall. All at once I went over and I do not remember anything for about 5 seconds.*

At first thinking that Leimkuehler was just drifting to cool off, George yelled at her to stand up. "When she didn't respond," George explains, "I jumped to my feet, screaming her name, and trying to get over to her when she caught the funnel that sucked her over the edge of the waterfall...she went over the top like limp spaghetti. I was horrified."

The re-circulating "eddy" water at the foot of the falls—again opaque due to recent rains—held Leimkuehler in a Maytag effect, recycling her in a static location, tumbling, tumbling, tumbling under water.

George scampered to the base of the falls and scanned for Leimkuehler. Nothing. She shallow-dived in and tried to pull herself along the bottom against the current to reach the re-circulating water where Leimkuehler must be. But, perversely it seemed, the creek swept George downstream. George tried again. Again no dice. She looked up at Kim and asked him if he had seen Leimkuehler.

Kim, in hysterics, sobbed, "No."

George, now as alarmed as it is possible for a human being to be, scanned the ledges for a less emotional helper. "Shut up!" she now hollered at Kim so that she could hear what other people were trying to yell down to her over the roar of the falls.

> *I must have been knocked slightly unconscious as I went over [Leimkue-hler sustained a fractured orbital bone and severe facial lacerations as she was knocked unconscious]. The next thing I knew I was under water and my leg was trapped in something. I could not see the top of the water and realized that I was trapped. I have had lifeguarding and CPR training and knew that if I took even one breath of water in I would fill my lungs with water and drown imme-diately. I kept saying to myself, 'Don't breathe, don't breath in.' As I was doing this I was also trying to reach up because I knew they did not know where I was, and if only I could get my arms high enough, someone would see them and pull me out. At this time I was not aware of any pain or fear. I kept thinking, 'I am not going to die like this, not today.' I quickly realized that they were not going to be able to reach me and I needed to get my leg free from the rocks it was wedged in. I pushed and pulled and finally pushed one last time very hard with my right leg and felt my leg come free. Then I passed out from lack of oxygen.*

No one, George realized in dread, had seen Leimkuehler emerge from the May-tag pool of the falls. George asked another client to stand guard at the foot of the pool to play "catcher" in case Leimkuehler floated out while George was under-water trying to crawl again. She saw an arm break the surface then vanish, then wondered if she had really seen it.

Someone twenty feet above yelled, "She's out!"

The Good Samaritan catcher scooped up Leimkuehler. George and another guide, Kam, raced over and carried Leimkuehler to lay her on her back on a shelf of Muav Limestone.

"If I thought I was horrified earlier," George admitted, "I was truly horrified now!" Leimkuehler was severely battered and bleeding. One of her front teeth had been shoved back into her mouth. Her face below her lip had been punctured and torn. The travertine had lacerated her face and body in a random broad assault. Far worse, she was not breathing. Neither Kam nor George could detect a pulse. Sylvia Leimkuehler now stared sightlessly upward, pupils fixed. She had, to George's hor-ror, "Doll's eyes."

George stared at her and thought, "Okay, cough and puke like they do in the movies." But nothing happened.

> *The next thing I felt was calmness and a sensation of floating but no aware-ness of my body. I saw faces above me in rows. They were faces of almost everyone I knew in my life including people on the trip. This seemed to go on forever until finally I could just see Kam and Tiffany's faces but nothing else, just black.*

"You're not going to die on my trip, not today," George hissed to herself. George sealed her mouth against Leimkuehler's torn lips and exhaled hard. "I was amazed at how easily her lungs inflated. And when her lungs deflated there was a terrible moan, empty and hollow, yet she was still unresponsive."

George inflated her again. This time Leimkuehler's "eyes flew open wide as her lungs deflated but her pupils were still unresponsive. I was yelling at her, 'C'mon, Silvie, BREATHE!' It took about five seconds and she drew in breath, closed her eyes, opened them again, pupils dilated and constricted...."

> Then I started to see more but I could not hear. They were yelling but I could not hear them or answer them. All of a sudden I felt like I was there again. I could hear them and see them and I felt tremendous pain all at once. For a couple of seconds I did not realize what had happened.

As Leimkuehler opened her eyes again, she said to George and Kam, "I had the strangest dream. I dreamt that you all were standing over me calling my name but I couldn't answer you."

As George listened to this, she admitted, "I could feel the hairs standing on end up and down my spine...."

> It all came back quickly though. I remember my face hurting and not being able to move my leg at all. I felt so scared and upset I could not understand what had happened. Tiffany kept talking to me and telling me to calm down, that I was fine. She was holding me the entire time. She never left my side [even after having been carried to the Muav ledges above the river for the helicopter evacuation]. Every once in a while I would feel as though my breathing was slowing and it might stop. I would start to panic but Tiffany would help me breathe by doing breathing exercises. I think that if she were not there to save me and breathe with me while we waited [1.5 hours] for the helicopter, I might not have made it.

The NPS medical evacuation helicopter arrived and carried Leimkuehler to Flagstaff Medical Center. Sylvia Leimkuehler not only was lucky in her "choice" of rescuers, but also in her doctor; the physician on duty upon her arrival was a plastic surgeon.

No surprise, this traumatic "flat-line," as-close-to-death-as-one-can-get-yet-regain-life, experience left an impression on Sylvia Leimkuehler:

> It changed my life in so many ways and it is not something I will ever forget or get away from. I still have nightmares and probably always will but I also

have an experience that very few people in the world have. I have been given a glimpse into death and what it feels like just in the first stages. Death is not scary or painful or anything. I am no longer afraid to die and I feel that I was saved and given the rest of my life for a reason and until that has been fulfilled I will be here.

A bizarre—and still unsolved—disappearance in Havasu Canyon occurred less than two weeks later on August 8, 1998. A sixteen-year-old boy, Robert Tarr, III was a client on a Wilderness River Adventures motor trip with his family. Young Tarr apparently vanished from an unknown location along Havasu Creek. He was last seen less than a quarter mile upstream from the mouth of Havasu and near the same falls where Leimkuehler almost drowned. And, indeed this falls could also have trapped young Tarr, as it had done to Leimkuehler. Instead, his disappearance ultimately may have been into the Colorado River at Havasu Rapid. Mysteriously, no one on this trip at Havasu Creek saw what happened to Tarr. And, except for one of his shoes found floating in the creek, even after more than 13 years since his disappearance, no trace of him has been found.

Havasu is so unearthly in its beauty that it beguiles some visitors' sense of self preservation. On a hot July 10, 1983, for example, five-time Colorado State Heavyweight Boxing Champion James Gouge, age 27, decided to cool off. He and several friends had been hiking in Havasu Canyon and had stopped at Havasu Falls, a place of ethereal beauty. Gouge told his friends he wanted to jump into the 25-foot-deep pool—from the level of the lip of the falls, 115 feet up.

Several of his fifteen companions tried to talk Gouge out of this idea. It was way too high, they insisted.

But Gouge remained convinced that this jump was too desirable a activity to avoid. He jumped the 115 feet. And landed on his back. The impact with the water killed him.

Fifteen years later, on July 16, 1998, David Matthew Kendig, age 41, had far better luck at Havasu Falls. Also known as Michael Lynn Jones, a.k.a "Coondog," the blond from Little Rock, Arkansas, had traveled to Havasu to visit a Rainbow Coalition event. Kendig, who reputedly had experience with cliff diving in Mexico, now found Havasu Falls to be irresistible. He swan-dived 115 feet into the blue-green waters successfully and emerged exhilarated. Next, about two miles downstream, Kendig stared in awe at Mooney Falls.

Kendig gazed off the travertine lip of the 196 foot plunge and studied his route. Yes, he was planning to dive off these falls too. Witnesses said Kendig walked to the lip and stared off. Next he backed away for his approach. Then he walked out to the edge again to recheck his planned dive repeatedly before satisfying himself that he had it figured out.

Finally he swan-dived off the dizzying lip of travertine in a seemingly slow motion, almost surrealistic descent of about two hundred feet. Kendig smashed to the bottom of the pool, 12 feet below the water's surface. Here his luck ran dry. He died almost instantly due to the collision. A doctor at Havasupai Village pronounced him dead at the scene. The doctor also reported possible drug use by Kendig prior to his dive.

Nine years later, on March 21, 2007 Flagstaff resident Christopher Phillip Burchett, age 22 was camping with a church group at Havasu. Burchett dived into a pool at the base of the Navajo Falls in Havasu Creek. He resurfaced briefly, then vanished. A rescue team recovered his body. He had drowned, but whether the cause was having been stunned or injured by impacting a boulder or travertine ledge under the falls during his dive or else being trapped by re-circulating water—or both—was never determined.

On June 30, 2010, only three years after Burchett drowned, Michael Allen, age 32, of Ogden, Utah was camping at Havasu with friends and family. Allen dived into Havasu Creek and swam under a pool located upstream of Mooney Falls. Everyone with Allen waited for him to surface. He never did resurface. Investigators suspected Allen experienced a loss of consciousness, possibly due to temporary entrapment underwater. He was swept over 196-foot Mooney Falls to his death and floated another 75 yards to lodge on a bank. Allen became the eighth known recreational victim to die in Havasu Creek.

Clearly the act of diving exerts an irresistible lure to many people. And as we have seen, this act exacts its toll. Yet what person learning to swim or dive has not heard the stern admonition: "Never dive into shallow water!" This parental admonition ranks up there with "Don't run with scissors;" "Don't play with matches;" and "Be careful with that! You could put your eye out!" At any rate, when it comes to diving, Grand Canyon may be the worst possible place even for shallow diving—and for the broken neck immediately afterward.

We would like to offer you the exact statistics on how many people have suffered paralysis from having dived into too shallow or boulder-studded water in Grand Canyon—in the Colorado, the Little Colorado, Havasu, and other streams—but the records do not allow a practical analysis. We can say the number of victims is heartbreakingly large. This is due to the reality that wherever water flows, so have boulders tumbled. And water often flows too murky to allow easy perception of these. And, of course, the rising and falling of flow levels of the Colorado also have beguiled many would-be divers with deceptively "inviting" stretches of water mined with shallow sandbars and nearly invisible boulders. Your parents were smart in their admonitions not to dive, but what they should have said is: "If you are in Grand Canyon, don't dive at all. Period."

In this chapter of freak accidents and mistakes we were missing something major. To fill in this gap I (Ghiglieri) sweet-talked Charles R. "Butch" Farabee, Jr. to tell us the story of what is likely most unique rescue in Grand Canyon history. Butch was the Park's coordinator for Search and Rescue missions and for the surprising mission described below. Butch, a veteran ranger of 34 years, also has earned the title as the National Park Service's premier historian of search and rescue missions and of ranger history in general. Here's his story....

During September, 1982 Patrol Ranger Dan Van Sice broke the passenger-side wind wing of a dust-covered clunker to enter it. He knew something was wrong here—the mystery was what. Van Sice had kept his eye on this vehicle parked now at the remote Grandview Trailhead for two days and nights. His inquiries on the license plate had revealed a registered owner, Mark S., but no report of the vehicle as stolen or needing repair. One significant further detail, Mark S. had not applied for a Backcountry Hiking Permit for an overnight hike.

Van Sice poked around inside the clunker and found a Grand Canyon National Park map with "Horseshoe Mesa" circled in ink. As clues go, this was a whopper. Moments later, he discovered a receipt from Babbitt's General Store. One purchase jumped out at him: a flashlight. Another whopper, or maybe a whopper junior. In the 1980s hikers did not normally carry a flashlight for a day hike—unless they were planning to enter a very dark place. Several caves existed below the rim here, including a popular one called Cave-of-the-Domes. Van Sice, a veteran search and rescue ranger, now sensed big trouble.

Had Mark S. chosen to explore Cave-of-the-Domes? It would not be surprising. It was relatively well known. This cave was first reported in *The Coconino Weekly Sun*, (Flagstaff) on May 28, 1896:

> *The latest discovery that has been made in the Grand Canyon will have the effect of materially adding to the interest and pleasure to be derived from a visit to this wonderful spot. This is an enormous cave, or series of caves, with two openings about 50 yards apart, containing numberless compartments. It has not been fully explored yet, but one compartment has been found to be 1,000 feet long and two others 300 feet long. One cut is 250 feet high and 75 feet wide, and the prismatic colors of the stalactite and stalagmite make those caverns a truly wonderful and absorbing scene. The caverns lead in every direction under the mountains, and there is no doubt that as soon as geologists become acquainted with the fact that such a cave is in existence crowds will attempt to explore its mysteries.*

An aside here, while serving as Assistant Chief Ranger and the Park's Search and Rescue Officer from 1981 to 1987, I recall seeing an official document stating that more caves existed in the 1.2 million-acre Grand Canyon National Park than in any other U.S. park. As an ardent caver and member of the National Speleological Society since I was 15 year old, I was impressed by this fact. Indeed, from its head to foot, the Canyon holds about 1,000 caves, mostly hidden in the thick Redwall and Muav limestones. Only 335 of these caves have been recorded. Far fewer yet, however, have been mapped or inventoried.

A few of the Canyon's caves have history—or even prehistory. In Western Grand Canyon, for example, Rampart Cave served for millennia as home to generations of the now extinct giant ground sloth (*Megatherium shastensis*). These creatures left behind tens of feet of stratified and mummified bones, fur, and dung (sadly— and stupidly—in the late 1970s this paleontological treasure trove was set afire and smoldered uncontrollably for years despite innovative attempts to extinguish it). Hundreds and hundreds of other caves still offer homes to the Canyon's 14 species of bats.

Ranger Van Sice phoned me his suspicions. Weirdly perhaps, I was sort of half-expecting it. I had wondered time and again why I had never heard of any SAR incident involving caves. (Even 30 years later I still never have found any records of either a cave rescue or search in Grand Canyon. Well, except for one.) Despite this dearth of SAR incidents, my interest in caving combined with my responsibility for Search and Rescue had already prompted me to plan for the real thing. In fact, a year before Van Sice broke into that clunker, I had located and asked several well-respected and dedicated Arizona cavers if they would consider making their services available should we need them. Search and rescue operations in a cave pose special challenges beyond what Grand Canyon normally throws at us. The claustrophobia and the all-encompassing darkness must be prepared for. It can prove a big mistake to take SAR personnel underground who do not want to be there. So I also figured out which SAR rangers on hand also possessed cave experience.

We had to weigh several alternatives for the mystery fate of Mark S. What were the odds that he had abandoned his car and simply left the Park? Or, if he was here in the Park, was he inside the Canyon? Near the river? In a mine shaft? In a cave? In Cave-of-the-Domes? Or instead had he merely suffered some mishap while scrambling in the open and now lay injured in some narrow tributary canyon? The list of possibilities went on.

We tried to weigh the odds and interpret our few clues. Our missing man probably had been out there somewhere for at least two days. If he had purchased his flashlight at the last moment, then what was the likelihood he also had equipped himself with sufficient water, food, map, first aid, clothing, and other survival gear?

The distance from Mark's car to Cave-of-the-Domes was about 3.5 miles. It also required a descent of 2,700 feet down a non-maintained trail. The cave sits in the top 100 feet of the Redwall, the largest limestone formation and arguably the most dramatic geological feature of Grand Canyon.

We mustered a ranger SAR team composed of myself, Dan Van Sice, Inner Canyon District Ranger Larry Van Slyke, Mike Ebersole (who had done his masters thesis on archeology of the Horseshoe Mesa area), Larry Frederick, Rick Mossman, and Paul Anderson (who ultimately would become President of the National Association of Search and Rescue). Every one of these guys was solid, reliable, and loved caves. Well, almost every one. Larry Van Slyke hated caves. But he did thrive on challenge.

Park pilot Tom Caldwell set us down on top of our suspected target number one, Cave-of-the-Domes (sadly Caldwell would be killed in a midair collision over Flagstaff on June 30, 2008 while piloting a medical transport). We faced a ten minute scramble down a sketchy social trail to the cave's entrance. This turned out to be the size of a refrigerator. Ebersole was the only one of us who had seen this cave before.

We each carried multiple sources of light, more even than the three that caving experts recommend. We also wore hardhats and carried 5-watt radios, first-aid equipment, climbing ropes and hardware, food, water, a sleeping bag, and a stretcher that fit onto a backpack. If events proved that we needed something more, the helicopter parked above us could get it.

Van Slyke and I were about to follow the first three searchers into the cave. As I again promised Van Slyke that, no, the ceiling would not cave in, my radio crackled.

"We found him, and he is alive!" Larry Frederick's voice said. "Repeat! He is alive and okay!"

This was good news, but I still wondered: Was he trapped under a rock? Stuck down a narrow crack? Nursing a broken leg? Did he need a stretcher carry?

"We can walk him out." Frederick added. As far as SAR missions go, this one had become even easier than that proverbial walk in the park.

Mark, our wayward adventurer, turned out to be a twenty-something guy from back East who was working here in the Park for a concession company. He possessed little outdoor experience. Indeed he had never before entered a "wild" cave. He simply had read something mentioning the Cave-of-the-Domes and thought it would be fun.

How did he prepare for his adventure? He bought a two-cell flashlight and asked for directions to the trailhead. He told no one about his plan. Oh, yeah, he also carried some water but drank most of it before reaching the cave.

Two days ago.

What went wrong? Within thirty minutes of his entering the cave, Mark dropped his flashlight. It broke. No amount of tinkering or shaking would bring it back to life.

This being his only source of light in the pitch black world he had penetrated, he became not merely blind but helpless. He had not kept track of the exact steps he had taken to get where he was, which was four rooms and about 150 feet into the cave. Nor had he, like Theseus in the labyrinth of the Minotaur, unravelled a thread to follow on his way back out.

Although he could not see his watch, he thinks he spent eight hours trying to feel his way out. He stumbled over rocks in the blackness. He slammed into sharp projections. He banged his head again and again. But he never found the small opening allowing him to exit this fourth room.

As he struggled in a growing nightmare for hour after hour to grope his way out of room number four, a warm and humid prison, sweat rolled off him.

Finally, frustrated, tired, dusty, hot, and dehydrated, he sat down. Sitting avoided the risk of further injury. On the other hand, he would never escape his self-created death-row prison by sitting here.

An overwhelming thirst set in. As nearly two days passed, it intensified to torture. More than a day ago he had dribbled his last drop of water down his aching throat. His defunct flashlight now regained a new, but desperate value. He could urinate into it then drink his urine.

He tried this. The taste disgusted him. He did not try it again.

If Ranger Dan Van Sice had not acted so assiduously in solving the riddle of the abandoned clunker, Mark S. ultimately would have become mummified in Cave-of-the-Domes. Some spelunker of the future would have happened upon his corpse one day, and then Mark S. would be listed in Table 7.

What did Mark S. do right and what did Mark do wrong? I wish I could be a "Glass-is-Half-Full" kind of a guy, but I am afraid I can't think of one thing he did right.

The lessons Mark teaches us? Enter Grand Canyon only when pre-armed with information. Once in the Park, seek advice and information from rangers and other authorities specific to your exact plans. At minimum, read the brochures and other written information. Mark's decisions were spontaneous. His subsequent actions proved ill-conceived. And remember: always tell someone where you are going and when to expect your return. At least leave a note inside your car.

In addition to taking food and *lots* of water, other possible essentials Mark should have carried include a map, compass, matches or lighter (flicking his Bic would have got him out of the cave), two spare lights, a whistle, signal mirror, poncho, and perhaps other survival equipment such as a multi-tool. Even though some of this gear might prove of limited use, some could have saved Mark's life. The mere packing of such gear forces one to think about the highly important questions, "What if?"

Speaking of "what if?" many miles east of Grandview, in the sacred territory of the Hopi, two thrill-seeking buddies also pushed the envelope too hard. Jonathan Bolin, age 45, and Joe Walker, age 32, both from California, drove to the South Rim on a windy May 9, 1993. They parked near the edge of the cliff. The two donned their parachutes there, about 1,000 feet above the floor of the Little Colorado River Gorge. Their quest was to BASE ("Buildings, Antennas, Spires, and Earth") jump into the Little Colorado Gorge all the way to that floor.

Like Butch Cassidy and the Sundance Kid, Bolin and Walker leaped together into space and dived down into the narrow gorge. A dazzling display of geology whirled past them as they plummeted toward bedrock. Each man deployed his chute successfully.

But the two men were so close to one another that their chutes entangled. Now whirling together and almost completely out of control, the lower talus slope 900 feet below the rim rushed up at them far too fast. Both men hit unyielding stone at high speed. The impact killed Bolin.

In closing this chapter, we are all too aware that it is a bit unlike the others in this book. It contains a few apparent acts of God back to back mixed with many acts of poor judgment. Hence its lessons are slightly more fatalistic. There is not much we can do about freak rock falls, for example, and only a few things we can do about bolts of lightning. But we can easily decide not to jump or dive 115 feet or 196 feet off the lip of a waterfall —or even dive off two feet off a perfect stretch of shoreline. We can also resist the urge to trundle rocks off high places and thus not endanger the living creatures below us. And we can just say no to BASE jumping with a buddy into the Little Colorado Gorge.

Table 7. FATAL ACTS OF NATURE AND FREAK ACCIDENTS AND ERRORS WITHIN GRAND CANYON (unless noted, all victims are discussed in text).

Name, age	Date	Location in Canyon	*Circumstances*

LIGHTNING

Blachley H. Porter, 18   July 25, 1895   Bissell Point (Comanche Point)
Porter was struck by lightning. Farabee, C. R. "B.", Jr. 1998. Death, Daring and Disaster Search and Rescue in the National Parks. *p.19.*

Daniel Mark Caesar, 21   May 13, 1993   Tanner Trail
Caesar of Rosemont, Pennsylvania was struck by lightning and killed while hiking. CPR by his two companions failed. Williams-Grand Canyon News, *May 20. 1993. Incident report #93-1137*

ROCKFALL

William H. Ashurst, 57   January 18, 1901   near Cremation Canyon
Ashurst was prospecting alone near a mineral claim. A rock fall (not mining related) pinned him, inflicting a lingering death. Billingsley, G.H., E.E. Spamer & D. Menkes. 1998. Quest for the Pillar of Gold the Mines & Miners of Grand Canyon, *p. 67.* Coconino Sun, *February 23, 1901.*

Charles Bell, adult   August 8, 1912   "Cape Horn" Bright Angel Trail
Bell and others blasting the face of the cliff on the Bright Angel Trail to open a tunnel set off five blasts. Only four exploded. After waiting 15 minutes, Bell volunteered to get dinner ready. While passing the hangfire charge, it exploded. The blast blew Bell off the edge of the cliff face to fall 80 feet. Coconino Sun, *August 9 &16, 1912.*

Rees B. Griffiths, 48   February 6, 1922   South Kaibab Trail
While building the South Kaibab Trail, foreman Griffiths of Utah removed a large projection of rock by detonating an enormous charge of dynamite. As he descended a rope past the slide a minute later to inspect the excavation, a mammoth boulder loosened by the blast rolled down, crushing and carrying Griffiths down to the rocks below. Smith, D. M. 1930. I Married a Ranger, *pp. 61-66.*

Masayuki Konno, 24   October 20, 1968   Bright Angel Trail 1 mile below rim
Konno, visiting from Tokyo, Japan with his fiancé—whom he was to wed in a few days—were walking beneath a recent rock slide. The two young lovers had just seen a mule deer. Abruptly a volley ball-sized rock from above struck Konno in the head, killing him within two hours. The rock slide and the fatal rock had been set into motion by kids on the rim who had been heaving off rocks with the goal of starting a rock slide of larger rocks. The boys succeeded. Letter to M.P. Ghiglieri from Vic Viera, January 31, 2002. Arizona Daily Sun, *October 22, 1968.*

Ralph R. Voss, 57   August 6, 1982   near Deer Creek Spring, (River Mile 136)
Voss, a swamper on a Hatch Expeditions' motor trip, became separated from his group as a solo hiker. Fifteen minutes later he was

found on trail lying pulseless. An autopsy revealed multiple broken ribs, a punctured lung, and tension pneumothorax—consistent with death to an impact from a large falling rock. Incident report #82-2540

Tom Gregory Standish, 32   July 21, 1990   Havasu Campground
Standish of Boulder City, Nevada was camping with his fiancé in a small tent by a ledge in the campground downstream of Havasu Falls to escape heavy monsoon rains. A boulder peeled off the cliff above and struck Standish in the head, killing him instantly. His fiancé emerged unscathed physically. Arizona Republic, *July 23, 1990.*

Rosalee Heaney, 33   May 19, 1992   Bright Angel Trail, below Mile 1.5
Heaney of Australia was hiking with three friends and heard loud reports of a rock loosened by recent heavy rains as it dislodged and fell from far above. A piano-sized rock hit Rosalee in passing, crushing her chest. Her respirations stopped almost instantly. Arizona Daily *Sun, May 20, 1992.* Williams-Grand Canyon News, *May 28, 1992. Incident report #92-1216*

Randal Thompson, 49   February 26, 1996   Tapeats Trail 1/3 mile from the Colorado
While working on the NPS Trail Crew in the first steep ascent chute of Tapeats Creek, a worker above Thompson of Arkansas lost control of a 400-pound rock. Upon hearing "rock!" Thompson, who was not wearing his glasses, hesitated, moved to the left, then back to the right, and crouched down. A 200-pound fragment of the block hit Thompson in the right scapula inflicting a fatal, crushing blow. Arizona Daily Sun, *June 12, 1996. Death, Randy Thompson, U.S. Department of the Interior Grand Canyon National Case Incident report #96-0818, August 6-18, 1996. Hansen, B. 2014.* boatmans quarterly review *27(3):pp.36-37.*

FREAK ERRORS & ACCIDENTS

Pete Hmaguulo, adult   April 5, 1947   Supai Village, Havasu
Hmaguulo died in his sweat lodge fire. Stephen Hirst, letter to Ghiglieri, May 1, 2012.

Ricky Manakaja, 2   1960   Havasu Creek
Richy had been left to play in an empty wash tub and to the care of his brother Roland, age 7, and sister Andrea, age 5. Ricky "escaped." Roland and Andrea followed his crawl/drag marks to the creek. Ricky is the only kown Havasupai child to have drowned. Stephen Hirst, letter to Ghiglieri, May 1, 2012.

Otis Brown, 40   June 27, 1965   Havasu Falls, Havasu Creek
While swimming under Havasu Falls, Brown of Van Nuys, California was caught then trapped in a "whirlpool" and drowned. Arizona Republic, *June 28, 1965.*

Christiane Haag, 22   July 10, 1972   Navajo Falls, Havasu Creek
Haag of Colmar, France eased herself into Havasu Creek at the

foot of Navajo Falls solo. She was caught by current and drowned.
Arizona Daily Sun, *July 29, 1972.*

Ted Grounds, 29

May 4, 1980   Long Mesa west of Havasupai
Grounds of Supai Village was hit by the tail rotor of Superior Avia-
tion helicopter on the ground when it unexpectedly rotated on its
axis. Grounds was about to ride on the chopper. (not discussed in
text) Arizona Republic, *May 13, 1980.*

Name unknown,

July 14, 1981   Havasu Creek
The Arizona Department of Public Safety Flagstaff logbook
records a helicopter extraction of a drowning victim from Supai on
this date but includes no details such as name or age of victim, or
the situation in which the drowning occurred. (not in text).

James Gouge, 27

July 10, 1983   Havasu Falls, Havasu Creek
Despite several of his 15 companions trying to dissuade him, Gouge,
a 5-time Colorado State Heavyweight Boxing Champion from
Lyons, Colorado, jumped 115 vertical feet into the 25-foot-deep
pool from the lip of Havasu Falls for fun. Gouge landed on his back,
fatally impacting against the water. Williams News, *July 14, 1983.*

Jonathan Bolin, 45

May 9, 1993   Little Colorado River Gorge
Bolin of Folsom, California and Joe Walker, age 32, of Corona,
California BASE jumped into the Little Colorado Gorge wearing
parachutes. The chutes entangled. The men lost control. Bolin died
impacting the talus. Arizona Republic, *May 11, 1993.*

David Matthew Kendig, 41
(a.k.a. Michael Lynn Jones,
a.k.a. Coondog)

July 16, 1998   Mooney Falls, Havasu Creek
Kendig was visiting a Rainbow Coalition event in Havasu and tried
some recreational diving. Reputedly experienced with cliff diving
in Mexico, Kendig dived off the 115-foot Havasu Falls and emerged
from the blue-green waters unscathed. He next tried the 196-foot
plunge off Mooney Falls. Witnesses said he studied the leap and
seemed undecided, but then swan-dived off. Kendig smashed to the
bottom of the pool, 12 feet deep, and died almost instantly due to
the collision. A doctor at Havasupai Village pronounced him dead
at the scene and reported possible drug use prior to Kendig's dive.

Robert Tarr, III, 16

August 8, 1998   Havasu Creek (or the Colorado River?)
While hiking with his family on a motor trip run by Wilderness
River Adventures, Tarr a computer whiz from Philadelphia, Penn-
sylvania became a solo hiker and vanished. He is suspected to have
drowned, either in Havasu Creek or the Colorado, but his body has
never been recovered. Incident report #98-2717

Colin Hoagland, 57

July 22, 2000   Colorado River near River Mile 260
                       "Sandbar Alley"
Hoagland of Meadview, Arizona was riding in an empty, 45-foot
commercial jet boat upstream from Pearce Ferry as the guest of the
boat pilot to pick up river trip passengers. The boat hit a sandbar
(the reservoir was at 1,199 feet, 23 feet below maximum) and

abruptly stopped. The sudden deceleration threw Hoagland and his stepson forward. Hoagland hit an aluminum bench ahead of him. The impact caused internal injuries and internal bleeding to the older Hoagland. The boat carried no radio. Rescue was via the happenstance passing of a private trip, but the time delay, 3+ hours, was too great. Hoagland died 90 minutes after collision while still stranded on the sandbar despite more than one hour of CPR performed on him. (not in text) Arizona Daily Sun, *July 24, 2000.*

Christopher Phillip Burchett, 22	March 21, 2007	Navajo Falls, Havasu Creek

NAU student Burchett of Milton, Washington was camping with a Christ Church of Flagstaff group and dived into a pool at the base of the falls, resurfaced briefly, then vanished, drowning. He had been "cliff jumping" with other members of the group. He was reportedly a weak swimmer, having learned only a year earlier. A rescue team recovered his body. Arizona Daily Sun, *March 23, 2007.*

Michael Allen, 32	June 30, 2010	Mooney Falls, Havasu Creek

Allen of Ogden, Utah was camping with friends and family. He swam under a pool located upstream of Mooney Falls but did not resurface. Investigators suspected Allen experienced a loss of consciousness, possibly due to temporary entrapment underwater. He was swept over 196-foot Mooney Falls to his death and floated another 75 yards to lodge on a bank. Grand Canyon News, *July 1, 2010.*

Kreg Harrison, Jr., 16	June 20, 2012	Mooney Falls, Havasu Creek

Harrison of St. George, Utah and of Boy Scout troop Green Valley 6 (Lord Scout Trooper 1800) was swimming directly into the plunging water at the base of the 196-foot falls and became recirculated in the recycling current and drowned. His 3 fellow scouts tried unsuccessfully to rescue him. CPR also failed. Coconino County Sheriff's Office Media Release, *June 21, 2012.*

Eiliv Ruud, 37	December 4, 2012	Salt Trail Canyon near Little Colorado Gorge, Navajo Nation

A celebrity, veteran BASE jumper with prior experience at the Little Colorado Gorge, Ruud of Foss Fallskjeriy, Norway made a 1,000-foot BASE jump into Salt Trail Canyon. When Rudd was about 500 feet from the floor, witnesses saw wind shove, then slam him into a canyon wall. Ruud's pilot chute then deployed, but his main chute failed. He spiraled downward and collided with a wall projection, died there, and was stuck until SAR responders later climbed to him (not in text). Arizona Daily Sun, *December 5, 2012,* Navajo-Hopi Observer *December 5, 2012*

David Stather, 41	January 24, 2014.	Little Colorado Gorge "near Grand Canyon"

Late in the afternoon, Stather of Calgary, Alberta, Canada decided to make a second BASE jump of the day off the rim in his wing-suit at a 45-degree angle while his 2 buddies watched. He failed to clear

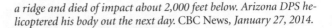

a ridge and died of impact about 2,000 feet below. Arizona DPS helicoptered his body out the next day. CBC News, *January 27, 2014.*

| Katherine Marie Newman, 54 | June 3, 2014 | Fern Glen camp, RM 168 |

Newman of Seattle, Washington was on day #5 of a commercial motor river trip run by AzRA when she sat down to eat dinner. The crew knew she was allergic to nuts. She started eating her "specially prepared" pesto but suffered immediate discomfort. She handed her plate to her husband, walked to her tent, and soon blew her whistle. When responders rushed to her, she was unconscious and blue. She soon died of anaphylactic shock despite two epinephrine injections 4 minutes apart and 100 minutes of CPR. The pesto mix, which Newman's husband had okayed, had contained cashews. Grand Canyon News Release, *June 5, 2014. Incident report #14047520*

<u>Chapter Eight</u>

Critters And Cacti

When the scheduled mule packer needed the day off from his run to Phantom Ranch, his friend, 48-year-old Eugene Waldroup offered to fill in. Waldroup was a native Arizonan and a lifelong cowboy. And although he was the Fred Harvey blacksmith, he felt plenty familiar with the duties of packer from his years of having been one. So, on September 27, 1968 Waldroup loaded his four pack mules with the typical supplies for Phantom Ranch: laundry, mail, food, and beer. Next he tethered the mules together in a string he could hitch to his saddle horn. At 6 a.m. he mounted the fifth and lead mule Nancy and set off down the South Kaibab Trail under a drizzling monsoon rain.

Waldroup knew the trail would prove wet, muddy, and slippery. These added up to far less than ideal conditions, especially considering the consequences of a mule losing its footing. True to expectations, the steep switchbacks in the "Chimney" immediately felt anything but secure under Nancy's iron shoes. The Chimney got its moniker, by the way, because it was blasted into the face of a nearly vertical, 300-foot-thick cliff of Kaibab Limestone. It was built into a steep natural chute wider at the foot and narrower at the top, tapering like a chimney. We owe the following details of Waldroup's "adventure" in the Chimney to his account told to Kathie Schulte in July 2006.

Within mere minutes, as Waldroup's caravan of five mules rounded an early and outward switchback, Nancy's hooves lost traction. Startled, she tried to spin to gain better footing in the greasy mire of the five-foot wide trail. But Nancy was top heavy with 200 pounds of rider, saddle, saddle bags, and a lead tether to four other mules. Instead of regaining her feet, they flew completely out from under her. Nancy and her rider foundered and thumped onto the edge of the trail. Then they toppled over it.

Meanwhile, safe above on the rim, final arrangements for a special ceremony that morning were being made to dedicate the newly completed Grand Canyon Hospital. This would be the biggest event of the year for the little Grand Canyon community when the state and national dignitaries converged. The South Rim's remoteness, combined with lots of visitors and residents, had quickly demanded a sophisticated medical facility. Grand Canyon's first tiny hospital was completed in 1922, three years after the Park itself. Now, 46 years later, the place stood in desperate need of an upgrade. But rather than renovate it, Congress appropriated money for the Department of Interior to build a new, state-of-the-art facility. This 22-bed medical center came with a dental office and a million-dollar price tag. It was considered the best facility of its kind within the National Park Service system. To recognize this new hospital, hands would be shaken, speeches given, and the traditional ribbon would be cut with over-sized scissors. Hopefully, the rain would stop to allow the ceremony to be held outdoors as planned.

Nancy's slip spurred Waldroup to yank his lead's tether to release the other mules and rescue them from being pulled off-trail to certain doom. Waldroup and Nancy, however, were trapped in an unstoppable fall. The only uncertainty remaining was how long and far they would fall before being killed by impact. Not very long, Waldroup figured.

No, his life did not pass before his eyes. Instead, he envisioned himself being crushed beneath Nancy's great bulk on the switchbacks below. Free-falling past the cliff face, Waldroup caught a last brief glance of Nancy falling next to him, a little farther out. A wild, terrified gaze filled her eyes as her legs flailed in the air for traction. Abruptly Waldroup slammed and ricocheted off something solid. Nancy disappeared from view.

At least a hundred people had gathered for the hospital dedication ceremony. Many locals arrived just to meet some of the impressive "Who's Who" in politics attending: Park superintendent Harold B. Stricklin, Governor of Arizona Jack Williams, and Secretary of the Interior Stewart Udall.

For a fleeting instant as Nancy and Waldroup had been airborne, dismay had overwhelmed him when he felt his favorite cowboy hat fly off. Not only was he about to be crushed to death, he also was about to lose his favorite hat. Next, a bit of bedrock rushed toward him, and he slammed against the Canyon wall. He bounced hard, then somersaulted and ricocheted again for about 60 feet. Finally he jerked to a jarring halt that left him dangling upside down.

Something had snared his right leg. Whatever it was felt as if it had nearly torn his leg clean off. But whatever it was also had saved his life. The searing pain in his thigh told him the agent of his rescue remained impaled in his leg. Waldroup squirmed and twisted to gain a glimpse of what anchored him to the wall.

"Well, I'll be damned," he thought. A projecting length of steel rebar used to secure logs onto the drop-off side the trail to prevent erosion had impaled his thigh. Waldroup hung off this rod impaled above infinity like a flag in the wind.

He looked down. Below him descended the remaining switchbacks, stacked nearly vertical for another 100 feet or so. Below those stretched 150 feet of steep talus slope. Below that slope yawned a cliff dropping 500 feet. He looked for Nancy. The poor but faithful mule was nowhere in view (sadly, she had fallen hundreds of feet farther to her death). Looking back up again, Waldroup felt relieved to see the rest of his mule string running back up the trail to the rim.

One person not in attendance at the gala opening ceremony for the new hospital was NPS maintenance worker Flore Estrada. He happened instead to be driving past the head of the South Kaibab Trail on his maintenance detail. Estrada saw something unusual this time, a string of loaded pack mules standing loose and unattended near the edge. What the hell? Estrada stopped, switched off the ignition, pushed the gearshift into granny, and exited his pickup. He joined the four mules. He scanned around for a wrangler but saw no one. He peered over the edge and called down. No one answered. Something was obviously wrong here. Estrada hitched the mules to a post then headed down the Kaibab....

A fella doesn't have many options in a predicament like this, Waldroup thought. And waiting for a Good Samaritan was not one of them. Waldroup knew he had to extricate himself from his predicament. And he had to do it now. If that rebar tore further through his leg, he'd quickly find out exactly where Nancy was.

Waldroup twisted and wriggled his body higher to pull himself up fully onto the trail. The rebar twisted in his thigh worse than any torture Torquemada had ever devised. Trembling with pain and exertion, Waldroup gasped then yanked his leg free of the meat hook. It revealed itself to be a mere five inches long. Blood geysered from his wound. Waldroup nearly fainted then and there.

Instead he forced himself to clinically survey his injuries. The gash in his thigh was crevasse-like, but his leg did not feel broken. He sported abrasions from head to toe and bled from a gash in his head. Almost miraculously he seemed to have escaped a serious spinal injury.

His hat was gone, making him feel half naked. He felt the bulge of his prized pocket watch in his vest. He tugged it out, expecting the worst. The thing was still ticking.

Inspired by this stalwart performance by his timepiece, he clambered to his feet. So far, so good. He stared back up the Chimney. He began limping toward the top, leaving a blood trail and filling his boot.

Estrada had descended only a few switchbacks down the trail when he spotted a blood- and mud-covered apparition staggering toward him. Estrada knew the fill-in wrangler needed medical attention *pronto*—before he collapsed. Estrada wedged his shoulder under Waldroup's to help him hobble up the switchbacks. On top, Estrada said, "I'll get you to the hospital in just a few minutes."

"Hold your horses," Waldroup protested.

Estrada stared at the battered, bleeding wreck of a wrangler and wondered if that blow to his head had caused internal damage.

"I may be a blacksmith," Waldroup told Estrada, "but I'm a cowboy first. I need my hat."

As Estrada thought this guy must have hit his head damned hard, Waldroup continued, "It can't be too far down the trail, can it? I'll just sit right here and wait for you."

"You want your *hat*?" Estrada decided not to argue. Everybody knew wranglers had hard heads. Hard to change an idea in there once it got wedged in tightly. At times their IQs seemed to match those of the animals they worked with.

Luckily Estrada discovered the runaway hat only a couple of switchbacks below the bloody rebar. He hiked again to the rim and jammed the hat onto Waldroup's head. Next he drove him three miles to the brand spanking new sickbay that had cost the taxpayers a pretty penny.

Neither man had ever been there before. Fortunately, the entrance proved obvious. Beyond it cars stood parked everywhere for the Grand Opening. Estrada joined them with his pickup and helped Waldroup out, wearing his hat.

Bloody and muddy and stinking of mules, the pair hobbled through the front door into the lobby. There reality struck and they stopped in their tracks. Muddy tracks.

Appalled gazes from stalwart citizens and dressed-to-the-nines muckity mucks bored into them. The pontificating politico at the podium quit speaking in the middle of his rehearsed speech. Stunned silence replaced rhetoric.

After a few seconds of silent gaping by the assembly, Dr. Rafael Garbayo ushered Waldroup and Estrada into the emergency room. Behind them the dedication ceremony resumed. But the wrangler's survival tale buzzed louder that day than details of the dedication itself. The mule wreck had stolen the show. Indeed, for hospital administrators and bureaucrats alike, Waldroup's untidy entry provided a serendipitous portent for the hospital dedication at Grand Canyon. *See? That's what this place is here for.*

Dr. Garbayo found Waldroup's thigh wound penetrated raggedly through the muscle down to the femur. Waldroup also had a big gash in his head. Garbayo cleaned and stitched both wounds, prescribed antibiotics, then drove Waldroup home. By 3 a.m. that morning, Waldroup's leg had swollen and turned red with infection. A neighbor drove him back to the hospital and phoned Dr. Garbayo. He arrived, removed his sutures, opened the wound again to the bone, and tried to cleanse it more thoroughly. He admitted Waldroup to the hospital and started intravenous antibiotics. He left the wound open this time because of the severity of the infection.

The next few days proved touch and go. It looked as if Grand Canyon might have its first one-legged blacksmith. Indeed, Waldroup overheard Dr. Garbayo discussing over the phone in the hallway with colleagues in Phoenix, "If the infection can't be stopped soon, I'll have to amputate the leg. I would prefer not to have to do it by myself."

Two doctors drove to the Canyon to help saw off Waldroup's leg. Fortunately, his infection finally began to improve. As it did, Garbayo pulled the wound edges together a little more each day until fully closing it a few weeks later. Waldroup was left with a foot-long scar but otherwise he made a full recovery. That winter would see him a back in the saddle and in one piece, sporting his favorite hat and with his pocket watch still ticking.

Of course, Waldroup's misadventure on the South Kaibab Trail was not the first mishaps with equines. This stalwart friend of mankind for the past few thousand years, the horse (or mule), often has experienced somewhat a raw deal from humans in Grand Canyon. The *Coconino Sun* on January 28, 1921 illustrates an example.

> *The first serious accident in the history of the Bright Angel Trail at Grand Canyon occurred Friday morning when three pack horses loaded with hay, grain, provisions, bedding, and 116 pounds of TNT for the construction camp at the foot of the trail, where the National Park Service is engaged in the erection of a bridge across the Colorado River, went over the wall of the canyon and perished on the rocks below.*
>
> *Among the horses was a black one recently acquired by Superintendent D. L. Raeburn. This horse was unaccustomed to the trail and had acted badly on a previous trip. In rounding the first curve immediately below the Kolb Brothers' studio it is supposed either that the pack slipped upon the horse or that he was accidentally prodded from behind, whereupon he turned, reared and plunged off of the trail.*
>
> *The three horses were roped together and in its mad plunge the black horse pulled the other two horses with it. The first horse to go over landed at the second turn, 208 feet below; the second horse landed at the fourth turn, 350 feet below; while the third horse did not stop until it had reached the sixth turn in the trail, about 650 feet from where it took the fatal plunge or within a few feet of the tunnel.*
>
> *The TNT did not explode....*

Oddly, in view of the danger of nearly every other means of getting into or out of or over the Canyon, the mules and the horses carrying people up and down on the Kaibab and Bright Angel Trails offer a near miracle of safety. On the other hand, among many hikers of the Bright Angel and Kaibab trails, mules are the Big Uglies. They hog the trail; they block the trail; they pee copiously at every switchback to create lakes of urine; and they poop prodigious piles of gooey green globs of odoriferous, foot-clinging nastiness all over the trail. Worse yet, the dudes who ride them don't have to grunt and huff and puff and suffer the virtuous pains and sweat of the far more noble hikers who haul themselves and their gear up and down these trails honestly on their own two Nikes.

If we set aside hiker envy of mule riders, we have to admit that riding a mule into the Canyon is a symbolic journey from the Old West. The rides possess an extraordinary allure. For city-slicker "dudes" yearning to play cowboy in an Old West setting, riding a mule down the Bright Angel Trail has no equal. For more than a century now, mules have been hauling supplies for miners, hauling construction materials and food for the Park Service and the Fred Harvey and Xanterra concessions, and so on. And for scores of years, they have carried dudes as well—and have done so with the best record of success.

In terms of fatalities, people do claim the mules have a perfect record with regard to riders who paid. The mules themselves, were they to be interviewed, might offer a slightly different definition of "perfect."

Consider March 25, 1991. It had snowed hard during the night. Then it snowed even more during the day. The wind howled, creating big drifts on the Bright Angel Trail. To cap it all off, fog set in, swirling with the wind-driven snow. Helicopter flights became unsafe. But for mule packer Stanley Sloan, these demons of winter were unavoidable. "Since I had to get supplies down to the inner canyon people, such as the rangers, trail crew workers and maintenance, I couldn't let the snow stop me."

Sloan prepared his mules with good winter shoes to prevent their sliding on the trail. Ominously, however, the trail itself had become not only hard to walk on, but hard even to see.

Sloan headed down the Bright Angel Trail. But he stopped after a few minutes to radio Dispatch to inform them of his intent and of the conditions on the trail. Sloan explains what happened from here:

> *What came next happened so fast that it was impossible to correct the chain of events. My #1 lead mule must have stumbled in a snowdrift. Next thing I knew we were being pulled toward the side of the trail. I guess the snow gave away and I felt the mule string falling. I bailed off the mule to save myself. I had a long lead rope to my first mule that went under my right leg to the saddle horn. After I bailed off, the rope came undone from the saddle horn. And Susan, my mule, didn't fall.*
>
> *By the time I got back on my feet and on the trail everything had already happened. All the mules were in a pile in a small wash below the trail. They had fallen 200 feet down the canyon.*

Sloan ran down the trail to find four of his mules amazingly alive, but all of them, having been tethered together and yanked off, were in bad shape. One of them, Gail, had a ten-inch laceration in her shoulder and was "in shock from the fall." Amazingly she—and she alone—survived, being well doctored by farrier Dan Cook.

No idle brag, the mule skinners running tourists down the Bright Angel Trail to Phantom Ranch do hold an apparently perfect record: No client among the half million or so taken during the past century has been killed while riding a mule. Those riding mules have been well chosen.

But they still obey the law of gravity. On June 17, 1951 Lee Smith and Lee Roberts were riding double as they headed down the Bright Angel Trail. Smith was a professional Fred Harvey Company guide/mule skinner. The mule that Smith and Roberts were riding was crowded off the trail by other mules. As all three of them dropped off the edge, Roberts leaped for safety. He survived. The mule and Lee Smith fell farther. The mule landed atop Smith. The mule survived. Smith was crushed to death.

Anyone in love with horses or mules would be quick to claim *they* are man's (or woman's) best friends. But what about man's "other" best friends? The ones that go woof woof?

Although it is not legal in the Park to hike below the rims with a dog, unless it is a service dog, lots of dogs on leashes mingle among tourists marveling at the view from the rim. At the crack of dawn on a crisp late winter morning in 2005 Park Superintendent Joe Alston felt happy to take a tail-wagging Bailey for a walk. Alston and his wife Judy had just agreed to dog sit for their son Josh during his visit from Scottsdale. And Bailey was hot to trot.

Alston had not done this sort of thing for quite a while. As an extra bonus, he anticipated, no one would be phoning him with difficult issues or shoving problematic reports under his nose while he was walking Bailey. Even so, Alston did not feel nearly as enthusiastic as Bailey. The young Border Collie/Shepherd mix was vibrating with anticipation to explore the unfamiliar neighborhood of Grand Canyon.

Alston looked out over the world famous landscape of buttes, pinnacles, and canyons that was his responsibility to administer. Winter had transformed it. The topography now glistened with a light dusting of snow as the sun crept up from behind the eastern horizon. It looked a perfect morning to stroll the rim.

Urgently sniffing and snooping, Bailey tugged the superintendent past El Tovar toward Hopi House. One serious obstacle to full olfactory satisfaction for Bailey was the 30-inch-high stone wall bordering the rim. Bailey darted back and forth, always stymied by this wall. When Bailey's frustration meter pegged out, she took Alston by surprise by leaping atop the wall then over it.

Welcome to Grand Canyon.

A split second late, Alston tugged Bailey's leash. The retractable leash was equipped with an unfamiliar locking device. As Alston fumbled with it, its nylon cord whizzed out with Bailey attached to the far end. It sounded like a lunker taking the bait. The cord burned through Alston's hand.

Bailey yelped and crashed through vegetation on the far side, diving into the void.

Alston braced for the yank certain to come when the leash went taut. On schedule, Bailey's fifty pounds jerked Alston against the wall. Would the mutt's collar slip off? If it did, there would be some interesting explaining to do.

The leash held taut. Gripping it, Alston peered over the edge. Ten feet below, Bailey thrashed and flailed like a tuna. She dangled by her neck and desperately pawed her hind feet for traction on a narrow ledge. Below her the Canyon yawned into infinity.

An experienced fisherman, Alston did what any angler would. He tried to reel her in. His tug, however, merely served to entangle Bailey more firmly into her scrub oak. Damn! A snag. He would need to scale the wall pronto and climb down to retrieve Bailey before he lost her.

Meanwhile, a group of bystanders eyed Alston suspiciously. One lady saw him about to climb over the wall. She hurried to him. "You're not going to climb down there, are you?"

"Yeah, I need to get the dog."

"Don't do it! Don't go!" she said, grabbing him. "It's too dangerous!"

"I'm fine, really! It's alright. Let me go. I need to get the dog." He started climbing over.

"No! No, don't do it!" She grabbed Alston more firmly.

"Just leave me alone," Joe said firmly. "I'll be fine!" Now he worried that this woman's good intentions might get Bailey killed—or get him killed. "Quit grabbing me. You're going to push me over!"

She released him and stalked off in a huff.

Good riddance, thought Alston in relief. Now, how in the hell am I going to get this damn dog? He scaled the wall focusing on keeping tension on the leash. Next he wedged himself down a crack then shimmied through the vegetation to Bailey. The dog acted overjoyed—and frantic. Bailey clawed at Alston for traction, like a drowning victim clambering aboard a rescuer.

A couple of bystanders now leaned over the wall above and offered assistance. Joe appreciated this. He hoisted his son's crazy cur and shoved her overhead into the hands of his helpers. Bailey plopped down on the safe side of the wall. Joe, now feeling a little frazzled, followed. Whew. Glad that's over…

"Hey, the rangers are coming!" someone said.

"Oh, great," Joe muttered. His original Good Samaritan had dialed 911.

Disheveled from hastily throwing on their uniforms, two rangers now skidded to a halt in surprise. They did a double take at the man and his mutt. One finally asked, "Is that you, Boss?"

"Yeah, it's me," Alston admitted sheepishly.

"We got this report of an old man over the edge…"

But maybe our focus here is too tame. After all, not only are mules and horses and dogs domesticated, they are pretty smart and, after all, harmless to visitors. Again, these animals have been friends to us for millennia (if only we could rise to the occasion and be as good to them in return). On the other hand, there exist other recondite and venomous creatures lurking in the Canyon salivating, many fear, over the prospects of nailing an unwary tourist….

It was a hot June night in 1976. Bruce Aiken and his wife Mary slept soundly. Their kids—four-year-old Mercy and one-and-a-half-year-old Shirley—slumbered on a mattress in the front yard just outside the door. Bruce was a New York native, a painter, and the NPS Roaring Springs pump house operator. He had grown to love their home here in the Canyon 4,000 feet below the North Rim. All he had to do to guarantee a continued life here was maintain the water pumps that shoved a small river of artesian water to the rims above, north and south of the Canyon. For three years since 1973, this home built in 1921 had been theirs. The little house stood surrounded by soaring cliffs that made it seem a child's toy. This idyllic setting proved an inspiration for Bruce's paintings. Moreover, it appeared a safe haven for his family. The kids could play outside without fear. No cars sped by, no hoodlums roamed the alleys, and no sex offenders preyed in this neighborhood.

A blood-curdling scream pierced the night. It was nearly 11:00 p.m. Everyone jolted awake. Little Shirley had screamed. Mary bolted out their door and grabbed her toddler. She looked her over feverishly. What could have spurred a scream like that? Mary found no obvious trauma. But Shirley continued to howl in pain.

Bruce searched the mattress and yard nearby. Nothing. Even so, he suspected the unseen culprit. Shirley had been stung by scorpion.

Inside the house Shirley's agitation increased. Mary held her closely, rocked her, and gently tried to console her. Nothing worked.

Bruce phoned NPS Dispatch. Even with Dispatch, little could be done. The Park helicopter would not fly during darkness. But Dispatch could get the Grand Canyon Clinic doctor on the phone.

The doctor soon phoned the Aikens. He instructed them about what might happen due to the scorpion's neurotoxic venom. It would be vital, he said, to keep Shirley's airway open.

Shirley's crying had become uncontrollable. Her wails emerged in crescendo waves of intensity as venom circulated through her tiny, twenty-five pound body. She acted agitated, restless and inconsolable. Drool dripped from her chin. Her eyes darted to and fro, fluttering and seeing nothing. Abruptly she launched into a grand-mal seizure. She bit her tongue. Hard. Blood and saliva foamed at the corners of her mouth. Her entire body stiffened and she arched her head and neck backward for more than an hour, crying uncontrollably in between seizures.

To Mary and Bruce, this seemed a nightmare worse than the one portrayed in THE EXORCIST.

Cottonwood Ranger Wayne Ranney, 22 years old and new to the inner Canyon, received a phone call shortly after 11 p.m. The ringing startled him. During his two months on the job, it had never rung this late at night. Groggy, he yanked the receiver. The caller was NPS Dispatch. The news of Shirley's situation instantly woke him. He gathered his wits. Could he assist? Wayne sprinted out the door.

As he jogged the mile and a half to the Aikens, a family that had fed him dinner almost every night, he wracked his brain for any good idea about how to help little Shirley. Did antivenom exist for a *Centruroides* sting? Ranney was a green and inexperienced NPS seasonal ranger hired as a reward for his working as a volunteer for six months since the fall of 1975. His experience with children was nil. His medical knowledge ditto.

On the other hand he did know what a scorpion sting could do. A month earlier, Wayne's old high school friend had visited at Phantom Ranch. A scorpion had zapped the 6-foot, 2-inch, 180-pound athlete on the sole of his foot. His own fault. He had stepped on it. Barefooted. That one sting, however, had incapacitated Wayne's buddy. The electrical pains shooting through the young man's leg had tortured him and kept him from bearing weight on his foot for 36 hours. What would that same sort of sting do an infant? Ranney shuddered.

Twenty five minutes later Wayne found Mary an emotional wreck clutching an inconsolably crying baby girl. Bruce was on the phone with the doctor. Mercy sat wide-eyed and tearful, terrified at the strange horrible thing happening to her little sister. Wayne took all this in and realized there was not a damned thing he could do to fix any of this. The most Ranney could provide was emotional support.

Two hours after the sting, Shirley's temperature had climbed to more than 102 degrees. Her pulse was so fast it was barely detectable as pulse at all. Her eyes roved sightlessly. The doctor had told Bruce to place ice packs in Shirley's groin to fight the fever and to reduce her runaway heart rate. Shirley continued to spasmodically arch her head and neck. Her eyes rolled back into their sockets, and she stiffened as if possessed by a demon.

Crying, Mary continued to hold Shirley tightly. She wiped the foamy, bloody froth off her infant's mouth and tried to keep her throat clear. As Mary rocked Shirley back and forth, the specter of losing her seemed to hover in the room as a palpable entity. Mary never prayed so hard in her life.

Four hours later, after 3 a.m. Shirley's epileptic posturing seemed to subside. Less foam formed around her mouth. She cried less. Was this because this tiny person's physical resources had been drained so drastically? Or was it instead because the venom was slowing denaturing?

Dawn came at 4:45 a.m. The NPS helicopter landed, packaged Shirley, and flew her and Bruce to Grand Canyon Clinic. Mary stayed with Mercy. During the next two hours the doctor injected the still-agitated Shirley with two shots of pheno-barbital, a standard therapy in scorpion envenomations to help control seizures and agitation.

By 8 a.m., Shirley seemed out of danger. Her breathing was good. Her fever and heart rate had dropped. Bruce asked for a flight back into the Canyon with Shirley to finally let her sleep. Back in Roaring Springs, Shirley did sleep—for 12 hours.

At 8 p.m. Shirley woke up to a Canyon sunset. She strolled out into the living room now crowded not just with her family but several concerned friends. They greeted the littlest scorpion sting survivor with a round of applause.

Maybe because the Southwest has a reputation as picturesque landscapes of wide vistas slithering and crawling with rattlesnakes and scorpions and tarantulas and Gila monsters in a sort of writhing, venomous wall-to-wall carpet of doom, many visitors to Grand Canyon expect to be assailed by some creeping menace. Little do they realize (as you do by now) that the most dangerous critter out there is a human being, maybe even oneself.

After spending thousands of days in the Canyon guiding commercial rafting clients and after spending thousands more days on the South Rim treating in-jured clients and other park visitors, we are convinced that the greatest irony in the emotional "contest" between visitors and the Canyon is their extreme fear of its venomous creatures as death-slaves of the Grim Reaper. As is clear in this book, the Canyon is a dangerous place. Its sheer, dizzying heights, its implacably power-ful river, its relentless and sometimes lethal heat, aridity, and penetrating cold, its exposure to lightning, and its labyrinthine maze of heart-breaking, "almost" routes and cliff-guarded cul-de-sacs that sap the final molecule of vitality from a hiker, all offer the biggest and most deceptive larger-than-normal-life array of fatal dangers of any place we know of. Amazingly, however, many people stare directly at these truly lethal dangers and worry instead about the Canyon's tiny nocturnal crawlers as its real dangers.

In defense of this fear of desert venom, it is true that there exist few among us, perhaps none, who have not witnessed a Hollywood rattlesnake kill a Hollywood actor, or a Hollywood scorpion kill a Hollywood actor, or a Hollywood spider kill a Hollywood actor. And as a monkey-see-monkey-do species, we humans learn from what we see. And we learn to fear, often in a paranoid way, those little slithering or crawling predators whose true mission is merely to furtively seek a modest meal of an errant insect under the cover of darkness so that they themselves do not become food for the raven or the hawk during daylight.

So how bad is it?

Of the ninety or so species of scorpions in North America, all but four of them exist naturally west of the Mississippi. Arizona hosts six of the potentially lethal ones. At least one of these, the bark scorpion *Centruroides exilicauda* (formerly called *sculpturatus*) seems not only to be the most common scorpion in the Canyon, but, in a bit of weird luck during the ecological draw, it also seems to be the most common nocturnal arthropod.

Inconveniently for anyone's peace of mind, the venom of the bark scorpion is the worst in North America. It's a complicated mixture containing at least fifteen protein toxins, all of which are neurotoxic, and some of which are 100,000 times as toxic as cyanide.

Moreover, the bark scorpion can control, via fine muscle command, the amount of venom it injects. No surprise, its sting in humans can produce a severe systemic reaction with respiratory distress, particularly in infants and toddlers. Hence that horrible episode with Shirley Aiken. But these scorpions are not Hollywood plot devices. In reality they are tiny predators equipped with poison evolved to kill very tiny prey and also to discourage predators.

Even the rattlesnakes here, of which the Canyon hosts several species, were designed by Mother Nature to kill small rodents not much bigger than a desert woodrat (*Neotoma lepida*)—not to slay pumas, bighorns, or human tourists.

How many of the Canyon's millions of human visitors have been killed by these toxic-nightmare scorpions? Although pediatric mortality records from the Ancestral Puebloans and Desert Culture hunters and gatherers before them have not yet been discovered among the petroglyphs scattered in the Canyon, recent historical records reveal the answer to be: None.

But a very rough estimate by Inner Canyon rangers is that about one in each 200 summer visitors who camp overnight is stung. Another informal Canyon statistic is that the record number of stings for any one victim by any one scorpion is thirteen, suffered by a woman desperately trying to squirm out of her snug sleeping bag after sting number one. Nearly all of the unlucky visitors who likely failed to follow the basic rule of shaking out all items of clothing or bedding before packing, wearing, or sleeping in them, however, experienced only minor neurological symptoms radiating upward from the short-lived pain of the sting itself. The savvy desert visitor, by the way, never unrolls his sleeping bag until the moment before he slides into it.

According to Arizona Poison Centers, several thousand Arizonans call in each year to report envenomations via scorpion stings. But the vast majority of victims never bother to call. Either way, none of those sting victims died. The last reliably documented fatality in Arizona due to a single episode of *Centruroides* sting occurred in 1964 and was of a small child. On the other hand, just a few years ago a woman in Tucson was stung by a scorpion for the second time in her life. During the first she had emerged unscathed. In the interim, however, her immune system had developed excessive antibodies to the scorpion's venom. Immediately after her second sting, she died of anaphylactic shock. Medically speaking, the risk of such a scenario playing out for the average person is miniscule. In short, for an otherwise healthy adult, a sting is more of a painful inconvenience than a threat to life.

So what happens if you are stung?

First, plan on a sleepless night. This sleep deprivation will be due to nerve pain then the sort of numbness and tingling one feels after "hitting one's funny bone" (the ulnar nerve) of the elbow. The stinging throb the venom causes will radiate, tingling and pulsating up your arm or leg or wherever else you were stung. You can confirm a sting by tapping on its site. A positive "tap test" usually exacerbates the painful tingling, sending it reverberating outward from the area. These symptoms usually peak in severity and radiation in 4 to 6 hours, after which they begin to dissipate. Two or three weeks may pass before all symptoms resolve.

But if scorpions are not the Canyon's big killers, then how many of the Canyon's millions of human visitors have been killed by the Canyon's black widow spiders, brown recluse spiders, killer bees, bumblebees, so-called "fire" ants, occasional Gila monsters, rabies, and all its other little venomous, noxious, and/or parasitic denizens?

None that we know of.

Nor has any visitor to the Canyon been seriously injured by any large mammal. There has been no mauling by a bear or big cat and no goring, kicking, or butting by a deer, elk, or bighorn sheep.

Okay, fine, but how many of the Canyon's millions of human visitors have been killed by all those species of rattlesnakes or coral snakes?

Again, none.

Not in Grand Canyon, anyway. Arizona as a state is a different matter. "Since 2002, Arizona has had about one snakebite death per year," says Jude McNally, managing director of the Arizona Poison and Drug Information Center, "that's up from 1985-2000, when there was a reported death about every five years."

One of the most recent deaths (October 10, 2007) was to a Paulden woman (Chino Valley/Prescott), 63-year-old Jackie Ledwell, who discovered a Mojave rattlesnake in her yard. The Mojave rattlesnake (*Crotalus scutulatus*) is a species that delivers a neurotoxic and hemolytic venom ten times more toxic than that of any other North American rattlesnake. In Arizona this slightly greenish (but variable in color) rattlesnake with bold dorsal diamonds and a distinct eye streak running rearward can be found in many different habitats and in a broad range of elevations across the western and southwestern two-thirds of the state, including more than half of Grand Canyon. Ledwell decided to kill the snake with a kitchen knife. Instead it nailed her. After the Mojave rattlesnake bit her, paramedics in Chino treated her then transported her to Flagstaff Medical Center. She died there the next day.

Rattlesnakes have also bitten people in the Canyon. For an agonizing example, consider Virginia Rice, age 32. On June 25, 1996 Rice and another member of a private river party had just swum to shore after the boat they were riding in had flipped in Lava Falls. Grateful to still be alive, Rice dragged herself out of the frigid current. She climbed a few feet above the racing river onto the rocks along the left bank. Again, preoccupied with her narrow escape from that swim in notorious Lava Falls—and now feeling emotionally that she was safe—Rice neither heard nor saw the snake that bit her. But she did feel a sudden sharp, searing pain in her left leg.

She looked down and saw a rattlesnake recoiling. Not only was Rice's action in spotting it too late, it also was too slow.

Before Rice moved away, the rattlesnake struck her again, biting her a second time on the same leg, just above the ankle.

The pain was immediate. Rice's leg swelled almost instantly due to the hemolytic effect of the venom. Blood oozed from the fang marks. Rice was appalled, shocked, depressed, and alarmed that she might not live to see another day. Drowning in Lava Falls suddenly seemed a far better way to shuck this mortal coil.

Once Rice managed to tell the other members of her party what had happened, they flagged down a commercial trip. The guides on it radioed out to an overflying aircraft to relay a message to NPS Dispatch for Rice's evacuation.

Two hours later, an NPS helicopter with Ranger Medics Marty Johnson and Matt Vandzura retrieved Rice then dropped her off at Grand Canyon Clinic. Rice's left leg was swollen and had hemorrhaged under the skin up into her groin. Her pain was excruciating. At Grand Canyon Clinic Myers and staff infused Rice with antivenin and pain medication then evacuated her to Flagstaff Medical Center. Rice eventually recovered.

Other people, though not many, have been bitten in the Canyon by different species of rattlesnakes (most of which have gone unidentified as to species). And while no one bitten has died, neither was any of them "improved" in any way by being injected with venom. Instead, many victims experience long-term problems due to the hemolytic effects in destroyed blood vessels. In short, rattlesnake bites remain serious business. And because most of us know this, most guides who work in the Canyon teach people the cardinal rule: "Never place any part of your body anyplace where you have not looked first."

Guides and most visitors in general also have imagined snake scenarios and tried to decide what to do about them to rescue themselves or their buddies.

I (Ghiglieri) had imagined several of these myself. But I had never imagined being a participant in one of the more challenging scenarios I ultimately ended up being called upon to "fix." Working a Tour West rowing trip in 1987, we had camped at, of all places, "Upper Rattlesnake Camp" (at River Mile 74 and named when a passenger on a much earlier river trip, who had been sitting on the porta potty, reached back for the toilet paper, and a rattlesnake bit him on the hand; amazingly, an identical incident would happen years later to another river runner reaching for the toilet paper at Tanner Camp). Anyway, a couple of hours after dark, I awoke when a lady on our trip appeared at the bow of my boat urgently calling my name. I asked her, "What's up?"

"A rattlesnake is coiled up on Barbara's chest. You've got to get it off before something happens."

Sure. A rattlesnake on Barbara's chest, I thought to myself. I've heard them all now. Rattlesnakes never coil up on someone's chest. That only happens in Gary Larson cartoons. But what if she was telling the truth? I suddenly realized I would need something—a tool—to remove said snake. With no more time to think, I grabbed a short folding shovel, a G.I. "E-tool."

I followed the agitated lady to her and Barbara's nearby camp spot. Sure enough, there she lay on her back. She was not quite all the way inside her sleeping bag. And despite the beam of my MagLite hitting her face, she was staring straight up into the starry heavens with the same permanent fixity of gaze as held by the inner golden coffin of young King Tutankhamen. On her chest a medium-sized rattlesnake had coiled.

Ever since having worked in rain forests and bush country of Central and East Africa populated with lightning quick mambas and absolutely lethal cobras, rattlesnakes have seemed to me far more like puppy dogs than true threats to life. Now, suddenly, this all changed. This rattlesnake's fangs were only a few inches from Barbara's carotid artery.

The handle on my E-tool seemed to have shrunk. Even so, it would have to do.

As I approached the snake, it abruptly felt less satisfied with its warm snuggling spot. It uncoiled. DO NOT, I tried to project mental commands to it (snakes being deaf), SLITHER TOWARD THIS WOMAN'S HEAD!

Instead it slithered slightly toward her left shoulder, opposite me and toward the river.

I circled around Barbara's feet to head it off. Gingerly, I slid the flat blade of the E-tool against Barbara's chest and under the snake's middle, but a bit forward. I knew that if I screwed this up, there would be hell to pay. Likely Barbara would be the one paying.

I lifted. The snake dangled off the E-tool but continued to slither forward. I carefully rotated the shovel to keep the snake balanced on it near mid-length. This worked. But again, the handle of the E-tool was less than 18 inches long. And if this snake fell off, I'd have to recapture it—in a very agitated state—in the dark. Or else no one in this camp would sleep tonight.

Conveniently, the Colorado flowed past only a dozen or so feet away. What do you do with a hot-blooded, cold-blooded rattlesnake? Yes, it fell off my E-tool into the cold river. By the way, this was a mistake on my part. Rattlesnakes rarely survive in the river because it cools them beyond their operational temperatures. Normally when I capture a snake in camp, I place it in a bucket for the night with a lid on it then release the snake in the morning just before we launch. Grand Canyon is a national park. The creatures living in it are fully protected by law—as they should be.

Again, and contrary to popular misconception, even when considering the time before antivenin was available here, there have been no documented human deaths to rattlesnake or coral snake bites in the Canyon. In the United States as a whole, a whopping 40,000 to 50,000 bites are reported yearly involving nearly every one of the 115 species of snake in the country. Roughly 7,000 of these bites are from one of America's 19-25 poisonous species. How many of those 7,000 poisonous bites in the U.S. per year kill the victim? About a dozen victims (1 in 500+) per year die. No surprise by now, 90 percent of bite victims are male. Moreover, 80 percent of bites known were inflicted on the victim's hand while he or she intentionally handled the snake. What this reveals is that most bites on humans are inflicted by the snake in justifiable self-defense. It also reveals that men, not women, are the primary threats to such snakes. These statistics also reveal again that one and only cardinal rule that a rational (non-snake-enamored) person needs to remember to avoid being bitten: Never put any part of your body—or your child's—anyplace where you have not looked in advance to check that it is not already a rattlesnake's or a scorpion's personal space.

To be perfectly truthful here, we have to admit that once upon a time in Grand Canyon a man did die because of a rattlesnake. This took place on September 13, 1933 in, of all places, Snake Gulch. On that date 43-year-old Francis Clem Cochrane of Los Angeles, California was hiking into the Canyon about 12 miles from Hatch cabin and heading down into Kanab Canyon. The goal of Cochrane and his buddy Gordon Smith, also of Los Angeles, was to descend to the Colorado to prospect for gold.

Cochrane's big problem (among a few) was his phobia of snakes, especially rattlesnakes. The inevitable finally did happen. A coiled rattlesnake rattled and struck toward Cochrane. But the snake never connected. It missed because Cochrane was not close enough. Even so, the little reptile frightened Cochrane so severely that he suffered a fatal heart attack.

Smith dutifully hauled Cochrane back to Kanab by mule back to a doctor. He confirmed by autopsy that Cochrane had literally died of fright without a fang mark on him.

Okay, if the little critters don't kill people in Grand Canyon, what about the big ones?

Eric York, age 37, of Shelburne, Massachusetts held a passion for studying the mountain lions (*Felis concolor*) of Grand Canyon. He blow-darted them with immobilization drugs to collar them with global positioning system radio collars. These allowed York between 2006 and 2007 to monitor via telemetry the movements of ten pumas among Arizona's population of about 2,500 lions. He noted many aspects of their ecology in the Park. He recorded what they ate, where each ranged in his or her 150 square-mile home range, which females had kittens, how they developed, and so on. Sadly, he also faced the dismal task of documenting the demise of his elusive subjects, often as victims of drivers hitting them on the highway and of hunters shooting them when the big cats exited the Park in search of food, territory, or a mate.

As often happens to a biologist specializing in fieldwork on large mammals, York began to identify with his subjects as a kindred species. No doubt they do need his friendship. Eric's focal animals are serious underdogs of public relations. Pumas are a species that has been reviled in North America as sneaking, cowardly killers whose presence signified for some people either the imperfection of God's creation or else the work of Satan. Many people today still hate them unreasonably.

Eric York's work as a National Park biologist at Grand Canyon and also in Alaska, California, Nepal, Chile, and Pakistan (on snow leopards, *Panthera uncia*) served to a small degree as an antidote to the defamations heaped upon big cats by the livestock raising industry, which in America has successfully lobbied Congress for more than a century to apportion tax money to try to eliminate *all* of America's large predators. As told well by Michael J. Robinson in *Predatory Bureaucracy The Extermination of Wolves and the Transformation of the West* (a book every American should read, but only with a strong stomach), American taxpayers have been paying for a hundred years—and continue to pay today—federal and state employees to systematically exterminate America's wildlife heritage for the imagined financial benefit of cattlemen (most often), sheepmen, and large agricultural conglomerates.

In Arizona alone, from 1947 to 1969 when legislators were paying bounties for dead mountain lions, the state paid out bounties to wildlife assassins for 5,400 pumas they killed. This killing ostensibly was to protect the profitability of cattle interests. Sheepmen, for example, generally shepherd their flocks, use guard dogs, and so on to protect their sheep. In contrast, cattlemen essentially abandon their pregnant cows, often on public lands (half of the western U.S. is public land, and cattle graze 70 percent of it), then cry wolf when their unattended livestock, which often ruins the habitat for the natural grazers and prey of pumas and wolves, falls prey to natural predators on public lands. In most cases the big cats had taken calves of domestic cattle (88 percent of all livestock kills between 1976 to 2005 were calves), especially it turns out, when the numbers of local mule deer had dropped to low levels due to overhunting by humans and habitat loss to developers and habitat deterioration due to overgrazing by cattle.

York's research helped to reverse the falsely maligned image of mountain lions and other big cats as spawn of the devil. The reality being—as nearly all wildlife biologists will readily attest—that the single most important agent that exists out there to keep herds of deer (*Odocoileus hemionus* and *Odocoileus virginianus*), elk (*Cervus canadensis*), bison (*Bison bison*), and other herbivores healthy and free of disease epidemics is our big predators culling their weak and sick. Pumas and wolves (*Canis lupus*) operate as "keystone species," the prime agents that fine tune a local ecology by enhancing biodiversity and reducing over-exploitation of habitats. Indeed, in Earth's oceans today the severe overfishing of predator species is leading to an explosion of trillions of stunted prey fish which are over-browsing their primary species of forage, causing ecological disruptions, and are heading for population collapses of magnitudes beyond biblical proportions.

At any rate, York's work to observe and understand the ecology of Grand Canyon National Park's mountain lions stands in stark contrast to older federal policies regarding predators. A prime example of the horrid management of the old days unfolded on the North Rim's Kaibab National Forest and Grand Canyon National Game Reserve (in 1919, it became a "Park") between 1906-1939, when Federal policy and Arizona policy aimed at eliminating *all* predators. D. Irvin Rasmussen notes in *Ecological Monographs* (July 1941, page 236) that in a misguided attempt to increase deer herds, 816 mountain lions were killed by government hunters, bounty hunters, and/or commercial trappers using hounds, leg-traps, snares, ropes, poisoned bait, bullets, and clubs. These hunters also killed all of the last 30 wolves alive in Northern Arizona plus 7,388 coyotes (*Canis latrans*), 863 bobcats (*Lynx rufus*), and an uncounted number of eagles, hawks, owls, and badgers (*Taxidea taxus*). They even shot wild horses (*Equus caballus*). Interestingly, one trapper/hunter named "Uncle" Jimmy Owens acted as the primary assassin during much of this era of slaughter. By the 1920s, Owens amassed a huge fortune in bounties paid to him over the corpses of slain wildlife. Owens was awarded the Grand Canyon Game Reserve Warden position in 1906. Over the next dozen years before the region gained National Park status, he used his position to personally kill most of those hundreds of mountain lions.

The results? The deer populations exploded and drastically over-browsed the entire region. Next deer starved to death by the thousands. Some scientists estimate tens of thousands. The survivors continued to breed, however, to the point where sport-hunting had to be augmented with government trapping and killing of deer. Now, nearly a century later, despite all game management efforts, the ecology of the Kaibab Plateau has yet to recover to its pre-1906 lush biodiversity.

Rarely mentioned but ecologically significant, pumas were not the Canyon's only big cats in those days. Donald F. Hoffmeister notes in his *Mammals of Grand Canyon* that jaguars (*Felis onca)* were rare but present around the Canyon, being seen in 1907 or 1908 "near the railroad about 4 miles south of the canyon rim" within current Park boundaries. This old male, the last one known in Northern Arizona, was tracked in snow, shot, and killed where it was dining on a dead colt.

This hideous history makes it all too tempting to most modern field biologists to want to belatedly befriend Mother Nature's beautiful big cats and wolves, our imperiled keystone predators, to make up for the century-long avalanche of misery we humans have inflicted on their species via wildlife "management" during America's ecological Dark Ages. But for Eric York this well-intentioned atonement for past slaughters went wrong.

During the last week of October, 2007 the mortality sensor on the collar of one of York's two radio-collared females, #P13, signaled that she had died. He inspected #P13's body. The 90-pound puma had died curled up with blood under her nose. York found puncture marks in her neck and abdomen. More sad, this female's three, 3-month-old, fuzzy, blue-eyed cubs, far too young to survive on their own, soon would starve in their den. In that York's mission was to understand the ecology of pumas in the Grand Canyon region, he decided to take #P13 home and perform a necropsy on her in his residence in the Park.

As noted by Cyndy Cole in the *Arizona Daily Sun* (November 10, 2007) and by Jackie Brown in the *Williams-Grand Canyon News* (November 20, 2007), within a couple of days, Eric York felt sick with a fever, headache, chest pain, and a cough that produced bloody saliva. Neither Eric nor anyone else recognized these symptoms for what they were: pneumonic plague, the most serious but least common form of plague. Eric's mother lion had been injured, yes, but she had died of plague. He had brought her—and it—home with him. Meanwhile, back in their den, #P13's young cubs died too. Indeed by now, seven of York's ten radio-collared pumas had died, again, most of them to human causes.

On the morning of November 2, Eric York was found dead in his trailer. The Centers for Disease Control soon confirmed York had died of pneumonic (a.k.a. "sylvatic") plague—a plague extremely similar to that which wiped out half of Europe a few times in the Middle Ages. Pneumonic plague is caused by the bacterium *Yersinia pestis*. It invaded North America by hitchhiking on fleas who in turn were hitchhiking on rats who in turn were hitchhiking on ships that tied up in San Francisco Bay around the year 1900. Plague now resides in—and decimates—several natural populations of wildlife species in North America and in Arizona at elevations above 4,500 feet. Locally sylvatic plague has made inroads in prairie dog (*Cynomys gunnisoni*) colonies, especially since 2006. Indeed many such colonies have sustained catastrophic losses to the point of being wiped out—and with them their extremely endangered specialist predator the black-footed ferret (*Mustela nigripes*).

If diagnosed quickly this virulent bacterium can be cured easily in people, pets, and other animals with antibiotics. And it can be prevented in people or cats or dogs or even prairie dogs and ferrets by an oral vaccine hidden in marble-sized peanut butter pellets developed by USGS epizootiologist Tonie Rocke. Notably, York's dying alongside his dead puma comprises the only documented case in Arizona history in which a human died due to a mountain lion.

As a local wildlife biologist, Eric York likely knew about plague. He should have considered plague as a possible contributory cause of death of his mama mountain lion. We mention this not to seem uncharitable to York's memory. On the contrary, we think he died a hero. We spell out this epidemiology only in hopes of emphasizing that Eric York's death should serve at minimum as a warning to the rest of us. Handling carcasses of wild animals that appear ill or have died due to a questionable cause is risky business.

Well, if the lions, tigers and bears are not a problem, what is?

On any summer day one can walk past the Fountain at Bright Angel Lodge—an epicenter for outward ripples of ice cream and fast food—and see not tourists but squirrels lined up to be fed by the hands of tourists. That this happens in front of NPS signs specifically saying not to do this seems a moot point. In the defense of the tourists dumb enough to feed these Arizona gray squirrels (*Sciurus arizonensis*) despite the Park's pointed warning signs, the little buggers do seem irresistible. These insatiable rodents are pudgy, big-eyed balls of fluff that charmingly bound up (or waddle up) to their intended mark sitting on the rim guard wall munching Double-Chocolate Chunk.

But it's a con game.

We are guessing that each "chosen" tourist thus approached feels special, like Dr. Doolittle, because the squirrel has selected him or her out of a throng of so many others. As a reward for this apparent "natural connection" between man and beast, the Dr. Dolittle in many of us offers the rambunctious rodent a nibble on a bit of sugar cone. Then maybe we add a second or third or fourth tidbit as a bribe for a photo-opportunity to prove to everyone back home that this intimate encounter with nature and this uncanny animal clairvoyance actually took place.

This usually proves the moment when the charming little pudgeball of fur metamorphoses into a ravenous beast. The transformation seems as abrupt as when the adorable little miners of Beryllium spheres in GALAXY QUEST turn into merciless predators sporting fangs the size of bananas. As the Arizona gray squirrel lunges for our proffered morsel, its shy, innocent, and darling persona dissolves into the attack of a fat, fearless, and aggressive rodent who had done all this before. The scene degrades into a mini feeding frenzy perpetuated by hordes of well-intentioned but irresponsible tourists. Due to the rodents' penchant for successfully duping then intimidating tourists, the chubby little guys actually become unhealthy. Like many of the humans feeding them, the squirrels too die younger from heart disease, cancers, and other problems related to obesity.

But most tourists conclude these rodent pan-handlers must be starving. The problem? All too often when these greedy furballs snatch bite after bite, they also chomp a chunk out of their benefactor's fingertip. And then Dr. Doolittle metamorphoses into a patient worried about rabies. How often does this happen? Two or three tourists each day report bites to rangers. Each victim is then referred to Grand Canyon Clinic for treatment.

What should you do if you are bitten? First, you probably deserved it. You or your kid should not have been feeding the squirrel. On the other hand, some squirrels have perfected the tactic of sneaking up behind their mark unseen then "purse-snatching" the goods. This is a common scenario on the rim, Indian Gardens, the South Kaibab Trail or at Bright Angel Campground. Here the Houdini-like squirrels magically pull your entire bag of Cheez-Its from your pack and scurry away, exhibiting impeccable timing in the process. Yes, many have learned how to unzip a pack. Others just bore through the nylon like a mechanical mole bent on drilling down to the core of the planet.

Whether getting bit is your own fault or not, what should you next worry about? The biggest concern, it turns out, is a minor risk of infection. Therefore treatment primarily consists of wound cleaning and a tetanus booster (if it has been more than ten years since one's last one).

What about rabies? The Centers for Disease Control (CDC) website notes: "Small rodents (such as squirrels, rats, mice, hamsters, guinea pigs, gerbils, and chipmunks,) and lagomorphs (such as rabbits and hares) are almost never found to be infected with rabies and have not been known to cause rabies among humans in the United States."

Why don't these small mammals transmit rabies? "—the most likely explanation," notes Dr. Jean S. Smith of the Division of Viral and Rickettsial Diseases at the Centers for Disease Control and Prevention in Atlanta, "is that [rodents] probably would not survive an encounter with an infected carnivore. It is also possible that they may lack a means of transmitting the virus within the species, because of mouth shape or some other factor, and so do not become significant reservoirs for the disease. There is not much fighting within the species that would lead to the bites that would spread the infection."

Among carnivores, however, rabies is always a possibility.

On October 5, 2002 45-year-old Sjors Horstman was winding up his fourteenth year as a volunteer in the park (or VIP) at Phantom Ranch. As the sun poised to rise above the rim he toted a couple of boxes to the mule duffle area to be packed out that morning. As he walked the trail east of the ranger station toward the trail crew bunkhouse a flash of movement flicked in the corner of his eye. Startled, Sjors spun for a better look.

It was a gray fox (*Urocyon cinereoargenteus*). Neither of the two species of foxes in Grand Canyon exists in high numbers. Most people never see them. So this encounter seemed unusual. What seemed far more unusual to Sjors right now was this fox was stalking him.

Although Sjors did not know it, this same little carnivore had been seen the night before. A hiker had mentioned to the interpretive ranger at the evening program that he had seen a fox acting "peculiar." The ranger did not think much about it. This would turn out to be a mistake.

Sjors sensed this fox's atypical behavior boded ill. What the heck could this fox be thinking? Closing in on Sjors, the adorable little creature circled him. Then it circled again. Each circle became faster and tighter.

Something, thought Sjors, is wrong with this guy.

The fox was not foaming at mouth as is commonly described for hydrophobic (rabid) carnivores. On the other hand, Sjors could see all forty-two of its teeth as they gnashed together menacingly.

Worried, Sjors rotated to remain facing his new-found admirer as it circled him. This odd tango of man and beast repeated for several spins before Sjors's dancing partner made a leap for his face.

Sjors flung one of his boxes at it. It connected. But the fox remained undaunted. Sjors nailed it with the other box. The fox did not act fazed. Instead it leaped again at Sjors's head. Luckily it seemed unable to jump that high.

Sjors countered this leap with a kick. Again the fox remained unimpressed. It resumed making tight little circles around the man. While Sjors spun too, he again tried to kick it. He not only failed to connect, he tripped over his own feet and landed on his back.

An "Oh, shit!" moment.

The fox instantly charged. It jumped onto Sjors's stomach. Teeth bared, it zeroed in on Sjors's face.

Sjors tightened his fists to avoid giving the fox something soft into which to sink its teeth. In a flurry of punches he landed a solid left jab then a right, knocking the fox several feet away with each.

After the second time, Sjors scrambled back to his feet as the crazed little mouse-eater resumed the circle dance. Suddenly it stopped in its tracks and arched its back in a weird cat-like pose.

Sjors hammered the little demon with a round house to the head. The animal bounced away, stood for a few seconds, then keeled over.

Was it dead? Or merely a technical knockout? Cautiously Sjors moved closer to investigate.

It was still breathing. Okay, a TKO. Good enough.

Sjors hurried back to the ranger station. Two hikers stood in front of the building.

"Get inside! There's a crazy fox out here. It's probably got rabies!"

Sjors phoned Dispatch. He was informed that Backcountry Law Enforcement Ranger Kathy Jean ("KJ") Glover was hiking down the trail toward him. She could shoot the fox. She would arrive in a couple of hours. "We'll radio her," the dispatcher added, "and make sure she's informed."

Sjors exited the ranger station to hurry upcanyon to the Phantom Ranch Canteen to warn everyone making the morning run with material for the compost pile. Before he had gotten far he heard the two hikers at the ranger station yelling to him.

"Hey! The fox is coming back your way!"

Sjors spun and ran back into the ranger station. He phoned Dispatch.

"Did you reach Kay Jay?"

"No. Not yet. She's probably turned her radio down and is not hearing the traffic."

"Well, tell her the fox is up again and roaming around."

Sjors ran outside to find the fox.

The fox had vanished.

"Awww…now where the hell is it?"

Sjors headed west of the ranger station and saw people on the main trail. They were photographing the fox.

He ran closer to warn them.

He arrived to see his nemesis sitting on the trail and looking as sweet and innocent as a puppy.

"Isn't it cute?" they asked.

"No it's not! It's sick and probably has rabies. You need to get out of here! Go back to the campground."

Suddenly the "puppy" attacked a rock. Then it gnashed at plants. It chomped an irrigation hose. Next it stalked in fast circles again. It chased its tail, trying to bite it. Abruptly it stopped doing all this and shifted back to puppy mode.

Then it keeled over as if playing dead.

Sjors realized something had to be done long before Ranger Glover arrived. He yanked his radio to call NPS water treatment operator Frank Corey.

"Frank, we got a problem."

"Okay. I'll stay here at the bridge at the upper campground and direct people heading your way away from the trail the fox is closest to. If the fox is near the creek, I'll send them on the trail by the cliff on the east side of the ranger station. If not, I'll let them use the creekside trail."

Sjors next radioed David Meyer, Phantom Ranch manager. Meyer agreed to monitor and direct traffic like Corey at the other end of the trail near the ranch and prevent people from heading down to the ranger amphitheater where the fox now was.

VIP Sjors decided to climb the roof of the ranger station to stake out the fox and direct tourist traffic.

These tactics of diverting human traffic worked for nearly two hours. Meanwhile the fox roamed freely.

Where the hell was Glover? She normally would have arrived at Phantom long ago. She still was not responding to radio calls.

On the South Kaibab Trail about a mile and a half from Phantom near Panorama Point Glover ran into the trail crew workers. Sjors had anticipated this encounter and had radioed the trail crew supervisor to tell Glover to "turn up her radio."

Now Dispatch was able to instruct Glover to shoot the fox but not in the head. Its brain would be needed for rabies testing. Glover hurried down the trail.

Meanwhile, back at the ranch, the fox entered the cabin area and settled in front of the shower house. Sjors followed and heard shower noises. Somebody was in there.

"Hey! Don't come out! There's a crazy fox by the front door. It probably has rabies. You need to stay inside!"

"Can you tell my husband?" an unseen woman's voice asked. "He's in cabin six."

Sjors banged on the door of cabin six. "Your wife is stuck in the shower because a rabid fox is blocking the door. You need to go to the canteen and wait there." The bleary-eyed husband (it was now 10:30 a.m.) looked perplexed.

The fox next approached the employee bunkhouse. A worker emerged. Upon witnessing the fox's bizarre antics, he made a quick about-face and bolted back into the bunkhouse.

Three and a half hours after Sjors first had been stalked by the fox, Glover arrived.

"Awww, this is sad," said Glover, a longtime animal advocate. "I know it's got to be done though, and it's not the best place for it. Okay. Let's clear everybody, Sjors. I'll shoot for the heart and lungs and be done with it."

Once everyone had been safely ensconced in the canteen and now craned their necks for a view, Glover drew her semiautomatic handgun and approached the fox. An experienced marksman, she aimed her pistol and fired. BLAM!

Sjors saw fur fly as the fox jolted back. Sjors relaxed for the first time in hours. Finally the poor thing was out of its misery. Yes, it was sad. But nothing else could be done. No living creature can be cured of rabies.

Sjors now stared at the dead fox and could not believe his eyes.

The fox rose from the ground like a movie Terminator and lunged toward Glover. Next it ran tight circles around her. Glover rotated to continue facing it. She calmly fired at the fox as she rotated in their dance. BLAM! BLAM! BLAM! BLAM! Half her shots went wild. But she hit it about every other shot. It continued circling, even with half its jaw shot away.

Finally it keeled over. Glover walked the few steps to it.

"Don't trust it!" Sjors shouted.

On cue, the ten-pound demon jumped up again and launched into attack mode.

Glover fired at it yet again, emptying her pistol. BLAM! BLAM! BLAM! She reloaded a full magazine. She shot again, hitting it twice. BLAM! BLAM! BLAM! BLAM!

Now, after nearly a dozen bullets, it dropped into the dust.

"Sjors, come over and tell me what you think?"

"One more shot. I don't trust it!"

Glover shot the inert mess of a fox a final time.

"Do I need a rabies shot?" Sjors asked me (Myers) a couple of hours later by phone and relaying the unbelievable tale of the fox that had terrorized Phantom.

"Hell yeah, you do! Go to the Flag Medical Center tomorrow and get started. Kay Jay too, with blood and saliva from the busted jaw and whatnot flying around."

The NPS chopper flew Sjors, Glover, and the fox carcass to Flagstaff. Shots began the next day. While Sjors didn't have any obvious bites and scratches from the fox itself, he did have multiple open scratches from the day before on his hands and legs from grass cuts gained while cleaning irrigation ditches in the campground. Any of these could allow for rabies transmission into his bloodstream. So as precautionary treatment Sjors received rabies immune globulin shots into the pre-existing scratches, a whopping and burning 17. Glover received three. Both continued the rabies series over several months.

Scuttlebutt has it that Sjors's little dancing partner was the first fox in Grand Canyon documented with rabies. Rabies kills up to 50,000 people per year worldwide. In the western United States skunks, bats, and foxes prove the most common hosts. From 1995 through 2011, the CDC reported 49 cases of human rabies (3 per year) in the U.S., 35 of those (71 percent) from likely bat exposure. Once a person is bitten, a series of six anti-rabies vaccinations are necessary. Receiving those shots within two weeks proves 100 percent effective. The protocols for rabies treatment were established by the U.S. CDC. They hold for Arizona and Coconino County. If a person has been exposed to a potentially rabid animal and that animal is available for testing (the fox at Phantom), then the patient should wait for the results of that testing before receiving any anti-rabies vaccines. There exists a safe window of up to 14 days prior to treatment, during which that testing can take place. If the attacker tests positive for rabies, the victim then should receive the vaccine series. If it tests negative, no anti-rabies shots are needed. If the animal is not available (if a bat bit a person then fluttered or crawled away), but exposure is pretty certain, then the bite victim should receive those shots.

If, after 14 days with no shots, signs and symptoms of rabies manifest, it is too late for the vaccine. The odds of survival are close to zero. Why only "close?" In 2004 the "Milwaukie Protocol" developed at the Children's Hospital of Wisconsin actually saved a bite victim with symptoms by putting her into a coma using ketamine to ward off rabies and protect the brain, midazolam to lessen ketamine's tendency to cause hallucinations, plus two antivirals: ribavirin and amantadine. Within six days the victim produced antibodies to rabies. After a month in the hospital she needed rehab to relearn how to talk, stand, walk etc. This Protocol does sound better than a death sentence, but note that of 41 rabies patients who have so far received it since 2004, only 6 have survived---and they required months to achieve a partial recovery.

Our intent with this chapter was to help illustrate what not to do when encountering Grand Canyon fauna (or flora). In short, do not approach, feed, pet, handle, rescue, or harass wildlife. Indeed veterinarians in Arizona are not allowed to practice on injured wild animals. Sad and unfortunate, but it is the law of the land.

While Grand Canyon's unique landscapes inspire aesthetic awe, some of the Canyon's denizens invisible to the naked eye instead inspire dread. Grand Canyon, for example, hosts one of the world's most deadly viruses.

It started as a mystery disease. In May of 1993 in the Four Corners area of the United States, for example, a cluster of deaths resulted from a mysterious respiratory illness. This invisible scourge spurred widespread fear across the Southwest. It also spawned a flurry of research by the Centers for Disease Control to identify its cause.

Because in the past such outbreaks had been episodic and poorly understood, the disease agent responsible for these strange deaths had earned multiple names. "Four Corners virus," "*Muerto* (Dead) Canyon virus," and "*Sin Nombre* (Without Name) virus" all were used to label what turned out to be the same incredibly tiny strand of RNA now known as hantavirus. Again, in 1993, hantavirus Pulmonary Syndrome (or HPS) caused a severe form of respiratory distress that led to 32 deaths among the 53 cases that year, a 60 percent mortality rate.

Why such a sudden epidemic? Oddly, the answer resides in weather. After years of drought, 1993's *El Niño* winter dumped heavy snows and rains. This water fostered bumper crops among native vegetation. The production of pinyon (*Pinus edulis*) nuts, for example, spiked. This bounty of food fueled a population explosion of deer mice (*Peromyscus maniculatus*) to a level ten times higher than a year earlier. These mice are the primary (but not sole) carriers of hantavirus.

As unlikely as it may seem, people become infected with hantavirus by inhaling the aerosolized droplets of deer mouse urine droplets or feces. How? Usually when the dried virus rises into the air as dust in areas where infected rodents have constructed their nests and middens. The act of sweeping a storage area or cabin where deer mice have nested can be enough to kill you. Merely being in such a place while a wind leaks in to raise dust can do the same thing.

Grand Canyon—and the Southwest in general—cannot claim a monopoly on this deadly virus. The CDC's website shows a total of 606 U.S. cases in several states beginning in 1993 through 2013, ranging from 11 to 48 cases per year. The overall case fatality rate for those 21 years was 36%.

One third of these people died. Hantaviruses around the world have been classified into one genus. Additionally, hantaviruses have been categorized as zoonoses, entities that transmit diseases from nature to man. In Sweden, for example, a hantavirus epidemic has existed since 1934. Hantaviruses can create two kinds of acute and severe illnesses, one affecting the kidneys, the other the lungs. Worldwide, the kidney-related disease form is far more common. But the pulmonary form has proved more deadly.

In July of 1998 a Grand Canyon river guide was camping on the left bank at river mile 19.5, upstream of North Canyon. While he lay sleeping under an overturned paddle raft as shelter from the rain, a mouse decided to traverse his body.

"In the middle of the night I was awakened by a mouse running around on top of me," says the guide, who remains anonymous. "Then I noticed a little moisture on my face—my startled reaction had caused it [now startled too] to urinate."

Gasping in surprise, the guide had inadvertently aspirated a few droplets of urine.

Weeks later he became very sick. Hospital tests confirmed the cause as hantavirus. He ended up in the intensive care unit. Fortunately, with supportive respiratory treatment, he recovered completely. Researchers later confirmed hantavirus in the 19.5 Mile Camp. Four of 42 mice captured there tested positive as carriers.

A few years later another infection occurred in the South Rim Village area. While tearing out an old carpet from a trailer for replacement, a worker was exposed to deadly "mouse dust" and contracted the virus. Luckily, he too survived.

Despite these survival stories, the seriousness of hantavirus should not be underestimated. The Canyon hosts nearly 27,000 river runners and 120,000 backcountry hikers each year. Mice exist in nearly all camps. Their numbers explode month by month as they scavenge food scraps or raid poorly stashed food. An odd piece of trivia, when aspens and related species of trees die out in a region (elk can and do wipe out aspens) and are replaced by other vegetation, populations of deer mice may triple. This leads to one of those intricate ecological situations where wolves and mountain lions help reduce hantavirus infections among people and other creatures. It goes like this: the predators reduce elk herds and also keep them from congregating for long in one area. This prevents the elk from utterly destroying stands of aspen, which they otherwise would do. Stands of aspen attract hikers but foster far lower populations of deer mice. Fewer deer mice mean far less hantavirus.

So far, little research has been conducted in the Canyon to reveal where hantavirus is and is not. Future research may clarify this. But don't hold your breath. Interestingly, as revealed by small mammal trapping studies conducted by Steven W. Carothers, deer mice probably are not native to the river corridor. Instead, the mice likely hitchhiked their way to river trip camps at the bottom of the Canyon aboard river boats, most likely ones trailered to Lees Ferry from deer mouse habitat such as Flagstaff, Kanab, and so on.

In the meantime the best advice is to avoid mouse burrows or den sites—commonly found under rocks, vegetation, logs, abandoned cabins, shacks, enclosed structures, and the mouths of caves. If your camp area seems suspicious, sleep in a zipped tent. It is also wise to take precautions to avoid attracting mice with food. Keep all food and trash in rodent-proof containers. Hang them out of reach.

What are the signs and symptoms of having contracting hantavirus?

"Flu-like" symptoms begin 1 to 6 weeks after exposure—long after one has left the Canyon behind. These symptoms include fever, muscle and body aches, a dry cough, and sometimes abdominal cramping and vomiting. These can last 2 to 15 days. This may be followed by a life-threatening respiratory distress or respiratory failure (Acute Respiratory Distress Syndrome, or ARDS). This acute condition may emerge as early as 24 hours after the onset of those flu-like symptoms, and it can look like severe pneumonia wherein the lungs become inflamed then fill with fluid. Respiratory distress becomes ever more acute and characterized by extreme shortness of breath and rapid and shallow respirations—even to the point where the victim's neck and rib muscles pull or retract inward with each labored breath, as if sucking on a straw. As oxygen levels drop, skin color, especially on the lips and fingertips, may turn to gray to bluish or mottled.

If you strongly suspect hantavirus, seek medical help *immediately*. And let the medical personnel *know* you suspect you have been exposed to hantavirus. *Insist* on tests. People outside the Southwest need to tell their doctors exactly what they suspect. Doctors practicing outside this region often will not think to test for the virus, even though it may exist in their state.

The bad news? No cure or no antibiotic therapy exists to combat hantavirus. Treatment is merely supportive and aimed at keeping oxygen levels up. Hospitalization is required, usually in a critical care unit with advanced life support measures. These include being placed on a respirator. Survival rate for ARDS *with* hantavirus is a dismal 60 percent.

During early June of 2009 in the Canyon a private group of river runners spent the night camping at river mile 137, also known as Pancho's Kitchen. The attraction of this location is a huge cliff shelter of Tapeats Sandstone. Every member of a river trip can sit comfortably beneath this natural overhang and, while watching thundering spectacles of the worst storms the monsoons can conjure, they remain warm and dry.

So can deer mice.

After the sun finally had set, one member of this trip, a Mary Frances Curran, in her fifties and from St. Paul, Minnesota, noticed (as had many other campers) the plethora of mice scurrying through camp on the beach and along the sandstone ledges. Shortly after the members of this trip had returned to their homes in other states, Curran felt pulmonary distress. On June 11, she entered a Minnesota hospital. She explained to her physician that she suspected she had hantavirus and that she may have gotten it in Grand Canyon.

Her doctor dismissed this possibility, notes Curran's brother Jim Curran, by telling her that hantavirus is so rare that it could be ruled out as the cause of her problem.

Curran died the next day. Postmortem testing revealed she had died of a hantavirus infection.

The location of her lethal exposure at Pancho's Kitchen remains guesswork based only on her group's sightings of mice.

We have covered a spectrum of dangerous—and not so dangerous—critters and microbes that pose some sort of potential threat to people. Happily, as you now have seen, a surprisingly few persons have died directly due to any of these creatures in Grand Canyon. Surprisingly, however, the same cannot be said about the relationship of plants with people in the Canyon.

In some tragic cases, even though common sense was well exercised, Mother Nature herself seemed to have been in a foul mood. During the night of August 27, 1970, for example, Raymond James Hock, age 52, was camped at the Supai Campground. While sitting at a picnic table that night, gusty winds tore off the top from a nearby Fremont Cottonwood tree (*Populus fremontii*). The tree top fell on Hock, killing him.

If treacherous trees seem a bit much, consider treacherous flowers. On the evening of March 24, 1971 Anthony Krueger, age 20, of Hutchinson, Minnesota quaffed a cup or two of the essence of the ten-inch-long white flower of *Datura*. Three of his buddies with him near Phantom Ranch also drank *Datura* tea. Krueger's first reaction was insomnia. The anticholinergic effects of the atropine-like alkaloids (including hyoscyamine, hyoscine, scopolamine and several others) of *Datura* have been characterized as making the person who ingested it as "hot as a hare, blind as a bat, dry as a bone, red as a beet, and as mad as a hatter." This brew of *Datura* induced all of this and more.

That night and the next day Krueger's behavior took a dive for the inappropriate. He talked for hours to inanimate objects and to nonexistent people—he also acted as if both were responding to him. He said his family was there. He said that his family was coming. He tried to lift huge, impossible boulders. He ate handfuls of dirt.

The following morning (March 25) Krueger went missing. His buddy Richard Wendt found him "running around on rocks and cactus plants." After this, Krueger's group members took turns watching him. Late that afternoon Barbara Jean Peters saw him in the area of the Silver Bridge and the old corral. She called him. Krueger came to her, admitting he thought she was a girl he had been chasing. Barbara looked around. No other girl was present. Even so, Krueger did seem more coherent to her now than previously. He asked her for water.

Michael R. Shrode, another buddy, joined them. Krueger told Shrode he wanted to camp on the beach (illegal) alone to "get his thoughts together." Peters and Shrode left Krueger alone to fetch him water and his gear. Shrode gathered Krueger's sleeping gear and canteen and brought it to the beach near the Silver Bridge where Krueger had said he wanted to sleep. But Shrode could not find Krueger.

Robert Vadas was a backpacker with two buddies who had linked up with Krueger's group during Krueger's *Datura* experience. Vadas adds that Krueger's group had felt "safe" taking drugs on the evening of March 24 because they thought all the rangers were gone from the Phantom Ranch area. No one in Vadas' group drank *Datura* tea, but they did feel somewhat responsible for the group who did. Three of the *Datura* group had slowly come out of their experience on March 25, but Krueger had not.

Vadas says he had seen Krueger around 6:30 p.m., about 5-15 minutes prior to his disappearance noted by Shrode. At the time Vadas was carrying a load of firewood (now illegal) across the Silver Bridge. But upon arriving at the area between the old stables and the Silver Bridge where he thought he had seen Krueger, Vadas no longer saw him. Vadas carried his firewood to the group's camp at the rock shelter site near Bright Angel Creek and up near the present Ranger Station. He asked people there, "Who is watching Krueger?" No one seemed to know. Barbara Peters seemed nonplussed. Several people started looking for Krueger. None found him. After Krueger proved un-findable for nearly 24 hours of fairly thorough searching, on March 26, Krueger's buddy Richard Wendt walked to Phantom Ranch and phoned the Park on the rim for help.

The accounts of Krueger's *Datura* experience by his buddies clash with the version told by Ranger Bob Cornelius. As Cornelius remembers it:

> *I discovered Krueger and several friends camped illegally on the boat beach. He was one of many* Datura *cases at the Canyon. He was obviously out of his mind. He brought himself to my immediate attention by eating substantial quantities of sand in my presence. He was willing to have a conversation with me. The first thing he asked was: Did you see all the cop cars down here last night? I of course said, "I sure did!" Since he was with friends, I got them all to move to the campground. I told his friends I wasn't going to arrest him, that I was worried about his welfare, but they needed to keep any drugs, including* Datura, *away from him. I told them they needed to keep a close eye on Krueger and they needed to keep him away from dangers, especially the river, until he recovered.*

About 20+ hours after he had drunk *Datura* tea, Krueger either had entered deliberately, or fell accidentally into, the Colorado River. *Datura* tea induces a serious thirst. And he had told his friends he wanted water. He might have been trying to drink the river. On the other hand, the last page of a book he had been reading mentioned "water gods." Krueger's buddies admitted he had been muttering off and on about "water gods," who, it might seem, were a bit like that nonexistent girl he had been chasing moments before he vanished.

Robert Vadas insists that neither Bob Cornelius nor any other ranger had been at Phantom Ranch on March 24 or 25. Furthermore, Vadas adds, Cornelius did not mention in his official incident report having been present at Phantom prior to his arriving by helicopter for the search on the morning of March 27. Why this discrepancy?

First, Vadas did not accompany the "*Datura*" group during their entire drug experience. Moreover, Krueger's three buddies also were high as kites as they stood and listened to Cornelius' warnings about watching Krueger. The likelihood that these buddies promptly forgot about Cornelius' brief visit along with forgetting most of their other hallucinations they were experiencing then is high. So from Vadas' experience it is unsurprising that Krueger's buddies might have said later, "Ranger? What ranger?"

But why did Cornelius not write up his encounter with the *Datura* trippers in his official report? After Krueger had gone missing, Cornelius became the ranger who managed the Park's search for him beginning on March 27. Had Cornelius later written officially about his having met the drug trippers days earlier and having warned them in reasonable, friendly terms to care for Krueger, but then noting that they had failed to do so, leading to Krueger's death, none of this would have helped Cornelius' career—or theirs.

This is because such mention also would have placed greater official guilt on Krueger's buddies. It would have been a "lose, lose" section of his report. Besides, Cornelius' mentioning his encounter with Krueger and his buddies would have shed no light on what actually happened to Krueger later, on the evening of March 26. Nor is this lack of mention strange. Nearly all NPS incident reports in those days focused almost entirely on the Park's *response* to an emergency rather than to preliminary details that occurred well before an emergency existed.

The Park search began on March 27 via helicopter with Ranger Bob Cornelius guiding the air search. It failed to locate any sign of Tony Krueger.

Five weeks later, around May 4, a group of hikers found a body, still wearing jeans, seven miles downstream in the fluctuation zone at Hermit Rapid. The hikers alerted the Park. On May 6, at Phantom Ranch Ranger Bob Cornelius asked Whale (Curtis Hansen), a river guide for Hatch River Expeditions for a boat ride to Hermit. Whale dropped off Cornelius and got the heck out of there, leaving the ranger alone to muscle and maneuver the decomposing body into a body bag then drag it up the beach 100 yards to the helicopter evacuation area. Dental records confirmed the body as Krueger's. Sadly, as we have seen, this would not be the last corpse in the river that Whale would encounter.

Nor would the huge trumpet-shaped blossoms of *Datura* fail to entrap other seekers of visions. Just a few years later, on August 28, 1977 Web Jones, age 26 quaffed a brew of *Datura* tea. He dropped dead hiking the Hualapai Hilltop Trail. Hopefully, he will be the last victim of the era of *The Teachings of Don Juan*.

"Killings" by plants are rare. Other than the tree limb fall and the *Datura* deaths, there have been no other known flora fatalities. On the flip side, has a Canyon plant ever "saved" a person's life? One pervasive idea about desert survival is drinking cactus juice can rescue a person in severe heat stress and dehydration. Many of us have heard about chopping open a California barrel cactus (*Ferocactus acanthodes*) the big species in Grand Canyon, mashing the pulp and drinking the juice to get water. As you may recall from Chapter 3, doomed hiker Bryce Gillies tried to claw his way into a barrel cactus in vain after he had trapped himself in Bonita canyon. Has this tactic ever worked?

No. Not that we know of. On the other hand, we do know of occasions where it made things worse. Consider, for example, Chief Ranger Howard B. Stricklin's *Monthly Report to the Superintendent* for May, 1955, dated June 4:

> *District Ranger Sylvester made a trip during the early morning hours of*
> *May 30 to Topocoba Hilltop and hiked down approximately 3 miles into Supai*

Canyon to take water to a Boy Scout group. The four boys and one scoutmaster had drunk all their water during the first five miles of hiking two days earlier, and after mixing water from a barrel cactus with fruit juice, they became ill. The boys were returned to Grand Canyon Village where they were able to send for funds to stay in the village for the remainder of the week.

The upshot? When it comes to hydration, forget cactus cocktails. Cactus pulp juice is not the nectar of the gods. Instead it tastes extremely bitter due to its heavy content of alkaloids. And that's the good news. If one is not already sicker than a dog beforehand, one likely will become so after trying to choke down this stuff, as discovered by desert survival expert Tony Nester's experiment of demolishing a centuries old, well-hydrated barrel cactus knocked loose by a flashflood. He salvaged six ounces of fluid from the whole thing by using a bandana as a sponge, then wringing it out repeatedly.

The juice comes out thick and soupy, just a little thinner than Elmer's glue. It tastes absolutely horrible, like sour milk. I had to meditate like a monk to keep it down. It made my stomach churn like a cement mixer.

Nester had to drink a couple of liters of water just to flush this "elixir" from his system. Hence, clearly, trying to drink cactus pulp "juice" when already sick and nauseated from dehydration would risk vomiting and becoming even more dangerously dehydrated. Moreover, the getting at the pulp, which is laden with moisture only after a series of good rains, demands an expenditure of energy and sweat. More moisture lost than gained. It's not like peeling a banana. Breaking open the tough outer "shell" of a barrel cactus requires a hatchet—or a chainsaw. By the way, plan on being cited for destruction of Park flora if you try this.

The weirdest example of a major backfire in trying to survive by sucking the moisture from cactus occurred in another national park. It unfolded in August of 1999 when two buddies—David Coughlin and Raffi Kodikian—arrived in New Mexico's Carlsbad Caverns National Park during their cross-country road trip from Massachusetts. Coughlin was about to enter a graduate program in the Donald Bren School of Environmental Science and Management connected to the University of California at Santa Barbara. Kodikian, his closest buddy for years, was a journalism graduate accompanying him on their last hurrah together before going separate ways in life. (Thickening this plot, the two men each had experienced a relationship with the same woman, Kodikian first, Coughlin second.) On August 4, the pair signed up for their overnight permit, Coughlin bought a topo map. Kodikian purchased three pints of water and a quart of Gatorade (instead of carrying the two gallons of water recommended by the Park). Next the pair drove five miles and parked Coughlin's car at the trailhead into Rattlesnake Canyon. From here they hiked more than a mile with their camping gear. They camped at sunset.

As Jason Kersten notes in his *Journal of the Dead a Story of Friendship and Murder in the New Mexico Desert*, no one had ever vanished in Carlsbad's 47,000 acres during its entire sixty-nine-year history as a park. But on August 8, after noting that a car had been parked for multiple days on the road at the trailhead, Ranger Lance Mattson decided to hike down and see if something was amiss. About half an hour later Mattson found Raffi Kodikian bivouacked 275 feet from the trail leading out of Rattlesnake Canyon to the paved road and also still within view of the cairns marking that trail.

Mattson gave the 25-year-old man a water bottle. Next he asked: "Where's your buddy?"

"Over there," Kodikian answered, pointing toward a long pile of rocks about thirty feet away.

As Mattson stared toward the stones but still failed to see a person near them, Kodikian added an explanation, "I killed him."

A moment later the young man added, "He begged me to do it."

Mattson's mind shifted into high gear as he stared at the macabre scene. The camp was a mess of scattered food wrappers and gear. Sitting under a semi-shredded tent, Kodikian, black-mustached and dressed only in shorts, bore superficial-appearing injuries to his forearms.

Only thirty feet away, David Coughlin apparently lay buried under a heap of boulders, some of them weighing more than fifty pounds each.

Kodikian added that he had stabbed Coughlin through the heart only six hours earlier.

Mattson wondered: What the hell had gone wrong here?

The short version is, after camping that first night, the two buddies could not relocate the trail to their car. They also felt that hiking cross-country out of the canyon via its sloping sides was impossible. As Jason Kersten notes further in his *Journal of the Dead*, in an attempt to find their way out they hiked up the side of Rattlesnake Canyon opposite from that which they had entered. The pair had rimmed out 700 feet above their bivouac site. Although they now found themselves in equally arid surroundings, they could see water towers and buildings off in the distance. Here, the two were about eight miles from the main highway. Kodikian said he did not feel that he had the energy to make that long a hike. Further complicating things, neither man was able to understand (or read) the topographic map Coughlin had bought. So the two men had scrambled back down to their makeshift camp. There they had stalled out and simply waited for Park Rangers to rescue them (their expectation of this was based on their being overdue as per the dates on their camping permit). To help this happen they built a small "SOS" from rocks on the canyon floor. Barring rescue, they would die where they were.

As their thirst grew ever worse, Kodikian said, and vultures circled overhead, the two friends finally forged a suicide pact as the ultimate escape from their dehydra-tion-incited misery. Coughlin's pain, he added, seemed to exceed his own.

As responding Chief Ranger Mark Maciha, a veteran of several very hot, dry national parks, would note to Ghiglieri, Kodikian's behavior during his first hour of rescue seemed incongruous. The self-admitted killer seemed far from incapaci-tated. Instead he seemed almost chipper. He chided the rangers and wisecracked, "My grandmother can fly a Blackhawk faster than those Army boys can." (Ranger Mattson had called for this SAR response from Fort Bliss). Maciha admitted that some of the details of that day still fail to quit flopping like beached fish. For one thing, Kodikian felt the need to urinate in the emergency room after his rescue ("how dehydrated could he have been?"). For another, the rocks Kodikian had used to bury his murdered buddy weighed fifty pounds: "If he had the strength to lift these rocks, why didn't they walk out?" Another strange fact was that Kodikian had been carrying in Coughlin's car a textbook on criminal justice, yet Kodikian had majored in journalism. Moreover, on the day of his rescue, Kodikian hired the most famous and successful murder defense attorney in New Mexico. Even more contributory to Ranger Maciha's chagrin, he never saw Kodikian exhibit remorse.

Kersten reports Kodikian went before the court for a hearing on second-degree murder. He decided to plea bargain and plead no contest, thus avoiding a jury trial.

An autopsy later revealed Coughlin to have been about 12 percent ("moderately") dehydrated, well short of a fatal level. His kidneys had still been functioning. Pos-sibly exacerbating his discomfort, however, Coughlin had been eating prickly pear fruits (genus *Opuntia*), some of them unripe. As we saw during Robert Billingsley's float below Crash Canyon in 1957, when not ripe, these *tunas* tend to spur painful and prolonged stomach cramps. Even so, Medical Investigator Dr. Dennis Klein con-cluded that had Coughlin not been stabbed, he would have lived quite a while longer.

The serrated edge of the stout, lock-blade knife found on scene, the investigation would reveal, was *still* sharp. It had been sharp enough to slice through Coughlin's chest and fatally sever his heart with two strokes—and it had remained sharp enough to sever Kodikian's wrists. The killer's failure to carry out his end of the suicide pact by slitting his own wrists, claimed the prosecutor, had not been through dullness of the blade but instead through Kodikian's lack of commitment to commit suicide.

Chief District Judge Jay Forbes, notes Kersten, found Kodikian guilty of vol-untary manslaughter and sentenced him to fifteen years in prison. Forbes then suspended thirteen of these. Kodikian ultimately served sixteen months in New Mexico State Prison near Santa Rosa before being released for good behavior.

According to Kersten's research, Kodikian's "mercy homicide" of David Coughlin is the only known case of one lost person killing another with dehydration agony as the putative primary ailment of the victim. Of course even this oddity begs the question of how two otherwise capable and intelligent young men could feel com-pelled to bivouac in the Chihuahuan Desert in summer and remain lost for days in a short, five-mile-long canyon that ended a couple of miles downcanyon by trail at Rattlesnake Springs and how they also decided to park themselves to die a mere 275 feet from the one-mile trail leading to their car and about eighty feet from the marker for that trail. For a deeper look at this classic example of being lost fatally in an American national park, we refer the interested reader to Kersten's book. At least one lesson here is: Take responsibility for *knowing and understanding* your route exactly—before you leave the pavement. And by the way, don't bother trying to use a cactus to save your life.

What we see in Grand Canyon is Mother Nature in her desert mood. How did this extreme dearth of water come to pass? During prehistoric eras, the region that would someday host Grand Canyon subsided many times as an inland sea. For eons the seas transgressed and regressed, often ruling supreme over this section of the continent. After the final sea retreated, the once lush coastal landscape slowly rose to become the world's second largest major plateau (Tibet is number one). Next, this rising plateau of the Four-Corners region eroded to form the most complex canyon system on Earth. To many people these extensive and confusing canyonlands appear to be barren desert, maybe even a worthless, lifeless wasteland.

The reality? Grand Canyon is home to 305 species of birds, 76 of mammals, and 35 of reptiles and amphibians, and 8 native fish. Millions of insects and arachnids creep, crawl, flit, and buzz within the Park. The Canyon hosts approximately 1,737 known species of vascular plants, 167 species of fungi, 64 species of moss, and 195 known species of lichen found within 129 vegetation communities living within the Park's boundaries. This tally offers only a glimpse into the ways that deserts are actually wonderfully diversified ecosystems containing thousands of life forms adapted to survive (and sometimes flourish) in arid harshness. Indeed, five of North America's seven life zones and three of the continent's four desert types are represented here.

In our opinion, the fauna and flora of Grand Canyon—and that of North America in general—constitute a major treasure of America's legacy. The Canyon's diverse life forms pose little fearsome threat to any of us. And even less threat to those who know what challenges to expect. Instead they enrich our lives in so many ways it would require several books to explain them all and to describe their ecological relationships. Our wildlife heritage not only deserves our respect, these many species need our help to escape the inimical actions of humans. Please do your best to protect them all.

Because when Grand Canyon was gazetted as a park the land included within it fell vastly short of being an intact ecosystem or even an intact watershed, Grand Canyon's biodiversity today exists at great risk. To safeguard it, the protected area must be expanded to exclude mining, logging, and livestock grazing. To help accomplish this, tell your congressman you want to him or her to vote in support of the Grand Canyon Wildlands Council's plan to re-designate 1.7 million acres of federal lands north and south of the Park as "Grand Canyon Watershed National Monument." A lot of wildlife will owe you big.

TABLE 8. FATAL ENCOUNTERS with FAUNA AND FLORA in GRAND CANYON. All are discussed in the text unless otherwise noted.

Name, age	Date	Location in Canyon	Circumstances
father of Jdwayvoo, adult	circa 1870	near Topocoba, Havasu	
	*A Havasupai hunter trapped a pair of **bighorn** rams on a ledge. One ram butted the hunter off the ledge. Ram and hunter fell fatally. (not in text) Leslie Spier, 1928. Havasupai Ethnography, p. 24.*		
Francis Clem Cochrane, 43	September 13, 1933	Snake Gulch (?), Kanab Canyon, 12 miles from Hatch cabin	
	*While prospecting, Cochrane was descending toward the Colorado River with fellow Los Angeles resident Gordon Smith when a **rattlesnake struck at him but missed**. The reptile frightened Cochrane so severely that he suffered a fatal heart attack, confirmed by autopsy.*		
Lee Smith, 50	June 17, 1951	near top of Bright Angel Trail	
	*Smith was a professional Fred Harvey Company guide/mule skinner. He was riding double with Lee Roberts. The **mule** they were riding was crowded off the trail by other mules. Lee Roberts survived; the mule and Lee Smith fell. The mule landed atop Smith, who was killed. The mule survived. The Coconino Sun, January 23 & 28, 1951.*		
Raymond James Hock, 52	August 27, 1970	Havasu Campground	
	*During a fread tornado-like storm, Hock and his illicit girlfriend sought shelter under a ledge. Hock spotted his camera on the picnic table and made a dash for it. The wind tore the top from a nearby cottonwood **tree**, which fell on Hock's head, killing him. Stephen Hirst, letter to Ghiglieri, May 1, 2012. Arizona Republic, August 29, 1970.*		
unidentified white male, adult	circa August 1970-72	Hualapai Hilltop, Havasu	
	*While staging for an Arizona Horsemen's Association ride led by Emery Henderson into Havasu, "a gentleman from the group was showing off, making his **horse** rear as he sat astride, when the horse toppled over backward. The horse came down on the gentleman and drove the saddle horn into the man's forehead before rolling off. He lay on his back with a big concavity in his forehead.... I remember him bleeding from his ears. He made words for about 10 seconds.... This deteriorated into gibberish, moaning, and then the lights went out. It all took no more than a minute." (not in text) Stephen Hirst, letter to Ghiglieri, May 1, 2012.*		
Anthony Krueger, 20	March 24/25, 1971	Phantom Beach (RM 88), flow: 9,000 cfs	
	*While camped with friends under a rock shelter near Phantom Ranch, Krueger of Bell Lake, Minnesota, drank a brew of **Datura** blossoms. Many hours later, after several inappropriate behaviors such as trying to lift impossible boulders, talking to nonexistent*		

*people for hours, and eating dirt, he (**no life jacket**) entered the river unwitnessed and drowned. Death was mitigated by* Datura *poisoning. His body was found by hikers weeks later and 7 miles downstream, at Hermit Rapid, washed ashore. (Not in drowning statistics, but instead counted here in "Critters & Cacti".)* Arizona Republic, *August 24, 1971. Personal communications from Robert E. Vadas & Robert E. Cornelius. Incident report #71-0180*

Web Jones, 26   August 28, 1977   Hualapai Hilltop Trail
Jones, a Havasupai, had ingested an effusion from blossoms of sacred **Datura** *and died from its toxicity on the trail.* Williams News, *September 19, 1977.*

Mary Frances Curran, 50s   June 12, 2009   uncertain, Pancho's Kitchen (RM 137)?
Curran went on a private Canyon river trip between May 14-29, returned home to St. Paul, Minnesota, felt pulmonary distress, and on June 11 entered a hospital. Despite informing her doctor about **hantavirus** *and him dismissing it as "too rare to consider," she died the next day of a* **hantavirus** *infection. The location of her exposure remains guesswork based only on sightings of mice. Our thanks to Tom Martin for tracking down the identity of Curran.* Coconino County Health Department, *June 22, 2009.*

Richard Fairfield Wilson, 80   August 2, 2011   Flagstaff Medical Center
Flagstaff resident Wilson, a dedicated local philanthropist, environmentalist, animal rights worker, and Ph.D. geologist with a Grand Canyon focus, was on a family rafting trip in the Canyon when he began developing a rapidly worsening **bacterial** *skin infection from multiple cumulative abrasions on his legs. After having delayed his medical evacuation for too many days in late July (very hot weather), wanting to make a run through Lava Falls (RM 179), he finally agreed to be airlifted out. His infection became critical. He died of systemic complications in Flagstaff Medical Center two days after his evacuation. (not in text)* Arizona Daily Sun, *August 4 & 7, 2011.*

Chapter Nine

Suicide

Ranger Angela Boyers knew she was not driving one of the fastest vehicles in the NPS fleet. But at least this Ford Expedition was equipped with a damned-good heater. For Boyers and District Ranger Michael Nash sitting shotgun, it helped take some of the sting out of spending this bitterly cold New Year's Eve on duty.

As the old cliché goes: It is a tough job, but someone has to do it.

On the other hand, tonight's near-zero cold was not about to dissuade the hard-core partiers from celebrating. Nor would it stop a few of them from getting into trouble.

As if to prove this hypothesis, only thirty minutes into the shiny new year of 2007, the crackling radio traffic announced trouble.

Boyers and Nash listened as Rangers Brandon Torres and John Evans restrained an intoxicated man who had just punched an intoxicated woman at the Maswik Bar.

Nash and Boyers looked at one another. It did not sound as if Evans and Torres would need backup as they tag-teamed their duo of drunks.

Maybe this bar scene would be the Canyon's only trouble tonight.

As Nash and Boyers resigned themselves to staring again through the Expedition's windshield at the four-way stop near the Backcountry Office and Maswik Lodge, a new silver 4-door Toyota Forerunner ran the stop sign.

Probably another drunk, Boyers thought. And he's sitting behind the wheel. She shifted into "drive" and followed the Toyota. Her headlights illuminated a Florida plate. This car had driven a couple of thousand miles to run this stop sign.

Boyers ran the license plate through Dispatch. Without waiting for the report, she flipped on her red and blue police lights.

Instead of pulling off the pavement to a stop, the Forerunner now accelerated.

Boyers followed it. Dispatch reported back that the license plate was for a 2003 Saab, not a new Forerunner. The vehicle was probably stolen. She flipped the switch to activate her siren. The Toyota pulled away faster. Boyers and Nash pursued in the Expedition.

The Forerunner continued to accelerate along the Entrance Road. Soon it and the Expedition sped at more 80 miles per hour through the 25-miles-per-hour area of Mather Point.

Both vehicles flashed across the 15 miles-per-hour crosswalk. Thank God, Boyers thought, no one is walking across it.

As the Expedition careened eastward along the road, Nash radioed for Ranger Shawn Cave to respond to their area. Cave was the only ranger on duty who was driving a Crown Victoria police cruiser, a vehicle capable of much more nimble pursuit.

Ahead of Boyers and Nash the Toyota turned abruptly onto East Rim Drive toward Desert View. It briefly fishtailed out of control in the loose gravel and snow on the shoulder of the road. Then it regained control.

Boyers knew no ranger was on duty tonight at Desert View. This lack offered the suspect racing ahead of them a chance to escape the Park onto the Navajo Reservation via the East Rim Entrance more than 20 miles ahead. Anywhere this driver encountered other traffic or wildlife along the next 50+ miles along Highway 64 he would pose a menace to people and wildlife both. Twice he passed cars in the no passing zone at speeds over 75 mph.

Boyers decided to pass the Toyota and get in front of it. Maybe she could block it. Or at least slow it down. But as she pulled her patrol car alongside the Forerunner it swerved into her Expedition in an attempt to run her off the road. Being forced northward off the wrong stretch of this road could mean driving into a thousand vertical feet of air.

To avoid re-enacting *Thelma and Louise*, Boyers braked hard and swerved to avoid a collision that could pinball them into the void.

This psycho, Boyers thought, is either going to kill us or somebody coming from the opposite direction. Boyers now pulled back to merely follow the speeding car along East Rim Drive at a safer 50 mph.

Off-duty Desert View Ranger Joe Florko in Grand Canyon Village heard Boyers' radio traffic. As Boyers and Nash reached Duck on a Rock overlook, Florko radioed her to be careful because the next 15 miles of East Rim Drive were icy and hazardous from snowmelt during the day now frozen.

Boyers and Nash backed-off from their high-speed pursuit. Boyers switched off the Expedition's red and blue lights and its siren. But she continued to follow.

Ahead, the Forerunner slowed to 50 miles per hour. It was proving easier to follow than anticipated due to its contrast against the snow shrouding the landscape.

At Twin Overlooks, the Toyota slowed further yet. It steered off the road into the overlook parking. Boyers pulled over too. The Toyota quickly took off again onto the main road. Again Boyers and Nash followed.

At Thor's Overlook, over eight miles from where the chase began, the Forerunner abruptly pulled in again. This time it stopped. The headlights of the Expedition illuminated a young man emerging from the Toyota's driver's door, the engine still running. He darted from the vehicle and sprinted toward the Canyon rim.

Without stopping or even pausing, the shadowy form in the headlight beams ran straight off the edge of the Canyon. It vanished into the icy black void.

"Holy shit!" Boyers and Nash asked each other in astonishment: "Did that just happen?"

Shawn Cave arrived just after the driver disappeared. Nash radioed their shocking observation to Dispatch. Next Boyers and Cave grabbed their rifles, while Nash his handgun, and then took up tactical positions outside their vehicle. Next Cave and Nash approached the vehicle while Boyers provided cover. Nash cleared the vehicle and shut the engine off, taking the keys. Waiting for further backup, the three discussed the possibility of the fugitive having jumped merely to a nearby ledge where he next could maneuver below the rim, or else climb back up to ambush them. Weirder things than this had happened in the Southwest.

Other rangers, Florko, O'Neil, and Morrison, also arrived and set up containment of the scene at both ends of the overlook. Boyers, Cave and Nash slowly moved forward to confirm that the running man did indeed sprint over the edge.

Boyers', Cave's and Nash's flashlight beams revealed footprints running from the car in the six inches of snow carpeting the landscape. The half dozen steps ended at the rim with no apparent break in stride.

Scything their flashlight beams into the blackness below, they could see nothing beyond a high angle scree slope of scrub oaks and pines except projections of naked ledges of Kaibab Limestone leading to a twelve-foot drop. Beyond that, nothing but darkness. It looked as if their fugitive had sprouted wings. The hour now was a little after 1 a.m. All three rangers hollered downward into the eerie silence of the void and waited.

No reply emerged from the void.

The rangers now called for the Park's technical rescue SAR team and Rescue 1. While they waited for the rescue team, Boyers began processing the car plates. They came back registered to a man we'll call Edward Lance Anderson, a 23-year-old from Florida. Was he the driver who had vanished? Boyers also found five suicide notes in the Toyota. Anderson had signed them all. Apparently he was down there below the rim somewhere, probably in a mangled heap. Each note he had written was addressed to Anderson's family members, including one to his sister that said, "I didn't want you to be the only one who has stolen a car." Ironically, Anderson's initial intent was to come to the Grand Canyon to commit suicide.

Had he succeeded?

It seemed almost impossible that he could have failed.

At 1:59 a.m., Search and Rescue Rangers Brandon Torres and John Evans arrived with technical rescue gear. Their drunken pugilist at the Maswik Bar had been secured. The two soon would find out whether or not the mystery driver of the Toyota had succeeded.

The expanding ranger crew rigged an anchor system for the technical rope rescue to Boyers' Expedition. Before rappelling off the rim, the rangers locked every one of its doors. It would fail to work out nicely if someone new to the scene decided to drive the Expedition to a new location while the two men dangled off it within the Canyon.

Rangers Evans and O'Neil rigged their harnesses and started their rappel down the 60- to 70-degree slope. They were carrying rifles in case the driver was armed or found hiding with an ambush in mind.

They immediately came upon a shoe, a black dress shoe, loafer style. Below this they located other footprints, then slide marks and broken branches leading to, then over, the twelve-foot drop. At this point, both rangers returned to the rim. This information the ranger team had gathered thus far allowed them to conclude the driver had continued to fall down into the Canyon as opposed to hiding or traversing out.

The Incident Commander now decided that Evans should prepare for a longer rappel into the Canyon. As Rangers on the rim illuminated Evans with flashlights, he disappeared below into the blackness.

At about 175 feet down, Evans heard a weak voice crying "help."

By now it was now 3:36 a.m. The suicidal driver of the Toyota had vanished over the edge more than two hours earlier. Evans continued rappelling downward, 200 feet, then 300 feet, then more than 500 feet. He continued to add yet more ropes to the system. He still had not reached the driver. At this point Nash requested additional rescue personnel for what likely would be a difficult extrication.

Due to the increasing vertical distance and thick vegetation, it was after 4:30 a.m. and about 600 feet below the rim when SAR ranger Evans finally reached the battered, 23-year-old jumper. He had bounced and tumbled, somersaulting in the snow and talus, all 600 feet. He finally had braked to an instant stop when a tree had caught him in his crotch.

"Do you have a gun?" Evans asked, shining his flashlight onto the driver's face.

"No," came a shaky reply through white vapor puffs and slightly labored breathing.

"Well, if you do and you're lying, remember, I'm on a rope and you're not."

Below the duo's 600-foot level yawned a 400-foot vertical drop.

Anderson confessed to Evans that he had stolen the vehicle two weeks ago from a Toyota dealership where he worked in Florida and come to the Grand Canyon to "jump off the edge." He also told Evans he could not move his legs. Evans did a quick physical assessment. Anderson could actually move his legs but was experiencing numbness and weakness in his extremities due to hours of lying in the snow in sub-freezing air. Anderson also appeared to have suffered a possible broken ankle and now sported a spectacular assortment of bruises and scratches. Miraculously, the would-be suicider had failed to self-inflict any life-threatening injury beyond the certainty of freezing to death if no rescue had come.

Adhering to precautions for a possible subtle spinal injury, Evans carefully loaded Anderson into a sleeping bag and waited for Ranger Torres who was being lowered with the litter. Rather than attempt to carry the 230-pound man by litter up to the rim, they would arrange for a "short haul" and lift him out by helicopter with the litter dangling beneath. This would be at first light. Until then, Anderson would remain securely strapped and lying in the litter, under the guard of Evans and Torres.

To battle hypothermia themselves, the two rangers would dance and perform calisthenics around the fugitive to avoid freezing.

Evans and Torres continued capering in their desperate antics to embattle the penetrating chill for nearly three hours, until well after dawn. In the interim Anderson, strapped immobile in the litter, became hypothermic despite the sleeping bag. His core temperature slid to 94 degrees.

No sunrise before had ever looked so beautiful, even to Anderson.

At 8:00 a.m. the Park helicopter short-hauled Anderson to the rim. There he was placed under arrest. An ambulance drove him to Flagstaff Medical Center (FMC). All told, the entire rescue and transport to save the life of a car thief who wanted to kill himself had lasted over ten hours, from shortly before 1 a.m. to 11:00 a.m., and took 19 NPS employees and one pilot to pull it off.

From FMC the Coconino County Sheriff's Department transferred Anderson to the county detention facility. Meanwhile Boyers arranged for the stolen Toyota to be towed to impound. Boyers' investigation eventually would reveal that Anderson had worked at a car dealership in Florida. He had placed his own license plates on this new 2006 Forerunner. Next he absconded with it and drove it across the continent. Interestingly, a phone call to the dealership would reveal the managers did not even realize their car was missing. Boyers also discovered that Anderson had recently experienced depression and had made a prior suicide attempt during a previous trip to Arizona a few months earlier.

Anderson was charged with Sale or Receipt of Stolen Property, Transportation of Stolen Property, Reckless Driving, Failure to Obey Traffic Control Devices, and Aggravated Assault (for forcing Boyers and Nash off the road). The National Park Service prosecuted him through the state of Arizona and Coconino County. Boyers testified before a Grand Jury.

On March 26, 2007, Edward Lance Anderson ultimately pled guilty to Unlawful

Use of a Means of Transportation (a class 6 felony) and Aggravated Assault (another class 6 felony).

The irony here is stunning. Dozens of visitors who wanted to live have accidentally fallen off the rim at Grand Canyon and died, while Anderson, who drove 2,000 miles with the sole intention to jump off and die, did jump off, tumbled 600 feet, and instead of dying survived with a mere sprained ankle and a sore crotch. One very important detail here: Anderson admitted to rangers that he had leapt off the edge with the full intent of committing a long-planned suicide, but when he saw the endless slope dropping into infinity below him, *he changed his mind instantly and decided he wanted to live. During his somersaulting descent he tried everything he could think of to arrest his fall. Indeed, his efforts did avert his original suicide plan.*

Many of us have wondered at one time or another how many victims of suicide leaps have changed their minds once they went into an accelerating freefall over the edge and off the rim into thin air. Clearly the answer is: Some definitely have changed their minds. But too late....

In early June of 2004, Timothy George Clam of Illinois arrived at Grand Canyon with a special mission in mind. He stopped at Papillon Airways tours at the Grand Canyon Airport in Tusayan, just outside the Park. There, on June 7, he purchased a $120 ticket for a helicopter air tour over the heart of Grand Canyon. The flight lifted off as scheduled, then returned a half hour later. But without Clam aboard. In fact he had never boarded the flight. For some reason, at the last minute he had changed his mind.

Two days later, Clam returned to the Grand Canyon Airport and walked up to Papillon's ticket counter again. He wanted to book yet another flight. This time he requested a front shotgun seat, next to the window. His request was denied due to issues of weight distribution involving the other passengers who already had booked. Clam exited the airport disappointed.

Clam returned to the airport the next day and booked with Papillon yet again. Three times is the charm, so to speak. This time Clam got his front, window seat.

This seat, of course, was the prime one. The best seat in the house. The other five passengers were buckled in separately in the aft compartment. Sitting up here, one feels like the pilot. This position is akin to the front car seat on a roller coaster. The view through the windshield bubble is so huge it provides one hell of a thrill.

The pilot lifted off and flew low across a forest of ponderosas. Abruptly the forest vanished and the world yawned open as if flying across some gigantic canyon on Mars. The views into an ever unfolding Grand Canyon gaping under a blue sky proved breathtaking. Clam craned his neck for an even better view.

During the return flight of the Papillon Airways Bell 206 (N1076T) at 7,500 feet (only 500 feet above the South Rim), two miles short of the rim, the aircraft passed over Dripping Springs.

Abruptly Clam quit gazing into the depths. Instead he reached for his seatbelt. He unclipped it. Moving fast, he yanked the helicopter door latch at his side. Next he shoved the door. Hard. The wind from the speed of the helicopter was pushing against the hatch. Opening it would not be easy.

The door cracked open. A rush of air and a deafening motor and rotor noise filled the cockpit.

Taken by surprise, Pilot Maria Langer stared at Clam. "What are you *doing*?" she screamed over the roar.

Oblivious to Langer, Clam shoved the door harder and began wedging his body into the narrow opening. He forced it farther outward beyond his seat.

Langer could barely believe her eyes. This guy was trying to exit her airship 4,000 feet above Dripping Springs. Was this for real?

Langer grabbed the waistband of Clam's trousers and tried to pull him back into his seat.

Clam lunged outward even harder, jerking Langer sideways and off center. Now Clam's feet dangled outside the helicopter above a dizzying drop. The helicopter lurched heavily.

Langer instantly realized she could either try harder to restrain Clam's exit but meanwhile lose control of her airship (and maybe crash) or else she could release him and regain control of the airship. Langer's mind also wondered: If this guy is this intent on killing himself, is he also willing to take her and her five other passengers with him?

Langer released Clam's waistband and fought to level her airship.

Still shoving the door open against the wind, Clam forced himself out of the cockpit. Abruptly he vanished into a freefall nearly a mile above the rugged terrain gaping below. Whizzing through empty air, Clam's body reached a terminal velocity of 120 to 200+ miles per hour (depending on his body orientation in the air) in about fifteen seconds. After another five to ten seconds he had dropped the entire 3,900 feet between the Bell 206 and the bare rock surface of Travertine Canyon near White Butte. He exploded upon impact.

Badly shaken, Langer and her five now terrified passengers continued to Grand Canyon Airport and landed. Terra firma never had felt so good before.

The body parts recovery of Clam required fifteen NPS personnel and several plastic bags. Taxpayers footed the bill.

The investigation revealed that Clam, a former U.S. Marine, had "experienced periods of serious depression and mental illness over a significant portion of his adult life." The Marine Corps had characterized Clam as having "schizotypal personality disorder," which led to suicide attempts.

One can only wonder what passed through Clam's mind during his nearly half a minute of freefall before his final impact. Perhaps he experienced intense regret, as Anderson (above) had done. Or, perhaps instead, his thoughts ran along the following lines…

"This is the best way out for you and for me. I'm going out peaceably and cleanly as possible. I love you all. Edward." After writing this, Edward jumped off.

No matter how you look at it, it is tough to find a silver lining on the cloud that a suicide leaves behind. In the U.S.A., a land infamous for its rates of murder, far more people—at least 30,000 and possibly up to 100,000—take their own lives each year. Suicides in America since 1999 to 2010 have soared 31 percent. The biggest "growth" sector is baby boomers facing financial problems and/or challenges with aging parents or difficult teenagers. This total vastly exceeds victims of murder (less than 12,000/year). In short, suicide is fairly common here— as it is in developed countries worldwide from Switzerland to Japan. And while America's rate of suicide may seem high, it is actually only a small fraction of the rates in Japan and many European countries. Even so, America's suicide rate remains high enough that psychologists continue to argue over suicide's causes. They list depression, alcohol and/or drug addiction, unstable or dysfunctional families, antisocial tendencies, serotonin deficiencies, race (middle-aged black women, for example, almost never commit suicide), cultural mores and codes of honor, economics, mental illness, and also a family history of suicide. Sheer hopelessness ultimately seems to prompt a person to commit the final tragic act.

Recent research, however, reveals a critical insight: When children at home are subjected to emotional abuse, a mentally ill primary family member, sexual abuse, a battered mother, physical abuse, substance abuse, and divorce (in descending order of impact), suicide attempts later sky-rocket compared to children not subjected. Such abuse seems to permanently repress or negate expression of a gene that regulates the brain's stress response such that cortisol production is not shut off after a stressful event. Such kids' stress-response systems become permanently altered so that they exist in states of constant stress due to pumped up levels of stress hormones.

What makes suicide in Grand Canyon an important issue are two unique aspects. First, the Canyon, especially its rims, offers a spectacular, sure-fire (almost), easy, and even a "Heaven-sent" opportunity to end it all. And, second, NPS rangers, Coconino County SAR personnel, professional guides, or even innocent bystanders in the Canyon who are called upon to try to rescue unsuccessful victims or to recover the bodies or body parts of ones who did succeed are often forced to expose themselves to highly significant dangers.

On June 15, 1980, for example, Edward Enzor Walters, age 36, wrote two elaborate suicide notes, one to his family and the other to the police. The first explained:

"—the show received horrible reviews from the critics, myself included. All I've managed to do in my life is to bring distress and worse to others. The bad habits I've learned have simply become too ingrained to change at this late date."

Were his body to be recovered, Walters asked further, do not send it back home to Troy, Alabama. Finally, after admitting that he could not interact successfully with people any longer, Walters concluded with the quote that opened this chapter: "This is the best way out for you and for me. I'm going out peaceably and cleanly as possible. I love you all. Edward."

Walters' letter to the police was twice as long. He explained who he was and how he had weighted himself down with heavy clothing and rocks and probably would never be found. But if he were, he added, check for dental records with his dentist (name and address provided). Once identified, he instructed the police whom to contact about his death and whom not to, providing more names and addresses. Then he explained what was good and not so good about his car and instructed the Coconino County Sheriff's Department to give it—and the food in the trunk—to someone deserving. Next he wanted the Sheriff's Department to find a worthy teenager for his camping gear, listing it and also a storage locker in New Mexico holding yet more stuff. The letter continued in the same last-will-and-testament vein—at great length with numerous requests of the police to attend to this and that detail of his unfinished business. Then he apologized to the police, admitting that he would not want their job (especially, one might conclude, when they are being saddled with "clients" like Walters). He closed with his explanation: "If I could have found another way for me or another place, I would have done so. Time just ran out."

What all of this reveals are the common threads of complete self-absorption and selfishness typical to suiciders. Apparently they often think they are solving other people's problems, not just escaping their own. How Walters "solved" everyone's problem was to weigh himself down with rocks in his pockets, walk out to the center of Navajo Bridge (River Mile 4.3), and jump off. He plummeted 470 feet to the Colorado River.

In September, about 100 days later, Tour West boatman Michael Harris reported by radio that a private river trip member, while kayaking, had spotted a rotting body wedged in driftwood against shore seven miles downstream near Soap Creek Rapid (River Mile 11.25). It was decomposing and stank, but it was wearing new hiking boots. Harris tethered the decomposing body to a tree with parachute cord.

But when NPS Rangers Sam West and Stephen Martin and Coconino County Deputy Steve Luckeson arrived by NPS chopper to evacuate the body, they could not find it. Finally the three SAR personnel helicoptered deeper into the Canyon to ask the original discoverer exactly where he had tethered the corpse. After being told the minute details, the rangers and deputy then located the body.

Because of fluctuating flows, the body had been exposed to air, ravens, flies, scorching sunlight, et cetera, repeatedly, then re-submerged. The decomposition was horrendous, and the recovery was anything but "peaceable and clean." The three SAR personnel managed to scoop and shovel Walters' maggot-ridden remains into two body bags for evacuation.

During early June in 1933, a botanical cactus expert from Riverside, California was scanning with his field glasses a nearly inaccessible ledge 600 feet below the rim of Shoshone Point in search of cactus. Instead he spotted a sun-bleached human skeleton. Deputy Sheriff Jack Harbin and Park rangers worked their way to the ledge. The deceased man's weather-bleached skeleton was wearing the rags of khaki pants, a white cotton shirt and apparent "sandals." Neither a coat nor hat was in evidence.

The skeleton had a .32 bullet lodged in his cranium from an entry hole just above and behind his right ear. In his pocketbook were 40 cents and nothing else. Beside the man lay a "cheap" H&R .32 revolver. No obvious clue existed to identify this victim of the .32 caliber bullet.

At this point the plot thickens considerably. Soon after this Shoshone Point discovery, Emery Kolb had donated a human skeleton to the Grand Canyon High School science lab. Years later the school acquired an articulated and mounted skeleton. It then returned the original skeleton to Kolb, who stowed it in a bundle inside a canvas boat Carl Rust had given him. Kolb hitched the boat up into the rafters in his garage. Upon doing so, Kolb joked to Art Gallenson, "When I die and somebody finds that skeleton, it's gonna cause a lot of commotion. …Take it to the school in Kanab, would you?"

Gallenson never took it.

Kolb died in his sleep in December of 1976, at age 95. The skeleton finally saw daylight again the next month. When Kolb's grandson Emery Lehnert dug it out of Rust's boat, Kolb's prophesy came true. The skeleton came back to life. Rumors grew like weeds that the bleached bones were those of Glen Hyde, whom Kolb must have murdered to rescue Bessie Hyde. Forensic anthropologist Walter Birkby, however, examined the skull and post-skeletal material and concluded they could not be the bones of Glen Hyde. "Period." Moreover, Birkby added, the trajectory of the .32 caliber bullet into the cranium suggested suicide, not homicide. So, again, who was the mystery skeleton?

In 2006 Bob Williamson donated to the Grand Canyon Museum Collection a set of 1933 photos taken by his father Ranger Robert R. Williamson of a skeleton. As noted by Allyson Mathis in *Canyon Views* (Spring 2009), these photos inspired Park Archivist Kim Besom in 2008 to research their provenance. Williamson, it turns out, was the investigating ranger in 1933 along with Deputy Sheriff Jack Harbin 600 feet below the rim at Shoshone Point who sorted out the skeleton discovered by that cactus botanist. Again, the original owner of that skeleton had committed suicide with that cheap H&R .32 caliber revolver a few years before 1933.

NPS Special Agent Joe Sumner, today an indefatigable cold case investigator for the Coconino County Sheriff's Department, compared the actual bones and the shoe (sandal-like), et cetera from Kolb's Studio with Williamson's several photos. Surprisingly, they matched perfectly.

But how had Kolb ended up with this skeleton from below Shoshone Point?

Joe Sumner probed deeper and found that Kolb had served on the Coconino County Coroner's jury representing Grand Canyon in the 1930s. This jury had reviewed the case of the mystery skeleton. When the verdict had proved to be suicide, Kolb likely had decided "waste not, want not" and had donated the bones to the high school.

Sumner is still trying to find an identity for this mystery skeleton, whose femurs reveal that he stood taller than six feet and whose mandible is missing its 3 right-side premolars and molars in an unusual pattern that suggests that the jaw either never had these teeth or had lost them as a very young child. Even with these forensic clues, however, we would not recommend holding your breath on discovering an identity after 80 years.

The upshot here? No known evidence ties Emery Kolb to the mysterious death of Glen Hyde, who most likely drowned in Mile 232 Rapid with his bride Bessie. On the other hand, the tie between Emery Kolb and Glen Hyde when he was alive has proved so intriguing that the latter's fate will likely remain forever connected to Kolb's warning to him that the Colorado River does not suffer fools without life jackets.

If the above story reads a bit like fiction, the next seemed even more so. Indeed, Osan Kang seemed a bit too strange even for fiction. He was born in 1913 in San Francisco of Korean parents. As an adult, Kang regaled listeners with tales of working with General MacArthur's intelligence staff during World War II in the South Pacific. In truth, Kang had passed a strict security clearance and had qualified as a language instructor—Korean, Japanese, Chinese, and English—for the U.S. Army. He worked for the Army off and on in California until 1961.

In the early 1960s, Kang registered as an older student at California's Reedley College. His fellow students found him dignified and charming. Student sponsors there, writes journalist Don Dedera, also found Kang "quick to borrow, free to spend, and slow to repay his loans."

As the 1960s became The Sixties, Kang's fortunes ebbed. He tried his hand at several trades—importing jewelry, investing in a radio and television station—but none produced profits. By 1965, Kang gained the sympathy of a Korean couple who ran a Washington, D.C. motel. The two respected and supported him. They even got him a job as a desk clerk at another motel.

But Kang's new employer soon fired him because he suspected that Kang was subletting his own free quarters to patrons and pocketing the rent instead of renting to them the employer's normal rooms.

Kang appeared next in February, 1967, in Las Vegas, where he was detained by deputies on a bogus check warrant from a Washington bank. The law released Kang when the Washington, D.C. bank informed them that they would not press charges. Kang stayed in Las Vegas for a month. He gambled heavily. He lost.

On March 24, Kang drove into Williams, 60 miles south of Grand Canyon, in a rental car from Las Vegas. There he tried to trade the car's jack for a tank of gas.

When this failed, Kang tried to borrow money from a local motel operator. The operator turned out to be a Williams policeman. He called Las Vegas and learned that the rental agreement for Kang's car stipulated that it was not to be driven out of Nevada. Even so, the rental firm said, they would not prosecute Kang.

The policeman then countered Kang's attempt to borrow money by offering him a meal of plain food and a night's lodging in a clean, open-door cell in the Williams jail.

Insulted, Kang refused.

Kang next made a bee-line for the Williams Hertz rental car agency. On the strength of Kang's identification card issued by a high-security government agency, Hertz rented Kang a replacement car, one with gas in the tank. While waiting for the car, Kang talked of being a language professor and of being married to a woman who was a missionary teacher in Korea. They had two children, he explained. He was on vacation, he added, and temporarily out of funds. He was, Don Dedera reports, "witty, courteous and talkative."

Hours later Kang drove the Hertz car at 40 miles per hour toward the edge of Lipan Point. Kang must have done his homework. Lipan Point is well east of Grand Canyon Village. But of all the lookout points and scenic vista points, Lipan stands out in two ways. It offers a fairly good approach route during which one can accelerate on a level roadway without many trees in the way and with no guard wall. And it offers a thousand vertical feet of air immediately over the edge of the South Rim.

Kang and Hertz launched out over the Canyon for several scenic seconds before those thousand feet evaporated into solid rock. No one spotted the twisted wreckage of the Hertz car for four days.

While Kang was the first person known to drive off the rim and commit suicide, he was not the first person to drive off the rim in a suicide attempt. During the evening of July 31, 1951 Blanche Mahape, a Hopi "girl" working at South Rim Village quarreled with her boyfriend. Their argument must have been a doozy because at 10:30 that night she climbed into her car and drove it past the Bright Angel Lodge. She continued driving purposely off the rim. Her car rolled and slid about 80 feet down the slope (she had missed an immediate vertical drop) before thick brush and trees stopped her car above a vertical plunge certain to prove lethal.

Rangers and Fred Harvey employees worked together immediately to retrieve Mahape before her car shifted and dropped off a vertical cliff, making all efforts instantly too late. The rescuers roped together and hauled the injured Mahape back up to level ground. Medical personnel at the Grand Canyon Hospital diagnosed her with a broken right arm, a few lacerations, and several bruises.

Significantly, while Mahape recovered in the hospital she changed her mind about committing suicide.

This latter tidbit of information is extremely significant when it comes to how final suicide is (as the permanent solution to a temporary problem). Again, most of us have wondered at one time or another whether, during those seconds of freefall, how many people who have made a suicide leap have changed their minds in mid-air about their desire to die. Mahape did.

A half dozen years after Kang's less-than-excellent adventure, on February 2, 1974, Hertz lost yet another car. Stephen S. Steiner, age 24 and Peggy J. Horner, age 31, drove to the South Rim on their prized motorcycle. Once there, they rented a Hertz Car. They then drove the rented Ford Pinto off the rim at high speed from Yaki Point. The car plunged an impressive 500 feet, ricocheted, then somersaulted another 1,000 feet before being crushed with its two occupants. The motorcycle, parked in a safe place, escaped unscathed.

A dozen years later, Richard McMillan, age 50, and Lynn Allen, age 30, rattled toward the South Rim in McMillan's 1965 International Scout. Behind the pair, in Los Angeles, police had just issued arrest warrants for the two for seven counts of child molestation.

McMillan and Allen had lived together for the past two years and had a previous record of a few violent crimes. The present police charges were that the pair had sexually molested Allen's 9 year-old daughter and 8 year-old son. The two children, who normally lived with their father and stepmother, had spent the weekend with McMillan and Allen. After returning home they told their stepmother, "We don't want to go back!" Then, with coaxing, they explained why.

Not long afterward, Allen's mother, the children's maternal grandmother, told Allen that the children had reported being molested and that the police were issuing warrants. This had prompted Allen and McMillan to flee east.

A quarter mile east of the Desert View junction at the east boundary of Grand Canyon National Park, McMillan turned off the highway toward the nearby South Rim. On July 10, 1986, witnesses saw McMillan cut in front of an on-coming vehicle then steer across 147 feet of Coconino Plateau, dodging trees and leaving a trail of debris. Next McMillan's Scout launched off the edge. It hit bedrock nearly 500 feet down.

Twenty-four years after Osan Kang's last drive and 17 years after Stephen S. Steiner and Peggy J. Horner rented their Hertz car and 5 years after McMillan and Allen blasted off the rim to grab 500 feet of vertical air, Hollywood treated us to a similar denouement in the otherwise charming 1991 "chick flick," *Thelma and Louise*. This Academy Award winning screenplay ends—maybe because writer Callie Khouri could not figure out any other way to reconcile the plot—with Thelma and Louise being surrounded hopelessly by platoons of male police, some of whom have been chasing them for at least half of the movie.

Yawning before Thelma and Louise and their convertible is a Southwestern canyon a lot like Grand Canyon (Hollywood used Deadhorse Point State Park outside Moab, Utah). Thelma and Louise have had so much fun—some of it very illegal (although they were provoked by men)—that, now that they have been herded into this apparent cul de sac, they can only envision their future as a sad, anticlimactic trip to jail. But, no; one other option remains still available....

Instead of going to jail, they could do what accused child molesters Richard McMillan and Lynn Allen had done. They could drive their car off the rim into space.

And so they do. In glorious slow motion. And somehow suicide seems a nice tidy end to coping with the problems that life throws daily into the faces of all of the rest of us who choose to go on with life's drudgery. In its defense, as is often the case in Hollywood, with *Thelma and Louise*, Hollywood was imitating life, specifically the drive-off-the-rim suicides mentioned earlier. But, as is even more often the case, life—and death—would soon imitate Hollywood.

The power of Hollywood has been known for years as an extremely effective model for shaping people's behavior—although the big studio lawyers are quick to point out that it is very hard to prove this in court. But consider an innocent example: when actor Clark Gable took off his white dress shirt in Frank Capra's 1934 Academy Award winner *It Happened One Night*, movie-goers were titillated to see that Gable was not wearing an undershirt. They were so titillated that for the next twelve months undershirt sales coast to coast plummeted to less than 50 percent of the numbers sold prior to that particular Gable movie.

No surprise, a quick look at Table 9 also reveals that after *Thelma and Louise* fictionally committed suicide by driving off the Grand Canyon-like rim, the same ball started rolling in reality on the South Rim.

1993, a year after *Thelma and Louise* came out in home rental video, became a bonanza year for emulators of *Thelma and Louise*. On January 15, 1993, Patricia Locke Astolfo, age 37, recently divorced and now too broke even to pay the Park entrance fee after driving from Texas, tried to drive her Chevy Suburban across the snowy shoulder of the road then off the South Rim at the Abyss. Despite the cynical saying in some Grand Canyon Village circles, "You just can't miss at the Abyss" (if success in suicide is one's aim), Astolfo did.

Her Suburban high-centered on a rock outcropping on the edge of the roadway a few yards before the rim and lurched to a halt against a boulder. The vehicle suffered substantial damage and not would not budge off the boulder.

This was not like *Thelma and Louise* at all. Astolfo, an investigation found later, had obsessively watched this video more than 50 times.

Astolfo opened the car door and walked a few hundred yards along the rim. Here she jumped off. Having chosen this spot in haste, she fell only 15 feet, hitting a ledge below. Painfully injured, she next crawled to the edge of this ledge and dropped off it another 25 feet onto a second ledge. Injured far worse, Astolfo crawled to a 75-foot precipice and dropped off its edge. She bounced again and ultimately dropped a total of 190 feet to her death.

Why had she done this to herself? Astolfo had been divorced for a month, was on medications for depression, and had just attempted suicide unsuccessfully in Texas.

Four months later, on May 8, Daniel McCourt drove an Enterprise rental car off Pima Point to his death. While any role of *Thelma and Louise* may remain hypothetical, McCourt did seem to possess a possible reason to drive off the edge. He was reportedly HIV positive. In 1993, being HIV positive usually was a grisly death sentence.

Later that same year, on November 19, Michael Balboa Swinger, age 19, sped his car around the parking lot at the South Kaibab Trailhead then aimed it directly off the edge. This motor plunge into thin air proved fatal. And it was the third copycat suicide drive-off plunge from the South Rim in 1993.

By June 13, 2009, when 57-year-old Gheorghe Chiriac of Apple Valley, California drove his blue Mazda 4-door behind the Thunderbird Lodge then accelerated off the South Rim to crash 600 feet below he became the thirteenth known drive-off victim using the eleventh known vehicle to plunge deliberately into Grand Canyon. A Native Romanian, Chiriac had allegedly just beaten his wife/girlfriend almost to death and was facing criminal charges of attempted homicide.

It's worth mentioning that nearly all non-suicidal people immediately seem to understand that even one drive-off is not merely a tragedy but a dangerous hazard for innocent bystanders that also incurs significant danger to search and rescue personnel who must descend to the scenes of impact to scoop up and bag body parts and evidence. Removing the vehicle itself incurs yet greater cost and risks. Again, almost everyone readily recognizes this reality except the suicidal people who decide to hell with everyone, I'm the only person who matters, and I want to drive (or jump) off the rim.

Only three days after Daniel McCourt imitated *Thelma and Louise* in late November of 1993, backpackers in the Canyon would report a collapsed hiker at the base of a 30-foot cliff below the west edge of the Grandview Trail and Horseshoe Mesa atop Cottonwood drainage.

The collapsed man they had found, Michael S. Walchle, had used his knife inside Crystal Forest Cave to slice his left antecubital fossa with three long slashes (at the inner side of the elbow) in a suicide attempt. He failed to sever his artery, but he had cut his brachial vein and had begun bleeding heavily. Contented with a job sort of well done, he fell asleep in the cave.

He awoke to daylight streaming into the entrance. Staring at the crust of blood painting his arm, he now felt stupid for still being alive. He also now experienced second thoughts and decided to hike back out of the Canyon for help. He tossed his "kinda dull" knife off the cliff. Earlier he had thrown away his driver's license so that his body could not be identified.

Although for eight years in the 1980s he had driven tours and worked a front desk job at the South Rim, he lately had been living in Las Vegas. He'd had a breakup argument with his girlfriend. She had thrown hot coffee on him. This proved to be the last straw. Depression and a feeling of worthlessness had driven him to reenter the Canyon one final time. But now, not far up from his reconsideration point, Michael felt dizzy and weak. He collapsed and slid down 30 steep feet of cliff.

This is where one of those backpackers witnessed him tumble. They helped him upward to Horseshoe Mesa. He explained that he had cut his arm in a fall. The backpackers handed off Michael to four other campers they met, all physicians. These new caretakers warmed up Michael, dressed his wound, and treated him for dehydration and hypothermia. Meanwhile two of them trekked up through a storm to fetch help.

NPS rangers hiked in that night and found the 30-year-old patient. When the rangers radioed Dispatch, the dispatcher on duty, Barb Brutvan, was suspicious of Michael's story of having cut himself during a fall. She prompted the rescuers to question Michael more closely.

A quick search revealed the sleeve of his jacket had sustained no tear during the alleged injury. This prompted a confession: Yes, he admitted, he had tried to commit suicide.

Why?

Because of that row with his ex-girlfriend. And also because he was a diagnosed bipolar with obsessive compulsive disorder and was suffering from post-traumatic stress disorder. Worse, he had quit taking his anti-depression medications. His risk factors were even more considerable than these would imply. He had been raised in a series of foster homes. Indeed, his sister and five other family members had committed suicide. It seemed to run in his genes. The cards, it would seem, were heavily stacked against him.

But his genes proved not to be his destiny. Fourteen years later Michael (who informed Ghiglieri of the details of his suicide attempt and its aftermath) is not only still alive, but successfully married and is the father of a young daughter. To fight his demons he assiduously sees his therapist and psychiatrist and takes his antidepressant meds.

His regret? "I wish I could have been a Park Ranger or someone who helps others instead of being a burden on others."

Although many episodes of suicide prove, upon investigation, to result from strange ways of thinking by the victim, this next example may prove the strangest at Grand Canyon. On January 5, 2010 college student Syu Jhih-Cheng leaped into space unwitnessed at the Abyss.

Rangers soon noted a vehicle parked unattended for two days in snow in the bus lane near the Abyss. Footprints led from it to the edge, but none returned. Helicopter-based searchers scoured the snowy cliffs and found University of Georgia student Syu's body 300 feet below the icy rim from which he had jumped. The question, of course, was: Why had he jumped?

Rangers found a copy of the *I-Ching* in Syu's backpack. The *I-Ching*, or *Yi Jing*, is among the oldest known written documents in the world. It is also known as the "Classic of Change." The origin of the *I-Ching* has been traced back in written form for 3,000 years. Some Chinese claim beyond this antiquity that it was passed down via oral tradition for 2,000 years earlier yet. The *I-Ching* remains a popular spiritual resource in Asia and elsewhere. It remains one of the fundamental books of Confucianism and one of the oldest forms of divination.

Syu seemed mired in mysticism. Rangers also found a white stuffed animal. Syu had slept with and obsessively carried this toy with him everywhere since his childhood. More interesting but recondite were Syu's own garbled, incomplete writings in Chinese.

Interpreted into English, these revealed that Syu of Taiwan believed his parents were not his true biological family. Instead, Buddha and the mountains were. Syu also wrote he "wanted to stay away from money, success, and women and wanted to be a superman." He wrote too that he believed he was above common people and he had been given a task—and also a promise—by the sky god. Once he finished this task he could return to immortality in the sky.

Indeed, Syu had gone a big step further by convincing himself he was immortal and he could skip the long step of attaining enlightenment via the teachings of Buddha. Instead Syu could leap forward by the act of sacrificing himself to the sky god in a very non-Buddhist manner and thus re-attain his previous immortality. Later, Syu seemed to believe, he could return to Earth as a god.

One might wonder why Syu was so eager to leap into the sky to meet this fate, especially when it appeared that he may not have completed the task the sky god had assigned to him.

The answer would prove more Earthly. Back at the University of Georgia, Syu was failing his graduate student courses. He had lost his assistantship. He also had been arrested (he was out on bail), and was facing five new arrest warrants for trespass, battery, threatening a witness, false imprisonment, and attempted sexual battery of a woman he was stalking.

Suicides Spurred By Canyon Experiences

In a few cases, the Canyon was not the opportunity for suicide, it was instead the precipitating factor.

An early example comes from a chapter "Lost Mines & Hidden Treasures" in George H. Billingsley, Earle E. Spamer, and Dove Menkes' book *Quest for the Pillar of Gold: The Mines & Miners of the Grand Canyon*. The story begins more than a century ago, when "Long Tom" Watson, a lone prospector who had combed Northern Arizona for gold, spent the winter in Flagstaff. He used old papers to start his fires. Among them he found a batch of letters, one envelope of which had an illegible address and had never been opened. Inside it Watson found a piece of brown wrapping paper with a note scrawled on one side and a map on the other. It had been written by a prospector to his brother.

The letter turned out to be the stuff of which dreams are made. The letter said he had found gold in Grand Canyon but he was also being followed by two men whom he suspected would rob him. To foil them he had filled a sack with his nuggets and hid it in a small cave behind a waterfall.

The next morning, the letter continued, the two men entered the prospector's camp. All three men had yanked their guns and fired at one another. The prospector had been hit and seriously wounded. Despite his wound(s), he managed to reach the rim. Someone had found him there and had hauled him to Williams (60+ miles south) to see a doctor. It was here the wounded and possibly dying man had drawn his map and written his letter.

"Long Tom" Watson waited until spring before trying to follow the map. Then he combed tributary canyons from Havasu to Tanner, eventually guessing that the waterfall the prospector had used must have been an ephemeral one that flowed only in the spring or during run-offs. On the Tanner Trail he heard water trickling. Following the sound he found a small waterfall nearby. Plunging through the water he found a rotting sack full of gold nuggets. Watson transferred many of these to his own sacks and pockets then plunged back out through the falls. But in doing this, he lost his footing, so the story goes, fell, broke his leg, hit his head, and lost consciousness.

The next day he managed to climb atop his burro and escape up the Tanner. Yet another Good Samaritan found Watson—more or less as the first one had found the original discoverer of the gold. This rescuer hauled him to a hospital 80 miles away in Flagstaff.

Four months later, Watson shared the secret of the gold behind the waterfall with "Doc" Scanlon. Scanlon proved interested. The two men entered the Canyon and combed the Tanner Trail area, now dry. Watson, however, could not relocate the region of the now-vanished waterfall no matter how hard they searched. "Watson, bitterly disappointed," write Billingsley, Spamer, and Menkes, "took his own life with his rifle near the Canyon rim." No one knows what happened to the nuggets or even to Doc Scanlon.

The above story may be apocryphal. It contains all of the standard elements of the "lost gold" tales that emerge in any mining region. On the other hand....

Although nearly every suicide is a tragedy, and all are depressing, a few are truly astounding. The following episode transcends even the astounding. This story begins in the mid 1980s, when Carolyn (now Carolyn Castleman) was floating the Colorado on a private trip a few miles downstream of Lava Falls. Their group decided to hike up the Whitmore Trail at River Mile 188.

An hour or so later, she was surprised to see a solitary hiker atop the trail about to ride off on his mountain bike while wearing a life jacket. For a hiker in such a remote part of the Canyon, she thought, this guy was not carrying much of anything he really needed—and why the life jacket way up here? But he was drinking a Coke and he did offer them a cold one. The hiker was tall and lean, with long hair but a receding hairline. Allegedly, he was old enough to be have been a draft-dodger (an episode that he alluded to later) during America's Vietnam conflict. Curious, Carolyn and her husband talked to him and heard his story.

"I'm riding over to Toroweap to swim Lava Falls," he explained.

He had done all of this before, he assured them. This time he had driven out to the head of Whitmore Wash in his International Scout, and was now about to pedal from Whitmore to Toroweap Overlook, and then would hike down the trail to the Colorado River at Lava Falls (River Mile 179.5). After his swim of Lava he would continue down the river nine more miles to the Whitmore Trail where he then would hike up and out to his Scout. From there he would drive to Toroweap to pick up his bike. This intrepid hiker identified himself as Lesley (a.k.a. Ed) Marr, from California.

Marr was in his mid-thirties, of average build, and somewhat unkempt, Carolyn thought, but he seemed friendly enough. So friendly, in fact, that she and her fellow river runners offered Marr a ride downriver to Diamond Creek instead of continuing his plan to bike, hike down, swim, hike back up to his vehicle, then drive home.

He gladly accepted.

Becoming better acquainted over the next few days en route to Diamond, Carolyn and her husband asked Marr if he wanted to come along on another float trip on the Green River. He did. And he had a good time on that trip as well. But he also showed some peculiar behavior. At times, for example, Marr chained his ammo box to himself to prevent its loss or theft. But what the heck? He seemed harmless enough.

The river runners also found out that Marr had a girlfriend. They invited Marr and this girlfriend onto the section of their next Canyon trip beginning at Phantom Ranch planned for the following year. Marr accepted yet again. They told Marr they would meet him and his girlfriend at the Phantom Ranch boat beach on a specific day in mid-June.

When that day came, Carolyn remembers floating toward the boat beach near Phantom Ranch. But only one person, a woman, waited on the beach. Lesley Marr was nowhere in sight. Moreover, the woman was very upset.

She introduced herself as Marr's girlfriend then told them what had gone wrong. She and Marr had hiked down the trail the night before and slept on the boat beach. Early that morning a ranger had approached them and told them they had camped illegally by being outside the campground. When the ranger next learned that the two campers had no permit at all for overnight camping, he said he was required to cite them for their violation of NPS backcountry rules.

Marr told the ranger that they were meeting a river trip. The ranger explained that was irrelevant. As this ranger wrote the citation, Marr became extremely irate and belligerent. The ranger warned Marr that he was treading on thin ice and could be arrested.

At this, Marr acted even more belligerently. Finally, the ranger did arrest him. Next the ranger discovered that Marr's I.D. cards showed two different identifications. One of them had to be false. The ranger handcuffed Marr and ordered him flown to the South Rim. Marr's girlfriend seemed somehow immune to all of this hassle and was simply left behind by both men on the boat beach. So she waited there for the river trip.

After explaining her story, the boaters still offered her a ride downstream with them as planned.

"No," she explained with genuine worry, "Ed would kill me if I went downstream with you."

Carolyn, however, took this statement not at face value but as hyperbole, and told her, "Well, the only other way out of here is by hiking back up."

Marr's girlfriend grimaced and said something to the effect of, "No way am I going to do that...."

Carolyn then told her, "If you're not going to come downstream with us, and you're not going to hike out, then the only other way out of here is by a medical evacuation."

The river trip continued downstream. Marr's girlfriend ended up exiting the Canyon neither by river nor by foot but instead from Phantom Ranger Station via a medical evacuation helicopter. She had somehow "hurt her ankle" after talking with Carolyn.

Up on the rim, NPS rangers released Marr from custody but issued a date for him to appear in Court before the magistrate at Grand Canyon in early July.

The date came. Marr never appeared. A warrant went out for his arrest.

At about this same time, Grand Canyon National Park Headquarters received a bomb threat targeting Superintendent Dick Marks and the head of Law Enforcement, Dave Swickard.

Hundreds of miles away at this same time (July 5, 1987) during early morning in downtown Twentynine Palms, California, two highway patrolmen tried to stop a driver for a traffic violation. When the driver of the International Scout failed to yield to them, the officers pursued him. During their pursuit, the officers observed the driver lighting a traffic flare inside the vehicle as he drove into Joshua Tree National Park.

When this fleeing subject approached that park's headquarters, he accelerated his vehicle through the parking lot and aimed it directly at the building's entrance.

The Scout crashed through a three-foot high retaining wall and lurched to a crunching stop.

The CHP officers stopped, took cover, and drew their weapons. They ordered the man in the Scout to place his hands on his head. Instead, the Scout's driver, still inside it, ignited yet another flare. The two CHP officers next heard the metallic clicks of a pump shotgun or rifle being loaded. Then they heard several shots.

Within seconds the interior of the Scout burst into flames.

Horrified, the CHP officers also saw the driver's head suddenly engulfed in flames. Even so, they again ordered him out of the car with his hands on his head. Soon the door of the Scout opened and the driver fell out of the Scout, collapsing onto the ground.

At significant risk (far higher risk than they knew at this moment), the two officers ran up and pulled the flaming driver away from the burning vehicle.

Seconds later, thousands of rounds of ammunition exploded inside it, along with several loaded guns, numerous bottles of compressed propane and acetylene, several cans of gasoline, and thousands of books of matches. The entire vehicle, they now realized in shock, had been loaded as a crudely designed car bomb.

The officers hospitalized the scorched driver of the exploded Scout. An investigation showed him to be Lesley Marr. Marr died from third degree burns over most of his body and from a self-inflicted .22 caliber gunshot wound to the head.

Yes, the bomb threat at Grand Canyon was confirmed to be linked to Marr. Marr's actions convinced law enforcement officials that he fully intended to kill several officials at the South Rim—along with himself as pilot of his car bomb. His *Kamikaze* trip to Grand Canyon National Park Headquarters to explode it and everyone inside it, however, had gone awry only because, en route, he had violated a routine traffic law.

So your mother was right: some hitchhikers can be real trouble.

What is the upshot on Canyon suicides? Several people apparently have traveled to Grand Canyon with the specific intent to commit suicide. At least 75 of them have committed suicide in ways in which their bodies have ended up below the rims. Considering that nearly a century has passed during which this sort of thing was possible, and also considering that as many as fifty million people have deliberately visited Grand Canyon, this suicide rate off the rims is remarkably low.

On the other hand, during 1993, the year after the Hollywood video *Thelma and Louise* was released, three people committed suicide in three independent copycat drive-offs from the South Rim; and two more people failed in their suicide attempts by foot. Almost one fifth of all 82 suiciders listed (thirteen of them, counting Patricia Astolfo) in Table 9 have done so by driving off the South Rim. These three in 1993 comprise a statistical anomaly. Throughout the entire 90-year period during which this type of suicide was possible, again, only those thirteen people have driven off in eleven vehicles (many of them rental cars). Thus the statistical "anomaly" of one quarter of all drive-offs occurring in 1993 is very likely a nonrandom product of these victims copycatting a Hollywood glorification of an internal-combustion-powered death-plunge suicide presented in Technicolor as a desirable means of exploring infinity.

Beyond copycatism, and as we have seen thus far in this book, men far more than women become victims of fatal mishaps in the Canyon. This also holds true for deliberate suicides. Of the 82 suiciders through 2014, 69 (84 percent) were men. Only 13 (16 percent) were women. The ages of both genders, however, were more or less similar. The range for women was 18 to 49 years old, for men 17 to 69 years old (or perhaps 72, if Ambrose Bierce truly died in the Canyon—see Table 9). The average age of both genders was about 37.

Suicide, however, shows an inverse seasonality to that of visitation—and also to that of all other types of fatal mishaps. Unlike accidental falls from the rims, 47 of the 80 suicides occurring during a known month (59 percent of the total) occurred during the six "off" months from October through March of low visitation to the Canyon. In contrast, with accidental falls from the rims the opposite pattern holds: 34 of those 56 victims (61 percent) fell during the six "summer" months of high visitation. But during the six "off" months, only 22 people (39 percent) fatally fell by accident. August was the peak month for accidental fatal falls, with 11 victims, versus October being the peak month for suicides, with 12.

How did most of the people commit suicide? Interestingly many of the early suicides were committed slightly below the rim by a self-inflicted gunshot (N=7) or even by hiking down to the river and leaping into it to drown (N=2). Apparently leaping off the rim did not seem an attractive option in those days. By the 1970s onward, however, leaping or driving off the rim became paramount.

The data available to us—we rarely got the opportunity to read the notes and letters that at least 19 known victims left behind—did not allow us to answer the question: Why did the majority of these Grand Canyon suicides happen? What were the most common motivations? We do know that depression is very common in victims, as is a history of early childhood abuse and/or neglect. More than a dozen victims had been diagnosed or hospitalized with psychiatric problems. A recent report in *The Lancet Psychiatry* noted that between 2000-2011, 45,000 suicides, 1 out of every 5 suicides in the world, were linked to joblessness. Common, too, in the Canyon was the fugitive factor. At least 13 victims were fleeing arrest by law enforcement (as in *Thelma & Louise*) when they drove or leaped off the rim.

In summary, while the suicide season in the Canyon occurs more during times of low visitation, the number of people who commit suicide in ways that deposit their bodies within Grand Canyon is less than most people might imagine. For perspective, for each known person who committed suicide listed in Table 9, five times more people than that were killed accidentally due to air crashes in and around the Canyon.

A recent analysis found that of all national parks west of the Mississippi, Grand Canyon experienced the greatest number of suicides between 2003 and 2009. But for additional perspective on this, note that more than 400 people are known to have committed suicide by leaping off Niagara Falls. Moreover, consider the Golden Gate Bridge running north from San Francisco. Since it was built in 1937 at least 1,600 people have leapt from it to commit suicide. Of course the human populations living near San Francisco and close to Niagara Falls is far larger than the number of people living near the isolated region around Grand Canyon. As Table 9 also reveals, however, a majority of victims traveled a thousand miles or more deliberately to Grand Canyon with the sole purpose of committing suicide here. How many potential victims changed their minds after they arrived and decided instead to live will remain forever unknown.

We may conjecture that the vista of Grand Canyon from either rim has proved so ethereal and is such a powerful reminder of how precious the gift of being alive on this planet is, that this spectacle has discouraged suicides among its five million visitors per year instead of facilitating them.

One final and unexpected development we wish to address is the reading material a few suiciders have chosen as their "guidebook." In November of 2002, for example, 35-year-old Clayton Cuppy redirected a family vacation from Disneyland to Grand Canyon. This occurred during a point in Cuppy's life when allegedly nothing good was happening, but something bad was. Ominously, after telling his mother, "Jumping off the rim is so unoriginal," Cuppy hiked down the Bright Angel Trail to Plateau Point and jumped off 600 feet. Rangers found a copy of *Over the Edge: Death in Grand Canyon* in Cuppy's backpack. At least two other people who committed suicide in the Park during the last decade also were found with a copy of *Over the Edge*. While other books might also be viewed as apparent literary accomplices in other Canyon suicides (such as the *I-Ching* with Syu in 2010 and a copy of German poet Goethe's *Faust* with George Lewis Kinsey in 1962), this remains a disappointing but not entirely unexpected development to Ghiglieri and Myers. (Oddly, no one committing suicide with *Over the Edge* has duplicated a suicide existing in the book.) Again, as this chapter and Table 9 both illustrate, many suiciders suffer from severe mental illness and have become extremely self-absorbed attention seekers. Many intentionally have committed suicide with dramatic flare only after ascertaining they had an audience. The few who have committed suicide while imagining they would "go down in history" by "getting into the book" most likely fit into this extreme, attention-seeking category. Here we would like to take pains to emphasize that this chapter is not meant to glorify suicide but to discourage it.

As most readers would by now agree, this book is plenty long even without a chapter on suicide. Indeed, we wish there was no need for one. The scope of this book, however, is to document all fatal events below the Canyon's rims.

Not all readers of this book agree with our take on suicide. Consider the opinion of one reader who wrote Myers the following email in July, 2010:

I enjoyed your book immensely, but was aghast at your plea at the end of the chapter on suicides to potential jumpers. While I can certainly appreciate how one can be enamoured of Grand Canyon and the heroics of the dedicated NPS rangers, whom I deeply respect, the audacity to pretend to possess the moral authority to dictate to others where or where not to die, while typical of the arrogance of many physicians, is unseemly.

Actually we do believe we possess—as you, too, possess—the "moral authority to dictate to others where or where not to die." Indeed, we firmly believe no one has the moral right to choose to violently murder oneself in a public place. And the laws of all fifty states in America agree with us on this. We firmly oppose this level of narcissistic selfishness on the part of anyone contemplating suicide due to the harm a public suicide does to those nearby. More specifically, we oppose suicides at Grand Canyon and all other national parks because of their impact on the innocent bystanders, acquaintances, family members, and others who are left not just with a sense of loss but also with lifelong nightmares from witnessing the unexpected suicide. Further, despite our attitude possibly seeming "unseemly," we oppose anyone deliberately creating a situation that forces Park EMS personnel to conduct costly investigations and to "clean up" and dispose of splattered blood, brains, and skin and ruptured organs, shattered bones, and sprayed vomit, urine, and feces from a high impact suicide. Several suicide notes written over the years have stipulated the authors' preference that NPS rangers leave the suicider's body wherever it falls. The rub here, of course, is that no Park visitors' experiences are enhanced by the sight and smell of a rotting corpse. Hence the need for body recoveries.

Thus we also oppose NPS personnel deliberately being forced to expose themselves to the additional extreme risk of recovering of body parts on incredibly dangerous terrain. No one possesses the right to endanger or ruin the lives of others—at high expense to taxpayers—simply to indulge themselves. Finally and foremost, we oppose the tragic aftermath of suicide, the devastating psychological mess and legacy of horror that suicide leaves. Again, it eternally haunts the parents, siblings, spouses, and/or children of the victim. Suicide lingers as a miasmic evil for generations.

Sadly, what most people who commit a spectacular suicide fail to understand in their self-absorption is: No one is dazzled by their actions. Pity is the very most they ever get.

If you are contemplating suicide, please do not come to Grand Canyon or any other public place to commit it—thus risking the lives of rescue personnel and sabotaging the mental well-being of others. Instead, seek help, call 911. The old aphorism that suicide is a permanent solution to a temporary problem is usually true.

And remember, changing one's mind in midair rarely works out.

Table 9. SUICIDAL DEATHS BELOW GRAND CANYON'S RIMS.			
Name, age	**Date**	**Location**	**Circumstances**
? Ambrose Gwinnet Bierce, 72	1914	below the South Rim?	

*The mysterious disappearance of former Civil War purple-heart veteran and noted journalist Bierce was under research by writer Scott Thybony. He has assembled a convincing case based on circumstantial evidence that Bierce detoured from a putative journey into Pancho Villa's Mexico and instead committed suicide within the Canyon at a years-long, pre-decided location, possibly by shooting himself with a new **German pistol** he admired.*

Unidentified man	circa 1930.	3 miles east of El Tovar, Shoshone Point, 600 feet below rim	

*During early June in 1933, a botanical cactus expert from Riverside, California was scanning with field glasses a nearly inaccessible ledge 600 feet below the rim for cactus and instead spotted the skeleton of a man. Deputy Sheriff Jack Harbin and Ranger Robert R. Williamson worked their way down to the ledge. The deceased man's weather-bleached skeleton was wearing the rags of khaki pants and a white cotton shirt and "sandals." No coat or hat. The skeleton had a **.32 bullet in his cranium** from an entry hole just above and behind his right ear. In his pocketbook was 40 cents and nothing else. Beside the man lay a "cheap" .32 revolver. This skeleton ended up becoming the mystery skeleton found in 1977 stashed in Carl Rust's boat in Emery Kolb's garage, giving rise to the rumor that the bones were the skeleton of river runner Glen Hyde who vanished in 1928.(see text) Coconino Sun, June 9, 1933. Canyon Views, vol 15(1), Spring 2009.*

Ida M. Rusk, 40-ish	June 1, 1933	Hermit Rapid (RM #95)	

*Rusk of Maywood, California had spent 3 months the previous summer camping at Grand Canyon. At the end of May, 1933, she traveled from home to stay the night at El Tovar where people found her rational. The next morning she hiked the Hermit Trail. Rusk reached the river at midday. There she ate lunch, smoked several cigarettes, took off her shoes, and tossed them in the Colorado. Next she **leapt into the river**, now flowing at flood stage, at the head of Hermit Rapid. The river swallowed her instantly. Rusk left a signed note at Santa Maria Spring: "If you are looking for me, don't look further. For I am heading for the river and am never coming back." Construction workers found her body 3-4 days later drifting near Hoover Dam. Her husband identified her. Coconino Sun, June 9, 1933. Superintendent's Report, 1933.*

James R. Willis, (a.k.a. Jack Way), adult	August 15?, 1948	between Yavapai & Yaki Points	

*Willis was considered "the finest packer that ever lived at Grand Canyon. He could take any object—no matter what its size or shape—and successfully pack it on a mule. He had apparently seated himself just beneath the rim...and taken **poison**." Willis had* *been an NPS packer from 1927-1933 but in 1948 had experienced a stroke which left him unable to get a job.* Superintendent's Report, *Sept. 4, 1948, p. 11.*

Charles Cuma, 48   June 27?, 1949   Kaibab Bridge over Colorado (RM #88)
*Mr. Charles Cuma, a new Professor of engineering at the University of New Mexico, but formerly an engineer for Chrysler, "left Albuquerque on June 26 after announcing his intention of hiking into Grand Canyon and **jumping off the bridge** [into the Colorado]. Park men on the trail and Harvey guides reported seeing the native Czechoslovakian hiking below Indian Gardens and no further trace of his was found. Word of his intended self-destruction did not reach the park until after he had gone down the trail. River parties going through the Canyon will be asked to look for any clues."* Arizona Daily Sun, *July 6, 1949.* Superintendent's Memorandum for the Director, *July 11, 1949, p. 9.*

Vernon Taylor, adult   November 23, 1951   below South Rim
"Vernon Taylor, Fred Harvey trail guide, committed suicide in the park on the night of November 23rd." The Superintendent's Monthly Narrative Report, *November 1951.*

Mildred Violet Allen, 40+   October 5, 1951   Maricopa Point
*Allen of Pasadena, California was sitting on the rim holding onto the bottom rung of a railing, when she suddenly shoved her body out in a suicide "**leap**" and away from the ledge and let go. She fell 400 feet. She left a suicide note.* Arizona Daily Sun, *October 8 & 13, 1951.*

Tony Pischke, 40   June 22, 1957   near Lookout Studio
*Pischke, a salesman from Phoenix and a former Fred Harvey Company butcher, was last seen walking alone along the rim. He wrote a suicide note and left it in a Bright Angel Lodge cabin he had rented. Pischke **jumped** off and fell 150 feet below the rim.*

George Lewis Kinsey, 33   December 7, 1962   "Duck-on-a-Rock," East Rim Drive
*Kinsey of Gary, Indiana was found on a ledge and with a **bullet hole** to the heart. A new, French-made 32-caliber automatic and a copy of the German poet Goethe's "Faust" ("On one's own initiative") lay next to him. Kinsey, an ex-U.S. Marine who fought in Korea was characterized as a "very sensitive and unstable" and a "moody sort of fellow who had been despondent."* Arizona Daily Sun, *December 8, 14 & 17, 1962.* Arizona Republic, *December 18, 1962.*

Marion Leroy Bates, 39   January 1965   a ledge below Hermit's Rest
*A hiker found Bates of Forest Park, Illinois in 1969 in a small crevasse under a ledge below rim, a .38 caliber revolver gripped in his skeletal hand. Death was due to **gunshot** wound.* Arizona Daily Sun, *April 7, 17 & 21, 1969.*

Osan Kang, 54	March 28, 1967 Lipan Point

*Kang of San Francisco and Washington, D.C. **drove** a Hertz rental car off an ideal "launch ramp" on the rim, plunging a clean 1,000 feet. Kang had been a very dignified and courteous small-time con man who had recently been down on his luck after several failed ventures. Kang's was the first known drive-off suicide at Grand Canyon. (see text)* Arizona Republic, April 2, 3 & 9, 1967.

Dorothy Dowdy, 49	October 1971 Mather Point

*Dowdy of Tucson, Arizona was found huddled under a ledge below the rim with a paper sack over her head and a **pistol shot** into her head. Still gripped in her hand was an automatic pistol. Dowdy had recently been released from a mental institution and was disturbing the other guests at the Bright Angel Lodge. Ranger Vic Vieira checked with her doctor, who assured Vieira that Dowdy was not a threat to herself, or anyone else, nor was she welcome back at the institution.* Arizona Daily Sun, April 4 &13, 1972.

Robin Ruth Myers, 18	November 3, 1972 Maricopa Point

*Myers of Janesville, Wisconsin was found by Dave Elston who noticed an orange stocking cap in the snow and yanked it out to reveal a frozen human head. Myers had a suicide note in her pocket. Hers was an unwitnessed apparent **jump**. She was a former mental patient with prior suicide attempts who walked away from her mental hospital.* Arizona Daily Sun, October 27, 1975. Arizona Republic, October 28, 1975. Letter to Ghiglieri & Myers from Dave Elston, February 2, 2015.

Stephen S. Steiner, 24 Peggy Jo Ann Horner, 31	February 3, 1973 Yaki Point

*Steiner of Baltimore, Maryland and Horner of Mount Joy, Pennsylvania drove to the Canyon on their prized motorcycle, rented a Hertz car in Tusayan, and, in apparent suicide pact (based on investigation), **drove it off the rim** at high speed, plunging 500 feet, hitting then ricocheting another 1,000 feet. (see text)* Arizona Daily Sun, December 17, 1974. Arizona Republic, December 17 & 21, 1974.

Gregory F. Bansberg, 32	October 13, 1978 behind Yavapai Museum

*Bansberg, a troubled Vietnam vet and Fred Harvey concession employee in maintenance from Youngstown, Ohio, was seen taking a few very deliberate "**giant steps over the rim** and into the Canyon."* Williams News, October 19, 1978. Incident report #78-7402

Edward Enzor Walters, 36	June 15, 1980 Navajo Bridge/Marble Canyon

*Walters of Chiefland, Florida wrote two long suicide notes on seven pages, weighted himself with rocks in his pockets, parked his car in the oncoming lane of Navajo Bridge, left his lights on and door open, exited, and **leaped** off Navajo Bridge. His body became visible, lodged under driftwood 100 days later and 7 miles downriver by a kayaker and was not a pretty picture. (see text)* Arizona Daily Sun, June 18 & September 25, 1980. Incident report #80-1884

Myung Sun Kim, 28

December 26, 1980　First Trailview Overlook
*Kim of Tustin, California stepped past the guard rail and ignored pleas of her family to step back from the rim. Seconds later, when her husband and other family members looked away, she **stepped out** and "fell" 300 feet. She was depressed over personal issues.* Arizona Daily Sun, *December 28 & 29, 1980. Incident report #80-4641*

Unidentified white male, 25–30

December 30, 1980　Pima Point
*The body of a young adult white male dead from having **fallen** was found well below the rim wearing a black leather jacket, blue Levis, and hiking boots. No I.D. Incident report #80-4677*

William Joseph O'Brien, 38

August 12–22, 1984　Mather Point
*O'Brien of Phoenix, Arizona had terminal cancer. He had informed his former wife and friend of his intent to **jump**, and then he did, falling 300 feet.* Arizona Daily Sun, *September 24 & 25, 1984. Incident report #84-2567*

Eric B. Lopez, 19

March 15, 1985　The Abyss
*Lopez, a U.S. Marine stationed at El Toro, California, **drove his car** off West Rim Drive near The Abyss and plunged 400 feet. He was the fourth suicide victim to die by driving off the rim (in the third vehicle).* Arizona Daily Sun, *March 17, 1985. Incident report #85-0281*

Laura Lynn Allen, 30
Richard Lee McMillan, 50

June 29, 1986　East Rim Drive past Yaki Point
*Double suicide. Allen of Lancaster, California was despondent over her disability, and also was about to be arrested for child molestation of her own children. She apparently formed a suicide pact with Richard McMillan of Taft, California, also about to be arrested for molestation of Allen's children. Witnesses saw the couple as McMillan **drove** his 1965 International Scout at high speed 147 feet off-road then off the rim to plunge 1,000 feet. (see text)* Arizona Daily Sun, *July 1 & 11, 1986.* Arizona Republic, *June 30 & July 2, 1986. Incident report #86-1748*

Peter K. Schrieber, 23

July 20, 1986　Toroweap Overlook
*Schrieber of Goleta, California wrote a note to his parents then **jumped** off 400 feet.* Arizona Daily Sun, *July 27, 1986. Incident report #86-2218*

Roy Bundens Jones, 38

January 22, 1987　Hopi Point, W beyond guardrail
*Two days after Jones of Albuquerque, New Mexico had **fallen** 1,000 feet down partially snow-covered and vertical terrain, he was discovered by a passenger of helicopter pilot John Parrish while making a routine maintenance flight. Jones apparently had been living out of his car. His post office box and telephone had been cancelled for lack of payment. Jones, apparently unemployed, died with $21 in his wallet. Undetermined reason for unwitnessed death, but likely suicide.* Arizona Daily Sun, *January 26, 1987. Incident report #87-0140*

Alan Heaton, 41

September 9, 1987   Point Imperial
Died of gunshot to head (details unclear). Incident report #87-3575

Michael Hope-Ross, 31

December 15, 1987   Yavapai Point
*Hope-Ross, an unemployed airline pilot living in Spain, left a journal indicating despondent but not quite suicidal thoughts. NPS concluded he **jumped** off, falling 500 feet. His family, however, notes that Ross had $30,000 in the bank and a girlfriend whom he was thinking of marrying. Arizona Daily Sun, December 21, 1987. Incident report #87-4572*

Roger Keeling, Jr., 19

April, 1987   ½ mile east of Hopi House
*On June 24, 1988 the discovery of a decaying victim who had **jumped** 300-500 feet with a suicide note in his pocket apologizing for the mess (that his body made?) and an item with "R.K." initials posed a mystery. A faded Amtrak ticket and a tape player were found on him with an acid rock tape. The body of this white male, 5 feet, 6 inches tall, was badly deteriorated after 14 months. His skull was crushed into fragments scattered by small animals. His hands had been mummified. He also was wearing a cloth brace for a broken collarbone. Identification eventually was made via dental records to reveal the victim as Keeling of Brea, California. Arizona Daily Sun, June 28 & July 7, 1988. Los Angeles Times, June 29, 1989. Incident report #88-unlisted*

John F. Zitko, 21

October 24, 1989   Yaki Point
*Zitko left home in St. Charles, Missouri on a "self-seeking" journey. He told his family, "You'll hear from me when I find myself." He **jumped** off. Arizona Daily Sun, October 25, 1989. Incident report #89-4967*

Mark Scott Clements, 33

October 26, 1990   The Abyss
*Clements of Sepulveda, California wrote a detailed several-page note then posted it, taped, to the guard rail. This note included an arrow pointing downward and instructions for whomever found the note to contact NPS rangers. Clements also tied a rope to his rifle and tethered it to the railing. When Clements **shot himself**, he fell off the rim. But his leg caught in the rifle tether he had rigged, and he fell less than ten feet, instead of hundreds. Clements had left several instructions that, among other things, his expensive assault-type rifle should be returned to his relatives. Williams News, November 1, 1990. Arizona Daily Sun, October 28, 1990. Incident report #90-4253*

Scott Beug, 17

September 14, 1991   Mather Point
*Beug was in trouble at school. He took the family car and firearms from his South Dakota home. He **jumped** off 250 feet. Incident report #91-3907*

Bruce Ciniello, 21

October 15, 1992   No Name Point
*Ciniello **jumped** off, falling 500 feet. Incident report #92-3812*

Patricia Locke Astolfo, 37

January 5, 1993　　The Abyss
Astolfo of San Marcos, Texas had viewed her **THELMA & LOUISE** *video obsessively many times.* **She tried to drive** *her 1986 Chevy Suburban off the edge of the rim but she had slammed it hard and fast atop a boulder, high-centering it and foiling her attempted drive-off. Astolfo opened the door and walked a few hundred yards along the rim. She* **jumped** *off 15 feet, hitting a ledge below. Injured, she crawled to its edge and dropped another 25 feet onto a second ledge. Injured worse, Astolfo crawled to a 75-foot precipice and dropped off its edge. She ultimately dropped a total of 190 feet to her death. Astolfo had been divorced for a month, on medications for depression, and had just attempted suicide in Texas. (see text). Incident report #93-0054*

Daniel McCourt, 32

May 8, 1993　　Pima Point
McCourt **drove** *a 1993 Nissan (an Enterprise rental car) off the South Rim. He reportedly was HIV positive (see text). Incident report #93-1071*

Michael Balboa Swinger, 19

November 19, 1993　　South Kaibab Trailhead
After racing his car across the parking lot, Swinger of Bakersfield, California then **drove** *it over the edge at about 30 mph. He hit 700–800 feet below. He left a suicide note. (see text)* Williams-Grand Canyon News, *November 25, 1993.* Arizona Republic, *November 20 & 21, 1993.* Chicago Tribune, *November 21, 1993. Incident report #93-4698*

Joseph Seitz, 34

May 1, 1994　　1/3 mile west of Hopi Point
Seitz **jumped** *off, falling 500 feet. Incident report #94-1060*

Christopher White, 25

December 30, 1994　　Powell Memorial
White wrote a suicide note then smashed his watch on the rim (as if to symbolically end his time). He next drew an arrow pointing toward the Canyon then he **jumped** *off, falling 540 feet. Incident report #94-5458*

Michael S. Gardner, 27

January 18, 1996　　Mather Point
Gardner of Kansas City, Kansas had stolen money from his fast food employer and gambled it. He arrived at the NPS entry station with too little to pay the entrance fee. So he parked—leaving his keys in his car—outside the Park, then walked several miles to Mather Point. He **jumped** *off, falling 250 feet. He had been reported as despondent prior to his jump but left no note.* Grand Canyon-Williams News, *February 28, 1996.* Arizona Daily Sun, *February 23, 1996. Incident report #96-0716*

Roberta Kay Beard, 21

March 1, 1997　　Worship Site, Rim Trail
Beard, a Fred Harvey employee, reportedly had been depressed. She walked off her job that night and **jumped** *off the rim. Incident report #97-0536*

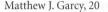

Matthew J. Garcy, 20

October 24, 1997   Cape Royal
*In a bizarre act of extreme emotional disturbance, Garcy asked a bystander to take his photo and to mail a letter on the front seat of Garcy's car. The bystander asked, "Why can't you mail it yourself?" Garcy said, "I'll show you why," then he handed his glasses to the bystander, took a few steps, and **jumped** off the North Rim, falling 400 feet. He left a 6-page suicide note. Incident report #97-4958*

? Steven Vincent Mylan, 20

after February 14, 1998   Little Colorado River Gorge (?)
*Mylan left his home in Mississauga, Ontario, Canada, and visited Rainbow Bridge in Glen Canyon (on February 14). A Navajo found Mylan's black 1991 Chevrolet Bareta parked with keys in the ignition at the jewelry stands at the Little Colorado Gorge Overlook and drove it for a few months until it broke down. On June 8, 1998, Mylan's car was found stripped and parked off State Route 64 for months. Interviews led to an unsuccessful search for his body in the Little Colorado Gorge. Mylan, who did not seem a good candidate for a suicide **jump (?)**, may have been a victim of foul play or of a scrambling mishap. North American Missing Persons Network.*

unidentified man, 40s

March 13(?), 1998   near Hopi House
*On April 13, someone spotted the body of a 6-foot, 4-inch, 281-pound, Caucasian man about 400-500 feet below the rim. Rangers found the man to have been dead "for weeks." The decaying corpse possessed no identification or personal property. The next day Ranger Bil Vandergraff rappelled to retrieve an "EMS" backpack, which contained a completely empty wallet (a common pattern among suiciders). Attempts to I.D. the man via fingerprints and/or his route of entry into the Park failed. This unwitnessed fall appears a probable suicide **jump**. Incident report #98-0928*

Andrew Gradzik, 42

April 23 (?), 1998   E of Yavapai Point
*On September 26, 2001, NPS SAR rangers recovering suicider Richard W. Gibbs (same day) discovered a nearby skeleton scattered over 200 sq. feet, 400+ feet below the rim. Dental records identified it as Gradzik, from Toronto, with a previous suicide attempt. He went missing from El Tovar on April 26, 1998 and likely **jumped**. On April 23, Gradzik had sent a postcard saying that he had met a man who offered to take him on "private hikes." A 14-day SAR in 1998 failed to locate him. Incident report #01-2976*

Murray M. Marshall, 51

November 19, 1998   Maricopa Point
*At 7:30 a.m., the Sprague family walking the rim found an untended walking cane, a half-empty Coors beer can, and a "snakelight" flashlight (switched "on" but now with its battery dead) wrapped around the safety railing and aimed at the Canyon. Another couple arrived and spotted a body atop of the Coconino Sandstone 483 feet below a rare unobstructed vertical drop. The victim who had **jumped**, Marshall, was a handicapped "missing person" of Cherry Log, Georgia. He had just pawned several items, including the title to his 1988 red Ford Ranger pickup with a camper shell, at*

"Superpawn" in Flagstaff. Murray had left his ex-wife in Georgia "with a lot of debt." No suicide note. Incident report #98-3805

Kahlil Williams, 28

February 2000   The Abyss
*A routine overflight on March 29 noticed a "new" vehicle about 1,000 feet below the rim. The pilot recommend an investigation. Searchers found Williams' body (he was from Phoenix) well above the car and 450 feet below the rim. Williams was the tenth **drive-off** suicider, using the eighth vehicle to be driven off. Incident report #00-0652*

Robert William van Rooden, 27   February 20, 2000   ½ mile east of El Tovar Hotel
*van Rooden's personal effects were found abandoned in his hotel room on February 20, but searchers below the rim found no body. An NPS overflight on March 31 spotted the body 250 feet below the rim as a suspected, but unproven suicide **jump**. Incident report #00-0382*

Brady Matthew Forrester, 20   October 18, 2000   First Trailview Overlook
*Forrester, reportedly "appeared to be bungee **jumping**" as he "swan-dived" off the rim, falling 300 feet. Identification took over one month. Victim had a pending warrant for his arrest. Incident report #00-3237*

Nakamura Yukitaka, 58?

? 2001   Grandeur Point
*Nakamura was a wanted man in Japan. Searchers found his remains scattered in snow in the Toroweap Formation below Grandeur Point on March 14, 2002. Unlike with other rim falls, the only broken bone of Yukitaka was the back of the head. Was this a hit/murder or a **jump**? Incident report #02-0593*

Richard W. Gibbs, 52

September 26, 2001   E of Yavapai Point
*Gibbs of California took a tour bus from Las Vegas to Grand Canyon Village. He was seen sitting on the edge of the rim. Witnesses saw (and videotaped) Gibbs **jump** off purposefully. He fell 400 feet. Incident report #01-2972*

Saifddin NoamanTaibjee, 35   November 7, 2002   Mather Point
*Plagued by schizophrenia, Taibjee of San Diego, California exited his Jeep Grand Cherokee after dark, left the door open, and used a flashlight to get to the guard rail. There he stripped off his clothes and dropped them. His naked body was found 400 feet below his **jump** by Ranger Greg Moore using a spotting scope. Incident report #02-3578*

Clayton Cuppy, 35

November 28, 2002   Plateau Point
*Cuppy had re-directed a family vacation from Disneyland to Grand Canyon. He had reached a point in his life where nothing good was happening. After telling his mother, "Jumping off the rim is so unoriginal," he solo hiked the Bright Angel Trail to Plateau Point and **jumped** 600 feet. In his backpack rangers found a copy of* Over the Edge: Death in Grand Canyon. *Incident report #02-3804*

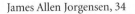

James Allen Jorgensen, 34   February 15 or 16, 2003   E of Quartermaster Canyon
*Jorgensen of Columbia, Tennessee apparently **drove** his Chevrolet
SUV off the rim as the eleventh suicide using the ninth vehicle,
plunging 600 feet.* Williams-Grand Canyon News, *March 11, 2003*

Timothy George Clam, 25   June 10, 2004   over White Butte into Travertine Canyon
*Clam of Illinois, had "experienced periods of serious depression and
mental illness during a significant portion of his adult life" The U.S.
Marines characterized Clam as having "schizotypal personality
disorder," which led to suicide attempts. On June 7 Clam purchased
a helicopter seat in Tusayan but did not use it. On June 9, he tried
to book a front "shotgun" seat on a Papillon tour helicopter but was
not offered a window seat. The next day he finally was sold that
seat, separate from the five other passengers behind. During the return flight of the Papillon Airways Bell 206 (N1076T) at 7,500 feet,
two miles from the rim, while passing over Dripping Springs, Clam
unclipped his seat harness, shoved open the door, and forced his way
out. Pilot Maria Langer grabbed the waistband of Clam's pants to
stop him from exiting but could not retain her grip and meanwhile
also fully control the Bell 206. Langer also began seriously wondering what sort of danger Clam would present to everyone in the
aircraft were she to succeed in keeping him aboard. She resumed
control of the airship. Clam **jumped**, vanishing into a freefall at 100
knots down 3,900 feet into Travertine Canyon. 15 people worked on
the body recovery. (see text) Incident report #04-2954*

Michael Alvarado, 37   September 13, 2005   below Yavapai Observation Point
*Alvarado of El Paso, Texas parked and **jumped** about 500 feet. He
left a suicide note. Incident report #05-4912*

Donald Roger Hansen, Jr., 56   December 23/24, 2005   Yavapai Point
*Witnesses watched Hansen of Huntington Beach, California make a
running dive off the rim then impact several seconds later in a cloud
of dust atop the Coconino Sandstone 600 feet below. Rangers found a
13-inch butcher knife under the driver's seat of Hansen's black Toyota
Corolla, a bag of documents regarding his Federal tax delinquency,
and a day planner in which he'd written the words "No help, Good
bye." Found on Hansen's 190-lb body was his Toyota key and a
"where you will spend eternity" medallion with a Biblical quote. Both
Hansen's wrists bore sutures from a recent failed attempt at suicide by
slitting his wrists. Incident report #05-6313*

Garret Patrick Barry, 24   May 15, 2006   Maricopa Point
*During an investigation of an abandoned Gregory backpack,
Ranger Brandon Torres found a bag of marijuana and a signed
letter inside: "Hi, I'm down in the Canyon. Maricopa Point!!!" Sure
enough, Barry of Salt Lake City, Utah had **jumped** 450 feet off the
rim with a suicide note in his pocket. Incident report #06-2165*

Cynthia Ann Fairham, 40   August 21, 2006   Angel's Window, Cape Royal, North Rim
*A blue Dodge Intrepid belonging to Fairham of San Lorenzo, Cali-
fornia had stood parked overnight with the door swung open and the*

*radio playing loud classic rock from FM 96.7. A 3-page suicide letter sat on the front seat. Its second sentence: "My body is on the right side of Angel Window." Footprints led to the edge. Ranger Devon McCauley saw the 115-lb blonde, recently separated from her husband and now back "into" methamphetamine and crack cocaine, 350 feet below an apparent suicide **leap**. Incident report #06-4997*

Henri Jean Bonin, 53

October 31, 2006   Mohave Point, The Abyss
*A routine helicopter flight spotted an Alamo red Chrysler Crossfire convertible 600 feet below the rim smashed on the Coconino, then a body above it, 539 feet below the rim. The 3,200-pound car contained more than $32,000 in Euros and U.S. cash in a brown canvas bag. The Crossfire also held a Northface backpack, 4 Snickers bars, and, strangely, a new Collins 2.5 -pound cutter pickax. The body has never been positively identified by French authorities. Bonin of France was into horse racing, he spoke weak English, and he had been diagnosed with fatal colon cancer. He had just blackmailed an ex-girlfriend with sex photos for cash. Bonin seemed mentally unstable in many ways and had exhibited a severe anger management problem, repeatedly swerving off-road into walls or into oncoming traffic to emphasize his point—at least once causing a head-on collision. Today, after Bonin's **drive-off** (as the twelfth victim using the tenth vehicle), the roads are safer. NPS (and Alamo) used an Aerospace KMAX helicopter to extract the Chrysler. Incident report #07-7105*

Eric L. Reddish, 24

April 2, 2007   Mather Point
*At 4:15 a.m., a Xanterra mule wrangler on the S. Kaibab Trail reported seeing a steady light below the rim and off-trail. Rangers rappelled 300 feet down and found Reddish of Milford, Delaware, a psychotherapy patient deemed suicidal via other evidence, but without a light. Reddish had **jumped**. The source of the light spotted by the wrangler remains a mystery. Incident report #07-1954*

Claudia Marisol Ramirez, 36

August 29(?), 2007   Walhalla Overlook, North Rim
*Claudia Ramirez of Lake Worth, Florida parked her rental car, left a suicide note projecting from the glove compartment, went to the rim, and **jumped** 350 feet in her bra and panties. Ramirez was a repeated mental health hospital inmate with a history of severe depression, but she refused to take meds. Ramirez had left a copy of* Over the Edge *in the car and had circled four previous suicide locations, none of which were Walhalla. On Ramirez's phone the background said: "Suicide is painless—it's only life that hurts." Incident report #07-7137*

Todd R. Delage, 44

January 19, 2008   Little Colorado Gorge overlook, MP280,
                         State Route 64, W of Dead Indian Canyon
*Delage quit his job, drove from Milbank, South Dakota then informed friends that he would travel until his money ran out then "jump off the Grand Canyon." He parked then **jumped**, bouncing 900 feet to wedge inside an inaccessible crack. Arizona Daily Sun, January 23 & February 28, 2008.*

Mihaly Szabo, 44

February 12(?), 2008   undeveloped viewpoint near Buggeln
*Szabo of Ypsilanti, Michigan drove a rental car to the picnic area,
arrayed his gear, then **jumped** 300 feet. Helicopter rangers found
a suicide note with him then winched up his body. Incident report
#08-0804*

Eric Joseph Stanley, 29

March 14, 2008   below 1st Trail View Overlook, W Rim Drive
*After imbibing alcohol, concession employee Stanley of Grand
Canyon Village, in financial difficulties, diagnosed bipolar, depressed,
and jealous, angrily argued with his girlfriend at 1:00 a.m. He told
her (witnessed): "No one is ever going to see me again" because, he
added, he was going to kill himself. At 2:00 a.m., "extremely angry,"
he left on foot toward on the icy rim above a "significant snowpack."
On April 4, a Peregrine Fund volunteer noted 5 condors on Stanley's
body 300 feet below an apparent **jump**. Incident report #08-1341*

Michael S. Wilson, 47

October 6, 2008   1st overlook on Desert View Drive
*Four witnesses reported seeing Wilson of Scottsdale, Arizona climbing
below the rim toward ever more dangerous ground. They asked Wilson if he needed help but he refused to answer. Instead he stood above
a precipice for 30-40 seconds then seemed to **purposely fall** then
bounce 250 feet to final impact. Wilson was a shy loner who worked
as an electrical engineer for a large defense plant and he was about to
be arrested for computer crimes. He also recently had been released
from 2-4 weeks in a psychiatric facility. Incident report #08-7144*

Richard Duane Jenkins, 58

October 22, 2008   just east of Yavapai Point
*Rangers responding to a report of an abandoned duffle bag 50
yards from the Yavapai Museum scouted below the rim and spotted
Jenkins, who had traveled from Chicago, Illinois to commit suicide,
300 feet below. Unwitnessed rim **jump**. Incident report #08-7517*

Robert Williams, 69

May 25?, 2009   ¼ mile south of Santa Maria Springs,
                     Hermit Basin
*On May 26, Williams of Surprise, Arizona was reported by his son as
overdue from a non-permitted, **solo** overnight hike. On June 2, VIP
Sueanne Kubicek spotted him 200 feet below the Hermit Trail ¼ mile
south of Santa Maria Spring where one must detour off-trail before
encountering vertical exposure. His backpack contained only "token,"
incomplete items for camping. Before Williams' hike, allegedly his car
was to be repossessed, he also had lost his job, and his girlfriend had
left him. He also had bought a new life insurance policy with his sons
as beneficiaries. All suggests a suicide **jump**. Incident report #09-3588*

Gheorghe Chiriac, 57

June 13, 2009   behind Thunderbird Lodge & near El
                     Tovar, South Rim
*At 6:00 a.m. native Romanian Chiriac of Apple Valley, California
drove his older blue Mazda 4-door off the rim to crash 600 feet
below. His body was found above 100 feet higher. Chiriac (the
thirteenth victim using the eleventh vehicle) had allegedly just
beaten his wife/girlfriend almost to death and was facing criminal
charges of attempted homicide. Incident report #09-5247*

Jhih-Cheng Syu, young adult male   January 5, 2010   The Abyss

> *Rangers noted a vehicle parked unattended for two days in snow in the bus lane. Footprints led from it to the edge, but none returned. Helicopter-based searchers found University of Georgia student Syu's body 300 feet below an icy rim from which he had **jumped unwitnessed**. In his backpack was a copy of the I-Ching, a white stuffed animal he had slept with and obsessively took with him <u>everywhere</u> since childhood, and his own garbled, incomplete writings in Chinese. Interpreted, these revealed Syu of Taiwan believed his parents were not his family, Buddha and the mountains were. He also wrote he "wanted to stay away from money, success, and women and wanted to be a superman." He wrote that he believed he was above common people and he was given a task—and a promise—by the sky god and that once he finished the task he could return to immortality in the sky. Syu had convinced himself he was immortal and could skip the long step of attaining enlightenment and instead leap forward by sacrificing himself to the sky god in a very non-Buddhist manner and thus re-attain his previous immortality. Later he could return to Earth as a god. In Georgia, Syu was failing his courses, had lost his assistantship, had been arrested previously, and was facing five new arrest warrants for trespass, battery, threatening a witness, false imprisonment and attempted sexual battery of a woman he was stalking. Incident report #10-0117*

Michael D. McMahon, 64   May 21, 2010   Mather Point

> *McMahon of Long Beach, California handed a bystander an envelope containing his car keys. Written on it was "Suicide, Give to Rangers." Witnesses at 05:38 a.m. next saw pediatrician McMahon run to the rim, hold his arms out perpendicularly, then **jump** off—despite their yells to him to stop. Searchers rappelled to find his body 610 feet below in the Coconino. Incident report #10-3027*

Kirby Porter, 50   July 12, 2010   Moran Point

> *Porter of Mechanicsville, Virginia was witnessed exiting his car and climbing over the retaining wall then lying on the edge of the Canyon rim. Witnesses called 911. Searchers the next morning found Porter's body 250 feet below. Earlier the previous day Rangers had approached Porter, who allegedly told them, "This is f---ing bullshit." Porter had seemed drunk. Rangers had left the man alone, as he was "doing nothing wrong." "Kirby was commonwealth attorney for Hanover County and came to national attention in 2006 when he skillfully assisted state and federal prosecutors with the prosecution of Washington, D.C. snipers John Allen Muhammad and Lee Boyd Malvo, who led a killing rampage that spanned multiple states." But after this, in 2007, Kirby had lost his job, and in 2010 his family home was for sale. A **jump?** Richmond Times Dispatch, July 13 & August 29, 2010. Incident report #10-4399*

Abraham Lorenzana, 30   September 2, 2010   Navajo Bridge/Colorado River

> *Well after evaluation in a mental hospital, Abraham Lorenzana of Long Beach, California and his mother, age 53, were driving to New York City and detoured off route to Navajo Bridge. Ranger*

*Dave Chapman received a call that a pile of clothes (shorts, t-shirt, underwear, and sandals) had been left on the pedestrian walkway on Navajo Bridge. Chapman responded and encountered the mother, who stated her son was missing. Abraham had a history of getting naked atop high places and of drug abuse and psychological depression. Members of a private river trip found Lorenzana's body 2 months later on November 3, near river mile 21. He had **jumped** off the bridge. Incident report #10-7225 and Coconino County Sherriff's Office case #S10-03196.*

Robert J. Friesen, 60-ish

2010   Hermit Creek drainage
In September, 2013 a river runner found a weathered wallet stuck in mud at Hermit Creek with Friesen's Tucson, Arizona ID inside. In February, 2014, someone else found human bones in the drainage identified via DNA analysis as Friesen's. In 2010, Tucson Police had listed him as a "missing person" after his sister in Texas could not contact him. Friesen was a USAF Vietnam vet, likely with PTSD, who refused VA treatment, had no job, was a "loner," car-less, phone-less, & often homeless and who avoided contact with his family for years on end. He exited his neat room at the Copper Cactus Inn and ended up in Hermit Creek. Cause of death unknown, hence not listed in suicide statistics or in Table 11. Tucson Police Dept. Missing Person Report, TPD # 1005250258. *Coconino County Medical Examiner's Office, pers. comm.* 2014 Annual Report, Branch of Emergency Services, GCNPS

Joseph Radford, 47 (pilot)

March 11, 2011   unknown location W of Scorpion Ridge
*Radford of Glendale, Arizona flew his "experimental" homebuilt (from a kit) RV-6 (N650RV) from Grand Canyon Airport at 8:30 a.m. westerly for a couple of minutes. Then he manually turned off his transponder, cutting the ability of radar to track him. He next made a hard right, north turn to **fly into a no-fly zone over Grand Canyon**. Radford's RV-6 next turned westerly and was seen by hikers flying illegally low over Scorpion Ridge. Next it vanished. Two days later a commercial pilot reported hearing transmissions from an ELB (emergency locator beacon) nearby and about 30 miles northwest of the airport. The next day Radford was reported as a missing person and a coordinated Coconino County Sheriff's SAR and Grand Canyon NPS search began. By now the ELB had stopped transmitting. (Background: Radford had seemed upset over relationship issues regarding a meeting time.) Various tactics for the air search continued for three weeks but found nothing. Not included in air crash statistics. Instead included in suicides stats. Incident report #11-????*

Robert T. Watson, 24

March 21, 2011   Below Shrine of the Ages/Park Headquarters
*Watson of White Plains, New York had an alcohol problem and was reported as missing on March 21. Watson had a history of depression and had written he was considering **jumping** off the rim. Watson's vehicle was reported abandoned in the Shrine of the Ages parking lot on April 6, which launched a search for him. His body was discovered via condor activity on March 25, 700 feet*

below the rim in a steep, narrow gully. It took until May 6 for 25
NPS personnel to safely extricate the corpse. Arizona Daily Sun,
May 21, 2011. Incident report #11-1445

James Owen Burt, 40   April 23, 2011   Navajo Bridge/Colorado River
Burt of Benson, Arizona was a cook at Marble Canyon Lodge
restaurant but was fired from his job that morning, possibly
alcohol-related. He walked to the bridge and **jumped** *off 470 feet*
to the river, witnessed by multiple people, San Pedro Valley News-
Sun, *May 12, 2011. Incident report #11-1747*

Ryan Thomas Cunningham, 28 August 5, 2011   Lookout Studio, South Rim Village
Cunningham of Gridley, California **jumped** *200 feet below the*
rim, witnessed. Grand Canyon National Park Information Center,
August 17, 2011.

James Olen Waibel, 52   October 25, 2011   Navajo Bridge
On November 17, Peregrine Fund volunteers noted exceptional
condor activity and 7 feeding ravens on a corpse 20 feet from the
river. Waibel of Glendale, Arizona had left a 'positive' 'goodbye'
suicide note to his parents then **jumped** *off the pedestrian Navajo*
Bridge, likely at night, unwitnessed, impacting talus. Incident
report #11-5136

Peter Reichner, 41   January 12, 2012   Near S Kaibab Trail, 1/3 mile from trailhead
The body of Reichner of Glenside, Pennsylvania was found next
to the Kaibab Trail below an unwitnessed fall. Reichner is not yet
designated a suicide versus an accidental fall, therefore he is not
considered a specific statistic yet due to his uncertain demise. Grand
Canyon News Release, *January 19, 2012.*

Shaw Joseph Ostermann, 47   April 16, 2012   Mather Point
Ostermann of Tempe, Arizona **jumped** *off the rim about 500 feet.*
Condors alerted Peregrine Fund volunteers. Grand Canyon News
Release, *April 27, 2012.*

Elizabeth Miller, 67   April 26, 2012   Trailview Overlook
Miller of Phoenix, Arizona **jumped** *off the rim 100 feet.* Grand
Canyon News Release, *May 2, 2012.*

Rommy Hugh Radford, Jr, 36   March 4, 2013   Twin Overlooks, Desert View Drive
At roughly 3:00 p.m., after leaving multiple suicide notes blaming
his ex-girlfriend, Radford of Virginia drove his 1999 white Honda
Civic off the rim in his 4th lifetime suicide attempt. Ejected from
the Honda early, he landed 400-450 feet down. His car tumbled to
550 feet. Using binoculars, Ranger Brian Bloom spotted Radford
in the snow. His arms were moving. Bloom rappelled to Radford's
exposed, dangerous position, heard him muttering, and assessed
his vitals. Minutes later, at 9:06 p.m., Radford died roughly 6 hours
after impact, as evacuation preparations were nearly complete. He
was the 14th known drive-off suicide victim using the 13th known
vehicle. Incident Report # 13-0890

Jody Kay McDaniel, 45   April 28, 2014   Mather Point amphitheater
*After her father(?) died in late 2012, McDaniel of Flagstaff, Arizona
became depressed, was placed on antidepressants, attempted suicide
via overdosing antidepressants (March 2014), then was taken off
them. She also was in financial difficulties. She drove to rim and
worked her way out, witnessed, scooting 15 yards down over 3-4
ledges to the farthest point. She sat on the final edge then fell (=*
jumped*) off 400+ feet. Incident report #14-031492*

Marc Buckhout, 42 or 36(?)   August 2, 2014   South Rim W of Grandview Point
*Buckhout of Glendale, Arizona hiked away from his family at about
4:30 p.m. and was not seen again until August 8 when his body was
discovered several hundred feet below an unwitnessed* **jump***. Buckhout considered Grand Canyon his "favorite place on earth" and
had become the 29th person to hike the Arizona Trail from Mexico
to Utah.* Grand Canyon News Release, *August 8, 2014. Incident
report #14088424*

If you are contemplating suicide, please do not come to Grand Canyon to commit it—thus
risking lives of rescue personnel and mental states of visitors. Instead, seek help, call 911 or the
suicide hotline at 800-273-8255.

Chapter Ten

Murder

The act of murder seems to plague every tribe from the Eskimos of the far north to the now-vanished Indians of Tierra del Fuego in the far south. Although rates of homicide vary greatly between nations, no nation exists without murders being committed within its borders. Sad to say, Grand Canyon proves no exception to this universal affliction. To avoid any confusion, in this chapter we want to point out that, unlike most of our reporting which thus far has been strictly limited to deaths below the rims, in this chapter on murders we also consider deaths on the rims.

The first known suspected murder happened in the Canyon nearly 1,000 years ago. Nicknamed "Tanner Man," for his discovery adjacent to the Tanner Trail 1.25 miles and more than 1,000 feet below the trailhead, he consists of the partial skeleton of a robust male Ancestral Puebloan about 5 feet, 4 inches tall. These remains were found under the shade of a Supai boulder exposed by natural erosion and overlaid with recent trash from hikers.

During the investigation in February, 1997 an inch-long, stone arrowhead was found by Yavapai County Sheriff's Dept. Captain (now Sheriff) Scott Mascher situated within the area of Tanner Man's chest cavity. Anthropologist Helen Fairly identified this projectile point as a "Parowan Basal Notched" style of 1000-1200 A.D. Note that in lacking side notches to firmly secure the arrowhead to its foreshaft, this type of projectile point is considered by many experts as an antipersonnel type of point rather than one designed for hunting game. Game hunting points are more often side-notched to secure the head firmly to the arrow's foreshaft. Elk, deer, bighorn sheep, and pronghorn lack opposable thumbs and cannot easily yank out a foreshaft piercing their bodies. In contrast, of course, humans can. Hence the design of an arrowhead for war which is only lightly secured to its foreshaft by basal notches for weak hafting so that when an enemy yanks the foreshaft from his body, the arrowhead remains embedded within him.

Nearby Tanner Man lay a perfectly circular, yellow travertine finger ring. His burial site was located a bit off the Tanner Trail above an even older Basketmaker III/Pueblo I midden of pot shards, a mano, etc. all near the 75-Mile Canyon saddle. After a forensic investigation by Anthropologist Laura C. Fulginiti of the Maricopa County Office of the Medical Examiner, she noted that Tanner Man was indeed a man, and maybe 40 years old. The Park decided Tanner Man was a likely prehistoric burial site rather than a forensic scene. But was it a post-homicide burial?

The next homicide we know about happened many centuries later. Of course the lack of a written history and the paucity and inaccessibility of an oral history of Indians in the region make an accounting of such events a very chancy enterprise. Even so, it is all we have to work with for the early era. During the 1920s Anthropologist Leslie Spier spent months among the Havasupai. Tribal elders told Spier about a running battle between 1860-1863 fought between them and an invading party of Yavapai raiders along the "Apache Trail" area east of and below Great Thumb Mesa. This Yavapai war party intent on raiding the Havasupai ran into greater defensive resistance than expected. Havasupai warriors, "Captain Burro" and "Captain Navajo," shot two of the Yavapai warriors then scalped and decapitated them. These scalps were retained for future scalp dances.

Only a year or two later, between 1863 and 1864, a dictatorial U.S. Brigadier General James H. Carlton masterminded and commanded a politically-motivated and apparently illegal scorched-earth war against the Navajo tribe. This led to the fruition of his obsessive and il-conceived scheme to relocate all of the 5,000 Navajos he estimated to be alive (those not already being held in slavery) via the "Long Walk" to a "reservation" at Fort Sumner (a.k.a. Bosque Redondo) on the Pecos River in east-central New Mexico. Each of the more than 400-mile Long Walks by captured or surrendered Navajos from Arizona to Fort Sumner in early 1864 resembled the Japanese-mastered Bataan Death March of American and Philippine troops during 1942. Each Navajo Long Walk was brutal. Along the way, unscrupulous New Mexicans stole Navajo livestock and captured straggling Navajos as slaves. Yet these Indians may have been some of the lucky ones, as historian Ruth Roessel (in the 1983 Smithsonian *Handbook of North American Indians, Vol. 10, Southwest* and in her 1973 *Navajo Stories of the Long Walk Period*) explains:

> *There were a few wagons to haul some personal belongings, but the trip was made on foot. People were shot down on the spot if they complained about being tired or sick, or if they stopped to help someone. If a woman became in labor with a baby, she was killed. There was absolutely no mercy.*

Even thoughabout 500 Navajos on the Long Walks died en route, by 1865 their numbers at Fort Sumner had swelled to 9,022. Ultimately 3,000 of these starved or died of disease. So, during the next three years (during which General Carlton was relieved of duty) before the Navajos were allowed to return to Dinetah (Navajoland), many Navajos fled into the most recondite alcoves of the canyonlands of the Colorado Plateau, to the foot of Navajo Mountain, or even into Apache territory—as many Navajos had done even earlier to escape persistent slave raiders operating out of New Mexico. A best estimate is 2,000–4,000 Navajos had also escaped capture and/or surrender to the Long Walks themselves during the 1863–1864 war. A few of these early refugees from Navajoland and later ones from Fort Sumner were desperate enough to flee into Tsechiikolh ("Red Cliff Canyon," a.k.a. Grand Canyon).

One young family—a man, his pregnant wife, and their young child—seeking this vast sanctuary had almost reached its safety. They were nearing the area of the South Rim from which, twenty years hence, Captain John T. Hance would build a trail down to River Mile 77 to facilitate his mining of asbestos. Now, in the 1860s, however, no trail had been built. Even so, the route Hance's trail would follow had already seen the passing of countless hundreds of Native Americans, from at least as far back as the Ancestral Puebloans a thousand years ago. It was still a good path.

This young Navajo family fleeing the U.S. Cavalry knew that the Inner Canyon would offer them refuge, at least for a few months. There would be bighorn sheep to hunt and several wild foods—honey mesquite, agave, prickly pear, and many other plants—to gather. It would not be an easy life. But it would at least be one distant from enemies and capture and possible death. Besides, everyone knew that no *bilagaana* (white man) could find his way into the huge, forbidding fastness of "Red Cliff Canyon." Yes, down there life would at least be safe.

But to enter this refuge without being tracked, the young Navajo man knew that he had to be thorough now. So he lagged behind his wife and child as they rode their horse ahead. As noted by James Peshlakai (in a personal communication to Ghiglieri), the young Navajo father brushed away their footprints and removed other signs of their passing. Later, he caught up with them at a part of the South Rim that whites would someday name Grandview. To his surprise and alarm, he found his wife, instead of riding their horse, sitting on the ground in tears and hugging their child to her pregnant belly, swollen almost to term.

Alert now, he scanned for the cause of his wife's despair. Ahead, in a place just north of the future site of Hull's cabin, he saw some strange Navajos squatting over his wife's murdered horse and butchering it for meat. Nearby stood a few more Navajos of a type the young man knew instantly to be bad men.

Without hesitation, the young husband raised his rifle, took careful aim, and fired at the man sitting atop a rock ledge and sharpening his knife. The other rogues spun in shock as their comrade crumpled to the ground mortally wounded. With barely a glimpse of the angry young husband, the brigands scattered and fled into the forest of pinyon pines and junipers.

The slain man, it turned out, was, among Navajos at least, public enemy number one by the name of *Aah'yi'd digish*. He was a murderous renegade Navajo robber who led a small gang of robbers and killers who preyed on members of their own people. He was infamous among the tribe as a very bad man. When eventually other Navajos—many of whom were also fleeing from Carlton's relentless U.S. Cavalry—learned of the death of this notorious robber and killer, they rejoiced. Now at least the tiny hidden enclaves of wilderness sanctuary remaining to them might be safe.

Having just killed public enemy number one and also having earned the gratitude of thousands of his people, however, did not free the young husband from a harsh reality: the disagreeable task of now butchering his family's slain horse. In such desperate times as these, nothing could be left to waste.

He also examined *Aah'yi'd digish's* body. He removed the dead man's medicine bundle. Later, as he and his family continued their hegira down into Red Cliff Canyon via the route that would ultimately become the Hance Trail, he stopped at a cave and hid his slain enemy's medicine bundle.

At this point we move into recorded history, but not necessarily *known* history. In the entire history of the exploration of western North America, very few expeditions emerge as such romantic and audacious high adventure as John Wesley Powell's 1,000-mile descent of the Green and Colorado rivers from Green River, Wyoming to and beyond the Grand Wash Cliffs at the foot of Grand Canyon. To borrow an apt cliché, this expedition was fraught with peril. So much peril that the crew disintegrated only two days from a successful completion. The biggest mystery concerning Powell's 1869 expedition—and concerning Grand Canyon history in general—is: What happened to crew members William H. Dunn, Oramel G. Howland and Seneca B. Howland once they hiked away from the river at Separation Canyon?

In reality, this infamous tragedy embodies two mysteries. Why did the Howland brothers and Dunn split from the expedition at all? And what happened to them after they did?

How important is it to solve this dual mystery? Well, even in the unlikely event that "Captain" John Moss did raft through Grand Canyon in three and a half days in 1861, and even if James White also drifted through on a succession of three rafts during about ten days in 1867, and even if the young Hopi warrior Tiyo had drifted through the Canyon in a hollow log a thousand years earlier yet (as Hopi legend tells it), Powell and his crew of eight were the first people of European descent to *explore* the Canyon, however briefly during their 26-day Canyon race against starvation.

For clues to unravel this tragic mystery we must look first to Powell's ability in 1869 to lead men when the chips were down. John Wesley Powell, the evidence shows, possessed many skills. But one he apparently lacked was the leadership ability of a Captain Meriwether Lewis or a Captain William Clark. These two commanded and orchestrated the most famous exploration of unknown wilderness on North America. They struggled up the Missouri River over horrendous portages then ran whitewater on the Pacific side to the coast. Then they managed the return trek to Missouri—all without losing a single man to accident or to violence during their two-year epic expedition. In contrast, in just a few months, the self-absorbed and one-armed (he lost his right arm in the Battle of Shiloh to a Confederate minié ball) J. W. Powell lost six men of his potential eleven to desertion and three of these to murder.

Again the mysteries lie in why and how.

The first clue lies in the events which occurred only sixteen days downstream from Green River, in the Canyon of Lodore. Here crewmembers Oramel G. and Seneca Howland and Frank Valentine Goodman missed their pull to shore alongside Powell's *Emma Dean*. Instead they rode their 21-foot *No Name* swamped and out of control into Disaster Falls. As described in several of the crewmen's journals on June 8, 1869, the *No Name* smashed into midstream boulders and disintegrated in successive collisions. The men aboard her barely escaped to a midstream island. Almost immediately this island began shrinking due to a rising river.

After a daring rescue by John Sumner, who rowed the *Emma Dean* across the Green to this island to scoop up the three castaways, the expedition reunited. The Howland brothers and Goodman emerged alive. Otherwise everything aboard the *No Name* except the barometers, thermometers, and a keg of whiskey was lost. Vanished to the bottom of the Green was one-third of the expedition's ten-month supply of food and equipment. With this went the three men's rifles, revolvers, clothes, bedrolls, and other personal gear.

Understandably, Major Powell felt upset about this huge loss. Goodman, now destitute, quit the trip afterward at his first opportunity, two weeks later at the Uinta River. But the esprit of this expedition suffered far worse. Jack Sumner would later write, "From this wreck commenced the many quarrels between Major Powell and O. G. Howland and Bill Dunn which caused so much trouble and finally terminated in their leaving the party and the murder of the Howland brothers and Bill Dunn. As soon as O. G. Howland got out of the boat [the *Emma Dean*] after the rescue, Major Powell angrily demanded of him to know why he did not land [but instead had run downstream of the *Emma Dean*]."

Two months later, on August 5, seven hundred miles out of Green River, Wyoming, Powell and his eight remaining stalwarts rowed their three surviving beat-up boats past the future site of Lee's Ferry to enter Grand Canyon. Having not spotted the Paria River, no one realized they had entered Grand Canyon. Thus emerged Powell's mistaken naming of this section of the Canyon "Marble Canyon." Powell loved this name so much that he had pinned this name on a canyon upriver. At Mile 29 below the Paria he decided to move this name to the unnamed canyon he was now floating. Only it was not unnamed. It was already called Grand Canyon on a railroad survey map drawn in 1868. Having not seen the Paria, Powell and his crew were lost.

Five days of rowing beyond the Paria carried Powell's crew to the Little Colorado (River Mile 61.5) and to the certain knowledge that they were in Grand Canyon. They also knew all too well they were starving on partial rations of bisquits, dried and moldy apples, a few beans, and plenty of black coffee. Deer and bighorn sheep seemed to have long since vanished from the river corridor. Hunting now proved fruitless. Even the fish had refused to bite for George Young Bradley, a consummate fisherman. Worse, the monsoons had begun. The men were now reduced to one blanket per two men and two or three wagon-tarps as shelter for all nine of them.

The explorers camped for three days at the Little Colorado River while Major Powell and his brother, Captain Walter Powell, geologized and tried to determine latitude and longitude. The Little Colorado, Bradley wrote, was "a lothesome [sic] little stream, so filthy and muddy that it fairly stinks." It frothed with sediment from the Painted Desert. Sumner called it "as disgusting a stream as there is on the continent....Half its volume and 2/3 of its weight is mud and silt."

As Bradley wrote on August 14, discontentment seethed here:

> *The men are uneasy and discontented and anxious to move on. If Major does not do something soon I fear the consequences, but he is contented and seems to think that biscuit made of sour & musty flour and a few dried apples is ample to sustain a laboring man.*

The expedition shoved off downstream. Sumner would later describe to explorer and historian Robert Brewster Stanton the grim side of this journey's final leg:

> *And if any men ever did penance for their sins we did a plenty for the next two hundred miles. To add to our troubles, there was a nearly continuous rain, and a great rise in the river, that created such a current and turmoil that it tried our strength to the limit. Starvation stared us in the face, weakened by hardships and ceaseless toil twenty out of twenty-four hours of the day. I felt like Job....A ceaseless grind of running or letting down rapids with lines, varied in places by making portages of boats and contents. The contents were a small item, but the boats were water-logged, and very heavy, and taxed our strength to the limit....* [and while heading downstream in general] *there was not much talk indulged in by the grim, clenched teeth squad of half starved men, with faces wearing the peculiar, stern look always noticed on the faces of men when forming for a charge in battle.*

In Powell's very brief journal he wrote little to nothing about this part of the journey. The little that he did write about at length later focused on geology, specifically the lava bracketing the Toroweap region around Lava Falls. Only much later yet, back in Washington, D.C., would Powell compose via dictation the semifictitious account which would be published as his "journal" of running the river. Meanwhile the only other surviving journals of the crew's Grand Canyon experience—the official one of Sumner and the secret journal, mostly optimistic, that Bradley wrote—do express undisguised disgust and impatience at their predicament with Powell in the Canyon. Interviews by letter of Sumner and of William Robert Wesley Hawkins conducted later by Robert Brewster Stanton (collected in his 1909, never published magnum opus*) and by William Wallace Bass* revealed a disintegrating expedition flirting with full mutiny.

What went wrong in Grand Canyon?

We owe most of what we know of this tangled tale to a series of sleuths including Stanton and Bass all possessing Canyon experience in their own right, having searched for clues for well over a century. It seems the conflict of wills and attitudes that had begun at Disaster Falls between Powell and Oramel G. Howland continued to fester. Powell had held Howland most responsible for the wreck of the *No Name*. Powell possibly may have been finding fault with Howland's map-making as well. Howland, in turn, found fault in Powell's decision-making regarding food resupplies at the Uinta Reservation in repeated, tit-for-tat spats. Sumner explains:

> *Major Powell was gone five days, and brought back a shirt tail full of supplies. I thought at the time it was a damned stingy or foolish scheme, as there was plenty of supplies to be had, to bring back such a meager mess for nine to make a thousand mile voyage through an unknown and dangerous cañon, but as I wasn't boss I suppose I ought to keep still about it.*

A bad relationship allegedly also began between Major Powell and William Dunn, the long-haired mountain man who, with Sumner, rowed Powell's *Emma Dean*.

Decades later, Hawkins' explained to Stanton his motive for writing: "I do not wish to cast any discredit on Major Powell's report or upon his memory of the Colorado expedition; but—in honor to Dunn and the Howland brothers—the account in the report, which accuses them of cowardice, I shall say that it is entirely wrong, and was perhaps made to cover up the real cause of their leaving. The state of Ohio never turned out a man that had more nerve than William Dunn."

Dunn, apparently the best (or most willing) swimmer of the crew, took the

---

* "The River and the Cañon: The Colorado River of the West, and the Exploration, Navigation, and Survey of its Cañons, from the Standpoint of an Engineer" and Bass' 1920 "Adventures in the Canyons of the Colorado By Two of its Earliest Explorers, James White and W. W. Hawkins with Introduction and Notes."

more risky posts perched on boulders in the river as the crew lined the boats along the edges of roughly 100 rapids. During one of these episodes, apparently in Grand Canyon, notes Hawkins, "the ropes happened to catch Bill Dunn under the arms and came near drowning him, but he managed to catch the ropes and come out." Still in Dunn's pocket from some previous chore was one of Powell's watches—among the last that worked. It appeared ruined.

At dinner Sumner remarked that Dunn (only Powell possesed a life jacket) had come close to drowning. Then (Sumner and Hawkins agree on this) Walter Powell "made the remark that it would have been but little loss." Major Powell was so angry at Dunn that he ordered him to pay $30 for the ruined watch then and there or else leave the trip and hike out of the Canyon. Depending on where this episode occurred, Dunn's easiest exit (to the south) could have demanded that he climb 4,600 feet up cliffs to the middle of a waterless nowhere. This "escape" would have been to the uninhabited and unexplored and nearly waterless Coconino Plateau, many miles even from Indian villages, much farther yet to a white settlement. How bleak one's odds of survival would be *if* one managed to gain the Coconino were described by Lieutenant Joseph Christmas Ives, who explored it and published his findings in his 1861 report.* Ives had struck across overland to the "Big Canyon" with a train of more than 100 mules plus soldiers and his invaluable Mojave guide, Ireteba. After visiting Western Grand Canyon at Diamond Creek (River Mile 226) and next flirting with exploring Supai as well, Ives had forged farther east to make sense of the confusing and arid terrain of the Coconino Plateau. After losing several mules due to dehydration, he finally turned south and concluded:

> *The positions of the main water-courses have been determined with considerable accuracy. The region last explored is, of course, altogether valueless. It can be approached only from the south, and after entering it there is nothing to do but to leave. Ours has been the first, and will doubtless be the last, party of whites to visit this profitless locality. It seems intended by nature that the Colorado River, along the greater portion of its lonely and majestic way, shall be forever unvisited and undisturbed. The handful of Indians [Hualapai and Havasupai] that inhabit the sequestered retreats where we discovered them have probably remained in the same condition, and of the same number, for centuries. The country could not support a large population, and by some provision of nature they have ceased to multiply. The deer, the antelope, the birds, even the smaller reptiles, all of which frequent the adjacent territory, have deserted this uninhabitable district....We start for the south with some anxiety, not knowing how long it may be before water will be met with again.*

*Report upon the Colorado River of the West, Explored in 1857 and 1858 by Lieutenant Joseph C. Ives. Corps of Engineers, Under the Direction of the Office of Explorations and Surveys, A. A. Humphreys, Captain Topographical Engineers, in Charge, by Order of the Secretary of War.

Not only was this the terrain that William H. Dunn would have had to face had he succeeded in hiking out of the Canyon, it was also the terrain that Major Powell *knew* Dunn would face. Powell, of course, had read Ives' 1861 *Report*—virtually the only modern exploration ever done in the region up to the time of Powell's own trip. Powell, however, intended to go Ives one better in the annals of exploration, and as time would prove, turn a profit on Ives' profitless locality.

Dunn responded to Powell's weird tantrum with, "A bird could not get out of that place."

Although the men thought Powell was joking, he soon convinced them he was serious.

As Hawkins tells it, Dunn told the Major, "He could not leave then, but that he would go as soon as he could get out."

Hawkins soon informed Powell that if Dunn were to leave, they would take a boat, and he, Hall, and Bradley would accompany Dunn downriver. This allegedly sobered Powell, who relented slightly. For as long as Dunn was to delay his departure from the trip, Powell allegedly demanded, he must pay a boarding fee of $30 (or $50) per month (Hawkins' and Sumner's letters disagreed over Powell's stipulated fee). Later Powell decided Dunn could pay the $30 for the ruined watch after the trip.

Sumner interceded and told Powell he could neither order Dunn off the trip nor compel him to pay for rations. Relationships apparently spiraled downward. For example, not much farther downstream, Hawkins noted in a far more serious allegation (made in 1919, to William Wallace Bass), that while lining a rapid Powell "saw his chance to drown Dunn."

—as Dunn was a fine swimmer, the Major asked him to swim out to a rock so the boat could swing in below. He made the rock all O.K. and was ready to catch the rope which was supposed to be thrown to him, so he could swing in the boat below, but the Major saw his chance to drown Dunn, as he thought, and he held the rope. That was the first time he had interfered in the letting of the boats around bad places, and the rope caught Dunn around the legs and pulled him into the current and came near losing the boat.

But Dunn held on to the rope and finally stopped in water up to his hips. We were all in the water but the Major and the Captain. Dunn told the Major that if he had not been a good swimmer he and the boat both would have been lost. The Major said as to Dunn that there would have been but little loss. One word brought on another, and the Major called Dunn a bad name and Dunn said that if the Major was not a cripple he would not be called such names.

Then Captain [Walter] Powell said he was not crippled, and started for Dunn with an oath, and the remark he would finish Dunn. He had to pass right by me and I knew he would soon drown Dunn, as he, so much larger could eas-

ily do. He was swearing and his eyes looked like fire. Just as he passed I caught him by the hair of his head and pulled him over back into the water. Howland saw us scuffling and he was afraid Cap would get hold of my legs. But Dunn got to me first and said, "For God's sake, Bill, you will drown him!" By that time Howland was there and Cap had been in the water long enough and Dunn and Howland dragged him out onto the sand bar in the rocks. After I got my hold in Cap's hair I was afraid to let go, for he was a very strong man. He was up in a short time, and mad! I guess he was mad! He cursed me to everything, even to being a "Missouri puke." I wasn't afraid of him when I got on dry ground. I could out-knock him after he was picked up twice.

He made for his gun and swore he would kill me and Dunn. But this talk did not excite me. As he was taking his gun from the deck of the boat, Andy Hall gave him a punch behind the ear and told him to put it back or off would go his head. Cap looked around and saw who had the gun, and he sure dropped his. This all happened before the Major got around to where we were. He soon took in the situation and came to me and made the remark that he would have never thought I would go back on him. I told him that he had gone back on himself, and that he had better help Cap get the sand out of his eyes, and that if he mon-keyed with me any more, I would keep him down next time...

Of this argument between Dunn and the Major, Sumner admitted, "I think the Major's one arm only saved him from a broken head, if nothing worse."

As Hawkins continues to tell it:

...Sumner and I had all we could do to keep down mutiny. There was bad feel-ing from that time on for a few days. We began not to recognize any authority from the Major. We began to run races with the boats, as the loads were almost gone. It was fun for the first two days but then the water began to get rough. Hall, Howland, and myself were in my boat. I had become an expert in bad rapids. We ran several that the other two boats were let over with ropes.

Sumner adds: "Major Powell did not run the outfit in the same overbearing manner after that. At a portage or a bad let-down he took his geological hammer and kept out of the way."

Many historians and biographers over the years—William Culp Darrah, Wal-lace Stegner, and David Lavender, to offer a few examples—who have wanted to present a squeaky clean and unblemished image of Major Powell as "Saint Powell of the Colorado" have either ignored Sumner's and Hawkins' testimonies disparag-ing Major Powell's leadership and also ignored all other evidence of Powell's nar-cissistic personality disorder (including accusations that the Powell brothers had attempted murder) or else they have discounted Sumner's and Hawkins' words as lies. Stegner, for example, agreed that Powell had done bad things in real life. But Stegner insisted to his editor that Powell was not going to "do" anything bad in Stegner's biography of Powell, *Beyond the Hundredth Meridian*. William Culp Darrah, in his *Powell of the Colorado* (page 141), utterly discounts what Hawkins and Sumner said after 1869. Darrah in essence accuses both men of lying due to bitterness toward Powell. Lavender, on page 16 of his *River Runners of the Grand Canyon*, explains away Sumner's and Hawkins' lengthy testimonies with a facile rhetorical question and an even more facile assertion of mental incompetency:

> *If they* [the events that Hawkins and Sumner wrote about] *did not occur, why did the two men invent them? Spleen perhaps. Though Powell gave the men the expedition's boats and what money he had at the end of the trip neither Hawkins nor Sumner felt he had received his due. The neglect festered, to find relief in wild tales to Stanton when the men were old and their memories fading.*

Previous "historians" who had fallen in love with Powell have used this "spleen" excuse to arrogantly label Sumner and Hawkins—men both loyal to Powell and courageous beyond these historians' abilities to comprehend—as liars. Yet Hawkins' and Sumner's multiple disclosures of Powell's decisions leading up to the Separation incident have been proved consistent. Did some genuine bone of contention exist for Sumner or Hawkins to support this facile excuse of "spleen" and "wild tales?"

The hand-written copy of Powell's original contract (the "AGREEMENT") for this trip hired only three of the nine men present for $75 each for the duration of the expedition. The men were also to be allowed time on their own to trap and prospect. All three of these hired men were to run the boats and work in all general capacities on the expedition from June 1, 1869, until, if needed, May 31, 1870. Dunn was also supposed to take twice-daily barometric readings and determine elevations of cliffs, et cetera. Sumner was to take readings with the sextant. Oramel G. Howland was contracted as the expedition cartographer to draw maps of the river canyons as the crew traversed them.

Apparently no other known record or contract written in 1868 or 1869 survives regarding what anyone else on the 1869 trip was to expect as payment. Hawkins, however, was the expedition's cook. He prepared every meal. He even washed Major Powell's one hand for him prior to meals and then served him his meals. No Powell scholar believes Hawkins did this gratis. Indeed, Hawkins wrote the following in 1907 to explain the arrangements Major Powell had made with him back in 1868 at Hot Sulphur Spring:

> *I told the Major that Sumner was thinking of selling his trading post, and in company with Dunn and myself, we were going to try the cañons as far as Cot-*

tonwood Island. That I had already packed my year's supplies in from Denver, to which the Major replied, "Those things are just what I want, also your mules and horses, I will buy them and pay you just what you can sell them for elsewhere." I told him I would think the matter over and let him know in the evening. In the meantime, he and Sumner arranged a trade for Sumner's supplies at his post. Later I went to the Major's camp and told him if we could arrange things and agree on a price for my animals, I would join his party. I showed him my bills and everything I had in stock, and he allowed me the price of the goods, and for packing them over the range, and he allowed me a fair price for three of my animals, but, for the other one, we could not agree upon a price, so I kept it, as it was a favorite of mine and had safely carried me through several Indian fights. After all was counted up, outside of 36 steel traps, it amounted to $960.00. The traps, he said, could be used that winter and, when we got to Cottonwood Island, we would replace them. He also offered me $1.50 per day for cooking for the outfit, and, when we got through our journey down the Colorado Cañon, he would pay our transportation back to where we were then, at Sumner's place. The Major added, "Now, as to the money you are to receive for your goods and horses, I expect to get it from the Government, and also to pay your transportation back," saying that he had money with him and that he would let me have what I needed during the trip, and that he would be responsible to me for the remainder, and he gave me a receipt for the amount due me at that time.

Sumner told me that he was to receive good prices for his supplies and stores, and good pay for his work, and that he would have several thousand dollars coming to him when he got through, and that he was to receive it all when he got to the end of the river journey. Later in the fall, Major Powell told me that if he could get the Government to appropriate $12,000., there would be $1,000 for each of us and $2,000 for himself for the trip.

When we got to the mouth of the Virgin River, the Major and his brother left us. I cannot tell how much money he paid to each one, but he gave each man some. He gave me $60, and Hall $60., and said that he would send us a government voucher for the rest, and also for what he was to pay me for the provisions and animals I sold him. As we had not come to Cottonwood Island, I asked him how about my traps, that he was to make good—there were 36 of them, and I had paid $3.00 apiece for them. "Well," says the Major, "they got lost on Green River." "Yes," I said, "but you agreed to make them good when we got to Cottonwood Island." Then he said he would allow me $2.50 for each trap, and would find out what the transportation was and send me a voucher for the whole amount—the voucher is still coming." [emphasis ours; the irony here is this was written four years after Powell had died.]

Hawkins did work for Powell again during the 1870s—though never again on a river. And Powell reassured Hawkins that he was still expecting government appropriations (which Powell did receive every year after 1870) and that he then would pay Hawkins. But Powell never did pay him.

Sumner's account mirrors Hawkins'. Sumner says he too was out more than $1,000 on equipment and supplies lost or used on the 1869 expedition for which Powell said he would reimburse Sumner after the expedition and after Congress issued him the money. At the Rio Virgin, Powell paid Sumner his $75 as originally contracted. But, as with Hawkins, Sumner mentions that Powell never reimbursed him that $1,000. Indeed Powell asked Sumner to accompany Powell on his second Colorado Expedition. Sumner, however, sent Powell word that he could not make it. Both Sumner and Hawkins likely felt to their dying days that Powell had welshed on his debts to them despite their loyalty to him and despite Powell having access to government funds. So maybe "spleen" is one way of expressing Hawkins' and Sumner's disappointment in Major Powell's capacity for keeping his alleged promises. Even so, none of this means that either Sumner or Hawkins would therefore fabricate lies about what happened during the 1869 expedition. Indeed, the only member of the expedition whom we *know* did fabricate lies about it was Major Powell himself, and he did so copiously in print.

Critics of Sumner's and Hawkins' accounts such as Darrah and Lavender point out further that Sumner's journal mentioned neither an attempted expulsion of Dunn, nor fights. But Sumner was writing his journal at Powell's behest to supplement Powell's own very weak one. Under such conditions Sumner could not have been expected to spell out in it any mistreatment by Powell of his crew—any more than Powell himself would have penned such admissions.

Sergeant George Y. Bradley's secret journal, however, also reveals no specifics about Powell versus Dunn. At first glance this lack seems to carry more weight. Bradley does say Powell was oblivious to the feelings of his crew toward him, and that these feelings were often unfavorable. He also mentions, on August 25, a boating accident that might have gotten worse had certain things happened differently. On a slightly different tack, despite Bradley's alleged (by some authors) "complaining" in his journal, Bradley obviously did not write about what most troubled him. For example, in his 22,000-word journal he only mentioned once, in passing, that the *No-Name* was smashed to splinters. Yet all historians consider this an extremely significant event during the expedition.

To better see this quirk of Bradley's, note how in all of his 22,000 words, he also *never* wrote the name "Walter" or otherwise said much of anything about Walter Powell, the demented man with whom Bradley spent three months rowing the *Maid of the Cañon*. Wanting to retain his sanity, Bradley never confided even to his secret journal the experience of traveling with Walter. Nor, we suspect, did he want to record any tantrums and abuses by Walter Powell's older brother, John Wesley.

Hawkins' and Sumner's interviews late in life were conducted independently hundreds of miles apart, months apart, years apart, and by different interviewers. Sumner's and Hawkins' accounts, despite being independent, agreed on Powell's mistreatment of Dunn, et cetera. In short, if these two separated men—both brave, capable, and loyal to Powell during the 1869 expedition—were lying to vent their spleen, they would have been doing so with a phenomenal coincidence of specific detail. They also would have been doing so very out of character. Historian Martin J. Anderson reminds us (in his "commentary" in Stanton's posthumous *Colorado River Controversies, 2nd edition*), "It is important to note there was no collusion between Sumner and Hawkins. They wrote their versions at different times from different places."

The upshot? By the time Powell's first trip entered his Great Unknown, it had begun to disintegrate. Somewhere in mid-Grand Canyon Hawkins and Hall began running *Kitty Clyde's Sister* independently of Powell's decisions. Until River Mile 239.5. At this point even Hawkins knew he should wait for Powell to catch up in the *Emma Dean.*

The rapid here looked appalling on August 27, 1869 (today it is silted in by Lake Mead). As Sumner remembers, the river narrowed to fifty yards wide. Here twin side canyons, mouth to mouth along a transverse fault, had doubly choked the Colorado and partially dammed it with flash-flood-generated debris flows. Cliffs on both sides appeared to preclude a portage. Lining the Z-shaped rapid also looked impossible due to a lack of footing. River Mile 239.5 is now called Separation Rapid because, after many hours of scouting it, Oramel Howland and William Dunn decided to exit the expedition by hiking up the north side canyon to seek the Mormon settlements many miles farther north. As Hawkins remembers it:

> When we came to the rapid where the Howland boys and Dunn left the party, we all looked at it, and Hall and I had our course picked out on that rapid for the morning. The Major and some of the other boys went across the river to look to see if there was any chance to let the boats over it by ropes...[the next morning] Bradley came up to the fire and I asked him if it was not coming to a show down. He said he could not understand the Major, but there was something going to happen. I did not know, or care, what happened, as I was sure Andy and Bradley would stand by me in anything that was reasonable....
>
> [After dividing the flour balls Hawkins had cooked] The Major, the Howland brothers, Dunn and Sumner went off to one side to hold another council. Bradley came over to where Andy Hall and I were standing and completely broke down and shed tears, and said such actions made him feel like a child again. By that time the Major came up to where we were standing and said, "Well, Billy, we have concluded to abandon the river for the present." Stating that on account of the scarcity of provisions, and as the rapids were getting more

severe, he thought the better thing to do was to abandon the river, as it could not be more than one hundred miles to some settlement in Utah, and that we could get a new supply of grub and return and complete our journey.

By that time all the boys were standing and listening to him. When he finished his say, I asked him if he would sell the boat to Andy and me, and he said if we would come back and finish the trip he would give us the boat. I told him I proposed to finish my part of it then, I said, "Major, you have always looked on Hall and me as being too young to have anything to say in your council, but Hall and I are going to go down this river whether you or any of the rest go or not," and I told him that if he left the river I would not think of following him one foot on land, that my mind was set. Then the Major said, "Well, Billy, if I have one man that will stay with me, I will continue my journey or be drowned in the attempt." I told him that Bradley, Hall and I had made up our minds to continue....

Sumner spoke up and said, "Stay with it, Billy, and I will be with you," and it did not take long to settle the rest of it. The Howland brothers and Dunn had made up their minds and would not change them. Of course we knew what was the reason Dunn left: as for fear, he did not possess it. As for the other two boys, they never showed any signs of fear. The older of the Howlands was in the boat with me since his boat [the No Name] *was wrecked.*

We all crossed over to the north side, hid our supplies and instruments [Sumner identified these as two barometers and some beaver traps]*, and left one boat for the boys. It is my opinion that if the Howland boys had not agreed to leave the river in the council I referred to, that they would have come with us, but they were sore the way Dunn had been treated....*

Sumner recalls this incident from a different perspective that first afternoon.

I talked with Major Powell quietly on the subject. He seemed dazed by the proposition confronting us. I then declared that I was going on by the river route, and explained my plans to him how to surmount the difficulty, which plans were carried out the next morning. I explained to the boys—the Howlands and Dunn—how we could pass the rapid in which they agreed—but what was below? We knew that we were less than seventy miles from the mouth of the cañon, but had no idea what kind of river we had to encounter below where we were.

As O. G. Howland appeared to be the leader of the three, and had fully made up his mind to quit as the rapids had become a holy terror to him, I saw that further talk was useless and [I] so informed Major Powell, and suggested we make duplicate copies of field notes, and give the men latitude and longitude and a draft of the location of the Mormon settlements as far as we knew. Major

Powell and I were up most of the night to get an observation, and he worked out the calculations while I kept a light burning for him with mesquite brush. At daylight we crossed back to the north side of the river and commenced to make the portage....

On the morning of August 28, 1869, the trip hastily split their guns, cash, food, and copies of the field notes, as Sumner said, between the three hikers and the six boaters. It is unclear whether or not Powell paid O. G. Howland and William Dunn their $75 each in wages, but it seems he may have. Powell did ask the hikers to tote a $650 barometer (or chronometer—accounts of this vary). The three also carried a batch of personal letters to be mailed, and Sumner's watch to go to his sister in Denver in the event Sumner drowned. Here too Major Powell abandoned his 16-foot *Emma Dean* tied on the north bank. It was damaged yet may have proved useful had the three hikers changed their minds.

That morning the three helped the other six men line and portage the two 21-foot oak boats partway down the rapid to a small eddy about forty feet long adjacent to the roaring rapid. Once both oak boats wobbled in this eddy, several of the men asked Dunn and the Howlands to reconsider. Hawkins explains:

Dunn held me by the hand and tears came into his eyes when he said he hated to leave Sumner and me; that we had had many a hard and daring time together before we ever saw the Colorado River. "But," he said, "Billy, you cannot blame me." I could not answer; I, for one time in my life, was hurt to the very heart, and in silence I shook his hand for the last time in this world. All this time Sumner and Hall were talking to the Howland boys.

The Major came into my boat [Kitty Clyde's Sister], and we started first, but when we struck the main current it was so swift that it sent us back in the eddy in the little cove. By this time things were getting interesting, and again Dunn and the Howland brothers said we would never make it. I said, "Watch my smoke this time." I told Hall to put all his strength in the oars and I would do the rest. The Major got a firm hold with his left hand and sat in the bottom of the boat. I headed for the lower side of the cove so as to strike the main current more on a downstream course than before. It was perhaps thirty feet from the mouth of the cove to the middle of the high waves which were over fifteen feet in height, but Hall had the boat under such headway that I could manage it with my steering oar [whether this "steering oar" refers to a running oar in a lock or instead to one braced against the stern remains unknown], so I caught the side of the main waves, then cut them for the other side, which we made all right, and landed below. Then came Bradley and Sumner and Captain Powell in the other boat.

We only took in, perhaps, thirty gallons of water in my boat; the other boat did not fare so well, as it struck the rapid too high up, but we got through all right, and we all landed and halloed to the other boys that we left on the rock to come, but they would not.

It was here that Major Powell took off his life preserver and handed it to me, saying he would have no more use for it and would make me a present of it. I told him he had better keep it on, but he said that any man who could come through the way I did between the rocks he felt safe with, and that he would make me a present of it. I thanked him, and said I would keep it to remember the Major and the daring trip and hardships through the entire length of the Colorado River cañons. I have the life preserver now in my possession, although it is unfit for use [38 years later] *by reason of age.*

Peace and good will to all men. W. R. Hawkins

Sumner watched Hawkins and Hall row Powell in *Kitty Clyde's Sister.* Here is his account.

*The first start was not successful, but the second time away they went as the current took hold of the bow and whirled the boat round in a flash, but shot her nearly across the river, and cleared the dangerous rock and fountain waves below. We watched them till they passed the two falls farther down, **and we saw them turn in and land** on a sandy beach a half mile beyond.*

We repeated the same tactics with the other boat and rounded in beside them. We waited for about two hours, fired guns, and motioned for the men [the Howlands and Dunn] *to come on, **as they could have done by climbing along the cliffs.** The last thing **we saw of them** they were standing on the reef, **motioning us to go on,** which we did. If I remember rightly, Major Powell states it was not as bad as it looked and we had run worse. I flatly dispute that statement. **At the stage of water we struck it,** I don't think there is one chance in a thousand to make it by running the whole rapid."* [emphasis either Stanton's or Sumner's]

Clearly, while it may have been fear of the river at this point that drove the Howlands and Dunn to hike out and to emphatically refuse to rejoin the other six below Separation Rapid, it was no longer fear of this rapid itself (Andy Hall's letter of 1869 suggests he felt certain Dunn and O. G. Howland were afraid of Separation Rapid), which now they could have hiked around. Visible downstream were some smaller rapids, but these appeared minor threats.

Interestingly, Powell would later write in his 1875 *Report* (page 100) and in his book *Canyons of the Colorado* (page 282) differently of the aftermath of running Separation Rapid:

*We land at the first practicable point below, and fire our guns, as a signal to the men above that we have come over in safety. Here we remain for a couple of hours, hoping that they will take the smaller boat and follow us. **We are behind a curve in the canyon and cannot see up to where we left them, and so we wait until their coming seems hopeless, and then push on.** [emphasis ours]*

In reality, the river corridor immediately downstream of Separation Rapid runs phenomenally straight for two miles. Bradley's and Sumner's and Hawkins' accounts of the men's final separation as being visible to one another seem more accurate (and perhaps less self-serving) than Powell's. Powell's true entire *journal* entry for that fateful day (from Ghiglieri's *First through Grand Canyon,* page 226) reads:

Boys left us. Ran rapid. Bradey [sic] *boat Broke. Camp on left bank. Camp 44.*

Was this brevity merely the result of Powell's awkwardness in the mechanics of writing due to having lost his right arm? Maybe. But on August 25, only three days before the Separation incident, the Major had penned 365 words in his journal #1 describing the new geology at the Toroweap/Lava Falls region. These 365 words, his longest entry during the entire trip, constitute 12.5 percent, or one-eighth, of Powell's entire two-month journal #1 from the Uinta to the Virgin River. Powell's average journal entry for the 45 days on which he wrote anything at all held 65 words. Hence his Lava entry was a record six-fold increase over his average, while his Separation entry three days later was only one fifth of his average. Or, looked at another way, Powell wrote 28 times more words to describe Lava than to describe the fateful events leading to the separation of the Howlands and Dunn from the expedition. Perhaps Powell was simply apportioning his words according to the subjects that he found most interesting. Perhaps instead, he was too stunned by events to write. Either way, Powell's "Boys left us" entry would be his final entry for the 1869 expedition. How and what he actually felt about this event we can only guess.

Thus ends our probe into mystery #1: Why did the Howlands and Dunn separate from the Powell expedition? They apparently left to escape Powell himself. And for Oramel Howland, the rapid. In so doing, however, their decision led to the worst case of bad timing in the entire history of global exploration.

Now we'll examine mystery #2: What happened to the Howlands and Dunn once they hiked out via Separation Canyon?

The six remaining river runners in the two boats ran six more miles of fast river. Then, mostly out of control, they survived a truly hair-raising, willy-nilly run down what Bradley considered the worst rapid of the entire trip, Lava Cliff. Ironically, the next day, Powell and his surviving five men rowed past the Grand Wash Cliffs, thus exiting Grand Canyon and escaping the last whitewater dangers.

Yet another day later, 99 days and a thousand miles out of Green River Station, Wyoming they rowed into the mouth of the Rio Virgin.

Here the Powell brothers decided to go north overland and catch the train back East. The other four men would row downriver to continue surveying a few more miles and beyond that, just for the hell of it. Before they separated, Major Powell asked the small Mormon community up the Rio Virgin to pass the word to help the Howland brothers and Dunn, were they discovered. Unfortunately, he did not take the time or use the money (even if this meant not paying Sumner $75?) to ask for, organize, accompany, and/or pay for a genuine search party. As time would reveal, this decision may have been a fatal one, and arguably the greatest single "mistake" or worst decision Powell would make in his life.

On September 8, twelve days after the morning of the Separation incident, the *Deseret Evening News* reported that the Howlands and Dunn had been helped by friendly Indians "almost five days ago," who "put them on a trail leading to Washington, in Southern Utah. On their journey they saw a squaw gathering seeds and shot her; whereupon they were followed by three Shebetts [sic] and killed."

Powell read this and also received a telegraph message in Salt Lake City, Utah, informing him that the Howlands and Dunn had been killed by Indians. No evidence exists to indicate that Major Powell, while still in Salt Lake City where he stayed until at least September 18, tried to make an earnest effort to investigate these murders or identify the bodies. Tellingly also, in Powell's 400-page *Canyons of the Colorado* he expresses no words of regret that Dunn and the Howlands had been murdered.

In 1870, however, Powell did return to southern Utah for more exploring. He visited the Uinkaret Indians, neighbors to the Shivwits Indians whose territory straddles the route the Howlands and Dunn would have taken. The Uinkarets requested for Powell an interview with the Shivwits. Jacob Hamblin, Mormon scout and proselytizer assigned by Brigham Young to guide Powell, interpreted for him the Shivwits' explanation of the fate of his three men. As Powell would later write, the Shivwits, Hamblin said, had met the three boatmen as they were trying to exit the Canyon. The Shivwits had helped them with food and directions. But after the trio continued on, Indians from the south side of the Colorado arrived and told the Shivwits that they were chasing some drunken miners who had abused and murdered a squaw. At this information, Powell says Hamblin explained, a few of the Shivwits pursued then ambushed the Howlands and Dunn, murdering them in retribution and in sympathy with these other Indians.

Hamblin gave a slightly different account than Powell's. The Shivwits, Hamblin said, had told him:

—*some of their friends from the other side of the river crossed on a raft and told them that miners on their side of the river abused their women.*

They advised them to kill the three white men who had gone back from the river, for if any mines were found in their country, it would bring great evil among them. The three men were then followed, and killed when asleep.

This same basic story of how and why Powell's three men who hiked out were killed by the Shivwits exists in every book discussing Powell's full journey. But even on cursory examination, it makes little sense. The full story of miners killing a squaw and Powell's three men being misidentified as these miners did not seem to surface until nearly a year after the Howlands and Dunn had been killed. This late breaking of this story is strange in light of the Mormons having reported a year earlier that the Shivwits had killed the Howlands and Dunn over a murdered woman. If the Mormons knew these Indians had killed these three whites for such a reason, why had they never during a year of opportunity asked for the details of exactly why? This lack was not because relations between the Shivwits and Mormons were too weak. The Mormons had baptized the tribe en masse into the LDS church seven years earlier, in 1862.

Indeed, this "We-killed-them-by-mistake-because-other-Indians-who-had-rafted-the-Canyon-came-and-told-us-that-they-were-bad-miners-who-shot-a-squaw" story seems improbable on many levels. The Howlands and Dunn were well-armed and experienced with Indians. The Indians were few and armed only with bows and arrows. Moreover, the two Indians who "confessed" were never arrested by the Mormons. Nor were any of the items carried by Powell's three men—their guns, Powell's chronometer or barometer, Sumner's watch, or the expedition's records—ever mentioned conclusively as having been recovered by the Mormons.

Besides, who were those bad miners who had allegedly perpetrated the rape-murder? Where did they come from and where did they go? This detail is even weaker. There exist virtually no written records of mining or prospecting activity for this region of Western Grand Canyon—which in 1869 was considered terra incognita for whites, including Jacob Hamblin himself. Claim records found by George Billingsley, E. E. Spamer, and Dove Menkes in their exhaustive history of Canyon mining *Quest for the Pillar of Gold: The Mines & Miners of the Grand Canyon* postdate Powell's 1869 trip. Indeed it was Powell's trip that gave the green light to pursuing riches in Grand Canyon.

Moreover, during the years 1867 to 1869, the Hualapai Indians living in Western Grand Canyon south of the Colorado were locked in a brutal war against the U.S. Cavalry. Lengthy scorched-earth campaigns by the army against the Hualapais finally fizzled out during 1869-1870. In short, 1869 was not a likely year for miners to have been prospecting in this region. As local historian Michael Belshaw—who followed on foot the Howlands' and Dunn's hike out Separation and noted a "Dunn" inscription atop Mount Dellenbaugh—explains (in the *Journal of Arizona History*, 1979):

That a small group of Indians or a solitary Indian from the South would be motivated to cross the river and carry the news to unrelated tribes is on the thin edge of probability. The story is less plausible because no mining had been carried out within a hundred miles of Shivwit territory [until 1872 in Kanab Canyon and in Grand Gulch] and should have been of little interest to them. Frederick S. Dellenbaugh reports that the Indians were incited by members of their own band, who reported outrages to the north....It is also most unlikely that the [Powell's] three men wantonly killed an Indian woman as reported in the Deseret News.

Is it impossible that there could have been any miners in this region at the end of August in 1869? No, but there have been few worse years in known history for a miner to survive—let alone prospect—in Western Grand Canyon. Even so, note historian Henry F. Dobyns and anthropologist Robert C. Euler (in the *Journal of Arizona History*, 1980) mining had been taking place since 1864, 60 air-miles south-southwest of the edge of Shivwits territory (about 100 miles by an overland route), and hence may not have been unknown in concept to the Shivwits. More to the point, Dobyns and Euler add, some Shivwits had moved south of the river to Pine Spring near camps of their trading partners, the Hualapai. These Shivwits could have been the "friends" who crossed the river to the north as Jacob Hamblin reported.

On top of all this, because the Hualapais had been very badly treated by the U.S. Cavalry, the Shivwits too may have looked upon any white men, including the Howlands and Dunn, as enemies. Hence the Shivwits remain likely suspects with plausible motives. Even today, some Shivwits Paiutes still admit things like "my grandfather (or my great uncle) was the one who killed Powell's men." Because this sort of claim, even though made with no supporting evidence (such as a gun or watch from the Howlands or Dunn) is one that adds stature and prestige to some Indian families, we must consider it with a grain of salt.

A few stories from southern Utah attempt to pinpoint not merely the Shivwits but also the specific scene of the crime and even the identities of the individual killers.

An early and quoted "sleuth" was Frederick S. Dellenbaugh. In his "history"* he recounts a scanty hybrid of Hamblin's and Powell's versions of the murders. Dellenbaugh also pinpoints a *tinaja* (a bedrock pool) in an intermittent drainage atop the Shivwits Plateau and southeast of Mount Dellenbaugh that he visited around 1875 as the murder site. From his imagination, it seems, he paints the men's demise:

---

*The Romance of the Colorado River: The Story of its Discovery in 1540, with an Account of the Later Explorations, and with Special Reference to the Voyages of Powell through the Great Line of Canyons. 1904. Frederick S. Dellenbaugh

The trail to the water leads down under a basaltic cliff which I visited six years later. As the unfortunate men turned to come up from filling their canteens, they were shot down from ambush. In consequence I have called this Ambush Water-pocket. The guns, clothing, etc. were appropriated by the Shewits [sic], and I believe it was through one of the watches that the facts first leaked out.

Dellenbaugh, however, offers no clues and cites no evidence whatsoever (spent cartridge cases, broken arrowheads, bones, etc.) to support his conclusion that Ambush Water-pocket was the scene of the crime or, indeed, that any ambush happened anywhere. He simply cites proximity to the route he believes the Howlands and Dunn had hiked then relies on his intuition.

Several years after 1869, Anthony W. Ivins explained the killings in the 1944 *Pioneer Stories Compiled under the Direction of the Presiding Bishopic for the Youth of the Church.* Based on what Ivins admitted were "somewhat obscure facts," he "surmised" that soon after the Howlands and Dunn were killed, a party of Shivwits arrived in St. George to trade several articles, including a watch. They said they had found these at an abandoned camp. Unfortunately, none of these articles have ever been found or identified. Nor were the Indians interviewed.

Sometime after 1869, Ivins bought the Mojave Land and Cattle Company, which itself claimed to have "bought" water hole rights from the Shivwits. But when Ivins brought in his herds, the Shivwits began hunting his stock as wild game. This led to the Shivwits being "relocated" at Ivins' request onto a reservation on the Santa Clara River. Among those gathered there "was one man who was a constant source of trouble. He was obstinate, uncontrollable, a constant mischief maker," Ivins writes. "He pretended to be possessed of supernatural power, was a medicine man, and pretended to see, in dreams and visions, the past, present and future. His name was Toab. We called him John."

Toab, Ivins continues, later murdered a fellow Shivwit, "George," in a dispute over water by beating him to death with a hoe. Toab was tried for this murder, Ivins writes, convicted, and sent to prison. The warden, however, asked Ivins to return him to his people. Because Toab was such a trouble maker, Ivins suspected Toab had been involved with the murder of the Howlands and Dunn, though Ivins offers no reasons or evidence for his concluding this beyond his own intuition.

In conflict with Ivins' story is, as historian LaVan Martineau notes in 1992 in *Southern Paiutes Legends, Lore, Language & Lineage,* Utah State Prison records show no record for Toab having been tried for, or convicted of, any murder. Instead they only show that Toab spent six days in prison from September 14-19, 1907 for stealing a horse.

Ivins writes further that, twenty years after the 1869 murders, he was riding the range a little east and north of the Parashant Ranch House and happened upon a small camp site. Although apparently nothing existed at this location to tie it to the

Howlands and Dunn, Ivins felt his intuition at work again: "Like a bolt from the blue the thought came—This is the spot where Powell's men were killed."

Much later, in 1923, after Toab had died, Ivins interviewed Old Simon—"the only man [Shivwit] remaining, who would have personal knowledge of the details of the tragedy." Old Simon allegedly told Ivins when "he was a big boy three white men came up from the river which flows through the Grand Canyon, and were killed by the Indians on Shivwit Mountain." Strangely, Ivins does not say that, 54 years after the crime, Simon said anything about which Indians had committed the murder or about their motive. Nor did Simon refer to the "three bad miners" story.

Even so, Ivins concludes that Powell's three men had followed an old Shivwits trail east of Green Spring Canyon. "It appears that," Ivins writes, filling in innumerable gaps in evidence by using his imagination, the three men were met by friendly Shivwits whose attitudes were turned sour because "Toab insisted that they be dealt with as enemies. Persuading two young Indians to go with him, he followed the men a short distance north east of the Para-shont [sic] Ranch House, which was built many years after, where they attacked them from ambush, and killed them." Although Ivins never offers any evidence at all for his ultimate "solving of the crime," not even testimony by Simon—and certainly no confession by Toab—Ivins, who besides having run cattle was a mayor of Saint George, had been appointed one of the high Council of Twelve Apostles by Joseph Smith, and was counselor to the First LDS Presidency, ends his report with this amazing summation:

> *It is interesting to know that the point marked by Simon as the spot where the tragedy occurred, is the exact locality where some invisible influence caused the writer to stop his horse and reflect, as before stated, and it was at that time that the resolve came to him some day to fix the responsibility for this needless and unjustifiable murder, where he always believed it belonged, on John To-ab [sic].*

In 2002, Frank M. Barrios, writing in *The Ol' Pioneer: A Magazine of the Grand Canyon Pioneers* but without citing his sources of information, tells a somewhat different story. Toab, Barrios writes, was living near the Wildcat Ranch on the plateau during the early part of the 20th century:

> *—and claimed to be a small boy in 1869 when the incident occurred. He once pointed to a nearby landmark [vaguely near Mount Dellenbaugh] and told local cowboy Jimmy Guerrero that this was the location where his people killed the men from the Powell expedition, claiming they begged and pleaded for mercy as his people killed them. Toab was said to be a scoundrel and the stated location where he says the ambush occurred may or may not be the place.*

For that matter, one might conclude, the rest of Toab's stated "history" may not be true as well. Clearly it is difficult, if not ludicrous, to conclude anything firm from either Ivins' or Barrios' or even Dellenbaugh's accounts—yet some historians do. In short, concluding that Toab ever laid eyes on the Howlands or Dunn, or whether any Shivwits, with or without Toab, killed them, remains precarious.

Which brings us back to Jacob Hamblin's story, as translated from the Shivwits, of bad miners abusing Indian women. Even with Toab's rumored report, Hamblin's story still seems concocted post hoc by the Indians to justify their killing and robbing innocent men. Or was it concocted instead by someone else to cover their own murder of the Howlands and Dunn?

Interestingly, despite the Shivwits' stories (as told by Hamblin or Ivins or Powell, who could not speak any Paiute dialect), the concept of Indians having killed the Howlands and Dunn seemed flimsy to Jack Sumner even in 1869. He later wrote to Stanton that, even while Powell's six were still inside Grand Canyon on their final and 98th day:

> *The boys discussed the conduct and fate of the three men left above. They all seemed to think the red bellies would get them sure; but I could not believe that the reds would get them, as I had trained Dunn for two years in how to avoid a surprise, and I did not think the red devils would make an open attack on three armed men. But I did have some misgiving that they would not escape the white double dyed devils that infested that part of the country. Grape vine reports convinced me later that that was their fate....*
>
> *....I heard about two months afterwards, while at Fort Yuma, California, that they [Mormon searchers] brought in the report that the Howland brothers and Dunn came to an Indian camp, shot an Indian, and ravished and shot three squaws. The Indians then collected a force and killed all three of the men. But I am positive I saw some years afterwards the silver watch that I had given Howland [to pass on to Sumner's sister]. I was with some men in a carousal and one of them had a watch and boasted how he came by it. I tried to get hold of it so as to identify it by a certain screw that I had made and put in myself, but it was spirited away and I never afterwards could get sight of it. Such evidence is not conclusive, but all of it was enough to convince me that the Indians were not at the head of the murder, if they had anything to do with it.*

Not only did Sumner feel "positive" about the watch being his, but back on August 30, 1869, when he, Hawkins, Hall, Bradley, and the Powell brothers arrived at the Rio Virgin, he also felt suspicious about the motives of at least one of the local whites they met there. This being only two or three days after the Howland brothers and Dunn had started their hike up Separation Canyon, Powell and the others explained to these friendly Mormons the three men's predicament, asking that help be sent if possible. During this request, as Sumner later complained in disgust:

>—but when Major Powell made the foolish break of telling them the amount of valuables the boys had, I noticed a complete change in the action of a certain one of the men. From a listless demeanor, he instantly changed to a wide-awake, intensely interested listener, and his eyes snapped and burned like a rattlesnake's eyes, particularly so as Major Powell told him of an especially valuable chronometer that he had paid six hundred and fifty dollars for.

Aside from this insight into which of Powell's priorities might be served by asking these Mormons to render assistance to Dunn and the Howlands, Sumner's observation also clarifies how a significant monetary motive quickly could have developed for a robbery-murder of the missing three men. It also offers a possible explanation for why nothing at all carried by the Howlands and Dunn was ever visibly recovered from the Mormons' friends, the baptized Shivwits, who had little use for chronometers, watches, or notes of river expeditions.

In 1919, Billy Hawkins, seventy years old, mentioned to William Wallace Bass, also old, that "some years afterwards [after 1869] I, with a party of some others, buried their bones [the Howlands' and Dunn's] on the Shewits Mountains, below Kanab Wash." Nothing else has been found regarding this burial. Nor has anyone found its location or that of the murders since. Nor, again, has any item the Howlands or Dunn carried been found—other than that watch Sumner felt certain was his.

Could the Howlands and Dunn have been murdered by Mormons for a simple robbery? Or maybe for something more?

That "something more" likely would be the same set of conditions that prompted the September 7, 1857 Mountain Meadows Massacre perpetrated in southern Utah. Indeed, without understanding this massacre, the murders of the Howlands and Dunn would make little sense.

In late summer of 1857, a wagon train of about 140 people from Arkansas crossed Utah from northeast to southwest. This train was led by one of the three Baker brothers—Captain John T., George W., and Abel Baker—but has been identified historically as the "Fancher party" after Alexander Fancher, its outspoken member. Within weeks rumors would spread that the Fancher train had trampled Mormon crops, shot a Kanosh Indian, stole Indian cattle, and may have poisoned a water hole that killed more cattle and more Indians. Mormon historian Will Bagley, however, notes in his exhaustive *Blood of the Prophets Brigham Young and the Massacre at Mountain Meadows* that no evidence exists to show that members of the Fancher train committed any of those alleged offenses. Instead, Bagley notes, the allegations were all mere rumors, folklore, and deliberate anti-Gentile propaganda.

Next, before leaving Utah, the Bakers and Fancher made the decision to camp at Mountain Meadows in southwestern Utah to fatten their oxen and hundreds of head of livestock before crossing the bleak Nevada deserts.

As is told in detail by Mormon Historian Juanita Brooks in her *Mountain Meadows Massacre* and half a century later more accurately by Will Bagley in *Blood of the Prophets*, Brigham Young's war stance against the U.S. and his religious stance of vengeance against Gentiles for the murders of Joseph Smith, Parley Pratt, and other Prophets led to a combined attack by southern Utah Mormons aided by Paiutes against the Fancher train. Young's tactics were to eliminate it and steal all its possessions. Brigham Young's larger strategic goal, however, was aimed at stopping all passage of emigrant trains westward through Utah.

Despite fierce fighting for five days, however, the well-armed Fancher party continued to withstand the siege.

To break this stalemate, the combination of Mormons and Indians, Brooks writes, enlisted John Doyle Lee, a prominent Mormon and the local Indian Agent, to act as intermediary. Lee, however, was subordinate to Major John M. Higbee of the Mormon militia. Higbee had orders from Isaac C. Haight to kill "all the immigrants who could talk."

Lee convinced the train to surrender their weapons.

If their surrender seems to make no sense, consider how the Arkansans by now were low on ammunition, many had been wounded, including women and children, and their prospects for escape looked bleak. Their draft oxen had been shot dead. Perhaps the Fancher party also worried that they might not reach the southern Sierra in time for a safe crossing unless they left Utah soon. Besides, the besieged wagon train had been isolated from their only source of water, a nearby spring. For whatever reasons, the Fancher party agreed to Lee's conditions.

The Mormons, Brooks and Bagley continue, convinced the fifty men of the train to separate from their wagons by a few hundred yards then formally surrender their arms. Next, as soon as each man handed over his gun, his Mormon counterpart shot him dead (some humane Mormons of this militia refused to commit murder, but others nearby did it for them). Meanwhile, Brooks (but not Bagley) writes, the Paiutes spent the next half hour murdering all the women and most of the children with knives and hatchets. They spared about eighteen of the youngest for adoption into Mormon families. After killing 120 people, the murderers stole everything the victims had owned, including $4,000 in gold held in a strong box. Indeed, this theft may have been a prime motive; as Mark Twain noted in his appendix in *Roughing It*, the Fancher Train was wealthy enough in goods, livestock, and cash to have excited the envy of many locals in Utah, both Indian and white.

Significantly, subsequent research and interviews with the surviving little children revealed that many of the "Paiutes" who murdered the women and children were actually Mormon whites painted and dressed as Indians. These killers had used guns and knives.

Most accounts, including Brooks' and Bagley's, however, pay only selective attention to the first investigation of the crime by Brevet Major James H. Carleton, U.S. Army, Captain 1st Dragoons. In 1859, Carleton received orders to investigate the loss, somewhere in Utah, of what was then known as the "Perkins" train, named because Perkins was the guide for the Bakers and Fanchers. Local whites, Carleton found as he attempted interviews, were less than coherent and very unhelpful. He did learn that Jacob Hamblin, Indian sub-agent for the Paiutes, had advised the train to camp at Mountain Meadows, which Hamblin owned (as a gift from the Mormon Church), to "recruit" (rest and fatten) the train's five hundred head of livestock.

Hamblin told Carleton that during Hamblin's absence, the wagon train had been wiped out. Hamblin returned to his summer ranch four miles from Mountain Meadows on September 18, 1857, to find "three little white girls [sisters Rebecca, Louisa, and Sarah Dunlap gathered by John D. Lee] in the care of my wife; the oldest six or seven years of age, the next about three, and the next about one. The youngest had been shot through one of her arms, below the elbow, by a large ball, breaking both bones and cutting the arm half off." Hamblin next told Carleton:

> The **Indians** have often told me that they made an attack on the emigrants between daylight and sunrise as the men were standing around their campfires, killing and wounding fifteen at the first discharge, which was delivered from the ravine near the spring close to the wagons and from a hill to the west....The **Indians** say they then run [sic] off the stock but kept parties at the spring to prevent the emigrants from getting to the water, the emigrants firing upon them every time they showed themselves, and they returning the fire. This was kept up for six or seven days. The **Indians** say they lost but one man killed and three or four wounded. At the end of six or seven days they say a man among them who could talk English called to the emigrants and told them if they would go back to the settlements and leave their property, **especially their arms**, they would spare their lives; but if they did not do so, they would kill the whole of them. The emigrants agreed to this and started back on the road towards my ranch. About a mile from the spring there are some scrub oak bushes and tall sage growing on each side of the road and close to it. Here a large body of Indians lay in ambush, who, when the emigrants approached, fell upon them in their defenseless condition, and with bows and arrows, and stones and guns and knives, murdered all, without regard to sex or age, except a few infant children, seventeen of which have been since recovered. This is what the Indians told me nine days after the massacre took place....When I buried the bones last summer, I observed that about one third of the skulls were shot through with bullets, and about one third seemed to be broken with stones....These are all the facts, within my knowledge.

When next Carleton interviewed Hamblin's 45-year-old wife, Carleton was impressed that Hamblin insisted on being present during the interview and he often prompted his wife on the events of the massacre, even though she had been nearby Mountain Meadows during the murders and he had been absent. She heard all the shooting, she said, for day after day, and watched the Indians pass and re-pass her house. She also saw John D. Lee several times, saying that he was trying to stop the hostilities. Carleton considered her a simple-minded woman who explained the world through the eyes of her husband. And Carleton doubted the honesty of that husband.

Next, Albert, Hamblin's Crow Indian helper and adopted son, told Carleton that he saw the Paiutes lying in ambush as Hamblin had described, with the emigrants *walking, women first, men second,* without wagons, toward them. The Indians then massacred all but a few children, Albert said, over the next half hour. Carleton later learned that two of the surviving children identified Albert himself as the man who had murdered their two sisters. Carleton found so many holes and inaccuracies in Albert's story that he considered him a liar and his account a worthless fiction.

Carleton next found a Paiute of the Santa Clara band named Jackson who admitted he was one of the attackers. Jackson said that John D. Lee had led a group of sixty Mormons, all painted and disguised as Indians (the costuming being done one mile from the spring at which the train was camped). "Lee and Haight," Jackson said, "led and directed the combined force of Mormons and Indians in the first attack—throughout the siege—and at the last massacre."

On May 25, 1859, Carleton finished his report. He noted how some of the local Mormons had a feud with anyone from Arkansas. The locals, he added, expressed no regret that 120 people from Arkansas had been murdered. More intriguing, Carleton found that several Cedar City Mormons said they held no doubt that Lee, Haight, and Higby "were the leaders who organized a party of fifty or sixty Mormons to attack this train," with many Indians as helpers. "The Mormons say," Carleton added, "the emigrants fought 'like lions' and that thy [sic] could not whip them by any fair fighting."

Carleton also heard from locals and from a dentist named Whitelock (at Camp Floyd who had interviewed a self-admitted Mormon participant in the massacre who fled to California and was suffering from post-traumatic stress disorder) that hostilities ended in the following way:

> *After some days fighting, the Mormons had a council among themselves to arrange a plan to destroy the emigrants. They concluded finally, that they would send some few down and pretend to be friends and try to get the emigrants to surrender. John D. Lee and three or four others, head men from Washington, Cedar and Parowan, (Haight and Higby from Cedar) had their paint washed off, and dressing in their usual dress, took their wagons and drove towards the*

emigrants' corral as if they were just travelling [sic] *on the road on their ordinary business. The emigrants held out a little girl toward them. She was dressed in white. Had a white handkerchief in her hand which she waved in a token of peace. The Mormons with the wagons waved one in reply and then moved on to the corral. The emigrants then came out—no* **Indians or others being in sight at this time***; and talked with these leading Mormons with the three wagons. They talked with the emigrants an hour, or an hour and a half, and told them that the Indians were hostile, and that if* **they gave up their arms***, it would show that they did not want to fight; and if they, the emigrants would do this, they would pilot them back to the settlements. The emigrants had horses which had remained near their wagons, the loose stock, mostly cattle, had been driven off, not the horses. Finally the emigrants agreed to these terms, and delivered up their arms to the Mormons with whom they had counseled. The women and children then started back toward Hamblin's house, the men following with a few wagons that they had hitched up. On arriving at the scrub oaks, &c., where the other Mormons and Indians lay concealed, Higby, who had been one of those who had inveigled the emigrants from their defenses,* **himself gave the signal to fire,** *when a volley was poured in from each side and the butchery commenced and was continued until it was consummated.*

The property from the Fancher train was then sold in Cedar City at public auction and called "Property taken at the siege of Sabastopol." When Carleton questioned the Paiutes along the Muddy River, whom the Mormons had fingered as the Mountain Meadows culprits, The Indians responded with, if *we* had done it, then:

Where are the wagons, the cattle, the clothing, the rifles, and other property belonging to the train? We don't have them. You will find these things in the hands of the Mormons.

Carleton added that Hamblin himself had told him that in 1855 the entire tribe possessed only three guns. How, Carleton asked rhetorically in his 1859 *The Mountain Meadows Massacre: A Special Report*, could they then, in 1857, have beaten fifty well-armed male emigrants?

Carleton and his men gathered up the bones of thirty-four of the victims at Mountain Meadows. He buried them in a mass grave. He next had built a rude conical monument fifty feet in circumference of loose granite. Atop this he placed a cross of cedar twenty-four feet high and inscribed it with the facts of the mass murder. In 1861 Brigham Young ordered this monument destroyed. Regarding forensics, how had these victims—the women and children 600 yards closer to Hamblin's cabin than the men—died? Carleton explains:

I observed that nearly every skull I saw had been shot through with rifle or revolver bullets. I did not see one that had been "broken with stones"....The scene of the massacre, even at this late day, was horrible to look upon. Women's hair in detached locks and in masses, hung in the sage bushes and was strewn over the ground...

Carleton was so disturbed by this mass murder and the devious means by which it had been committed that he characterized the Mormons as "Latter Day Devils."

Revealingly, on August 23, 1999, while excavating for the construction of a new monument at Mountain Meadows, a backhoe's claw accidentally disinterred 2,602 bone fragments in a mass grave of at least 28 victims of the massacre. Due to politics, forensic biologist Shannon Novak at the University of Utah's Medical School was restricted in her analysis of the original damage inflicted on the cranial fragments of 18 victims to one single 25-hour Marathon of forensic examination. She carried this out from September 9 to 10, 1999, before being required to return the bones to Shane Baker, archeologist at Brigham Young University. What Novak discovered during those 25 hours of study opened a Pandora's Box.

For starters, she found that at least five of the men had been shot in the head while facing their executioners. More troubling, Novak found that one child between the ages of ten and fifteen had also been shot through the top of the head. Two children, age four and seven, had been beaten to death. Most revealing, however, was the following: Novak found *no* evidence whatsoever of any Indian-specific attacks on any of the victims—no arrow wounds, no knife or hatchet wounds, and no evidence of scalping.

This lack not only corroborates the Indians' own stories, as told in 1859 to Carleton, that they had not been principals in the massacre but instead local whites had painted their faces and done most of the killing themselves. It also helps explain why local whites would have been even more highly motivated to keep all details about this massacre absolutely secret forever.

Hence, despite several federal investigations over the years after 1858, by 1869 no one had been arrested, tried, or punished for the mass murder at Mountain Meadows. Even so, the U.S. government still wanted answers. Was Jacob Hamblin's explanation of the Shivwits having killed Powell's three men a cover-up to hoodwink Powell? Was Hamblin reliable? John D. Lee, who worked with and around Hamblin for years, later referred to him as "Dirty-Fingered Jake" and as a habitual liar. These disparaging remarks were made in the context of Hamblin having testified against Lee during Lee's trial regarding his role in the Mountain Meadows Massacre. Lee found Hamblin's testimony ironic in that it was at Hamblin's cabin, with Hamblin's first wife, that the Mormon militia stayed the night before murdering the Fancher train at Mountain Meadows, also Hamblin's property. Lee's "dirty fingers" allegation may have been in reference to Hamblin having ended up with a share of the loot from that massacred train hidden in that same cabin.

John Doyle Lee was found guilty during this trial and was executed in 1877 by firing squad. As the only person ever arrested or tried for the Mountain Meadows Massacre, Lee obviously had been sacrificed as a scapegoat.

"Scapegoat," however, does not mean "innocent." Indeed, as noted by Will Bagley (page 263), Lee's 19th wife Ann Gordge reported that when one of the Fancher train's surviving children saw Emma Lee all dressed up after the massacre, the girl said Emma was wearing her mother's dress (as loot from the pirated Fancher train). John Doyle Lee, said wife Ann Gordge, "reached down, took the child by the head and bent her back and cut her throat from ear to ear, then threw her body in a well nearby. This I saw with my own eyes."

After this, Ann Gordge divorced Lee.

The question regarding the fates of the Howland brothers and Dunn remains: But what might Hamblin have been covering up, if anything, with his Shivwits story?

What *really* happened to the Howland brothers and Dunn?

"New" information on this surfaced via a fluke discovery made by Wesley P. Larsen, professor emeritus and former dean of the College of Science at Southern Utah University. In the early 1980s, Larsen purchased the old historic house built by John Steele in Toquerville. Steele, born in Ireland in 1821, was an accomplished explorer of southern Utah and northern Arizona. Steele was also a Parowan judge, a mayor, and a county recorder.

Larsen, also a Mormon, had sifted through a trunk of old documents and letters John Steele's great grandson Gary Callister had turned up. Larsen found among them a letter, verified as authentic, written to John Steele in 1883 by William Leany, apparently in response to a letter Steele—by then an old man—had written to him suggesting it was time for them both to confess to and repent their sins.

William Leany, born in 1815, was a Parowan city council member and Harrisburg water master. He had fallen from the church's graces, however, in 1857 when he gave food to William Aiden, one of the members of the doomed Fancher party soon to be massacred at Mountain Meadows. Leany had given William Aiden food because he was the son of Dr. S. R. Aiden, who had saved Leany's life earlier in Tennessee from an anti-Mormon mob while Leany was on a church mission. For this minor repayment for saving Leany's life by giving food to an "enemy" (as the Fancher's train had been dubbed in Utah prior to its obliteration), local Mormon Barney Carter ambushed Leany at night on his own front porch. He broke a picket-like club over Leany's head, fractured his skull, and left him for dead. Leany failed to die. But years passed before he recovered.

No surprise, Leany's 1883 letter back to Steele was anything but repentant. He had nothing to repent, he said, adding that his accusers were "drunken, adulterous, murderous wretches." Leany continued:

—God shall bear me witness that I am clean of all of which they [President Erastus Snow and others] *accuse me & they guilty of all that I accuse them & much more....And I cannot see that for me to confess to a lie would make me more worthy or they less guilty & here let me say that my object is & has been to stay the overwhelming tide of thieving whoredom murder and Suicide & like abominations that threaten to desolate the land & you are far from ignorant of those deeds of blood from the day the picket was broken on my head* **to the day those three were murdered in our ward & the murderer killed to stop the shedding of more blood**....*As the old Prophets said of the blood & violence in the city & blood tondreth blood if that was not fulfilled in* **the killing of the three in one room of our ward** *please say what it was & for all this & much more unrighteous dominion shall we be cast out of the land....Be assured that I will, God being my helper, clear my skirts of the mobbing, raking, stealing, whoredom, murder, suicide, lying, slander & all wickedness & abominations even in high places.* [emphasis ours]

Larsen admitted to writer Scott Thybony that Leany's letter had led him to suspect Powell's three men must have hiked across Shivwits land and have been seen and brought to Toquerville, the county seat and local center of Church authority. Only weeks earlier in 1869—Larsen also found out—Brigham Young had warned faithful Mormons that there would soon come yet another attempt by Gentiles to invade Utah. To avoid being attacked by surprise, the Latter Day Saints posted sentries at passes leading into southern Utah.

Hence, the Howland brothers and Dunn likely *would have been spotted* as they hiked north. Next they would have been brought to Toquerville.

Leany's letter mentioned to Steele, "*our ward.*" Larsen looked into this and found Leany and Steele had shared a ward between 1869 and 1874. Leany also mentioned "*in one room of our ward.*" Apparently the only ward then with more than one room was in Toquerville.

Larsen next wondered if Leany could have been referring to some other three people murdered or killed. So he searched the records of 1869 for the local region of southern Utah. Only one trio had been killed in 1869, the Howland brothers and Dunn. But why?

As late as 1869, the year was one of prejudice against Mormons, of federal investigation concerning the as-yet-unsolved Mountain Meadows Massacre, of Mormon paranoia about being punished, and of Mormon vigilance against federal spies. Into this climate of paranoia wandered three very beat-up and starving river runners from a river whose name was synonymous with impossibility. The Howlands and Dunn would have been doubly suspect given their improbable, perhaps unbelievable, story. Therefore, they were lying to cover up something. Something like being federal spies.

The three, Larsen suspected, might have been killed outright and robbed once they were brought to Toquerville even without sanction from higher church authorities.

If so, then word of their execution soon would have reached Salt Lake City in a message to the effect that "we just executed three federal spies whose cover story was that they had just boated Grand Canyon." Such a message would have arrived at virtually the same time as word from John Wesley Powell at the Rio Virgin reached Salt Lake saying that three of his men had hiked north from Western Grand Canyon and would need assistance. Together these two messages would have caused instant turmoil.

Larsen suspects church authorities quickly sent word back to Toquerville commanding that the executioner himself must be executed and the entire crime be covered up completely to avoid further bloodshed. Leany's passage in his 1883 letter, "*& the murderer killed to stop the shedding of more blood*," suggests too that this is what happened. Larsen suspects further that the blame for the three killings was officially placed on the Mormons' Indian allies (who also took the blame for the Mountain Meadows Massacre and for other deeds committed by Mormon militias who dressed up like Indians to assassinate enemies). As with the booty looted from the Fancher train, nothing that the Howlands and Dunn had been carrying has surfaced except Sumner's watch, which likely was pocketed by accomplices at the scene of the crime. These accomplices later had exhibited the poor judgment to boast of this where Sumner could overhear.

Indeed, the "discovery" that the Indians had killed the Howlands and Dunn was announced by Mormons only about ten days after the killings supposedly happened. How would they have known this so soon from the isolated Shivwits who had so little contact with whites? Was it via Anthony Ivins' vague rumor of Indians trying to sell booty, or instead by other Indians simply showing up to report a murder, a report that might seriously screw up their lives? No, says Larsen, it was Mormons. And after the cover-up that "Indians did it," Larsen also suspects everyone involved was sworn to a blood oath "covenant of silence" similar to that sworn after the Mountain Meadows Massacre.

In Hurricane, Utah, Wes Larsen told Thybony that, while this scenario was the only one that seemed to account for all the facts as he knew them, he wanted to corroborate his hypothesis with more evidence. Larsen had a friend who submitted for him a request to examine documents from that era in the Mormon Archives.

Larsen waited there for an hour. The chief archivist finally demanded to know on whose authority Larsen could view such documents. Larsen said, "Well, I'm a Mormon." The archivist denied Larsen access and told him to leave.

"I guess you have to be a *good* Mormon," Larsen wryly told Thybony, the irony being that earlier, during the heat of that day, Larsen had steadfastly refused a cold beer because of his religion.

Thybony asked Larsen if he was worried about repercussions from the church if he published what he had put together.

"Hell yes, I'm worried."

But Larsen did not give up. An important missing piece to this puzzle was who, specifically, had murdered the Howlands and Dunn and then was executed himself. Larsen dug deeper. Soon it seemed clear to him that the murderer was Eli N. Pace. Pace was a son-in-law of John D. Lee and had killed all three, Larsen reckoned, to protect Lee from the three, federal men coming out of "nowhere." Pace died on January 29, 1870 (five months after the Howlands and Dunn) under suspicious circumstances, shot with a revolver positioned to suggest he had fired it.

Soon after the Howlands and Dunn were murdered, Brigham Young would send John D. Lee to the confluence of the Paria and Colorado rivers to build and run a ferry—Lee's Ferry. Not only was the ferry necessary to colonize northern Arizona, its desolate location might isolate Lee from federal marshals.

Just before Larsen and Thybony parted company, Larsen answered Thybony's question of why he had gone to such trouble to investigate the killings of the Howland brothers and Dunn.

"If these were Mormons who did it," Larsen answered, "and the Paiutes got the damn blame for everything, it's...it's...." He stopped. Later he admitted, "I only wish I'd felt this way fifty years ago."

Wes Larsen published his findings in *Canyon Legacy #17* (in 1993).

To further complicate matters, however, in 2003 historian Don Lago noted how Richard Fryer had murdered his estranged wife Theresa, their infant son, and Thomas Batty in 1875 in Toquerville. A sheriff's posse then shot Fryer. These four killings, Lago suggests, may instead be the murders that William Leany had referred to in his letter to John Steele. These killings, however, do not accord with Leany's "*the killing of the three in one room of our ward.*"

Each of us now must weigh the existing evidence and arrive at our own conclusion. Did the Shivwits murder the Howlands and Dunn in Grand Canyon? Or did whites do so beyond it? You decide.

But first consider what we've held back until now. While Wes Larsen was the main detective recently for more than a decade to solve this crime, John Colton Sumner had somehow "known" the culprits a century earlier. In 1906, Sumner wrote a long letter to his old friend Lewis Keplinger (this letter, also discovered by historian Don Lago and published in 1992 in the *boatman's quarterly review*, volume 15, #2), is reproduced in full under the fate of *John "Jack" Colton Sumner* in Ghiglieri's *First through Grand Canyon: the Secret Journals and Letters of the 1869 Crew who Explored the Green and Colorado Rivers.* Be that as it may, Keplinger had previously asked Sumner what had happened to each member of the 1869 crew. Sumner explained what he knew of each man's fate then dropped the big bombshell (one with a long-delayed detonation fuse because the letter has remained hidden and unread for so long in the Kansas State Historical Society's Keplinger Collection). In it Sumner tells Keplinger:

> —*the two howlands* [sic] *and Dunn were killed. Powell states by Indians & I Say Killed by the Mormons, Part of the Same old 'Mountains Meadows' massacre gang.*

Fifteen years passed after the demise of the Howland brothers and William Dunn before another murder apparently took place at Grand Canyon. We owe the discovery of this, as you'll see, cryptic account to National Park Service historian and former Ranger Charles R. "Butch" Farabee, Jr., who uncovered it in the *Arizona Champion* (February 21, 1885):

> *A San Francisco hoodlum recently visited the Grand Canyon of the Colorado in company with a party of respectable citizens of Flagstaff. On arriving at the brink of the awful yawning chasm and gazing with dizzy delight on the enchanting miniature world far below, he assumed the striking of attitude of a Prescott tragedian, his manly breast swelling out like an enraged cobra, and in stentorian tones shouted, "Zamuel! Zamuel! —a single soul, a single year; a hundred souls, a hundred years"—when he was reminded of the fact that the beautiful natural panorama before him was no "black crook" show, and that Zamuel did not reign there, but that the great chief of the Supais might entertain him, whereupon he shouted lustily for the main guy of the Canyon dwellers "great mogul of the Supai hear my prayer; almost thou pursuiest me to become a bug-eating member of your carmine-tinted horse thieves. Bring hither the reddest, greasiest maiden in your tribe that she may welcome the pale-faced stranger from the Golden Gate; I would live forever in your beautiful home, after which you can make me up into tobacco signs; I will unfold—" But he didn't. Two of the party seized him, and with a harlequin maneuver, he was hurled far over the cliff, and his body whirred to the bottom, ten thousand feet below, and presently the reverberation of a "dull thud" was wafted to the ears of the avenged spectators above.*

Yes, we agree, it is hard to know exactly what to make of the above news flash. Whether it is more or less true or instead utterly bogus remains as clear as mud.

On nearly the last night of the last trip of 1971, a 20-day run operated by Grand Canyon Expeditions, trip leader Rick Petrillo regaled his passengers around the campfire with the unsolved mysterious disappearance of Glen and Bessie Hyde (see Chapters 5 & 9). As usual, Petrillo's small audience was captivated and intrigued by the Hydes' reckless bid for stardom then their mysterious fate. Later, as the boatmen on this trip, George Billingsley, O. C. Dale, and Regan Dale, sat around the fire the tables turned.

A little old lady on the trip, Liz Cutler, announced that she had a confession to make. Billingsley already had been impressed by this woman. She frequently seemed to know more about the Canyon than she should have for a first timer. This time she dropped a bombshell. She said she knew some of what had happened during the Hydes' fateful journey because she had known them.

When pressed about how this could be, she confessed that she knew them because she was Bessie Hyde.

O. C., who considered Liz a good-humored trickster, asked something like, "Well, if you're Bessie, where's Glen?"

Liz became serious. Glen, she said, had changed when he got on the river. He was no longer the man she had fallen in love with. He had become abusive, she explained. "He was a son of a bitch who beat me all the time." Liz (a.k.a. Bessie) explained that she had wanted to quit the river at Hermit, but Glen had forced her into the boat. She knew, she said, from Emery Kolb that the worst rapids—232-Mile, Separation Rapid (River Mile 239.6), and Lava Cliff Rapid (River Mile 246)—were downstream of Diamond Creek. So Diamond represented her last chance to escape. That night above Diamond, their 42nd night on the trip, they had camped on the south side of the river. Fearing now for her life, she had waited until Glen fell asleep. Then she took a knife and stabbed him to death. She then pushed his body into the river. Next she re-loaded the boat and shoved it into the river too. At dawn she hiked a few miles down to Diamond Creek and then hiked the 23 miles out to Route 66 where she caught a bus to a new life.

Pausing for a moment, Liz re-gathered herself. She reached into her pocket and retrieved a small pocketknife. "And this," she said, displaying it, "was what I did him in with."

The Dale cousins told us (Ghiglieri) they never took Liz seriously. But Billingsley, with his scientist's take on the world around him, thought to himself (and to Marty Anderson, Ghiglieri, and Scott Thybony), "You never know..."

How possible was Liz's story?

Emery and Ellsworth Kolb, Jim Brooks, Rollin C. Hyde, and Deputy Sheriff John Nelson visited Diamond Creek on Christmas Eve of 1928 to search for Glen and Bessie. Weeks later, the elder Hyde and Nelson had hiked upriver. More than a dozen miles upstream of Diamond lay an abandoned campsite. Because the river level was dropping into winter, nothing had washed away. The beach held footprints, an empty jar of home canned lima beans from Idaho and an empty can. Someone suspiciously exactly like the Hydes had camped there recently, and the route from there to Diamond, while not easy, was walkable.

So if Liz was Bessie, why did she come back and why would she confess to murder? When asked why she came back, Liz answered, "Because I loved him so much." When asked why she confessed, she said, "I've lived my life. And no one is going to believe my story anyway."

Was this because it was so outlandish? Or because it was in fact untrue and Liz knew no one would take it seriously?

Strangely, no one followed up on Liz's story for years. In the meantime the plot thickened. On December 11, 1976, Emery Kolb finally died. We say "finally" because he had been living on the South Rim since 1902, and had shown up there as an adult. He died at age 95. Indeed Emery still holds the record for length of residence at the South Rim's Grand Canyon Village, nearly 74 years. He also holds an even more interesting record. In 1911–1912 he and his brother Ellsworth had each built a boat and had rowed them during an epic trip from Green River, Wyoming, to beyond the foot of Grand Canyon. During parts of this trip they had taken moving pictures. The two spliced together a movie. Emery showed it daily and narrated it live, and later via audiotape, at the South Rim Kolb Studio from 1912 to 1976. It was, and still is, the longest running movie of all time. At any rate, when Emery Kolb died, his studio was jammed with the impedimenta of ages.

As workers cleared it out they found a canoe-type boat (given to Kolb by David Rust) hiked up to the rafters. They lowered it. Inside the boat were canvas bundles. One contained a set of old clothes. The other held the skeleton of a man. The skull, stored inside a coffee can, had a bullet hole in the temple. Inside the skull a .32 bullet had lodged against the opposite side. Someone said, "Hey, that looks like it could be Glen Hyde."

At this time Bruce Babbitt was Governor of Arizona. The skull was clearly of a person who had been murdered—or committed suicide—hence it became state's evidence in an unsolved crime. Governor Babbitt was a Canyon-phile of the first order. Nothing Canyonesque was beneath his interest. And the skeleton of a murder victim in Emery Kolb's Studio promised to be a kind of Canyon Rosetta Stone. Who knew what mysteries from the past it might translate? A special forensic investigation of the skeleton and the clothes began.

Norm Tessman, Curator of the Sharlot Hall Museum in Prescott, examined the clothes. Yes, they were 1920s vintage, or maybe 1930s. But the belt buckle included with them did not match the one worn by Glen Hyde in Emery Kolb's or Adolph Sutro's photos of the honeymooners.

Forensic anthropologist Walter H. Birkby in Tucson examined the bones and the skull for architecture and degree of suture closure (for age). The skeleton seemed to have lain exposed to the elements for at least a year before being gathered into a more protective environment. Yes, the hole was a bullet hole. And the slug inside the cranium was from an H & R .32 caliber revolver. The trajectory of the bullet suggested homicide or suicide.

The cranial sutures suggested the skull was a 23-year-old man's. Moreover, Birkby's anthropomorphic measurements revealed the eye orbits to be angled wrong for what Glen Hyde looked like in life. The cheek bones were too wide. The chin was too square. "These bones that were submitted for analysis," Birkby reported, "are not the bones of Glen Hyde. Period."

On top of these anthropometrics was credibility. Birkby scoffed, finding the notion "preposterous that he [Emery Kolb] would off somebody and then keep the damn body around."

But why would anyone suspect Kolb to have Glen Hyde's skeleton to begin with? The chain is weak but seductive enough to raise an eyebrow. First, Western historian Michael Harrison was a young NPS ranger in 1928 in Grand Canyon. He explained to one of us (Ghiglieri) that Emery Kolb almost completely sequestered Glen and Bessie Hyde after they reached the South Rim Village.

Second, Emery Kolb had badgered Glen to take his own life jackets. When Glen refused them, Kolb suggested that Glen at least take something else to provide floatation, such as inner tubes from the Fred Harvey Stable. Glen Hyde refused both suggestions.

Third, Emery's daughter, Edith, was a young woman of twenty, much like Bessie only more Western and outdoorsy. Edith, in fact, was the first woman ever (at age 15) to run a Grand Canyon rapid, Hance Rapid, with a whopping drop of 30 feet, in her dad's boat when he was the head boatman of the 1923 U.S. Geological Survey Expedition in Grand Canyon. In Bessie, Emery may have seen his daughter Edith, entwined with some idiot egotist in a stubbornly dangerous stunt to achieve stardom regardless of the risk to the woman he bullied along while refusing to allow her a life jacket. Rescuing Bessie was, in a golden-rule sort of way, rescuing Edith.

The plot really thickens when the next rumor is added. Around the end of November, 1928, at the time when Glen and Bessie were to pass Diamond Creek and soon make their quick run to Needles, Emery is rumored to have disappeared from the South Rim. Supposedly, the rumor goes, he went to Peach Springs then down to Diamond Creek to try one last time to save Bessie's life (and Glen's) with his life jackets.

At Diamond Creek the two men found one another so irritating that they got physical and somehow Glen came out the loser.

In which case Bessie (a.k.a. Liz) would have not knifed Glen, she instead would have been the beneficiary of Emery's rescue. And her confession in 1971 would have been a cover for Kolb, her rescuer, who still lived at the South Rim.

From Diamond, Bessie and Emery Kolb could have gone out to Route 66, her to a new life and him back to the rim....(with Glen Hyde's body?)

No, the skeleton being that of Glen Hyde really does not make much sense, does it?

As you might remember from Chapter 9, in early June of 1933, that botanical cactus expert from Riverside, California had spotted a sun-bleached skeleton 600 feet below the rim of Shoshone Point. Soon after this, Emery Kolb had donated a human skeleton to the Grand Canyon High School science lab. Years later the school acquired an articulated and mounted skeleton. It then returned the original skeleton to Kolb, who stowed it in a bundle inside a canvas boat Carl Rust had given him. Kolb hitched the boat up into the rafters in his garage. Upon doing so, Kolb joked to Art Gallenson, "When I die and somebody finds that skeleton, it's gonna cause a lot of commotion. …Take it to the school in Kanab, would you?"

Gallenson never took it.

When Kolb died in December of 1976, the skeleton finally saw daylight again the next month. And when Kolb's grandson Emery Lehnert dug it out of Rust's boat, Kolb's prophesy came true. The skeleton came back to life. Rumors grew like weeds that the bleached bones were those of Glen Hyde, whom Kolb must have murdered to rescue Bessie.

As noted in Chapter 9, in 2006 Bob Williamson donated to the Grand Canyon Museum Collection a set of 1933 photos taken by his father Ranger Robert R. Williamson of a skeleton. As noted by Allyson Mathis in *Canyon Views* (Spring 2009), these photos inspired NPS Archivist Kim Besom in 2008 to research their provenance. Williamson, it turns out, was the investigating ranger in 1933 along with Deputy Sheriff Jack Harbin 600 feet below the rim at Shoshone Point who sorted out the skeleton discovered by that cactus botanist. Again, the original owner of that skeleton had apparently committed suicide with that H&R .32 caliber revolver a few years before 1933.

Also as mentioned in Chapter 9, NPS Special Agent Joe Sumner, today an indefatigable cold case investigator for the Coconino County Sheriff's Department, compared the bones and the shoe, et cetera from the boat in Kolb's Studio with Ranger Robert R. Williamson's photos of the 1933 skeleton found below Shoshone Point. They matched perfectly.

Kolb had served on the Coconino County Coroner's jury representing Grand Canyon in the 1930s that had reviewed the case of the mystery skeleton. When the verdict had proved to be suicide, Kolb likely had decided "waste not, want not" and had donated the bones to the high school.

The upshot? No known evidence ties Emery Kolb to the mysterious death of Glen Hyde, who most likely drowned in Mile 232 Rapid with his bride Bessie.

Even so, when one of us (Ghiglieri) asked Bruce Babbitt in late 1988 what, exactly, that forensic investigation had actually found, he paused, looked puzzled, and answered, "What ever did happen with that, anyway."

What about Liz? Did she have a life before 1928? Two river sleuths dogged her early trail. In the 1980s, writer and river runner Scott Thybony finally called Liz Cutler (a.k.a. Bessie) to interview her. Yes, she remembered the trip very well. She described details the boatmen themselves had forgotten: bad runs in Horn Creek Rapid, a girl who broke her arm and had to be evacuated, and the broken lower unit on O. C.'s motor. But when Thybony asked Liz what she knew about the Glen and Bessie Hyde story, "She drew a complete blank." She even denied having told the story." Thybony told us (Ghiglieri) "I'm not Bessie. [she said on the phone] I don't even know the name, 'Hyde.'"

Not long after this, river sleuth and Dock Marston protegé Martin J. Anderson became intrigued by this same enigma. He researched both Bessie and Liz back to each one's birth certificates. As Anderson noted to Ghiglieri, Bessie was born Bessie Haley in Washington, D.C. on December 29, 1905, and lived later in Parkersburg, West Virginia. She attended college with Earl Helmick, whom she secretly married on June 4, 1926, and she majored in art at Marshall College in Huntington, West Virginia. Liz Cutler was born on December 2, 1909, in Pomeroy, Ohio, (maybe 40 miles from Parkersburg) as Elizabeth Arnold. After Bessie abandoned Earl and was attending the California School of Fine Arts in San Francisco, Liz was attending the fourth annual Arnold family reunion at Rock Springs Fairground. What, then, are the chances that Bessie escaped the Canyon, assumed Liz Cutler's identity, and then grew four inches taller?

Infinitesimal.

What are the chances that Liz herself as a late teenager had read in the local newspapers about the romantic and mysterious Grand Canyon disappearance of local girl Bessie Haley/Hyde in 1928?

Pretty good.

Was Liz an impostor? Not really. Girls just want to have fun.

But being charged with murder in Arizona isn't much fun.

Marty Anderson also contacted Earl Helmick. In the past, Helmick had refused to talk to people about Bessie. And to Anderson, he was only slightly more open. When he asked Helmick what he thought about the stories going around that Bessie was alive ("Unsolved Mysteries" at this time was airing a television pseudo-documentary on Bessie and Glen), he simply said: "No, she is dead."

When the Kolb brothers and Brooks found the Hydes' scow, Bessie's purse was still aboard it. Inside her purse was a couple of dollars. Had Bessie killed Glen and decided to hike out, would she have left her money behind?

Maybe.

No one who knows the Canyon's history doubts that there exist untold—and maybe untellable—tales of murder that unfolded in real life below its rims. The inaccessibility of so many parts of this gigantic labyrinth lends itself to converting a run of the mill homicide into the "perfect" murder. "Perfect" in that the location of the victim and the details of what happened to him or her may remain hidden for eternity. The Canyon is the dry rock version of the middle of the ocean.

Despite this seeming convenience to the potential murderer, murder within the Canyon almost never happens. Considering that more than half a million people have run the Colorado River in Grand Canyon, and well over a million more people have hiked or camped within it, the very low number of known murders in the Canyon is impressive. Yet on the rims and plateaus, homicides and suicides, both successful and attempted, have been far more frequent (see Tables 9 & 10).

In mid-June of 1927, for example, Bert Lauzon, custodian of the Bright Angel Trail and constable at Grand Canyon, received a strange warning from the sheriff's office of Okmulgee, Oklahoma. Five men, the sheriff warned, were reportedly traveling in a Buick, Packard, and a Studebaker to Grand Canyon around June 20. Their intent was to rob the Grand Canyon payroll. The sheriff's warning included names and descriptions and even photos of the five would-be robbers. Instantly NPS rangers were on the alert.

Late in the morning on June 23, notes the *Coconino Sun* (June 24, 1927), a Buick sedan drove into Grand Canyon National Park. Leo Smith, the registry officer, recognized its driver as Matthew Kimes, one of the "bad five" from Okmulgee. Kimes of Bristow, Oklahoma was truly a hard case. At age 21, he had already been convicted of bank robbery and murder in Oklahoma.

Smith passed word ahead that Kimes—driving the Buick with its owners George Keady and his wife—was approaching the Village. At 2:30 p.m., Coconino County Sheriff John Parsons spotted the 5' 8", 170-pound Kimes near a Bright Angel cottage. Parsons told Kimes to come with him to the administration building. Both men climbed into the Buick. But as Kimes drove down the hill by El Tovar, he said, "The brakes won't hold!"

As he shot past the building he reached down and yanked the emergency brake. When his hand came back up, however, his fingers were wrapped around the butt of a Colt .45 revolver. Parsons grabbed Kimes' hand and the gun. For an amazing 15 minutes the two men fought all over the interior of that Buick. They piled into one seat, wrestled their way to the next seat then slid onto the floor.

During this epic car-shaking frenzy, Curley Ennis, the garage foreman for Fred Harvey Company, happened along. He reckoned the two men were drunks locked into an impressive argument. But when Ennis looked into the car, the muzzle of the .45 swung into his face.

"Get away," someone commanded. Ennis then recognized Parsons' face under the steering wheel.

At this same moment George Cravey, the trail foreman, joined Ennis and also peered into the jiggling Buick. The .45 now swung into his face.

Bizarrely, neither Ennis nor Cravey could manage to get into a position to haul Kimes off of Parsons. So the two desperate men in the car—one trying to kill, the other fighting for his life—continued to weave and wrestle and grunt around the inside of the Buick. Finally Ennis ran to the garage for his gun. En route he heard three shots, then five more.

Kimes had broken out of Parsons' grip, exited the Buick, and run. Now Parsons had a chance to grab his own gun. He fired twice at Kimes. Ordinarily Parsons was a dead shot. But his hands had been torn by the hammer of Kimes' gun while wrestling over it and were now bleeding and unsteady. Both of Parsons' shots missed Kimes.

Kimes spun and fired several times back at Parsons. His shots also missed.

Kimes next ran to the rim near Verkamps store and dropped over the edge onto a sloping descent. Within ten minutes, at least thirty Grand Canyon residents carrying rifles or pistols deployed themselves along the Rim Trail in a semi-circle reaching from El Tovar to Yavapai Point. Ennis and Cravey tracked Kimes through a myriad of other tracks. They too dropped off the rim. They saw where Kimes had dug his heels into the steep slope, loosening some gravel.

Three hundred feet down they hit the rim of a cliff falling off several hundred feet. At this same instant they spotted Kimes, about twenty feet away.

"I give up," Kimes said. "I know when I've had enough."

This sounded good. But maybe too good. Ennis and Cravey could only see Kimes' left hand. Both pursuers ducked behind bushes. Then Ennis saw that Kimes' right hand was also up. Ennis kept his rifle aimed at Kimes while Cravey went up and took Kimes' Colt. Every chamber of the revolver had been reloaded.

Kimes and the Keadys were placed under arrest. Kimes was sentenced to prison by the state of Oklahoma. Kimes somehow escaped prison. On December 1, 1945, while still on the run from prison, Matthew Kimes was hit by a truck. He died later of his injuries.

A quarter century later, on January 22, 1977, one of the most heinous murders in Canyon history was committed. At midday a Park visitor found Dr. Michael A. Sherman and his wife Charlotte H. Sherman, both age 28, in the front seat of the car parked at Powell Memorial. Both had been shot in the head by a .22 caliber firearm less than an hour earlier. The apparent motive for the double homicide was minor robbery. The Shermans of Arlington, Virginia had been moving from the East to Norton Air Force Base in California with their possessions, which the killer left mostly intact. This senseless murder devastated the Shermans' parents and siblings for the rest of their lives. The murder weapon has not been found. This case is the only one known in a U.S. national park of a midday murder in a public attraction area. In 2011 the Shermans' murder remained an active cold case with a "very extensive file" and awaited results from a vastly improved forensic science. We have our fingers crossed on this one.

Fifteen years after the heinous murder of the Shermans, during the summer of 1992, hundreds of law enforcement personnel stormed Grand Canyon during the largest manhunt in the history of the state of Arizona. The fuse for this explosion of manpower at Grand Canyon was lit as an almost unrecognized fizzle on June 26.

The sun had just set. NPS Patrol Ranger Donny Miller (who told his story to Myers) sat in his patrol car and wondered why a frantic boy was running across the parking lot of Babbitt's General Store and waving to flag him down. Nothing all evening had seemed unusual. Until now. Well, no rest for the wicked.

Obviously panicked, the boy now had trouble getting his words out. Miller tried to be patient. He reassured the boy that he should calm down and just speak clearly. He had to understand him to be of any help.

The boy pointed across the parking lot and blurted, "You've got to stop him, he's taking my Dad! He's kidnapping my family!"

Shocked, Miller turned and saw that the boy was pointing to a car parked next to an R.V. with Texas plates fifty yards away. Several people stood nearby. It seemed as if they were merely talking. As Miller started to drive over to investigate, the boy yelled, "He's got a gun!"

As Miller approached the R.V. he possessed not the foggiest idea that here, in Babbitt's parking lot, he was about to play a long game of touch tag with public enemy number one. Miller was about to become Wile E. Coyote. The Roadrunner was waiting just a few yards away.

Six weeks earlier, on May 12, convicted Winslow bank robber and child molester Danny Ray Horning, age 35, had been about to stand trial—with his brother—for their parts in the mutilation-dismemberment murder of catfish farmer and alleged marijuana dealer Sam McCullough, age 40, near Stockton, California in 1990. But Horning had sneaked out of his cell in Florence State Prison in southern Arizona and into the infirmary. There he donned a white medical coat. He pinned onto it a forged photo identification card. Then he hefted a medical bag. Successfully posing as an orderly, Danny Ray Horning walked out of the prison unchallenged—leaving behind four consecutive life sentences unserved.

He fled Florence on foot into the desert.

To re-arm, he burglarized a nearby ranch, exiting it with a Ruger Blackhawk .44 magnum revolver. Then he returned to Florence. Two days later he hitched a ride to Tucson. There he planned, then carried out, an armed robbery of the Valley National Bank. Now well-funded as well as armed, Horning hitched a ride toward Flagstaff. The law enforcement bureaucracy had issued a BOLO (Be On the Look Out) bulletin for Horning. Despite the massive manhunt organized in southern and central Arizona (even the U.S. Border Patrol was on the lookout for him), for the next three weeks Horning not only remained at large, he left no trace of his whereabouts.

Finally, on June 3, a USFS Fire Prevention Officer recognized Horning near Blue Ridge Reservoir, 75 miles southeast of Flagstaff. Horning vanished before law officers arrived, beginning a trend that would embarrass Arizona law officers again and again in the next several weeks.

Two days later, Horning was spotted south of Mormon Lake. Arizona Department of Corrections set a dog team on his trail. Horning eluded them too and vanished again.

On June 10, Governor Fife Symington declared a state of emergency in Arizona to help release state funds for counties participating in the search for Horning.

Two days later Horning burglarized several homes and stole a 1980 Chevy 4-wheel drive pickup truck in Pine, Arizona, 90 miles southeast of Flagstaff. In some victims' homes Horning left notes of apology for his thefts. He also left a note for police telling them to send his backpack to his parents and to stop following him!

Victim Richard Lynd (away from home on vacation) lost from his Pine cabin his favorite pickup truck, a .22-caliber rifle and ammunition, a chainsaw, a 13-inch color television, food, sleeping bags, a tool box, dress clothes, and even Lynd's electric razor. "It's kind of weird," Lynd reported, "the stuff he took."

Lynd's son-in-law was first to the cabin. The break in was immaculately done with a neatly slitted window screen, "I'll say one thing for him," the son-in-law said, "he's probably about the neatest burglar I've ever seen." Then he added, even so, "We're down to our last truck. I hope he doesn't come back."

From Pine, Horning drove to Socorro, New Mexico. It seemed he would now flee the Southwest. What was Danny Ray Horning's ultimate goal? Was he planning to flee the U.S. and head to Mexico, Canada, or the Caribbean?

More than a month after his escape, on June 21, a citizen in Payson, Arizona, reported seeing Horning driving Lynd's stolen pickup. But before law officers arrived in Payson, Horning was already driving over Chavez Pass to Meteor Crater and onto Interstate 40.

In Flagstaff, a police officer spotted Horning on Lake Mary Road. The officer pursued him onto a remote USFS dirt road south of Mormon Mountain. Horning abandoned the stolen truck and fled on foot into the forest, successfully vanishing yet again.

Several days later, Horning made his way to Flagstaff. There he stalked the Little America Truck Stop in search of potential hostages. Not finding the "right" ones, he went deeper into town. A local police officer stared Horning in the face, scrutinizing him. Horning nonchalantly walked past him, then ducked into a nearby hotel.

Capitalizing on a Hollywood-style coincidence, Horning spotted a fire down the street and reported it to the desk clerk in the hope that the emergency call would divert that suspicious officer outside. Having successfully eluded the officer with this ruse, Horning waited outside the Circle Q western wear store on Route 66 to scout for victims.

He did not have to wait long. He soon kidnapped Adam Lakritz, age 43, and Kathryn Falk, age 39, both Flagstaff residents, as they tried to drive away from the Circle Q. Horning escaped with Lakritz driving his white Ford Taurus—with the gun barrel of that stolen .44 magnum prodding him in the ribs.

Now, on June 25, six weeks after his escape, he forced his two hostages to drive him on a circuitous 330-mile route to the South Rim of Grand Canyon. En route, in between bragging about the big .44 magnum in his belt and boasting about his "lifestyle" of crime, Horning told his hostages that he would kill any policeman who tried to pull them over. He also informed them that his goal was to kidnap an affluent family with a motor home and to hold them hostage.

Even more amazingly, after driving 150 miles to Kingman, then backtracking 180 miles to Grand Canyon through Williams (where the hostages withdrew $1,500 from their bank account for him), all without arousing suspicion, Horning and both hostages spent the night unchallenged at El Tovar Hotel! Here at the South Rim Village was where Horning planned to hijack that expensive motor home and kidnap its affluent owners for that fat ransom.

Being organized, he had prepared in advance a wordy, detailed and bombastic tape recording of his ransom demands. His tape revealed, among other things about Horning's character, that he intended to kidnap and hold six hostages for a $1 million ransom plus his freedom and that of his older brother (Jerry Dewayne Horning, serving time in Florence for sexual misconduct with a minor and also awaiting that trial for murder). On June 26, Horning pulled into the parking lot at Babbitt's General Store....

As Ranger Donny Miller slowly drove his cruiser toward the Texas R.V., he expected a domestic violence situation. He radioed his imminent investigation of the "panicked" boy's report of a felonious man with a gun. Miller had never received the APB about Horning, but he did know of the situation. He had even cut Horning's photo from the local newspaper and was keeping it in his back pocket. Still, not in his wildest dreams had he imagined what was about to happen next.

Near the R.V. Miller saw three people standing close together. He guessed they were the boy's family. Next to a nearby car stood a man wearing a baseball cap pulled low over his strawberry blond (no longer dark brown) hair. The uplifted collar of his windbreaker concealed his face, now clean-shaven. This man stared at Miller, but he neither moved nor showed any expression. A man and a woman in their mid-thirties (Adam Lakritz and Falk kidnapped in Flagstaff) sat rigid and staring straight ahead in the back seat of the man's car.

Miller stopped his NPS cruiser by the car.

About a mile away, off-duty NPS Rangers John Piastuck, Keith Lober, and Chris Fors were enjoying a party for a co-worker at a friend's house when they heard Miller's call about a man with a gun at Babbitt's. Piastuck and Fors ran to Piastuck's car and jumped in. Lober ran to his vehicle. Both cars accelerated toward Babbitt's.

Miller stepped halfway out of his patrol car and told the man with the baseball cap to step to Miller's side of the vehicle. At the same time Miller tried to ready his shotgun. Horning raised his right hand over the roof of the car and aimed the .44 Ruger at Miller.

Miller ducked back into his car and tried to shift it into reverse. But the boy had just run up behind him. So, instead, Miller chambered a shell in his shotgun and radioed that the man did have a gun. Next Miller asked for backup. He drew his own handgun but did not fire it because the parking lot was crawling with people.

A bullet from Horning's .44 would have penetrated Miller's cruiser like a hot knife through butter. But Horning, too, did not fire.

Escape, not a gun duel, was his priority. Horning jumped back into the car containing his two hostages and accelerated it across the parking lot. He raced past Yavapai Lodge and drove into the parking lot by the Shrine of the Ages and the Visitor Center. Miller pursued at high speed. This parking lot too was crowded. An evening ranger interpretive program had just ended. Horning streaked between tourists ambling back to their cars. Abruptly he must have thought that the parking lot looked too much like a cul de sac. Horning tried to turn back on the main road. His right front tire dropped into a ditch. The hubcap flew off and rolled onward in an escape of its own.

Rangers Piastuck and Fors raced past all this on the main road. Horning saw them. He fired one shot at their vehicle. It missed. Lober, right behind Piastuck and Fors, saw Horning's gun arm and the muzzle blast. He swerved his vehicle toward Horning's to block his exit onto the main road.

Horning swerved around Lober and accelerated down the main road toward El Tovar Hotel. Miller spun around in pursuit.

Horning blurred past El Tovar and the Bright Angel Lodge on Village Loop at seventy miles per hour. Normally thirty is pushing it. Seconds later Horning missed the hairpin turn. He lost control and crashed into the West Rim Drive traffic gate. The driver's window exploded. Shattered glass flew everywhere, striking tourists lined up at the gate. The car skidded to a stop.

About fifteen yards behind it, Miller too screeched to a halt. Miller stepped out with his shotgun and yelled at Horning to step out of his car. Bystanders stared open-mouthed.

Horning slammed his gearshift to reverse, jockeyed the car, and maneuvered through the barricade. Then he accelerated up the hill past Bright Angel Trailhead on West Rim Drive. He aimed his Ruger out his shattered window and fired two rounds back at Miller. Tourists hit the dirt en masse.

Miller tore after him through the broken barricade.

Horning spun around and, just as his woman hostage ducked, fired two more rounds out the back window at Miller, blowing the glass into flying shards. Miller saw the muzzle flash and for an instant thought that it was the dome light and that one of the hostages was trying to escape out the back door. Miller backed off so as not to run over this escaping hostage.

No one jumped out. But next, as Miller passed Hopi Point and then rounded a blind corner in delayed pursuit, he saw Horning standing on the road about 45 yards away, outside the car stopped in the middle of the road. As Horning frantically yanked at a backpack to get it out of the car, Miller slammed on his brakes and skidded sideways to a stop.

Miller and Horning stared at one another for a split second. Then Horning raised his gun and fired at Miller.

Miller ducked down in his car and grabbed his shotgun. As he emerged with it,

Horning's shadowy figure vanished into the woods.

Rangers Piastuck, Fors, and Lober caught up. They exited their vehicles, took cover, and surrounded Horning's car with the two Flagstaff hostages still in it. To no avail. Horning had apparently crawled back around them to the rim and then followed the Rim Trail eastward, either back toward the Village or into the Canyon itself via the Bright Angel Trail. NPS personnel and other law enforcement officers suspected that Danny Ray Horning had indeed dropped into the Canyon, possibly in search of more hostages.

The day after Horning vanished into the dark, June 27, Grand Canyon National Park set up a dozen roadblocks manned by law enforcement officers. Over the next several days, hundreds of law enforcement personnel—NPS rangers, State Police, Sheriff's Deputies, and FBI—swarmed into and over the Park in an intensifying manhunt for Danny Ray Horning.

This same day hikers told police they saw a man who matched Horning's description in the newspaper walking down the Bright Angel Trail into the Canyon.

At this same time one of us (Ghiglieri) was running a commercial rowing trip. We had just camped at Cremation Creek (River Mile 87) preparatory to sending most of our clients up and out of the Canyon the next morning via the Bright Angel Trail beginning at River Mile 89. NPS rangers at Phantom gave us (Michael Fabry, Rob Pitagora, Liz Hymens, Chris Dippold, and me) the lowdown. This lowdown was a big question mark surrounded by a lot of embroidery consisting of the many possible tactics that Danny Ray Horning might or might not be about to adopt in his next hostage-taking location. Roads and trails, including the Bright Angel, were being patrolled. But people could still leave.

If they could avoid Horning.

We in the OARS' crew argued over what to tell our people who were hiking on their own up the Bright Angel Trail. Was ignorance bliss? Or was it better to inform our people to stay in one group for security? Luckily, two of our trainees running the baggage boat on this trip were Flagstaff Police sergeants Ray Martinez and Chuck Martin. Their advice was prudence is better than bliss.

Our passengers hiked out as planned. Luckily their experience added nothing new to the Horning saga.

But he was still out there somewhere, either in the Canyon with us or on the rim. Again, roadblocks blocked every road. Search dogs and SWAT teams roamed the Village and the pine woods around it. Residents had been warned to lock their doors and windows and to stay inside. This included a nervous Myers with his young family. Becky Myers decided they finally had to begin locking their doors. Becky borrowed a proffered pistol from a neighbor. The cops prowling everywhere proved unnerving. This was not the Grand Canyon I (Myers) thought I knew. Many of us kept loaded weapons at hand. Trails into the Canyon were closed to entry while armed searchers scoured below the rim.

Three days after Horning's wild escape from Ranger Miller, Horning reappeared on the South Rim and struck again. Two tourists from Oregon, Jana Cerny, age 21, and Zdenek Kel, age 29, had pulled their overheated station wagon into the Grandview parking lot at about 7:00 p.m. As Cerny peered under the hood of her 1978 Chevy Caprice, Horning approached her unseen and said, "Get into the car. You have to help me."

Kel told Horning, "The car is broken; it won't run."

"I'll fix it for you," Horning said as he pulled "his" Ruger .44 magnum out from behind his back.

"I'm not going anywhere with you," Kel said. "If you want to shoot me, shoot me right now."

Horning hesitated. Kel yelled at Cerny, "Run!" Then he started to run himself.

Horning pointed his gun at Kel. Kel froze in his tracks. Then Horning aimed it at Cerny. She also stopped. "I thought he would shoot me," she said "But he didn't. Then I started to run."

Then Kel ran as well. Both ran down the road.

Horning jumped in the station wagon and drove it after them, chasing them down the road. He pulled up even with Cerny and looked her in the eyes. Horning commanded her, "Get in the car."

"I was really scared," Cerny admitted. She slowed her running speed and glanced behind her. She saw Horning looking in the rearview mirror. Maybe he was spooked by another car, she surmised. "He stepped on the accelerator and took off as fast as he could."

As he accelerated away, Kel and Cerny hid in the woods. They emerged later to flag down a Ford Bronco driving by.

The next day Park rangers found the couple's car smashed into a tree. Cerny was upset, mostly about not being warned: "When we entered the park, nobody told us to watch out for a fugitive."

Horning continued to elude everyone. Having learned evasion lessons during his eleven-month stint in U.S. Army reconnaissance in the late 1970s, he now used every trick he could remember. He walked in circles to confuse the hounds tracking him. He traveled during the day when he could be careful enough in choosing his path as to leave no tracks. Even so, to escape the Coconino Plateau, Horning needed a vehicle—he also wanted those affluent hostages as his ticket to paradise.

Despite these hundreds of law officers from ten law enforcement agencies and their helicopters, hounds, and high-tech impedimenta, Horning continued to elude capture. Now, in fact, he could watch his 385 pursuers, the platoons of Coyotes, and listen to the statements they made on TV—at least he would have been able to were he still dragging around that 13-inch TV he had stolen in Pine.

Even more weird, due to his outrageous Roadrunner-like success in escaping these government Coyotes, Horning was becoming a sort of folk hero, a real-life

Rambo. A survivalist who could—and did—survive for yet another week despite seemingly impossible odds. The land and the elements were his allies. His outwitting hundreds of cops eager to nail him seemed miraculously easy.

On July 4, Horning struck yet again twenty-five miles east of the Village at Desert View. Unnoticed amidst a small crowd of visitors at Desert View Lookout, Horning squatted down between cars. There he pulled his gun on and abducted two British medical students. He forced Sally Edwards and Caroline Young, both age 27, to sit up front in their rented Nissan Sentra and chauffeur him. Horning "back-seat" drove them toward the Village, then south on U.S. 64. Horning chose the Fourth of July, he explained to his captives to stun them with his intellect, precisely because it was the busiest time he could imagine for Park rangers to deal with.

Horning faced three roadblocks. The first one, the terrified hostages later said, was easy for him. But at the second roadblock south of the Park in Valle (a.k.a. Flintstone Village), an Arizona Department of Public Safety Officer asked Horning to step out of the car.

Danny Ray Horning stepped out.

"Please remove your straw hat."

Horning did so. And while the officer compared a photo of Horning to the real thing, his two hostages in the front seat sat in rigid terror. They were not only so paralyzed with fear that they could not bring themselves to tip off any of the officers manning the roadblock, they were so scared that they would not even talk to each other.

"Please open your trunk," the officer asked.

Horning popped it open. The trunk's interior did not look suspicious. "Is there anything wrong, officer?" Horning asked innocently.

The officer shook his head and thanked Horning then let him and his hostages drive onward. Horning, it seems, by having changed his clothes, shaved, and bleached his hair, no longer resembled Horning.

Ten miles north of Williams, near Red Lake, Horning pulled off Highway 64. About ten minutes from the road he tied both of his hostages to a tree.

"Please don't shoot us," the women begged.

Horning told Edwards and Young that he did not want to hurt them but that he did need at least 30 minutes to get away. Horning left both women tied to that tree—with their luggage and so on piled nearby. He next drove south to I-40 then headed east toward Flagstaff and Walnut Canyon National Monument. He still hoped to steal an R.V. and to kidnap some newer and richer hostages.

While passing through Flagstaff, he was spotted by a state patrolman who gave chase. This patrolman lost Horning, but another officer, an explosives technician, picked him up.

Horning fired at the officer. One bullet penetrated the officer's trunk and a bag full of detonation equipment. Luckily, none of it exploded.

Horning lost control during his high-speed escape and crashed at high speed onto rocks south of Flagstaff after using the Rocky Park exit off I-17. Again like the Roadrunner, he ran into the woods. And despite his carrying a large case, he vanished yet again.

The next day, July 5, a woman residing in the Village of Oak Creek (south of Sedona) spotted Horning as he borrowed a garden hose to guzzle water. The woman grabbed her gun then her phone. She dialed 9-1-1 for the Yavapai County Sheriff's Department.

Yavapai Deputies and Border Patrol officers using a bloodhound zeroed in on a deck perched on a nearby hill. They stealthily advanced on it.

Curled up in exhaustion under the deck, stolen .44 magnum in hand, lay Danny Ray Horning, the Roadrunner, asleep.

A Border Patrol Agent pointed a gun at Horning's head and said, "If you move, you're dead."

"It was a really fun chase," Horning told officers. "I really enjoyed it....I wish I could do this every week."

Danny Ray Horning found himself back in Florence. This time there would be no visit to the dispensary. The woman with a gun near Sedona who'd had her eye on her garden hose had just ended, after 54 days, the largest single manhunt in the history of Arizona. This massive and protracted manhunt sought a blue-collar felon whose admitted goal was simply to extort a few innocent but rich people at gunpoint, and, by threatening to murder them, gain the leverage to free his brother from prison and to steal the money he needed to live the good life. After his capture, Radio Station KFYI interviewed Horning, who spelled out his simple plan:

> *After I would have gotten a million dollars and my brother, I would have gone out of the country, most likely to Mexico, and I'd have hired about ten different families, men, wives, and kids. I would have set them up for life and lived in a nice little ranch and whenever I would have wanted something I would have given them the money and they could go get it for me.*

In yet another interview, with KTAR Radio, Horning admitted to robbing the bank in Tucson and to kidnapping all of his hostages, but he denied murdering Sam McCullough.

Two years later, however, Horning failed to convince a California jury of this. In 1994, Danny Ray Horning stood trial in San Joaquin County Superior Court for shooting Sam McCullough in the head in 1990. McCullough had apparently caught Horning burglarizing his home. Allegedly, Horning (being a "neat" burglar) methodically sawed off McCullough's head and limbs and stuffed them all into plastic bags, which he later dumped into a gully called Burns Cut.

Indeed, before his incarceration in, and escape from, Arizona State Prison in

Florence, Horning had been captured in Winslow, Arizona on March 22, 1991 after he robbed a bank there using a gun he had stolen from his victim, McCullough.

After hearing all testimony, including pretty solid evidence, on July 15, the jury convicted Danny Ray Horning of first-degree murder. Judge William R. Giffen was so impressed with the "dastardly" cold-blooded execution style of the murder that he sentenced Danny Ray Horning to the death penalty.

"It's been four years of hell," admitted McCullough's wife, Carol, and the mother of his two sons. "The only peace that I find is that Danny Ray Horning can't do this to someone else."

Smirking, Horning walked out of the courtroom saying, "*Que sera*'" (What will be...).

A month later, while waiting on San Quentin Prison's lengthy death row in a segregated cell where "he's not allowed to be around anybody," Danny Ray Horning was stabbed three times by an unknown assailant. He survived but was in critical condition. Horning's brother, Mark Anthony Horning, also said, "He wasn't there long enough to make enemies. He wasn't there long enough to get into any trouble. I think it was a contract hit."

If so, someone had to return their fee. Years later Danny Ray Horning still sat on death row. And, as many hundreds of other murderers sentenced to death in California are doing, Horning too awaited developments on his lengthy appeal process. As of mid-2011, he was still waiting.

Brain cancer and lung cancer. Sometimes nature is too cruel, reflected Robert Merlin Spangler, age 67, as he lay in his bed during early fall of 2000 in the Grand Junction home of himself and his fourth wife, Judith. Learning that your cancer has metastasized and that you have only months to live is shocking, to put it mildly.

A lot of things were about to end. One of them, his sojourns into Grand Canyon. Among other things, Spangler seemed something of a Canyon addict. His second wife, Sharon Spangler, had ignited his passion for the vast majesty of Grand Canyon. She was so entranced with the Canyon that she wrote the popular 1986 book *On Foot in the Grand Canyon: Hiking the Trails of the South Rim.* In this book, Sharon acknowledged: "My husband, Bob Spangler, took photographs, helped me to remember things, encouraged me through the rough times, and, being an accomplished writer, offered suggestions to make the text read better."

Cancer or not, you could not buy memories and accomplishments like these.

Robert Spangler had met Sharon (then Sharon Arst Cooper) in 1976 when she applied for a job with the company he worked for. He had been impressed by her. At the time, however, Spangler was married to someone else. This did not prove to be a roadblock for Spangler. He started an affair with her in 1976, while still being married to Nancy Spangler (maiden name Stahlman) since 1955, for more than twenty years. Robert and Nancy had moved from Iowa to Arapaho County,

Colorado, where, by 1976, Spangler had landed a good job as a public relations manager for American Waterworks. Robert's and Nancy's two children, David and Susan, were now 15 and 13 years old.

Two years later, however, a horrifying disaster shattered Robert Spangler's picture perfect suburban life. On December 30, a neighbor and friend of young Susan Spangler stumbled upon a grisly tableau writ in incomprehensible gore in the Spanglers' Colorado home. Spangler's son David, now age 17, lay dead in his bed with a .38 caliber bullet in his chest. Susan, only 15, lay slain in her bed with a bullet wound to her back. Downstairs, sprawled their mother, Nancy, age 45, shot in the head with the same revolver. Close at hand investigators found a typed suicide note signed with Nancy's initials.

Despite a lack of gunshot residue on Nancy hands and the presence of it on Spangler's hand, investigators ultimately concluded that this tragedy had been a double homicide-suicide by the distraught mother.

Less than a year following this hideous tragedy, in 1979, Robert married Sharon. Although Sharon was not fond of children, she did love landscapes. Sharon had gone on two river trips in the 1970s and fallen in love with Grand Canyon—and now with Robert. She combined these two loves during their honeymoon wrap-up by beginning an avocation of hiking off the South Rim. She tackled the Hermit Trail with her new husband, who, as she confessed admiringly, was "a natural athlete" on a trail that left her stumbling. In the 1970s era of free-love-and-love-nature-too, Bob and Sharon Spangler's hand-in-hand sojourns into the Seventh Natural Wonder of the World seemed to prove that love indeed conquers all.

For years, at odd intervals and locations of Sharon's choosing, the two hikers became an ever more entrenched part of the Canyon landscape. We can imagine it: Robert, trim and bald-headed and with a thick white beard, striding along confidently, and Sharon, with her hiking diary, becoming ever more adept on the treacherous terrain.

Surprisingly, however, in 1988, Sharon and Robert Spangler divorced after a bitterly fought contest over their financial assets. Sharon had been on medication for years to control severe anxiety attacks, suicidally inclined, that had manifested themselves during her relationship with Spangler.

A year later, in 1989, Donna Sundling, a mother of five grown children and a well-liked bookkeeper for Warrior Oil Company, decided to shoot for greater happiness by taking a risk. She answered a personals ad. The ad had been placed by Robert Merlin Spangler. Almost immediately, Spangler swept Donna off her feet.

On August 18, 1990, Robert Spangler married yet again, this third time to Donna Sundling. They moved to Durango where Spangler became a country music disc jockey for KRSJ-FM and developed a following. Spangler was a paragon, it seems: trim, healthy, cheerful, and a giver. He officiated at soccer and basketball games. Spangler, however, had quit visiting Grand Canyon during his first two years with Donna. Then, abruptly, his passion for Grand Canyon fired originally by his now ex-wife, Sharon, resurged even as his relationship with Donna seriously deteriorated due to a lack of mutual interests.

One fly in this ointment, however, was that Donna was afraid of heights. Robert chipped away at Donna's fear by convincing her that the Canyon was truly so important to him that he could not bear her not sharing it with him.

On Easter Sunday, April 11, 1993 Donna and Robert Spangler finally hiked the Grandview Trail and beyond. The views were stupendous. But, suddenly, disaster struck. Spangler explained later to NPS rangers that while he had his back turned to adjust his tripod for a photo of Donna standing on the rim of a Redwall cliff along the Page Springs Trail, she somehow had fallen off. Maybe, he speculated, a freak gust of wind had stolen her balance. He had heard nothing, he added, possibly because his hearing aid had been turned off. As Robert Spangler explained during an interview:

We were only maybe a hundred yards up that trail [Page Springs] when, on one of these switchbacks, came this beautiful sunrise morning—Easter sunrise, as a matter of fact. We decided to stop and take one last picture back down the Canyon and at the area that we had been....I turned around and she was gone. She wasn't there. And I can only surmise that she, you know, adjusted her pack, or got it out of balance, or she moved slightly and stepped on a rock that rolled under her feet, something. At any rate, she just went over the edge, and about 200 feet down....The Canyon didn't take her life. God didn't take her life; it just happened. Those things occur. When you are in a place that does have precipitous terrain, the possibility is always there.

Despite Spangler's reasonable explanation, some of Donna Sundling's friends kept the case of Robert Merlin Spangler and his vanishing wives on a back burner. Although no actual evidence implicated Spangler, to Donna's friends the history of violent death among those closest to him reeked.

Next, despite Sharon's divorce from Spangler, after Donna's tragic accident in Grand Canyon, Sharon moved back into his attractive Durango home, reportedly in a now platonic relationship. Disaster soon struck again. In October of 1994, Sharon Spangler, age 52, also died tragically of an overdose of anti-depression meds combined with alcohol. Although initially suspicious of foul play, investigators concluded that, based on "strong evidence," Robert Spangler had "nothing" to do with Sharon's death. On the other hand, she died in his presence in the hospital, alone with him. Immediately afterward Spangler gained $20,000 from the event of her death. Beyond this largess, he no longer was required to pay her $500 per month alimony.

Perhaps this helps explain the apparent situation in which Spangler later thought of his Grand Canyon Sharon in the most positive of lights. Consider Spangler's March, 1998, tribute to Sharon reveals almost nothing but respect for her:

> *But I think the main reason she was here was to discover the remarkable nature of the Grand Canyon and to translate her experiences in such an interesting, informative and persuasive manner that thousands of others, with similar surprise, would find themselves drawn there, too.*
>
> *The book was her crowning achievement and I am so proud of her, so glad to have participated in its creation. Sharon had in mind to do a second book, one that would dig into the delights of hiking on the North Rim. But it never came to pass. She was the victim of an insidious disease that didn't show much, but was consuming her through the years. We were together in Durango, Colorado, when she died October 2, 1994.*
>
> *I have continued to hike the Canyon, delighting especially in communicating with other aficionados and helping newcomers get started. I love guiding first-timers and experiencing their thrills and joy as Sharon and I first experienced it all those years ago.*
>
> *I miss her very much, but like so many of you, I have her book to remind me not only of her, but how much she helped popularize this place we love so much. What a wonderful, talented, creative woman was Sharon Spangler, one of the Grand Canyon's most eloquent friends.*

In 1994, Arapaho County Sheriff's investigator Paul Goodman heard about Donna Spangler's 1993 fatal fall in the Canyon and felt queasy about it. To Goodman, as to others, something just did not add up. But, if a crime had been committed, it had apparently been a perfect one. Goodman could not put his finger on any piece of evidence that implicated Robert Spangler. Only...Only the reports of the rangers who had interviewed Spangler after Donna had fallen to her death continued to haunt him. Spangler had, they agreed, seemed less distraught than what one might expect for a man losing his wife in such a hideous way. On the other hand, Spangler seemed to some rangers an honest man who seemed to tell his story of loss forthrightly.

Even so, another NPS ranger working at Grand Canyon, Beverly Perry, also felt queasy about writing off Donna Spangler's death to accidental causes. Something was wrong here. Perry felt certain. Only how would she ever get proof?

Goodman next heard about Sharon Spangler's suspicious death by overdose.

Goodman recalled too the grisly 1978 case in which Robert Spangler's two teenaged children were brutally murdered and his wife allegedly committed suicide. This horror had occurred during Goodman's rookie year with the Sheriff's Department.

Goodman saw so much smoke in all this that his mind refused to believe the nonexistence of a fire. But, again, no real evidence existed to reveal that fire.

In August of 1998, Spangler renewed an acquaintance with Judith Hilty in Grand Junction, Colorado. They wed, Spangler's fourth trip to the altar, two years later, at nearly the same time that the news and symptoms of his cancer metastasizing surfaced. Judith didn't care that their months together might be few, she cared only that they be together. But the invading growth inside Spangler changed almost everything in his view of life.

Almost everything.

With the Grim Reaper now breathing down Spangler's neck, he began telling his friends and neighbors that he had only months to live. As they brought him cakes and pies in sympathy, he told his friends bravely that he expected that death "will treat me about as quickly and gently as one could hope."

By 1998, under a push by Assistant U.S. Attorney Camille Bibles, an Arizonan who also had long suspected that Donna Spangler's demise had resulted from murder, an inter-departmental team was assembled to monitor Spangler. This team included National Park Service Criminal Investigations Special Agent Beverly Perry, Flagstaff FBI Agent Leonard Johns, and Arapaho County's Officer Paul Goodman. The team had full FBI resources at its disposal. When routine FBI monitoring of Spangler caught his medical tests indicating cancer, the team knew they had to act immediately.

"We just knocked on his door," Goodman explained. "He didn't seem surprised…"

Under two days of very sophisticated interviewing of Robert Merlin Spangler masterminded by Agent Johns, Spangler soon matter-of-factly confessed to an astonishing list of heinous misdeeds—then he signed his confession.

"It was his [Spangler's] opinion," reported Arapaho County Undersheriff Grayson Robinson, that "he was a model citizen and a good human being except during two days of his life when he did something terrible."

When Spangler entered court in Grand Junction at the end of September, 2000, he walked in jauntily and winked at his new wife Judith, who, at this point, still refused to believe his confession was real. On October 7, 2000 the FBI transferred Spangler to a federal holding facility in Florence, Arizona, to stand trial for the first degree murder of Donna Spangler committed in Grand Canyon.

An additional window into Spangler's narcissistic mind exists in his letter to the FBI asking to keep his confession quiet so as not to sully his reputation.

What about those "two days of his life when he did something terrible?"

One of them happened in 1978, long after Spangler had decided that his suburban life with Nancy and their two children was no longer the life he wanted now that he had met and formed a relationship with Sharon, his co-worker at American Waterworks. Spangler had moved out of his family's house earlier in 1978 then had moved back in during October. This move back to Nancy was anything but promising. Instead, it was simply a tactic Spangler was using to engineer his permanent exit from his family.

On the pretext, he admitted, of saying that he wanted to write a Christmas note, he convinced his now estranged wife Nancy to initial a blank piece of paper. Then he typed her bogus suicide note on it. Later he told Nancy that he had a surprise for her downstairs in the basement, but that she first had to sit in a chair and cover her eyes. Once she complied with his conditions, he shot her in the forehead with his .38 handgun. Then he left the note nearby.

He next gunned down his 15-year-old daughter Susan by shooting her in the back as she slept in bed, killing her instantly. Finally he entered his 17-year-old son's, David's, room and shot him in the chest as he tried to rise, alarmed at having heard the shot that had killed his sister. Spangler's quick shot failed to kill his son. The wounded boy turned to stare in shock at his father. Robert Spangler now rushed forward and smothered the critically wounded teenager with a pillow until he too was dead.

Then he left his house and drove to a Burger King for a hamburger then visited a movie theater on University Avenue to watch the animated version of *Lord of the Rings*.

Later that morning, at 10:30, Susan's boyfriend Timothy Trevithick tried to visit her but found no one responding to his knock on the front door. He circled the house but found all the doors locked. Puzzled, he climbed inside via the basement window. Not seeing Nancy, he ascended the stairs to Susan's bedroom and found her not asleep, as he expected, but murdered. Shaken, he phoned the police.

When Robert Merlin Spangler returned to his family's house later that day the place was crawling with the Arapahoe County Sheriff's officers and crime scene personnel. An officer took Spangler in for questioning. As mentioned earlier, the sheriff's department fell for the bogus suicide note and also fell for the psychopath's glib alibi despite the presence of gunshot residue on his hand. Being a well-practiced pathological liar paid off yet again for Spangler.

As the years afterward had passed, Sharon Spangler, whose relationship with Robert Spangler had begun two years prior to the murders of his first family, had begun to suspect that her new husband had played a role in them. Then, at some point, according to at least one of Sharon's close friends at Grand Canyon, she knew. Indeed, during late 1987 Sharon placed a 911 call to the police to tell them she was afraid of Robert Merlin Spangler. She next fled to a local grocery store to hide from him. Less than six months later the couple filed for a divorce in which Spangler was required to pay Sharon $500 per month alimony and $150,000 in cash. Meanwhile Sharon's hideous knowledge likely metamorphosed into, as Robert Spangler himself put it, that "insidious disease that was consuming her through the years."

As time passed, that event on Robert Spangler's other day of doing "something terrible"—Easter Sunday of 1993, when that "gust of wind" on the Page Spring

Trail below the Grandview Trail "maybe" pushed Donna Spangler to her death, likely also nudged Sharon Spangler over her own edge. With Robert Spangler still in the house and with her, Spangler's ghastly misdeeds likely nudged Sharon so hard that she swallowed a fatal overdose of alcohol and drugs.

What about that gust of wind in Grand Canyon that blew Donna Spangler, who was deathly afraid of heights, from atop a cliff to plunge almost two-hundred feet to her death?

Robert Merlin Spangler confessed to Agent Johns and Deputy Goodman and Special Investigator Perry a new and different explanation. It was not wind after all. It was instead Spangler again adjusting his life circumstances ("as quickly and gently as one could hope") with a big shove over the edge. He and Donna's relationship had stopped being rewarding to him many months earlier. So in Grand Canyon Spangler saw the opportunity for yet another perfect crime—and the perfect solution to his lack of contentment.

He waited until he and Donna had reached the upper section of the Page Springs Trail in the Redwall Limestone where it offers a guaranteed lethal exposure. He knew from his hikes with his second wife Sharon that no perfect vertical exposures remained above this trail. It was here that it had to happen, or not at all.

Upon reaching this perfect spot, Robert Merlin Spangler walked up to his wife Donna and, facing her face to face, simply shoved her off the cliff to plummet 160 feet to her death. What terrified and dismal thoughts passed through Donna's shocked mind during her long plunge toward the jagged rock below no one will ever know.

Afterwards Spangler hiked out. Then he stood in the back of the line at the NPS Backcountry Office to patiently wait his turn. When it finally came, he told the ranger that his wife had accidentally fallen to her death off the Page Springs Trail.

"It was easier," Spangler later explained his murderous decision to Johns in the summer of 2000, "than getting a divorce."

Indeed Spangler later returned on a hike to the exact scene of his crime where Donna had smacked at high speed onto jagged bedrock and been smashed to a pulp. He built a small cairn or "shrine" there housing a Ziplok baggie containing some sort of personal note. What thoughts passed through his demented mind at this time likely would best be not known.

On December 27, 2000, Robert Merlin Spangler entered a plea of guilty to the premeditated murder of Donna Sundling Spangler. Ever the narcissist, he requested of the presiding federal judge that his ashes be scattered in Grand Canyon after his death to cancer. The judge turned to Spangler and read him the riot act, saying that Spangler was one of the most heinous, depraved, despicable and undeserving slime on the planet. The judge added that he would do all in his power to *prevent* Spangler's ashes from being scattered in Grand Canyon.

Spangler reportedly shrank silently into his seat in the courtroom.

After Spangler's conviction, yet more of his dark and nasty secrets emerged into the light. In 1944, for example, at age 11, Robert Merlin Spangler was strongly suspected of having murdered a classmate who had offended him. The murdered boy was found under suspicious circumstances drowned in a quarry pool.

It gets worse. Much later in life, in 1986 when Spangler was 53 years old, he visited the 92-year-old man, Merlin Spangler, who had become his father by adopting Spangler as an infant. Within 2 days after Robert's arrival in Ames, Iowa, Merlin, who had been in good health, suffered a severe fall. When the elder Merlin died two weeks later from his injuries sustained during that fall, Robert Merlin Spangler inherited enough money from his adopted father's estate to retire.

On August 5, 2001, Spangler died of cancer in prison. Did it "treat" him "quickly and gently?" At times, as we have seen, Mother Nature can seem cruel and uncompromising. Yet at other times, even at her worst, she may seem not half cruel enough. As it turned out, Spangler would die slowly in Federal Corrections Medical Center in Springfield, Missouri.

While murders within Grand Canyon have happened at a rate just above not-at-all, sadly, a few innocents *have* met an untimely death within this, the most spectacular of the World's Seven Natural Wonders. Tomomi Hanamure decided to celebrate her 34th birthday in the same way she had been doing for years—by flying from Japan and hiking into Grand Canyon. After doing a lot of research, Hanamure decided the best way this time to do this would be to trek down to Supai Village then hike down Havasu Creek—instead of again hiking the Bright Angel Trail to Phantom Ranch. Hanamure flew from her home in Kanagawa, Japan then started her hike on May 8, 2006 from Hualapai Hilltop.

Hualapai Canyon proved enchanting, just what she had imagined. After checking into the Supai Lodge that same afternoon, she felt impatient to see more of the Canyon. So, during late afternoon she left the Lodge with the intent of walking the trail two miles or so to Havasu Falls.

Somewhere during this two-mile walk that has been made uneventfully by hundreds of thousands of hikers over the years, Hanamure vanished.

A maid discovered Hanamure's personal gear and un-used bed in the morning. She alerted the management, who alerted the Bureau of Indian Affairs police then the Coconino County Sheriff's Department Search and Rescue Team. Within a day, more than forty searchers from multiple agencies were combing the region of Havasu Creek downstream from Supai. Days passed, however, and no sign of Hanamure surfaced. This was proving to be a rough search demanding major bushwhacking. Literally no one interviewed admitted having seen Hanamure.

Finally, on May 13, one young Havasupai man, Randy Redtail Wescogame, told the official searchers near Navajo Falls he thought he had found the body.

After the Marathon of searching thus far, Wescogame's announcement seemed too good to be true—except for the "body" portion of the message. The searchers followed Wescogame through thick streamside greenery to a recondite pool below a place called Fifty-Foot Falls about 1 mile north of the village. Yes, there was something floating there just under the blue-green water that looked like a body.

An FBI team retrieved everything in the pool, including Hanamure and her backpack. Hanamure's pants had been yanked back on haphazardly and remained unfastened. The rest of her looked like a prop for a slasher movie.

Identifying Hanamure proved relatively easy. She sported a small tattoo on her left foot of the Japanese symbol for "flower." She had told friends this tattoo would identify her if anything happened. Sadly, something did.

The autopsy proved a nightmare even for a medical examiner used to seeing the results of violent death. Hamamure had been stabbed 29 times, 20 of them to her head and neck. Her hands bore defensive slash wounds gained by trying to ward off a 3-inch knife blade used in a frenzy of stabbing to murder her. Several of her wounds could have killed her. But the one that severed her left carotid artery was enough. The wounds Hanamure sustained revealed that the 5-foot, 140-pound Japanese woman had put up a determined fight, moving, dodging, and blocking her much larger attacker...but in the end she had succumbed.

On May 11, the FBI offered a reward of $5,000 for information relating to the murder of Hanamure.

On December 5, a federal grand jury indicted Randy Redtail Wescogame for a five-count charge of murder. The indictments charged the 6-foot, 200-pound Wescogame with kidnapping, murder, and robbery of Hanamure's credit cards, cash, cell phone, camera, et cetera. Meanwhile the tribal government banned news media from the reservation for a 12-day period of mourning.

Even without Wescogame's surprising—and suspicious—location of Hanamure's corpse, he would have been a prime suspect in her disappearance. His first documented act of violence was at age 8 in grammar school—reacting against other kids harassing him when his father, a tribal policeman, had been sent to prison for raping a female inmate. At age 10, Randy had beaten a girl younger than himself. At age 13 he was hooked on methamphetamine. For at least five years Wescogame had been in trouble for juvenile violence. He had spent 3 years in various facilities in the Arizona juvenile justice system, having been released from Arizona's Queen Creek facility on February 26, 2006, his 18th birthday.

Back in Supai on May 31, Wescogame again assaulted a fellow tribal member. Unfortunately the law enforcement "system" in Supai did not act to prosecute him, partly because the jail there had no staff (despite tribal tourism bringing in about $2.5 million per year).

Former BIA agency Superintendent Bob McNichols (retired in 2005) spent 28 years working with the Havasupai. In 2007, he said: "Every family on the reservation is affected by drugs and alcohol, and that leads to other abuse, sexual assault, and violence....Very little crime is ever reported. Victims don't report it because they know the perpetrator could be back in the house immediately. The [two] cops don't write up all the incidents because they know they will never be prosecuted." The situation is so bad that elders among the 650-person tribe who have asked in vain for several years for better law enforcement have decided they would like to build an apartment complex encircled by a gated security fence intended to keep out young Havasupai high on methamphetamine.

On September 18, 2007 Randy Redtail Wescogame pled guilty to the second degree murder of Tomomi Hanamure in a plea bargain that guaranteed him a life sentence without parole. He made this plea to avoid a federal trial for first-degree murder which would lead, if convicted, to the death penalty. Wescogame had lured Hanamure off the main trail into seclusion by offering to show her "secret" waterfalls that tourists never see. His intent was premeditated rape, murder, and robbery.

"Have you *ever* known anyone like me?" Maverick demanded pointedly.

I (Myers) thought about it for a second. No, I hadn't.

"Here, check my pulse," he added before I could answer, shoving his arm under my nose. His arm now blocked the book I was signing. "My blood pressure's perfect too, you know. I bet you don't have any patients like me. I have a doctor friend in Salt Lake City who says he wants to analyze my heart after I die to see why it was so exceptional. I only weigh 130 pounds. I don't have any fat. I'm in the best shape of my life. I just hiked across the Canyon again."

For the umpteenth time.

Indeed, Maverick was unlike anyone I had ever known. In several ways. I had known him as a patient since he had moved to Grand Canyon nearly a decade earlier. He had been in reasonable shape then. Now, however, he had attained phenomenal athletic condition. His 5-foot 6-inch frame stood svelte after shedding 40 pounds. More to the point, how many 80-year olds could hike across the Canyon rim to rim even once, let alone a record 106 times during one year? Twice a week for the entire year he had walked across the Canyon, south to north and back again. At 21 miles a pop, and with an average of 5,000 feet of elevation gain, Maverick had hiked nearly 2,300 miles and climbed an astonishing 1,130,000 feet in elevation. Almost unbelievable....

Even though I considered Maverick eccentric and self-absorbed, one of those *Well, enough about me. So, what do you think about me?* types, I usually sort of enjoyed his one-sided "conversations." During these I would listen to him praise himself and expound on his simple-minded Canyon exploits. I found his enthusiasm for hiking Grand Canyon inspiring but his affinity and bravado for repeated crossings seemed oddly amusing. It was like listening to someone brag about watching a 24-hour *Twilight Zone* Marathon but one that simply repeated the one and only episode that featured him.

Now, however, Maverick's self-congratulatory rambling was going over the top.

It was August 1, 2007 and I was in the midst of a book signing at the Grand Canyon Association's Canyon View bookstore. Sitting beside me was Elias Butler, my co-author for *Grand Obsession: Harvey Butchart and the Exploration of Grand Canyon*. A line had assembled in front of our table. Maverick had just appeared out of nowhere and wedged himself in front of a woman named Ellen whose copy I was signing.

"Yeah, you're pretty darn amazing, Maverick," I admitted without patronizing him. "One of a kind, that's for sure."

I shifted my attention briefly back to Ellen, patiently waiting to get her book signed since before Maverick had interrupted. Her look of irritation seemed to be growing more acute.

Before I could get a word in to thank her for buying our book, Maverick interrupted again, "So is this book about hiking?"

My pen stopped again and my focus shifted back to him. "Yeah, it's about Harvey Butchart and his hiking in the Canyon. Do you know about him?"

Harvey Butchart stood tall as Grand Canyon's foremost explorer on foot, having bushwhacked 12,000 miles below the rim over nearly half a century of nosing after new routes.

"No, not really," he harrumphed. "But I did find someone to write *my* biography after you said you couldn't. He's a guy who hiked with me. The book's going to be called '42 Miles with Maverick.' It'll be a great inspiration to a lot of people. I'm sure it will sell well, maybe even be a *New York Times* bestseller. But, of course, I don't want to make any money off it. Nope. Any profit would go into reprints of the book, and I'd especially like to use proceeds to fund a non-profit for underprivileged youth to learn about Grand Canyon so they can experience it. But some of the money might go toward making a movie about my life and Canyon hiking as well."

Ellen looked ready to bail on me.

"Oh, I'm sorry, Ellen," I said. "This is Maverick. He hikes the Grand Canyon a lot, crossing it more than any other person I know of. Maverick is a local legend."

Ellen eyed him curiously. Her annoyed look softened a bit as she studied Maverick, now looking smug.

"Heck, Maverick, maybe you should be signing this book instead of me," I joked.

Maverick glanced at me then reached for my pen.

"I'm just kidding, Maverick," I said, only a little surprised that he was actually going to do it. Now *he* wore Ellen's annoyed look. "Awww, Maverick, you'll be having one of these for yourself before you know it," I blurted, trying to avert any fallout from this emotionally fragile man. "And you'll get writer's cramp from all the signing. Well, I better get busy here. Nice talking with you, Maverick."

"Yeah, okay. Fine," he grunted before sauntering away.

Once he was out of earshot and our line had cleared, I leaned toward Eli and whispered, "Geez. I don't know how Shirley stands that guy. What an ego."

Seconds later I felt a tap on my shoulder. I turned to see Shirley Gaudreau, Maverick's wife, wearing a pained look.

"I'm sorry about Maverick," she offered. "I don't know why he does that."

Had she overheard me? Shirley knew better than anyone that the recurrent culprit for Maverick's increasingly unrestrained flamboyance was his ever-expanding ego. After all, she was married to the guy. Looking at her now I saw she felt even more embarrassed than I did. Her eyes now signaled her humility, a sharp yet sweet contrast to her husband's hubris. Her concern for the decorum of our book-signing session was genuine.

Not for the first time, I felt sorry for her.

"It's okay, Shirley. No worries. I know Maverick tends to get excited about this stuff."

"Well, thanks," she said. "And thanks for coming to sign. It's good to see you again."

"Ditto, Shirley. You take care."

"I absolutely refuse to act my age," was one of the mottos by which Maverick lived. He wore this same phrase emblazoned on his commemorative T-shirts once his Canyon hiking notoriety kicked in. He also started making yellow baseball caps advertising "I am Maverick." "Maverick," however, was his born-again identity. Originally he had been born Laurent Osias Gaudreau in Ludlow, Massachusetts on May 8, 1926 of French-Canadian ancestry. He reportedly had been stricken with polio before kindergarten, spending half a year confined to a bed before suddenly regaining his ability to walk. He later had joined the Air Force and served as an x-ray technician in the Pacific. He stayed in the Philippines for close to fifteen years with a local woman. Later yet he entered the teaching profession as an instructor for children with reading disabilities. He also became addicted to alcohol.

Unattached again, he moved to Denver where he taught. He also joined the military reserves. Eventually he recovered from alcoholism as a member of Alcoholics Anonymous. Later, while living in Moab, Utah and attending another A.A. meeting, Gaudreau adopted the handle "Maverick." He had hiked in Colorado and elsewhere in the West since the 1950s. He also had hiked the Canyon a few times over three decades, at the end of which he abruptly became infatuated with the place. Footloose and single, Maverick wrangled a job as a food server at the Maswik Cafeteria in 1998. For Laurent "Maverick" Gaudreau life was about to begin at 72.

Within a year he set for himself a personal challenge to hike the rigorous rim-to-rim—or "R2R" as it is known within Canyon hiking circles. Typically done on the Canyon's main hiking highway, the Kaibab Trail system, an R2R is a 21-mile hiking Marathon. This trek includes no bushwhacking or route finding or challenging terrain. It follows a well-maintained trail that resembles a wide, eroded sidewalk. Even so, hiking the Kaibab is not for the weak in spirit or body. Maverick not only completed his first R2R, he did it in 19 hours, unusual for age 73. Maverick's co-workers and friends acted stunned. Spurred by this, Maverick tackled more R2Rs, finishing each hike faster than the last.

Word of his ever faster hikes rippled across the Grand Canyon hiking community—with Maverick himself acting as his own primary and indefatigable public relations man. He thrived on peoples' astonishment. With each additional R2R he completed, he and his public seemed to grow more inspired. Maverick eventually whittled his Canyon crossing down to 10 hours and 40 minutes. For comparison, the world record for a person on foot is well under 4 hours. For further comparison, one of Eric York's radio-collared young female pumas (#05) dropped off the South Rim, descended trail-less terrain, swam the Colorado, and climbed to the North Rim in 8 hours. At any rate, people wondered how this guy in his 70s could do what reduced many 20-somethings to blobs of quivering, exhausted jelly!

Laurent Gaudreau reveled in the attention and admiration people now lavished on him. Finally, he was somebody. The warm buzz his notoriety imbued in him felt even better than those first couple of shots of good whiskey in the old days.

Shirley was a 60-year-old divorced mother and grandmother when she arrived at Grand Canyon in 1996, having escaped a verbally and physically abusive relationship in Fresno, California. For Shirley the Canyon offered an antidote to having endured a rough childhood and an even rougher marriage that had lasted far too long. Always a hard worker, Shirley worked several Canyon jobs before settling in with the Grand Canyon Association as a sales clerk at the Books & More Bookstore in Canyon View Information Plaza.

Infallibly kind and thoughtful, she regularly toted apples to feed the mules at the nearby stables. She possessed a quick wit and a reputation for a snappy rapport with tourists. She often approached one by saying, "Have you ever met a bag lady?" Then she would pull a bag over her head and extend her hand to say hi. Shirley always wore a bear-fetish necklace. She frequently asked customers, especially young men, if a hug from a bear-chested woman might persuade them to buy a GCA membership. Then she'd give them a hug. Shirley became the record-selling leader in membership sales.

Even more important than this, notes Shirley's supervisor Patty Brookins, Shirley proved such a positive influence with so many visitors over the years that she inspired them to develop a far more intimate connection with Grand Canyon. Several visitors who developed a relationship with her—remember she was "just" a sales clerk—returned to the Canyon committed to contribute to the Association's projects and so on. Shirley, in a sense, expanded these peoples' lives and fostered in them a more positive and direct connection with the natural world.

By most accounts Shirley's life improved after she met the little French-Canadian R2R-er. "She chased me until I caught her," Maverick would say to explain how they got married in 1999, a year after they met. Shirley tagged along with Maverick on his hikes until problems with bunions confined her to walks to the rim. Shirley told people her husband had "silver hair and legs of steel," adding that he was a good and kind-hearted man. Shirley called Maverick her "Sweetie," and she meant it. Between her relationship with the Grand Canyon Association and with her Sweetie, Shirley entered the happiest period of her life.

A home on the South Rim serves as an obvious benefit for any hiker obsessed with setting Canyon records. For Maverick to retain his new identity and expand his stardom it remained vital for him to live on the South Rim. A few minutes out his front door he could set off down a trail. The Catch-22 here is: Living on the South Rim requires that one be employed in a tourist job to qualify for housing, which typically is owned by a concession company. Yet Maverick also realized that to keep repeating his Canyon crossings and setting new records, he needed far more free time than any job would allow. Hence, in early 2004, at age 78, he quit his job. Shirley, who loved her job, kept working. Thus they could retain their housing on the rim, and Maverick was positioned to hike all the way to that Hollywood biography.

His goal for the year? Thirty rim-to-rim hikes. He streamlined his traverses for efficiency. He carried a 15-pound pack containing two liters of water. His R2R hiking routine entailed leaving the South Rim early in the morning, hiking 6.5 miles down the South Kaibab Trail, crossing the Black Bridge, and continuing past Phantom Ranch up the North Kaibab Trail to camp at Cottonwood Campground, 5 miles below the North Rim and 16 miles from where he had started. On day two, he would hike to the North Rim then back to Cottonwood, spending a second night there. On day three he would depart Cottonwood at 3 a.m., hoping to hit the Phantom Ranch Canteen when it opened at 8 a.m. to buy refreshments. Finally he would plod upward to the South Rim.

Maverick achieved 42 crossings that year. He reveled in local accolades. He emerged hell bent on breaking his own record. In 2005, he shot for 45 crossings. He made them all. In 2006 he decided he would accomplish 80 crossings to match his 80 years—a record he hoped never would be broken. To pull this off he would hike every week for an entire year, no matter what the weather or circumstances or how he was feeling, those 21 miles across the Canyon then back again to rack up two more R2Rs. He allowed his usual three days for each round-trip hike. After each he would rest a day or two before doing it all again. Before the clock struck midnight on December 31, 2006 Maverick had completed a record 106 R2Rs.

Maverick followed this feat by achieving another personal record for seeking media attention. He sought interviews from several newspapers and a couple of television newscasts. In 2007 he expanded his business of self-promotion with his T-shirts, hats, pens, and business cards advertising he was Maverick, an age-defying inspiration to all. He soon expanded his name to "Rim-to-Rim Maverick." Strangers began writing and emailing him. Rangers in the NPS Backcountry reservations office were queried by tourists about "Maverick." He began taking reservations for people he encouraged to accompany him on his cross-Canyon hikes. The ones who completed the hike went home wearing a T-shirt announcing, "I went all the way with Maverick."

His personal sales campaign proved such a success that people now sought him for his advice on how live, how to be happy. Maverick appeared to be a unique, happy, healthy octogenarian who had embraced then overcome the process of aging, itself normally a depressing and terrifying reality for many people. He seemed to have conquered every adversity of life by sheer will. He had overcome his alcohol addiction. He had metamorphosed into a self-created guru in love with life and living it to the fullest. "I'm happier and healthier," he proclaimed, "than I've been in my 80 years."

Everything was coming up roses. Maverick embraced his new public persona as "teacher." "I certainly need to find out what allows me to be in that state of mind," he said, "so I can pass it on to other people."

Maverick eventually found a way to pass on his "secret." To reach a larger audience, in 2008 Maverick began writing a weekly gratis column for the *Grand Canyon News* called "Maverick's Musings." He added a blog to the paper's website, grandcanyonnews.com. He and Shirley often shared this regular column. Maverick focused on inspirational and self-help topics while Shirley chronicled life in Grand Canyon Village.

Titles from his first writings included: "Self-love a powerful force" and "Positive thinking sets you free." Interestingly, a common topic in his articles was anger. His anger. Indeed, during his first column (on May 29, 2008) in his "Self-love" article he wrote:

> *I would like to dwell on a subject that causes misery both in our lives and the lives of others that could be somehow connected between love and hate. Anger, perhaps, stems from our inability to completely control both ourselves and the outside world. We get angry at our significant others and our co-workers.... First comes our decision to do something about anger. Then an easy and fast way to deal with it is the thought process called taming your demons....*

A few months later another Maverick article appeared titled "Rage can be hazardous to your health." Here he wrote, "I would like to make the case for helping ourselves more effectively with anger and rage. For the sake of simplicity, I will label rage as being angry enough to cause physical harm to others....I believe that once we can accept responsibility for our anger, we are on the road to controlling it."

Four months later Maverick offered his first clue as to why anger management applied to him. On January 20, 2009, within a span of 10 minutes around 11 p.m., he submitted a flurry of articles to his blog "Maverick's Musings/Mentors." In one of these last submissions he admits to having experienced, at least in his "previous" life, problems with anger. In his "Reflecting on the value of not getting angry" Maverick admits:

> *I am very proud to report to you what happened on Thanksgiving night. When I came in the door after spending an evening at a friend's house watching a film, I discovered that Buddy, our lovable mutt, has soiled several places on the floor. The old* **Maverick** *would have gone on a tirade and hit the poor dog. This time, my emotions didn't budge and I accepted responsibility for the situation. It was my responsibility to either not have been gone so long, or to remove both his water and food while I was away. I hope you see the value of not getting mad or at least taking a time-out to reflect on the course of action that would not be detrimental to the other parties concerned....*

Two weeks later, at 12:30 a.m. on February 5, 2009, NPS dispatch received a frantic 911 call. The caller reported he just shot his wife at their Pinion Park home. He identified himself as Maverick, giving no further information. He then set the phone down still active. As emergency-response rangers raced to the scene, the dispatcher heard repeated shots ring out over the earpiece.

Rangers surrounded Maverick's and Shirley's house, unsure what they would find hidden under the shroud of midnight. The scene seemed as quiet as the grave. Buddy stood silently on the porch. The Rangers knocked then entered a scene of inexplicable carnage.

As Shirley had reposed asleep in bed Maverick had shot her in the head with a rifle. The rangers saw no evidence that she had struggled or confronted her killer.

Next, Maverick had apparently reclined beside Shirley's corpse. He had positioned his rifle muzzle under his chin and shot himself.

These deaths were investigated as a murder/suicide, but Park investigators gave no motive. An investigation would reveal that Maverick, who had not previously owned a firearm, had purchased his rifle recently. Why would "Rim-to-Rim Maverick" pre-meditatively murder his wife then commit suicide?

Clearly anger management had been an issue in Maverick's past. Less clear is why. Almost certainly it had emerged as a bigger problem while he acted under the influence of alcohol. But no evidence suggests he had dropped off the wagon. If rage or anger had motivated Maverick, what could have sparked it? Again, the NPS reported no motive.

A plausible motive did exist but it was based only on rumor. It was rumored that Shirley had cleaned out—or had merely *appeared* to clean out—her locker at the Grand Canyon Association the day before this tragedy. Investigator Chris Smith reported this rumor as false. Shirley's supervisor Patty Brookins confirmed this as false too, noting that on her last day at work (February 5) Shirley seemed happier with life and with her job than anyone. When Brookins, a wonderful friend of Shirley, had offered her a ride home that evening, she answered cheerfully, "Oh, no thanks, my Sweetie is coming to pick me up."

But this rumor continued to appeal to some Canyon residents because it seemed to explain a clear motive for Maverick's heinous murder. The logic goes like this: Had Shirley broached the idea of retiring with Maverick on the night of February 5, it would have raised the specter for Maverick of losing their housing in the Park and with it his lifestyle and celebrity status. This prospect, some believed, would have sent him into a rage.

How valid is this hypothesis? Shirley's daughter Diane Caldwell and her husband Victor had tried recently to convince Shirley and Maverick to move closer to them and their son in California. But Shirley had told her daughter, "I love my job. I love the canyon. I love where I'm at." Even one day prior to Shirley's murder she had sounded fine on the phone to Caldwell. "There was no history of violence or anger," notes Caldwell (*Arizona Daliy Sun*, February 9, 2009). "This man treated my mom like a queen…that's what is so unreal about this."

Moreover, Shirley had repeatedly insisted she was never going to press Maverick to quit hiking. Instead she had acted supportive and left his hiking decisions up to him.

Shirley had experienced no reported issues with depression or suicidal tendencies. Instead she not only acted happy, she was happy. All of her life she had been a strong and hard-working woman who had overcome adversity from childhood onward and emerged from her adversity cheerful if not downright spunky. Was it conceivable that Shirley had begun experiencing secret issues with major depression and suicidal ideations unbeknownst to her friends and family and co-workers to the point where she would have entered into a suicide pact with Maverick? Everyone who knew her says no; Shirley loved her life at the Canyon.

A far more plausible culprit here is a sudden change having occurred in the mindset of the person who pulled the trigger.

Bruce Aiken was a 33-year resident and artist of the Inner Canyon based at Roaring Springs who worked as the NPS Pump House operator on the North Kaibab Trail. Aiken crossed paths below the rims with Maverick more than a hundred times. Aiken does not think Maverick's state of mind seemed what anyone would term "healthy." Instead, Aiken recalls that shortly after Maverick began gaining notoriety for his hiking:

—something went really, really wrong with him. Whether it was an underlying, undiagnosed mental condition, I'm not sure. He was single minded and hungry for attention. The more he got, the more he wanted. And he never wanted to talk about anything other than himself. And he wasn't into the Canyon. It was just about setting an unbeatable record of crossings. He wanted to get in

the Guinness World Book of Records. *That was it. In fact, whenever I ran into him, the absolute first words, sometimes the only words, that came out of his mouth were what number of hike he was on. I'd see him and say, "Hey, Maverick." His response would be "fifty-six" or whatever number he was on. Maverick would also be on the trail all hours of the day and night, in all types of weather. I remember running into him, literally running in to him, on the North Kaibab Trail near the Needle's Eye at 1:30 in the morning. It was pitch black. I had a headlamp on and I was coming around the narrow section by a cliff next to a shear drop. Out of nowhere was this old man with no headlamp clinging to the cliff face. It startled me and I said, "Maverick! Is that you?!" His reply was, "Number forty-six." My wife Mary and I considered him harmless, but we both knew he was a kook.*

In short, Maverick was not having a love affair with Grand Canyon. He was having a love affair primarily with Maverick. He appeared indifferent to the Canyon's geology, history, exploration, or ecology. The Canyon merely offered him a grand stage upon which to perform his stunt—much like juggling or sword-swallowing but in his case manically repeated R2Rs that would win applause from his audience. He was Evel Kneivel without a motorcycle.

Nor were the Aikens alone in their assessment that all was not well upstairs with Maverick. Linda Popp of Tusayan also logged many long miles of hiking with Maverick. But the two had drifted apart because Popp wanted to explore other trails beyond the rim-to-rim system (*Arizona Daliy Sun*, February 9, 2009).

He was trying to get into the Guinness Book of World Records. *That was what he was trying to do. He handed out business cards along the trail with his name and the line "inspire to perspire." Generally, he wanted friends to seek out time with him, instead of him calling them. And he hoped to be on the Oprah Winfrey show....Something about him had changed. Several people would say he was getting maybe senile because they saw him and they knew that he knew them and he acted like he didn't know them* [Popp found herself included in this non-recognition of friends by Maverick]...*there was some sort of change, like he wasn't himself.*

Indeed, many who knew Maverick noted his behavior at times had become erratic and inconsistent. Dementia can lead to unpredictable and sometimes aggressive or defiant behavior. Maybe Maverick had fallen into its grip. For example, he and Shirley had volunteered to work for the NPS policing the trail. Just one backcountry ranger, Chuck Sypher, however, agreed to patrol with Maverick. No other ranger would have him. "He already had a reputation of having a pretty big ego and attitude and was hard to instruct," noted Sypher. "Eventually we had to kick him off our volunteers list because he wouldn't listen and kept trying to do his own thing."

His obsession and obstinance infused his interactions with other hikers. For example, the last time I (Myers) witnessed Maverick in the Canyon it was in 2007 and I was hiking. Ahead of me were nearly ten other people, friends and family, heading single file down the South Kaibab Trail to celebrate New Year's Eve. A couple I know well was bringing up the rear of this hike. Abruptly, one by one, those hiking in front peeled off to one side of the narrow trail near Windy Point, as something unseen ascended. The woman near me at the rear had turned her head toward her husband when a short, white-haired old guy with his head lowered in a cartoon posture of a walking man in the grip of utter determination closed in on her. Without pausing or allowing the woman to step aside, he rammed his head squarely into her chest in a head butt that knocked her off her balance.

"Uphill," he barked in anger, "has the right of way."

"I'm so sorry," the head-butted woman said apologetically.

The old man, without breaking stride, grunted and trudged upward.

"What a little jerk," her husband muttered.

"Hey," she whispered, seconds later, "That was Maverick!"

Spinning to scan back up the trail, he and I both felt shocked and disappointed to see she was right. It was Maverick.

The couple shrugged. I heard them chalk it up to Marverick having become a grumpy old man.

Maverick also butted heads with the Park Service. During one of several episodes, when Maverick was camping in the Canyon where he was not permitted, a ranger ticketed him.

"He tried to push the limits of his local celebrity status," noted Ranger Bil Vandergraff, "feeling he should be able to come and go as he pleased because he was Maverick."

This ticketing came after Maverick had been given several previous warnings instead of citations. Maverick, a prime example of narcissistic personality disorder if there ever was one, became indignant about the ticket and challenged it. He lost.

Instead of having to pay a fine, however, he was ordered to perform several months of community service and to "stay out of trouble." During his community service he bragged that he had beaten the ticket.

Later, radio shows including *Backpacker* and *Growing Bolder* interviewed Maverick. He said he had signed a contract with *Go-Lite* backpacking gear as a spokesman. Go-Lite created a pack specifically for Maverick. It weighed only one pound. Maverick also planned to go into business with a friend selling special nutrition bars advertised as a basis for Maverick's success. Mike Freeman, the director of retail for Xanterra at the South Rim, recalls how Maverick insisted on Xanterra displaying a life-size cutout of himself—like one of John Wayne or Marilyn Monroe or Darth Vader—in their shop to accompany the nutrition bars. "He was way into self promotion, but even for him the life-size cutout was over the top," noted Freeman. "He had a hard time taking no for an answer and got pretty indignant about it."

Maverick also sought financial support for a proposed "encore" hike retracing Colin Fletcher's legendary mega trek from Havasu to Nankoweap, a saga immortalized in *The Man Who Walked through Time*. Maverick, the self-proclaimed minimalist, estimated this backpacking trip would require a whopping $10,000 to $20,000. Aside from the fact that several hundred dollars seems more realistic, it is clear that Maverick wanted to do something that surpassed his string of R2Rs. But the realistic odds of his completing the arduous 250-mile "length-of-the-park" hike while possessing virtually no off-trail experience were remote. He was a walker, after all, not a hiker, not a route finder, not a scrambler, and not even a guy who understood how the Canyon's geological formations facilitated or forbade routes. The exorbitant and likely unattainable "fee" he quoted may actually have been his dignified way to exit a hiking disaster that would have sullied his "iron man" persona. A moot point, the trip never happened.

In short, not having arranged an encore to one up his R2Rs likely proved depressing for Maverick. Depression was indeed an issue for him. Many of Maverick's and Shirley's friends knew the couple had begun psychological counseling in 2007. Maverick often mentioned it. Local Grand Canyon dentist Dr. Mark Draugel and his wife Nancy recall Maverick's excitement over revelations he had gleaned from an anger management workshop. (Maverick, by the way, had appeared at the Grand Canyon Clinic around this time with an armory of framed photographs of himself and instructed everyone to hang them on the walls of the clinic and dental facility.) "Shirley's previous husband had physically abused her," Maverick now explained his fascination to Draugel. "And while I've never laid a hand on her, there's something about the way she had responds to me at times that makes me feel like I could do the same."

Alcoholics are known for exhibiting addictive, dependent behavior even after they quit, by substituting one addiction for another. In Maverick's case, the Canyon seems to have replaced booze. The "rush" of each hike, especially in his mega year of 2006, acted as an addictive drug, one he apparently could not get enough of. Yes, it was therapeutic. It triggered a release of endorphins acting as natural antidepressants. His manic and compulsive hiking likely helped him better control any tendency toward depression or anger. So too did the accolades and admiration people lavished on him for being an octogenarian iron man. Hiking the Canyon and being recognized as famous for it ultimately became his twin drugs of choice, ones he depended upon to "tame his demons." Shirley had become his enabler by holding down her job, earning money, and ensuring a home at the Canyon and a launch pad for fame for him on the rim.

At 11:11 p.m. on January 20, 2009, Maverick had submitted what would become his final, and highly revealing, blog, "Working for a positive attitude."

> *I'm excited writing this week's column because of what I have discovered about myself. As you know, I have been working on learning to love Shirley unconditionally. It wasn't long before I discovered it was just not working...*

— *Rim to Rim Maverick*

Maverick did not elaborate on why he found Shirley impossible to love unconditionally. He did, however, end his blog with: "Controlling your thoughts and emotions will make a significant difference in the quality of your life."

Meanwhile, something predictable but undesired was happening to Maverick and it was happening fast. This guy whose persona revolved around not acting his age was aging. People who saw him on the trail during these last days noted that he stumbled and seemed increasingly less capable of hiking. No doubt Maverick more than anyone else realized he was deteriorating. Instead of beating old age, now old age was beating him. Indeed Patty Brookins feels convinced that Maverick's deterioration haunted him with the looming specter of failure in his manic quest to take his fame to the next higher level. There would be no slot on Oprah, no biography, no Maverick franchise, no Hollywood movie of his life. In short, he was losing it and he knew it. From now on it would all be downhill.

Hence the most plausible explanation for Maverick's inexcusable final action is that he had decided to depart life while still in possession of his fame and accolades and before he nose-dived into a pitiful has-been. This likely explains why so late in life he abruptly decided to buy a firearm, the choice of suicide means for American men. Maverick's next likely thought process proved to be his most sick and tragic. Patty Brookins suspects Maverick imagined that Shirley could not live without him. Therefore she should come with him.

I (Ghiglieri) asked Patty Brookins what she thought Shirley might have said (hypothetically) in response to Maverick had he asked her, "Hey, I've decided to commit suicide; I know you can't live without me, want me to kill you too?" Brookins adamantly responded that there was absolutely no chance Shirley would have said "yes, kill me too." For that matter, there also was no way, Brookins added, that Shirley could not have lived without Maverick. She loved her life and not only was quite capable of living without Maverick, she had created relationships with many others and the Canyon itself that continued to be immensely rewarding and fulfilling to her. In short, she would have wanted to live and would have done fine on her own.

Obviously Maverick failed to "control his thoughts and emotions" well in his final hour. He loaded his new rifle. He aimed it at Shirley's head. He pulled the trigger. She would not have to live without him. What an ego.

When Shirley had discussed her marriage, it usually was in positive terms. "We have a wonderful life up here," she once had said. "We both love what we do, and we have a nice place to live in. I always say, 'I'm going to die here.'"

Maverick's legacy? He achieved a level of Grand Canyon immortality that will exceed what he desired. His record of 106 R2R Canyon crossings at age 80 likely never will be surpassed by anyone of any age. (Who in their right mind would want to?) His iron man hiking and defiance of aging inspired many people, especially seniors. On the flip side, whatever merits his example might have exemplified evaporated in a single moment of intense and inexcusable selfishness. Had he taken only his own life, he may have been regarded as a tragic hero sadly disturbed by mental illness. But his cold-blooded murder of his incredibly supportive wife, a gentle woman whom virtually everyone liked, was a despicable act of cowardice and selfishness and of a sick psyche.

"I'm happier and healthier than I've been in my 80 years," Maverick had claimed. "I certainly need to find out what allows me to be in that state of mind, so I can pass it on to other people."

We can only hope he didn't.

Table 10. MURDERS WITHIN GRAND CANYON OR ON ITS RIMS. A question mark prior to a victim's name indicates some degree of uncertainty that death was due to homicide.

Name, age	Date	Location	Circumstances
? "Tanner Man," 35-40	1000-1200 A.D.	Tanner Trail 1.25 miles below trailhead	

The partial skeleton of a robust male Puebloan about 5' 4" tall was found under a Supai boulder exposed by natural erosion and overlaid with recent trash from hikers. During the investigation in February, 1997, an inch-long, stone arrowhead of the "Parowan Basal Notched" style of post-1,000 A.D. was found by Yavapai County Sheriff's Dept. Captain Scott Mascher situated in the area of the chest cavity. The burial site was located a bit off the Tanner Trail above a Basketmaker III/Pueblo I midden of pot shards, a mano, etc., all near the 75-Mile Canyon saddle. The deceased, the Park decided, was a likely prehistoric burial site rather than a forensic scene. But was it a post-homicide burial? (see text) Incident report #97- 0147

Name, age	Date	Location	Circumstances
unnamed Yavapai man unnamed Yavapai man #2	between 1860-1863	"Apache Trail" area E of Great Thumb Mesa	

A Yavapai war party intent on raiding the Havasupai ran into greater defensive resistance than expected. Havasupai warriors, "Captain Burro" and "Captain Navajo," shot two of the Yavapai then scalped and decapitated them. These scalps were retained for future scalp dances. (see text) Leslie Spier. 1928. "Havasupai Ethnography." Anthropological Papers of the American Museum of Natural History *29(3):81-392.*

Name, age	Date	Location	Circumstances
Aah'yi'd digish, adult Navajo male	1864–68	north of the site of the future Hull's cabin at Grandview	

The husband of a Navajo refugee family from the Long Walk found the infamous outlaw/brigand Navajo, Aah'yi'd digish, in the act of butchering the horse that the husband's pregnant wife had just been riding. The husband shot and killed the man who had stolen, slain, and butchered this horse. (see text) This story came via Tony Hillerman and James Peshlakai as personal communications (to Ghiglieri).

Name, age	Date	Location	Circumstances
William H. Dunn, under 30 Oramel G. Howland, 36 Seneca B. Howland, 26	? August 30– September 3, 1869	uncertain location either between Mount Dellenbaugh and Parashant Wash or Toquerville, Utah	

Dunn and the Howland Brothers separated from J. W. Powell's first exploration down the Grand Canyon Colorado on August 28, 1869, and hiked north. The three were murdered. (see text for story and references)

Name, age	Date	Location	Circumstances
? unnamed hoodlum, adult	1885?	South Rim somewhere	

An unnamed "hoodlum" was allegedly executed by a group of Flagstaff's "respectable citizens" by tossing him off the rim into the Canyon. (see text) Arizona Champion, *February 21, 1885.*

Archimedes McClurg, adult   Fall 1894   Navajo Spring (5 miles S of Lees Ferry)
McClurg, of Denver, Colorado and a self proclaimed Mormon missionary intending to "preach the gospel of salvation to the sinners" of Flagstaff, passed through Lees Ferry in fall, 1894. In mid October of 1894, Seth B. Tanner and some Navajos found McClurg's body— with a bullet hole through the chest and his pockets turned inside out—partially buried by rocks and sand. McClurg was buried at Lees Ferry. Reilly, P. T. 1999. Lees Ferry from Mormon Crossing to National Park. Logan, Utah, Utah State University Press. pp. 139 & 487.

? Elsie Reed, adult woman   July 5, 1924   S Rim, Buggeln Ranch near Grandview
During a resurgence of the Ku Klux Klan and of bootlegging gangs of concession employees at the South Rim, Elsie Reed was shot in late June, 1924. Rumor had it that Elsie's relationship with Martin Buggeln, for whom she worked as a maid at his ranch house, had become overly close and that her husband Frank had complained. A man named Shirley—a Fred Harvey transportation manager and a champion of Buggeln—had engaged in a fistfight with Frank Reed over this Elsie issue. This left Frank lying insensible on the ground. Some witnesses reported that Elsie, seeing this and feeling guilty, had entered the ranch house and used Buggeln's .32 caliber six-gun in his bedroom to shoot herself in the left breast. She lived for several days and appeared on the mend but died suddenly after drinking the contents of her hot water bottle (after having been warned by the doctor not to drink much fluid). Despite a lack of powder burns, the Coroner's jury ruled her death as a suicide, based on very garbled witnesses. In contrast, Assistant Superintendent George C. Bolton (a member of that jury) and Coconino County Sheriff Campbell believed Elsie instead had been murdered by her diminutive husband Frank Reed "in a fit of temper and shame" over her relationship with Buggeln. Information source for this is a July 5, 1924, letter by George C. Bolton, Assistant Superintendent, GCNP.

Milo "Sonny" Craig Jaycox, 2   July 28, 1927   near home in Grand Canyon Village
Ten minutes after Milo's mother, Mrs. Milo Jaycox of Grand Canyon Village saw him playing, he vanished. A troubled local, Raymond Sandoval, age 12, confessed to killing Milo but told twelve different versions of disposing the body, none of which were true. After Sandoval's father talked to him, he denied all wrong doing. Several weeks later, Milo's body was found in the woods 2+ miles from the Canyon with its skull fractured by a blow to the back of the head. Sandoval was sentenced to the state reformatory until age 21, then went on to a life of crime. Coconino Sun, July 29, August 5, & December 9, 1927.

? Glen R. Hyde, 29   December 1, 1928   ? between Diamond Creek and Mile 237
Homicide is one hypothetical but unlikely explanation of Hyde's otherwise unsolved mysterious disappearance. (see text of Chapters 5, 9 & 10 for story and references)

George Wilson, 65   June 26, 1935   Marble Canyon gas station
Wilson was shot by one of three armed robbers—Albert White, age 19, Carl White, age 17, and Carl Cox, age 29—on June 23. He died

three days later. Albert White was convicted of 1st degree murder, but escaped jail. He was shot and killed near Bitter Springs during his escape attempt.

Mary Hunsaker, adult
Norman Bennett, adult
Ray Goodman, 44 (suicide)

December 28, 1950   Grand Canyon Village at Bennet's home
Ray Goodman, a 44-year-old Fred Harvey concession employee and dishwasher at Bright Angel Lodge, asked Mary Hunsaker of Mesa, Arizona, while a dinner guest at the Bennets' house, to go to dinner with him. She declined. Goodman (misnamed, it proved) immediately shot Norman Bennett of Grand Canyon Village in the head with a .22 revolver. He next emptied his revolver into Hunsaker's chest. He reloaded but told Norman Bennett's wife that he would spare her if she stayed still. Goodman then walked into the woods and shot himself in the head. Coconino Sun, December 30, 1950.

Bert Brown, adult

July 15, 1951   outside El Tovar Hotel
Bert Brown, a "disabled" WWII veteran from Pecos, Texas, plus John Paul Harris and Charles Read entered El Tovar, robbed the desk clerk at gun point of $12,000, then fled. A law officer shot Brown fatally in the heart in front of El Tovar. Read and Harris were cought 30 miles N of Flagstaff. Coconino Sun, July 19, 1951.

? Connie Smith, 15

summer, 1957   Skinner Ridge, 10 miles SW of Grand
                Canyon Village
On the morning of July 16, 1952, after a fight with other girls in her tent at Camp Sloane in Salisbury, Connecticut that had left her nose bloodied, 10-year-old Connie Smith of Newcastle, Wyoming walked out of the camp then vanished while hitchhiking on U.S. Route 44 to Lakeside, Connecticut. Smith was the granddaughter of former Wyoming Governor Nels Smith and daughter of cattleman Pete Smith. A man later determined a "mental case," made a self-admitted bogus confession to police that he had picked up Connie Smith and later drove her to Arizona where his partner killed her. This suspect's motive for confessing was to get admitted into a mental health program. Later, convicted murderer William Redmond also confessed to murdering Smith. Despite his passing a lie detector test, he was not believed. Virtually nothing is known for certain of what Smith did for the 5 years after her kidnapping. Her body was found by two hunters from Yuma on October 31, 1958, dead since approximately the summer of 1957. The skull was positively identified via dental records. "There's only one chance in a million," insisted Flagstaff dentist John Stilley, that the skeleton is not Connie Smith. Smith's clothing was found a significant distance from her body, suggesting high odds of foul play. Arizona Daily Sun, November 22, 23 & 26, 1962. "A Camper Walks away, Picks Daisies and Vanishes," The Hartford Courant News Library.

Winona B. McComas, 49

September 17, 1964   near Hermit's Rest
McComas of Albuquerque, New Mexico was shot behind her right ear with a .22 rifle by her estranged ex-husband Ralph McClendon, age 61, who then shot himself, but survived. Arizona Daily Sun, September 19, 1064.

Addie Lee Venturini, 46   February 27, 1972   Red Butte (6 miles S of National Park)
Thomas J. Smith, 48 (suicide)   *After a Relief Fire Dispatcher entered the fire observer's cabin and found it in disarray and spattered with blood, searchers found the body of Addie Lee Venturini (a drug-addicted mother of five and from Jackson, Mississippi). She had been dragged to a nearby cliff then tossed fifty feet to the bottom. An autopsy revealed that she had been stabbed 42 times with an ice pick, beaten with a wrench, and shot several times with a .22 pistol. She had been traveling with Thomas J. Smith, age 48. On April 11, Smith's 1966 Buick was found not far off. Smith was lying nearby, face down with a .22 bullet wound to his right temple.* Arizona Daily Sun *March 6 & 7 & April 13 &14, 1972.*

Michael A. Sherman, 28   January 22, 1977   Powell Memorial
Charlotte H. Sherman, 28   *A Canyon visitor found both Shermans at mid-day shot in the head by a .22 caliber firearm less than an hour earlier. The apparent motive for the double homicide was minor robbery. The Shermans of Arlington, Virginia had been moving from the East to Norton A.F.B. in California with their possessions, which the killer left mostly intact. This senseless murder devastated Dr. Sherman's parents and siblings for the rest of their lives. The murder weapon has not been found. This case is the only one known in a U.S. national park of a midday murder in a public attraction area. In 2011 the Shermans' murder remains an active cold case with a "very extensive file" and awaits results from a vastly improved forensic science. (see text)* Arizona Daily Sun, *January 24, 1977.* Arizona Republic, *April 27, 1977. Personal communications by Investigator Joe Sumner (to Ghiglieri). Incident report #77-0146*

unidentified Uqualla boy   circa 1983   Supai Village, Havasu
   The Uaualla boy was shot by Havasupai Galen Crook. Stephen Hirst, letter to Ghiglieri, May 1, 2012.

Gertrude Marshall, adult   August 27, 1983   Supai Village, Havasu
   Marshall of Supai was shot to death by her estranged common law husband Wayne Paya after she told him she was leaving him due to his alcohol problem. He served 10 years in prison. Stephen Hirst, letter to Ghiglieri, May 1, 2012.

Robert Leeds Layne, Jr., 35   June 8, 1984   El Tovar Hotel
   A Fred Harvey Company mule wrangler, Robert Hinckle, age 36, was arguing with his girlfriend in the piano bar when an uninvolved tourist, Layne, tried to intercede by saying something like, "Hey, leave the woman alone." The wrangler pulled a .357 magnum revolver and shot the Good Samaritan tourist fatally. Incident report #84-1335

Robert E. Diggs, 23   August 7, 1986   Victor Hall/Fred Harvey employee housing
   Diggs, a Fred Harvey concession employee, was slain by a gunshot wound to the throat inflicted by a fellow Fred Harvey employee. Incident report #86-2505

? un-identified American Indian, adult	**August/September 1986　riffle at River Mile 231.8** *Boatmen Shane Murphy and Chris Peterson were running a 2-boat Canyoneers trip. At Mile 231.8 Murphy saw trash in the riffle and retrieved what turned out to be a severed head of long-haired male Indian—allegedly as witnessed by Sir Randolph Finnes, who said: "Yes, it looked like a dead man to me." Murphy, surprised, dropped the head. Peterson saw it too and reported it to Meadview NPS. Rangers never found it. Murphy's lost find remains an unsolved mystery. But Peterson added: "There was talk of a murder on the Havasupai reservation, the body cut-up and thrown in the river." This incident remains officially in the "unfounded" category. Incident report #86-3407*
Donna K. Spangler, 59	**April 11, 1993　Page Springs Trail in the Redwall below Horseshoe Mesa** *Based on the confession of her husband, Robert Merlin Spangler, then age 61, he shoved Donna Spangler of Durango, Colorado into the abyss to avoid the inconvenience of a divorce. She fell 160 feet. After signing his confession to murder, Robert Spangler requested an NPS permit to have his ashes spread over Grand Canyon. U.S. District Judge Paul G. Rosenblatt ordered the NPS to deny this permit. During a strong wind in the Canyon, you will not have to worry about sipping the ashes of a serial killer in your tea. (see text)* Spangler, D. *1986.1989.* On Foot in the Grand Canyon Hiking the Trails of the South Rim. *Boulder: Pruett.* Arizona Daily Sun, *April 13, 1993, October 5, 2000 & March 1, 2001.* Grand Junction Sentinel, *October 5, 2000.* Denver Post, *October 6 & 8, 2000.* Las Vegas Review-Journal, *March 13, 2001. United States District Court District of Arizona plea agreement #CR-00-0968-PCT-PGR, December 27, 2000, Phoenix, Arizona, U.S. Courthouse. Incident report #93-0764*
Antonio Castillo, Jr., 31	**December 13, 1996　Tusayan** *Castillo was an invited guest at a Christmas party at a local motel when Harry Manchee, age 58, heavily intoxicated, stabbed him in the chest. Manchee had mistaken Castillo for someone who had admonished Manchee earlier to stop harassing some of the women present. Castillo died less than a half hour later at Grand Canyon Clinic due to a severed internal thoracic artery. Manchee was convicted of second-degree murder. Incident report #96-6039*
? Maria Sophia Edovist, 24	**August 23, 1997　Tuweep Overlook** *Edovist of Sweden was found 600 feet below the cliff at the Tuweep Campground. Her body had seriously torqued on impact, but forensics seemed to indicate she had died well before going off the cliff. One interpretation is Edovist was strangled, either deliberately or as a sexual turn-on. Her death remains "highly suspicious." Edovist's boyfriend who had been with her departed Arizona for Sweden within a couple of days and is predicted unlikely to return to the U.S.A., a capital punishment nation. Incident report #97-3801*

? Sandra Marie Elizondo, 18   February 20, 2001   Rim Trail near Grandeur Point
*Elizondo of Ontario, California was seen 20 feet from the rim by
two couples walking the Rim Trail. When the couples returned
maybe 10-20 minutes later, Elizondo's personal items were still
there. Also, close to the edge, were one of her shoes now with a
broken strap, her sunglasses, and a black button torn loose. But
Elizondo had vanished. The 5' 4", 100-lb woman's journal entry for
that day indicated no discontent with life. Indeed she was planning
to soon head home to begin a happily anticipated career as a flight
attendant for America West Airlines. SAR rangers found her body
360 feet below the rim. Her hand still gripped a pair of purple knit
gloves. Above her on the rim a couple of deep imprints from the
heels of her 2-inch, platform shoes appeared in soil adjacent to the
rim, suggesting a sudden abrupt movement of her body prior to her
fall. Investigator Joe Sumner noted (to Ghiglieri): "We worked the
homicide angle pretty hard but could not find any evidence."* Arizona Daily Sun, *March 2, 11 & 13, 2001.* Grand Canyon-Williams
News, *June 20, 2001. Incident report #01- 0299*

Kim Suzette Quanimptewa, 30   June 12, 2001   Trailer Village, Grand Canyon Village
*Concession employee Quanimptewa, a native of the Hopi village,
Hotevilla, was found hidden under a bed and stabbed to death and
covered with a bedspread. A search of the residence of suspected
Navajo assailant and concession employee, Jeremiah Becenti, age
21, revealed a bloody Buck knife and clothing, etc. Becenti plead
guilty to first degree murder. Motive was unknown but this brutal
murder occurred during a drunken "party."* Arizona Daily Sun,
September 11, 2001. Grand Canyon-Williams News, *June 20,
2001. Incident report #01-1586*

Tomomi Hanamure, 34   May 8, 2006   Havasu Canyon, 1+ mile north of Village
*Hanamure of Yokohama, Japan vanished while hiking from
Havasupai Village en route to Havasu Falls. SAR teams failed to
find her. She was found 5 days later in a shallow eddy below a
waterfall by local teenager Randy Redtail Wescogame. She had been
stabbed 29 times. Her hands, arms, and wrists showed cuts and
bruises consistent with self defense. Forensics suggest she was raped.
On September 18, 2007, Randy Wescogame pled guilty to 2nd
degree murder to avoid the death penalty from a 1st degree conviction. (see text)* Doughtery, J. 2007. Problems in Paradise. High
Country News, *Vol. 39(10): 10-15. May 28.* McGivney, A. 2007.
Freefall. Backpacker, *June, pp.75-84 & 106-107 & 115.*

Shirley Gaudreau, 73   February 5, 2009   South Rim Pinion Park trailer park
Laurent Osias "Maverick"   *Apparently while asleep in bed, Shirley was shot in the head with
 Gaudreau, 82 (suicide)   a rifle by her husband, self-styled Canyon hiking hero and former
concession employee Laurent "Maverick" Gaudreau. He was
obsessed with setting records for rim-to-rim hikes and with extreme
self-promotion. His motive may have been that he was deteriorating in his ability to live up to the extreme reputation he had manically woven around his persona and wanted to exit life before life
let him down. He may have also believed (very likely in error) that*

his wife Shirley would not have wanted to live without him. After murdering Shirley, Laurent phoned 911 then shot himself fatally. (see text) Hollenhorst, J. 2006. Octogenarian crosses Grand Canyon 106 times. KSL.com, December 19. Arizona Daily Sun, October 18, 2006 & February 6 & 7, 2009. Grandcanyonnews.com February 17, 2009. Personal communications from Patty Brookins (to Ghiglieri). Incident report #09-0708

Jace Dehaven, 11
Jersey Dehaven, 6
Anthony Dehaven, 35
  (suicide)

October 3, 2011   South Rim Entrance Station
Anthony Dehaven of Woodbury, Minnesota shot to death his son Jace and daughter Jersey, lit their RV on fire then shot himself, thus denying his estranged wife Angela Elizabeth Velasquez her children and even an open casket funeral. Grand Canyon News, *October 18, 2011.*

Epilogue

What Have We Learned From All This?

After all is said and done, what people die in Grand Canyon? And when, where, how, and why do those particular people die? We cracked this multifaceted mystery a decade ago when the first printing of *Over the Edge: Death in Grand Canyon* hit the bookstores in 2001. Indeed we thought we had answered all these questions well enough to equip everyone with the information they needed to prevent tragic recurrences. Beyond this, the decade following 2001 coincided with a vast expansion of access to information via internet search capabilities. These spew an avalanche of facts and data and statistics and advice and tips about everything—including safely hiking, boating, and exploring Grand Canyon. All these data reside a mere fingertip away and require minimal effort to access. The past decade has also seen an explosion in the availability of cell phones, smart phones, satellite phones, global positioning devices, and personal locator beacons useful to varying degrees within the Canyon to facilitate a rescue when a visit does turn sour. Moreover, the SAR system at Grand Canyon has become one of the most sophisticated and efficient on Earth. It responds successfully to hundreds of emergencies within the Canyon yearly. It seems everything needed to prevent fatal errors and every technology needed to rescue those in trouble are cutting edge. In short, the safety net for explorers in Grand Canyon is the best it has ever been. By far.

Yet, somehow, all this has proved to be not enough.

Our biggest revelation since the first printing of *Over the Edge* is that some people who visit the Canyon never will be reached no matter what information resides within their grasp. Sadly, in the decade since the book appeared and multiplied to a quarter million copies and despite all the other means of accessing safety information, well over 100 more people have cashed in their chips below the rims. In 2009 alone, a record ten hikers died. Why? Not to place too fine a point on it, they died due to laziness, arrogance, ignorance, and poor judgment. And due also to reckless behavior spurred by testosterone. For these same reasons, we suspect, yet more new names will be added to future printings of this book.

Even so, we remain convinced *Over the Edge* has helped preserve some people's lives. People have told us how the book has influenced their decision-making and judgment in a good way. These individuals are not listed in this book. No one will ever know the exact number of disasters *Over the Edge* helped avert. A disaster that never occurred cannot be measured.

On the other hand, it remains almost as difficult to measure or identify before-hand the levels of ignorance residing in the minds of visitors that subsequently lead to their self-destruction. We suspect that if the majority of the 100+ new entries in this book had read it before they dropped below the rim, they too would have avoided being listed here.

The disturbing growth trends in fatality categories during the decade from 2001 to 2011 include disproportionately more: 1. hikers falling below the rim, 2. hikers succumbing to heat, 3. private boaters drowning, and 4. people making suicide jumps. On the other side of the coin, fewer people have fallen off the rims accidentally, and fewer have died in aircraft crashes than during the previous three decades up to 2000. These differences seem significant.

So what are we to do? The mass phenomenon of people seeking adventure for its own sake is a fairly recent one. Why do we do it? Adventure writer Sebastian Junger says we do it because modern society has been "designed to eliminate as many unforeseen events as possible, [but] as inviting as that seems, it leaves us hopelessly under utilized." This lack of purpose is where the idea of "adventure"—being any situation in which the outcome is not entirely within our control—comes in. "Threats to our safety and comfort have been so completely wiped out," Junger concludes, "that we have to go out of our way to create them."

Indeed, in our preoccupation with safety, "adventure" (as defined by *Webster's Dictionary* as an enterprise in which one faces real hazard) has become such a highly desired commodity that it has become profitably marketable in almost every form. Lethal trips up Everest titillate us so much that some of us even shell out $65,000 to go there and get frostbite, breathe from an oxygen tank, and generally experience insane misery—just so our lives suddenly will have some meaning, some definition, some bragging rights.

But for American society in general it well can be argued that, in our generations-long quest for security, we have domesticated ourselves. We train and hire specialists to do nearly everything for us so that we do not face taking the risk of doing it ourselves. We hire police to protect us from sociopaths, contractors to build our houses, farmers to grow or raise our food, programmers to battle computer viruses, Ralph Nader to make our cars and skies safe, guidebooks to keep us on the safe routes, and Hollywood to flash vicarious yet extremely dangerous adventures in our faces so that we don't risk experiencing anything like the real thing in order to jack up our adrenaline levels. If Hollywood pales, we still have organized sports, with lots of rules for safety and referees to enforce them. We've laced our social lives into a network wherein rights and wrongs are defined by hundreds of thousands of laws. And we have airbags and parachutes and orthopedic surgeons and seat belts and life vests and helmets to protect us when something does go wrong. If all of these fail, we call one of those lawyers we see on daytime TV and sue somebody. In short, we are what would be referred to in biology as a domesticated species. We are no longer wild *Homo sapiens*. Instead, psychologically, many of us have become sheep. Baaa....

As sheep—or, if you prefer, domesticated *Homo sapiens* (*Homo sapiens domesticus* or perhaps *Homo sapiens touristicus*)—many of us now make the habitual and unquestioned assumption that somebody else is supposed to be watching out for our best interests for us. We blindly follow the rest of the flock and assume that the sheepherder, wherever he is, is keeping his eye peeled for the wolves.

The average of 3,380 SAR operations yearly to rescue visitors in U. S. national parks reveals this sort of lack of self-responsibility is all too obvious. And, as we've seen, it all too often proves lethal. As Lee H. Whittlesey reports in *Death in Yellowstone*, between the time Yellowstone became a national park in 1872 until 1995, over 300 people died in it traumatically, mostly due to their own errors. As with the twice as many traumatic fatalities in Grand Canyon too, these casualties teach us vital lessons in survival. Perhaps the first of these lessons, Whittlesey notes, is: "**Nature demands of us that we pay attention.**" More often than not, however, this lesson goes unheeded. Every day, Whittlesey says, someone enters a wilderness area unprepared.

Certainly this is true in Grand Canyon. But what should we do to fix this situation? Law students do exist who firmly believe that every possible location in the American West where someone might die accidentally should be labeled with warning signs. *Every* location. But even after posting several billion signs, these places would still be dangerous to people who failed to think—or even to read the signs. Should we then try to pave, pad, sanitize, declaw, and defang American wilderness so that those of us who have no respect for its reality will not be able to hurt ourselves in our blissful ignorance and arrogance? In our current era, a time during which money-chasing lawyers and irresponsible jurors have nearly abolished the legitimacy of the concept of self-responsibility for the consequences of one's own personal actions, this question is a complicated one.

Making federal wilderness so "safe" that mentally and/or physically unprepared people are guaranteed to survive in it unscathed is a tort lawyer's dream come true. This is because making the world safe cannot be done, yet lethal human foolishness is unlimited. Meanwhile wilderness itself offers an infinite number of opportunities for someone to carelessly hurt him or herself. Hence, if a mandate did exist to force an attempt to make wilderness safe, America's one million lawyers would be assured of litigation income forever. Thus the logical answer seems to be to bar all human entry by land, water, or air into U.S. wilderness.

Crazy? Maybe. But the question of the degree to which federal or state governments should be required to change anything in wilderness involves several complicated issues of legality, morality, value, and practicality. The 1916 U.S. National Park Organic Act dictates that the NPS must leave national parks in their natural state, unchanged and unencumbered to the future enjoyment of posterity. So, no one is legally allowed to "fix" national park wilderness to make it safe. Instead, the NPS and state park systems are legally required only not to be negligent in safeguarding visitors. Mainly this safeguarding consists of forewarning people of common dangers in a systematic, easily understandable way through warning pamphlets, signs, radio broadcasts, and so on. Unfortunately, warnings that 999,999 people out of a million agree are quite clear and useful, number 1,000,000 does not bother to read or understand or heed and, in his ignorance, kills himself. Here, again, is the lawyer's bread and butter.

Each "frivolous" suit forces the government to install more warning signs, erect more railings, pave more trails, forbid any step off the trail, continually lower and restrict visitor access, and in general treat most people as something less capable than a blind cow. Many of us find this trend to be very negative when it comes to enjoying a visit to a national park or other natural area. Yet because protecting the ignorant or foolish from their own mistakes is an endlessly spiraling arms race between NPS administrators and human stupidity, NPS restrictions will only increase in this endless war to protect people too lazy or naive to protect themselves.

Nor can the NPS bring more resources to bear on this war. As mentioned above, making federal wilderness safe is both illegal and impractical (to put it mildly) even if funds were unlimited, which they are not. Worse, in today's downwardly spiraling economy, shortfalls in the NPS budget will lead to increasing backlogs in maintenance, resource management, construction, and land acquisitions. Hence the NPS has no choice but to employ the cheapest possible weapons in this war. Unfortunately, the cheapest weapon is simply restricting the places that a visitor can visit— not in constructing 2,757 miles of safety railings that some people would climb past anyway.

Beyond the questions of legality and practicality lie even more important questions of morality and value. As has become increasingly clear in the past fifty years, the human population on this planet is exploding to 7 billion. Humanity is not an endangered species (yet). Meanwhile wilderness—and merely pleasant and quiet natural scenery—is shrinking as people co-opt every scrap of unprotected landscape for economic use. Our shriveling wilderness not only contains, and is vital to the survival of, uncounted endangered species, wilderness itself is an endangered environment. Many of us insist that not only do we have a moral obligation to preserve such species, such habitats, and such ecosystems, we also are guilty of committing murder if we do not. Therefore, sanitizing and "human-proofing" the wilderness is not only illegal, impractical, and ultimately impossible, morally it is unconscionable ecocide.

Where does that leave us? Morality and practicality each dictate that, in the question of man versus protected wilderness, the onus is on humankind to assume the personal responsibility to prepare its members for all of the environmental challenges wilderness poses to the visitor. If a prospective visitor is unwilling to show the wilderness and his fellow humans this respect, he should stay out of the wilderness. Instead, he should rent the video.

Most of the five million people each year who drive or fly out of their way to visit Grand Canyon—a World Heritage Site and one of the most impressive of the World's Seven Natural Wonders—do not do so because they have been assured that it has been made as safe as (or safer than) their local neighborhood park. Instead they come to experience a truly inspirational chunk of wilderness. Few of them want to see it "improved" or "safety-proofed." Again, it is our job to safeguard ourselves by respecting the natural world, and most of us know this.

This respect is at the root of our love for wilderness. We know that wilderness is not only something bigger than all of us, it is also the source of all of us. It molded much of our own nature. Our ancestors survived in wilderness for millennia only by respecting its impersonal dangers. Our psyches were molded by these dangers and also by the rewards the wilderness offers to those who pay attention. In essence, we are surviving great-great-grandchildren of the wilderness. Our five senses were fine-tuned by its demands. To see its vastness, hear its thunder, smell its springtime, and to feel the bite of its winds, the heat of its sun, and the chill of its rains brings us back to our childhood, to our very roots.

Most of us know, however, that the wilderness in turn cares not a whit for us. It reciprocates neither our fascination nor our love for it. If we fail to respect its dangers, we realize, not only might those dangers hurt us, they may kill us—or an innocent child who's depending on us.

Most of us would have this relationship be no other way.

The take-home lesson here—one obvious in the first eight chapters of this book—is the people who die traumatically in Grand Canyon die mainly, almost universally, due to their own or their guide's poor judgment. It is impossible for the rest of us to protect them fully from these personal failings. We can only hope to do our best to inform people of the real dangers the Canyon wilderness poses and always will pose.

Forewarned, it becomes the personal responsibility of each of us to avoid killing ourselves—and thereby also avoid tacitly accusing the wilderness of being our murderer. We hope this book does just that, forewarn each of us of the dangers the Canyon poses. Forewarned enough, perhaps we and our vanishing wilderness will both survive.

Table 11. SUMMARY OF ACCIDENTAL and NONACCIDENTAL DEATHS WITHIN GRAND CANYON or (on plateaus), 1860 to September, 2012. No victim is counted in more than one category. [Kids] = number within total who were less than 18 years old.

Type of Mishap	Male Victims	Female Victims	Total Victims	[kids]
Falls from the rims	41	15	56	[7]
Falls within the Canyon	49	10	59	[4]
Dehydration/heatstroke	33	10	43	[4]
Heat & heart attack	36	3	39	[0]
Cardiac, not heat-related	12	3	15	[0]
Hyponatremia	1	1	2	[0]
Cold (hypothermia)	6	-	6	
Flashfloods on tributaries	8	6	14	[2]
Drowning while:				
Boating	34	5	39	[1]
Crossing the river	20	-	20	[1]
Swimming:				
Near Phantom Ranch	12	-	12	[2]
Miles 0 to 87 & 90 to 277	8	1	9	[3]
Accidentally falling in	6	2	8	[0]
Mysterious disappearance	6	3	9	[1]
Aircraft Down fatally (N=64)				
Within Canyon:				
Commercial (N=18)	137	80	217	
Private (N=14)	29	13	42	
On adjacent plateaus:*				
Commercial* (N=9)	25*	24*	49*	
Private* (N=23)	47*	24*	71*	
Freak Accidents & Errors:				
Lightning	2	-	2	[0]
Natural rockfall	3	1	4	[0]
Mistakes in judgment	15	2	17	[1]
BASE jumping	3	-	3	[0]
Critters & Cacti				
Muleback or horseback	2	-	2	[0]
Bighorn sheep	1	-	1	[0]
Natural treefall	1	-	1	[0]
Datura ingestion	2	-	2	[0]
Hantavirus or bacteria	1	1	2	[0]
Unknown cause**	4	0	4	[0]
Totals, accidental deaths	472 (75%)	156 (25%)	628	[26=4%]
Suicide below rims	69	13	82	[0]
Homicide (definite and possible)	9+14*	5+8*	14	[4*]
Grand total below the rims:	550	174	724	[24]

* Not included in totals for within Grand Canyon.
** Friesen, Ott, Uqualla & Welch

RULES of SURVIVAL (and PREVENTION): a CHECKLIST

1. Always tell a reliable friend in advance where you are going (your "plan A").

2. Set a specific time (or date) when you plan to re-contact this friend after you return to confirm with him or her that you have safely returned.

3. Should you fail to report in, your friend must know your pre-arranged trigger time when he or she should set in motion a search and rescue mission for you.

4. If where you plan to visit is new to you, do your homework in advance to learn how to prepare for its challenges, topography, and so on. Under-estimating challenges and/or over-estimating one's own abilities have led to a very high number of bad results. Never hike, climb, scramble, ride, spelunk, swim, or boat beyond your ability or level of skill or preparedness.

5. Stick to your plan A unless you can contact your reliable friend to alter your original destination with him or her. Retreating from your plan A, should it prove dicey, is always okay and sometimes is the key to survival.

6. Never short cut an established route or trail.

7. If a trail or route in a guidebook or web site is listed as requiring a specific number of hours or days to cover, then it is a bad idea to cut shorter those times in your planning.

8. Hiking or otherwise penetrating wilderness solo has proven far more hazardous than doing the same activity with a buddy. Two heads usually are far better than one.

9. Stay hydrated but do not flush the electrolytes from your body by excessive drinking. You should drink only enough water to maintain the same, normal output of urine you normally experience.

10. Try to hike from water to other water. For waterless destinations bring "extra" water. Cache extra water partway along your return route. Always know where and how you can find more water.

11. Protect yourself from summer sun; wear a hat and light-colored clothes, use sun screen.

12. During summer, plan to fully avoid hiking or horseback riding during the hottest times of day (10 am-4 pm).

13. Rivers, creeks, and flashfloods all can pose serious potential dangers. Educate yourself on all the perils of moving water before entering any. Never dive into water you have not previously checked for adequate depth and clearance from boulders. In desert canyons during monsoon season or winter weather beware of flash floods.

14. Do not toy with rattlesnakes, scorpions, tortoises, or other desert wildlife. And if you slip and fall, don't grab a cactus to arrest your fall (because when the pain prompts you to let go of it, you will fall anyway).

15. Never rely on a cell phone as your sole safety and survival kit.

16. Be prepared to counter adverse outcomes by contemplating in advance "What if" scenarios and by carrying a lightweight survival kit. What items should be included in this kit? We're glad you asked....

SURVIVAL ESSENTIALS, a second CHECKLIST

1. A topographic map of the region you plan to enter. This should not be a scale of 1/250,000 showing major cities and highways. Instead your map(s) should be of your target region and at a scale of 1:24,000 or a smaller ratio yet. As map and compass expert Bjorn Kjellstrom notes, a topographic map acts in many ways as a magic carpet to carry a traveler over terrain, but only if it is the correct map for the terrain you have chosen. Lack of an appropriate map too often has proven fatal. Indeed, if you want to master topographic maps and the art of orienteering , we recommend you read Kjellstrom's classic guide: *Be Expert with Map and Compass.*

2. An orienteering compass for orienting your map and yourself. Silva and others make many usable intermediate models. Yes, most GPS units and smart phones offer compasses that point north. But no savvy outdoorsperson counts on his or her cell phone or GPS unit to work flawlessly or its batteries to last indefinitely or the GEO satellites to be contactable in narrow canyons or beneath forest cover. A physical compass is invaluable, even if you know next to nothing about using it.

3. A GPS unit (Garmin, Magellan, or others) can be pre-programmed with waypoints and your destination(s) using coordinates gained from reading your map or guidebook before you ever leave the pavement. A GPS unit can also point you back to your vehicle (if you way-pointed your vehicle's parking spot). But even when downloaded with an appropriate topographic map a GPS unit still does not provide the quality of essential help that a hard copy map does. Yet a GPS unit can prove an extremely useful, perhaps lifesaving, tool. Remember spare batteries.

4. Enough water to carry you to your ultimate destination, whether this be your parked vehicle or a guaranteed re-supply source en route. Which is better--- bottles versus bladders with feeder hoses? Because we have seen many bladders rupture and/or leak via malfunctions or mishaps and leave its owner high and dry (and in danger of dehydration), we recommend hard containers of BPA-free plastic or stainless steel.

5. Water purification tablets and/or a lightweight water filter for water that could save your life but appears "icky." With dehydration and potential heat stroke looming, any water is appropriate to drink. Overly fastidious victims who thought otherwise have died of dehydration. Water equals life. Even dirty water.

6. A good quality multi-tool or Victorinox Swiss Army knife with saw, knife blade, tweezers and/or pliers, and so on. The potential uses for such tools for survival or while lost or delayed or injured are innumerable. Being able to yank out cactus spines alone makes such a tool invaluable.

7. A headlamp with spare batteries (or, better yet, a second headlamp). The ability to travel after nightfall can prove life-saving. The inability to do so due to lack of a headlamp has prompted fatal decisions to continue hiking during the maximum heat of daylight.

8. A Bic-type lighter and a waterproof match case of matches. Also a similar case containing instant tinder: cotton balls impregnated with vasoline. Although other means of starting a fire exist, an emergency (especially in wet weather) is no time to try your hand at learning them. The ability to build a fire after nightfall when lost, delayed, or injured can provide warmth, an improved sense of self-control, and a beacon to searchers or SAR personnel. One of us managed a midnight technical canyon rescue solely because the victim merely flicked his Bic once while injured and walled out within a trail-less canyon while carrying neither survival gear nor headlamp. Do not, however, ignite a wildfire.

9. A small police-type whistle for signaling distress and your position.

10. A signal mirror. You'll want the real thing made of glass from an outdoor store. How effective a signal mirror is at reflecting sunlight for miles is mind-blowing. Moreover they are simple and fun to learn how to use.

11. A lightweight space blanket or poncho or equivalent for use as shelter or cover during an unexpected bivouac.

12. Emergency food, preferably loaded with calories and salt. This stash can consist of salted peanuts and/or power bar-type products, but should be durable and plentiful.

13. A small roll of Gorilla tape (not duct tape). You can create this by "re-rolling" about 6 feet of Gorilla tape around a Sharpie marker. The marker also can be used to leave messages to lost companions or searchers.

14. A small first aid kit containing bandaids, athletic tape, Ace bandage, a cravat or two (if you can find them), a needle or tweezers, a small magnifying glass, plus Benadryl, Betadine, ibuprofen, and so on. If you are allergic to specific insect stings or other environmental hazards, carry your epinephrine injector.

15. Oh yeah, don't forget your cell phone (or satellite phone). But, again, do not pretend that either can serve you as a replacement for the above list. We recommend against using a SPOT type device unless it's engineered to allow two-way text messaging for precise communication with potential rescue personnel.

Continuing Research

As we explained at the onset of this book, finding all of the information and then determining whether or not this information is accurate regarding fatal episodes in Grand Canyon is an unending task. If you possess personal knowledge of any episode at odds with what we have written, or instead know of an episode that we have missed, we would appreciate your information. One of our top priorities here is that this book be accurate. High accuracy makes its lessons that much more reliable. If you wish to share any information you possess, please contact us by letter via Puma Press, P.O. Box 30998, Flagstaff, AZ 86003 USA, or by email at: pumapress1@gmail.com.

Deer Michael P. Ghiglieri,
Thomas M. Myers.
My name is Lars Schumitz
I am nine years old. Me my
cousin read death and the
Grand Canyon and reinacted
the deths in the pool. I'm
a big fan of the book I have
some ideas that you should
make, deth and the Grand Canyon
the movie, deth and the Grand
canyon toy's and death in the
Grand canyon the video game.
pleas let me know if you like
my ideas.
                    Love,
                        Lars

Lars Schumitz, 2011

Author's Profiles

Michael P. Ghiglieri grew up at Lake Tahoe, Nevada as the great grandson of a forty-niner, served as a U.S. Army platoon sergeant during the Vietnam era, and then earned his Ph.D. in Ecology in 1979 from the University of California at Davis for his pioneering research on wild chimpanzees in Kibale Forest, Uganda. In addition to teaching university courses in primate behavior and ecology and in human evolution and ecology, he has directed several semesters-overseas centers focusing on sustainable resource management (in Kenya, the Turks & Caicos, Palau, Far North Queensland, and on Vancouver Island), and has worked as a wilderness river guide and EMT. Since 1974, he has guided more than 676 commercial whitewater trips and also guided treks in Ethiopia, Java, Kenya, Papua New Guinea, Peru, Rwanda, Sumatra, Tanzania, Turkey, and the USA. These include 163, 2-week rowing or paddling trips through Grand Canyon and more than 48,000 miles on 40 different river runs overall, a few in the Canyon as an NPS ranger. He has guided several Kilimanjaro ascents and Kenyan foot safaris. Ghiglieri lives in Flagstaff, Arizona, is happily married, has three grown children and two grandchildren, and has authored documentary screenplays and seven books (two on wild chimpanzees) and, with his wife Susan, is a volunteer for the Coconino County Sheriff Department's Search and Rescue Teams.

Tom Myers has worked in the Grand Canyon region as a rural family and emergency physician since 1990, and currently serves as medical advisor for Grand Canyon National Park. A dedicated explorer of the Canyon backcountry since his late teens, he also works as an occasional river guide and hiking guide. With a B.S. degree in history from Northern Arizona University and an M.D. from the University of Arizona, he has a special interest in Grand Canyon human history and wilderness medicine. His first book *Fateful Journey: Injury and Death on Colorado River Trips in Grand Canyon*, with Larry Stevens and Chris Becker, dispelled many of the myths about the perceived risks of river running in Grand Canyon. His third book, *Grand Obsession: Harvey Butchart and the Exploration of Grand Canyon*, with Elias Butler, won the National Outdoor Book Award for biography in 2008. He and his wife Becky have three children and live in Flagstaff.

To Order Copies of Puma Press Books:

Photocopy this page and fill out your order. Please print legibly.

Please send_____copies of *OVER THE EDGE: DEATH IN GRAND CANYON*, $25.95 softcover (if being shipped to an Arizona address, please add $2.11 sales tax per copy)   subtotal =_____

Please send_____copies of copies of *OFF THE WALL: DEATH IN YOSEMITE*, $24.95 softcover (if being shipped to an Arizona address, please add $2.11 sales tax per copy)   subtotal = _____

Please send_____copies of *FIRST THROUGH GRAND CANYON: The Secret Journals and Letters of the 1869 Crew Who Explored the Green and Colorado Rivers*, $19.95 softcover (if being shipped to an Arizona address, please add $1.62 sales tax per copy)   subtotal = _____

Shipping & Handling: please add $3.00 for the first book, $1.00 for each additional book.   shipping subtotal =

TOTAL = $ _____

Order via our website: **pumapress.org** or
Enclose your check or money order for the total above payable to:
    Puma Press, P.O. Box 30998, Flagstaff, AZ 86003 USA
    Thank you for your order. Please allow 3 weeks for delivery

---

SHIP TO ADDRESS (please print)

_____

STREET

_____   _____   _____

CITY   STATE   ZIP CODE

_____

NAME

Index